Lecture Notes in Computer Science   13635

More information about this series at https://link.springer.com/bookseries/558

Eric Pardede · Pari Delir Haghighi ·
Ismail Khalil · Gabriele Kotsis (Eds.)

Information Integration and Web Intelligence

24th International Conference, iiWAS 2022
Virtual Event, November 28–30, 2022
Proceedings

 Springer

Editors
Eric Pardede
La Trobe University
Melbourne, VIC, Australia

Pari Delir Haghighi
Monash University
Melbourne, VIC, Australia

Ismail Khalil
Johannes Kepler University Linz
Linz, Austria

Gabriele Kotsis
Johannes Kepler University Linz
Linz, Austria

ISSN 0302-9743   ISSN 1611-3349   (electronic)
Lecture Notes in Computer Science
ISBN 978-3-031-21046-4   ISBN 978-3-031-21047-1   (eBook)
https://doi.org/10.1007/978-3-031-21047-1

Preface

This volume includes the papers presented at the 24th International Conference on Information Integration and Web Intelligence (iiWAS 2022), which was organized in conjunction with the 20th International Conference on Advances in Mobile Computing & Multimedia Intelligence (MoMM 2022). Due to safety concerns as well as other restrictions preventing travel and gatherings, it was decided to organize iiWAS 2022 as a virtual conference.

iiWAS is one of the leading international conferences for researchers and industry practitioners to share their new ideas, original research results, and practical development experiences in all information integration and Web intelligence related areas. The submitted papers were reviewed in a mixed peer review process by at least two reviewers based on their originality, clarity, relevance, contribution, and impact. This year, the accepted papers are published by Springer in their Lecture Notes in Computer Science (LNCS) series. LNCS volumes are indexed in the Conference Proceedings Citation Index (CPCI), part of Clarivate Analytics' Web of Science; Scopus; Ei Compendex; Google Scholar; DBLP; etc.

iiWAS 2022 attracted 97 submissions from 31 countries. After a rigorous review process we accepted 26 full papers and 25 short papers, yielding an acceptance rate of 25% for the regular paper category. The dominant research focus of submitted papers was artificial intelligence and machine learning. The accepted papers presented advances and innovations in an array of areas such as the Internet of Things, virtual and augmented reality, and various business applications.

This year we had three distinguished keynote speakers, Antonio Liotta from the Free University of Bozen-Bolzano, Italy, Janika Leoste from Tallinn University of Technology, Estonia, and Robert Wrembel from Poznan University of Technology, Poland. We also had our second World ABC (Artificial Intelligence and Big Data Convergence) Forum with world-renowned speakers, which was hosted by Won Kim from Gachon University, South Korea. The abstracts of the keynote talks of Janika Leoste and Robert Wrembel, as well as the Forum abstract, are included in this volume.

We would like to express our sincere gratitude to the iiWAS 2022 participants, dedicated authors, Program Committee members, keynote speakers, session chairs, organizing and steering committee members, and student volunteers for their continuous and generous support and commitment that made this event a success.

We are looking forward to seeing this conference grow further over time, and expecting more researchers, scientists, and scholars to join this global platform to share and discuss their ideas, findings, and experiences.

November 2022

Eric Pardede
Pari Delir Haghighi
Ismail Khalil
Gabriele Kotsis

Organization

Program Committee Chair

Eric Pardede — La Trobe University, Australia

Steering Committee

Gabriele Kotsis — Johannes Kepler University Linz, Austria
Ismail Khalil — Johannes Kepler University Linz, Austria
Pari Delir Haghighi — Monash University, Australia
Dirk Draheim — Tallinn University of Technology, Estonia
Syopiansyah Jaya Putra — Universitas Islam Negeri, Indonesia

Program Committee

Ali Alwan — Ramapo College of New Jersey, USA
Toshiyuki Amagasa — University of Tsukuba, Japan
Idir Amine Amarouche — University of Science and Technology Houari Boumediene, Algeria
Masayoshi Aritsugi — Kumamoto University, Japan
Karim Benouaret — Université Claude Bernard Lyon 1, France
Devis Bianchini — University of Brescia, Italy
Marco Antonio Casanova — PUC-Rio, Brazil
Barbara Catania — University of Genoa, Italy
Cindy Chen — University of Massachusetts Lowell, USA
Soon Ae Chun — City University of New York, USA
Alfredo Cuzzocrea — University of Calabria, Italy
Deborah Dahlm — Conversational Technologies, USA
Vincenzo Deufemia — University of Salerno, Italy
Bettina Fazzinga — University of Calabria, Italy
Matteo Francia — University of Bologna, Italy
Luca Gagliardelli — University of Modena and Reggio Emilia, Italy
Enrico Gallinucci — University of Bologna, Italy
Jorge Lloret Gazo — Universidad de Zaragoza, Spain
Manolis Gergatsoulis — Ionian University, Greece
Dion Goh — Nanyang Technological University, Singapore
Sven Groppe — University of Lübeck, Germany
Francesco Guerra — Università di Modena e Reggio Emilia, Italy

Giovanna Guerrini	University of Genoa, Italy
Sami Habib	Kuwait University, Kuwait
Takako Hashimoto	Chiba University of Commerce, Japan
Sergio Ilarri	Universidad de Zaragoza, Spain
Yasunori Ishihara	Nanzan University, Japan
Peiquan Jin	University of Science and Technology of China, China
Dan Johansson	Umeå University, Sweden
Sangwoo Kang	Gachon University, South Korea
Anne Kao	Collinear Group, USA
Anne Kayem	Hasso Plattner Institute, Universität Potsdam, Germany
Carsten Kleiner	Hannover University of Applied Sciences and Arts, Germany
Naoko Kosugi	Takasaki University of Health and Welfare, Japan
Michal Krátký	Technical University of Ostrava, Czech Republic
Petr Kremen	Czech Technical University in Prague, Czech Republic
Hind Lamharhar	Mohamed V University, Agdal, Morocco
Anne Laurent	University of Montpellier and CNRS, France
Wookey Lee	Inha University, Japan
Qiang Ma	Kyoto University, Japan
Elio Masciari	Federico II University of Naples, Italy
Michele Melchiori	University of Brescia, Italy
Ronaldo Mello	UFSC, Brazil
Marco Mesiti	University of Milan, Italy
Lars Moench	Fern Universität in Hagen, Germany
Francesc Munoz-Escoi	Universidad Politècnica de Valencia, Spain
Akiyo Nadamoto	Konan University, Japan
Brahim Ouhbi	Moulay Ismail University, Morocco
Elaheh Pourabbas	IASI-CNR, Italy
Massimo Ruffolo	ICAR-CNR, Italy
Johannes Sametinger	Johannes Kepler University Linz, Austria
Marinette Savonnet	University of Burgundy, France
Erich Schikuta	University of Vienna, Austria
Sucha Smanchat	King Mongkut's University of Technology North Bangkok, Thailand
Bala Srinivasan	Monash University, Australia
Emanuele Storti	Università Politecnica delle Marche, Italy
Jeff Tan	IBM Research, Australia
Vicenc Torra	Umeå University, Sweden
Traian Marius Truta	Northern Kentucky University, USA

Harald Wahl	University of Applied Sciences Technikum Wien, Austria
Yousuke Watanabe	Nagoya University, Japan
Edgar Weippl	University of Vienna, Austria
Werner Winiwarter	University of Vienna, Austria
Muhammad Younas	Oxford Brookes University, UK
Yan Zhu	Southwest Jiaotong University, China
Qiang Zhu	University of Michigan, USA
Marcin Zimniak	Leipzig University, Germany
Ester Zumpano	University of Calabria, Italy

External Reviewers

Bernardo Breve	University of Salerno, Italy
Gaetano Cimino	University of Salerno, Italy
Stefano Cirillo	University of Salerno, Italy
Matthew Damigos	Ionian University, Greece
Houyi Du	University of Michigan, USA
Ramon Hermoso	University of Zaragoza, Spain
Eleftherios Kalogeros	Ionian University, Greece
Abderrahmane Kiouche	University of Lyon 1, France
Jianguo Lu	University of Windsor, Canada
Gang Qian	University of Central Oklahoma, USA
Zheni Utic	Georgia Southern University, USA

Organizers

Institute for
Telecooperation

Abstracts of Keynote Talks

Data Integration, Cleaning, and Deduplication: Research versus Reality

Robert Wrembel

Poznan University of Technology, Poland

Abstract. In business applications, data integration is typically imple-mented as a data warehouse architecture. In this architecture, heteroge-neous and distributed data sources are accessed and integrated by means of an Extract-Transform-Load (ETL) layer. This layer runs ETL processes whose tasks include: data integration and homogenization, data cleaning, and deduplication. At the end of an ETL process, homogeneous and clean data are uploaded into a central repository - a data warehouse. Designing such processes is challenging due to the heterogeneity of data models and formats, data errors and missing values, multiple data pieces representing the same real-world objects. As a consequence, ETL processes are very complex, which results in high development and maintenance costs as well long runtimes.

To ease the development of ETL processes, various research solutions were development. They include among others: (1) ETL design meth-ods, (2) data cleaning pipelines, (3) data deduplication pipelines, and (4) performance optimization techniques. Despite the fact that these solu-tions were included in commercial ETL design environments and ETL engines, there are still multiple open issues in this research and techno-logical area. Moreover, the application of these solutions in commercial projects reveals that they frequently do not fit business user requirements.

In this talk, I will provoke a discussion on what problems in ETL design one can encounter while implementing ETL pipelines. The pre-sented findings are based on my experience from research and commer-cial data integration projects for a financial sector, healthcare sector, and software development sector. In particular, I will cover the following: (1) challenges in designing ETL processes, (2) faulty data and cleaning, (3) deduplicating large row-like data, and (4) open problems in optimizing ETL processes.

Are Telepresence Robots Here to Stay?

Janika Leoste

Tallinn University of Technology, Estonia

Abstract. The praised and cursed hybrid education seems to become reality at least in higher education in the upcoming years. The biggest threat we have seen so far is the low engagement of the remote students when they are mediated via a teleconferencing system as they tend to be forgotten by the professor while the physical students are in class. This, of course, leads to incomplete learning gains. Another threat the remote learners tend to experience is the social isolation because it is difficult to immerse yourself to another location when you do not control your senses and body-movement at that other location. Based on my recent research, I will contemplate whether a telepresence robot could cultivate a stronger feeling of social presence and enable richer communication that is more similar to that of an in-person communication.

Forum

2022 Second Annual World AI-BigData Convergence (ABC) Forum

Won Kim

AI Vice President of Gachon University, South Korea

Abstract. In this Second Annual World AI-BigData Convergence (ABC) Forum, six world-renowned speakers from both academia and industry have discussed the issues and problems surrounding the vision of Artificial Intelligence (AI) and Big Data confluence and propose ground-breaking solutions with a full awareness of potential benefits and risks.

The objective of this World Forum is to explore the current status and R&D opportunities and issues in the convergence (or confluence) of AI and BigData from a data centric perspective. The objective of the ABC initiative, as defined by Prof. Won Kim in his keynote for iiWAS-2021 last year, is to help propel the current smart data processing to the next level. The ABC vision is based on advancing both AI and Big Data through fuller uses of data and through AI and big data leveraging each other. The fuller uses of data include the use of higher quality data and multimodal data for both AI and Big Data.

As expected, the forum was a very informative, productive, and exciting Forum.

Contents

Keynotes

Data Integration, Cleaning, and Deduplication: Research Versus Industrial
Projects 3
   Robert Wrembel

Aspects of Using Telepresence Robot in a Higher Education STEAM
Workshop 18
   Janika Leoste, Sirje Virkus, Tiina Kasuk, Aleksei Talisainen,
   Katrin Kangur, and Piedad Tolmos

Business Data and Applications

An Analysis of Data Modelling for Blockchain 31
   João Vicente Meyer and Ronaldo dos Santos Mello

Sharing Semantic Knowledge for Autonomous Robots: Cooperation
for Social Robotic Systems 45
   Sara Comai, Jacopo Finocchi, Maria Grazia Fugini, Theofilos Mastos,
   and Angelos Papadopoulos

Exploiting Named Entity Recognition for Information Extraction
from Italian Procurement Documents: A Case Study 60
   Angelo Impedovo, Emanuele Pio Barracchia, and Giuseppe Rizzo

bNaming: An Intelligent Application to Assist Brand Names Definition 75
   José Vieira, Rodrigo Rocha, Luis F. Pereira, Igor Vanderlei,
   Jean Araujo, and Jamilson Dantas

Discovering Conditional Business Rules in Web Applications Using
Process Mining 90
   Hamza Alkofahi, David Umphress, and Heba Alawneh

Comparison of Job Titles for Specific Terms: Investigating "Data Science" 98
   Abdulkareem Alsudais, Abdullah Aldumaykhi, and Saad Otai

Generating Smart Contracts for Blockchain-Based Resource-Exchange
Systems 104
   Kushal Soni and Olga De Troyer

Analysis of Country Mentions in the Debates of the UN Security Council 110
  Raji Ghawi and Jürgen Pfeffer

Data Mining

A Comparative Performance Analysis of Fast K-Means Clustering
Algorithms 119
  Christian Beecks, Fabian Berns, Jan David Hüwel, Andrea Linxen,
  Georg Stefan Schlake, and Tim Düsterhus

Mining Twitter Multi-word Product Opinions with Most Frequent
Sequences of Aspect Terms 126
  C. I. Ezeife, Ritu Chaturvedi, Mahreen Nasir, and Vinay Manjunath

An Analysis of Human Perception of Partitions of Numerical Factor
Domains 137
  Minakshi Kaushik, Rahul Sharma, Mahtab Shahin, Sijo Arakkal Peious,
  and Dirk Draheim

Fast Top-k Similar Sequence Search on DNA Databases 145
  Ryuichi Yagi and Hiroaki Shiokawa

Graph Data and Knowledge Graph

GN-GCN: Combining Geographical Neighbor Concept with Graph
Convolution Network for POI Recommendation 153
  Fan Mo and Hayato Yamana

Network Topology to Predict Bibliometrics Indices: A Case Study 166
  Vincenza Carchiolo, Marco Grassia, Michele Malgeri,
  and Giuseppe Mangioni

A Neural Network Approach for Text Classification Using Low
Dimensional Joint Embeddings of Words and Knowledge 181
  Liliane Soares da Costa, Italo Lopes Oliveira, and Renato Fileto

Tree-Based Graph Indexing for Fast kNN Queries 195
  Suomi Kobayashi, Shohei Matsugu, and Hiroaki Shiokawa

IoT and Machine Learning

An Object Separated Storage Framework Towards Spatiotemporal Point
Data Fast Query 211
  Jin Yan, Zhiming Ding, and Shuai Zhang

Streaming Augmented Lineage: Traceability of Complex Stream Data
Analysis 224
  Masaya Yamada, Hiroyuki Kitagawa, Salman Ahmed Shaikh,
  Toshiyuki Amagasa, and Akiyoshi Matono

A Web Application for Experimenting and Validating Remote
Measurement of Vital Signs 237
  Amtul Haq Ayesha, Donghao Qiao, and Farhana Zulkernine

Neural Kernel Network Deep Kernel Learning for Predicting Particulate
Matter from Heterogeneous Sensors with Uncertainty 252
  Chaofan Li, Till Riedel, and Michael Beigl

Ontology and Semantic Web

Comparative Ranking of Ontologies with ELECTRE Family
of Multi-criteria Decision-Making Algorithms 269
  Ameeth Sooklall and Jean Vincent Fonou-Dombeu

Machine Learning Selection of Candidate Ontologies for Automatic
Extraction of Context Words and Axioms from Ontology Corpus 282
  Mohammed Suleiman Mohammed Rudwan
  and Jean Vincent Fonou-Dombeu

WAPITI – Web-based Assignment Preparation and Instruction Tool
for Interpreters 295
  Bartholomäus Wloka, Yves Lepage, and Werner Winiwarter

Performance and Optimization

Optimization Heuristics for Cost-Efficient Long-Term Cloud Portfolio
Allocations 309
  Maximilian Kiessler, Valentin Haag, Benedikt Pittl, and Erich Schikuta

Latency-Aware Inference on Convolutional Neural Network Over
Homomorphic Encryption 324
  Takumi Ishiyama, Takuya Suzuki, and Hayato Yamana

PR-MVI: Efficient Missing Value Imputation over Data Streams
by Distance Likelihood 338
  Savong Bou, Toshiyuki Amagasa, Hiroyuki Kitagawa,
  Salman Ahmed Shaikh, and Akiyoshi Matono

Discovering Relational Implications in Multilayer Networks Using Formal
Concept Analysis   352
   Raji Ghawi and Jürgen Pfeffer

Inexpensive and Effective Data Fusion Methods with Performance Weights   367
   Qiuyu Xu, Yidong Huang, and Shengli Wu

GPU Accelerated Parallel Implementation of Linear Programming
Algorithms   378
   Ratul Kishore Saha, Ashutosh Pradhan, Tiash Ghosh,
   Mamata Jenamani, Sanjai Kumar Singh, and Aurobinda Routray

Towards Explaining DL Non-entailments by Utilizing Subtree
Isomorphisms   385
   Ivan Gocev, Georgios Meditskos, and Nick Bassiliades

Query Optimization in NoSQL Databases Using an Enhanced Localized
R-tree Index   391
   Aristeidis Karras, Christos Karras, Dimitrios Samoladas,
   Konstantinos C. Giotopoulos, and Spyros Sioutas

Handling Exit Node Vulnerability in Onion Routing with a Zero-Knowledge
Proof   399
   Nadav Voloch and Maor Meir Hajaj

Privacy and Security

An Accurate, Flexible and Private Trajectory-Based Contact Tracing
System on Untrusted Servers   409
   Ruixuan Cao, Fumiyuki Kato, Yang Cao, and Masatoshi Yoshikawa

Bilateral Bargaining for Healthcare Data Sharing   415
   Svetlana Boudko and Wolfgang Leister

Modifying Neo4j's Object Graph Mapper Queries for Access Control   421
   Daniel Hofer, Aya Mohamed, and Josef Küng

Recommendation Systems

A Recommendation Method for Recipes Containing Unskillful Elements
Using Naïve Bayes Classifier to Improve Cooking Skills   429
   Xinyu Liu and Daisuke Kitayama

Extraction of Complementary Topics Based on Phrase Importance
and Co-occurrence in Technical Blogs 435
  Masaru Hakii and Daisuke Kitayama

Feature Relevance Analysis of Product Reviews to Support Online
Shopping 441
  Fumiya Yamaguchi, Felix Dollack, Mayumi Ueda, and Shinsuke Nakajima

Annotation System for Dialogue Datasets of Older Adult's with Photos
and Storytelling 447
  Seiki Tokunaga, Shogo Takata, Kazuhiro Tamura,
  and Mihoko Otake-Matsuura

Evaluation Axes for Automatically Generated Product Descriptions 453
  Kenji Fukumoto, Risa Takeuchi, Hiroyuki Terada, Masafumi Bato,
  and Akiyo Nadamoto

Similarity Measures and Metrics

CISQA: Corporate Smart Insights Question Answering System 463
  Le Duyen Sandra Vu, Jamal Al Qundus, Johannes Jung, Silvio Peikert,
  and Adrian Paschke

Symmetry Metrics for Pairwise Entity Similarities 476
  Alex Romanova

A New Method to Measure Similarity of Words in Japanese Twitter Based
on Related Images 489
  Zhelin Xu, Atsushi Matsumura, and Tetsuji Satoh

Topic and Text Matching

Hybrid Phishing URL Detection Using Segmented Word Embedding 507
  Eint Sandi Aung and Hayato Yamana

A Scheme for News Article Classification in a Low-Resource Language 519
  Hailemariam Mehari Yohannes and Toshiyuki Amagasa

Expertise Computation for Automatic Reviewer Assignment 531
  Divya Kwatra and Vasudha Bhatnagar

Detection of Hot Topics Using Multi-view Text Clustering 548
  Maha Fraj, Mohamed Aymen Ben Hajkacem, and Nadia Essoussi

Virtual Reality/Augmented Reality

Interactive Visualization of Comic Character Correlation Diagrams
for Understanding Character Relationships and Personalities 561
  Kanna Miyagawa, Yutaka Morino, and Mitsunori Matsushita

Two Case Studies on Guiding Human Behavior Using Virtualization
Technologies in Distributed Virtual Shopping Malls 568
  Taku Watanabe, Yuta Matsushima, Risa Kimura, and Tatsuo Nakajima

Central Figures in the Climate Change Discussion on Twitter 575
  *Anil Can Kara, Ivana Dobrijevic, Emre Öztas, Angelina Mooseder,
  Raji Ghawi, and Jürgen Pfeffer*

E-Tracer: A Smart, Personalized and Immersive Digital Tourist Software
System 581
  *Alexandros Kokkalas, Athanasios T. Patenidis,
  Evangelos A. Stathopoulos, Eirini E. Mitsopoulou, Sotiris Diplaris,
  Konstadinos Papadopoulos, Stefanos Vrochidis, Konstantinos Votis,
  Dimitrios Tzovaras, and Ioannis Kompatsiaris*

Author Index 589

Keynotes

Data Integration, Cleaning, and Deduplication: Research Versus Industrial Projects

Robert Wrembel[✉][iD]

Poznan University of Technology, Poznan, Poland
robert.wrembel@cs.put.poznan.pl

Abstract. In business applications, data integration is typically implemented as a data warehouse architecture. In this architecture, heterogeneous and distributed data sources are accessed and integrated by means of Extract-Transform-Load (ETL) processes. Designing these processes is challenging due to the heterogeneity of data models and formats, data errors and missing values, multiple data pieces representing the same real-world objects. As a consequence, ETL processes are very complex, which results in high development and maintenance costs as well as long runtimes.

To ease the development of ETL processes, various research and technological solutions were development. They include among others: (1) ETL design methods, (2) data cleaning pipelines, (3) data deduplication pipelines, and (4) performance optimization techniques. In spite of the fact that these solutions were included in commercial (and some open license) ETL design environments and ETL engines, there still exist multiple open issues and the existing solutions still need to advance.

In this paper (and its accompanying talk), I will provoke a discussion on what problems one can encounter while implementing ETL pipelines in real business (industrial) projects. The presented findings are based on my experience from research and commercial data integration projects in financial, healthcare, and software development sectors. In particular, I will focus on a few particular issues, namely: (1) performance optimization of ETL processes, (2) cleaning and deduplicating large row-like data sets, and (3) integrating medical data.

Keywords: Data integration · Data warehouse · Data lake · Big data · Extract transform load · Data processing workflow · Data processing pipeline · Data quality · Data deduplication · ETL performance optimization

1 Introduction

Topic *data integration* (DI) has been researched and developed since 60s, but a substantial interest of research communities on the topic started in years 2000. Figure 1 shows the number of publications available on the DBLP service on topic *data integration* within 1971–2022. Moreover, another DI topic, i.e., *ETL, cleaning, and provenance* became researched by the DOLAP community

E. Pardede et al. (Eds.): iiWAS 2022, LNCS 13635, pp. 3–17, 2022.
https://doi.org/10.1007/978-3-031-21047-1_1

(i.e., International Workshop On Design, Optimization, Languages and Analytical Processing of Big Data) since 2001. This was the 2nd most popular topic in the period 1998–2018 of the history of the DOLAP workshop [85].

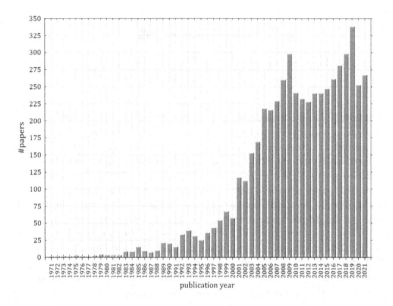

Fig. 1. The number of publications per year on topic *data integration* (based on DBLP: dblp.uni-trier.de), in years 1971–2021

In early 80s, two fundamental virtual DI architectures were developed, namely *federated* [13,25] and *mediated* [83]. Both of them share a common feature of physically storing data only in original data sources (DSs), which are typically heterogeneous and distributed. These data are integrated on demand by a software layer located between a user and the DSs. This layer, composed of a few software components, is responsible for: (1) transforming source data models into a common integration model (frequently the relational one), (2) decomposing user queries into sub-queries and routing them into appropriate DSs, (3) transforming the sub-queries into executable code snippets for each DS, (4) transforming and integrating results of the sub-queries. The main difference between the federated and mediated architecture is that the first one is used to integrate databases and it uses more software components in the intermediate layer than the mediated one. The mediated architecture is applied to integrating not only databases but also other types of DSs.

A virtual DI architecture is advantageous for building a system that needs to access fresh data. However, the architecture has some drawbacks, i.e., (1) time overhead of transforming queries and data, (2) network transmission delays, (3) unavailability of data sources. These drawbacks motivated the development of an industry standard DI architecture, called a *data warehouse* (DW) [39,82].

In the DW architecture, the integration is implemented by means of the so-called extract-transform-load (ETL) layer [81], where ETL processes are run to integrate data. They are responsible for: (1) ingesting data from data sources and storing them in an intermediate staging area, (2) transforming heterogeneous data into a common data model and schema, (3) cleaning, normalizing, and eliminating data duplicates, (4) loading data into a persistent repository, i.e. a DW. DW architectures are very well applicable to storing and processing row-oriented data.

The widespread of big data [16,41,77] called for the development of other architectures capable of integrating, storing, and processing data of an arbitrary complexities and sizes [5]. Such architectures are commonly known as a *data lake*. Both of them are typically deployed in a cloud. An interest of research communities in big data integration boosted the number of papers published on this topic since 2000 (cf. Fig. 1, which includes papers also on big data integration).

A data lake (DL) is a repository that stores a vast amount of heterogeneous data ingested from DSs in their original formats [56,67,80]. Next, the content of the DL is processed by ETL processes to build cleaned, homogenized, and integrated data repositories [40]. Further, these data are unified either on-the-fly in the so-called *logical* or *virtual* data warehouse [24,48,68,78] or are homogenized and uploaded into a physical data warehouse, often deployed in a cloud architecture [37,44,71,76]. Finally, in a *hybrid DL-DW* architecture [73] some DSs are stored in an on-premise architecture whereas some other DSs are physically integrated and stored in a private-public cloud eco-system.

Another classification of DI systems, orthogonal to the aforementioned one, was presented in [79]. It distinguishes: (1) a *federated architecture*, which supports multiple homogeneous storage, based on the same data model and one access interface (query language), e.g., Mariposa, TSIMMIS, Multibase, (2) a *polyglot*, which supports multiple homogeneous storage using one data model, and multiple access interfaces (SQL-like, procedural), e.g., Spark, (3) a *multistore*, which supports multiple heterogeneous storage (multiple data models) and one access interface (query language), e.g., HadoopDB, Polybase, and (4) a *polystore*, which supports multiple heterogeneous storage (multiple data models) and multiple access interfaces (SQL-like, procedural), e.g., BigDAWG, Polypheny, CloudMdsQL, Estocada.

Notice that, in all of the aforementioned architectures data are moved from source systems into an integrated system via a sequence of processing tasks (steps), bearing different names, e.g., ETL - in data warehouse architectures, data processing pipeline - in data science, or data wrangling, or data processing workflows (DPW) [46,66] (further in this paper, we commonly call these sequences of processing tasks either ETL or DPW).

Even though methods for developing ETL processes have been researched and developed for decades and were included in commercial (and some open license) ETL design environments and ETL engines (e.g., [28,30]), the task of designing and managing ETL processes is difficult and time costly. In this area, there still exist a few interesting and difficult problems to be solved.

In this paper, I'm presenting my subjective point of view on the challenges on designing ETL processes, based on my experience gained from projects in financial, healthcare, and software development sectors. The particular challenges addressed in this paper include: (1) performance optimization of ETL processes, (2) cleaning and deduplicating large row-like data sets, and (3) integrating heterogeneous medical data.

2   Challenge 1: Performance Optimization of ETL/DPW

DPWs are complex workflows composed of dozens to thousands of tasks. They ingest and process large volumes of data of various structures. For these reasons, reducing DPWs execution times is crucial for the whole data integration architecture. Designing DPWs is supported by multiple commercial [28] and open license tools [45]. However, the support from these tools for optimizing such designs is very limited. Further in this section I'm discussing DPW optimization techniques applied in industry and in research. I'm also giving a subjective opinion on the still open issues in this area, based on my cooperation with a corporate software house on the topic of DPW optimization ingesting data from NoSQL data sources.

2.1   Techniques Used in Industry

Typically, in order to reduce execution time of DPWs companies apply:

- hardware vertical scaling (i.e., increasing the number of CPUs, the size of RAM, adding specialized hardware like FPGAs) [50,59] or horizontal scaling (i.e., adding new nodes, either physical or virtual, to a cloud architecture);
- parallel processing either by data or task parallelism [3,4];
- task orchestration (a.k.a. reordering), called *push down* or *balance optimization*; *push down* consists in moving the most selective tasks towards the beginning of an ETL process (towards or into data sources) to reduce a data volume (I/O) as soon as possible [36]. IBM extended this technique into the *balanced optimization* [35,49], where some tasks are moved into DSs and some are moved into a DW to be executed there.

Unfortunately, tasks orchestration has to be done manually by a DPW designer, as neither of the tools supports a designer in this work.

2.2   Approaches Used in Research

To alleviate the difficulty in task orchestration, some research approaches propose techniques for automatic orchestration, e.g., [42,51,74,75]. Unfortunately, a typical search space of all possible valid orders of tasks is too large to be fully searched (it is a problem of exponential complexity). The problem of searching the space of all possible valid reorderings, is similar to searching the space of query execution plans in the query optimization problem. Thus, techniques used in query optimization (a cost model, execution plan, searching the space of execution plans) could be adapted to DPW optimization. However, DPW optimization has its intrinsic challenges. First, a cost model of the whole DPW is very complex, since it is composed of cost models of individual tasks, each of which itself can be very complex. Second, the cost model of a particular task may be unknown if the task is treated as a black box. Typically user-defined functions – UDFs are used in DPWs and they are treated as black boxes. Thus, developing a DPW optimizer is yet to come.

Another challenge is to figure out the most efficient parallelization schemes for a given DPW task or the whole DPW [3], especially when DPWs use user-defined functions. An orthogonal approach is to cache intermediate data to use them by multiple tasks within the same DPW or by different DPWs, e.g., [31].

2.3   UDFs in DPWs

On top of the aforementioned challenges, processing of big data adds new challenges to the already difficult DPW optimization problem. Big data are ingested into a DPW in variety of complex data formats. This often requires implementing dedicated pieces of software to process such data, since adequate out-of-the-box tasks are frequently unable. As mentioned before, such pieces of software, implemented as UDFs, are often treated as black boxes. A black box does not expose its internal processing logic to a DPW engine. Moreover, UDFs are frequently executed as external components to a DPW engine. As a consequence, neither task orchestration or cost-based optimization can be applied to such components, since in order to optimize a DPW with black boxes, a workflow execution engine must know UDF performance characteristics, i.e., resources being used, execution time, and semantics of the UDFs. For this reason, it seems to be crucial to develop methods for learning performance characteristics of black-boxes and develop methods for discovering their internal logic (i.e., opening a black-box).

Several approaches to discovering semantics and performance characteristics of a software component have been developed. Some of them are based on annotating a software component with hints or rules that allow to figure out automatically some characteristics of the software [33,34,65]. Other approaches collect performance characteristics (typically, CPU, I/O, memory usage) during a normal execution of a software piece or during an excessive testing phase. Then, based on the characteristics, various model building techniques are used, cf. [84] for a survey.

A promising direction towards opening a black box is to combine code annotation techniques, with performance characteristics analysis by ML algorithms. Additionally, we advocate for extending these techniques with discovering patterns of resource usage. To this end, time series analysis algorithms can be applied.

2.4 Final Remarks

Although some algorithms were proposed by the research community for orchestrating DPW tasks, these solutions are quite complex (both technologically and computationally), which makes them difficult to apply to large DPWs. Only a simple form of orchestrating, namely the push-down and balanced optimizations were included in some commercial DPW environments. Both of the techniques are based on a simple rule that moves the most selective tasks towards the beginning (push-down) of a DPW or towards the beginning and/or the end of a DPW (balanced). In both cases, if possible and if such a re-ordering reduces execution time, some tasks can be moved to a data source or data destination. Nonetheless, there are no performance models that would assess whether a push-down or balanced could reduce execution time of a DPW. This has still to be done manually by a DPW designer, based on pilot experimental assessments. Furthermore, a sill open issue is how to efficiently and automatically implement a given DPW task in a data source or data destination, given some hardware and software characteristics of given storage systems.

A step further is to allow to execute the push-down and balanced optimization for NoSQL storage. The works towards building some methods and knowledge on this topic has recently started, e.g., [9,10].

Even though some methods for developing DPWs have been proposed in the research literature (cf. [2]), they focus on separated phases of a DPW development life-cycle, e.g., separate methods have been proposed for designing a logical DPW model, separate approaches have been proposed for optimizing a DPW execution. Unfortunately, an end-to-end approach to design, development, optimization, and deployment of DPWs has not been proposed yet, either for standard on-premise architectures or cloud architectures.

An initial work towards this goal has been proposed in [66] where we presented a standardized approach to this problem. The approach is based on a 3-layer architecture: a conceptual DPW design, a logical design, and a deployment model. The approach opens new direction of research in DPW design methods, e.g., (1) conceptual DPW design model and language, (2) intelligent (cost-based, machine learning-based) optimization methods of DPWs, (3) methods for translating a conceptual model into a logical model and finally into a deployment model.

3 Challenge 2: Identifying Duplicate Customer Records

Financial institutions (FIs) apply data governance strategies and use the most advanced state-of-the-art data integration, data management, and data engineering software to manage data collected by their day-to-day businesses. However, these advanced technologies do not prevent from collecting and storing some faulty data – mainly with typing errors, outdated, and duplicated, e.g., [73]. Such data mainly concern customers, both individuals and institutions. Further in this section I'm focusing on data deduplicating customer records, based on my experience from running a project for a bank. I'm also giving my subjective opinion on the difficulty of applying research solutions to a commercial project in the financial sector.

3.1   Standard Data Deduplication Pipeline

The research community has proposed a standard data deduplication pipeline (DDP), which has been used in multiple research data deduplication projects, e.g., [21,26,47,62,63]. This DDP includes four basic tasks, namely: blocking, block processing, entity matching, and entity clustering.

The blocking task (a.k.a. indexing) divides records into groups, such that each group is likely to include duplicates. This task aims at reducing the quadratic computational complexity of data deduplication. The block processing task (a.k.a. filtering) eliminates from groups records that do not have to be compared, thus further reducing processing time. Entity matching (a.k.a. similarity computation) computes similarity values between record pairs being compared, based on some similarity measures. Finally, entity clustering merges pairs of similar records into larger groups. These groups of similar records are typically represented as graphs, whose nodes are records and labeled edges represent similarity values.

Despite the fact that the standard DDP covers the whole deduplication process, it is based on three important assumptions (or limitations), which are discussed in this section.

Assumption 1: Cleaned Data. The standard DDP assumes that data delivered to the pipeline are clean (e.g., no null values, no spelling errors, homogenized full names and abbreviations). Unfortunately, this assumption in real projects cannot be guaranteed, especially in the financial sector. In a large financial institution (FI), cleaning and deduplicating applies to several millions or dozens of millions customer records. Each customer is described by at least 20–30 core attributes that are used in the deduplication process. Inevitable typos, missing values, inconsistent values exist in attribute values storing personal data, institution names, and addresses. On top of it, some unique IDs include erroneous values. For large data sets it is impossible to perfectly clean all erroneous data (at least within a reasonable time). Moreover, by regulations, even known erroneous customers data cannot be cleaned without an explicitly permission of a customer. Getting such permissions from millions of customers in a finite time frame is impossible. For this reason, only simple cleaning is possible, like: (1) removing leading or trailing erroneous characters from customers addresses, (2) removing obvious typing errors from first names, (3) removing obvious typing errors from street and city names, or (4) homogenizing street names and zip codes. For this reason, in practice, the deduplication pipeline has to be applied to data that have undergone only basic cleaning.

Assumption 2: DDP Testing. Most of the methods used in the standard DDP were verified on either small real data sets, e.g., bibliographical with 32000 records [7,22,43,69,72], restaurants - 500 records [22,43], movies - 5000 records [72], patients - 128000 records [32], or on data sets generated artificially [7,23]. The exception is [52] where the authors discuss reproducibility experiments on data set of 2M rows. This size, however is still at least one order of magnitude smaller than the size of data deduplicated in real industry projects.

Assumption 3: DDP Parameter Tuning. Some tasks in the standard DDP are guided by parameters, whose settings typically have impact on the deduplication process efficiency and quality. These tasks are as follows:

- Selecting attributes used for dividing records into groups - such attributes are crucial for co-locating similar records close to each other.
- Selecting attributes whose values will be compared in record pairs - these attributes must allow to identify real world objects, ideally they should contain error-free not null values, and their values should not change over time.
- Selecting the most adequate similarity measures for given attributes - the literature lists well over 30 different similarity measures for text data, e.g., [20,57], where different measures are applicable to specific text data, e.g., [1,12,19,20]. Moreover, in Python packages there are available more than 40 implementations of these measures [11]. Notice that some measures are implemented in different packages. As a consequence, their similarity values and computation time differ when run on the same data. A challenge here is to select the most adequate measure to given text values being compared.
- Defining importance (weights) of compared attributes - some attributes contribute more to record similarity than others; for example, last name is more important (usually more clean and not null) than an email address (frequently null and changing in time). For this reason, similarity values of compared attributes must be weighted, but setting adequate weights is not trivial.
- Defining similarity thresholds for matching, probably matching, and non-matching records - these thresholds impact the number of true positives and false negatives. Again, setting an adequate values of these thresholds is challenging. It is typically based on experiments, expert knowledge, and an iterative tuning process.
- Selecting a method for comparing records - it impacts the performance of the whole process. Two frequently used methods include: hashing and comparing in a sliding window. However, defining the size of the sliding window is challenging. Too small window may prevent from discovering all potential duplicates, whereas too large window will cause time overhead caused by comparing non-matching records.
- Selecting an algorithm for building graphs of similar records - multiple algorithms were proposed for this step and they differ in complexities and output produced. Again, selecting the right algorithm for a given data set is challenging.

3.2   Machine Learning in Data Deduplication Pipeline

Some tasks in the DDP can be run with the support of machine learning (ML) techniques, e.g., blocking [27,54], selecting similarity measures and thresholds [8], matching similar records [55,61]. If the pipeline applies ML, it is assumed that there exists a set of training records tagged as: true matches, probable matches, non-matches. It is tacitly assumed that the set is large enough for a given ML problem. Unfortunately, in a large FI it is impossible to create such a training set with a sufficient number of samples, because of the volume of data to be processed by the pipeline is very large. For an original data set composed of 10M of records, a training data set of a reasonable size should include at least 10% the original set. In reality, such a large number of training records is impossible to be created by experts. For this reason, in practice, only small training data sets are available. As a consequence, produced ML models may offer poor prediction capacities.

To overcome this problem, a weakly supervised learning is suggested, e.g., [58]. Its overall idea is to build a set of representative rules for tagging records, based on a sample data set. Iterative rule testing and tuning is necessary, before constructing a production set of rules. Next, the rules are applied to automatically tag new records. Assuming that these records are tagged correctly, a large training set is produced for a ML algorithm (e.g., classification). A model is learned from this automatically tagged data set. Once the final model is built, it is applied to the remaining non-tagged data set.

However, manually building rules for the weakly supervised learning is difficult and very time expensive, as a representative set of rules for a data set composed of 1M customer records may reach a few hundreds. Managing such a large set of rules by a human is impossible. This is the main limitation of the weakly supervised approach.

Other approaches suggest to use in a DPP unsupervised learning techniques, e.g., [6,29], active learning techniques, e.g., [15,18,38,53,70], or BERT-based techniques [60,64].

3.3   Final Remarks

First of all, a DDP applied in an industrial project has to fulfill some requirements of a company w.r.t. to techniques and software used, e.g.:

- a DDP has to accept partially dirty data, since it is impossible to perfectly clean millions of rows within a limited time;
- processed data must be accessible either from a relational database or from files (csv, xls); for verification purposes by company experts, discovered sets of duplicates are preferred to be delivered in a spreadsheet format (typically Excel);
- developed algorithms and models have to be easy to implement by the IT staff, ideally they should be based on out-of-the-box software components;
- algorithms, models, and software developed in a DDP have to be intuitive and understandable by a company technical IT;

- the whole DDP has to be efficient, since it will be applied to at least several millions of rows;
- the produced software has to be deployable in an IT architecture used by a company (specific hardware and software);
- only licensed software can be used (especially in banks and other financial institutions); if a software is open licence, then it has to be certified by a security department - this fact limits the set of tools and libraries that can be applied.

Second, of all, it must be stressed that the exact number of duplicated records is unknown for a big company. Typically, only some rough estimates are known. For this reason, it is impossible to verify whether all duplicates were found. This industrial reality is distant from the research reality.

Finally, a substantial problem in using supervised ML algorithms in a DDP is that adequately large training data sets are typically unavailable. Even though, such data sets can be produced by the weakly supervised learning, the quality of these sets may be far from being perfect. As mentioned before, these sets are produced by a tagging system that depends on rules. These rules do not cover the whole original data set and are created by humans, thus are error-prone.

Aging of values, e.g., addresses, telephone numbers, email addresses, makes the data deduplication problem even more challenging. For example, two customer records having the same first and last names but different addresses may be either two different physical persons or the same person who changed the address. To the best of my knowledge, none of the DDP developed so far takes this phenomenon into account.

4   Challenge 3: Integrating Medical Data

Medical data linked to patient personal data are typically stored in a healthcare information system (HIS) [14]. Multiple commercial and open licence HISs are available on the market. As in other business domains, multiple HISs are used in the same medical center, and therefore data integration is pertinent to such systems as well. In this section I'm outlining a common IT landscape and problems that it causes. These observations are based on my experience of being a consultant in a big private hospital.

A common landscape in hospitals is that they have deployed multiple heterogeneous HISs, delivered and deployed by different software houses. These systems are closed, as the result of policies of software houses. As a consequence, they do not allow to migrate data and it is almost impossible to make them interoperable at a reasonable monetary costs. Such an environment is inefficient w.r.t., systems performance and human performance.

Medical data include a plethora of formats, like: (1) structured electronic patient medical record, (2) partially structured or unstructured short and long texts, e.g., medical interviews, (3) multiple types of medical images, typically in the DCOM format, e.g., X-ray, CT, MRI, ultrasound. Medical images are typically stored in a picture archiving and communication system (PACS) [17], but again, usually multiple PACS from different vendors are deployed in the same hospital, making the interoperability challenging.

The highest priorities of a hospital management are to: (1) make their internal systems interoperable within the same hospital, (2) make the systems interoperable between multiple medical centers, (3) provide an integrated repository of all data collected with in a hospital, in order to obtain a $360\,°C$ view on a patient. To this end, a data lake and a data warehouse architectures need to be deployed. As mentioned before, integrating structured data has been researched and developed for decades. However, much less have been achieved so far in the area of warehousing medical images. In this context, multiple challenges are still waiting to be solved, including: (1) providing efficient storage for medical images, (2) providing tools for efficient searching large repositories of images, (3) providing tools for correlating, medical images, structured medical records, and unstructured data on a patient.

References

1. Alamuri, M., Surampudi, B.R., Negi, A.: A survey of distance/similarity measures for categorical data. In: International Joint Conference on Neural Networks (IJCNN), pp. 1907–1914 (2014)
2. Ali, S.M.F., Wrembel, R.: From conceptual design to performance optimization of ETL workflows: current state of research and open problems. VLDB J. **26**(6), 777–801 (2017). https://doi.org/10.1007/s00778-017-0477-2
3. Ali, S.M.F., Wrembel, R.: Towards a Cost model to optimize user-defined functions in an ETL workflow based on user-defined performance metrics. In: Welzer, T., Eder, J., Podgorelec, V., Kamišalić Latifić, A. (eds.) ADBIS 2019. LNCS, vol. 11695, pp. 441–456. Springer, Cham (2019). https://doi.org/10.1007/978-3-030-28730-6_27
4. Ali, S.M.F., Wrembel, R.: Framework to optimize data processing pipelines using performance metrics. In: Song, M., Song, I.-Y., Kotsis, G., Tjoa, A.M., Khalil, I. (eds.) DaWaK 2020. LNCS, vol. 12393, pp. 131–140. Springer, Cham (2020). https://doi.org/10.1007/978-3-030-59065-9_11
5. Azzini, A., et al.: Advances in data management in the big data era. In: Goedicke, M., Neuhold, E., Rannenberg, K. (eds.) Advancing Research in Information and Communication Technology. IFIP AICT, vol. 600, pp. 99–126. Springer, Cham (2021). https://doi.org/10.1007/978-3-030-81701-5_4
6. Bhattacharya, I., Getoor, L.: A latent Dirichlet model for unsupervised entity resolution. In: SIAM International Conference on Data Mining, pp. 47–58. SIAM (2006)
7. Bilenko, M., Kamath, B., Mooney, R.J.: Adaptive blocking: learning to scale up record linkage. In: IEEE International Conference on Data Mining (ICDM), pp. 87–96 (2006)
8. Bilenko, M., Mooney, R.J.: Adaptive duplicate detection using learnable string similarity measures. In: ACM SIGKDD International Conference on Knowledge Discovery and Data Mining, pp. 39–48 (2003)
9. Bodziony, M., Morawski, R., Wrembel, R.: Evaluating push-down on nosql data sources: experiments and analysis paper. In: International Workshop on Big Data in Emergent Distributed Environments (BiDEDE), in conjunction with IGMOD/PODS, pp. 4:1–4:6 (2022)

10. Bodziony, M., Roszyk, S., Wrembel, R.: On evaluating performance of balanced optimization of ETL processes for streaming data sources. In: DOLAP. CEUR Workshop Proceedings, vol. 2572, pp. 74–78 (2020)
11. Boinski, P., Sienkiewicz, M, Bebel, B., Wrembel, R., Galezowski, D., Graniszewski, W.: On customer data deduplication: Lessons learned from a r&d project in the financial sector. In Workshops of the EDBT/ICDT Joint Conference. CEUR Workshop Proceedings, vol. 3135 (2022)
12. Boriah, S., Chandola, V., Kumar, V.: Similarity measures for categorical data: a comparative evaluation. In: SIAM International Conference on Data Mining (SDM), pp. 243–254 (2008)
13. Bouguettaya, A., Benatallah, B., Elmargamid, A.: Interconnecting Heterogeneous Information Systems. Kluwer Academic Publishers (1998). ISBN 0792382161
14. Brook, C.: What is a health information system? DataGuardian (2020). http:// digitalguardian.com/blog/what-health-information-system
15. Brunner, U., Stockinger, K.: Entity matching on unstructured data: an active learning approach. In: Swiss Conference on Data Science SDS, pp. 97–102 (2019)
16. Ceravolo, P., et al.: Big data semantics. J. Data Semant. **7**(2), 65–85 (2018)
17. Charles, M.: Pacs. TechTarget. http://searchhealthit.techtarget.com/definition/ picture-archiving-and-communication-system-PACS
18. Chen, X., Xu, Y., Broneske, D., Durand, G.C., Zoun, R., Saake, G.: Heterogeneous committee-based active learning for entity resolution (HeALER). In: Welzer, T., Eder, J., Podgorelec, V., Kamišalić Latifić, A. (eds.) ADBIS 2019. LNCS, vol. 11695, pp. 69–85. Springer, Cham (2019). https://doi.org/10.1007/978-3-030-28730-6_5
19. Christen, P.: A comparison of personal name matching: techniques and practical issues. In: International Conference on Data Mining (ICDM), pp. 290–294 (2006)
20. Christen, P.: Data Matching - Concepts and Techniques for Record Linkage, Entity Resolution, and Duplicate Detection. Springer, Data-Centric Systems and Applications (2012)
21. Christophides, V., Efthymiou, V., Palpanas, T., Papadakis, G., Stefanidis, K.: An overview of end-to-end entity resolution for big data. ACM Comput. Surv. **53**(6), 127:1–127:42 (2021)
22. Cohen, W.W., Richman, J.: Learning to match and cluster large high-dimensional data sets for data integration. In: ACM SIGKDD International Conference on Knowledge Discovery and Data Mining, pp. 475–480 (2002)
23. de Souza Silva, L., Murai, F., da Silva, A.P.C., Moro, M.M.: Automatic identification of best attributes for indexing in data deduplication. In: Mendelzon, A. (ed.) International Workshop on Foundations of Data Management. CEUR Workshop Proceedings. vol. 2100 (2018)
24. Dremio. The next-generation cloud data lake: An open, no-copy data architecture (2021). http://www.hello.dremio.com/wp-the-next-generation-cloud-data-lake.html
25. Elmagarmid, A., Rusinkiewicz, M., Sheth, A.: Management of Heterogeneous and Autonomous Database Systems. Morgan Kaufmann Publishers (1999). ISBN 1-55860-216-X
26. Elmagarmid, A.K., Ipeirotis, P.G., Verykios, V.S.: Duplicate record detection: a survey. IEEE Trans. Knowl. Data Eng. **19**(1), 1–16 (2007)
27. Evangelista, L.O., Cortez, E., da Silva, A.S., Jr. W.M.: Adaptive and flexible blocking for record linkage tasks. J. Inf. Data Manage. **1**(2), 167–182 (2010)
28. Gartner. Magic quadrant for data integration tools (2022)

29. Gheini, M., Kejriwal, M.: Unsupervised product entity resolution using graph representation learning. In: SIGIR Workshop on eCommerce @ ACM SIGIR International Conference on Research and Development in Information Retrieval. CEUR Workshop Proceedings, vol. 2410 (2019)
30. Hameed, M., Naumann, F.: Data preparation: a survey of commercial tools. SIGMOD Record **49**(3), 18–29 (2020)
31. Heidsieck, G., de Oliveira, D., Pacitti, E., Pradal, C., Tardieu, F., Valduriez, P.: Distributed caching of scientific workflows in multisite cloud. In: Hartmann, S., Küng, J., Kotsis, G., Tjoa, A.M., Khalil, I. (eds.) DEXA 2020. LNCS, vol. 12392, pp. 51–65. Springer, Cham (2020). https://doi.org/10.1007/978-3-030-59051-2_4
32. Hernández, M.A., Stolfo, S.J.: Real-world data is dirty: data cleansing and the merge/purge problem. Data Mining Knowl. Discov. **2**(1), 9–37 (1998)
33. Hueske, F., et al.: Peeking into the optimization of data flow programs with mapreduce-style udfs. In: International Conference Data Engineering (ICDE), pp. 1292–1295 (2013)
34. Hueske, F., et al.: Opening the black boxes in data flow optimization. VLDB Endowment **5**(11), 1256–1267 (2012)
35. IBM. IBM InfoSphere DataStage Balanced Optimization. (IBM Whitepaper, Accessed on 18/03/2019)
36. Informatica. How to Achieve Flexible, Cost-effective Scalability and Performance through Pushdown Processing. http://www.informatica.com/downloads/pushdown_wp_6650_web.pdf
37. Ryan, U.B.J.: A comparison of cloud data warehouse platforms, 2019. Sonora Intelligence. http://www.datamation.com/cloud-computing/top-cloud-data-warehouses.html
38. Jain, A., Sarawagi, S., Sen, P.: Deep indexed active learning for matching heterogeneous entity representations. VLDB Endowment **15**(1), 31–45 (2021)
39. Jarke, M., Lenzerini, M., Vassiliou, Y., Vassiliadis, P.: Fundamentals of Data Warehouses. Springer (2003)
40. Jemmali, R., Abdelhédi, F., Zurfluh, G.: Dltodw: transferring relational and nosql databases from a data lake. SN Comput. Sci. **3**(5), 381 (2022)
41. Jin, X., Wah, B.W., Cheng, X., Wang, Y.: Significance and challenges of big data research. Big Data Res. **2**(2), 59–64 (2015)
42. Karagiannis, A., Vassiliadis, P., Simitsis, A.: Scheduling strategies for efficient ETL execution. Inf. Syst. **38**(6), 927–945 (2013)
43. Kejriwal, M., Miranker, D.P.: An unsupervised algorithm for learning blocking schemes. In: IEEE International Conference on Data Mining, pp. 340–349 (2013)
44. Kerner, S.: Top 8 cloud data warehouses, 2019. Datamation (2019). http://www.datamation.com/cloud-computing/top-cloud-data-warehouses.html
45. King, T.: Top 12 free and open source etl tools for data integration. Solution Review (2019). http://solutionsreview.com/data-integration/top-free-and-open-source-etl-tools-for-data-integration/
46. Konstantinou, N., Paton, N.W.: Feedback driven improvement of data preparation pipelines. Inf. Syst. **92**, 101480 (2020)
47. Köpcke, H., Rahm, E.: Frameworks for entity matching: a comparison. Data Knowl. Eng. **69**(2), 197–210 (2010)
48. LaPlante, A.: Building a unified data infrastructure, 2020. O'Reilly whitepaper
49. Lella, R.: Optimizing BDFS jobs using InfoSphere DataStage Balanced Optimization. IBM Developer Works white paper (2014)

50. Lerner, A., Hussein, R., Ryser, A., Lee, S., Cudré-Mauroux, P.: Networking and storage: The next computing elements in exascale systems? IEEE Data Eng. Bull. **43**(1), 60–71 (2020)
51. Liu, X., Iftikhar, N.: An ETL optimization framework using partitioning and parallelization. In: ACM Symposium on Applied Computing, pp. 1015–1022 (2015)
52. Mandilaras, G.M., et al.: Reproducible experiments on three-dimensional entity resolution with jedai. Inf. Syst. **102**, 101830 (2021)
53. Meduri, V.V., Popa, L., Sen, P., Sarwat, M.: A comprehensive benchmark framework for active learning methods in entity matching. In: SIGMOD International Conference on Management of Data, pp. 1133–1147 (2020)
54. Michelson, M., Knoblock, C.A.: Learning blocking schemes for record linkage. In: National Conference on Artificial Intelligence and Innovative Applications of Artificial Intelligence Conference, pp. 440–445 (2006)
55. S. Mudgal, S., et al.: Deep learning for entity matching: a design space exploration. In: SIGMOD International Conference on Management of Data, pp. 19–34 (2018)
56. Nargesian, F., Zhu, E., Miller, R.J., Pu, K.Q., Arocena, P.C.: Data lake management: challenges and opportunities. VLDB Endowment **12**(12), 1986–1989 (2019)
57. Naumann, F.: Similarity measures. Hasso Plattner Institut (2013)
58. Nodet, P., Lemaire, V., Bondu, A., Cornuéjols, A., Ouorou, A.: From weakly supervised learning to biquality learning: an introduction. In: International Joint Conference on Neural Networks (IJCNN), pp. 1–10 (2021)
59. Owaida, M., Alonso, G., Fogliarini, L., Hock-Koon, A., Melet, P.: Lowering the latency of data processing pipelines through FPGA based hardware acceleration. VLDB Endowment **13**(1), 71–85 (2019)
60. Paganelli, M., Buono, F.D., Baraldi, A., Guerra, F.: Analyzing how BERT performs entity matching. VLDB Endowment **15**(8), 1726–1738 (2022)
61. Paganelli, M., Buono, F.D., Pevarello, M., Guerra, F., Vincini, M.: Automated machine learning for entity matching tasks. In: International Conference on Extending Database Technology EDBT, pp. 325–330 (2021)
62. Papadakis, G., Skoutas, D., Thanos, E., Palpanas, T.: Blocking and filtering techniques for entity resolution: a survey. ACM Comput. Surv. **53**(2), 31:1–31:42 (2020)
63. Papadakis, G., Tsekouras, L., Thanos, E., Giannakopoulos, G., Palpanas, T., Koubarakis, M.: Domain- and structure-agnostic end-to-end entity resolution with jedai. SIGMOD Record **48**(4), 30–36 (2019)
64. Peeters, R., Bizer, C.: Dual-objective fine-tuning of BERT for entity matching. VLDB Endowment **14**(10), 1913–1921 (2021)
65. Rheinländer, A., Heise, A., Hueske, F., Leser, U., Naumann, F.: Sofa: an extensible logical optimizer for udf-heavy data flows. Inf. Syst. **52**, 96–125 (2015)
66. Romero, O., Wrembel, R.: Data engineering for data science: two sides of the same coin. In: Song, M., Song, I.-Y., Kotsis, G., Tjoa, A.M., Khalil, I. (eds.) DaWaK 2020. LNCS, vol. 12393, pp. 157–166. Springer, Cham (2020). https://doi.org/10.1007/978-3-030-59065-9_13
67. Russom, P.: Data lakes: purposes, practices, patterns, and platforms (2017). TDWI white paper
68. Russom, P.: Modernizing the logical data warehouse, 2019. TDWI white paper. http://tdwi.org/articles/2019/10/14/dwt-all-modernizing-the-logical-data-warehouse.aspx
69. Sarawagi, S., Bhamidipaty, A.: Interactive deduplication using active learning. In: ACM SIGKDD International Conference on Knowledge Discovery and Data Mining, pp. 269–278 (2002)

70. Sariyar, M., Borg, A., Pommerening, K.: Active learning strategies for the dedu-
    plication of electronic patient data using classification trees. J. Biomed. Inf. **45**(5),
    893–900 (2012)
71. ScienceSoft. Data warehouse in the cloud: features, important integrations, success
    factors, benefits and more. http://www.scnsoft.com/analytics/data-warehouse/
    cloud
72. Shen, W., Li, X., Doan, A.: Constraint-based entity matching. In: Nat. Confer-
    ence on Artificial Intelligence and Innovative Applications of Artificial Intelligence
    Conference, pp. 862–867 (2005)
73. Sienkiewicz, M., Wrembel, R.: Managing data in a big financial institution: con-
    clusions from a r&d project. In: Workshops of the EDBT/ICDT Joint Conference.
    CEUR Workshop Proceedings, vol. 2841 (2021)
74. Simitsis, A., Vassiliadis, P., Sellis, T.K.: Optimizing ETL processes in data ware-
    houses. In: International Conference on Data Engineering (ICDE), pp. 564–575.
    IEEE Computer Society (2005)
75. Simitsis, A., Vassiliadis, P., Sellis, T.K.: State-space optimization of ETL work-
    flows. IEEE Trans. Knowl. Data Eng. **17**(10), 1404–1419 (2005)
76. Soliman, M.A., et al.: A framework for emulating database operations in cloud data
    warehouses. In: International Conference on Management of Data (SIGMOD), pp.
    1447–1461 (2020)
77. Stefanowski, J., Krawiec, K., Wrembel, R.: Exploring complex and big data. Int.
    J. Appl. Math. Comput. Sci. **27**(4), 669–679 (2017)
78. Friedman, N.H.T.: Data hubs, data lakes and data warehouses: how they are dif-
    ferent and why they are better together. Gartner (2020)
79. Tan, R., Chirkova, R., Gadepally, V., Mattson, T.G.: Enabling query processing
    across heterogeneous data models: a survey. In: IEEE International Conference on
    Big Data, pp. 3211–3220. IEEE Computer Society (2017)
80. Terrizzano, I.G., Schwarz, P.M., Roth, M., Colino, J.E.: Data wrangling: the chal-
    lenging yourney from the wild to the lake. In: Conference on Innovative Data
    Systems Research (CIDR) (2015)
81. Thomsen, C.: ETL. In: Encyclopedia of Big Data Technologies. Springer (2019)
82. Vaisman, A.A., Zimányi, E.: Data Warehouse Systems - Design and Implementa-
    tion. Springer, Data-Centric Systems and Applications (2014)
83. Wiederhold, G.: Mediators in the architecture of future information systems. Com-
    puter **25**(3), 38–49 (1992)
84. Witt, C., Bux, M., Gusew, W., Leser, U.: Predictive performance modeling for
    distributed batch processing using black box monitoring and machine learning.
    Inf. Syst. **82**, 33–52 (2019)
85. Wrembel, R., Abelló, A., Song, I.: DOLAP data warehouse research over two
    decades: trends and challenges. Inf. Syst. **85**, 44–47 (2019)

Aspects of Using Telepresence Robot in a Higher Education STEAM Workshop

Janika Leoste[1,2(✉)] , Sirje Virkus[2] , Tiina Kasuk[1], Aleksei Talisainen[1] ,
Katrin Kangur[1], and Piedad Tolmos[3]

[1] Tallinn University of Technology, Tallinn, Estonia
janika.leoste@taltech.ee
[2] School of Digital Technologies, Tallinn University, Tallinn, Estonia
[3] Universidad Rey Juan Carlos, Calle Tulipán, s/n, Móstoles, 28933 Madrid, Spain

Abstract. Telepresence robots (TPRs) are becoming increasingly popular in education as they support social presence (an important component of human communication) of teachers and students. This paper presents the results of a study that explored the challenges of using a telepresence robot in a higher education STEAM workshop through the eyes of a teacher, telepresence robot mediated persons and physically present students. We identified crucial aspects that need to be addressed when involving telepresence robots in the hybrid teaching and learning process. The perspectives of using TPRs were mostly positive. However, technical support and changes in classroom practices are needed for successful use of TPRs in the teaching and learning process. Although TPRs enable greater social presence, the technology is still novel and its successful implementation requires more research, focusing on applying effective pedagogical design principles and adapting the environment accordingly to the conditions necessary for the successful operation of the TPRs. The TPR's passenger option did not yield positive results in our research. This caused the participants to become detached from what was happening in the classroom, feel unable to control the situation, and supported social presence even less than using teleconference-based distance learning methods.

Keywords: Telepresence robot · Social presence · Distance learning · Hybrid teaching · Emergency remote learning

1 Introduction

Synchronous hybrid learning is a technology-rich approach to deliver comparable, shared, and collaborative learning experiences to face-to-face and online participants in real time [1]. A synthesis of ten years (1996–2008) of research on online learning suggests that hybrid learning, combining the methods of face-to-face and online learning, is the most promising approach to higher education [2, 3]. However, a challenge to successfully implementing hybrid instruction is that social presence (i.e., students' ability to project their personal characteristics into the learning space) is reduced with potential negative effects on student engagement, persistence, and academic achievement [3].

E. Pardede et al. (Eds.): iiWAS 2022, LNCS 13635, pp. 18–28, 2022.
https://doi.org/10.1007/978-3-031-21047-1_2

For example, remote virtual students sense being easily forgotten by those physically present, they miss the informal pre- and after-lesson classroom conversations and they sometimes feel the need to apologize when they want to contribute to what is happening in the physical space [4]. One way to deal with these challenges is to use Telepresence Robots (TPRs) in the teaching and learning process. In this paper, we examine the various challenges of TPR use in a synchronous hybrid higher education STEAM workshop and discuss addressing these in order to contribute to successful implementation of TPRs in the teaching and learning process.

Telepresence is defined in this study as the feeling of being fully present at a remote location away from one's own physical location. Telepresence uses technology to create, based on a real physical location, a simulated or virtual environment for the telepresent user [5]. A telepresence robot is a remote-controlled movable wheeled device, equipped with speakers, microphones, a screen, cameras, sensor-assisted motion control, and other interactive features, which are especially designed for communicating and collaborating remotely [6, 7]. A remote user can log into the TPR to control it via a computer, tablet or smartphone and to experience the on-site surroundings on the screen. The users' face is projected directly onto the TPR's screen that allows the on-site persons to interact with the TPR-mediated person (TMP) face-to-face, creating a remote telepresence [8].

TPRs are becoming increasingly popular in education [9, 10] due to their cost effectiveness (based on savings in time and traveling costs), the possibility of using them during certain emergency remote learning situations [11], and their ability to enable enhanced communication and social presence [12, 13]. Garrison [14] describes social presence "*as the ability to project one's self and establish personal and purposeful relationships.*" Several authors have noted that compared to video-conferencing solutions, TPRs offer several advantages, including improved social presence [4, 15, 16]. Participants interacting via a TPR experience a greater sense of togetherness and being together in one room [17]. In addition, TPRs can enable otherwise impossible interaction with the remote environment [18] during the emergency remote learning situations [11]. The results of [19] imply that although students who used TPRs experienced a stronger sense of social presence, their interaction partners perceived them as more robotic (i.e., robomorphism). However, the negative effects of robomorphism were compensated by the positive effects through social presence.

The perspectives of using TPRs in education are mostly positive. Previous research on TPRs in education has shown that TPRs can promote social interaction and collaborative learning through incorporating the social dimension into the learning process, enabling students to participate in-person in teamwork and navigate through remote learning environments [8]. Bell et al. [4] demonstrated that the mobility of TPRs is essential to create a sense of physical presence. Cheung et al. [20] highlighted the benefits in implementing TPRs at the Michigan State University: (1) Persistence and retention – TPRs help students remain successful in their classes by providing an easy option to overcome challenging circumstances; (2) Student empowerment – TPRs empower students who experience setbacks and other serious life challenges, allowing them demonstrate their commitment to learning; (3) Comparable learning experiences – TPRs facilitate active participation and peer interactions during class; (4) Easy implementation – TPRs offer a flexible, affordable, and simple solution that is relatively easy to implement by students and instructors; (5) Minimal impact on instructors – although instructors require some training to integrate the system into their classroom, its actual use is typically easier than extending deadlines, changing assignments, or scheduling alternate exam days; and (6) Empowerment for student-support personnel – TPRs enable immediate, short-term assistance for students who were experiencing temporary setbacks, empowering personnel to help students who may have had no other options. Through improved social presence, TPRs can improve learner engagement, interest, confidence, motivation in classroom settings, by allowing teachers to teach lessons and students to participate in classes from anywhere [8].

The main drawbacks are the technological and functional shortcomings of TPRs such as their connectivity issues, maneuverability, the quality of audio/video, power consumption and battery, adjustable height, system stability, low-speed control, and motion control for slopes and sudden inclines. More work is required to improve the safety of TPRs [13]. Some research findings have shown that teachers may resist the use of TPRs due to perceived inconsistencies with their existing teaching and learning practices and perceived usefulness [21, 22]. Convincing teachers to adopt new technologies requires a good understanding of teachers' perspectives [23]. Introducing a new technology and the accompanying methods into the existing teaching practices of the universities requires introducing the technology to the teaching staff, gathering their feedback and preparing an implementation plan that takes into account the needs of the teaching staff [8].

Based on the above, this research aimed to identify the crucial aspects that need to be addressed when involving telepresence robots in the hybrid teaching and learning process. The research process was guided by the following research question:

What are the aspects of a TMP attending a hands-on higher education STEAM workshop, as perceived by TMPs, PPSs and physically present teachers?

This case study describes the experience of using a telepresence robot in a STEAM workshop, the challenges that were encountered and possible remedies to some of these challenges, and the lessons that were learned along the way.

2   Method

The study sample was made of three different sub-groups: (a) Physically Present Students (PPSs); (b) TPR-mediated persons (TMPs); and (c) a teacher conducting the workshop. The sub-sample of PPSs consisted of 10 Higher Education Master's degree level students who participated in the first workshop of the course "Robot integrated learning in the early childhood and primary education" in Tallinn University, Estonia. Six of the students were from Estonia and four were Erasmus exchange students from Germany and Switzerland. The TMPs were three authors of this paper: one from Spain and two from Estonia. One of the TMPs controlled the TPRs movement and her face was displayed on the robot's screen. The other two TMPs were using the TPR as "passengers" – they were able to see the robot's video stream, hear the primary TMP and classroom discussion. However, they were not able to control the robot's movement, their faces were not shown and it was agreed that they did not talk (in order to avoid confusing the PPPs). All the students saw a TPR for the first time, while two Estonian researchers had been using TPRs for a month for their research group meetings and the Spanish researcher had gotten three short training rounds on manipulating the robot. The teacher, who conducted the workshop, was from Estonia and she is one of the authors of this paper. She had more than six months of experience of using TPRs in different teaching, learning and meeting situations. The teacher was also an expert on the topic of the lesson.

The four-academic-hour STEAM workshop took place on a Saturday afternoon in September 2022, in Tallinn University's EDUSPACE research lab (Fig. 1). The TPR used in the study was the Double 3 TPR with automatic obstacle detection, regulated height and battery life of about 3 h. The tables and chairs of the lab were re-arranged by the teacher to free maximum floor space for the TPR to move while maintaining a comfortable group-work setting for four groups of students.

Fig. 1. The workshop setting in EDUSPACE.

The workshop was divided into 8 sections:

- getting to know each other;
- introducing the whole course content;
- a mini lecture about digital storytelling;
- learning to use the Ozobot educational robot and to design educational activities for early-childhood education;

- teamwork on designing an educational activity with the Ozobot robot (each student group had a table to use in the same room);
- short break;
- presentations of the teamwork, involving active movement in the room;
- mini lecture about the technical features of various educational robots;
- instructions about the homework.

The TPR robot was already working when the PPSs started to arrive at the lab. The TMP greeted them and tried to have some social small talk. There was no specific place determined for the TPR to stand during the workshop. In addition, no specific instructions were given to the TMPs, except to take part in the workshop activities as a student.

At the beginning of the workshop, the experiment was introduced to the PPSs and their oral permission to conduct the experiment (including being accompanied by the TPR-mediated students and filling in a survey about their perceived comfort) was asked. At the end of the workshop, a Microsoft Forms survey was sent to all PPSs to understand their perceptions about having a TPR-mediated co-student in the workshop. In addition, semi-structured Zoom interviews were conducted with the three TMPs and the physically present teacher two days after the workshop, in order to understand the different aspects of using a TPR robot in the workshop. The interviews were recorded and transcribed. Two researchers applied qualitative content analysis on the interview content, researching the common themes, and negotiating the differences.

3 Results

Our research question was "What are the aspects of a TMP attending a hands-on higher education STEAM workshop, as perceived by TMPs, PPSs and a physically present teacher?" To answer this question, we used PPSs' perceptions, gathered via an online query, and semi-structured interviews with TPMs and the teacher.

Most PPSs (9 students out of 10) felt comfortable when interacting with a TPR-mediated person: *"It was the first time I have seen a telepresence robot, so in the beginning I was quite confused. In the end I got used to it and respected the robot as a member of our group."* (ID 17).

Half of them (5) considered contacting robot-mediated persons easy, while the other half either had not formed their opinion on this matter or (one person) found it difficult (due to robomorphism): *"Sometimes it was difficult to communicate with the person, and sometimes I forgot that there was another person in the room behind the robot."* (ID 19).

In addition, more than half of PPSs (6) were able to understand when the TMP wanted their attention, whereas three of them had not formed their opinion on this or (one person) were not able to understand it: *"Couldn't answer the question about how well I could tell when a person was trying to contact me, as I never once noticed an attempt to contact me."* (ID 13).

The content analysis of the interviews of TMPs and the teacher revealed that all of them had used modern videoconferencing-based distance learning methods in their teaching practices. None of the TMPs had significant previous experience with TPRs, while the teacher had been experimenting with TPRs for about half a year. Based on the results of the analysis, we identified the following areas of challenges, benefits and limitations: (a) implementation challenges; (b) technical difficulties; (c) aspects related to social presence; and (d) various benefits.

TMPs and the teacher identified four main **implementation challenges**. All of them found that using a TPR in the lessons requires initial training, in-site support, and that most probably some time for getting adjusted to the technology is needed: *"I think that it is not very easy just to bring a robot to your class if you have no previous knowledge and experience of how to use it. It's like each technological tool."* (ID 2).

In addition, using TPRs could require teachers to either slightly adjust or, in some cases, radically change their teaching methods to keep the attention of PPSs, while allowing TMPs to participate: *"There may be some questions in the class and you have to remember all the time that you have to actually do things so that the students are also comfortable. But it also requires planning in the learning process, which tools to use."* (ID 3).

The teacher, who had more experience with teaching with TPR, highlighted the importance of preparing the classroom for using TPRs. These preparations include planning the activities in a way that the TPR-mediated students could participate as actively as possible, making sure that the needed driveways were free of cables or other obstacles, providing a charging station with longer activities, etc.: *"Since I have previous experience that it is not easy for the robot to move around between the tables, I planned with my colleague how the room could be arranged. We moved these desks next to the walls, so that there would be a lot of free space in the middle, so that this robot could move freely to everyone. I thought about where to place the charging socket. We picked up all the wires from the floor so that the robot would not get tangled in the wires."* (ID 4) These additional tasks contributed to the increase of the teacher's cognitive load.

The TPM's and the teacher identified various **technical difficulties** when using TPRs in teaching and learning. The TPR's audio quality was sometimes problematic, as it picked up the noise of the robot's motors, making it difficult to understand the discussion in these moments. This problem was more strongly perceived by the TPMs in the passenger role as they had no way to control the robot's movements, and, in addition, they heard the voice of the TPR's driver TPM at significantly higher volume than the classroom discussion: *"That I noticed that I had to constantly change the volume because I wanted to hear what was going on in the classroom, but at the same time, the person who was there [the TPR's driver], he was talking too loudly, so that it was necessary to intervene like that."* (ID 3).

Next, it was quoted that the visibility through the eyes of a TPR was not good enough to read what was written on the whiteboard, or to follow what the PPSs were doing during the teamwork: *"I saw only the left side of the whiteboard, so the right side was unreadable. It was some kind of lightning problem, so when the robot went closer, I still didn't see it."* (ID 2) Some TMPs speculated that these problems could be solved by adjusting the lighting conditions in the classroom or by using different teaching methods (for example, by sending the information directly to TPR-mediated students).

The Double 3 TPR that was used in the experiment lacks hands, limiting thus the ability of TMPs to participate in hands-on activities. This deficiency was noted by all the TMPs. In addition, the TPR was unable to participate in physical activities meaningfully (e.g., dance, jump): *"Another negative thing was that we had active movement, that, well, we have this early education stuff, that, well, we dance and sing with (toy) robots. Then you have to think about where this (telepresence) robot would be, since it obviously can't jump there? I don't think you can spin either."* (ID 4).

Also noted by all the TMPs were the interruptions in being present in the classroom, due to bad internet connection or the robot shutting down because of the low battery. It was especially difficult for the TMPs in the passenger role, as they could not do anything to re-establish the connection: *"For us the class was over when the battery ran out."* (ID 3).

Using a TPR provided the TMP who was driving the robot with better **social presence**, compared to using teleconference-based distance learning methods: *"For me, the most positive is the feeling that I was there, I was really there."* (ID 1) It was possible to move around the room or even to visit other rooms and to start conversations with people by just moving closer to them. However, compared to the traditional way of being physically present in the room, using a TPR involved some challenges. It was difficult to navigate in narrow spaces, especially as it was difficult to estimate properly the distance between objects or other people, as perceived by a student: *"As a person, I didn't feel her being present in class and it was strange when she was sometimes too close."* (ID 20) In addition, in a quieter classroom, the robot could disturb other students with its motors' noise or login ringing.

Social presence of the TMPs in the passenger role was problematic at least, as none could see them and, in addition, they could not see each other: *"I didn't see <NAME>. I knew that <NAME> had to be within the robot, but I didn't feel that she was there. Nobody introduced me, nobody knew that I was there. I hadn't any possibility to add something to the discussion. If we talk about social presence, then I didn't feel that I was present (at all)."* (ID 2).

Against the background of these several challenges listed above, the question arises as to which **benefits** TPRs offer. In the opinion of the teacher (ID 4), some of the benefits are apparent when weighed against the teleconference-based distance learning method. There is less cognitive load when checking if all students are following the lesson and it is easier to set up the room for the lesson. In addition, TPRs can enable education better in certain scenarios, for example, providing simulated physical presence for people with disabilities. In addition, in other scenarios, using TPRs can lead to savings in paid time and travelling expenses, for example, allowing teachers to give lessons at rural schools. As put by a TMP (ID 2): *"Each Monday we have these meetings and it takes time to go there and back. During this (travel) time I can do a lot of useful things, (for example) to write scientific articles and so on. I think that it saves a lot of time and also if you are really in some other country, you can also give your lectures to your students if you are not there. Also if there are some kind of illnesses, or such kinds of things, I think."*

Our results indicate that TPRs are accepted by students relatively easily. TPRs could allow saving time and money, and they would provide their users with good social presence in cases where physical participation is obstructed. However, some technical difficulties need to be addressed in the interest of smooth user experience. In addition, these technical challenges require teachers to spend more time preparing the classroom, and cause additional cognitive load when conducting lessons.

4 Discussion and Conclusion

This study explored the aspects that emerged from the use of TPRs in conducting a STEAM workshop in a higher education institution. In particular, we examined the general reaction of students to having a TPR in their class, the experience of TMPs who took part in the workshop via the TPR, and the feedback from the teacher who set up and conducted the workshop.

From the point of view of the students, it was considered convenient to participate in a class where TPRs is used. However, at least half of the PPSs in our experiment did not feel comfortable when making contact with a TMP or being approached by them. One participant in our experiment found that such contact could even be uncomfortable or alienating. The students' discomfort may have been influenced by the fact that they were unfamiliar with the TMP in our experiment. It would probably have been easier for the students to interact with the TMP if it had been another course mate they already knew or their teacher. However, this and similar challenges can be caused by wrongly chosen social distance. It is difficult for a TMP to estimate properly the distance between their robotic body and a physically present person. This can lead to unintentional violation of social norms [24]. However, the more time a TMP can spend in a given environment, the more accurate their estimates will be. To avoid these types of situations, it might be good to improve the TPR user interface with the ability to turn on distance numbers between objects and subjects in social and personal distance.

One of the major benefits of TPRs is providing their users with social presence – i.e., being socially present for their peers. In our experiment, we noticed that at least the person who was controlling the TPR felt that way. However, it was also found that TPR's "passenger" feature which allows multiple people to use a single TPR robot, should be used with caution, as it can lead to a sense of detachment from what is happening in class, a feeling of helplessness in controlling the TPR, and is likely to result in a less social presence than distance learning methods based on teleconferencing. On the other hand, there could be situations where the passenger feature is valuable – for example, if a teacher borrows a TPR from a local school to visit a local museum while she is on a trip. In this case, more students could benefit from a visit to the museum.

Using robots in teaching is not as simple as unboxing a TPR and starting to use it. The physical space must be configured to meet the characteristics of the TPR, creating movement corridors for the TPRs, offering the possibility to charge during the lesson (i.e., the charging socket must be located in a place where a TMP can observe what is happening in the lesson), and ensure a stable Internet connection. It is also necessary to provide the TMPs with digital/electronic possibilities that allow them to overcome the difficulties of not being able to write on the auditorium's blackboard or express their emotions using body language. In these cases, it could be appropriate to use a digital board and some additional devices that help them express themselves in a richer way – or allow them to take part in classroom discussions without interrupting others, allowing them to pose their questions to the teacher or to other students (i.e., simulate raising their hand). In addition, the TPR should have the ability to notify the audience if there is a problem with the TPR (such as a lack of battery power) in order to allow the TMP to continue attending the class, even if it is (e.g.) in a charging station. Our results also suggest that when conducting hands-on teaching and learning activities such as a STEAM workshop, TMPs need to be provided with appropriate beforehand training on controlling the TPR's different cameras and using zoom-in to better follow the hands-on activities. TMPs also need training to adjust the TPR's sound levels to suit group-work, informal conversation or presentations, and training to use the TPR microphone's boost options to hear better in different communication situations. In addition, TMPs need to become aware of the robot's battery life and plan using the charger to avoid battery drain. Teachers should also consider changing their teaching methods somewhat, especially in the classes that involve some physical activity or teamwork, in order to ensure that the TPR-mediated students could take part in the classroom activities similarly to PPSs. The presence of the TPR can sometimes disturb the concentration of physically present learners, e.g., due to the noise generated when the TPR moves. At least some additional rules should be introduced that ensure a proper classroom environment for teaching and learning (e.g. the TMPs could be asked to stand still while someone is speaking to the audience). To put it shortly, implementation of TPRs should follow a pre-planned innovation implementation process [25].

There is a need to think through the scenarios when the use of TPRs makes sense. Presumably, the TPRs can be almost useless when the whole educational institution is in distance mode, as their prices (about 7000 EUR per unit) do not justify providing all students with TPRs. After all, someone still has to be present to ensure charging and, if necessary, rescue intervention (e.g., if the robot falls down). On the other hand, the robot could support individual students or teachers who are not able to participate on site for good reasons. These reasons could involve COVID-like infectious diseases, permanent or temporary mobility disability, or participation from far away (from another city, country or rural area). In these cases, it is probably necessary to provide the TMPs with an assistant (e.g., a support student) who would carry the TPR over thresholds and stairs.

Our experiment provides an overview of the challenges and various aspects that must be taken into account when using a TPR. However, the sample of the experiment was rather small, and the TPR-mediated participants were not students but members of the research team. It was also a one-time experiment, where the lack of previous experience probably played some role in the students' attitude towards the TPR or in the TMPs' ability to handle the robot. Many of these limitations have been removed in a study that the authors are currently conducting at Tallinn University of Technology. We are using eight TPRs from October to November 2022 to allow students and teachers to participate in at least 30 regular lessons of the Information and Communication Technology and Social Sciences curricula. This currently conducted study should bring more understanding to the use of TPRs in higher education teaching and learning.

References

1. Cain, W., Bell, J., Cheng, C.: Implementing robotic telepresence in a synchronous hybrid course. In: 2016 IEEE 16th International Conference on Advanced Learning Technologies (ICALT) (2016)
2. Means, B., Toyama, Y., Murphy, R., Bakia, M., Jones, K.: Evaluation of evidence-based practices in online learning: a meta-analysis and review of online learning studies. U.S. Department of Education (2010)
3. Gleason, B., Greenhow, C.: Hybrid education: the potential of teaching and learning with robot-mediated communication. Online Learn. J. **21**(4), 159–176 (2017)
4. Bell, J.: Telepresence robots give distance students their own seat at the table. EdTech: Technology Solutions That Strive Education. EdTech (2017). https://edtechmagazine.com/higher/article/2017/03/telepresence-robots-give-distance-students-their-own-seat-table
5. El-Gayar, O., Chen, K., Tandekar, K.: Multimedia interactivity on the Internet. In: Pagani, M. (eds.) Encyclopedia of Multimedia Technology and Networking. Idea Group Inc., Hershey (2005)
6. Tuli, T.B., Terefe, T.O., Rashid, M.M.U.: Telepresence mobile robots design and control for social interaction. Int. J. Soc. Robot. **13**(5), 877–886 (2021)
7. Vaughn, J., Shaw, R.J., Molloy, M.A.: A telehealth case study: the use of telepresence robot for delivering integrated clinical care. J. Am. Psychiatr. Nurses Assoc. **21**(6), 431–432 (2015)
8. Leoste, J., Virkus, S., Talisainen, A., Tammemäe, K., Kangur, K., Petriashvili, I.: Higher education personnel's perceptions about telepresence robots. In: Computational Intelligence Advances in Educational Robotics (to be published, 2022)
9. Conti, D., Di Nuovo, S., Buono, S., Di Nuovo, A.: Robots in education and care of children with developmental disabilities: a study on acceptance by experienced and future professionals. Int. J. Soc. Robot. **9**(1), 51–62 (2017)
10. Reis, A., Martins, M., Martins, P., Sousa, J., Barroso, J.: Telepresence robots in the classroom: the state-of-the-art and a proposal for a telepresence service for higher education. In: Tsitouridou, M., A. Diniz, J., Mikropoulos, T.A. (eds.) TECH-EDU 2018. CCIS, vol. 993, pp. 539–550. Springer, Cham (2019). https://doi.org/10.1007/978-3-030-20954-4_41
11. Davey, R.: Telepresence robotics: an overview, AZO Robotics (2021). https://www.azorobotics.com/Article.aspx?ArticleID=414
12. Hickenbottom, K.G.: Almost Like Being There: Embodiment, Social Presence, and Engagement Using Telepresence Robots in Blended Courses (Doctoral dissertation, Seattle Pacific University) (2022)
13. Adalgeirsson, S.O., Breazeal, C.: MeBot: a robotic platform for socially embodied telepresence. In: 2010 5th ACM/IEEE International Conference on Human-Robot Interaction (HRI) (2010)
14. Garrison, D.R.: Online community of inquiry review: Social, cognitive, and teaching presence issues. J. Asynchronous Learn. Networks **11**(1), 61–72 (2007)
15. Shin, K.W.C., Han, J.: Children's perceptions of and interactions with a telepresence robot. In: 2016 11th ACM/IEEE International Conference on Human-Robot Interaction (HRI) (2016)
16. Keller, L., Pfeffel, K., Huffstadt, K., Müller, N.H.: Telepresence robots and their impact on human-human interaction. In: Zaphiris, P., Ioannou, A. (eds.) HCII 2020. LNCS, vol. 12206, pp. 448–463. Springer, Cham (2020). https://doi.org/10.1007/978-3-030-50506-6_31
17. Newhart, V.A., Warschauer, M., Sender, L.: Virtual inclusion via telepresence robots in the classroom: an exploratory case study. Int. J. Technol. Learn. **23**(4), 9–25 (2016). https://doi.org/10.18848/2327-0144/CGP/v23i04/9-25
18. Wernbacher, T., et al.: Trine: telepresence robots in education. In: Proceedings of INTED2022 Conference (2022). https://doi.org/10.21125/inted.2022.1653

19. Schouten, A.P., Portegies, T.C., Withuis, I., Willemsen, L.M., Mazerant-Dubois, K.: Robo-morphism: examining the effects of telepresence robots on between-student cooperation. Comput. Hum. Behav. **126**, 106980 (2022)
20. Cheung, D., Dykeman, T., Fell, C.: Using telepresence robots to support students facing adversity. Educause Rev. (2018). https://er.educause.edu/articles/2018/6/using-telepresence-robots-to-support-students-facing-adversity
21. Karypi, S.: Educational robotics application in primary and secondary education. A challenge for the Greek teachers' society. J. Contemporary Educ. Theory Res. **2**(1), 9–14 (2018)
22. Khanlari, A.: Teachers' perceptions of using robotics in primary/elementary schools in Newfoundland and Labrador (Doctoral dissertation, Memorial University of Newfoundland) (2014)
23. Miles, M.B., Huberman, A.M., Saldaña, J.: Qualitative Data Analysis: A Methods Source-book. Sage Publications, Los Angeles (2018)
24. Hall, E.: The Hidden Dimension. Anchor Books Editions, New York (1966)
25. Leoste, J., Heidmets, M., Ley, T., Stepanova, J.: Classroom innovation becoming sustainable: a study of technological innovation adoption by Estonian primary school teachers. Interact. Des. Archit. J. **47**, 144–166 (2021). https://doi.org/10.55612/s-5002-047-008

Business Data and Applications

An Analysis of Data Modelling for Blockchain

João Vicente Meyer⬤ and Ronaldo dos Santos Mello^(✉)⬤

Universidade Federal de Santa Catarina, PPGCC, Florianópolis, Brazil
1994meyer@gmail.com, r.mello@ufsc.br

Abstract. The popularity of blockchains has been steadily rising since the end of the 2001–2010 decade. Its original focus was the creation of a distributed trustless system for a digital currency. Bitcoin was the first widely used blockchain. However, many more have been further created: Ethereum, Solana, Hyperledger Fabric, IOTA, to name a few. Due to it, blockchain networks and its properties are being scrutinised by data scientists. This topic is known as blockchain analysis. However, analysis' tasks are hard to be accomplished over multiple blockchains. Even though most have similar concepts, each one has its own data modelled differently. As a consequence, scientists end up needing to do rework in order to apply similar analytics in more than one blockchain network. In fact, blockchain data modelling is an open issue. This paper researches the state-of-the-art on this issue. We also present a comparative analysis of the related work and suggest some directions for future researches.

Keywords: Blockchain · Data model · Ethereum · Bitcoin

1 Introduction

With the popularity of blockchain technologies, the world has seen the imagination of developers flourish with its many applications. Blockchain originated as a way to decentralise finances, with Bitcoin being the biggest and most successful example. However, with the advent of smart contract-based blockchains, like Ethereum, we have witnessed the creation of decentralised autonomous organisations (DAO), like Aragon[1], Maker[2] and The DAO[3], as well as decentralised exchanges, such as Uniswap[4], and full virtual worlds, like Decentraland[5].

Unfortunately, new technologies come with new and innovative ways to trick their users. The pseudo anonymity given by blockchains make them useful for illegal activities, most commonly ransomware and ponzi schemes. There are already many studies describing techniques for fraud detection [5], and de-anonymisation

---

[1] https://aragon.org.
[2] https://makerdao.com.
[3] https://github.com/blockchainsllc/DAO.
[4] https://uniswap.org.
[5] https://decentraland.org.

E. Pardede et al. (Eds.): iiWAS 2022, LNCS 13635, pp. 31–44, 2022.
https://doi.org/10.1007/978-3-031-21047-1_3

[19,30]. However, most studies focus on specific algorithms crafted for a single blockchain network. Although different blockchain implementations have different inner workings, the data they generate and the transactions between accounts are very similar. An unified data model would allow researchers to create algorithms that could be executed in different blockchains effortlessly and without rework for each different one.

Additionally, the research topic of blockchain analysis[6] [1,31], shows us that (old) new problems, such as fast data querying and management, arise from the volume of data generated by blockchain networks, where data is often *churned* in order to extract extra information from it. Some examples of applications are: (i) Detecting accounts used by the same user; (ii) Detecting account behaviours; (iii) Account clustering; (iv) Wealth movements; and others. Again, an unified data model would make algorithms for the aforementioned analysis work for multiple blockchains and would let researches focus more on the analysis itself instead of implementation details for manipulating different blockchains.

The main contribution of this paper is an original survey on the topic of blockchain data modelling. Even though there are surveys on the broad topic of blockchain, this study is the first one that focuses on how researchers are tackling data modelling issues in order to make blockchain information easier to understand and manipulate.

The rest of this paper is organised as follows. Section 2 introduces blockchain networks and some common blockchain data model concepts. Section 3 discusses surveys related to blockchain, and Sect. 4 describes the considered research protocol to select the state-of-the-art on the subject, as well as the search results. Section 5 summarises the selected studies. Section 6, in turn, accomplishes an analysis on the studies, and Sect. 7 is dedicated to the conclusion and suggestions for future research directions.

2   Background

This section presents some concepts that are related to this paper. It includes a basic description of a blockchain network, as well as short descriptions of the most popular ones. It also describes common blockchain data model concepts and the relationships among them.

2.1   Blockchain

Blockchains are peer-to-peer networks comprised of nodes that agree on an append-only data structure, usually a linked hash list. It is also commonly referred as an append-only *distributed ledger*. Figure 1 shows an example of such a structure. Each item appended to the ledger contains the hash of the previously appended one. This makes possible to verify all the data in the blockchain by analysing the hashes for each block. Trying to modify any data in the mid-

---

[6] Sometimes referenced as "blockchain analytics".

dle of this structure would result in the need to recalculate the hashes for all subsequent blocks.

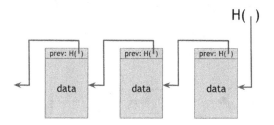

Fig. 1. A representation of a blockchain structure [18].

The technology of blockchain comes from the early 1990s[7] as a way to prevent tampering in time stamping digital files [7]. However, blockchains, as we know them today, first appeared in the Bitcoin paper of Nakamoto [17]. The crucial difference between modern blockchains and the one devised in the 1990s s is its network distribution and how the nodes agree between themselves using multiple consensus algorithms.

Newer networks, such as Ethereum [4], have popularised the use of smart contract-based blockchains. Smart contracts were first conceptualised by the work of Szabo [28]. It is based on the idea that if some network can agree on random pieces of data to be added to the list of blocks, then it can also validate computer program executions. Smart contracts provide a new paradigm where participants do not need to rely on any centralised third parties to "force" the execution of the contract's *clauses*. The whole network act as the "enforcer".

Some works also describe blockchains as a distributed append-only database management system (DBMS) [16]. However, it lacks many features of common DBMSs, such as powerful query processors. The reason behind this trade off is usually due to performance requirements. For the network to work, there is no need for complex queries. Instead, every value is identified by a key, usually a hash of the data being accessed. As a result, solutions make use of powerful key-value stores, most notably LevelDB[8], used by Bitcoin, Ethereum and Hyperledger Fabric[9].

2.2 A Blockchain Data Model

Most blockchains can be boiled down to very few concepts: blocks and transactions. Other ones, like accounts and balances, can be derived from attributes on these two entities. Figure 2 shows a data model using UML [20]. Although it

---

[7] It was not called "blockchain" back then.
[8] https://github.com/google/leveldb.
[9] Hyperledger Fabric also allows the use of CouchDB, a document-based DBMS.

is based on the Ethereum blockchain, the same concepts are also considered by Bitcoin and many other blockchains. The *AccountState* entity holds the state of an account, like its current balance, with *Account* representing the account itself. In some cases, *Account* is modelled as an identifier/hash on the transactions and blocks. In turn, the *Blockchain* entity represents the whole state of the network itself, being composed of the state resulting after applying all transactions, in order, to the initial state of the network.

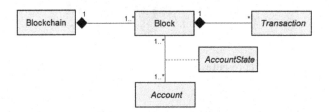

Fig. 2. The conceptual model of Ethereum [20].

In short, accounts usually represent users in the network. They are identified by their cryptographic public key's hash. A transaction is usually an operation, like a transfer of assets or a smart-contract interaction, and it is performed between two accounts. Finally, a block is a set of transactions. A block, if valid, is appended to the blockchain by all the participating nodes.

3   Related Work

There are some studies related to blockchains in the literature. However, even with the big interest in blockchain, no previous study focusing on blockchain data modelling had been found. Some recent ones are detailed next.

The work of Huang et al. [10] performs a thorough analysis of many blockchain surveys and its subjects, like consensus algorithms, data mining, applications and others. It also has a section about analytical modelling techniques for better understanding of blockchains. This section elaborates on strategies used to model data on blockchains for further analysis. Examples are graph-based model, stochastic model and queueing theory. However, the survey does not go into details about the concepts modelled by each technique. It concludes that surveys directed to *"theoretical modellings"* is a lack in the literature.

The survey from Przytarski et al. [25] consists on examining the query processing capabilities of blockchains. It researches for common application domains for blockchain systems, like logistics, health data management and others. It categorises data in the blockchain as *object types* and reviews the query capabilities of blockchain systems and current approaches on tackling lacking areas. In suggests that a *"standardised data model is needed that can be applied on all of these systems"*, but it does not define any.

Finally, Fekete et al. [6] surveyed the use of blockchain concepts adapted to distributed databases. Although this work performs a thorough analysis on the pros and cons of *Centralised Ledger Technologies (CLT)*, it does not consider data modelling. It focuses on the behavioural properties of blockchains, and not what composes it.

4 Research Protocol

This section describes the considered research protocol and its results. The chosen protocol is the systematic literature review (SLR) methodology [11]. It comprises a set of ordered steps: (i) Definition of research questions; (ii) Definition of the search string; (iii) Definition of inclusion and exclusion criteria. These steps are performed as a way to direct the research and provide a well-defined process for the review. The first step defines a set of questions that we hope to find answers to. These questions are the starting point of the SLR. We propose the following ones: (i) What are the main data entities in a blockchain? (ii) What are the most important attributes in blockchain data entities?

Once defined the research questions, the next step is to define a search string. We initially tried a few sets of keywords, such as "blockchain data model" and "blockchain model". However, strings with the keyword "model" resulted in works related to modelling *systems* based on blockchain and not in the data model itself, which is the focus of this research. Nonetheless, the search string *"blockchain AND (query OR model)"* was chosen because its results looked more promising.

Usually, queries performed on bibliographic DBs return too many results. This way, we provided a set of inclusion and exclusion criteria in order to filter out researches that are not related or important to this survey. For inclusion: (i) English and Portuguese only; (ii) Performance of data access in popular blockchains is discussed; (iii) Use cases for fast blockchain data querying is discussed; (iv) Entities and relationships in the blockchain domain are described. As for exclusion: (i) Focus on economic aspects of crypto coins; (ii) No performance considerations. We do not consider the year of publication as an exclusion criterion because blockchain data management is a relatively new research topic. So, there are not old-fashioned works.

We submitted the search string to a set of bibliographic DBs. The sorting mechanism on each bibliographic DB was the default one provided. Results are shown in the *Total results* column of Table 1. Next, we narrowed down the result set to make the research viable. Based on the inclusion and exclusion criteria, we applied the following filters: (i) Selection of the first 25 results of each DB; (ii) Title filtering; (iii) Abstract filtering; (iv) Fully reading.

Table 1 also shows the 13 selected papers after applying each of the aforementioned filters. Additionally, two other studies were included as suggested by the reviewers of this paper. They are detailed in the next section.

Table 1. Search results and selected papers.

Database	Total results	Start	Title	Abstract	Full
DBLP	24	24	22	13	9
Google Scholar	28.000	25	8	3	3
IEEE Xplore	150	25	4	3	1
Springer Link	2.013	25	4	1	0

5   State-of-the-Art Overview

The work of Bartoletti et al. proposes a tool, using Scala, for general purpose analytics on Bitcoin and Ethereum blockchains [2]. It allows the synchronisation of views of blockchain data to MongoDB or MySQL DBMSs. The tool was tested using Bitcoin and both DBMSs. However, the authors failed to compare the performance of their solution against other approaches, and do not go much deep into the data modelling part for each blockchain. Nevertheless, by looking into the tool's source code[10], it is possible to see the data entities used for each one. Both of them have representations for blocks, transactions and in-chain scripts[11]. Besides, the authors also include some data specific to each blockchain, like Bitcoin input/output transactions, and *ERC20* and *ERC721*, which are widely used in some Ethereum's smart contracts.

The work of Li et al. introduces *EtherQL* [14]. EtherQL is a REST service that synchronises Ethereum blockchain data, such as accounts, blocks and transactions, into a MongoDB instance. The authors validate their implementation by performing aggregate and range queries unavailable at LevelDB when used by the Ethereum blockchain network. The results show that EtherQL is almost twice as fast in all tests. As expected, the authors focus on the concepts available only at the Ethereum data model. By checking the source code[12], we can check the considered concepts: blocks, transactions, accounts and smart contracts.

The work of Xu et al. discusses the creation of an *Educational Certificate BlockChain (ECBC)* [32]. ECBC has a very specific use case, i.e., the emission of educational certificated by trusted parties. The transactions are modelled with a sender, receiver and some extra metadata, such as issuance timestamp. The senders are usually educational institutions, and receivers are usually students. The authors deemed efficient querying as a requirement for ECBC. In order to reach this requirement, they proposed the *MPT-Chain*, a combination of Merkle and Patricia Trees indexing data structures. The experimental evaluation suggests that queries are fast when using this approach. However, the authors did not compare their results with any other available solution. The data models

---

[10] Blockapi - https://github.com/blockchain-unica/blockapi.

[11] However, for Ethereum's smart contract models, the authors include data that is not standard because they use a third party API (https://etherscan.io/) to fetch data for Ethereum.

[12] EtherQL - https://github.com/LeonSpark/EtherQL.

described in this work differ from the previous ones. They are custom built for the proposed solution. Most entities are common sense, like blocks, transactions and accounts, but the attributes available on transactions, for example, differ from common blockchain networks, it follows a data model defined by *Open Badges* specification[13].

The work of Bragagnolo et al. proposes *Ethereum Query Language (EQL)*, an SQL-like language, and a tool to execute it [3]. The tool allows its users to perform complex information fetching from Ethereum. In order to make queries faster, the authors propose a binary search tree index. The tests show a decrease in performance when using the tool. Yet, the expressiveness of queries is the main point here. It allows users to easily fetch range and aggregate data from blockchains using SQL queries. The entities that can be queried by the tool[14] are: blocks, transactions, accounts and smart contracts.

The work of Pratama and Mutijarsa leverages EtherQL [24]. The authors developed an improved REST interface for Ethereum data whose data model represents accounts, blocks and transactions, as well as their attributes. They accomplished load tests and concluded that their implementation, when compared to Ethereum's native clients, has lower throughput.

In contrast to previous works, the proposal of Han et al. develops a *Quorum*[15] client that stores smart contract transactions in an embedded SQLite DB [8]. It allows the use of complex SQL queries. Their evaluation against LevelDB made use of range queries, which are not available in LevelDB. The results show a speedup of over 16 times. The only supported entity is transaction of smart contracts, but the authors do not detail it. Besides, the SQL queries used in its performance test were not elaborated besides *"INSERT"* and *"SELECT"*.

The work of Linoy et al. proposes a tool for querying Ethereum block data by using SQL and Hadoop as the underlying processing layer [15]. It uses an in-memory B^{+} Tree that indexes the block's and transaction's ids. Hadoop's MapReduce tasks are used to find and return data concurrently and in a distributed way. It allows range and aggregate queries, and the experimental evaluation suggests that the tool performance improves linearly with the addition of more nodes to the system. The available entities for querying are blocks and transactions.

A middleware called *Verifiable Query Layer (VQL)* is introduced by the work of Peng et al. [22]. It reorganises Ethereum blocks and transactions into a MongoDB instance in order to provide ways to make query results verifiable. The authors show that the throughput of MongoDB is higher than Ethereum's client, but they did not perform more complex queries, like range and aggregate queries. The considered entities are also blocks and transactions.

The work of Qu et al. introduces an approach to enable spatio temporal queries over a blockchain [26]. Blocks are defined as a set of transactions where each one contains geographical coordinates (latitude and longitude) together

---

[13] https://openbadges.org/.

[14] As seen in the source code: https://github.com/smartanvil/UQLL.

[15] An Ethereum-based blockchain with enterprise features, such as customizable consensus algorithms and permissioned transactions.

with timestamps and the public key of the entity that generated the data. It stores the transactions in a Merkle KD tree that provides fast geographical queries such as range query, K-nearest neighbours, bounded K-nearest neighbours, and ball-point query. Tests were performed considering two types of queries: *SCAN time-space*, which filter time and later space; and *SCAN space-time*, which filter space first. The results show that the custom data structure outperforms common scans on the blockchains, being three times faster.

In a similar way to the work of Linoy et al., the work of Trihinas introduces *Datachain*, an open source framework for querying and manipulating data from blockchain networks [29]. The author's implementation works with Hyperledger and BigchainDB[16]. Unlike Bitcoin, which only considers a data model based on the crypto currency, the *asset* is the smallest data unit of Datachain. An asset can be anything, tangible or intangible. This way, the model is entirely customizable for the use case of the network. However, the author defines the minimum requirements for common blockchain transactions: *sender address, receiver address* and *asset address*. The implementation allows users to query data using easier and well-established interfaces, such as common Python libraries (numpy, pandas, etc.) and SQL. The evaluation shows that Datachain does not perform better than querying data directly from Hyperledger and BigchainDB. Yet, the framework implements an *async* mode that lets many parts of the underlying queries be performed in parallel, which incurs in a bigger throughput compared to the usage of the original clients directly.

Ledgerdata Refiner is proposed by the work of Zhou et al. [33]. It is a library that extracts data from Hyperledger and parses them to be organised and stored in common DBMSs. The tests considered PostgreSQL DBMS and focused on data ingestion and not in query performance. They demonstrated that the synchronisation between the blockchain and the DBMS is quite fast. The entities synchronised are Hyperledger's blocks and transactions.

The work of Ozdayi et al. is the result project of a competition hosted by *Multichain*[17] [21]. Multichain is a Bitcoin compatible blockchain with extra features such as data streams. Those streams allow users to store arbitrary data into the blockchain's transactions. The authors focus on creating ways to query this arbitrary data more efficient. They define a set of reverse indexes and bucketization techniques. The reverse index is used to quickly find all data related to a user, for example. The bucketization, in turn, is used for range queries. At last, the implemented approach proved to be less efficient than querying data indexed in a relational DBMS, like SQLite. The queried entities, although not explicitly mentioned, can be inferred. The streams are stored in the blockchain's transaction. The transactions, as this blockchain implementation is based on Bitcoin, are stored in blocks. So it is safe to infer that those are, at least, the entities the authors considered when modelling their approach.

The work of Ren et al. describes a custom-built data structure called *dual combination bloom filter (DCOMB) index* [27]. The authors define DCOMB

---

[16] https://www.bigchaindb.com.
[17] https://www.multichain.com/.

as a probabilistic data structure for efficient insertion and query that can be constructed using the hash power of available hardware designed for data mining. It enables the conversion of all the computing power of blockchains, specially *proof of work*, to be used for query processing. However, the authors say that it could be adapted for more generic cases. They use DCOMB to quickly find blocks and query their transactions based on indexed fields. They also present an experimental evaluation demonstrating that their implementation is much faster than other techniques, such as indexing blockchain data into a known DBMS, like MySQL. A drawback of this work is the lack of a data model description. It only emphasises that the data model contains timestamps.

The study of Kruijff et al. [12] creates a set of blockchain ontologies based on Bitcoin. The first one is the *datalogical* ontology. It maps the data from the blockchain entities. The second one is the *infological* ontology. The blockchain and its entities are viewed as a distributed ledger. For example, a transaction modifies the state of the distributed ledger. The last one is the *essential* ontology, where it is modelled the "business logic" of the blockchain. For example, the transfer of assets from one party to another. The authors define a generic ontology for blockchain data. However, the authors do not consider other blockchains and did not validate their results.

The article of Ugarte-Rojas et al. [9] defines an ontology for three blockchain networks: Bitcoin, Ethereum and Hyperledger Fabric. They map the following entities and their attributes: blocks, transactions, accounts and smart contracts. Although the study makes a thorough analysis of the data models of these networks, the study does not specify an unified model.

Next section analyses the works summarised here.

6 Analysis

Most works agree that the prevalent entities used in blockchains are blocks, transactions and accounts. In fact, most of the proposals consider the entities implemented in existing blockchains, like Bitcoin, Ethereum and Hyperledger Fabric. Nevertheless, there is no focus on data requirements' analysis for the blockchain domain.

Unfortunately, not all works define the entities explicitly, i.e., blockchain data models are presented in a tangential way. For some of them, we had to search for the source code, if available, and check what entities were implemented there. However, many works do not provide the source code. In this case, we had to infer entities based on the broad descriptions or tests reported. Table 2 shows the entities considered by each work. As stated before, blocks and transactions are the basic ones. Accounts, in turn, are usually an address with a balance count, and can be derived from the whole list of blocks. However, for performance issues, some blockchain data models keep an updated list of all accounts and their balances separately.

It is worth mentioning that all studies make use of the transaction entity. This is due to the fact that the transaction contains the core information of

Table 2. Considered data entities.

Work	Block	Transaction	Account	Smart contract	Ledger
Bartoletti et al. [2]	X	X	X	X	Bitcoin Ethereum
Li et al. [14]	X	X	X	X	Ethereum
Xu et al. [32]	X	X	X		Custom
Bragagnolo et al. [3]	X	X	X	X	Ethereum
Pratama et al. [24]	X	X			Ethereum
Han et al. [8]		X		X	Quorum
Linoy et al. [15]	X	X			Ethereum
Peng et al. [22]	X	X			Ethereum
Qu et al. [26]	X	X	X		Custom
Trihinas [29]	X	X	X		Hyperledger
Zhou et al. [33]	X	X			Hyperledger
Ozdayi et al. [21]	X	X			Multichain
Ren et al. [27]	X	X			Custom
Kruijff et al. [12]	X	X	X	X	Bitcoin
Ugarte-Rojas et al. [9]	X	X	X	X	Bitcoin Ethereum Hyperledger

the distributed ledger, which usually is an account sending assets to another account. Some studies also consider smart contracts as an entity [2,3,8,9,12,14]. This is the case of some blockchains, like Ethereum and Quorum, where smart contracts are widely used.

We also point out other interesting features we found in the works. Most of them agree that blockchain querying is not optimal. Some of them propose solutions that make use of readily available DBMSs, such as MongoDB, PostgreSQL and MySQL, which run besides the original blockchain and duplicate their data in a structured manner. Table 3 shows the works that consider DBMSs. A data migration from LevelDB, a key-value storage solution, to some DBMSs, like MongoDB and PostgreSQL, is supported by some works [8,14,22,24,33]. However, the authors do not propose a conversion process between the source and target data models of the DBMSs. Instead, they simply store the data format returned by the tools they use, like a third party API (e.g., Etherscan[18]) or native blockchain clients (e.g., Ethereum's geth[19]). This process could be improved by creating suitable data models for the entities and its relationships in order to make better use of the DBMS logical structure.

Also, the consideration of popular DBMSs sounds a good approach to make data easily accessible by interested parties. Of course, the chosen DBMS should suit the information to be retrieved. For example, if only data regarding specific blocks, transactions and accounts is sufficient, without any aggregation, a key-value store is suitable. If aggregations are needed, like comparing transactions

---

[18] https://etherscan.io/apis.
[19] https://geth.ethereum.org/.

Table 3. Considered DBMSs and query interfaces.

Work	DBMS	Query interface
Bartoletti et al. [2]	MongoDB and MySQL	
Li et al. [14]	MongoDB	EtherQL (REST API)
Xu et al. [32]		
Bragagnolo et al. [3]		Ethereum Query Language (EQL)
Pratama and Mutijarsa [24]	MongoDB	REST API
Han et al. [8]	SQLite	
Linoy et al. [15]		SQL + Hadoop
Peng et al. [22]	MongoDB	
Qu et al. [26]		
Trihinas [29]		SQL + Python libraries
Zhou et al. [33]	PostgreSQL	
Ozdayi et al. [21]		
Ren et al. [27]		
Kruijff et al. [12]		
Ugarte-Rojas et al. [9]		SPARQL

executed in a specific time window, document and relational DBMSs can be considered. Additionally, if more complex information is desired, like following the flow of transactions as funds are transferred between multiple accounts, we can select a graph-based storage solution. So, depending on the use case, a specific DBMS can be chosen.

An important point to pay attention is that all works adopt one kind of blockchain topology, the single linked list, as shown in Fig. 1. In this topology, each block holds a single parent and a single child, generating one long chain with no bifurcations. Bitcoin and Ethereum, for example, use it. However, newer blockchains have adopted another topologies. Iota [23], for example, is a graph-based blockchain where blocks can have multiple parents and each block can contain a single transaction, as exemplified in Fig. 3(a). Another example is Nano [13], a blockchain consisted of multiple connected linked lists where each list represents the transactions of one user (see Fig. 3(b)). The dotted lines represent a "link" or a send/receive transaction. Although these blockchains are not as popular as its counterparts, they still hold the common entities, like blocks and transactions, but modelled in a different way.

Table 3 also summarises the querying interfaces adopted by the selected works. Some authors had developed libraries [29] aiming at making blockchain data searchable in a more expressive way. Also, the usage of SQL or SQL-like languages [3,9,15] provide a well-known standard to query data, and the adoption of REST interfaces [14,24] offer a well-versed way to communicate with data in the world of the Web.

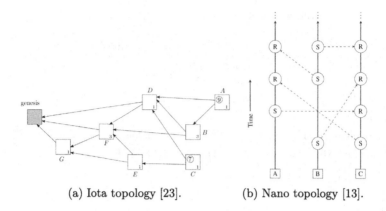

(a) Iota topology [23].   (b) Nano topology [13].

Fig. 3. Examples of unusual blockchain topologies.

7 Conclusion and Research Directions

Blockchain data management and analysis still is an open issue. However, its use cases are very relevant. Fraud detection, wallet de-anonymization, transactions and inter-chain analysis are just the simpler ones. Native blockchain clients are not well equipped to perform such tasks.

On following this context, this paper presents the state-of-the-art regarding blockchain data modelling. We see the usage of well-established technologies, such as different DBMSs, to better store, index and query blockchain-related data, as well as common interfaces, like REST and SQL, to facilitate interaction with native clients. It highlights the importance of combining the best of those worlds to design blockchain data management solutions.

Nevertheless, we failed to find a work that details a *blockchain data modelling process*, including the usage of typical DB design methodology starting by a conceptual model and moving to a logical model to be further implemented over a DBMS. As described in Sect. 5, DBMSs with different data models are considered (e.g., document, key-value and relational), but there is no focus on how their corresponding logical and physical schemas are designed. One promising research direction in this context is to propose a *polystore design methodology* so that different logical models, as well as related DBMSs, could be considered for maintaining parts of a conceptual schema for blockchains. The choice for one or more DB model could be guided by the representation of entities and relationships, as well as the expected workload over them.

There is also the lack of a *common conceptual data model for blockchains*, i.e., a consensual set of concepts that properly represent blockchain data. As stated before, we have some blockchain network schemas, like Bitcoin and Ethereum, that are used as baselines for many works. However, these works do not worry about the design of a single interface for querying data for multiple blockchains and provide inter-chain relations based on a consensual data model. One example could be to link different accounts in different networks. It would be useful for fraud detection programs to identify possible inter-chain frauds.

Finally, another relevant research issue would be a *comprehensive comparison of DB technologies* for storing and querying blockchain data. Many selected works consider relational DBMSs, but we also see MongoDB as another choice. An interesting analysis could be a performance and query expressiveness evaluation in the context of a common blockchain data model. Different DBMSs with different data models could be considered, including the graph-oriented ones, as mentioned before. Which one is faster? Which one enables the search for more useful information? These are relevant questions that the DB research community should answer.

References

1. Akcora, C.G., Dixon, M.F., Gel, Y.R., Kantarcioglu, M.: Blockchain data analytics. Intell. Inform. Bull. **19**(2), 4–10 (2018)
2. Bartoletti, M., Lande, S., Pompianu, L., Bracciali, A.: A general framework for blockchain analytics. In: 1st Workshop on Scalable and Resilient Infrastructures for Distributed Ledgers, SERIAL@Middleware, pp. 7:1–7:6. ACM (2017)
3. Bragagnolo, S., Rocha, H., Denker, M., Ducasse, S.: Ethereum query language. In: 1st International Workshop on Emerging Trends in Software Engineering for Blockchain, WETSEB@ICSE, pp. 1–8. ACM (2018)
4. Buterin, V., et al.: Ethereum White Paper (2014). https://ethereum.org/pt/whitepaper/
5. Chen, W., Zheng, Z., Cui, J., Ngai, E., Zheng, P., Zhou, Y.: Detecting ponzi schemes on ethereum: towards healthier blockchain technology. In: World Wide Web conference, pp. 1409–1418 (2018)
6. Fekete, D.L., Kiss, A.: A survey of ledger technology-based databases. Future Internet **13**(8), 197 (2021)
7. Haber, S., Stornetta, W.S.: How to time-stamp a digital document. In: Conference on the Theory and Application of Cryptography, pp. 437–455. Springer (1990)
8. Han, J., Kim, H., Eom, H., Coignard, J., Wu, K., Son, Y.: Enabling SQL-query processing for ethereum-based blockchain systems. In: 9th International Conference on Web Intelligence, Mining and Semantics, pp. 1–7 (2019)
9. Hector, U., Boris, C.: BLONDiE: Blockchain Ontology with Dynamic Extensibility. CoRR abs/2008.09518 (2020)
10. Huang, H., Kong, W., Zhou, S., Zheng, Z., Guo, S.: A survey of state-of-the-art on blockchains: theories, modelings, and tools. ACM Comput. Surv. (CSUR) **54**(2), 1–42 (2021)
11. Kitchenham, B.: Procedures for Performing Systematic Reviews. Keele, UK, Keele University **33**(2004), 1–26 (2004)
12. de Kruijff, J., Weigand, H.: Understanding the blockchain using enterprise ontology. In: Dubois, E., Pohl, K. (eds.) CAiSE 2017. LNCS, vol. 10253, pp. 29–43. Springer, Cham (2017). https://doi.org/10.1007/978-3-319-59536-8_3
13. LeMahieu, C.: Nano: a feeless distributed cryptocurrency network (2020). https://www.exodus.com/assets/docs/nano-whitepaper.pdf
14. Li, Y., Zheng, K., Yan, Y., Liu, Q., Zhou, X.: EtherQL: a query layer for blockchain system. In: Candan, S., Chen, L., Pedersen, T.B., Chang, L., Hua, W. (eds.) DASFAA 2017. LNCS, vol. 10178, pp. 556–567. Springer, Cham (2017). https://doi.org/10.1007/978-3-319-55699-4_34

15. Linoy, S., Mahdikhani, H., Ray, S., Lu, R., Stakhanova, N., Ghorbani, A.: Scalable privacy-preserving query processing over ethereum blockchain. In: IEEE International Conference on Blockchain, pp. 398–404. IEEE (2019)
16. Mazlan, A.A., Daud, S.M., Sam, S.M., Abas, H., Rasid, S.Z.A., Yusof, M.F.: Scalability challenges in healthcare blockchain system - a systematic review. IEEE Access **8**, 23663–23673 (2020)
17. Nakamoto, S.: Bitcoin: a peer-to-peer electronic cash system (2008). https://www.debr.io/article/21260-bitcoin-a-peer-to-peer-electronic-cash-system
18. Narayanan, A.: Bitcoin and Cryptocurrency Technologies: A Comprehensive Introduction. Princeton University Press (2016)
19. Nick, J.D.: Data-driven De-anonymization in Bitcoin. Master's thesis, ETH-Zürich (2015)
20. Olivé, A.: The conceptual schema of ethereum. In: Dobbie, G., Frank, U., Kappel, G., Liddle, S.W., Mayr, H.C. (eds.) ER 2020. LNCS, vol. 12400, pp. 418–428. Springer, Cham (2020). https://doi.org/10.1007/978-3-030-62522-1_31
21. Ozdayi, M.S., Kantarcioglu, M., Malin, B.: Leveraging blockchain for immutable logging and querying across multiple sites. BMC Med. Genomics **13**(7), 1–7 (2020)
22. Peng, Z., Wu, H., Xiao, B., Guo, S.: VQL: providing query efficiency and data authenticity in blockchain systems. In: 35th International Conference on Data Engineering Workshops (ICDEW), pp. 1–6. IEEE (2019)
23. Popov, S.: The Tangle (2018). https://assets.ctfassets.net/r1dr6vzfxhev/2t4uxvsIqk0EUau6g2sw0g/45eae33637ca92f85dd9f4a3a218e1ec/iota1_4_3.pdf
24. Pratama, F.A., Mutijarsa, K.: Query support for data processing and analysis on ethereum blockchain. In: International Symposium on Electronics and Smart Devices (ISESD), pp. 1–5. IEEE (2018)
25. Przytarski, D., Stach, C., Gritti, C., Mitschang, B.: Query processing in blockchain systems: current state and future challenges. Future Internet **14**(1), 1 (2021)
26. Qu, Q., Nurgaliev, I., Muzammal, M., Jensen, C.S., Fan, J.: On Spatio-temporal Blockchain Query Processing. Futur. Gener. Comput. Syst. **98**, 208–218 (2019)
27. Ren, Y., Zhu, F., Sharma, P.K., Wang, T., Wang, J., Alfarraj, O., Tolba, A.: Data query mechanism based on hash computing power of blockchain in internet of things. Sensors **20**, 207 (2020)
28. Szabo, N.: Formalizing and securing relationships on public networks. First Monday **2**(9) (1997)
29. Trihinas, D.: Datachain: a query framework for blockchains. In: 11th International Conference on Management of Digital EcoSystems, MEDES, pp. 134–141. ACM (2019)
30. Turner, A.B., McCombie, S., Uhlmann, A.J.: Analysis techniques for illicit bitcoin transactions. Frontiers Comput. Sci. **2**, 600596 (2020)
31. Vo, H.T., Kundu, A., Mohania, M.K.: Research directions in blockchain data management and analytics. In: 21st International Conference on Extending Database Technology, EDBT, pp. 445–448. OpenProceedings.org (2018)
32. Xu, Y., Zhao, S., Kong, L., Zheng, Y., Zhang, S., Li, Q.: ECBC: a high performance educational certificate blockchain with efficient query. In: Hung, D., Kapur, D. (eds.) ICTAC 2017. LNCS, vol. 10580, pp. 288–304. Springer, Cham (2017)
33. Zhou, E., Sun, H., Pi, B., Sun, J., Yamashita, K., Nomura, Y.: Ledgerdata refiner: a powerful ledger data query platform for hyperledger fabric. In: 6th International Conference on Internet of Things: Systems, Management and Security (IOTSMS), pp. 433–440. IEEE (2019)

Sharing Semantic Knowledge for Autonomous Robots: Cooperation for Social Robotic Systems

Sara Comai[1], Jacopo Finocchi[1]([✉]), Maria Grazia Fugini[1], Theofilos Mastos[2],
and Angelos Papadopoulos[2]

[1] DEIB - Politecnico di Milano, Milan, Italy
{sara.comai,mariagrazia.fugini}@polimi.it,
jacopo.finocchi@mail.polimi.it
[2] KLEEMANN HELLAS SA, Kilkis, Greece
{t.mastos,ag.papadopoulos}@kleemannlifts.com

Abstract. In social robotic systems, robots interact with humans to collaborate for different tasks. In this paper we consider industrial scenarios, where a shop floor can be reconfigured and specific tasks can be assigned to robots that operate as assistants to human operators. We propose to use a Knowledge Representation approach to describe the human-robot interaction. In particular, the conceptual framework based on the Generalized World Entities paradigm is adopted to capture both the physical entities of the system and events, situations, behaviours as well as the relationships among them. The paper applies the methodologies to some real case studies of the Kleeman manufacturer to automated bending machine procedures and intra-shop floor transportation with automated guided vehicles.

Keywords: Knowledge representation · Social robotic systems · Intelligent manufacturing systems

1 Introduction

When physical and digital objects interact with the environment in a complex way, as in robotics, smart manufacturing, and Internet of Things (IoT) applications, it is of great benefit, if not crucial, that the various involved systems (devices, applications, humans, and so on) can *cooperate*. More and more often, cooperation among Cyber-Physical Systems (CPSs), e.g., for collaborative automation in smart manufacturing, or in sustainable agriculture, smart cities, multimodal intelligent transportation systems, and so on is proposed to be obtained via *shared knowledge layers* that can be accessed at a semantic level [1]. In fact, knowledge allows, for instance, path planning control for simulation of tasks [2], IoT semantic interoperability [3], or Semantic-aware Cyber-Physical Systems (SCPSs) that enable semantic machine-to-machine [4].

In particular, a level of semantic knowledge can provide *autonomous robots* [5] involved in manufacturing shop floors with advanced cognitive skills and with the ability to perform goal-oriented autonomous behaviours based on intensive and shared knowledge, in the interaction with a dynamic environment. This is especially true for *social robotic systems* designed to *interact with humans* as assistants at workplaces and homes, or to collaborate with humans in industrial settings [6].

The above considerations claim for the adoption of forms of Knowledge Representation (KR) about the subjects, objects and the environment, as well as about the tasks involved in a smart environment. A common knowledge-enabled approach to robot programming is to represent these terms using ontology languages [7]. Moreover, the choice of an appropriate KR enables knowledge interoperability and sharing, as shown also in [8] for cloud robotic scenarios. Another up-to-date issue in robot-human interaction in manufacturing systems regards re-allocating work tasks at run time, when changes are needed, or when unexpected events occur, so achieving *adaptivity* in robots' behaviour, while keeping a healthy level of awareness and comfort in human workers in work areas.

This paper discusses how KR can enable and enhance the deployment of reconfigurable production systems employing *mobile autonomous robots*, which move around in manufacturing systems across the shop floor to undertake different operations while acting safely as assistants to human operators. It also presents a proposal of a KR system specification that supports the achievement of goals such as *autonomy* in robot task performing and decision-making, improved robot-human interaction, or enhanced adaptive behaviour of robots. Our proposal focuses on *methods and tools to optimally design and plan* the *activities* involving the cooperation between humans and robots using shared KR. In such scenarios, the ability to perform the steps of *acquiring, storing and sharing* knowledge to semantically support the system capability to operate in an open, modular, reusable and reconfigurable way is a core issue. These three steps are the issue tackled in this paper.

A key objective of our framework is to reach a level of awareness of human activity that requires interaction with robots, to enable human and context aware cognitive and social capabilities on robots, and to facilitate the interaction and relaxed collaboration with human workers within shared fenceless environments. This knowledge is gathered via a modular *perception layer* implementing *context-aware functionalities*. It allows autonomous planning of the most proper corrective or preventive actions of robots, to operate and collaborate with humans in a safe and comfortable way.

In this paper, we present a KR approach to treat social robots issues using a semantic framework that describes the interaction level. In Sect. 2, we review related work. In Sect. 3, we describe the general framework of Generalized World Entities (GWEs) for social robots, while in Sect. 4 we introduce two case studies where the approach is being applied. Finally, in Sect. 5 we draw our conclusions.

2   Related Work

In the robotic field, KR has become a primary concern [9, 10]. A review of projects that use ontologies as a KR tool to support robot autonomy and classifying the different approaches with respect to the scope of the ontology, the supported cognitive capabilities and the application domain is described in [11]. The ontological-based reasoning framework presented in [12] includes the modeling of the environment, and a sensory module to perceive the objects and assert the ontological knowledge: in particular, they show abilities to query knowledge about the geometric reasoning and robot capabilities to solve the planning of manipulation tasks. The significance of the semantic level in the interaction with the environment was also highlighted in the IoT field, for example in [13].

A systematic survey given in [6] identifies several different techniques and applications of the ontology-based knowledge base systems to autonomous robots that are working in domestic, hospital and industrial sectors. In the context of Industry 4.0, [14] presents the current state of ontologies and reviews both existing ontological frameworks and ontological standardization efforts in this field, including those related to robotics and automation that play an important role.

A manufacturing environment is very heterogeneous, but ontologies allow modelling sensory information in Human-Robot-Interaction tasks [15], social robot services [15], but they also enable dynamic communications with Automated Guided Vehicles (AGVs) that must be adapted to changing operating conditions [16].

Different approaches try to represent and reason on information that includes the environment, people, objects, relations between objects and humans, like in [18]. Among the examined approaches, [19] presents a conceptual framework based on the GWEs paradigm [20]. This technique, further detailed in [21], extends the standard IoT approaches [17] to broaden the universe of the entities that can be considered when automatizing a sensor-monitored environment.

The GWEs approach is currently implemented in terms of the Narrative Knowledge Representation Language (NKRL), which is both a KR language and an inferential engine [22]. In recent years, different studies have been using NKRL in robotics for collaborative and human-aware robot applications in dynamic environments, such as [23] and [24].

3   The GWEs Approach for Social Robots

The proposal outlined in this paper is to use the GWEs representation illustrated in [21] and implemented through the NKRL language, to meet the needs of KR required by an autonomous robots industrial application.

3.1   Overall Framework

Our proposed framework for robotic applications is being designed in cooperation between the two organizations of the authors and which is part of a larger framework that is being designed by an academic/industrial consortium. The framework aims to support the continuous design of production lines in flexible manufacturing systems exploiting a set of AI Tools.

Our solution is developed around the conceptual architecture depicted in Fig. 1.

More in detail, we aim at developing a modular *perception layer* implementing context-aware functionalities for robots and machines to recognize humans, what they are doing, what they are going to do, how they feel, where they are located, and so on.

This knowledge, gathered by analyzing and processing raw data coming from IoT sensors, devices and wearables, along with the perception, recognition, localization and tracking of surrounding environment and objects, will allow planning the most

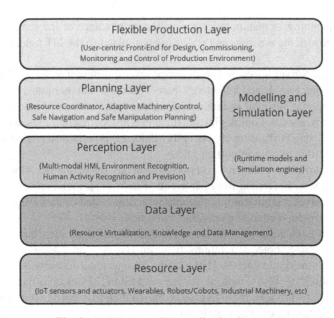

Fig. 1. Architecture of the application framework

proper corrective (or even preventive) actions to operate and collaborate with humans in a safe, relaxed and comfortable way. The establishment of a natural communication between humans and robots will also allow human workers to adjust the robot behaviour at runtime, and to enhance the quality of the user experience related to the physical collaboration.

The system collects knowledge about the identification and recognition of the human activity, attitude, mood, feelings, and level of stress, the comfort, health status and happiness. The analysis of this information should allow us to derive knowledge to model and predict human-to-human or robot-to-human interaction, so facilitating cooperation in work environments.

The system being studied tracks the evolution of the physical, emotional and cognitive aspects of the worker, which may affect his/her mood, feelings and happiness. In fact, these aspects are extremely more dynamic and require continuous evaluation (implicit and explicit) as well as attention to changes and drifts of the state of well-being with the aim of proposing targeted interventions to help the worker. In particular, the aim is to adapt the production process to human characteristics and needs, and not vice versa.

The system implements a user-centric multimodal interaction system, which enables ambient collaboration between humans, robots, machinery, and tools. It will deliver a hierarchical interaction communication network including projective, optical see-through and hand-held devices, supported by a centralized software platform that will analyse the environment state and select the optimal communication source, considering the current human state and activity.

The implemented autonomous and adaptable behaviours of robots and machines to properly support humans in their work - also improving in precision, safety, trust, and comfort - will be pursued by exploiting a deep analysis, modelling and prediction of the human behaviour, feeling and level of stress. AI, combined with the GWEs approach and with natural communication and social sciences precepts, will be used to pursue such objective.

A modular safety controller will provide a robust safety control system aligned with current safety standards and legislations coupling the latest trends in certified safety equipment with low-level robot controller through safe I/O signal exchange. Innovative safety concepts will be implemented and tested based on the requirements of each industrial pilot case and the collaboration needs. These involve, without excluding others, workspace monitoring, power and force limiting applications, robot movement monitoring and control, collision avoidance and detection. The implemented safety logic will ensure the triggering of the required safety function(s) at each point of the execution when needed. Being human-centered, our system exploits the capabilities provided by existing components and methods.

3.2   Overview of the GWEs Approach

GWEs [21] is a conceptual framework employed for the representation of high-level, structured and spatio-temporally denoted information.

This approach allows representing and modelling in a unified way both *observable entities*, like physical objects, humans, robots, sensors, actuators, and entities at *higher levels of abstraction*, corresponding to situations, actions, events and behaviours that involve lower level entities and their relationships. Consequently, it enables us to deal with both physical and higher-level entities using a coherent set of computational tools, thanks to a unique conceptual representation of the world used for modelling the GWEs of both types.

The remarkable progress made by IoT in recent years left some shortcomings in the *semantic and cognitive aspects,* especially when moving to a higher abstraction level or dealing with dynamic situations. A limited ability to deal with time varying environments, to generalize objects and events at the conceptual level and to infer hidden relationships, reduces the capabilities to handle complex situations, like those happening in a smart manufacturing environment.

In traditional approaches, the W3C languages for KR, like RDF and OWL, show a limited expressiveness and give a direct support only for binary relations, whilst n-ary relations are more effective to describe real application scenarios.

Moreover, OWL follows an open world assumption paradigm, whilst many industry-oriented applications adopt a closed world assumption.

GWEs are based on an ontological representation of the world, but where classical ontologies express properties as binary relations, the GWE paradigm requires the use of *n-ary structures*, which allow to describe the semantic relations in a more concise and more expressive way.

The use of this unified approach is aimed to the possibility of:

- Getting rid in a general way of the *interoperability problems* that notably affect the IoT domain. The use of a *unique KR language,* ontology-based, for entities of any origin and level of conceptual complexity guarantees the *semantic scalability* by allowing for smooth integration of information coming from multiple, distributed and heterogeneous sources.
- Systematically bridging the *semantic gap* between the values collected at the sensor level (i.e., at the sub-symbolic level) and their representation in conceptual, semantic format (i.e., at the symbolic level).
- Implementing advanced inference techniques. This is linked with the possibility of representing in a *smoothly integrated* way both the *objects* and the *contexts* where these objects are immersed.

3.3 Applying the GWEs Approach

As previously mentioned, the NKRL tools can be used to implement the GWEs conceptual paradigm, providing both a KR formalism and an operational environment, built up thanks to several European projects.

The NKRL environment provides two kinds of tools, which natively support an n-ary semantic model:

- A structured "representation of the world", that is ontology-based and is general enough to deal in a unified way with objects, human beings, robots, sensors, events, situations, behaviours and their relationships;
- A set of inference rules with the corresponding inference engines, that work at different levels of granularity.

The environment provides also inferencing services, that range from the direct questioning of a knowledge base of NKRL formal structures to the execution of high-level inference procedures. The connections and interactions are dealt with making use of Higher Order Logic structures, where a predicate can take one or more other predicates as arguments, obtained from the reification of generic occurrences, that is based on the use of symbolic labels.

NKRL is based on the definition of *templates*, useful to express structured GWEs as instances of conceptual entities that correspond to multi-layered concepts. NKRL templates and their instances are n-ary structures consisting of several triples of the "predicate - functional role - argument of the predicate" form. Attribute types are used to supply additional information with respect to the basic ternary structure.

In such a way, a formalized scenario or use case can be represented by blocks of NKRL code.

This representation allows us to obtain a formal description of full "narratives" as logically structured associations of the constituting elementary events.

An n-ary representation allows us to coherently assemble within a single symbolic structure the information that is different, even if conceptually related, in particular the various arguments of the predicate introduced by the functional roles. The notion of functional role is used to denote the logical and semantic function of the entities representing the arguments of the conceptual predicates, involved in the different elementary events.

3.4   GWEs Adaptability in a Dynamic Context

The GWEs paradigm is particularly effective in a dynamic context, also for its adaptability to changes, due to its predisposition to update and increase the stored knowledge through a dynamic correspondence of the observed entities with the conceptual ones, formally defined in the model.

In a manufacturing environment, as stated in the introduction of the paper, the need arises to adapt the robot/human actions along the process to react to changes and events, so making the architecture adaptive to the environment.

In order to implement a full recognition and categorization of GWEs to have reactions to the environment at run time, represents a significant improvement with respect to the state of the art. In fact, there is no guarantee in general that the information available in the external environment be sufficient to perform the *recognition tasks* in an adequate way, even in presence of a complete ontology.

For instance, sensing and inferencing might not be capable of fully categorizing a shop floor object (e.g., an aluminium sheet of square format) and as such, leading then to the existing instances AL_1 or IRON_SHEET_1 instead of the correct AL_SHEET_1 that we want to specify. Our world model must thus be sufficiently powerful to elaborate on *lacking information* associated with the provisional descriptions of the GWEs with its own stored knowledge.

When *stored knowledge is not sufficient* for depicting a complete state of the environment, sensors can be pro-actively directed to get missing information – when this is possible of course, e.g., when sensors are mounted on a mobile robot.

Moreover, the world model must be sufficiently flexible to allow for the creation of new conceptual entities in case of impossibility of associating the description of an external incoming entity with an existing ontological entity.

The recognition/categorization activities will be performed in two subsequent phases.

1. Categorization of background input entities: the raw descriptions of the input entities pertaining to an (extended) physical objects category will be matched with the conceptual entities included in the background (standard) component of the world model introduced above. This will be done using a semantic-based reasoning system able to unify the low-level features (properties/attributes) attached initially to the input entities with the semantic properties of the general concepts included in this background component. This conceptual unification activity will be integrated with the usual, algorithmic machine learning techniques used to recognize an object through a comparison of the associated features with those of standard objects stored in a database. In some tasks, like those relative to patrolling and search and rescue, this process could exploit a representation of the environment to help matching the physical entities detected by sensors to the general concepts. When the match succeeds with a reasonable probability degree, the GWE is created and a new instance of the corresponding concept is added to the corresponding branch of the model.

This procedure is equivalent to semantically annotating input entities (input sensor data) with concepts associated with standard ontologies. We can note its correspondence with recent semantic approaches devoted to mitigate, in an IoT context, the interoperability problems originated by the use of multiple competing application level protocols. In fact, a scalable IoT architecture should be independent of any difference among the various messaging protocol standards and should provide, on the contrary, integration and translation between them.

2. Categorization of foreground input entities: the procedures developed in a GWEs framework for recognizing the external entities represented by contexts, events, situations, circumstances – i.e., for identifying the corresponding conceptual entities described in the dynamic/foreground component of the world model – represent a step towards the progressive generalization of the IoT paradigm. They consist mainly in a reasoning process based, in general, on the results of the previous process of recognition of the physical/static/background GWEs. Let us consider an IoT system formed of sensors of different types (cameras or RFID, contact switches and pressure recognition tools). These could be used to hypothesize the presence of a GWE of an event of the "Move:ForcedChangeOfState" type.

The "Move:" templates are used in NKRL to represent the transmission of some complex entity whose content is described by one or more predicative occurrences. The "Move:ForcedChangeOfState" template is used when an agent entity (SUBJ) moves an object entity (OBJ, such as a physical object, information entity, process, etc.) from an initial state to a final one.

Before being able to add a new instance (a new GWE) of an event of this type to the dynamic component of the world model, we must:

- Identify the possible concept/instances that are candidate to fill the SUBJ(ect) and OBJ(ect) properties, i.e., the functional roles associated with the MOVE predicate that identifies the general conceptual category of this event.
- Verify that these potential fillers satisfy the constraints associated with the above roles. This means to verify that, e.g., a GWE labelled in the previous background categorization phase, really corresponds to an instance of the human_being or robot_ concepts in the static/background component of the world model. A constraint of this type is associated, in fact, to the filler of the SUBJ(ect) role in the NKRL "Move:ForcedChangeOfState" template. In the same way, the filler of the OBJ(ect) role must be a GWE instance of the artefact_ concept, etc.
- Verify the global coherence of the new dynamic/foreground GWE with respect to the global situation we are dealing with. This means verifying that this GWE really corresponds to the content of a message addressed to the same subject or, in a subsequent phase, to an action carried out by the subject as a consequence, e.g., of the previous message.

4   Case Studies

In this section, we will show how to adopt a KR based on the GWEs paradigm to achieve some of the goals described in our system.

To validate the methodology and the feasibility of the framework, its application will be tested in two specific case studies at KLEEMANN, one of the most important lift manufacturers in the European and global market. Founded in 1983 in Kilkis, Greece, KLEEMANN is producing all types of residential or commercial passenger and freight lifts, escalators, moving walks, accessibility and marine solutions, parking systems and components and exporting its products to more than 100 countries. KLEEMANN plans to automate its production operations to accommodate larger orders in order to meet the continuously growing market trends. Currently, manual material manipulations and intra-shop floor transportations constitute an inhibiting factor that holds this initiative back. Therefore, KLEEMANN seeks the automation of a) its production line (e.g. bending machine procedures/re-configuration) and b) its intra-shop floor logistics that will improve the production flexibility, adaptability and expandability and will enable KLEEMANN to meet its strategic goals. At KLEEMANN's shop floor, two case studies will be developed to realize a human-robot collaboration and an automated logistics solution through the demonstration of a pilot experiment.

Through these two case studies, the framework is expected to prove the ability to automate KLEEMANN's bending machine procedures and intra-shop floor transportations with the collaboration of humans with robots and AGVs. These two case studies were selected after a workshop with the Group Manufacturing Manager and the Group Health, Safety and Maintenance Manager. The reason for selecting these cases is because they constitute an intra-shop floor supply chain.

4.1 Case Study 1: Bending Machines Workstation

Current Industrial Challenges. Correct metal sheet bending provides consistency of final products and ensures safety to the workforce. For KLEEMANN this is a critical manufacturing procedure, which is required to meet its customer needs and expectations. It is therefore important to ensure that metal sheet bending is carried out according to adequate quality and safety standards. Due to the dynamic nature of the physical properties of the raw materials, the lack of automated bending procedures (rolling procedure) and the lack of rapid reconfiguration of the bending machine's parameters, some quality issues may occur. The physical properties of materials such as metal sheets, may vary and their processing may cause delays in the production line, which significantly decrease productivity and increase the fatigue of human workers since their effort is dedicated to manually re-configure the parameters of the bending machine. This results in lower quality end products, delays in the production line which ultimately increase manufacturing costs and safety risks, while simultaneously decrease customer's satisfaction and loyalty. Currently, as shown in Fig. 2, most of the tasks are based on manual manipulations by the operator when the metal sheet is processed on the bending machine, (e.g. orientation, lift, holding steady).

Expected Results. The robotic solution is expected to pick up metal sheets (up to 6 kg) and in collaboration with the machine operator, place them to be rolled at a specific point of the bending machine. From the production order, specific parameters of the machine are set-up. Depending on the bending result, a camera will check if specific bending characteristics (e.g. metal sheet angle) are correct. In case of discrepancies,

Fig. 2. Operator in front of the bending machine

the developed solution, which takes data from the camera, will rapidly reconfigure the parameters and press the same metal sheet and provide a quality check. This is a circular iterative process until the result is acceptable. Over time, in the proposed solution some modules will learn from the produced datasets and will provide a default of the machine parameters to reduce (re)configuration deviations. In this way, the solution will be trained to recognise material qualities, connect them with specific suppliers, etc., so that the best possible result is achieved by reducing the programming effort and configuration time. With the developed solution, the parameters of the bending machine will not need to be changed manually during production. As a result, a reduction of manual material manipulation and defective bended metal sheets-quality improvements are expected. Simultaneously, a reduction of machine re-configuration time with the usage of AI and robotics is expected and this will ultimately increase productivity.

4.2   Case Study 2: Intra-shop Floor Transportation

Current Industrial Challenges. After the bending process, the half-finished parts are either placed on a storage shelf or transported to the next workstation (Fig. 3). Regarding the transportation of metal sheets from the warehouse to the bending machine and other workstations, the procedure includes the following steps:

a) metal sheets *transportation* with forklifts (on pallets) to the bending machine from the warehouse;
b) metal sheet pallets *placing* in the left side of the bending machine (see Fig. 2);
c) *bending and placing* of the half-finished parts in a pallet on the right side of the bending machine (see Fig. 2); and
d) operator's *request of a forklift* to collect the bended parts and transport them to other workstations (e.g. painting, assembly) or to the half-finished products warehouse. The above-mentioned manual manipulations of the metal sheets and the current intra-logistics procedures with manually driven forklifts also cause significant delays in the production.

Expected Results. AN intra shop floor logistics automation solution will be developed, that will deploy AGVs to connect the warehouse with the bending machine workstation.

Fig. 3. Two bending machine workstations and intra-logistics transportation (forklift)

With the application of the proposed solution, the transportation of the pallets from the warehouse to the workstation will be performed with an autonomous guided vehicle.

The outcomes of the developed solution are expected to reduce the usage of manual driven forklifts and increase the productivity with the usage of AGVs in the shop floor transportations.

4.3   Example of Use Case Specification in GWEs

In this section, we provide an example of the GWE approach in a scenario of cooperation among sensors, robots and human operators. The formalism is applied to an industrial context, namely an intra shop floor logistics automation environment, related to the use-cases we presented above.

A situation is presented where a bending machine operator requests that an AGV bring a new load of metal sheets to the workstation. In a GWE model, the involved real-world entities, such as sensors, humans and robots, are represented by digital instances (like OPER_1 or SENSOR_1), denoted with a binary model where the properties are expressed as a relationship linking an individual and a value.

The elementary events, states and situations have instead a formal representation through a symbolic structure where information is expressed by the functional roles of the various arguments of a single predicate. In NKRL, these events can be expressed as instances of conceptual entities that correspond to multilayered *templates*, representing structured GWEs.

In our case, we can define *two structured GWEs*, as detailed in Table 1.

The GWE kle2.1.c04 describes how, on 11/3/2022, at 11:30, the bending machine operator sends to the automated logistic control centre a request that is described in the GWE kle2.1.c05. On 11/3/2022, at 11:30, the control centre must provide the reload of the bending machine number 1, sending an AGV to transport a new metal sheets pallet from the warehouse to the workstation.

NKRL templates are *n-ary* structures formed of several triples in the form "predicate - functional role – argument". The triples have the predicate in common ("MOVE" in our example). Additional information, such as the deontic modulator "obligation" employed in kle2.1.c05 (to denote the *necessity* of reloading the bending machine tray) are supplied by *attributes or determiners*. The attributes "date-1" and "date-2" introduce the *temporal information*, suitable for all elementary events.

Table 1. Examples of high-level GWEs.

kle2.1.c04	MOVE	SUBJ	OPER_1
		OBJ	#kle2.1.c05
		BENF	AGV_CENTRAL
		MODAL	MESSAGE_1
		date-1:	11/03/2022/11:30
		date-2:	
Move:StructuredInformation			
kle2.1.c05	MOVE	SUBJ	AGV_CENTRAL
		OBJ	BENDING_TRAY_1: (empty_, loaded_)
		{obligation}	
		date-1:	11/03/2022/11:30
		date-2:	
Move:ForcedChangeOfState			

The *semantic labels,* like "kle2.1.c05", give names to the GWE structures. This *reification* is important for the semantic labels can be used to *associate* several independent GWEs together, to give a formal representation of complex real world scenarios. This association in NKRL is called *completive construction.*

To further detail the situation, we can add the specification that the operator is sending the request when an appropriate sensor device (such as a weight scale or a smart camera) reports that the tray is empty. Table 2 shows the kle2.1.c03 structure, describing the event where the sensor device detects that the left side tray of the bending machine is empty and notify it to the human operator.

Table 2. GWE of the sensor device notification.

kle2.1.c03	PRODUCE	SUBJ	SENSOR_1
		OBJ	SPECIF (BENDING_TRAY_1 empty_)
		BENF	OPER_1
		MODAL	AUDIO_MESSAGE
		date-1:	11/03/2022/11:30
		date-2:	
Product:Assessment			

We also introduce another linking modality of NKRL that is the *binding construction,* where several *symbolic labels* denoting elementary events are collected into a list as *arguments* of a particular *binding operator.*

In our case, we are using the "CAUSE" operator: (CAUSE s_1 s_2) means that the event denoted by the symbolic label s_1 finds its origin in the event denoted by s_2. A new structured GWE, labelled as kle2.1.c02, provides a binding construction like (CAUSE kle2.1.c04 kle2.1.c03), where kle2.1.c04 denotes the operator's request to the automation central and kle2.1.c03 is represented in Table 2, could be used to indicate that the operation (kle2.1.c04) has been caused by the sensor device notification (kle2.1.c03).

As a final summary, we can assemble all the formal structures introduced above and represent the general structured GWE under a tree format, in Fig. 4.

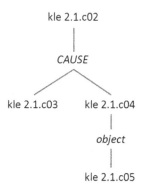

Fig. 4. Tree representation of the sample scenario fragment.

The top level consists of a "CAUSE" binding construction, while its continuation is represented by two structured GWEs: the first one denotes the operator's request following the sensor notification of the empty tray; the second one denotes the AGV intervention to carry a new metal sheets pallet from the warehouse to the workstation.

The process formalization could be of course extended and enriched adding further specifications, for example denoting for how long the warehouse robot must await an available AGV before proceeding to satisfy the operator's request and taking a new metal sheets pallet from the shelf.

5   Concluding Remarks

The present work proposes a data cooperation framework for social robotic systems that will be applied in a real-world shop floor. The proposed solution is preliminary discussed with lift industry experts, who evaluated the concept and the expected outcomes and benefits for the lift industry. Overall, we estimate that the proposed framework has the potential to reduce manual material manipulation, re-configuration time and improve quality characteristics.

As future work, we plan to apply the methodology to different case studies to derive knowledge to model and predict human-to-human or robot-to-human interaction. We also plan to build a digital twin to simulate different usage scenarios and validate the proposed approach for improving cooperation in work environments.

Other elements that can constitute added value are Social Elements regarding behaviour, acceptance, sustainability in the development of the framework and participatory design tools that involve various categories of users. Moreover, we are considering security, privacy (GDPR compliance) and ethics in the design of the platform to keep into consideration elements that protect humans and obey to the normative in terms of security, safety, risk prevention and healthy aging.

Acknowledgements. This work is partially supported by the H2020 "Working Age" Project https://www.workingage.eu under grant agreement No. 826232 and by the "Seamless" Regional Project in the context of the Smart Cities Programme.

References

1. Lu, Y., Asghar, M.R.: Semantic communications between distributed cyber-physical systems towards collaborative automation for smart manufacturing. J. Manuf. Syst. **55**, 348–359 (2020)
2. Schramm, J., Andelfinger, U., Fischer, H., Rausch, A.: Semantically valid integration of development processes and toolchains. Systems **10**(2), 40 (2022)
3. Larioui, J., El Byed, A.: Towards a semantic layer design for an advanced intelligent multimodal transportation system. Int. J. Adv. Trends Comput. Sci. Eng. (2020)
4. Li, J., Sun, L., Zhan, W., Tomizuka, M.: Interaction-aware behavior planning for autonomous vehicles validated with real traffic data. In: Dynamic Systems and Control Conference, vol. 84287. American Society of Mechanical Engineers (2020)
5. Sakai, T., Nagai, T.: Explainable autonomous robots: a survey and perspective. Adv. Robot. 1–20 (2022)
6. Mahieu, C., Ongenae, F., De Backere, F., Bonte, P., De Turck, F., Simoens, P.: Semantics-based platform for context-aware and personalized robot interaction in the internet of robotic things. J. Syst. Softw. **149**, 138–157 (2019)
7. Manzoor, S., et al.: Ontology-based knowledge representation in robotic systems: a survey oriented toward applications. Appl. Sci. **11**(10), 4324 (2021)
8. Pignaton de Freitas, E., et al.: Ontological concepts for information sharing in cloud robotics. J. Ambient Intell. Human. Comput. 1–12 (2020)
9. Schlenoff, C.I., et al.: Agile Industrial Robots (2022)
10. Paulius, D., Sun, Y.: A survey of knowledge representation in service robotics. Robot. Auton. Syst. **118**, 13–30 (2019)
11. Olivares-Alarcos, A., et al.: A review and comparison of ontology-based approaches to robot autonomy. Knowl. Eng. Rev. **34** (2019)
12. Diab, M., Akbari, A., UdDin, M., Rosell, J.: PMK - A knowledge processing framework for autonomous robotics perception and manipulation. Sensors **19**(5), 1166 (2019)
13. Palo, H.K.: Semantic IoT: the key to realizing IoT value. In: Pandey, R., Paprzycki, M., Srivastava, N., Bhalla, S., Wasielewska-Michniewska, K. (eds.) Semantic IoT: Theory and Applications. SCI, vol. 941, pp. 81–102. Springer, Cham (2021). https://doi.org/10.1007/978-3-030-64619-6_4
14. Sampath Kumar, V., et al.: Ontologies for Industry 4.0. Knowl. Eng. Rev. **34**, E17 (2019)
15. Azevedo, H., Belo, J.P.R., Romero, R.A. OntPercept: a perception ontology for robotic systems. In: Proceedings of the 2018 IEEE Latin American Robotic Symposium, 2018 Brazilian Symposium on Robotics (SBR) and 2018 Workshop on Robotics in Education (WRE), Joao Pessoa, Brazil, pp. 469–475 (2018)

16. Cupek, R., Fojcik, M., Gaj, P., Stój, J.: Ontology-based approaches for communication with autonomous guided vehicles for industry 4.0. In: Wojtkiewicz, K., Treur, J., Pimenidis, E., Maleszka, M. (eds.) ICCCI 2021. CCIS, vol. 1463, pp. 485–497. Springer, Cham (2021). https://doi.org/10.1007/978-3-030-88113-9_39
17. Chang, D.S., Cho, G.H., Choi, Y.S.: Ontology-based knowledge model for human-robot interactive services. In: Proceedings of the 35th Annual ACM Symposium on Applied Computing, Brno, Czech Republic, pp. 2029–2038 (2020)
18. Dimitropoulos, K., Hatzilygeroudis, I.: Context representation and reasoning in robotics-an overview. In: Virvou, M., Tsihrintzis, G.A., Tsoukalas, L.H., Jain, L.C. (eds.) Advances in Artificial Intelligence-based Technologies. LAIS, vol. 22, pp. 79–92. Springer, Cham (2022). https://doi.org/10.1007/978-3-030-80571-5_6
19. Amarilli, F., Amigoni, F., Fugini, M.G., Zarri, G.P.: A semantic-rich approach to IoT using the generalized world entities paradigm. In: Managing the Web of Things, pp. 105–147. Morgan Kaufmann (2017)
20. Zarri, G.P.: Using a high-level conceptual model as a support for the generalized world entities (GWEs) paradigm. In: ICIST 2020 Proceedings of the 10th International Conference on Information Systems and Technologies, Article No. 39, pp. 1–8 (2020)
21. Zarri, G.P.: IoT semantic modeling using the GWE (generalized world entities) paradigm. In: Rocha, Á., Adeli, H., Reis, L.P., Costanzo, S. (eds.) WorldCIST'18 2018. AISC, vol. 745, pp. 549–560. Springer, Cham (2018). https://doi.org/10.1007/978-3-319-77703-0_54
22. Zarri, G.P.: Knowledge representation and reasoning according to an advanced n-ary model. In: 2019 Third IEEE International Conference on Robotic Computing (IRC), pp. 373–376. IEEE (2019)
23. Lyazid, S.: Internet of robot things in a dynamic environment: narrative-based knowledge representation and reasoning. In: Hara, T., Yamaguchi, H. (eds.) MobiQuitous 2021. LNICS, Social Informatics and Telecommunications Engineering, vol. 419, pp. 520–526. Springer, Cham (2021). https://doi.org/10.1007/978-3-030-94822-1_33
24. Abdelkawy, H., Ayari, N., Chibani, A., Amirat, Y., Attal, F.: Spatio-temporal convolutional networks and n-ary ontologies for human activity-aware robotic system. IEEE Robot. Autom. Lett. **6**(2), 620–627 (2020)

Exploiting Named Entity Recognition for Information Extraction from Italian Procurement Documents: A Case Study

Angelo Impedovo$^{(\boxtimes)}$ ⓘ, Emanuele Pio Barracchia ⓘ, and Giuseppe Rizzo ⓘ

Niuma s.r.l., Via Giacomo Peroni 400, 00131 Rome, Italy
{angelo.impedovo,emanuele.barracchia,giuseppe.rizzo}@niuma.it

Abstract. Both large and medium-sized companies are concerned with maintaining good procurement relationships with their preferred suppliers and engaging previously unknown ones. To this end, potentially interesting suppliers are periodically monitored and evaluated by interacting with them via e-procurement platforms. Such a task rapidly becomes time-consuming and error-prone since buyer-side users ask documents of different types to suppliers, before manually evaluating the compliance status of every single document. To overcome this problem, we integrated Information Extraction capabilities, based on supervised Named Entity Recognition (NER), in the EPICS e-procurement platform. The solution has been evaluated both quantitatively and qualitatively on real-world procurement documents. Results show that the proposed approach is able to achieve good information extraction accuracy concerning different procurement document categories written in the Italian language.

Keywords: Information extraction · Named entity recognition · E-procurement · Supply-chain management

1 Introduction

Nowadays, in the global supply chain scenario, every large and medium-sized buyer company (*buyer* hereafter) wants to maintain good relationships with their suppliers over time. In fact, well-reputed suppliers compliant with internal and external quality requirements are less likely to negatively impact the overall business performance of the buyer. For instance, a timely supplier that sends the requested goods to the buyer is less likely to slow down the production lines. Otherwise, if this does not happen, the production lines will wait for the materials to come, leading to increased costs.

Unfortunately, suppliers are not in a steady state. Well-reputed suppliers at a given time-point may not remain that way in the future and, vice-versa, not well-reputed suppliers may become acceptable. This is often due to i) the dynamic nature of the global supply chain, and ii) the dynamic economic and

E. Pardede et al. (Eds.): iiWAS 2022, LNCS 13635, pp. 60–74, 2022.
https://doi.org/10.1007/978-3-031-21047-1_5

geo-political worldwide scenario. Clearly, the performance of suppliers may be affected by different internal and external features such as, for instance, the risk exposure, the sustainability indices, the market share, etc.

Consequently, buyers need to periodically evaluate whether the performances of known suppliers are still compliant with internal and external quality requirements. To this end, buyers request documents and information to suppliers through e-procurement platforms [7]. With the term *e-procurement* we refer to the digitization process of the procurement of goods and services undertaken by the buyer company, starting from the publication of a call for tenders to the payment, through the use of ICT facilities like online bidding, auctions, and so on. The benefits e-procurement platforms offer are manifold, including, but not limited to i) improved interaction efficiency between procurement actors, ii) enhanced productivity, by spending the time saved thanks to process automation, on strategically meaningful functions and tasks, and iii) increased spend awareness.

However, although the supplier evaluation and selection is a crucial task in the procurement domain, it has only been implemented with traditional technologies, leaving the burden of evaluating thousands of suppliers on procurement office employees. In fact, since procurement operations are often regulated activities, buyers and suppliers attribute considerable efforts in i) evaluating the document compliance of suppliers and ii) keeping a good document compliance status by updating overdue documents, respectively. The situation worsens considering that data generated by the interactions between buyers and suppliers comes at high volume (thousands of suppliers per buyer) and is arranged in documents that are digitally stored in e-procurement platforms. Clearly, procurement office employees become rapidly overloaded of information, causing an imprecise and error prone supplier evaluation. For instance, even a single overdue document (e.g., an outdated ISO-9001 certification) may represent a sufficient condition for a buyer to exclude a supplier from participating to a call for tenders. Therefore, e-procurement platforms equipped with Artificial Intelligence capabilities may greatly support procurement office employees in their daily work, opening the possibility of a real smart procurement.

As a first step towards smart procurement, our main claim is that equipping e-procurement platforms with Information Extraction capabilities helps the users in collecting the information required for evaluating the document compliance status of suppliers. As far as we can tell, there is no previously documented use-case concerning the adoption of Information Extraction technologies in the e-procurement domain. Therefore, we investigate how Information Extraction techniques based on Named Entity Recognition (NER) support the procurement office employees in capturing relevant information from structured, semi-structured and unstructured procurement documents. However, training NER models from scratch can be infeasible because: i) on the one hand, procurement documents are private and not publicly accessible, thus limiting the construction of large authorized corpora, and ii) on the other hand, NER methods require hundreds of thousands of documents from general purpose unbiased text corpora.

To tackle this issue, we claim that fine-tuning existing pre-trained NER models on few procurement documents is a viable solution instead of training new models from scratch on large corpora. Therefore, the contributions of this paper are manifold:

- we discuss how NER-based Information Extraction capabilities have been integrated into the EPICS e-procurement platform [7] developed by Niuma s.r.l.;
- we empirically evaluate the performance of 3 NER models trained on relevant procurement document categories;
- we qualitatively discuss the explainability of the information extraction models w.r.t. some real-world documents.

This paper is organized as follows: Sect. 2 introduces the relevant literature on Information Extraction with NER from documents, Sect. 3 presents the preliminary notions before stating the NER problem, while Sect. 4 discusses the peculiarities of the proposed application as well as the methodological approach. Then, Sect. 5 illustrates the experimental design and the quantitative results, Sect. 6 briefly discusses the results of a qualitative analysis on some extracted information. Finally, Sect. 7 draws some concluding remarks.

2   Related Works

Information Extraction (IE) is an *umbrella* term to denote processes that take unseen texts as input and produce, using a fixed format, unambiguous data as output. According to [19], there are several tasks under the label of IE such as, for example, *Named Entity Recognition* (NER), which aims at identifying *named entities*, that is tokens or groups of contiguous tokens from text considered relevant (e.g., the name of a person, organization, or location). The literature proposed sundry approaches for solving the problem which can be either supervised, semi-supervised or unsupervised methods.

Concerning supervised methods, several traditional methods such as Decision Trees [16], Maximum Entropy Models (ME) [3] and, in particular, Conditional Random Fields (CRF) [11] have been widely used to solve the problem. In [2], a NER system based on Hidden Markov model has been proposed to identify and classify names, dates, time expressions, and numerical quantities. Moreover, in [17], the authors developed a multilingual NER system by using C4.5 decision tree and AdaBoostM1 learning algorithms. In [10], the authors proposed a two-stage approach for NER combining two CRF classifiers where the latent representation of the output of the first CRF is given as an input to the second.

Among the semi-supervised methods, [1,12] exploited unlabeled data to generate additional features in order to improve the predictiveness of other NER methods. In a recent work [13], the authors solve the Information Extraction problem in the equipment support field, adopting a semi-supervised approach to deal with the presence of few labeled samples and a huge amount of unlabeled ones. The adopted approach consists of a BI-LSTM (Bi-directional Long Short

Term Memory) and a linear CRF to identify the weaponry equipment names. A different approach is the one adopted in [4], whose authors proposed a combination of semi-supervised and adversarial learning to solve the Information Extraction problem.

Finally, unsupervised methods have been also employed to solve NER problems using, for example, syntactic pattern matches [6], entity disambiguation [15] or cycle-consistency learning [8].

Despite the growing interest for IE with NER, to the best of our understanding, no previous documented attempts of NER on supply chain and procurement documents can be retraced in the known literature. However, NER has been exploited as a useful tool for extracting information from other kinds of document. In particular, [9] used BiLSTM-CRF for extracting custom named entities from a corpus of manually annotated call center transcripts. Similarly to our purposes, the authors i) tried to extract information for privacy law compliance purposes, ii) manually annotated a transcript corpus with custom named entities. Complementarily, [5] adopts LayoutLM, a pre-trained Transformer specialized in business documents, for extracting information from expense receipts, invoices, and purchase orders. In [20], the authors proposed an unsupervised approach to extract named entities from biomedical text resorting to terminologies, corpus statistics and syntactic knowledge. Lastly, [18] relies on the BERT language model for extracting information from free-form curriculum vitae documents.

3   Basics and Problem Statement

Let $D = \{d_1, d_2, \ldots, d_n\}$ be a corpus of n documents, each represented as the ordered sequence $d_k = \langle t_1, t_2, \ldots, t_{|d_k|} \rangle$ of $|d_k|$ tokens t_m, and let $\mathcal{S}$ be a finite set of labels. Each token $t_m \in d_k$ is labeled with a value $s(t_m) \in \mathcal{S}$. The text chunk between i and j, from $d \in D$, is the sequence of subsequent tokens $d[i, j] = \langle t_i, t_{i+1}, \ldots, t_j \rangle \subseteq d$, where $i, j \in \mathbb{N}$ and $1 \leq i \leq j \leq |d|$. A chunk $d[i, j]$ is coherently labeled with label $s(d[i, j]) = s$ iff $s(t_l) = s \; \forall l \in [i, j]$.

Solving an information extraction problem on a document $d \in D$ means to pull out only the chunks $d[i, j]$ that are coherently labeled as $s(d[i, j]) = \alpha$, where α is a user defined parameter used to filter out uninteresting information. Typically, this is done by i) labeling every token $t \in d$ with the membership class $s(t)$, ii) segmenting d into non-overlapping chunks $d[i, j]$ coherently labeled as $s(d[i, j])$, and iii) selecting only those where $s(d[i, j]) = \alpha$. Therefore, characterizing the class membership map at token level $s(\cdot)$ solves the problem. s takes the vector-based representation of tokens t as input and computes the class label $e \in \{0, 1\}$, where a result of 1 denotes a token that is part of relevant information, 0 otherwise.

The aforementioned general problem can be further specialized, by tweaking the class membership map, depending on the nature of the extraction criteria. In the case of NER, the extracted chunks are named entities. In particular, named entities are denoted by a proper name and instantiate a given category (e.g., the "New York City" chunk denotes an instance of the CITY category). Consequently, the tokens should be categorized according to the most appropriate category. Specifically, let $\mathcal{E} = \{\bot, e_1, \ldots, e_h\}$ be a finite set of h categories (hence, $\mathcal{E} = \mathcal{S}$), then the membership map classify tokens t as $s(t) \in \mathcal{E}$. The tokens where $s(t) = \bot$ are not part of named entities.

However, the theoretical map s is unknown in advance and is estimated from a training corpus of documents, whose tokens are labeled over $\mathcal{E}$. Therefore, it is necessary to infer the map $\hat{s}$ that best approximates s over the training corpus, that is:

$$\arg \min_{\hat{s}} \sum_{\forall d \in D, t \in d} I(\hat{s}(t), s(t)) \tag{1}$$

where $I(\cdot, \cdot)$ is a function whose result is 1 if $\hat{s}(t) \neq s(t)$, 0 otherwise. However, estimating $\hat{s}$ is not straightforward: it is possible that semantic/syntactic phenomena (e.g., multiple appearances of a term in the same document, synonymy, etc.) make the role of a term in the document ambiguous. In these cases, deciding the most appropriate category depends more on the linguistic context, the document language and the terms close to the considered token, rather than on the token itself.

4   Application Scenario: Document Management in EPICS

One of the main contributions of this paper is the employment of NER methods as a viable approach for extracting useful information from procurement documents (requested from buyers to suppliers as long as they periodically interact on e-procurement platforms). To this end, we equipped the EPICS platform [7], an e-procurement software system developed by Niuma s.r.l., with NER models that have been trained for targeting specific document categories. Specifically, the EPICS platform adopts a Robotic Process Automation (RPA) for managing documents requested from buyers to suppliers at the qualification stage, as depicted in Fig. 1.

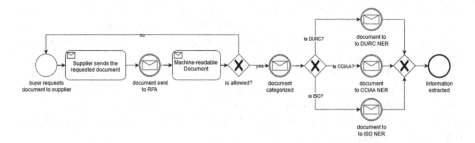

Fig. 1. Document management RPA pipeline in the EPICS platform

The pipeline gets invoked whenever the supplier uploads the document, hence answering the document request from the buyer user. Firstly, documents are

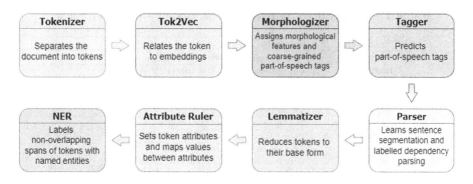

Fig. 2. SpaCy components of pre-trained model employed in the experiments

converted into a machine-readable format and filtered for anomalies: anomalous documents get discarded, and the buyer requests them anew. On the contrary, allowed documents are categorized and sent to the most appropriate NER model based on their category.

In order for our platform to support the majority of end-users, we queried our systems to spot the most requested document categories. Then, we devoted our attention to developing NER models compatible with such documents, which are i) DURC documents, ii) CCIAA documents and iii) ISO certifications.

According to the Italian regulation, a DURC ("*Documento Unico di Regolarità Contributiva*") is the document declaring, by stating exclusively the tax code of the party to be checked, the state of being up to date with payment contributions in respect of INPS and INAIL authorities. The CCIAA documents, instead, include several sub-categories such as CCIAA certificates and "visure camerali", and provide information on any Italian company listed in the business register held by the Chamber of Commerce, Industry, Crafts and Agriculture (*Camera di Commercio, Industria, Artigianato e Agricoltura*). Lastly, the ISO certifications are statements of approval, from a third party, that a company is conform to one of the international standards developed and published by the International Organization for Standardization (ISO). Among the procurement documents, the majority of ISO certifications include, but are not limited to, ISO-9001, ISO-14001 and ISO-27001 certifications.

Concerning the method used to deal with the information extraction problem on procurement documents, in this paper, we decided to leverage the NER training facilities available in SpaCy 3[1]. In particular, due to the limited number of available documents in our possession, it would be hard for us to train an effective and efficient NER model from scratch. Therefore, in this work, we relied on NER models made available off-the-shelf by SpaCy, pre-trained on Italian general-purpose documents, in order to fine-tune them on procurement documents. The pre-trained models are NLP pipeline including various components, which are reported, for the sake of the space, in Fig. 2.

---

[1] http://spacy.io.

Table 1. Custom named entities used to annotate the different corpora

Corpus	Named entity	Description
DURC	DURC_NO	Unique identifier of the document
	REQUEST_DATE	Date of request for the document
	DUE_DATE	Date by which the document is valid
	VALIDITY_DAYS	Validity days of the document
	TAX_CODE	Unique company identifier
ISO	ISO_STANDARD_NO	The ISO rule object of the certification
	ISO_CERTIFICATION_NO	Unique identifier of the ISO certification
	RELEASE_DATE	First release date of the certificate
	VALIDITY_DATE	Date from which the certificate is valid
	DUE_DATE	Date by which the document is valid
	COMPANY_NAME	The certified company name
	IAF_SUBJECT	Code or description of the company's business
CCIAA	CCIAA_NO	Unique identifier of the document
	RELEASE_DATE	Release date of the document
	CCIAA_LOC	Location of the issuing authority
	TAX_CODE	Unique company identifier
	PEC	Company certified e-mail
	REA_NO	Registration code to the Economic and Administrative Index

To exploit the prior knowledge of the pre-trained SpaCy models, we decided to conduct a fine-tuning process of the model, limiting it to the only *NER* component of the pipeline, to adapt and train it to recognize our custom named entities.

5 Experiments

Given the three most requested document categories reported in the previous section, we quantitatively evaluate the performance of the NER models by trying to answer the following research questions:

RQ1. How accurate is the proposed approach on the considered corpora?
RQ2. How fast does the training procedure converge on the considered corpora?
RQ3. How much time does the training procedure require to fit the models over the considered corpora?

In particular, we sampled the 600 most recent ISO documents, CCIAA documents and DURC documents from our systems. Moreover, since users upload documents to the EPICS platform either as scanned or digital pdfs, we equally represent both scanned and digital documents in each corpus. Then, a team of expert users was instructed to manually annotate the three corpora for the NER task, using the Doccano tool[2] and the BILOU annotation scheme. We remark that the annotation process required more than one annotation pass to reach the desired inter-annotator agreement. Table 1 reports the named entities taken into account during the labeling process.

Experiments have been performed on machines equipped with Intel(R) Core (TM) i7-10750H CPU @ 2.60 GHz, 16 GB RAM, Nvidia RTX 2070 Max-Q Design

---

[2] https://doccano.github.io/doccano/.

Table 2. Macro-avg f1-score over the named entities on the DURC, ISO and CCIAA corpora, when tuning i) the pretrained model, ii) the dropout rate, iii) the learning rate.

SpaCy model	Learning rate	Dropout rate	DURC	ISO	CCIAA
it_core_news_sm	0.01	0.35	0.917	0.736	0.929
		0.50	0.924	0.734	0.934
	0.001	0.35	0.929	**0.742**	**0.943**
		0.50	**0.930**	0.741	0.941
it_core_news_md	0.01	0.35	0.922	0.713	0.899
		0.50	0.895	0.719	0.896
	0.001	0.35	0.919	0.731	0.931
		0.50	0.917	0.730	0.932

GPU. The code has been executed in Jupyterlab 3.0.12 environment, running with Python 3.8 on top of the Windows 11 Pro (21H2) operating system.

5.1 Selecting the Most Accurate NER Models

Before evaluating the accuracy at the entity level, we performed model selection based on a grid search. In particular, we fine-tuned the NER components of 2 pre-trained SpaCy language models, namely it_core_news_sm and it_core_news_md, by varying the learning rate (0.01 and 0.001) and the dropout rate (0.35 and 0.50). We fixed the number of training epochs to 200 with early stopping patience to 10 epochs. The f1-score, at each of the 8 points from the grid, is macro-averaged over the entities in a 5-fold cross-evaluation, leading to the execution of 40 training processes for each corpus.

The results in Table 2 show, on average, a reduced f1-score on the ISO corpus for the DURC and CCIAA corpora. In particular, fine-tuning the it_core_news_sm model, with a learning rate of 0.001 and setting the dropout rate to i) 0.35 for the ISO and CCIAA, and ii) 0.50 for the DURC corpus, always results in the best accuracy. An aspect worth mentioning is that, on the considered corpora, the size of the pre-trained model does not seem to affect the predictive performance of the fine-tuned models.

5.2 Entity-Level Accuracy of the Best NER Models

We used the most accurate model from the previous section to evaluate the extraction accuracy in terms of precision, recall and f1-score at entity-level (see Table 1).

Fine-tuning it_core_news_sm with a learning rate equals to 0.001 and a dropout rate equals to 0.50 resulted in a model that performs considerably well on the DURC corpus. Since all the most recent DURC documents share the same document template (thus leading to an easy learning problem) the aforementioned one is an expected result. However, the low f1-score on the DURC_NO is due to a certain amount of scanned DURC documents in the training corpus. In these cases, the OCR cannot correctly recognize the corresponding tokens from such documents. Consequently, expert users agreed to leave unclear entities not annotated.

Table 3. Macro-avg (5 fold cross validation) f1-score, precision, recall per entity.

Corpus	Named entity	NER		
		F1-score	Precision	Recall
DURC	DUE_DATE	1.000	1.000	1.000
	DURC_NO	0.666	0.667	0.666
	REQUEST_DATE	0.997	1.000	0.993
	TAX_CODE	0.948	1.000	0.917
	VALIDITY_DAYS	1.000	1.000	1.000
ISO	COMPANY_NAME	0.614	0.662	0.574
	DUE_DATE	0.867	0.870	0.869
	IAF_SUBJECT	0.430	0.373	0.506
	ISO_CERTIFICATION_NO	0.832	0.879	0.790
	ISO_STANDARD_NO	0.905	0.880	0.933
	RELEASE_DATE	0.827	0.831	0.825
	VALIDITY_DATE	0.725	0.710	0.744
CCIAA	CCIAA_LOC	0.973	0.990	0.958
	CCIAA_NO	0.887	0.895	0.878
	PEC	0.895	0.892	0.900
	REA_NO	0.972	0.979	0.967
	RELEASE_DATE	0.967	0.994	0.943
	TAX_CODE	0.968	0.989	0.950

Surprisingly, fine-tuning `it_core_news_sm` with a learning rate equals to 0.001 and a dropout rate equals to 0.35 resulted in a model performing quite decently on the ISO corpus. It is worth mentioning that, in this case, we were expecting worse results. Indeed, i) `it_core_news_sm` is a pre-trained model for the Italian language while the ISOs are inherently multi-language documents (Italian-English), and ii) the ISO certifications do not share the same document template, which on the contrary is determined by the certification authority. However, although being acceptable in extracting the most relevant entities (`ISO_CERTIFICATION_NO` and `ISO_STANDARD_NO`), the model is not so good at extracting `IAF_SUBJECT`.

Finally, fine-tuning `it_core_news_sm` with a learning rate equals to 0.001 and a dropout rate equals to 0.35 resulted in a model that performs adequately on the CCIAA corpus. As for the ISOs, we also expected worse results in this case. We remark that the CCIAA corpus collects a balanced set of documents that differs in their document templates, in particular: i) the CCIAA certificates are always single-column scanned documents (and, therefore, originate noisy text due to OCR errors), and ii) the CCIAA "visure camerali" which, on the contrary, are always multi-column digital documents. Despite this, the model has an acceptable accuracy (Table 3).

5.3 Training Convergence of the Best NER Models

We now discuss how the three models fit the data and how fast the fine-tuning converges to a stable cumulative loss. The fine-tuning may proceed for, at most,

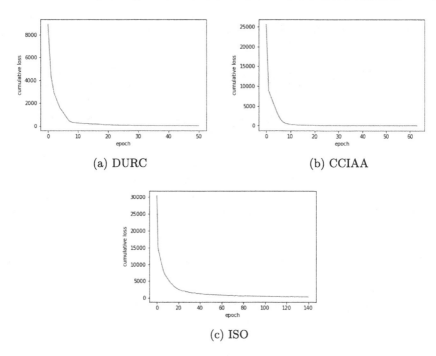

Fig. 3. Training cumulative loss over the epochs of the selected NER models

200 epochs trying to minimize the cumulative loss computed on the training data. In particular, the fine-tuning stops whenever: i) it reaches the maximum number of allowed training epochs, or ii) the cumulative loss does not decrease for 10 subsequent epochs.

Ideally, the fine-tuning starts by registering high cumulative losses at the first training epochs before converging at values approximately equal to 0. However, depending on the available data, it is possible for the training to converge at minimum losses that are still considerably large (thus, indicating the necessity of more refined training corpora). For instance, results in Fig. 3 show high cumulative losses in the initial epochs: less than 10.000 in the DURC corpus, more than 25.000 in the CCIAA corpus, and more than 30.000 in the ISO corpus, respectively. Such differences are due to the different nature of documents. As previously discussed, DURC documents share the same template, thus giving place to the lowest initial loss. The same does not hold for documents from the CCIAA and ISO corpora that share a more elaborate document template, thus giving place to increased initial losses. However, despite the initial peaks, the losses rapidly converge to thousands (ISO) or below 100 (CCIAA and DURC).

As for the convergence speed, in the case of DURC and CCIAA, the training stops within 70 epochs. However, this is not the case for the ISO corpus. The training stops at approximately 140 epochs due to the already mentioned high variability of both language and document templates.

5.4   Training Times on the NER Models

Results in Table 4 show the training times (in seconds) measured while per-forming the experiments on the three corpora. Concerning the adopted pre-trained SpaCy models, using `it_core_news_md`, which is a more complex lan-guage model than `it_core_news_sm`, resulted in increased training times. This is an expected result since the model, being pre-trained on more data than `it_core_news_sm`, is more resilient in forgetting prior knowledge, therefore need-ing more time to adapt to new data. When looking at the values of learning rate, results show that a learning rate equals to 0.01 leads to lower fit times. An aspect worth mentioning is that high values leads to fast optimization process, and, con-sequently, low training times. Lastly, analyzing the impact of the dropout rate parameter, it is possible to notice that generally low values yields to low training times.

When looking at the training corpus, it is evident that fine-tuning a NER model on the DURC corpus requires significantly reduced training times. On the contrary, fine-tuning a NER model on the ISO corpus requires consider-able effort. Such is an expected result because i) DURC documents are single-language documents sharing the same template, and ii) ISO documents are inher-ently multi-language with no standard layout. Finally, fine-tuning a model on the CCIAA corpus leads to training times always between those required on the DURC and ISO corpora: this is an expected result because CCIAA documents are single-language (differently from ISO documents) and more complex than DURC documents.

Finally, fine-tuning a model on the CCIAA corpus leads to training times always between those required on the DURC and ISO corpora: this is another expected result because, unlike ISO documents, CCIAAs are single-language documents with a common layout for presenting information but, at the same time, they are more complex to process than DURC documents.

6   Qualitative Analysis

Since NER models are inherently not explainable, performing a direct qualitative evaluation of the predicted named entities is not straightforward. Therefore we evaluate them using SHAP (SHapley Additive exPlanations) [14]. SHAP offers a model-agnostic and game-theoretic framework (based on Shapley values) to explain the output of any machine learning model seen as a black box.

Figure 4 shows the information extracted from a previously anonymized pri-vate DURC document. Tokens marked in red as "outputs" denote extracted information, and tokens marked in red/blue as "inputs" are the features that contributed positively/negatively to a prediction, i.e., the extraction of "INAIL_26221111" as `DURC_NO` in the case of Fig. 4. Considering the extrac-tion of the DURC_NO entity, the SHAP-based analysis suggests that the top contributors to the extraction are i) the DURC number itself, ii) the tokens in the initial portion of the document, and iii) the ones in the central part. The contributor tokens act as anchors in the phrasal context since they are always

Table 4. Training times (in seconds) on the DURC, ISO and CCIAA corpora, computed when tuning i) the pretrained model, ii) the dropout rate, and iii) the learning rate.

SpaCy model	Learning rate	Dropout rate	DURC	ISO	CCIAA
it_core_news_sm	0.01	0.35	94	609	448
		0.50	119	591	440
	0.001	0.35	179	963	669
		0.50	191	1182	884
it_core_news_md	0.01	0.35	119	476	511
		0.50	105	595	442
	0.001	0.35	192	962	713
		0.50	206	1147	985

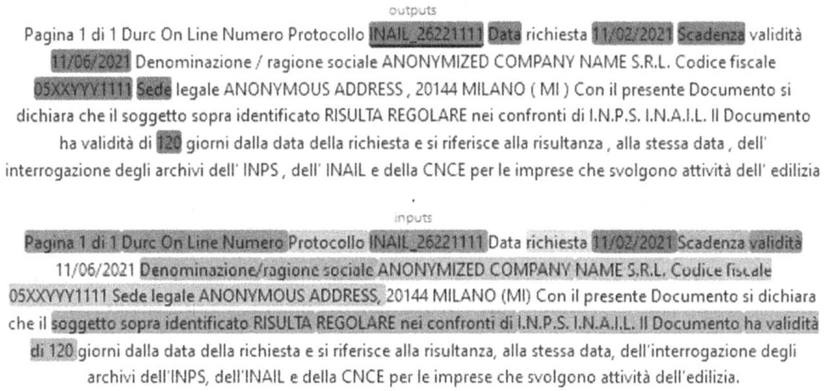

outputs

Pagina 1 di 1 Durc On Line Numero Protocollo INAIL_26221111 Data richiesta 11/02/2021 Scadenza validità 11/06/2021 Denominazione / ragione sociale ANONYMIZED COMPANY NAME S.R.L. Codice fiscale 05XXYYY111 Sede legale ANONYMOUS ADDRESS , 20144 MILANO (MI) Con il presente Documento si dichiara che il soggetto sopra identificato RISULTA REGOLARE nei confronti di I.N.P.S. I.N.A.I.L. Il Documento ha validità di 120 giorni dalla data della richiesta e si riferisce alla risultanza , alla stessa data , dell' interrogazione degli archivi dell' INPS , dell' INAIL e della CNCE per le imprese che svolgono attività dell' edilizia

inputs

Pagina 1 di 1 Durc On Line Numero Protocollo INAIL_26221111 Data richiesta 11/02/2021 Scadenza validità 11/06/2021 Denominazione/ragione sociale ANONYMIZED COMPANY NAME S.R.L. Codice fiscale 05XXYYY1111 Sede legale ANONYMOUS ADDRESS, 20144 MILANO (MI) Con il presente Documento si dichiara che il soggetto sopra identificato RISULTA REGOLARE nei confronti di I.N.P.S. I.N.A.I.L. Il Documento ha validità di 120 giorni dalla data della richiesta e si riferisce alla risultanza, alla stessa data, dell'interrogazione degli archivi dell'INPS, dell'INAIL e della CNCE per le imprese che svolgono attività dell'edilizia.

Fig. 4. Correct extraction of "INAIL_26221111" token as DURC_NO entity. (Color figure online)

included in DURC documents (except for the DURC no). On the contrary, variable parts in blue contribute negatively to the extraction as they add noise to the training set.

Figure 5 shows how the model incorrectly extracts the "Scadenza" token as a REQUEST_DATE. The SHAP-based analysis depicts that, approximately, the features that correctly contributed to the extraction of DURC_NO (mostly the tokens in the initial portion of the document) are sometimes positive contributors to such an incorrect extraction. As for the negative contributors, similarly to the previous example, they are composed of the noisy parts of the documents. Therefore, we can hypothesize that the positive contributors are more responsible for the final prediction than the negative ones, leading to identifying "Scadenza" as relevant information worth being extracted as REQUEST_DATE.

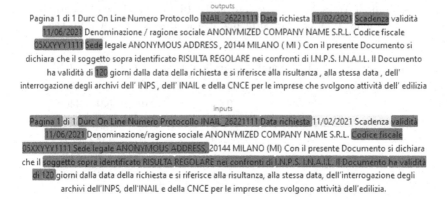

Fig. 5. Incorrect extraction of the "Scadenza" token as REQUEST_DATE entity.

7 Conclusions

In this paper, we proposed an application of Information Extraction techniques, based on supervised Named Entity Recognition, on procurement documents requested by Italian companies to their suppliers via the EPICS e-procurement platform developed by Niuma s.r.l.. Instead of training NER models from scratch on large datasets, we fine-tuned three pre-trained models for the Italian language on different corpora. Each corpus contains 600 documents (DURCs, CCIAAs, and ISO certifications) that were previously manually annotated by human experts.

We evaluated the performance of the three models from both a quantitative and qualitative standpoint. In particular, we discussed i) the accuracy, the training time and the convergence speed, and ii) the SHAP explanations, respectively. The two evaluations have shown promising results, although more curate training corpora than the one used are needed. To this end, future research directions involve the study of training algorithms that i) require a reduced amount of documents, and ii) are less sensitive to noise in the training data.

Acknowledgements. The EPICS (*E-Procurement Innovation For Challenging Scenarios*) project has been co-funded by *Programma del Regolamento regionale della Puglia per gli aiuti in esenzione n. 17 del 30/09/2014 (BURP n. 139 suppl. del 06/10/2014) titolo II capo 2 del regolamento generale aiuti ai programmi integrati promossi da medie imprese ai sensi dell'articolo 26 del Regolamento.*

References

1. Ando, R.K., Zhang, T.: A framework for learning predictive structures from multiple tasks and unlabeled data. J. Mach. Learn. Res. **6**, 1817–1853 (2005). http://jmlr.org/papers/v6/ando05a.html

2. Bikel, D.M., Miller, S., Schwartz, R., Weischedel, R.: NYMBLE: a high-performance learning name-finder. In: Fifth Conference on Applied Natural Language Processing, pp. 194–201. Association for Computational Linguistics, Washington, DC, March 1997. https://doi.org/10.3115/974557.974586, https://aclanthology.org/A97-1029

3. Borthwick, A., Sterling, J., Agichtein, E., Grishman, R.: Exploiting diverse knowledge sources via maximum entropy in named entity recognition. In: Charniak, E. (ed.) Sixth Workshop on Very Large Corpora, VLC@COLING/ACL 1998, Montreal, Quebec, Canada, 15–16 August 1998 (1998). https://aclanthology.org/W98-1118/

4. Chen, H., Yuan, S., Zhang, X.: Rose-NER: robust semi-supervised named entity recognition on insufficient labeled data. In: The 10th International Joint Conference on Knowledge Graphs. IJCKG 2021, pp. 38–44. Association for Computing Machinery, New York (2021). https://doi.org/10.1145/3502223.3502228

5. Douzon, T., Duffner, S., Garcia, C., Espinas, J.: Improving information extraction on business documents with specific pre-training tasks. In: Uchida, S., Barney, E., Eglin, V. (eds.) DAS 2022. LNCS, vol. 13237, pp. 111–125. Springer, Cham (2022). https://doi.org/10.1007/978-3-031-06555-2_8

6. Etzioni, O., et al.: Unsupervised named-entity extraction from the web: an experimental study. Artif. Intell. **165**(1), 91–134 (2005). https://doi.org/10.1016/j.artint.2005.03.001

7. Impedovo, A., Barracchia, E.P., Rizzo, G., Caprera, A., Landrò, E.: EPICS: pursuing the quest for smart procurement with artificial intelligence. In: Epifania, F., et al. (eds.) Proceedings of the 1st Italian Workshop on Artificial Intelligence and Applications for Business and Industries (AIABI 2021) Co-located with 20th International Conference of the Italian Association for Artificial Intelligence (AI*IA 2021), Online, Originally held in Milan, Italy, 30 November 2021. CEUR Workshop Proceedings, vol. 3102. CEUR-WS.org (2021). http://ceur-ws.org/Vol-3102/paper3.pdf

8. Iovine, A., Fang, A., Fetahu, B., Rokhlenko, O., Malmasi, S.: Cyclener: an unsupervised training approach for named entity recognition. In: Laforest, F., et al. (eds.) WWW 2022: The ACM Web Conference 2022, Virtual Event, Lyon, France, 25–29 April 2022, pp. 2916–2924. ACM (2022). https://doi.org/10.1145/3485447.3512012

9. Kaplan, M.: May I ask who's calling? Named entity recognition on call center transcripts for privacy law compliance. In: Xu, W., et al. (eds.) Proceedings of the Sixth Workshop on Noisy User-generated Text, W-NUT@EMNLP 2020 Online, 19 November 2020, pp. 1–6. Association for Computational Linguistics (2020). https://doi.org/10.18653/v1/2020.wnut-1.1

10. Krishnan, V., Manning, C.D.: An effective two-stage model for exploiting non-local dependencies in named entity recognition. In: Proceedings of the 21st International Conference on Computational Linguistics and 44th Annual Meeting of the Association for Computational Linguistics, pp. 1121–1128. Association for Computational Linguistics, Sydney, Australia, July 2006. https://doi.org/10.3115/1220175.1220316, https://aclanthology.org/P06-1141

11. Lafferty, J.D., McCallum, A., Pereira, F.C.N.: Conditional random fields: probabilistic models for segmenting and labeling sequence data. In: Brodley, C.E., Danyluk, A.P. (eds.) Proceedings of the Eighteenth International Conference on Machine Learning (ICML 2001), Williams College, Williamstown, MA, USA, 28 June–1 July 2001, pp. 282–289. Morgan Kaufmann (2001)

12. Liao, W., Veeramachaneni, S.: A simple semi-supervised algorithm for named entity recognition. In: Proceedings of the NAACL HLT 2009 Workshop on Semi-Supervised Learning for Natural Language Processing, pp. 58–65. SemiSupLearn 2009. Association for Computational Linguistics, USA (2009)

13. Liu, C., Yu, Y., Li, X., Wang, P.: Named entity recognition in equipment support field using tri-training algorithm and text information extraction technology. IEEE Access **9**, 126728–126734 (2021). https://doi.org/10.1109/ACCESS.2021.3109911

14. Lundberg, S.M., Lee, S.: A unified approach to interpreting model predictions. In: Guyon, I., et al. (eds.) Advances in Neural Information Processing Systems 30: Annual Conference on Neural Information Processing Systems 2017(December), pp. 4–9, 2017. Long Beach, CA, pp. 4765–4774 (2017). https://proceedings.neurips.cc/paper/2017/hash/8a20a8621978632d76c43dfd28b67767-Abstract.html

15. Nadeau, D., Turney, P.D., Matwin, S.: Unsupervised named-entity recognition: generating gazetteers and resolving ambiguity. In: Lamontagne, L., Marchand, M. (eds.) AI 2006. LNCS (LNAI), vol. 4013, pp. 266–277. Springer, Heidelberg (2006). https://doi.org/10.1007/11766247_23

16. Sekine, S., Grishman, R., Shinnou, H.: A decision tree method for finding and classifying names in Japanese texts. In: Charniak, E. (ed.) Sixth Workshop on Very Large Corpora, VLC@COLING/ACL 1998, Montreal, Quebec, Canada, 15–16 August 1998 (1998). https://aclanthology.org/W98-1120/

17. Szarvas, G., Farkas, R., Kocsor, A.: A multilingual named entity recognition system using boosting and C4.5 decision tree learning algorithms. In: Todorovski, L., Lavrač, N., Jantke, K.P. (eds.) DS 2006. LNCS (LNAI), vol. 4265, pp. 267–278. Springer, Heidelberg (2006). https://doi.org/10.1007/11893318_27

18. Vukadin, D., Kurdija, A.S., Delac, G., Silic, M.: Information extraction from free-form CV documents in multiple languages. IEEE Access **9**, 84559–84575 (2021). https://doi.org/10.1109/ACCESS.2021.3087913

19. Xiao, L., Wissmann, D., Brown, M., Jablonski, S.: Information extraction from the web: system and techniques. Appl. Intell. **21**(2), 195–224 (2004). https://doi.org/10.1023/B:APIN.0000033637.51909.04

20. Zhang, S., Elhadad, N.: Unsupervised biomedical named entity recognition: experiments with clinical and biological texts. J. Biomed. Inform. **46**(6), 1088–1098 (2013). https://doi.org/10.1016/j.jbi.2013.08.004, https://www.sciencedirect.com/science/article/pii/S1532046413001196, special Section: Social Media Environments

bNaming: An Intelligent Application to Assist Brand Names Definition

José Vieira[1], Rodrigo Rocha[1,2]($\boxtimes$), Luis F. Pereira[1], Igor Vanderlei[1],
Jean Araujo[1,3], and Jamilson Dantas[4]

[1] Agreste Federal University of Pernambuco UFAPE, Garanhuns, PE, Brazil
`{rodrigo.rocha,luis-filipe.pereira,igor.vanderlei,`
`jean.teixeira}@ufape.edu.br`
[2] Federal University of Alagoas UFAL, Maceió, AL, Brazil
[3] Federal University of Sergipe UFS, Aracaju, SE, Brazil
[4] Federal University of Pernambuco UFPE, Recife, PE, Brazil
`jamilson@cin.ufpe.br`

Abstract. Relevant branding projects start with a significant name, so the naming process is essential for creating a successful brand. However, not everyone has access to branding experts to guide this naming process. This paper proposes an accessible solution that makes a technical evaluation of brand names, supporting and helping people to decide the best name for their business. For this, our work aims to develop a mobile application that uses machine learning models trained on a database created by naming experts that evaluates many brand names accordingly to ten technical criteria. Thus, we provide a mobile application that makes the machine learning models accessible to the user in a simple way, allowing him/her to make rational decisions based on technical knowledge. Furthermore, we demonstrate the accuracy of our models on predicting the evaluation of the brand names. For the vast majority of the evaluation criteria, our application automatically generated a score matching with the output given by the branding experts within a positive/negative deviation of one point in more than 80% of the cases. Finally, an MVP is developed that already presents satisfactory results.

Keywords: Naming · Machine learning · Neural network · Mobile application

1 Introduction

Brand Naming is the process of choosing the more attractive name for a brand (company, product, or service). In Marketing, the naming strategy consists of creating or identifying a brand's ideal name. Such a name should be capable of fully representing and symbolizing the essence and personality of its products [1–3]. The Brand Naming process involves several steps and concepts, requiring creativity, in-depth study of the company and its consumers, analysis, and focus on the potential customers [1,4]. The constitution of a good name for a business is a critical factor contributing to its success [1–5].

The definition of a new brand name is one of the many challenges for the success of a business [1,6–8]. Nevertheless, several factors turn the naming process into a difficult task, such as lacking technical and rational criteria and insufficiency of creativity [2,3,8,9]. The cost of hiring branding experts is another factor that challenges the naming process [10]. Therefore, the solution presented in this work targets small businesses with few technical and financial resources, such as small companies, self-employed professionals, and general entrepreneurs. We propose an intelligent tool that supports the Brand Naming process using neural networks [11,12], and machine learning [13] concepts. The system is built based on marketing and business literature criteria to ensure the users will name their brands and products following a more rational and technical process. No works were identified in the literature involving the concepts of branding name definition and Neural Networks, as well as Vector Representation of Text, Embedding Layer and Text Classification.

Our platform assign scores to brand names suggested by the user based on his/her business segment. Different neural networks were trained to be specialized in a specific naming criteria such as *creativity*, *memorization*, *simplicity*, and *originality*. From the scores provided by each neural network, a final score is computed for the given brand name.

This paper is organized as follows: Sect. 2 presents the main background concepts adopted in this paper; Sect. 3 explains the methods used in the development of the solution, showing and describing the proposed system in details, including the architecture and the system design. Section 4 presents the machine learning models; Sect. 5 presents the evaluation of the results; Finally, Sect. 6 brings the final remarks, with last conclusions and future works.

2   Background

This section describes three fundamental concepts needed to understand the essential elements of the proposed solution: the Vector Representation of Text, Embedding Layer and Text Classification.

2.1   Vector Representation of Text

Since neural networks commonly receive valued numerical inputs, some treatment is necessary for the adequate processing of data by neural networks. As an alternative, seeking a numerical representation for the input texts is essential. An efficient way to represent text is through vector representation [14–16] with the application of the Tokenization technique [17–19]. In this case, for each word of the text, a token is associated with an integer, replacing the sequence of words with the sequence of tokens e obtaining a vector of integer values representing the initial text. Another alternative would be through a representation matrix using the One-Hot Encoding technique, in which it would be a sparse matrix with each row of the matrix representing a word of the text and only one element per row has the value 1, with the position of that element dictating which word that line represents [20–22].

However, it should be noted that both approaches entail efficiency limitations in machine learning models. The first approach brings a problem that can make neural networks inefficient. Depending on the size of the universe of words considered in the problem, it is possible to work with a large range between the integer tokens. This would require a great effort from the neural network to train weights that balance this large scale of input values, thus putting the model's learning ability and efficiency to the test. On the other hand, the second approach is not considered efficient because it deals with sparse vectors, where there is a large volume of data, but few of the data have a relevant representation. This makes it difficult for the weights of the networks to learn because, since they work with a product between the weights and the input data, with the vast majority of the input data being 0, a good part of the learned weights would be canceled out. Thus, it also hinders the model's learning ability and efficiency.

Given the deficiency of these two approaches, a decision was made to use a dense fan representation in this work. For this, an Embedding layer is used in the neural network, which will be detailed in the next section.

2.2   Embedding Layer

The Embedding Layer is a layer implemented by Keras API[1] in order to solve the problems mentioned in the previous subsection. This layer is usually used in natural language processing problems, being able to represent words in vectors of dense real values with a fixed size, becoming more efficient than the One-hot Encoding technique in a large set of words [23,24]. This approach basically works by learning weights through training the model and representing the input words in a dense array of real values of a pre-established size. Thus, making the neural network model more efficient compared to using the techniques presented in the previous section.

In this work, the embedding layer generates a dense array of real numbers with size 3 for each character of a branding name. As a result, our data representation resulted from the embedding layer is much smaller then the one that would be generated via One-hot Encoding. Therefore, we may also use a Neural Network composed of much fewer weights and parameters that is well suited scenarios where the amount of data available for training is limited.

2.3   Text Classification

Text classification (bag of words) is a classic text processing problem in the machine learning universe [14,15,25–28]. This concept is correlated with the problem in question, where names are classified instead of words. However, with an adaptation to this problem, a greater similarity can be achieved using each

---

[1] Available in: https://keras.io/.

word as an element of the bag of words vector if the characters that compose the word were used. This way, the tokenizer would replace each character with a name, not a word.

The traditional bag of words consists of a fixed-size vector, where each position of the vector represents the occurrence of a given the word in the input text. Thus, when processing the text, the number of occurrences of each word is considered in the vector. This vector will be the input for the predictions of text classification of the neural networks in question.

3   The Proposed Intelligent System

As described in the Introduction, this proposal aims to help users (entrepreneurs, self-employed professionals, or organizations) evaluate and decide when defining names for their products and businesses. In this way, from a simplified query, the user informs the name option and its business segment. Then, through a set of neural networks, the system evaluates the informed name in ten different criteria, producing data to assist and support the definition of the new business name.

The ten criteria that the system evaluates are respectively: Creativity, Spelling, Memorization, Originality, Popularity, Potential, Pronunciation, Simplicity, Sonority, and Concept. For each criterion, the system evaluates the name, assigning an integer grade between 1 to 5. It also informs a grade average that summarizes an evaluation and general score for that name. Table 1 presents these criteria, which are used to assist the user in interpreting and receiving the results. It should be noted that some of the criteria are subjective.

Table 1. Description table of the evaluated criteria

Criteria	Description
Creativity	Evaluation of the level of creativity
Spelling	Verification of writing ease level
Memorization	Classification of the degree of memorization of the proposed name
Originality	Qualification of the suggested name originality
Popularity	Popularity evaluation
Potential	Verification of the name potential as a brand (subjective criterion)
Pronunciation	Verification of the pronunciation's level of ease
Simplicity	Classification of simplicity and complexity
Sonority	Qualification of the sound of the presented name
Concept	Concept evaluation (subjective criterion)

The name evaluation will be done through machine learning models using neural networks that were trained using a database formulated by experts to evaluate the quality of brand names. This strategy considers as input for the models the brand name and the market segment that the brand will act, taking into account ten pre-defined segments that the user can select that best suit their brand. In this approach, each criterion presented has a specific neural network trained to be an expert in evaluating a given criterion of a name, and all networks have the same morphology.

This approach was developed in two parts, the mobile application, and the API. Figure 1 presents the architecture of this work's proposal, with the details that make up each implemented part, involving all the main structures and elements used in its operation.

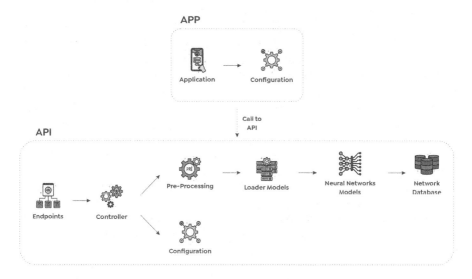

Fig. 1. Proposed architecture for the two application modules.

On the left side of Fig. 1, the mobile application module is illustrated, which follows an MVC pattern in which there are visual elements that interact with the entire system. This module comprises the layer responsible for calling the application's API and, finally, a layer with the application's basic settings.

On the right side of Fig. 1, the API architecture is presented as the system's core. The initial requests received by the API are handled by the endpoints, which are integrated with the API's control layer, where it manages such requests and performs the prediction of machine learning models. In control, the configuration data and the machine learning models are received, with weights and hyperparameters stored in the network database. There is a Model layer described as Neural Network Models, which contains the morphology of the application models. In the Loader Models layer, the application loads and instantiates the models and entities necessary for its operation. Finally, Pre-Processing is the layer that handles the inputs coming from the application, checking the validity of the data and processing them so that the neural networks consume them. In the following two subsections, briefly, more details about mobile application and API implementation are presented.

3.1   Mobile Application Implementation

The system was initially developed as a mobile application. However, considering the scenario that can/should go to other architectures besides mobile, this environment was modeled in a segmented way, transferring to an API the centrality of the system's functionalities, being the application, the front-end of the system. Thus, allowing portability to any platform or integration with other applications.

Flutter[2], a hybrid framework for mobile development, was used for the mobile application, compiling a single code for the two main operating systems of mobile devices, Android and IOS. The main purpose of this architecture, where the application is a user interaction layer, is to allow the API to be responsible for the entire kernel of the system.

As the application's proposal aims at simplicity, it starts with the splash screen feature and follows a direct flow, requesting the input of user names and segments. Then, the user is directed to a sequence of screens, each presenting important information for a better understanding of the system and its operation.

As illustrated in Fig. 2, the system asks the user for the name and market segment of the brand that wants to carry out that evaluation. Once the fields are filled in, the evaluate button is activated, and, when selecting to carry out the evaluation, the user is directed to a loading screen until, finally, the screen with the evaluation result is displayed.

3.2   The Development of the API

The main responsibility of the API is to have an environment for executing the neural network models. In this way, the API was built using the Flask microframework in Python since the machine learning models used in this work are also written in the same language, using, in this case, the TensorFlow[3] and Keras frameworks.

The API has a simple structure, with an interface where it implements the endpoints and all the structure and base settings of the API. This interface makes contact with the control layer, where the solution kernel is implemented. In this control layer, the API starts and all the neural network models already trained are loaded, as well as all the structures and hyperparameters necessary for the correct execution of the models, leaving them ready to perform the evaluations whenever the API is requested.

---

[2] Available in: https://flutter.dev/.
[3] Available in: https://www.tensorflow.org/.

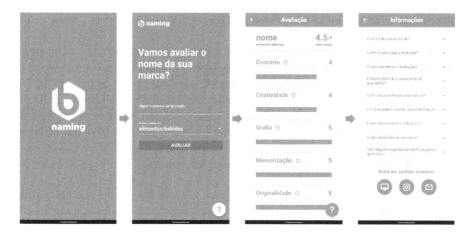

Fig. 2. Example of the application's main screens.

In this layer, there is also the implementation of the pre-processing of the requested names, where the entire process of tokenization and padding of the names submitted for evaluation by the API is carried out.

As this is an initial release of the application, the API was deployed on Heroku, which provides a pre-configured system with support for Python-Flask applications, facilitating the configuration and deployment process and thus making it possible to generate the initial release and test all the features of the APP.

The API has two simple endpoints, a simple GET, which is a way to start the API because, as we use Heroku, the application shuts down to save resources after a certain period of inactivity. So, this GET method is requested whenever the APP is opened on some device, initializing the start process in the API while the user interacts with the application. This reduces the waiting time for the evaluation when the second endpoint is activated as a POST method and then sends a JSON with the name and market segment presented by the user. It then returns a JSON with the criteria and their respective scores.

4   Proposed Machine Learning Models

This section presents the main elements of the work that represent computational intelligence, such as the construction of the database for training the machine learning models and the adopted machine learning models.

4.1   The Database Construction

For the construction of the database used for training and testing the machine learning models of this work, four marketing professionals were selected to assist the process, with technical knowledge and direct involvement in the name evaluation service.

This base was formed by 1,000 brand names, followed by their respective market segments, in this case: food/beverages, automotive, consumer goods, energy/fuel, entertainment, finance, logistics, services, technology, or retail. With this number of brands and segments, marketing professionals evaluated this information independently and subjectively through a spreadsheet shared between the evaluators involved. The selection was based on the ten criteria already described above, with the base objective being impartial, avoiding tendencies towards a single professional criterion, for example. This base is available in https://bityli.com/PHBUXDI.

After labeling the databases, the information from the four worksheets was compiled, resulting in a new worksheet with the average evaluation rounded off by the four experts. Since each criterion has its specific neural network, the database was segmented into ten bases, where each one has the evaluation of a specific criterion to train and test the machine learning models. Notably, this base was used for training and testing the models. Then, each of the ten bases was randomly divided into three sets, the training, the validation, and the test sets. These sets are useful for training and testing neural network models. In such a manner, the training set had 80% of the total data, and the validation and test sets each had 10% of the total data.

4.2   Data Pre-processing

The TensorFlow and Keras frameworks were used to build the machine learning models, given that they provide a good environment for such purpose.

As these are machine learning models for text evaluation, the problem in question works with unstructured data. Therefore, the first task is to process the input texts for a representation to be used in neural network models since the model inputs are always numerical values. Unlike what was mentioned in Sect. 2.1 about vector approaches, and because these more classic forms are not such efficient vector representations, this work sought to work on a dense vector representation form, thus favoring the performance of neural networks. Therefore, there is a sequence of steps in text processing to arrive at the vector representation.

In the tokenization first step, the Tokenizer structure provided by Keras was used. However, for this specific application, it created tokens for the letters instead of creating tokens for words since the evaluated texts are names. Then, the tokenizer was trained in the training database to learn the tokens of the letters present in this base. So, for every new entry, the first step is to transform the name received into a vector with the respective tokens of the letters that compose the name. To better contextualize, Fig. 3 illustrates the flow of steps performed for pre-processing and prediction in the learning models.

From the token vector, padding is performed on the vector, a step that consists of standardizing the size of the input vector for the neural network model. As the input names can have any size, but the models are designed to receive

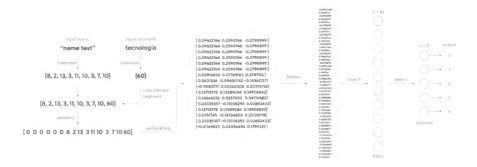

Fig. 3. Example of the pre-processing and propagation execution flow of the neural network model.

a fixed-size vector, this padding step is necessary. In order to arrive at an adequate padding size, the results of various sizes were tested. In this sense, size 15 presented the best performance and was used as the standard size. With that, the token vectors became size 15, and for those with smaller sizes, it will be completed with 0, and if larger, data that exceeds it is ignored. It is important to note that the vector is filled in reverse order. When performing the padding, the token of the first letter of the name will be the last element of the vector, and if necessary, to complete the padding vector with 0, the assignments will be in the first positions.

After padding, one more element is concatenated to the vector, which is a token that represents which of the ten market niches this entry name belongs to so that the market segment is considered at the time of name evaluation. Thus, increasing the vector of size to 16, where the 16th element represents one of the ten market niches considered by the solution.

Even with a standardized size, the limitation of the sparse vector and also that of the large range of tokens persists since brand names such as "HP," which is from the technology sector, would be evaluated as a vector of 16 elements, while only the three latter values would be different from 0. Furthermore, in the case of big names, there would be no sparse vector, but the difference in the size of the tokens could be a problem for the performance of neural network models. In this sense, the Embedding layer is used, as a layer of neurons that learns weights to result in dense vectors with concentrated values, thus facilitating the performance of neural networks.

4.3 The Machine Learning Models

The processing of the input names according to their vectorial representation can be conducted in two folds: following the classification or regression approaches. Using classification models, a discrete output score from 1 to 5 is assigned to each input vector associated with a name. Using regression models, a real value from 1 to 5 is generated as the score for each input.

5   Experimental Study

In this section, we present and compare results using both the classification and regression approaches. The classification model evaluated is composed of an embedding layer that maps each dimension of the input vector of size 16 into three new dimensions. As a result, a matrix 16×3 is generated. This data is then flattened to be given as input of two dense layers. The first is composed of ten neurons and activated by ReLU, and the last is composed of 5 neurons (one for each class) and activated by Sigmoid.

We generated the regression model from the classification network by replacing the Sigmoid in the last layer with a ReLU and adding a final layer composed of a single neuron without an activation function.

A classification and a regression network were trained for each of the ten evaluated criteria discussed previously in this paper. In such a procedure, the data in the training set were used to update the model's weights, and the validation set was used to track the network performance over unseen data. Only the weights associated with the best accuracy in a validation set were saved to prevent the training from overfitting the model weights to the training data causing a loss of generality over unseen data. Finally, we report the model's accuracy in the last test set in this section.

Figure 4 shows the loss decay for the training and validation sets during the training stage of classification networks to learn to scoring the *memorization* and *simplicity* criteria. After the 25th epoch, the ascending validation loss clearly shows that the models over-fit the training data. By saving the model weights associated with the lowest validation loss, we ensure no over-fitting in our model with unseen data.

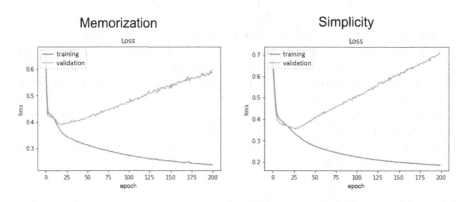

Fig. 4. Loss decay during the training stage for learning the *memorization* and *simplicity* criteria.

All the networks were trained for 200 epochs; their weights were updated according to the Adam optimizer with a learning rate equal to 25×10^{-4}. In

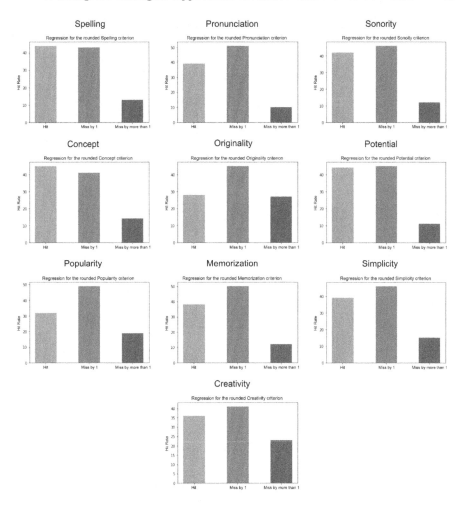

Fig. 5. Results obtained using the regression models.

the classification approach, the Binary Cross Entropy (BCE) was used as a loss function. The Mean Squared Error (MSE) was used in the regression approach as a loss function.

Results in Figs. 5 and 6 show the accuracy rates obtained by regression and classification models, respectively. Each graph in Figs. 5 and 6 is relative to different classification criteria for the brand names in the test set. On each graph, the first bar indicates the rate of samples in the test set at which the scores were assigned correctly, the second bar indicates the rate of errors by positive or negative deviations of one point around the correct score, and the third bar indicates the more significant errors.

The analysis of Figs. 5 and 6 show that the classification and regression models performed quite close on the score assignment for branding names. However,

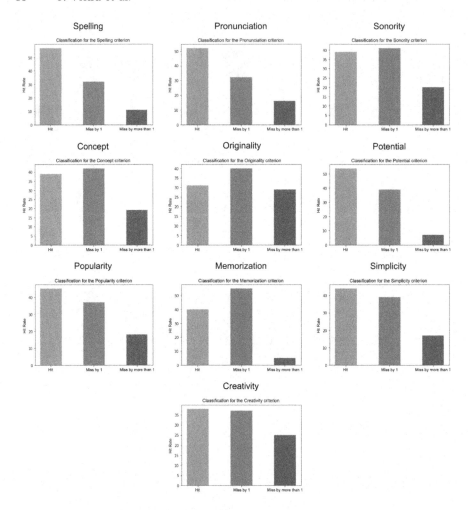

Fig. 6. Results obtained using the classification models.

the classification models presented significant superior performance in criteria like *memorization* and *potential*.

Some criteria, like *originality* and *creativity*, presented a higher prediction challenge. In such cases, the rates of significant errors were higher than 20%. For all the other evaluation criteria, the rates of significant errors were below 20%.

6   Final Remarks

The naming process is fundamental in any brand's initial phase, but it is necessary for almost all businesses. A good brand is based on the concept of a name representing it in the market. Thus, such a naming process is a critical step for the design of new brands. Unfortunately, the services of brand naming experts are not easily accessible due to financial costs, making this service unreachable for small businesses. This way, our work proposed an intelligent system that can aid entrepreneurs in creating and defining names for new brands.

In this work, the literature suggests that simpler models such as Decision Trees or Naive Bayes will generate hit rates lower or at maximum equal to those observed with Neural Networks. However, through Neural Networks, it is possible to more easily identify and circumvent problems during training such as over-fitting. Thus, the developed system is based on machine learning models, trained in a database built by experts. In a simplified way, it provides a technical evaluation under ten criteria. The application has a neural network for evaluating each criterion. We ensure an easy-to-use service by offering users access to those models via a mobile application.

Furthermore, we demonstrated the accuracy of the score prediction proposed using neural networks for classification and regression. For the vast majority of the evaluation criteria, our application automatically generated a score matched with the output given by the branding experts within a positive/negative deviation of one point in more than 80% of the cases.

This approach involves computational intelligence concepts and is intended for those who work offering services, brands, and products in general. In future work, a larger database will be evaluated to retrain and develop new models looking for more accurate results. Finally, some system implementations, such as a WEB interface, should be implemented to access the learning models.

References

1. Chiranjeeb, K., Doglas, W.L.: Observations: creating effective brand name: a study of the naming process. J. Advert. Res. **37**(1), 67–75 (1997)
2. Bhat, S., Kelley, G., O'Donnell, K.: An investigation of consumer reactions to the use of different brand names. J. Prod. Brand Manag. **7**, 41–50 (1998)
3. Ruffell, B.: The genetics of brandnaming. J. Brand Manag. **4**, 10 (1996)
4. Rubio, N., Villaseñor, N., Yagüe, M.: The role of private label tiers and private label naming strategies in the relationship between private label brand equity and store loyalty. J. Prod. Brand Manag. **29**(1), 124–138 (2019)
5. Choi, L., Huddleston, P.: The effect of retailer private brands on consumer-based retailer equity: comparison of named private brands and generic private brands. Int. Rev. Retail Distrib. Consum. Res. **24**, 59–78 (2014)
6. Martinez, J.: The magic of 'great' linked to product names. J. Brand Manag. **23**, 03 (2016)
7. Kara, S., Gunasti, Ross, W.T.: My brand identity lies in the brand name: personified suggestive brand names. J. Brand Manag. **27**, 09 (2020)
8. Arora, S., Kalro, A., Sharma, D.: A comprehensive framework of brand name classification. J. Brand Manag. **22**, 05 (2015)
9. Andreas, B., Eisingerich, C.: Whan Park, Deborah J. MacInnis. Brand Architecture Design and Brand Naming Decisions. Routledge, London (2016)
10. Kenagy, J.W., Stein, G.C.: Naming, labeling, and packaging of pharmaceuticals. Am. J. Health-Syst. Pharm. **58**(21), 2033–2041 (2001)

11. Undefinedniegula, A., Poniszewska-Marańda, A., Popović, M.: Study of machine learning methods for customer churn prediction in telecommunication company. In: Proceedings of the 21st International Conference on Information Integration and Web-Based Applications and Services, iiWAS2019, New York, NY, USA, pp. 640–644. Association for Computing Machinery (2019)
12. Tomihira, T., Otsuka, A., Yamashita, A., Satoh, T.: What does your tweet emotion mean? Neural emoji prediction for sentiment analysis. In: Proceedings of the 20th International Conference on Information Integration and Web-Based Applications and Services, iiWAS2018, New York, NY, USA, pp. 289–296. Association for Computing Machinery (2018)
13. Eddamiri, S., Zemmouri, E., Benghabrit, A.: Graph embeddings for linked data clustering. In: Proceedings of the 20th International Conference on Information Integration and Web-Based Applications and Services, iiWAS2018, New York, NY, USA, pp. 122–128. Association for Computing Machinery (2018)
14. Grzegorczyk, K.: Vector representations of text data in deep learning. CoRR, abs/1901.01695 (2019)
15. Liu, N., et al.: Text representation: from vector to tensor. In: Fifth IEEE International Conference on Data Mining (ICDM 2005), p. 4 (2005)
16. Dumais, S., Platt, J., Heckerman, D., Sahami, M.: Inductive learning algorithms and representations for text categorization. In: Proceedings of the Seventh International Conference on Information and Knowledge Management, CIKM 1998, New York, NY, USA, pp. 148–155. Association for Computing Machinery (1998)
17. Grefenstette, G.: Tokenization, pp. 117–133. Springer, Dordrecht (1999). https://doi.org/10.1007/978-94-015-9273-4_9
18. Mohan, V.: Text mining: open source tokenization tools: an analysis. Adv. Comput. Intell. Int. J. (ACII) **3**, 37–47 (2016)
19. Mullen, L.A., Benoit, K., Keyes, O., Selivanov, D., Arnold, J.: Fast, consistent tokenization of natural language text. J. Open Source Softw. **3**, 655 (2018)
20. Pham, D.-H., Le, A.-C.: Exploiting multiple word embeddings and one-hot character vectors for aspect-based sentiment analysis. Int. J. Approx. Reason. **103**, 1–10 (2018)
21. El Affendi, M.A., Al Rajhi, K.H.S.: Text encoding for deep learning neural networks: a reversible base 64 (tetrasexagesimal) integer transformation (rit64) alternative to one hot encoding with applications to Arabic morphology. In: 2018 Sixth International Conference on Digital Information, Networking, and Wireless Communications (DINWC), pp. 70–74 (2018)
22. Kumar, N., Bhatia, M.S., Aggarwal, A.: Speech-to-text conversion using GRU and one hot vector encodings. PalArch's J. Archaeol. Egypt/Egyptol. **17**(10), 7110–7119 (2020)
23. Khrulkov, V., Hrinchuk, O., Mirvakhabova, L., Oseledets, I.V.: Tensorized embedding layers for efficient model compression. CoRR, abs/1901.10787 (2019)
24. Hrinchuk, O., Khrulkov, V., Mirvakhabova, L., Orlova, E., Oseledets, I.: Tensorized embedding layers. In: Findings of the Association for Computational Linguistics: EMNLP 2020, pp. 4847–4860, Online. Association for Computational Linguistics, November 2020
25. Simanjuntak, D.A., Ipung, H.P., Lim, C., Nugroho, A.S.: Text classification techniques used to facilitate cyber terrorism investigation. In: 2010 Second International Conference on Advances in Computing, Control, and Telecommunication Technologies, pp. 198–200 (2010)

26. Yao, L., Mao, C., Luo, Y.: Graph convolutional networks for text classification. In: Proceedings of the AAAI Conference on Artificial Intelligence, vol. 33, no. 01, pp. 7370–7377 (2019)
27. Kowsari, K., Meimandi, K.J., Heidarysafa, M., Mendu, S., Barnes, L., Brown, D.: Text classification algorithms: a survey. Information $10(4)$ (2019)
28. Alcamo, T., Cuzzocrea, A., Bosco, G.L., Pilato, G., Schicchi, D.: Analysis and comparison of deep learning networks for supporting sentiment mining in text corpora. In: Proceedings of the 22nd International Conference on Information Integration and Web-Based Applications and Services, iiWAS 2020, New York. Association for Computing Machinery (2020)

Discovering Conditional Business Rules in Web Applications Using Process Mining

Hamza Alkofahi[1]([✉]), David Umphress[2], and Heba Alawneh[3]

[1] Jordan University of Science and Technology, Irbid 22110, Jordan
`hoalkofahi@just.edu.jo`
[2] Auburn University, Auburn, AL 36849, USA
`david.umphress@auburn.edu`
[3] Princess Sumaya University for Technology, Amman 11941, Jordan
`h.alawneh@psut.edu.jo`

Abstract. Advances in web frameworks input validation shifted the attacks towards exploiting applications' business logic. The absence of accurate business rules representation expanded the logical vulnerability surface. We propose an accurate and efficient approach for discovering the business logic of real-world web applications utilizing the dynamic behavior. Our solution discovered conditional business rules defined over one-to-one and one-to-many implicit dependency relations. Moreover, minimized the negative effect of substitute relations. Our results indicate a high precision in recovering positive long-distance dependency relations from the observed behavior.

Keywords: Process mining · Dependency mining · Web application · Knowledge extraction · Business rules · Business logic vulnerability

1 Introduction

Web technologies have revolutionized building and deploying solutions in various fields such as e-commerce, healthcare, e-education, and cloud services. However, as web applications grow in features and popularity, their complexity increases accordingly. Role management and decision-making processes of web applications are defined through business rules that formalize the system's intended behavior. Therefore, neglecting or failing to maintain these business rules throughout the system development increases the chance of faulty application logic over time as the system implementation diverges from its specifications. The code becomes the only documentation source available in case of outdated business rules, opening the door for potential Business Logic Vulnerability (BLV).

Web applications BLVs are hard to detect, as they are (unlike traditional injection attacks) uniquely tailored to the targeted system [4]. Detecting BLVs requires sufficient knowledge of the underlying application business logic to compare the observed against the expected behaviors. In the absence of a formal specification of the expected behavior, detecting BLVs becomes infeasible. However, Heuristic approaches [2,3] can be used to recover a subset of the business rules or system specifications.

This research proposes a novel mining approach for detecting dependency-based conditional business rules in web applications. Our solution is a black-box-based approach that uses HTTP traces generated during normal execution. It neither requires knowledge of the source code nor modifying it, limiting the overhead on the application performance.

2 Background

Condition business rules are assertion rules in the form of if-then statements [7], which, when resolved to true, activates a particular business logic. We refer to them as "if-then business rules," which are standard in web applications and enforced through business logic. If-then business rules are encoded into the application business logic using direct and indirect user input (inferred values), user session state (based on the usage behavior), and other data forms.

There are two types of dependencies to be considered during process mining, explicit and implicit [5]. Explicit dependencies are the number of times a task follows another over all the traces in the event log. Implicit dependencies represent indirect relations between tasks (events), where one's execution depends on the occurrences of another(one-to-one) or others (one-to-many relation) in the same trace. If the implicit dependency relies on the presence of one or more tasks, the relationship is considered positive, but if it relies on the absence of one or more tasks, it is said to be a negative implicit dependency [6].

When mining for implicit dependencies, detecting substitute relations can be challenging. In such cases, the implicit dependency is distributed across two or more tasks, where the occurrence of a single task satisfies the dependency. For example, If D substitutes E, and A implicitly depends on E, then A implicitly depends on D as well. Frequency-based metrics [5,8] can be used to detect such dependencies. However, these methods can only identify a segment of the implicit dependency or miss the dependency altogether.

Preliminaries: This research expands on and improves the capability of Flexible Heuristic Miner (FHM) in detecting implicit dependencies [8]. FHM is a mining algorithm that constructs a dependency graph as the means by which to discover the most likely process. We reused some (items 1 and 2 below) and introduced another (items 3) of the relation definitions employed by FHM for constructing causal dependency tables [8]. Let W be a workflow log over T, where T^* is all possible traces over the process activities composed of tasks T, such that $W \subseteq T^*$ and $\delta \in T^*$:

1. $a >_W b$ iff there is a trace $\delta = t_1 t_2 t_3 ... t_n$ and $i \in \{1, ..., n-1\}$ such that $\delta \in W$ and $t_i = a$ and $t_{i+1} = b$ (direct successor).

2. $a >>>_W b$ iff there is a trace $\delta = t_1 t_2 t_3 ... t_n$ and $i < j$ and $i, j \in \{1, ..., n\}$
   such that $\delta \in W$ and $t_i = a$ and $t_j = b$ (forward direct or indirect successor).
3. $a <<<_{W'} b$ iff there is a trace $\delta = t_1 t_2 t_3 ... t_n$ and $i > j$ and $i, j \in \{1, ..., n\}$
   such that $\delta \in W$ and $t_i = a$ and t_i is the first occurrence of a and $t_j = b$
   (backward unique direct or indirect successor).

3 Methodology

In this section, we propose our solution for mining positive long-distance dependency relations with the presence of substitute relations. Our focus will be on discovering one-to-one and one-to-many implicit dependencies in web applications, with substitute relations of length two (pairs).

3.1 Step1: Building the Dependency Graph

The first step in FHM is building the dependency graph (DG). Graph nodes represent tasks connectable with others through edges based on their causal dependency. Because the number of relations between tasks can be large, a frequency-based metric is used to measure the strength of the relationship to determine included edges. FHM defines several different dependency measures [8]. We used some (Eqs. 1 & 2) and introduced another as in Eq. 3.

Equation (1) quantifies the direct dependency relation between two tasks a and b, such that $|a >_W b|$ is the number of times a was directly followed by b in $W \subseteq T^*$. The term, $\Rightarrow^l_W$, in Eq. (2) calculates the direct or indirect followed-by relation between tasks (a.k.a., long-distance dependency), such that $|a >>>_W b|$ is the number of times a was directly or indirectly followed by b in $W \subseteq T^*$, and $|a|$ is the count of time a was executed in $W \subseteq T^*$. Duplicate patterns are considered when constructing the forward long distance relation $(>>>_W)$ table, as tasks can be performed multiple times in a single trace. Such patterns also contributes to the final value of $|a >>>_W b|$ and $|a|$.

$$a \Rightarrow_W b = \left(\frac{|a >_W b| - |b >_W a|}{|a >_W b| + |b >_W a| + 1} \right), \; if \; a \neq b \tag{1}$$

$$a \Rightarrow^l_W b = \left(\frac{2 \left(|a >>>_W b| \right)}{|a| + |b| + 1} \right) - \left(\frac{2 \, Abs(|a| - |b|)}{|a| + |b| + 1} \right) \tag{2}$$

In real-world web applications, usually, the dependency must be completely satisfied once per session. However, Eq. 2 can detect part or fail to detect the entire implicit dependency. For example, a user only has to *login* to the system once per session to have access to the logged-in user's functionalities. To address this, we introduced a new dependency measure capable of discovering a wide range of long-distance relations illustrated in Equation (3).

Equation (3) defines a direct and indirect backward long-distance dependency measure $(\Rightarrow^l_{W'})$ based on the first occurrence of the target task, where only the preceding tasks are considered. $|a <<<_{W'} b|$ is the number of times b directly or indirectly preceded a based on the first occurrence of a only, and $|a'|$ is the number of traces in which a occurred at least once. The goal is to avoid duplicate long-distance relations per trace and focus on the initial dependency of each task.

$$a \Rightarrow^l_{W'} b = \left(\frac{2 \, (|a <<<_{W'} b|)}{|a'| + |b'| + 1} \right) \tag{3}$$

3.2 Step2: Detecting Substitute Relations

A long-distance dependency can be non-straightforward one-to-one relation, as a task can depend on executing one from a set of tasks, known as a long-distance substitute dependency relationship. For illustration, we focus on detecting pairs of tasks. However, this approach can also detect longer substitute relations

First, we search for all the tasks $C \subseteq T$ that have the potential to participate in a substitute relation with every task in T. For task $c \subseteq C$ to be considered a candidate, the number of times it is directly or indirectly executed before $t \subseteq T$ based on the first occurrence ($|t <<<_{W'} c|$) must be less than $|t'|$. Otherwise, it is not a candidate, as substitute relation can not exist if the candidate task matches or exceeds $|e'|$. The search culminates by returning a (possibly empty) list of candidate tasks (C) for every task in T.

After detecting all candidate tasks (C) for every task in T, we proceed by creating pairs of tasks with potential substitute relations. All possible pairs in C are tested and only those that meet the selection criteria are considered. Two tasks (a and b) are considered to have a potential substitute relation with respect to e only if the following conditions are met:

- As defined in Eq. (4), both a and b must have a dependency score with t greater or equal to the long-distance dependency threshold (default $= 0.1$).
- The number of times a and b happened before t based on their first occurrence must be equal or very close to the number of times t' was executed. As shown in Eq. (5), the substitute ratio is computed and evaluated with an error margin of ± 0.1.
- The lift score of $a \Rightarrow^l_{Lift'} b$ and $b \Rightarrow^l_{Lift'} a$ should be less than 1 and as close as possible to zero. A lift score < 1 indicates a negative dependency or a substitute effect, thus the closer the score is to zero the stronger the effect. In Eq. (6), the lift score ($\Rightarrow^l_{Lift'}$) is computed based on the first occurrence, then compared to the lift threshold (default $= 0.15$).

$$t \Rightarrow^l_{W'} a \geq \mathbf{LRD\_THR} \ \wedge \ t \Rightarrow^l_{W'} b \geq \mathbf{LRD\_THR}, \ \textit{such that } a \neq b \tag{4}$$

$$\mathbf{Substitute\_Ratio}^t_{ab} = \frac{|t <<<_{W'} a| + |t <<<_{W'} b|}{|t'|}$$

$$\mathbf{MAXEM} \geq \mathbf{Substitute\_Ratio}^e_{ab} \geq \mathbf{MINEM}, \ \textit{such that } a \neq b \tag{5}$$

$$a \Rightarrow^l_{Lift'} b = \left(\frac{support_{a<<<_{W'}b}}{(support_{a'})(support_{b'})} \right) = \left(\frac{\left(\frac{|a<<<_{W'}b|}{|W|} \right)}{\left(\frac{|a'|}{|W|} \right) \left(\frac{|b'|}{|W|} \right)} \right)$$

$$\left(a \Rightarrow^l_{Lift'} b \leq \textbf{LIFT\_THR}\right) \wedge \left(b \Rightarrow^l_{Lift'} a \leq \textbf{LIFT\_THR}\right), \; such \; that \; a \neq b \tag{6}$$

Lastly, we assesses all the candidate pairs with substitute relations and generates a final list per task of the actual substitute relations. This is done by evaluating each candidate with all other candidates in the same list to make sure their direct and long-distance dependency scores were below the threshold (default direct $= 0.6$, long $= 0.6$). The main goal here is to eliminate any candidate pairs that directly or indirectly depend on one another, as tasks associated with a substitute relation should not appear at the same time and trace.

3.3   Step3: Mining Positive Long-Distance Dependencies

Early detection and handling of involved substitute relations is a critical step to successfully detect long-distance dependency relations. The strength of such relations that are defined based on substitutionally associated tasks are lower, due to the effect of substitute relations among tasks. Using measures like $\Rightarrow^l_W$ fails to detect some or all of dependencies due to low scores. To prevent distributing the frequency in the first place, we resolved the substitute relations by merging tasks into a single task. Take, for example, $W = \{A\underline{B}FEA^5, G\underline{C}GEH^8,$ $D\underline{B}HDE^7\}$, where $\textbf{E}$ depend on the occurs of B or C. Therefore, B and C have a substitute relation which to resolve, both B and C are merged to form a new task $"BC"$. Hence, W becomes $= \{A"BC"FEA^5, G"BC"GEH^8, D"BC"HDE^7\}$.

After resolving all the substitute relations in the event log (W), we iterates over all tasks in $E' \in T$, searching for relations between tasks based on the first occurrence of the target task (e). The relation selection criterion is based on the existence of a backward long-distance dependency relation between a and b, which is determined by the number of times b happened before the first occurrence of a and $(|a <<<_{W'} b|)$ is greater or equal to $|a'|$. A task can have multiple long-distance dependency relations. Thus, all relations are stored into a list data structure. Finally, a map of all detected relations per task is returned.

4   Evaluation

To evaluate our proposal, we created a Petri net model following the specifications of osCommerce. We used the Petri net simulator to generate synthetic workflow logs satisfying modeled specifications and simulating real users' behavior. We evaluated the capability of our proposal in re-discovering if-then business rules using dynamic behavior only. We also compared our solution with other dependency-based mining algorithms, such as FHM.

4.1   The Dataset

The synthetic event logs used in this evaluation were automatically generated using CPN Tools. We exported the simulated event logs in the XES format. The used Petri net model was based on the mapping scheme in our previous proposal

[1] and the specification of a popular open-source e-commerce shopping website named OsCommerce (version 2.3.4.1). The total number of positive long-distance dependency relations in the Petri net model was 34 distributed as follows, admin role: 13, guest role: 3, registered-user role: 18. In all roles, the total number of dependencies (an event depended on by another event) was 153.

4.2 Substitute Relations

To evaluate our system's ability in detecting substitute relations, we defined the Petri net model to generate traffic illustrative of substitute relations between two tasks. The substitute relation defined in the model was based on the transition from one role to another (sign in vs. sign up). Although the login page scenario is more probable, the user's role in both cases changes from guest to registered user delivering the same effect and implying a substitute relation between them.

Table 1. The discovered substitute relations

Role	Page	Observed substitute relations
Registered	logoff.php:GET:200	login.php:POST:302 $\Leftrightarrow$ create_account_success.php:GET:200
	account.php:GET:200	
	orders_history.php:GET:200	
	payment_methods.php:GET:200	
	. . .	

Table 1 shows that one substitute relation in the registered user role was discovered. The relation was defined between the "login.php:POST:302" and the "create_account_success.php:GET:200" tasks. A total of twelve unique tasks observed the same relation during the execution, whereas the total number of task classes under the registered user role was eighteen. Hence, more than 50% of the classes in the registered user role supported this substitute relation. The results illustrate our approach's ability to discover all the substitute relations in the provided event log, even with unequal frequency distribution in the tasks participating in the relationship.

4.3 Positive Long-Distance Dependency Relations

The user behavior in OsCommerce and our simulation Petri net model was restricted differently based on the user role. Restrictions were determined either by event transition (e.g., the login page can be reached through the index page) or by actual business rules of the application (e.g., only registered users can place orders). We considered both types of restrictions as they define how a system is used. Our focus was only on long-distance relations rather than direct relations.

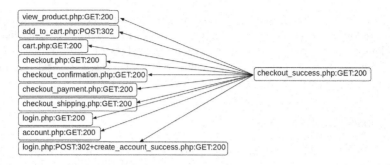

Fig. 1. A long-distance relation with all the tasks it depends on

A total of 13 long-distance relations were discovered in the admin role with an average number of dependees of 4. For the registered user role 18 relations (one can be seen in Fig. 1) were detected and a dependee average of 5. A total of 3 relations were detected for the guest role with a mean of truly detected dependee around 3. The result shows that our proposed solution was able to discover all positive long-distance relations along with all the dependees tasks these relations depend on.

Lastly, we compared our approach with the FHM in detecting long-distance dependency relations using the same synthetic event logs. The FHM only detected a single long-distance relationship with the long-distance threshold set to as low as 10%, while using our approach, all long-distance relations were detected along with all their dependees. Thus, we can conclude that our novel approach discovered positive long-distance dependency relations and vastly improved compared to the FHM.

5   Conclusion

We presented our novel approach for detecting if-then business rules defined based on implicit dependencies. Our initial analysis showed that the current frequency-based metrics are limited when detecting implicit dependencies, especially in discovering long-distance relations depending on tasks of substitute relations. Our proposed approach presented a capable solution of discovering conditional business rules defined over one-to-one and one-to-many implicit dependency relations. The results of our evaluation indicated a high precision in recovering positive long-distance dependency relations from the observed behavior even with the presence of substitute relations.

References

1. Alkofahi, H., Umphress, D., Alawneh, H.: Preparing HTTP traffic for process mining. In: 2022 13th International Conference on Information and Communication Systems (ICICS), pp. 142–148. IEEE, June 2022

2. Chaparro, O., Aponte, J., Ortega, F., Marcus, A.: Towards the automatic extraction of structural business rules from legacy databases. In: 2012 19th Working Conference on Reverse Engineering (WCRE), pp. 479–488. IEEE, October 2012

3. Normantas, K., Vasilecas, O.: A systematic review of methods for business knowledge extraction from existing software systems. Baltic J. Mod. Comput. (BJMC) **1**(1–2), 29–51 (2013)

4. Pellegrino, G., Balzarotti, D.: Toward black-box detection of logic flaws in web applications. In: NDSS, February 2014

5. Wen, L., Wang, J., Sun, J.: Detecting implicit dependencies between tasks from event logs. In: Zhou, X., Li, J., Shen, H.T., Kitsuregawa, M., Zhang, Y. (eds.) APWeb 2006. LNCS, vol. 3841, pp. 591–603. Springer, Heidelberg (2006). https://doi.org/10.1007/11610113_52

6. Wan, Q., An, A.: Efficient mining of indirect associations using HI-mine. In: Xiang, Y., Chaib-draa, B. (eds.) AI 2003. LNCS, vol. 2671, pp. 206–221. Springer, Heidelberg (2003). https://doi.org/10.1007/3-540-44886-1_17

7. Hay, D., Healy, K.A., Hall, J.: Defining business rules-what are they really. The Business Rules Group, vol. 400 (2000)

8. Weijters, A.J.M.M., Ribeiro, J.T.S.: Flexible heuristics miner (FHM). In: 2011 IEEE Symposium on Computational Intelligence and Data Mining (CIDM), pp. 310–317. IEEE, April 2011

Comparison of Job Titles for Specific Terms: Investigating "Data Science"

Abdulkareem Alsudais[(⊠)] [iD], Abdullah Aldumaykhi, and Saad Otai

College of Computer Engineering and Sciences, Prince Sattam bin Abdulaziz University,
Al-Kharj 11942, Saudi Arabia
a.alsudais@psau.edu.sa

Abstract. The ability to analyze a single term or phrase and generate its most relevant job titles and their similarities can be beneficial for organizations and government agencies. In this paper, we propose a framework that relies on a corpus of job postings for a single term and utilizes several text mining techniques to discover insights. The main outcome resulting from the application of our framework is a matrix and clusters representing the textual similarities between the job titles. To trial our framework, we studied the term "data science" and collected a corpus that consisted of 9,439 online job postings that contained the term. Our analysis identified 12 job titles and compared their similarities, allowing us to posit several important conclusions for data science and related fields.

Keywords: Data science · Job postings · Text similarity · Semantics

1 Introduction

In recent years, scientists have used text mining and NLP methods to study specific topics using corpora that consist of job postings [1, 2]. Two areas of focus for such studies have been identifying skills [2–4] and comparing similar job titles [5–7]. Many of these studies target emergent concepts and disciplines such as "big data" [8, 9] and "data science" [6, 10]. These terms represent a challenge to government agencies, academic institutions, and organizations, all of which may benefit from knowing how to define such terms. One way to understand these terms is to use text mining methods on corpora of job postings (i.e., online job postings that use these terms). In this paper, we propose an automated text mining framework that can be used to develop an understanding of the most advertised job titles for a selected search term and identify their similarity. To demonstrate the effectiveness of our framework, we apply it to a dataset of job postings containing the term "data science." A prominent issue in the field of data science concerns widespread disagreement regarding its scope and definitions [11, 12]. Moreover, several researchers have studied defining the term [11, 13–15]. Recent works have also studied the term by analyzing relevant job postings [4–7, 10, 16]. According to Jiang and Chen [6], "no consensus has been established for data science skills and job titles." Thus, analyzing job posts that use the term could help clarify some of the misconceptions about the term and provide an overview of how it is currently interpreted in industry.

E. Pardede et al. (Eds.): iiWAS 2022, LNCS 13635, pp. 98–103, 2022.
https://doi.org/10.1007/978-3-031-21047-1_8

2 Methodology

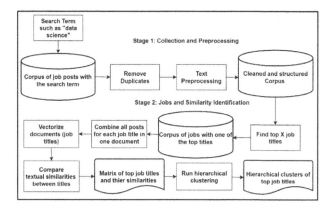

Fig. 1. The stages and steps in the framework

2.1 Data Collection and Text Preprocessing

Figure 1 demonstrates the stages and their main steps. The first step in the framework is to collect a dataset of job postings based on a specified search term. Job postings that include the search term are retrieved and included in the subsequent analyses. Once the corpus is constructed, the next step is to perform text preprocessing on the postings. The objective of this step is to process a corpus in order to remove or fix certain patterns in the texts that might negatively affect the quality of the desired results and to prepare the corpus for subsequent steps. The activities completed in this step often depend on the unique characteristics of the corpus. In summary, preprocessing steps are determined by the corpus and the structure of its text. Our "data science" corpus required certain preprocessing steps that may not be needed for other corpora that consist of job postings.

2.2 Jobs and Similarity Identification

After cleaning and preparing the corpus, the next step is to identify the most frequent job titles or roles advertised for within the corpus. This step is accomplished by determining a specific number of top titles (e.g., the 10 most frequent job titles) or a threshold of posts (e.g., all job titles with at least 20 job posts). Following this step, a group of the top "X" number of job titles can be specified. Once the most frequent job roles are identified, the next step is to measure the similarity between the job titles. The main objective of the similarity identification step is to process the texts of the most frequent job titles and determine the textual similarity between each pair of job titles. This permits the identification of the most similar jobs for each job title. To complete this, all the job posts for each of the selected job titles are combined in one document. Next, the textual similarity between pairs was calculated. The similarity between job titles is calculated by 1) generating the TF-IDF values for words in each job title, and 2) calculating the cosine similarity between jobs using these TF-IDF values. The result of this is a matrix with the job titles and their similarities, which can be used to identify the average similarities between jobs and to cluster jobs with high similarity. When cosine similarity and TF-IDF are used to compare documents, the values generated range from 0, when the two documents have nothing in common, to 1, when the two documents are identical. The final task in this stage is to cluster the jobs using an agglomerative (bottom-up) hierarchical clustering algorithm. The objective of hierarchical clustering is to generate clusters that are connected and organized in a hierarchical structure. The clusters can then be visualized using a dendrogram. Clustering algorithms rely on similarity metrics that can be used to determine the relatedness of input values. In our framework, we use the similarity values from the similarity matrix to create a hierarchical clustering representation that relies on the relationships between the jobs. This allows us to illustrate the clusters using a dendrogram that shows the jobs in a tree-like visualization.

3 Experiment and Results

3.1 Data Collection

We collected a corpus of job postings containing the term "data science." To provide a global perspective on data science, we specified three countries (Saudi Arabia, the United Kingdom, and the United States) and retrieved all job posts that included the term. We used three websites for the data: Glassdoor, Indeed, and LinkedIn. We collected our data from August 20th, 2020, to September 30th, 2020, ultimately compiling a full dataset that consisted of 9,439 job posts. To confirm the accuracy of our dataset, we processed a random sample of postings and confirmed that they do indeed exist on the websites. Unsurprisingly, most of the posts were from the United States (75%). Subsequently, we performed preprocessing steps to prepare the corpus.

3.2 Identifying Top Data Science Job Titles

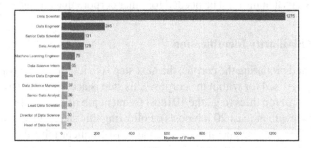

Fig. 2. Most frequent job titles for "data science"

The first step in the second stage of the approach is to find the most frequent job titles. For this, we processed all 9,439 job postings and extracted all the unique job titles. Then, we counted the number of posts that were in the corpus for each unique title. We then selected all the job titles with 30 or more posts. After finding 12 job titles that met this condition, we searched and removed duplicates from the subset. In the end, this process yielded 12 job titles, those in which the term "data science" appears most frequently. The results are in Fig. 2. For subsequent steps, we will use this subset of 2,117 posts.

3.3 Comparing Job Titles

	Data Scientist	Data Engineer	Senior Data Scientist	Data Analyst	Machine Learning Engineer	Data Science Intern	Data Science Manager	Senior Data Analyst	Senior Data Engineer	Director of Data Science	Head of Data Science	Lead Data Scientist
Data Scientist	1.00	0.93	0.97	0.94	0.79	0.86	0.92	0.91	0.90	0.90	0.89	0.93
Data Engineer	0.93	1.00	0.90	0.93	0.69	0.79	0.84	0.90	0.97	0.86	0.86	0.87
Senior Data Scientist	0.97	0.90	1.00	0.91	0.80	0.85	0.92	0.89	0.87	0.90	0.88	0.93
Data Analyst	0.94	0.93	0.91	1.00	0.67	0.82	0.85	0.94	0.90	0.86	0.84	0.87
Machine Learning Engineer	0.79	0.69	0.80	0.67	1.00	0.69	0.72	0.64	0.65	0.69	0.67	0.75
Data Science Intern	0.86	0.79	0.85	0.82	0.69	1.00	0.81	0.79	0.76	0.79	0.77	0.80
Data Science Manager	0.92	0.84	0.92	0.85	0.72	0.81	1.00	0.84	0.82	0.90	0.88	0.89
Senior Data Analyst	0.91	0.90	0.89	0.94	0.64	0.79	0.84	1.00	0.88	0.83	0.81	0.85
Senior Data Engineer	0.90	0.97	0.87	0.90	0.65	0.76	0.82	0.88	1.00	0.84	0.84	0.84
Director of Data Science	0.90	0.86	0.90	0.86	0.69	0.79	0.90	0.83	0.84	1.00	0.90	0.89
Head of Data Science	0.89	0.86	0.88	0.84	0.67	0.77	0.88	0.81	0.84	0.90	1.00	0.89
Lead Data Scientist	0.93	0.87	0.93	0.87	0.75	0.80	0.89	0.85	0.84	0.89	0.89	1.00

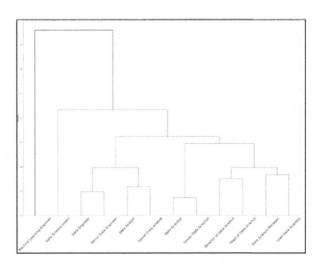

Fig. 3. The matrix of job titles and their similarity

Fig. 4. The jobs and their hierarchal clusters

Having identified the most frequent job titles, the next step was to measure their similarity. We first combined all posts for each job title in one document, producing 12 documents in total. For the documents, we generated TF-IDF representations using the library Scikit-learn. We experimented with several settings for the model, as results obtained from TF-IDF are sensitive to such modifications We used the default stop words list from the library to remove stop words. After we generated the document vectors for job titles, we compared the vectors using the cosine similarity implementation in Scikit-learn. The final output was a matrix with the job titles and their similarities (Fig. 3).

The matrix presents several notable findings. First, each job title with a second title for "senior" roles of the same title (i.e., "data analyst" and "senior data analyst") had the highest similarity with the senior role. This finding provides an assurance that our approach is capable of accurately identifying the similarity between jobs. Second, the four leadership positions—director, head, lead, and manager—share a high level of similarity, but have a lower level of similarity with the rest of the roles. Third, "machine learning engineer" had the lowest similarity with other job titles. To confirm, we calculated the average similarity for each job title. And indeed, the position had the lowest average, with 70.6%. Finally, our results suggest that the positions of "data analyst" and "data engineer" are very similar. However, it is important to note here that this analysis only compares the job posts for the two titles when the posts included the search term "data science."

The final step in this phase was to generate hierarchal clusters for the jobs using the similarity matrix. To do this, we used the hierarchal clustering implementation in the library Scipy. We used the "complete" [17] method to generate the clusters, which are displayed in Fig. 4. As the figure illustrates, "machine learning engineer" appears disconnected from any of the other job titles. As expected, all the job titles with a "senior" role level appear clustered along with the initial job title. Additionally, all four data analyst and data engineer job titles were clustered together. Similarly, all four leadership positions (e.g., "director of data science" and "data science lead") were connected in one cluster. Finally, all six job titles with "data scientist" or "data science" in the name appear in one large cluster. In the end, this hierarchal clustering representation provides a clear overview of the different job titles and their level of relatedness.

4 Conclusion

In this paper, we proposed a framework for the identification and comparison of job roles for a search term. We believe our approach is most impactful when used to investigate an emergent term. However, the framework can also be leveraged to study the current trends and occupations of more traditional terms. Our work still has several limitations. First, we have focused on the application of our framework to only one topic, "data science." Second, this current framework does not incorporate any longitudinal aspects. Third, our analysis of data science-related job posting adds other related job titles such as "data analyst" and "data engineer," but only includes job postings from these titles that include the search term "data science." Thus, while our investigation attempts to compare these related jobs, it only includes posts for other job titles that are likely to be similar due to their inclusion of the search term. These limitations point to potential directions for future work. For example, an update on the approach to include longitudinal aspects could be beneficial and productive. Such an empirical investigation may allow us to discover how data science is changing. Alternatively, it is possible that the term has "converged," and thus its utilization in postings will remain similar, even after a long period of time.

References

1. De Mauro, A., Greco, M., Grimaldi, M., Ritala, P.: Human resources for Big Data professions: a systematic classification of job roles and required skill sets. Inf. Process. Manag. **54**(5), 807–817 (2018)
2. Chang, H., Wang, C., Hawamdeh, S.: Emerging trends in data analytics and knowledge management job market: extending KSA framework. J. Knowl. Manag. **23**(4), 664–686 (2019)
3. Verma, A., Lamsal, K., Verma, P.: An investigation of skill requirements in artificial intelligence and machine learning job advertisements, Ind. High. Educ. (2021)
4. Meyer, M.A.: Research and Applications Healthcare data scientist qualifications, skills, and job focus: a content analysis of job postings. J. Am. Med. Inform. Assoc. **26**(March), 383–391 (2019)
5. Halwani, M.A., Amirkiaee, Y., Evangelopoulos, N., Prybutok, V.: Job qualifications study for data science and big data professions, Inf. Technol. People (2021)
6. Jiang, H., Chen, C.: Data science skills and graduate certificates: a quantitative text analysis. J. Comput. Inf. Syst. 1–17 (2021)
7. Michalczyk, S., Nadj, M., Maedche, A., Gröger, C.: Demystifying job roles in data science: a text mining approach. In: Twenty-Ninth European Conference on Information Systems (ECIS 2021) (2021)
8. Debortoli, S., Müller, O., vom Brocke, J.: Comparing business intelligence and big data skills a text mining study using job advertisements. Bus. Inf. Syst. Eng. (October) (2014)
9. Persaud, A.: Key competencies for big data analytics professions: a multimethod study. Inf. Technol. People (2019)
10. Radovilsky, Z., Hegde, V., Acharya, A., Uma, U.: Skills requirements of business data analytics and data science jobs: a comparative analysis. J. Supply Chain Oper. Manag. **16**(1), 82–101 (2018)
11. Ullman, J.D.: The battle for data science. IEEE Data Eng. Bull **43**(2), 8–14 (2020)
12. Fayyad, U., Hamutcu, H.: Toward foundations for data science and analytics: a knowledge framework for professional standards, Harvard Data Sci. Rev. 1–33 (2020)
13. Cao, L.: Data science: a comprehensive overview. ACM Comput. Surv. **50**(3), 1–42 (2017)
14. Ramzan, M.J., Khan, Inayat-Ur-Rehman, S.U.R., Khan, T.A., Akhunzada, A., Naseeb, C.: A conceptual model to support the transmuters in acquiring the desired knowledge of a data scientist. IEEE Access **9**, 115335–115347 (2021)
15. Saltz, J.S., Grady, N.W.: The ambiguity of data science team roles and the need for a data science workforce framework. In: 2017 IEEE International Conference on Big Data (BIGDATA), pp. 2355–2361 (2017)
16. Wu, D., Lv, S., Xu, H.: An analysis on competency of human-centered data science employment. Proc. Assoc. Inf. Sci. Technol. **57**(1), e219 (2020)
17. Murtagh, F., Contreras, P.: Algorithms for hierarchical clustering: an overview, II. Wiley Interdiscip. Rev. Data Min. Knowl. Discov. **7**(6), e1219 (2017)

Generating Smart Contracts for Blockchain-Based Resource-Exchange Systems

Kushal Soni[✉] and Olga De Troyer

Computer Science Department, Vrije Universiteit Brussel, Brussels, Belgium
{Kushal.Soni,Olga.DeTroyer}@vub.be

Abstract. Blockchain technology allows to store data in a secure and decentralized manner. The combination of blockchains with smart contracts allows for a novel range of applications. However, the creation of such applications requires IT skills, which introduces a burden for businesspeople that would like to incorporate blockchains combined with smart contracts in their business processes. To overcome this issue in the context of resource exchange across organizations and customers, we developed a framework that allows businesspeople to generate blockchain applications for such resource exchanges, without requiring any programming or blockchain knowledge. In this paper, we elaborate on the module that generates the smart contracts necessary to implement the specifications of use cases. In the current implementation, smart contracts are generated for Solidity, which is a smart contract language supported by many blockchain implementations, but this is not a limitation of the approach.

Keyword: Blockchain · Smart contract generation · Generic framework · Business people · Resource exchange

1 Introduction

With blockchain technology, data is stored in a decentralized manner using a group of computers and servers, called nodes. Full nodes keep a copy of the blockchain database, which consists of a series of linked blocks, each containing a number of transactions expressing operations that result in changes of data. Each node maintains its own copy by adding each block that has been mined (or validated) successfully to their own blockchain (after verifying its correctness) by means of a consensus algorithm that is followed. As a result, all nodes end up with the same copy of the blockchain; nodes with a different blockchain are declined by the network ensuring the integrity of the data. Furthermore, the lack of a single authority is one of the main advantages of a blockchain network, as it gives full control to the person owning the data [1–3].

Bitcoin is the first and most popular application built on top of blockchain technology [4]. However, with the help of smart contracts, the potential of blockchain technology goes beyond a means of payment. Smart contracts are pieces of program code that run under certain programmed conditions. Once deployed on a blockchain, the logic of the contracts cannot be changed. Currently, smart contracts need to be programmed. While this is justified for complex applications, for more common cases, this creates a technical burden for businesses. An example of such a case is the exchange of resources across organizations and their customers. To allow non-IT skilled people to set up a blockchain application with smart contracts for the exchange of resources, without the need to rely on programmers, we proposed a framework that generates the application including the smart contracts, automatically and tailored for the use case at hand. Note that the framework could also be used by ICT-companies to speed up the process of creating such applications. The web application of the framework that allows a non-IT skilled person to specify the requirements for a use case, has been described in [5]. Here, we focus on the generation process of the required smart contracts.

Related work in the context of the generation of smart contracts exist. Some works propose a more high-level specification formalism, such as the use of natural language specifications ([6] and [7]), a custom specification language ([8] and [9]), "Petri Nets" ([10]), or models [11]. Although this seems to be less complex than using existing smart contract languages, these specifications can still be very technical and in general these approaches still seem to require smart contract developers. Frameworks are presented in [12–14], and [15]. In [12], the context is limited to Smart Contracts from Internet Of Media Things (IoMT). The framework presented in [14] allows to generate smart contracts in Solidity for Ethereum, but the use cases are limited to registries. In [13], an ontology approach is used that allows for a broad range of applications, but implies the need for an ontology expert. The tool presented in [15] is quite powerful but its expressiveness could be too technical for non-IT skilled people.

2   Framework and Generation of Smart Contracts

To ease the development of blockchain applications involving smart contracts for the exchange of resources by non-IT skilled people (like business-level people), we propose a framework that allows to generate blockchain applications supporting use cases that deal with the exchange of resources across organizations and end users. An easy-to-use browser interface (provided by the Use Case Specification module) allows the user to enter the information about the use case, i.e., organization-specific details and requirements (see [5] for details). Based on this information, several smart contracts are generated, which can then be deployed on a blockchain of choice (e.g. Ethereum [16]). In addition, for the actual exchange of resources between the organizations and the end users, an application is generated. By relying on blockchain technology and when using a public blockchain, the resulting resource-exchange application will guarantee true ownership of resources for end users. Now, we elaborate on the generation of the smart contracts.

On purpose, the Use Case Specification module does not use blockchain terminology but concepts that are understandable by businesspeople (referred to as user concepts). These user concepts are translated into the smart contract concepts as follows. Wallets are used to identify users (i.e., end users and owners of organizations) involved in the resource exchange. For each organization involved, a smart contract is generated that will allow owners (i.e., people that are appointed to represent the organization in the use case) to execute transactions on behalf of the organization. These contracts will also enforce the rules specified for the use case, such as the financial settlements. Every resource type is implemented with a smart contract (a token contract) that controls the ownership of each of the individual tokens of a specific type. The logic for the types of operations that can take place in the use case are stored in a smart contract. With the help of "if" and "then" constructs, organizations can specify (a set of) rules to specify operation(s) that should occur when a (set of) operations have occurred. The logic to execute these "rules", as well as the rules themselves, is also stored in a smart contract. The contracts in our current implementation are generated for Solidity[1] (a smart contract language supported by many blockchains such as Ethereum [16] and Polygon [17]). Implementations for other smart contract languages (e.g., Rust[2]) can always be added.

Now, we give more details about the actual contracts that are generated. First, for each organization, an **Organization Contract** is generated that keeps track of the individual properties of the organizations. Second, a **Token Contract** is generated for each resource type involved in the use case. These contracts keep track of the total token supply (in case of an ERC-20 token) and of the ownership of each individual token. Next, a contract, called **OrganizationsController,** for keeping track of all organizations involved in the use case and to deal with the communication between the different organization contracts, is generated. Then, a library (containing reusable code), called the **Rules Library,** that contains all the logic that is required to define and store rules is generated. Additionally, a library to define and execute transactions is generated as well (called the **Transaction Library**). Finally, a contract, called **Controller,** is generated that facilitates the communication between all blockchain users and the other contracts. This contract acts as the main controller of all contracts. It is responsible for executing all user interactions in the use case, e.g., if an end user wants to transfer tokens to an organization or if an owner of an organization wants to transfer tokens to an end user[3] or another organization. In addition, it also stores all token types involved, and the allowed transaction types and rules. The function "checkAndExecuteRules" verifies whether any specified rule should be executed.

We illustrate the working of the contracts with an example. Figure 1 illustrates how resources (i.e., tokens) are transferred from an organization to an end user. In this example, organization A has one owner "Mark" who initiates a transfer (in name of organization A) of a number of tokens of type 1 to end user John (a customer). To transfer resources for organization A, a call of the "transfer" function of the Controller is needed, which checks whether Mark (the sender) is indeed in the list of owners of organization A (through the OrganizationsController Contract) and then calls the "transfer" function of the "Transaction" Contract. This function will check whether the proposed transaction matches the "allowedTransactionTypes" and will then call the "transfer" function of the OrganizationsController Contract, which calls the "transfer" function of the contract of

---

[1] https://docs.soliditylang.org/.

[2] https://www.rust-lang.org/.

[3] Transactions between end users (i.e., outside the use case system) are always possible and do not require interaction with any of the above specified contracts. This ensures that end users possess true ownership of their resources.

the organization that transfers resources (in this case organization A). Then, the contract of organization A calls the "transfer" function of the Transactions Contract. This function will check whether the proposed transaction matches the "allowedTransactionTypes" and will call the "transfer" function of the token contract. If all checks pass, an actual transfer of the tokens of type 1 to the wallet of John (the receiver) takes place. After the transfer, the Controller Contract checks whether any rules should be executed.

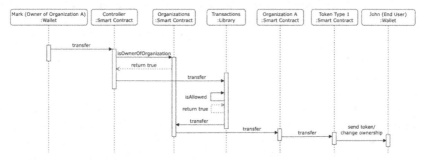

Fig. 1. Example scenario of transfer of tokens from an organization to an end user

3 Limitations

The framework currently supports the generation of smart contracts for Solidity. Although this is one of the most popular smart contract languages that can be used by a wide variety of blockchain networks, the possibility to generate contracts in other languages would give more flexibility. Implementations for other smart contract languages can be added, as the type of specifications used in the Use Case Specification module are independent of the smart contract language or blockchain used.

We verified the soundness of the generated smart contracts by writing tests for one use case. The tests mainly included the execution of several transactions and defined rules. Only transactions corresponding to defined transaction types were executed, and all "THEN" statements were executed for each set of "IF" statements in a rule (i.e., all rules were being executed correctly). As a result, all defined tests passed successfully. In future work we will investigate how we can generate tests for different use cases.

At the moment, the framework does not allow users to make changes to the specifications of a use case once the blockchain application has been generated and deployed. Ideally, one should be able to make certain changes to the applications after deployment, of course only under certain conditions and restrictions. For instance, it is possible that some organizations want to join an existing resource-exchange platform. In that case, it may also be necessary to review certain rules and settlements. However, ideally this should not affect the working of the already deployed application. This is the subject of future work.

Although the contracts were developed with efficiency in mind, we believe that still some work can be done to make the contracts more resource-efficient, resulting in faster execution of transactions and less gas fees (means of payment for transactions). Of course, this also greatly depends on the type of blockchain running the contracts.

For now, the involved transaction fees for deploying the generated contracts, and interacting with the contracts after deployment, should be covered by the initiator of the transaction. In some cases, it might be desired that some organizations (participating in the use case) should be accountable for such costs. Therefore, the initiator could sign a message to give permission to certain organization(s) for spending his funds (under certain conditions), instead of initiating the transactions himself. However, this requires further investigation as this might introduce more centralization into the system.

4   Conclusion

In the context of a framework that allows organizations to generate blockchain applications for the exchange of resources between them and their customers, we discussed the automatic generation of smart contracts to perform the needed transfers of resources but also to check and execute associated actions, e.g., to accomplish financial settlements between organizations. The resulting application consists of several smart contracts and libraries that are generated based on the high-level information specified for a use case through an intuitive web application. These high-level specifications are only using concepts that are understandable by businesspeople. Currently, the smart contracts are generated for Solidity, which runs on many popular blockchains. However, the generation process can be extended to support other languages and platforms as well.

We explained the mapping from the conceptual concepts used for the specifications and tailored towards non-IT skilled people, onto the technical concepts used in blockchain and smart contracts technology. We also explained the different types of contracts generated as well as their role and functionality. The exchange of resources by means of these smart contracts is illustrated with an example.

As part of future research work, we will investigate if and how the framework could generate verification tests for the generated smart contracts and how to allow to make changes to a deployed use case application. Furthermore, we plan to further optimize the generation process to generate blockchain applications that are more cost-efficient.

References

1. Scherer, M.: Performance and Scalability of Blockchain Networks and Smart Contracts (2017)
2. Underwood, S.: Blockchain beyond bitcoin. Commun. ACM. **59**, 15–17 (2016). https://doi.org/10.1145/2994581
3. Chauhan, A., Malviya, O.P., Verma, M., Mor, T.S.: Blockchain and scalability. In: Proceedings 2018 IEEE 18th International Conference Software Quality Reliability Security Companion, QRS-C 2018, pp. 122–128 (2018). https://doi.org/10.1109/QRS-C.2018.00034
4. Nakamoto, S.: Bitcoin: a peer-to-peer electronic cash system – whitepaper. https://bitcoin.org/bitcoin.pdf. Accessed 21 July 2021
5. Soni, K., De Troyer, O.: Specifying blockchain-based resource-exchange systems by business-level users using a generic easy-to-use framework. In: Arai, K. (ed.) Proceeding of the Future Technologies Conference (FTC), (vol. 2, pp. 36–54). (Lecture Notes in Networks and Systems, vol. 560). Springer (2022). https://doi.org/10.1007/978-3-031-18458-1

6. Regnath, E., Steinhorst, S.: SmaCoNat: smart contracts in natural language. Forum Specif. Des. Lang. 2018-September (2018). https://doi.org/10.1109/FDL.2018.8524068

7. Frantz, C.K., Nowostawski, M.: From institutions to code: towards automated generation of smart contracts. In: Proceedings IEEE 1st International Workshop Foundation Applications Self-Systems, FAS-W 2016, pp. 210–215 (2016). https://doi.org/10.1109/FAS-W.2016.53

8. He, X., Qin, B., Zhu, Y., Chen, X., Liu, Y.: SPESC: a specification language for smart contracts. In: Proceedings International Computer Software Application Conference, vol. 1, pp. 132–137 (2018). https://doi.org/10.1109/COMPSAC.2018.00025

9. Zhu, Y., Song, W., Wang, D., Ma, D., Chu, W.C.C.: TA-SPESC: toward asset-driven smart contract language supporting ownership transaction and rule-based generation on blockchain. IEEE Trans. Reliab. **70**, 1255–1270 (2021). https://doi.org/10.1109/TR.2021.3054617

10. Zupan, N., Kasinathan, P., Cuellar, J., Sauer, M.: Secure smart contract generation based on Petri Nets. In: Rosa Righi, R.D., Alberti, A.M., Singh, M. (eds.) Blockchain Technology for Industry 4.0. BT, pp. 73–98. Springer, Singapore (2020). https://doi.org/10.1007/978-981-15-1137-0_4

11. Lu, Q., et al.: Integrated model-driven engineering of blockchain applications for business processes and asset management. Softw. Pract. Exp. **51**, 1059–1079 (2021). https://doi.org/10.1002/SPE.2931

12. Allouche, M., Mitrea, M., Moreaux, A., Kim, S.K.: Automatic smart contract generation for internet of media things. ICT Express. **7**, 274–277 (2021). https://doi.org/10.1016/J.ICTE.2021.08.009

13. Choudhury, O., Rudolph, N., Sylla, I., Fairoza, N., Das, A.: Auto-generation of smart contracts from domain-specific ontologies and semantic rules. In: Proceeding IEEE 2018 International Congress Cybermatics 2018 IEEE Conference Internet Things, Green Computing Communication Cyber, Physical Social Computing Smart Data, Blockchain, Comput. Inf. Technol. iThings/Gree, pp. 963–970 (2018). https://doi.org/10.1109/CYBERMATICS_2018.2018.00183

14. Tran, A.B., Xu, S., Weber, I., Staples, M., Rimba, P.: Regerator: a registry generator for blockchain. In: 29th International Conference on Advanced Information Systems Engineering (CaiSE2017), Essen, Germany. pp. 81–88 (2017)

15. Tran, A.B., Lu, Q., Weber, I.: Lorikeet: a model-driven engineering tool for blockchain-based business process execution and asset management. In: 16th International Conference on Business Process Management, Sydney, Australia, p. 5 (2018)

16. Home | ethereum.org. https://ethereum.org/en/. Accessed 02 June 2022

17. Polygon. https://polygon.technology/. Accessed 04 June 2022

Analysis of Country Mentions in the Debates of the UN Security Council

Raji Ghawi$^{(\boxtimes)}$ and Jürgen Pfeffer

School of Social Sciences and Technology, Technical University of Munich,
Munich, Germany
{raji.ghawi,juergen.pfeffer}@tum.de

Abstract. In this paper, we present a dataset of country mentions within the debates of the UN Security Council (UNSC). Using the corpus of the UNSC debates [6], we extract country mentions from the speeches and link them to the country of the speaker, creating a who-mentions-whom network at country level. This data can be used to identify geopolitical change events over time by tracking the evolution of number of country mentions over time, and detecting peak points.

Keywords: Security council · Event detection · NER

1 Introduction

The United Nations Security Council (UNSC) is the premier forum in international politics. Through its decisions, mandated operations and enforcement actions the Council directly influences the present and future state of international peace and security. The UNSC is composed of five permanent (the P5) and ten non-permanent members (six before 1966). The UNSC meets regularly in a public format allowing for the global public to follow key debates and votes. Studying the substance of these debates therefore gives insights into developments of historical importance [6].

Schönfeld et al. [6] compiled a dataset of all public UNSC debates over a 25-year period from 1995 until 2019. As the unit of analysis, the dataset includes each individual speech contribution made by a participant of a public UNSC meeting, enabling a variety of qualitative and quantitative text analysis.

In this paper, we build upon the dataset of UNSC debates [6], and use it to construct a dataset of country mentions within the UNSC debates. We extract country mentions from each speech, and we associate the mentioned country as well as the country of the speaker with their ISO code obtaining a standardized representation of the countries. This enables as to create a dataset of country-country mentions at speech level, which can be then aggregated at different levels: meeting-level, country-level, and yearly level. This dataset[1] complements ongoing efforts to advance text-as-data research on political texts [1,6] and to systematize text-based and automated analyses of international conflicts [2].

---

[1] Available at https://github.com/rajighawi/UNSC-Country-Mentions-Dataset.

© The Author(s), under exclusive license to Springer Nature Switzerland AG 2022
E. Pardede et al. (Eds.): iiWAS 2022, LNCS 13635, pp. 110–115, 2022.
https://doi.org/10.1007/978-3-031-21047-1_10

By adopting the *country* as the unit of analysis, the dataset enables a variety of applications and analysis. This includes for instance detecting geopolitical events through observing the number of country mentions over time, identifying the peaks and using them as indicators of events. The paper is organized as follows. Section 2 describes the process of constructing the dataset, including the extraction of mentioned countries, and the normalization of country names. Section 3 presents the detection of geopolitical events as peaks on the timeseries of country mentions. Section 4 concludes the paper.

2   Constructing the Dataset

The official meeting protocols of the UNSC are publicly available at the website of the UN as well-structured PDF-documents. Schönfeld et al. [6] compiled a corpus of single speeches from the UNSC meeting protocols between 1995 and 2019. The process consisted of extracting raw text from PDF-documents, cleaning it up; then splitting up raw text into distinct speeches; and labeling speeches by speaker's names and countries (or affiliations). For every speech, metadata regarding the speaker, the speaker's nation or affiliation, and the speaker's role in the meeting is given. Overall, the dataset covers 5,507 public meetings and includes 77,815 individual speech contributions. We use this corpus and its associated metadata as the basis blocks to construct our dataset of country mentions.

In order to extract country names mentioned in the UNSC speeches, we apply Named Entity Recognition (NER) [4], which locates named entities and classifies them into categories, such as: Person, Location, Organization, etc. In particular, country names are mainly classified under the category GPE (Geo-Political Entity), but also as location (LOC) or organization (ORG); hence we retain only entities of those three categories. From the 77K speeches, in total NER identified 1.8 million entities of these three categories (53K without duplicates).

With the results returned by NER, we face several challenges. First, not all of the recognized entities are country names, where most of them are cities, organizations, or other types of locations. Second, the country name can appear in different forms. Third, even when a recognized entity is about a country, it is not purely a country name, i.e., a country can appear in an entity in various ways. Fourth, some recognized entities comprise more than one country. To solve such challenges, we conduct the next step: normalization of country names.

In order to solve the aforementioned challenges, we need a standard representation of countries. For this purpose, we use the ISO 3166–1 alpha-3 codes to represent countries[2]. A table of country ISO codes is openly available online[3] which associates each country name with its code. From this table, we take the country name and split it into k-shingles, i.e., substrings of length k [3] (we use $k \in \{2, 3\}$). and we find the frequency of each k-shingle obtaining a bag (multiset) of k-shingles (representing the country name) which is then associated with the country ISO code making a *reference dictionary*.

---

[2] https://www.iso.org/iso-3166-country-codes.html.

[3] https://en.wikipedia.org/wiki/ISO_3166-1_alpha-3.

We then match the recognized entities with the countries in this reference dictionary: First, we check whether the entity has an exact match with a country name. If there is no exact match for an entity, we conduct an approximate search. In this step, we apply the k-shingle tokenization onto the recognized entity and thus represent it as a bag of k-shingles (similarly to what we did with the reference dictionary of countries). Then, we calculate the similarity between this bag and all the bags of the countries in the reference dictionary. If the similarity to any country exceeds a certain threshold, we mark that country as a candidate match for the entity. If an entity has multiple candidate matches, we retain only the one with the highest similarity score. The similarity between k-shingles bags is calculated using Jaccard similarity measure of bags [3]. For bags B_1 and B_2 the Jaccard similarity is defined as:

$$J_B(B_1, B_2) = \frac{|B_1 \cap B_2|}{|B_1 \uplus B_2| - |B_1 \cap B_2|}$$

where $B_1 \uplus B_2$ and $B_1 \cap B_2$ are respectively the bag union and the bag intersection of B_1 and B_2; an element that appears n times in B_1 and m times in B_2 appears $n + m$ times in $B_1 \uplus B_2$, and appears $\min(n, m)$ times in $B_1 \cap B_2$.

Entities having exact match are associated with their matching ISO codes (for example, Pakistan, Slovakia, and Uruguay); whereas entities with approximate matches are revised manually. In this step, if an entity indeed corresponds to the candidate matched country, then it is associated with it. Otherwise, it either corresponds to a different country, and in that case it is associated with that correct country, or the entity is not a country and in that case it is just discarded. This manual verification also reveals the cases where an entity corresponds to more than one country, and in this case, it is associated with all of them.

To this end, we obtain a list of entity-country matches that comprises 1,804 unique entities corresponding to 212 distinct countries (represented as ISO codes). Then, those country entities are joined with the speeches where they were extracted from, and the frequency of mentions per speech is also calculated. Thus, we obtain a *speech-country-mentions* table which consists of three fields: code, speech-id, and frequency, and comprises 232,729 rows.

Similarly to recognized entities, we applied the process of country name normalization onto the countries of the speakers (in speeches metadata). Hence, we were able to associate the corresponding ISO code of the speaker country to 72,701 speech among the overall 77,815 speeches (93%). For the rest of speeches (∼5K), the speakers were not country representatives, but were representatives of the UN or other guest organizations.

After normalizing the country names, we join the two tables: speech-country-mentions and speaker-countries, based on the speech-id. Hence, the resulting table comprises: speech-id, meeting-id, year, speaker country, mentioned country, and number of mentions. This *speech country-country mentions* table consists of 211,237 rows (155,969 rows excluding self-mentions, i.e., when the speaker country and the mentioned country are the same).

We then aggregate this table by grouping it by *year*, *speaker country*, and *mentioned country*, and finding the number of meetings, number of speeches, total number of mentions, as well as the average number of mentions per speech and per meeting. This *country-country-mentions* table represents mentioning relations between countries on a yearly basis. It consists of 57,977 rows (25,323 excluding self-mentions).

3   Detecting Geopolitical Events

Table 1 shows an excerpt of the *country-country-mentions* table, sorted by number of mentions. We can see for instance that, in 2003 (the year when USA invaded Iraq) USA mentioned Iraq 406 times in 22 different speeches over 20 meetings. Another example, is in 2014 (the year when Russia occupied Crimea from Ukraine) Ukraine was mentioned by Russia 360 times.

Clearly, there is a relation between the number of mentions about a country, and geo-political events related to that country. Thus, we can exploit this data to detect geo-political events by observing the number of mentions over time, and identifying the peaks as indication of events.

Table 1. Top 5 country-country-mentions by number of mentions.

Year	Speaker country	Mentioned country	No. of meetings	No. of speeches	No. of mentions	Avg. mentions per	
						Speech	Meeting
2003	USA	IRQ	20	22	406	18.45	20.3
2014	RUS	UKR	31	54	360	6.67	11.6
2014	USA	UKR	28	37	289	7.81	10.3
2014	LTU	UKR	31	32	266	8.31	8.6
2018	USA	IRN	42	47	240	5.11	5.7

This dataset can be regarded as an edge list of a country-country network, in which the nodes are countries and the edges indicate the mention relationship among countries. This network is (1) *directed* from speaker country towards mentioned country; (2) *weighted*, where each edge is equipped by different measures of strength, such as number of mentions, speeches, and meetings; and (3) *temporal* as edges are observed on a yearly scale.

Using the country-country-mentions table, we project it only on the mentioned country and the year, and aggregate the different attributes: numbers of mentions, speeches, and meetings. This would add a new attribute, which is the number of speaker countries. As shown in Table 2, the most mentioned country was Iraq in 2003 (when it was invaded by USA) with 3,434 mentions by 104 different countries in 484 distinct speeches in 55 different meetings. Other top mentioned countries include: Ukraine in 2014 (Russian occupation of Crimea), Congo in 2001 (escalation of the Second Congo War, and Israel in 2002 (a large-scale military operation in the West Bank).

Table 2. Top 5 Country Mentions

Year	Country	#Meetings	#Speeches	#Mentions	#Countries
2003	IRQ	55	484	3434	104
2014	UKR	53	471	2593	36
2001	COG	55	341	2121	42
2002	ISR	47	430	1919	62
2018	AFG	47	251	1807	42

With this table, for any given country, we can construct a timeseries about the number of mentions (or any other attribute) over time. This kind of time series is useful for detecting geopolitical events. Intuitively, when there is a geopolitical event about a country, e.g., a military conflict, it would be intensively discussed at the UNSC, and that country would increasingly be mentioned in the debates. That is, there is a clear correspondence between peaks on the mentions time-series of a country and geopolitical events related to that country. Therefore, the problem of detecting geopolitical events is reduced to detecting peaks on the timeseries of country mentions.

In order to detect peak points on the timeseries of country mentions, we use a simple algorithm presented in [5]. Let $T = x_1, x_2, \cdots, x_N$ be a given uniformly sampled time-series containing N values (i.e., the time instants are assumed to be 1, 2, ..., N). Let x_i be a given i^{th} point in T. Given an integer $k > 0$, let $N_k^+(i) = \langle x_{i+1}, x_{i+2}, \cdots, x_{i+k} \rangle$ the sequence of k right temporal neighbours of x_i i.e., k points immediately following the ith point x_i in T. $N_k^-(i)$ is defined similarly as the set of k left (previous) temporal neighbours of x_i. The spikeness of point x_i can be defined as the average of the signed distances of x_i from its k left neighbours and k right neighbours:

$$S_k(x_i) = \frac{1}{2}\Big(\sum_{x_j \in N_k^-(i)} \frac{x_i - x_j}{k} + \sum_{x_j \in N_k^+(i)} \frac{x_i - x_j}{k} \Big)$$

The peak function S computes its value at each point using the local window (context) of size $2k$ around that point. All points where the peak function has a positive value are candidate peaks. We rule out some of these locally detected peaks using a simple rule: A given point x_i in T is a peak if $S_k(x_i) \geq \theta$, where θ is a user-specified (or suitably calculated) threshold value. A simple post-processing involves removing peaks if they are "too near" to each other (e.g., within the same window of size k). We use $k = 3$ and $\theta = 100$.

Using this algorithm, we were able to detect 182 peak points over the time-series of the 212 countries. This makes a table of *events*, each comprising a year, a country, and number of mentions.

With automatically identified peaks, a manual annotation is needed to associate each peak point of a country with the event(s) happened in that point in time (year). Figure 1 shows the timeseries of the top 5 most mentioned countries, with the major peaks on them associated with the geopolitical events that happened at those points in time. This includes: USA invasion of Afghanistan and Iraq in 2002 (late 2001) and 2003, respectively; Israel military operations in the West Bank and Lebanon in 2002 and 2006, respectively; Russian occupation of Crimea in 2014, escalation of the Second Congo War in 2001, and peace negotiations in Afghanistan in 2018.

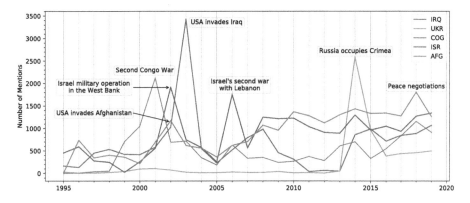

Fig. 1. Timeline of events about top 5 mentioned countries

4 Conclusion

Based on the UNSC debates corpus, we construct a dataset of country mentions within the UNSC debates. The dataset is used to detect geopolitical events through identifying peaks on the timeseries of country mentions over time. Directions of future work include: (1) analyzing the interests of countries, particularly permanent members, through observing their most mentioned countries over time; and (2) comparing permanent-, non-permanent members, and non-members of the UNSC in terms of their behavior of mentioning other countries.

References

1. Grimmer, J., Stewart, B.M.: Text as data: the promise and pitfalls of automatic content analysis methods for political texts. Polit. Anal. **21**(3), 267–297 (2013)
2. King, G., Lowe, W.: An automated information extraction tool for international conflict data with performance as good as human coders: a rare events evaluation design. Int. Organ. **57**(3), 617–642 (2003)
3. Leskovec, J., Rajaraman, A., Ullman, J.: Mining of massive datasets, chapter 3, finding similar items, pp. 68–122. Cambridge University Press, 2nd edn. (2014)
4. Nadeau, D., Sekine, S.: A survey of named entity recognition and classification. Lingvisticae Investigationes **30**, 3–26 (2007)
5. Palshikar, G.: Simple algorithms for peak detection in time-series (2009)
6. Schoenfeld, M., Eckhard, S., Patz, R., Meegdenburg, H., Pires, A.: The UN security council debates (2019). https://doi.org/10.7910/DVN/KGVSYH

Data Mining

A Comparative Performance Analysis
of Fast K-Means Clustering Algorithms

Christian Beecks[1]($\boxtimes$), Fabian Berns[1], Jan David Hüwel[1], Andrea Linxen[1],
Georg Stefan Schlake[1], and Tim Düsterhus[2]

[1] University of Hagen, Hagen, Germany
{christian.beecks,fabian.berns,jan.huwel,
andrea.linxen,georg.schlake}@fernuni-hagen.de
[2] University of Münster, Münster, Germany

Abstract. Data clustering is a fundamental and widespread problem in computer science, which has become very attractive in both scientific communities and application domains. Among the different algorithmic methods, the *k-means algorithm*, and its prominent implementation, the *Lloyd algorithm*, has developed into a de facto standard for partitioning-based clustering. This algorithm, however, turns out to be inefficient on very large databases. In order to mitigate this efficiency issue, several *fast k-means algorithms* for ad-hoc and exact data clustering have been proposed in the literature. Since their inner workings and applied pruning criteria differ, it is difficult to predict the efficiency of individual algorithms in certain application scenarios. We thus present a performance analysis of existing fast k-means algorithms. We focus on simple interpretability and comparability and abstract from many implementation details so as to provide a guide for data scientists and practitioners alike.

Keywords: Data mining · Clustering · Performance evaluation

1 Introduction

Data clustering is a fundamental problem in computer science [7], which aims to divide data objects into clusters such that similar data objects are placed into the same cluster whereas dissimilar data objects are separated into different clusters. Although different clustering paradigms and algorithmic methods have been proposed in the last decades [29,30], partitioning-based methods, which aim to divide a dataset into mutually disjoint clusters, have developed into one of the most prominent clustering approaches due to their simplicity in terms of interpretability and implementability. In fact, these clustering methods are implemented in many state-of-the-art data analysis tools [20].

Among the broad variety of clustering algorithms [29], the *k-means algorithm* [10,18,19,27] has evolved into one of the most influential clustering algorithm [25, 28]. While the term k-means algorithm is explicitly attributed to MacQueen [22],

---

The experiments underlying this paper have been conducted by Tim Düsterhus during his time at University of Münster.

it has been initially proposed by Steinhaus [26] in 1956 and first applied to data clustering by Forgy [15] in 1965. Today's well-known implementation is the *Llyod algorithm* [21], which dates back to 1982.

With the advent of growing data sources and the increasing need for efficient clustering methods, many *fast k-means algorithms* [12–14,16,17,24] have been proposed. They aim at computing an exact data clustering with significantly less computational effort. These algorithms do not require any kind of precomputation and are thus directly applicable to any application scenario.

In this paper, we present a comparative performance analysis of fast k-means algorithms for exact data clustering. Unlike existing investigations of this kind [24], our approach is to provide a conceptually simple overview and evaluation of existing algorithms and pruning criteria without elaborating the underlying theoretical concepts in detail. We focus on simple interpretability and comparability and abstract from many implementation details so as to provide a guide for data scientists and practitioners alike.

2   K-Means Clustering Problem

Given a set of data objects $X \subset \mathbb{R}^d$ of size $n = |X|$, a set of initial cluster centers $C \subset \mathbb{R}^d$ of size $k = |C|$, and a function $a : X \to C$ that assigns each data object $x \in X$ to its nearest cluster center $a(x) \in C$, the objective of the *k-means clustering problem* is to minimize the sum-of-squared error function $J(C, a|X) = \sum_{x \in X} L_2(x, a(x))^2$ where L_2 denotes the Euclidean distance [11].

The minimization of the function $J(C, a|X)$ corresponds to the determination of an optimal set of cluster centers C and an assignment function a which implies a data partitioning for the given dataset X such that the intra-cluster variance is minimized. Finding a global minimum of J is shown to be NP-hard [9,23].

As finding a global minimum of J becomes practically infeasible for an increasing size of X, the function J is often approximated in two alternating phases. While the first phase *optimizes the assignment function* a by minimizing $J(C, a|X)$ for constant C, the second phase *updates the set of cluster centers* C by minimizing $J(C, a|X)$ for constant a. Iterating these two phases gives us the *Lloyd algorithm* [21], whose pseudo code is shown in Algorithm 1.

Algorithm 1. k-means clustering

1: **function** LLOYD(X, C, a)
2:     $J_{new} \leftarrow \infty$
3:     **repeat**
4:         $J \leftarrow J_{new}$
5:         $a \leftarrow \text{UpdateAssignment}(X, C)$
6:         $C \leftarrow \text{UpdateCenter}(X, a)$
7:         $J_{new} \leftarrow J(C, a|X)$
8:     **until** $J_{new} \geq J$
9:     **return** (C, a)

The Lloyd algorithm converges within a finite number of steps and reaches a local optimum. Its computation time complexity lies in $\mathcal{O}(n \cdot k \cdot d)$, since updating the assignment function a by means of the method $UpdateAssignment(X, C)$ [line 5] requires the comparison of each data object with each cluster center, i.e., the computation of $L_2(x, c)^2$ for every $x \in X$ and $c \in C$. The number of distance evaluations, which grows linearly in both data size n and number of cluster centers k, is a major bottleneck of the Lloyd algorithm.

3   Fast K-Means Algorithms

The major objective of fast k-means algorithms is to reduce the number of distance evaluations in the method $UpdateAssignment(X, C)$. The main idea is to *approximate distances and to safely exclude cluster centers* from the assignment process. For this purpose, each data object $x \in X$ is assigned (1) an *upper bound* $u(x)$ on the exact distance of x to its nearest cluster center $a(x)$, such that $u(x) \geq L_2(x, a(x))^2$ holds and (ii) a *lower bound* $l(x|c)$ on the exact distance of x to a cluster center c, such that $l(x|c) \leq L_2(x, c)^2$ holds.

3.1   Basic Pruning Criteria

Lower-and-Upper-Bound (LU) Pruning Criterion: Given a data object x, *cluster center c can be safely excluded* if its minimum distance $l(x|c)$ to data object x exceeds the maximum distance $u(x)$ of the nearest cluster center from x, i.e. if it holds that $u(x) < l(x|c)$.

Besides the distance approximations between data objects and cluster centers, the exact pairwise distances $L_2(c, c')^2$ between two cluster centers $c, c' \in C$ can also be used for pruning.

Center-Center (CC) Pruning Criterion: Given a data object x, *cluster center c can be safely excluded* if the maximum distance $u(x)$ of the nearest cluster center from x is below the distance to the hyper-plane between the nearest cluster center $a(x)$ and cluster center c, i.e. if it holds that $u(x) < \frac{L_2(a(x), c)^2}{2}$.

While the pruning criteria above makes explicitly use of distances between cluster centers, another approach consists in utilizing an arbitrary reference point $r \in \mathbb{R}^d$, in order to exploit distance deviations. Frequently, the origin $0 \in \mathbb{R}^d$ is used as reference point.

Reference-Point (RP) Pruning Criterion: Given a data object x, *cluster center c can be safely excluded* if the maximum distance $u(x)$ of the nearest cluster center from x is below the distance between data object x and cluster center c with respect to reference point r, i.e. if it holds that $u(x) < |L_2(r, x)^2 - L_2(r, c)^2|$.

3.2   Algorithms

The **Elkan algorithm** [14] maintains one upper bound and k lower bounds for each data object and applies the **LU** and **CC** pruning criteria for each combination of data object and cluster center. The **Hamerly algorithm** [16] maintains one upper bound and a single lower bound on the distance to the second closest cluster center for each data object. It also applies the **LU** and **CC** pruning criteria, but the **CC** criterion is only applied globally based on the minimum distance between any two cluster centers $(u(x) < \min_{c,c' \in C} \frac{\mathrm{L}_2(c,c')^2}{2})$. The **Drake algorithm** [13] maintains one upper bound and a dynamic number of lower bounds for each data object and solely applies the **LU** pruning criterion. The **Annular algorithm** [17] is a strict extension of the Hamerly algorithm that additionally exploits the **RP** pruning criterion, where the origin $0 \in \mathbb{R}^d$ is selected as reference point such that the criterion simplifies to $u(x) < |\|x\| - \|c\||$. The **Exponion algorithm** [24] is also a strict extension of the Hamerly algorithm that makes use of a tighter **CC** pruning criterion. This criterion is modified with regard to the second closest cluster center c' as follows: $u(x) < \frac{\mathrm{L}_2(a(x),c)^2}{2} - \min_{c' \in C \setminus \{a(x)\}} \frac{\mathrm{L}_2(a(x),c')^2}{2}$. The **Yingyang algorithm** [12] follows a different approach and additionally divides clusters into groups. For each data object, one upper bound on the distance to the nearest cluster center and multiple lower bounds on the distance to the second closest cluster within each group are maintained.

The algorithms differ in the way the basic pruning criteria are exploited. While the algorithms **Elkan**, **Hamerly**, and **Drake** are based on distances between data objects and cluster centers as well as on distances among cluster centers, the algorithms **Annular**, **Exponion**, and **Yingyang** make use of additional information to improve the pruning performance. Nonetheless, it is worth mentioning that all of these fast k-means algorithms result in the same exact (non-approximate) clustering than the Lloyd algorithm.

4   Performance Analysis

In this section, we provide the results of our performance analysis of fast k-means algorithms, which is carried out on the following benchmark databases: The **s1** database [1], the **house16h** database [2], the **colormoments** database [3], the **birch** [1] database, the **kddcup04** database [1], the **conflongdemo** database [1], the **covtype** database [4], the **mnist784** database [5], and the **uscencus** database [6]. More information can be found on the corresponding websites.

All algorithms have been implemented in C++14 based on the Standard Template Library (STL) without external libraries and evaluated on a single-core 2.1GHz Intel Xeon CPU with 16GB main memory.

The primary evaluation criterion that we employ in our performance analysis is *real time*, i.e. wall clock time, needed for computing a clustering based on a *k-means++* [8] initialization. In order to increase legibility of the results and comparability of individual algorithms, we aggregate the measured run time values by means of the concept *rank*, which indicates how often a particular algorithm is outperformed by other algorithms. The lower the rank, the better the performance and vice versa.

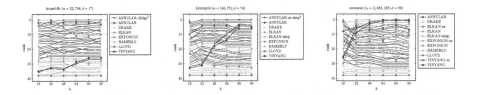

Fig. 1. Ranking of average clustering times for different data sets.

The results are shown in Fig. 1 as a function of the clustering size k. The results for the (small) **house16h** database indicate that (i) the Llyod algorithm is consistently outperformed by any other algorithm, (ii) the Exponion algorithm shows the highest performance for a small number of cluster centers, and (iii) the Annular algorithm outperforms all other approaches in case the clustering size is greater than or equal to $k = 48$. The results for the (medium) **kddcup04** database indicate a similar superiority of the Annular algorithm. It is worth noting that the Yingyang algorithm and the Elkan algorithm both improve with increasing clustering size k, and that the latter shows the highest performance for a clustering of size $k = 16$. Increasing the size of the database emphasizes this effect, as can be seen for the (large) **uscencus** database. The rankings indicate that both algorithms Elkan and Yingyang achieve the highest performance across all clustering sizes except the clustering of size $k = 16$, where the Exponion algorithm shows superior performance.

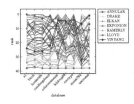

Fig. 2. Ranking of average clustering times based on a cluster size of 96. The data sets are sorted in ascending order based on the product of data set size and dimensionality.

The complete results for all combinations of algorithms and databases are summarized in Fig. 2. As can be seen in this figure, the performance of individual clustering algorithms strongly depends on the database, respectively its size and dimensionality. Every fast k-means clustering algorithm, nonetheless, is able to outperform the conventional Lloyd algorithm. In addition, the Annular algorithm is appropriate for small-to-moderate databases while the Yingyang algorithm increases in efficiency with increasing database complexity. For very large databases, such as the **uscencus** database, the performance of the Elkan algorithm increases. We thus conclude that the choice of clustering algorithm depends on the inherent properties of the database, e.g. size, dimensionality, and non-randomness structure, and that there is no clear overall winner.

5 Conclusions

In this paper, we have addressed the problem of efficient data clustering by means of the k-means algorithm. To this end, we have investigated the major state-of-the-art fast k-means algorithms. Our performance analysis reveals that different algorithmic methods are to be preferred in certain application scenarios but that there is no clear overall winner.

References

1. http://cs.joensuu.fi/sipu/datasets/
2. http://funapp.cs.bilkent.edu.tr/DataSets/
3. https://archive.ics.uci.edu/ml/datasets/corel+image+features
4. http://archive.ics.uci.edu/ml/datasets/covertype
5. http://yann.lecun.com/exdb/mnist/
6. http://archive.ics.uci.edu/ml/datasets/us+census+data+(1990)
7. Arthur, D., Manthey, B., Röglin, H.: Smoothed analysis of the k-means method. J. ACM **58**(5), 1–31 (2011)
8. Arthur, D., Vassilvitskii, S.: k-means++: the advantages of careful seeding. In: SODA, pp. 1027–1035. SIAM (2007)
9. Blömer, J., Lammersen, C., Schmidt, M., Sohler, C.: Theoretical analysis of the k-means algorithm – a survey. In: Kliemann, L., Sanders, P. (eds.) Algorithm Engineering. LNCS, vol. 9220, pp. 81–116. Springer, Cham (2016). https://doi.org/10.1007/978-3-319-49487-6_3
10. Bock, H.H.: Clustering methods: a history of k-means algorithms. In: Brito, P., Cucumel, G., Bertrand, P., de Carvalho, F. (eds) Selected contributions in data analysis and classification. Studies in Classification, Data Analysis, and Knowledge Organization. Springer, Heidelberg (2007). https://doi.org/10.1007/978-3-540-73560-1_15
11. Deza, M.M., Deza, E.: Encyclopedia of distances. In: Encyclopedia of distances. Springer, Heidelberg (2009). https://doi.org/10.1007/978-3-662-52844-0
12. Ding, Y., Zhao, Y., Shen, X., Musuvathi, M., Mytkowicz, T.: Yinyang k-means: a drop-in replacement of the classic k-means with consistent speedup. In: ICML. JMLR Workshop and Conference Proceedings, vol. 37, pp. 579–587 (2015)
13. Drake, J., Hamerly, G.: Accelerated k-means with adaptive distance bounds. In: 5th NIPS Workshop on Optimization for Machine Learning, vol. 8 (2012)
14. Elkan, C.: Using the triangle inequality to accelerate k-means. In: ICML, pp. 147–153. AAAI Press (2003)
15. Forgy, E.W.: Cluster analysis of multivariate data: efficiency versus interpretability of classifications. Biometrics **21**, 768–769 (1965)
16. Hamerly, G.: Making k-means even faster. In: SDM, pp. 130–140. SIAM (2010)

17. Hamerly, G., Drake, J.: Accelerating lloyd's algorithm for k-means clustering. In: Celebi, M.E. (ed.) Partitional Clustering Algorithms, pp. 41–78. Springer, Cham (2015). https://doi.org/10.1007/978-3-319-09259-1_2
18. Hans-Hermann, B.: Origins and extensions of the k-means algorithm in cluster analysis. J. Electronique d'Histoire des Probabilités et de la Statistique Electron. J. History Prob. Stat. **4**(2), 14 (2008)
19. Jain, A.K.: Data clustering: 50 years beyond k-means. Pattern Recognit. Lett. **31**(8), 651–666 (2010)
20. Kriegel, H., Schubert, E., Zimek, A.: The (black) art of runtime evaluation: are we comparing algorithms or implementations? Knowl. Inf. Syst. **52**(2), 341–378 (2017)
21. Lloyd, S.P.: Least squares quantization in PCM. IEEE Trans. Inf. Theory **28**(2), 129–136 (1982)
22. MacQueen, J.: Some methods for classification and analysis of multivariate observations. In: Proceedings 5th Berkeley Symposium on Mathematical Statistics and Probability, vol. 1, Statistics, pp. 281–297. University of California Press (1967)
23. Mahajan, M., Nimbhorkar, P., Varadarajan, K.R.: The planar k-means problem is NP-hard. Theor. Comput. Sci. **442**, 13–21 (2012)
24. Newling, J., Fleuret, F.: Fast k-means with accurate bounds. In: ICML. JMLR Workshop and Conference Proceedings, vol. 48, pp. 936–944. JMLR.org (2016)
25. Olukanmi, P., Nelwamondo, F., Marwala, T.: Rethinking k-means clustering in the age of massive datasets: a constant-time approach. In: Neural Computing and Applications, pp. 1–23 (2019)
26. Steinhaus, H.: Sur la division des corps materiels en parties. Bull. Acad. Polon. Sci. CL. III, **IV**(12), 801–804 (1956)
27. Steinley, D.: K-means clustering: a half-century synthesis. Br. J. Math. Stat. Psychol. **59**(1), 1–34 (2006)
28. Wu, X., et al.: Top 10 algorithms in data mining. Knowl. Inf. Syst. **14**(1), 1–37 (2008)
29. Xu, D., Tian, Y.: A comprehensive survey of clustering algorithms. Annals Data Sci. **2**(2), 165–193 (2015)
30. Xu, R., Wunsch, D.: Survey of clustering algorithms. IEEE Trans. Neural Netw. **16**(3), 645–678 (2005)

Mining Twitter Multi-word Product Opinions with Most Frequent Sequences of Aspect Terms

C. I. Ezeife[1($\boxtimes$)], Ritu Chaturvedi[2], Mahreen Nasir[1], and Vinay Manjunath[1]

[1] School of Computer Science, University of Windsor, 401 Sunset Avenue, Windsor, ON N9B3P4, Canada
{cezeife,nasir11d}@uwindsor.ca
[2] School of Computer Science, University of Guelph, Guelph, Canada
chaturvr@uoguelph.ca
https://cezeife.myweb.cs.uwindsor.ca

Abstract. Given a corpus of microblog texts from a social media platform such as Twitter (e.g., "the new iPhone battery life is good, but camera quality is bad"), mining multi-word aspects (e.g., battery life, camera quality) and opinions (e.g., good, bad) of these products is challenging due to the vast amount of data being generated. Aspect-Based Opinion Mining (ABOM) is thus a combination of automatic aspect extraction and opinion mining that allows an enterprise to analyze the data on relevant features of products in detail, saving time and money. Existing Twitter ABOM systems such as Hate Crime Twitter Sentiment (HCTS) and Microblog Aspect Miner (MAM) generally go through the four-step approach of obtaining microblog posts, identifying frequent nouns (candidate aspects), pruning the candidate aspects, and getting opinion polarity. However, they differ in how well they prune their candidate features. This paper proposes a system called Microblog Aspect Sequence Miner (MASM) as an extension of Microblog Aspect Miner (MAM) by replacing the Apriori algorithm with a modified frequent sequential pattern mining algorithm based on CM-SPAM to also enable mining multi-word aspects more efficiently. The proposed system is able to determine the summary of most common aspects (Aspect Category) and their sentiments for a product. Experimental results with evaluation metrics of execution time, precision, recall, and F1-measure indicate that our approach has higher recall and precision than these existing systems on Sanders Twitter corpus dataset.

Keywords: Twitter sentiment analysis · Aspect based opinion mining · Sequential pattern mining · Topic modeling

This research was supported by the Natural Science and Engineering Research Council (NSERC) of Canada under an Operating grant (OGP-0194134) and a University of Windsor grant.

© The Author(s), under exclusive license to Springer Nature Switzerland AG 2022
E. Pardede et al. (Eds.): iiWAS 2022, LNCS 13635, pp. 126–136, 2022.
https://doi.org/10.1007/978-3-031-21047-1_12

1 Introduction

Twitter is a microblogging social media service that allows users to send small elements of content such as short sentences, individual images, or video links called 'tweets' to their followers or clients. Almost all tweets are available and readily extractable, making it possible to compile vast Twitter information and sentiments for research [10]. Even though a person can only create a message of 280 characters or less, this "limitation" or "feature" has not reduced users' activity. As of January 2020, Twitter has more than 340 million dynamic clients inside a given month, including 100 million clients daily. Clients's origins are widespread, with 77% from outside the United States and sending out more than 500 million tweets every day. The Twitter site positioned thirteenth universally for activity and reacted to more than 15 billion API calls every day. Sentiment analysis and opinion mining are complex problems in social media, owing to the massive amount of data created by humans and robots [4]. We use the body of text from Twitter (Microblog) because: i) Microblogs contain information about only one topic due to their limitation, ii) Before making a purchase, consumers increasingly use social media, such as microblogs, to perform independent research, iii) Consumers are more likely to provide updates on the performance of items over their lifespan on microblogs and in real-time. Research on Opinion mining is generally categorized as document-level, sentence-level and aspect-level. When twitter users tweet opinions, the polarity of their opinion is not necessarily based on the entire subject of the tweet, rather, the opinion is on a certain aspect of the tweet. Opinion on a subject or item without specific aspects are of limited use. Multi-word aspects such as "picture quality" prove to be more useful than single-word aspects. This research focuses on using sequential patterns of words to improve extracting multi-word aspects of tweets.

1.1 Some Closely Related ABOM Systems

Table 1 presents a summary of some closely related existing ABOM systems with some limitations that the proposed system in this paper addresses. Three systems summarized in this table are: (i) Twitter Aspect Classifier (TAC) [7], which does not filter neutral statements (with no positive or negative opinions), does not consider multi-word aspects (such as Switchbot Camera). (ii) Microblog Aspect Miner (MAM) [2], which can filter out neutral statements (such as "a review sentence that consists of "cameras""). MAM still does not consider multi-word aspects such as Switchbot Camera. (iii) Hate crime Twitter Sentiment (HCTS) [12], which although can identify multi-word, but has the shortcoming of not retaining the order for the classification of tweets. It also still stores redundant single aspects. For example, it still stores life as a possible single candidate aspect without identifying the multi-word aspect "battery life".

1.2 Paper Problem Definition and Contributions

Problem Statement: As defined by [8], opinion is a quintuple (a set of five items), (e,a,s,h,t) where e is the target entity, a is the target aspect of entity e on which

Table 1. Closest existing ABOM systems on microblogs

System	Method used	Example aspects	Limitations
Twitter aspect classifier (TAC)	Pointwise mutual information (PMI)	S1: Switchbot and camera	Not handle neutral multi-word aspects
Microblog aspect miner (MAM)	Apriori algorithm, K-Means	S1: Switchbot S2: cameras	Handles neutral words, Switchbot camera
Hate crime twitter sentiment (HCTS)	Association rule mining	Switchbot camera Switchbot camera life	Not retain aspect order, keeps redundant ones

the opinion has been given, s is the sentiment of the opinion on aspect a of entity e, while h is the opinion holder, and t is the opinion posting time; sentiment s can be positive, negative, or neutral. Here, e and a together represent the opinion target. With the given definition, we define our problem as follows: Given a set of microblog posts about item P (e.g., iPhone), the main task is to identify P's k significant aspects (Single and Multi-word aspects) and to generate a summary of sentiments expressed based on the aspect.

A multi-word aspect is represented as a_n, where a is the aspect and n is the number of words in the aspect. For example, a multi-word aspect such as "battery life" is represented as a_2 to denote that there are two words in this multi-word aspect. The symbol a_1 represents one single word aspect. The main contributions of this paper are to: i) use sequential patterns to increase accuracy of mining single and multi-word aspects (such as "operating system") in microblogs retaining the order of words in them. ii) remove all single redundant aspects that are not meaningful. In order to achieve this, we propose a system called MASM (Microblog Aspect Sequence Miner), which takes nouns as input generated from the part of speech (POS) tags to extract single and more importantly, multi-word aspects (sequences) based on a user minimum support threshold. Our system removes redundant features by checking that no superset noun phrase appears together in any sentence with the single aspect word for it to be retained (e.g., manual, manual mode, manual setting will cause manual to be pruned).

1.3 Outline

Sect. 2 provides other relevant related work. Section 3 presents the new proposed Microblog Aspect Sequence Miner (MASM), Sect. 4 provides example application of MASM to a problem. Section 5 reports the results of our experiments and Sect. 6 provides concluding remarks and future work.

2 Other Related Work

An example opinion is: "The strap is really horrible and obstructs the way of parts of the camera all the time". Effective opinions will be useful when predicting the orientation of opinion sentences. From this example, "horrible" is an effective opinion of the strap. In the early system of FBS: Mining and summarizing customer reviews [5], a five step approach was used to mine product characteristics from customer evaluations, detect sentiment opinions, and summarize explicitly expressed elements' outcomes. The main five tasks consist of:

1. Performing Parts of Speech tagging of the sentence so words are marked as nouns, noun phrases, etc. Example: "I am absolutely in awe of this camera" yields: ('I', 'PRP'), ('am', 'VBP'), ('absolutely', 'RB'), ('in', 'IN'), ('awe', 'NN'), ('of', 'IN'), ('this', 'DT'), ('camera', 'NN').
2. Frequent Feature (aspect) Identification: This consists of generating frequent itemsets (aspects) from all reviews using an algorithm like Apriori algorithm and these are called candidate aspects.
3. Feature Pruning used to remove unlikely features through compactness pruning (keeping only feature phrases) or redundancy pruning (removing single words).
4. Opinion Word extraction by finding a positive, statistically significant relationship between adjectives and features.
5. Opinion Summarization: According to the opinion sentence orientations, related opinion sentences are classified into positive and negative categories for each discovered feature. A count is determined to illustrate how many reviewers offer positive/negative views of the feature. The output is a summary of the reviews such as: (e.g., picture quality (has positive adjectives 253 and negative 6 , camera size: positive 103 and negative 10).

This method and others tend to develop too many non-aspects and neglect low-frequency aspects. They require multiple thresholds to be manually calibrated, making it impossible to port them to another dataset. Also, none of these systems perform multi-word aspect mining.

3   The Proposed Microblog MASM Miner

The proposed Microblog Aspect Sequence Miner (MASM) algorithm accepts input data of an entity product name (e.g., iphone) that serves as a search query to the Twitter API and produces the output of a ranked list of relevant aspects of the product with summary of opinions expressed on them, that includes both single and multi-word aspects (e.g., Phone cases (negative 4, positive 1; Screen negative: 4; Battery life positive: 3).

Steps of the Proposed MASM Algorithm
Input: Twitter comments or Text data of a given product, p

Output: set of relevant single and multi-word aspects A of product p with number of positive and negative opinions on each a in A

Step 1: Preprocessing of Tweets: In this step, sentences extracted from tweets are cleaned such that words that are not likely regular nouns are removed (e.g., nouns such as email addresses).

Step 2: Classification of tweets into Subjective or Objective Sentences: In this step, the overall sentiment of the sentence is obtained using a lexicon. A lexicon is a collection of entries containing information on words (or word stems); information about a word can include its part(s) of speech, spelling variants, inflectional variants, encoded syntactical information, and so on. In this step, only the subjective sentences are passed on further for feature (aspect) extraction. VADER ([6]) is a lexicon and rule-based sentiment analysis method built for analyzing sentiment from social media with more than 9000 lexical words, which was used in this step for sentence level sentiment analysis. For example, with the review The iPhone is super cool, the rating by Vader for the sentence is 67% as Positive, 33% as Neutral and 0% as Negative. The lexicon ratings for each word in VADER is super (2.9) and cool (1.3) with total of 4.2. The compound score is used to determine the sentence opinion, where the sentence compound valence score (s) is computed as: $s = x/\sqrt{x^2 + \alpha}$ where x = sum of word valence scores, and α = Normalization constant (default value is 15). So, for the above example, $s = 4.2/\sqrt{4.2^2 + 15} = 4.2/5.71 = 0.735$

Step 3: Frequent Noun/Noun Phrase Identification: The MASM applies CM-SPAM algorithm [3] on the remaining nouns to find all multi-part noun phrases which are frequent, e.g., photo quality and LCD display. To accomplish frequent phrase mining, we modify the algorithm so that the position of words in the sentences are considered. Mining semantically meaningful phrases allows to change the granularity of text data from words to phrases. It also improves the power and efficiency of unstructured data manipulation. For example, consider a text dataset with two sentences: i) S1 = machine learning is a field of computer science. ii) S2 = machine learning gives computer systems the ability to learn. Although two Sequential Patterns X1 = machine, learning and X2 = machine, computer are found in both S1 and S2, X2 is less meaningful than X1 due to the large gap between machine and computer. In other words, the two words machine and computer are in two different contexts. We believe that if we restrict the distance between two neighboring elements in a sequential pattern, then this pattern is more meaningful and discriminative. We define a sequential pattern satisfying a gap constraint as follows.

Definition of Gap Constraint and satisfaction: A gap, g is a positive integer, g = 4. Given a sequence of aspects, consisting of m events $e_1, \ldots, e_m$ (aspects). Each event can have an instance or occurrence o such that sequence is S = $\{e_1, \ldots, e_m\}$ and an occurrence of each event e_i is marked as $e_i^o = \{i_1, \ldots, i_m\}$ of a subsequence X with occurrence marker i_k in sequence S. If the occurrence gap between X and any other event e_z is $i_k + 1 \leq i_k + 4(\forall_{i_k} \in (1, m1))$, then we say that this instance, o satisfies the 4-gap constraint and thus, the two events can be joined as multi-word sequence. If at least one occurrence of X satisfies the 4-gap constraint, we say that X satisfies the 4-gap constraint. Note that we consider the subsequences with length 1 (i.e., they contain only one symbol) to satisfy any 4-gap constraint. Let us consider an example sequential dataset with four sequences given in (sequence id: sequence) format next. (S_1 :{c, a, g, a, a, g, t}), (S_2: {t, g, a, c, a, g}), (S_3: {g, a, a, t}), (S_4: {a, g}). Assume that gap constraint g = 1 and minimum support δ = 0.7. The subsequence X = ag is contained in three sequences S_1, S_2, and S_4, and it also satisfies the 1-gap constraint in these three sequences. Thus, its support is sup (X, 4) = 3/4 = 0.75. We say that X = ag is a sequential pattern since sup (X, 4)$\geq \delta$.

Step 4: Candidate Aspect Pruning: In this step, the frequent patterns of nouns and noun phrases identified from step 3 are mined using the sequential pattern mining algorithm, CM-SPAM ([3]). This is multi word aspect extraction with CM SPAM algorithm where word Gap constraint = 2 and the extracted pattern is represented as a = a_1 x a_2 x a_3 x ... x a_n. It is able to preserve the order and meaning of the phrases. Example frequent noun phrases are "phone cases" and "battery life". In the second phase of this step 4, phrase embeddings are discovered using Sqn2Vec-SIM model ([9]) which uses information of both single

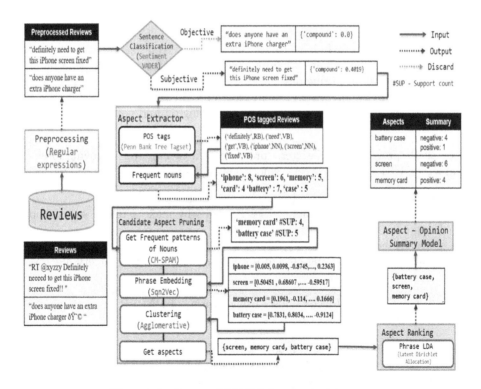

Fig. 1. The Proposed MASM System Architecture

symbols and sequential patterns (SPs) of a sequence simultaneously. Thereafter, sequence aspects are clustered to remove redundancies.

Step 5: Aspect Ranking and Summary: Using Latent Dirichlet Allocation (LDA) ([1]), a Bayesian model is used to rank sequence aspects based on the following guidelines: (i.) Choose a topic mixture for the document (over a fixed set of K topics). (ii.)Identify each word in the document by: first picking a topic, then using the topic to identify the word itself. LDA then seeks to backtrack from the document to discover a set of themes that are likely to have created the collection, assuming this generative model for a collection of documents. The architecture of the proposed MASM system is provided as Fig. 1.

4   An Application of the Proposed MASM System

This section presents an example processing of some sample Twitter posts on iphone to mine relevant sequences of single and multi-word aspects using the proposed MASM algorithm. Steps of the Proposed MASM System are:

Step 1: Data collection is done through Twitter API.
Four example tweets processed are:

   i. RT @xyzzy Definitely have to get this iPhone screen fixed!!
   ii. @_kaliblaze iPhone 6 are a pain for phone cases I mean why make a phone so thin & not bring out
  iii. does anyone have an extra iPhone charger
  iv. RT ElaineBaldwin86: lol at my iphone cutting off and not cutting back on @ 89% battery

Step 2: Preprocessing of Twitter - pre-processed tweets after removing foreign characters, URLs, RT (Retweet), emoticons, and such.

   i. definitely have to get this iphone screen fixed
   ii. iphone are a pain for phone cases i mean why make a phone so thin not bring out
  iii. does anyone have an extra iphone charger
  iv. lol at my iphone cutting off and not cutting back on 89% battery life

Step 3: Obtain the Subjective posts using Sentiment VADER

  (i) definitely have to get this iphone screen fixed
  (ii) iphone are a pain for phone cases i mean why make a phone so thin not bring out
 (iii) lol at my iphone cutting off and not cutting back on 89% battery life

Step 4: Tokenization and Stopword Removal will produce the following pre-processed posts.

(i) 'definitely', have, 'get', 'iphone', 'screen', 'fixed'
(ii) 'iphone', '6', 'pain', 'phone', 'cases', 'i', 'mean', 'make', 'phone', 'thin', 'bring'
(iii) 'laughing', out, loud, 'iphone', 'cutting', 'cutting', 'back', '89%', 'battery', 'life'

Step 5: single word Aspect extraction (Pos tagging) CM SPAM ([3]). The following words satisfy frequency requirements.
iphone: 3, phone: 2, get: 1 screen: 1, battery: 1, 'life: 1', cutting: 2 pain: 1, cases: 1, back: 1.

Step 6: Multi word aspect Extraction CM SPAM algorithm. (Gap constraint = 2). Represented by a = a_1 x a_2 x a_3 x ... x a_n (Tables 2 and 3).

Table 2. Result of multi word extraction

SN	Frequent noun phrases	Support count
1	Phone cases	1
2	Battery life	1

Table 3. Aspect ranking

SN	Dominant_topic	Topic_name
1	Topic 1	Phone cases
2	Topic 2	Screen
3	Topic 3	battery life

Step 7: Significance Score with Statistical Significance. using Input: Dataset D + Support Count done.

Step 8: Phrase LDA (Aspect Ranking) to answer question, which most common aspect people are talking about? phone cases with negative opinion 4 and positive opinion 1 , Screen with negative opinion 4 and positive opinion 0 or Battery life with negative opinion 0 and positive opinion 3? (Table 4).

Table 4. Aspect opinion summary

SN	Aspect of iphone	Opinion
1	Phone cases	Negative: 4 positive: 1
2	Screen	Negative: 4
3	Battery life	Positive: 3

5   Experimental and Performance Analysis

This section presents two different datasets widely used in Twitter sentiment analysis literature. We chose datasets that are: (i) publicly available to the research community, (ii) carefully annotated, giving a credible set of judgment over the tweets, and (iii) utilized to test multiple sentiment analysis algorithms. Tweets in these datasets have been annotated with different sentiment labels. Dataset is Sanders Twitter Corpus [11]; Number of Tweets is 5,113; Number of Negative tweets is 572; Number of Neutral tweets is 2,333; Number of Positive tweets is 519; while the Number of Irrelevant tweets is 1,689. The Sanders dataset consists of 5,113 tweets on four different topics (Apple, Google, Microsoft, Twitter). One annotator manually labeled each tweet as either positive, negative, neutral, or irrelevant concerning the topic. The annotation process resulted in 572 negative, 2,333 neutral, 519 positive, and 1,686 unrelated tweets. The Sanders dataset is available at https://github.com/zfz/twitter_corpus. To collect Twitter data, researchers typically use the freely available API endpoints for public data. There are two different APIs to collect Twitter data. (i) The Representational State Transfer (REST) API provides information about individual user accounts or popular topics and allows for sending or liking Tweets and following accounts. (ii) The Streaming APIs are used for real-time collection of Tweets. In this paper, we used 100,000 tweets from 4 different products as our text corpus. The products are Apple, Microsoft, Google, and Twitter. Apple and Microsoft were chosen because they are among the most talked-about products on Twitter. We obtained English tweets from Twitter throughout the month. (June 2021 July 2021).

Experimental Setup: The following tools are used in this experiment. (1) Java Programming Language (Eclipse), (2) Preprocessing using Regular Expression, (3) CM-SPAM algorithm used, (4) Python Programming Language (Google Colab), (5) Twitter API (Tweepy) for crawling the data from Twitter, (6) NLTK for tokenization, stopword removal, POS tagging, (7) Spacy for Sentiment VADER, (8) Latent Dirichlet Allocation, and (9) Graphs and Visualization.

Evaluation metrics for Aspect Extraction: We evaluate our proposed model MASM aspect extraction process with three close algorithms of MAM, HCTS and TAC with three performance metrics such as: Precision, Recall and F1-measure. Precision: We calculate the precision to identify the proportion of extracted aspects which are true over the total number of extracted aspects. We calculate the recall to identify the proportion of true aspects extracted by the system.

$$Precision = |ExtractedAspects \cap TrueAspects|/|ExtractedAspects|$$
$$Recall = |ExtractedAspects \cap TrueAspects|/|TrueAspects|$$
$$F1 - Measure = (2 * Precision * Recall)/(Precision + Recall)$$

Runtime Comparison: The experiments consisted of running all the algorithms on each dataset while increasing the minimum support threshold until algorithms became very easily executable or a clear winner was observed. For each system, we recorded the execution time, the percentage of candidates pruned by the proposed algorithms and the same size of candidates reviews and aspects.

Results of Aspect Extraction: From Table 5, we can easily see that MASM is performing better than the three other related systems. (i) The precision of all the four systems is very close because precision as defined is the percentage of extracted aspects as true to the total number of extracted aspects. So, the percentage of all the 4 systems are similar in extracting the relevant aspects. Also, we can see that MAM and MASM have slightly higher precisions the reason being, we remove the neutral statements. If we compare the results of MAM and MASM, MASM has higher. (ii) The recall of MASM compared to all the other systems is relatively higher because we remove the redundant aspects and considers the sequences of aspects which is in the order.

Table 5. Evaluation results with different systems for Sanders Twitter Corpus

Systems	Precision	Recall	F1-Measure
TAC	78.5	46.8	58.6
MAM	81.2	61.0	69.66
HCTS	77.9	76.6	76
Proposed MASM	82.5	79.8	81.12

6   Conclusions and Future Work

This paper proposes a hybrid approach Microblog Aspect Sequence Miner (MASM), which generates multiple word sequences of aspects related to a product. As input, MASM takes in raw unprocessed tweets and first classifies the tweets at the sentence level to determine whether they express any opinion or not. We clean posts before sentiment analysis. Then, we identify frequent nouns and noun phrases using a known sequential pattern mining algorithm (CM-SPAM) [3] to determine possible aspects. This work improves existing MAM aspect mining system [2] (that does not mine multi word sequences) techniques to generate high-quality phrases using Sqn2Vec [9] sequential pattern mining algorithm. Aspect Categorization is an essential task that represents opinion targets or what people talk about in opinions. In this study, we modified the known topic model Latent Dirichlet Allocation (LDA) [1], to discover which categories these aspects belong. Experiments demonstrate that the proposed approach works better in obtaining relevant aspects of a product with more precision. Getting feedback on these identified elements may also provide business owners insight into what their consumers think of their company. This aids business intelligence and decision-making by answering questions such as, "What portion of my product do consumers like?" and "What part of my rivals' goods do they not like?" Some of the future work of the system include: 1) Identifying aspects in different languages is still a significant limitation of this work. Also we did not work on the order between the words for example: battery power life and battery life power. 2) Extending to other platforms (Google, Apple, and Microsoft and on different domains such as political, restaurants, and environment such as Amazon reviews and Yelp reviews, where the length of each review is higher compared to microblogs.

References

1. Blei, D.M., Ng, A.Y., Jordan, M.I.: Latent dirichlet allocation. J. Mach. Learn. Res. **3**, 993–1022 (2003)
2. Ejieh, C., Ezeife, C.I., Chaturvedi, R.: Mining product opinions with most frequent clusters of aspect terms. In: Proceedings of the 34th ACM/SIGAPP Symposium on Applied Computing, pp. 546–549 (2019)
3. Fournier-Viger, P., Gomariz, A., Campos, M., Thomas, R.: Fast vertical mining of sequential patterns using co-occurrence information. In: Tseng, V.S., Ho, T.B., Zhou, Z.-H., Chen, A.L.P., Kao, H.-Y. (eds.) PAKDD 2014. LNCS (LNAI), vol. 8443, pp. 40–52. Springer, Cham (2014). https://doi.org/10.1007/978-3-319-06608-0_4
4. Giachanou, A., Crestani, F.: Like it or not: a survey of twitter sentiment analysis methods. ACM Comput. Surv. **49**(2), 1–41 (2016)
5. Hu, M., Liu, B.: Mining and summarizing customer reviews. In: Proceedings of the ACM SIGKDD International Conference on Knowledge Discovery and Data Mining - KDD 2004, p. 168177 (2004)
6. Hutto, C., Gilbert, E.: Vader: a parsimonious rule-based model for sentiment analysis of social media text. In: International AAAI Conference on Web and social media, vol. 8, no. 1 (2014)
7. Lek, H.H., Poo, D.C.: Aspect-based twitter sentiment classification. In: 2013 IEEE 25th International Conference on Tools with Artificial Intelligence, pp. 366–373 (2013)
8. Liu, B.: Sentiment Analysis and Opinion Mining. Morgan and Claypool Publishers, San Rafael (2012)
9. Nguyen, D., Luo, W., Nguyen, T.D., Venkatesh, S., Phung, D.: Sqn2Vec: learning sequence representation via sequential patterns with a gap constraint. In: European Conference on Machine Learning and Principles and Practice of Knowledge Discovery in Databases, Dublin, Ireland, vol. 11052 (2018)
10. Pak, A., Paroubek, P.: Twitter as a corpus for sentiment analysis and opinion mining. In: Proceedings of the Seventh International Conference on Language Resources and Evaluation (LREC 2010) (2010)
11. Sanders, N.J.: Sanders-Twitter Sentiment Corpus. Sanders Analytics LLC (2011)
12. Zainuddin, N., Selamat, A., Ibrahim, R.: Hybrid sentiment classification on twitter aspect-based sentiment analysis. Appl. Intell. **48**, 1218–1232 (2017)

An Analysis of Human Perception of Partitions of Numerical Factor Domains

Minakshi Kaushik$^{(\boxtimes)}$, Rahul Sharma , Mahtab Shahin ,
Sijo Arakkal Peious , and Dirk Draheim

Information Systems Group, Tallinn University of Technology, Akadeemia tee 15a,
12618 Tallinn, Estonia
{minakshi.kaushik,rahul.sharma,mahtab.shahin,
sijo.arakkal,dirk.draheim}@taltech.ee

Abstract. In Machine learning (ML), several discretization techniques
and mathematical approaches are used to partition numerical data
attributes. However, cut-points retrieved by discretizing techniques often
do not match with human perceived cut-points. Therefore, understanding
the human perception for discretizing the numerical attribute is important for developing an effective discretizing technique. In this paper, we
conduct a study of human perception of partitions in numerical data
that reflects best the impact of one independent numerical attribute
on another dependent numerical attribute. We aim to understand how
expert data scientists and statisticians partition numerical attributes
under different types of data points, such as dense data points, outliers,
and uneven random points. The findings lead to an interesting discussion
about the importance of human perception under distinct kinds of data
points for finding partitions of numerical attributes.

Keywords: Discretization · Partitioning · Numerical attributes · Data
mining · Machine learning · Human perception

1 Introduction

Discrete values are significantly used in statistics, machine learning, and data
mining. Moreover, to find the intervals of numeric attributes, several discretization techniques are presented in the literature [6,12,13]. However, these techniques are unable to find the ideal intervals with appropriate ranges and it is
still difficult to get an ideal discretizer.

Humans can easily visualize the ideal partitions and even the number of com-
partments in extreme situations (like step-functions). However, in some other
unusual cases, e.g., mixed data point, uneven random data points, the partition
ranges completely depend on data experts' perceptions and opinions. Perceptual conception is an important factor in developing an automated measure for

This work has been partially conducted in the project "ICT programme" which was
supported by the European Union through the European Social Fund.

discretizing numerical attributes. However, in the state of the art discretization techniques, human perceptions and observations are overlooked.

We conduct this study to identify the typical patterns of human perception in partitioning numerical attributes. We have also presented an order-preserving partitioning method to find the partitions of numerical attributes that reflect best the impact of one independent numerical attribute on a dependent numerical attribute [10]. We aim to investigate the impact of data points' features on human perception when partitioning numerical attributes. We mainly focus on data point density, the effect of outliers, uneven random distribution, and linear function while performing perceptual analysis. We set four hypotheses related to the data points of partitions that can influence human interpretation. The human responses are collected through several experiments with data scientists and machine learning experts. We used nine synthetic and three real-world datasets to create a series of graphs for the experiment. This study's concept is inspired by previous studies on partial conditionalization [3,4], association rule mining [16,19], and numerical association rule mining [11,20]. These articles cover the discretization process as an important stage in numerical association rule mining. Earlier, we have also presented a tool named Grand report [15] and a framework [17,18] for the unification of ARM, statistical reasoning, and online analytical processing.

The paper is organized as follows. In Sect. 2, we discuss related work. We formulate hypotheses in Sect. 3. Then we describe the design of the experiment in Sect. 4. We perform analysis and present the results in Sect. 5. We finish the paper with a conclusion in Sect. 6.

2 Related Work

Many studies have used human perception to evaluate various techniques. These studies primarily focused on visual perceptual analysis. However, they are not completely related to discretization. For example, Etemadpour et al. [5] conducted a perception-based evaluation of high-dimensional data where humans were asked to identify clusters and analyze distances inside and across clusters. Demiralp et al. [2] used human judgments to estimate perceptual kernels for visual encoding variables such as shape, size, color, and combinations. The experiment used Amazon's Mechanical Turk platform, with twenty Turkers completing thirty MTurk jobs. In [1] authors also evaluated bench-marking clustering algorithms based on human perception of clusters in 2D scatter plots. The authors' main concern was how well existing clustering algorithms corresponded to human perceptions of clusters. Our work is also related to considering human perceptions when discretizing numerical attributes.

3   Hypotheses

In this study, we want to see if the distances between the data points matter or if other characteristics influence human perception when finding the cut-points to partition a numerical attribute. We make the following hypotheses, which investigate how different aspects affect humans' partitioning process.

- H1: We expect that the density of data points influences the response.
- H2: We expect that outliers influence human responses.
- H3: Linear data functions will be partitioned using the mean of the function.
- H4: Random distribution of data points influences the responses.

4   Design of Experiment

We provide a set of graphs and discussed them with our team to create a diverse collection of graphs with different data points. Finally, twelve graphs were selected to be shared with humans to partition the data, as given in Fig. 1. These graphs are obtained from nine synthetic datasets (D1 to D9) and three real-world datasets (D10 to D12). The synthetic datasets (D1 to D9) consist only of two numerical attributes. The graph D10 is drawn from a real-world dataset DC public government employees [8]. It contains 33,424 records of DC public government employees and their salaries in 2011. This dataset is sourced from the washington times via freedom of information act (FOIA) requests. The dataset D11 is the Heart Disease dataset [7] and is sourced from the UCI machine learning repository. This dataset has 13 attributes and 303 records. We used attribute {Age} and {Cholesterol} for drawing the graph. The graph D12 is drawn from New Jersey (NJ) school teacher salaries (2016) [14] sourced from the New Jersey (NJ) Department of Education. It contains 138715 records and 15 attributes. We have only taken the initial 23000 rows from the dataset. We are interested in the column {experience_total} and {salary}. A copy of all these datasets is available in the GitHub repository [9]. We designed a Google form with a number of graphs (Fig. 1) and questions to get responses from individuals and their perceptions on discretization. The Google form was distributed to fifty DS/ML experts and non-experts to estimate the number of partitions and the ranges of these partitions to determine the cut-points. Respondent identity (name), email addresses, domain expertise (DS/ML expert or non-expert), the number of partitions observed, and the ranges of each partition were collected together and compiled after the experiments.

5   Analysis and Result

Two of the fifty responses submitted via the Google form were incomplete, therefore, they are not included in the analysis. We classified expert and non-expert responses from the remaining forty-eight responses into two categories. Table 1 illustrates the comparison of human perception to identify the number of partitions between the DS/ML experts' responses and non-expert people. We received 60% responses from DS/ML experts and 40% of answers from non-expert people.

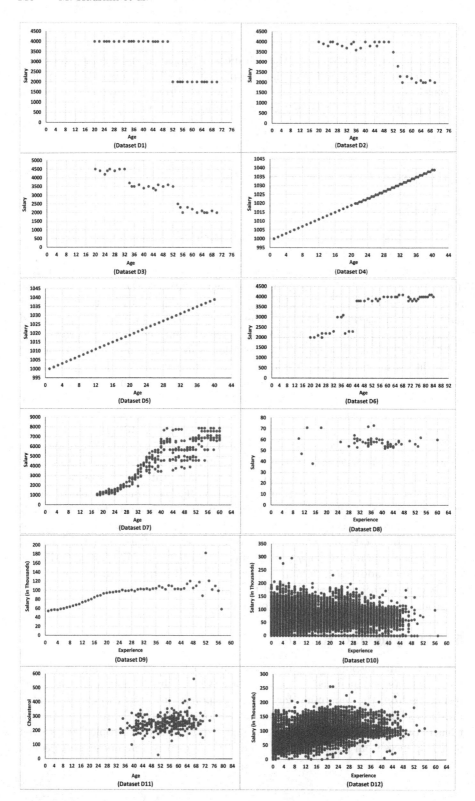

Fig. 1. Graphs for datasets D1 to D12.

5.1   Step-Function

In a *Step function f*, the domain is partitioned into several intervals. *f(x)* is constant for each interval, but the constant can be different for each interval. The different constant values for each interval create the jumps between horizontal line segments and develop a staircase, which is also known as a step function. The datasets D1, D2 and D3, are examples of step functions. We can also include D6 for the example of the step function. For datasets, D1 and D2, most responses from both categories (experts 93.3%, 73.3% and non-experts 90%, 60%) were for two partitions, and for dataset D3, three partitions were identified by contributors (expert 93.3% and non-experts 100%). The dataset D6 received maximum responses for four and five partitions, which indicates D6 as a step function. Humans identified partitions based on dense regions of data points. As for datasets D1 and D2, two dense regions were identified. However, for D3 and D6, three and four dense groups were identified, respectively. Hypothesis H1 confirms for datasets D1, D2, D3 and D6.

5.2   Linear Function

A linear function is a straight line between one independent and one dependent variable. The datasets D4 and D5 are examples of linear functions. The dataset D4 has more dense data points on another side of the slope and received a total of 60% of responses (see Fig. 2) for two partitions, which means contributors split the data points based on the mean of the function and identified two partitions. However, in contrast, dataset D5 did not receive any responses for two partitions and got a total of 92% responses for no partition. We argue that there is insufficient ground for selecting cut-points when a continuous variable is distributed uniformly in the environment, so splitting would be pretty random. Hence, contributors did not identify any partition for dataset D5. The hypothesis H3 confirms for dataset D4 but contradicts for D5. Here we can notice that H1 is also true for D4 and partially true for D5.

Table 1. The comparison of human perception to identify number of partitions based on their profile.

Resp.	P	Datasets											
		D1	D2	D3	D4	D5	D6	D7	D8	D9	D10	D11	D12
DS/ML Experts (60%)	No				33.3%	93.3%					40%	53.3%	40%
	2	93.3%	73.3%	0%	53%	0%	13.3%	60%	33.3%	73.3%	40%	26.6%	26.6%
	3	6.67%	26.6%	93.3%	13.3%	6.6%	26.6%	20%	66.6%	26.6%	6.66%	20%	6.66%
	4			6.66%			26.6%	20%	0%	0%	6.66%	0%	20%
	5						33.3%				6.66%		6.66%
Non-experts (40%)	No				20%	90%					40%	60%	20%
	2	90%	60%	0%	70%	0%	30%	40%	60%	60%	30%	30%	30%
	3	10%	40%	100%	10%	10%	0%	40%	30%	30%	20%	0%	30%
	4			0%			40%	20%	10%	10%	0%	10%	10%
	5						30%				10%		10%

Resp: Responders; P: number of partitions

5.3   Uneven Random Function

The datasets D7 to D12 fall under the uneven, randomly scattered plot category. We found that responses from both categories were opposite for graph D8. Out of the total responses for D8, 33.3% responses of DS/ML experts marked two partitions and 66.6% responses of experts marked three partitions; however, 60% of non-experts marked two partitions, and only 30% marked three partitions. Overall, 52% responses favor three partitions, and 44% of responses identify two partitions. In this case, experts include the scattered data points and consider them as one partition, and the remaining dense data points are identified as two more partitions. However, non-experts observed two partitions, one with a dense and the other with a scattered group of data points. The same situation occurs with dataset D9; here, a total of 68% of responses identified two partitions, one with the dense data points and the second with the scattered data points. Hypothesis H1 is also confirmed by the datasets D8 and D9. Datasets D10, D11, and D12 received high responses for no partition compared to other partitions. For the dataset D10, 40% contributors responded with no partition, and for the rest of the contributors, some random cut-points were marked for two, three, four, and five partitions. Similarly, for the dataset D11, 56% responses are favored for no partition, and the rest of the responses are answered for two, three, and four partitions. The dataset D12 encountered the same situation where 32% contributors responded with no partition, and 68% contributors marked some random cut-points for two, three, four, and five partitions. For these cases, hypothesis H4 confirms, but H2 contradicts, as outliers do not influence human response (case of datasets D8, D9, and D11). Hence, it proves that humans have no clear perception of these types of datasets and they are unable to identify cut-points.

The percentage of responses of each partition for each dataset is demonstrated in Fig. 2. Datasets D5, D10, D11 and D12 received high responses for

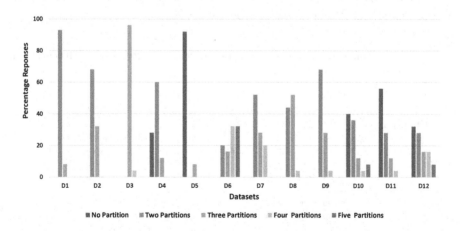

Fig. 2. Percentage responses of partitions for each dataset.

no partition compared to other partitions. Hence, it proves that humans have no clear perception of these types of datasets, and they are unable to identify cut-points. It is important to note that datasets D5 and D6 have similar appearances, but both datasets received different cut-points responses because of the distribution of their data points. D6 has not received any responses with no partition, and D5 has not gotten any responses with two partitions. For the datasets D1, D2, D4, D7 and D9, mainly two partitions were suggested by contributors. We find that the density of partitions has a substantial impact on perception during a visual interpretation. The random distribution of data points and linear function also influence human perception. However, outliers do not affect human judgement. After analyzing Table 1, we also reach the conclusion that the opinions of experts and non-expert responders do not make a huge difference, except in some situations.

6   Conclusion

The main objective of this research is to analyze the human perception of partitioning the numerical attribute. In this paper, we analyzed the perception of DS/ML experts and non-experts by providing them a series of graphs with numerical data. The analysis gives us insights that the perceptions of experts and non-experts while partitioning the numerical attribute are not much different. However, the data points' features influence most of the outcomes. Therefore, human judgment plays a vital role in developing an automated approach for partitioning numerical attributes with the best cut points. In future work, we plan to assess the accuracy of our proposed measures by comparing the outcomes of human perceptions.

References

1. Aupetit, M., Sedlmair, M., Abbas, M.M., Baggag, A., Bensmail, H.: Toward perception-based evaluation of clustering techniques for visual analytics. In: Proceedings of VIS2019 - IEEE Visualization Conference, pp. 141–145 (2019)
2. Demiralp, Ç., Bernstein, M.S., Heer, J.: Learning perceptual kernels for visualization design. IEEE Trans. Visual Comput. Graph. $20(12)$, 1933–1942 (2014)
3. Draheim, D.: Generalized Jeffrey conditionalization: a frequentist semantics of partial conditionalization. Springer, Cham (2017). https://doi.org/10.1007/978-3-319-69868-7
4. Draheim, D.: Future perspectives of association rule mining based on partial conditionalization. In: Proceedings of DEXA'2019 - the 30th International Conference on Database and Expert Systems Applications, LNCS, vol. 11706, p. xvi. Springer, Cham (2019). https://doi.org/10.1007/978-3-030-27615-7
5. Etemadpour, R., da Motta, R.C., de Souza Paiva, J.G., Minghim, R., de Oliveira, M.C.F., Linsen, L.: Role of human perception in cluster-based visual analysis of multidimensional data projections. In: Proceedings of IVAPP -International Conference on Information Visualization Theory and Applications, pp. 276–283 (2014)

6. Garcia, S., Luengo, J., Sáez, J.A., Lopez, V., Herrera, F.: A survey of discretization techniques: taxonomy and empirical analysis in supervised learning. IEEE Trans. Knowl. Data Eng. **25**(4), 734–750 (2012)
7. Janosi, A., Steinbrunn, W., Pfisterer, M., Detrano, R.: Heart Disease. UCI machine learning repository (1988)
8. Kalish, M.: DC public employee salaries (2011). https://data.world/codefordc/dc-public-employee-salaries-2011
9. Kaushik, M.: Datasets (2022). https://github.com/minakshikaushik/LSQM-measure.git
10. Kaushik, M., Sharma, R., Peious, S.A., Draheim, D.: Impact-Driven Discretization of Numerical Factors: Case of Two- and Three-Partitioning. In: Srirama, S.N., Lin, J.C.-W., Bhatnagar, R., Agarwal, S., Reddy, P.K. (eds.) BDA 2021. LNCS, vol. 13147, pp. 244–260. Springer, Cham (2021). https://doi.org/10.1007/978-3-030-93620-4_18
11. Kaushik, M., et al.: A systematic assessment of numerical association rule mining methods. SN Comput. Sci. **2**(5), 1–13 (2021)
12. Kotsiantis, S., Kanellopoulos, D.: Discretization techniques: a recent survey. GESTS Int. Trans. Comput. Sci. Eng. **32**(1), 47–58 (2006)
13. Liu, H., Hussain, F., Tan, C.L., Dash, M.: Discretization: An enabling technique. Data Min. Knowl. Disc. **6**(4), 393–423 (2002)
14. Naik, S.: NJ teacher salaries. (2016). https://data.world/sheilnaik/nj-teacher-salaries-2016
15. Arakkal Peious, S., Sharma, R., Kaushik, M., Shah, S.A., Yahia, S.B.: Grand reports: a tool for generalizing association rule mining to numeric target values. In: Song, M., Song, I.-Y., Kotsis, G., Tjoa, A.M., Khalil, I. (eds.) DaWaK 2020. LNCS, vol. 12393, pp. 28–37. Springer, Cham (2020). https://doi.org/10.1007/978-3-030-59065-9_3
16. Shahin, M., et al.: Big data analytics in association rule mining: A systematic literature review. In: Proceedings of BDET 2021- International Conference on Big Data Engineering and Technology, pp. 40–49. ACM (2021)
17. Sharma, R., et al.: A novel framework for unification of association rule mining, online analytical processing and statistical reasoning. IEEE Access **10**, 12792–12813 (2022). https://doi.org/10.1109/ACCESS.2022.3142537
18. Sharma, R., Kaushik, M., Peious, S.A., Shahin, M., Yadav, A.S., Draheim, D.: Towards unification of statistical reasoning, OLAP and association rule mining: semantics and pragmatics. In: Database Systems for Advanced Applications. DASFAA 2022, LNCS, vol. 13245. Springer, Cham (2022). https://doi.org/10.1007/978-3-031-00123-9_48
19. Sharma, R., Kaushik, M., Peious, S.A., Yahia, S.B., Draheim, D.: Expected vs. unexpected: selecting right measures of interestingness. In: Song, M., Song, I.-Y., Kotsis, G., Tjoa, A.M., Khalil, I. (eds.) DaWaK 2020. LNCS, vol. 12393, pp. 38–47. Springer, Cham (2020). https://doi.org/10.1007/978-3-030-59065-9_4
20. Srikant, R., Agrawal, R.: Mining quantitative association rules in large relational tables. In: Proceedings of ACM SIGMOD 1996 - International Conference on Management of Data, pp. 1–12 (1996)

Fast Top-k Similar Sequence Search on DNA Databases

Ryuichi Yagi[1]([✉]) [iD] and Hiroaki Shiokawa[2] [iD]

[1] Department of Computer Science, University of Tsukuba, Tsukuba, Japan
yagi@kde.cs.tsukuba.ac.jp
[2] Center for Computational Sciences, University of Tsukuba, Tsukuba, Japan
shiokawa@cs.tsukuba.ac.jp

Abstract. Top-k similar sequence search is an essential tool for DNA data management. Given a DNA database, it is a problem to extract k similar DNA sequence pairs in the database, which yield the highest similarity among all possible pairs. Although this is a fundamental problem used in the bioinformatics field, it suffers from an expensive computational cost. To overcome these limitations, we propose a novel fast top-k similarity search algorithm for DNA databases. We conducted experiments using real-world DNA sequence datasets, and experimentally confirmed that the proposed method achieves a faster top-k search than baseline algorithms while keeping high accuracy.

Keywords: Top-k similarity search · DNA database · Edit distance

1 Introduction

We address the top-k similar sequence search problem for DNA sequence databases. A DNA sequence can be regarded as a long chain composed of four characters, "A", "C", "G" and "T", each of which represents a nucleic acid. Given a DNA database composed of DNA sequences, it is the problem to find the most similar k pairs in the database. Since the similar sequense search is helpful to estimate DNA functionalities, this problem has become an important building block for basic biological research, medical diagnosis, and bioinformatics [1–5].

Although the top-k search is effective, it requires expensive computational costs to handle large-scale DNA databases. A DNA sequence can be regard as a string. Hence, it is a natural choice to use an Edit distance [6] to evaluate a similarity between two sequenses. However, an Edit distance computation typically incurs $O(m^2)$ time, where m is the length of DNA sequence [6]. Thus, it is difficult to evaluate the distance for all possible sequence pairs in a database.

In this paper, we propose a partition-based algorithm that effectively approximates the Edit distance to solve the problem quickly. The existing approach incurs at least $O(tm)$ time to compute the Edit distance. To avoid such expensive cost, we employ sequence partitioning approach into the Edit distance computation. Our extensive experiments using real-world DNA databases showed that our partition-based algorithm is up to two times faster than the bounding approach while keeping at least 91% accuracy.

E. Pardede et al. (Eds.): iiWAS 2022, LNCS 13635, pp. 145–150, 2022.
https://doi.org/10.1007/978-3-031-21047-1_14

2 Preliminary

Problem Statement: We denote a DNA database as $S = \{S_1, S_2, \ldots, S_n\}$, where S_i ($1 \leq i \leq n$) represents a DNA sequence. Recall that each sequence S_i is a chain of four characters "A", "C", "G", and "T". We denote the number of sequences as $|S| = n$, and the length of S_i as $|S_i| = m_i$, which counts up the number of characters in S_i.

We address the problem to find top-k similar sequence pairs included in a DNA database. Let P_k be a set of k sequence pairs in S^2, and $ED(S_i, S_j)$ be the Edit distance function that evaluates a similarity between S_i and S_j. The problem is formally defined as follows:

Definition 1. *(Top-k similar sequence pair search (kSSPS)) Given an integer $k \in \mathbb{N}$ and a DNA database S, kSSPS is a problem to find a set of k sequence pairs $P_k \subset S^2$ such that P_k minimizes $\sum_{\langle S_i, S_j \rangle \in P_k} ED(S_i, S_j)$.*

Edit Distance Computation: Edit distance [6] is a similarity function that measures the difference between two sequences. Given a pair of sequences S_i and S_j, $ED(S_i, S_j)$ counts the number of character insertions, deletions, and replacements that are required to convert S_i to S_j, and vice versa.

In order to efficiently compute an edit distance, the dynamic programming algorithm is generally used [6]. Let us consider two sequences $X = x_1 x_2 \ldots x_m$ and $Y = y_1 y_2 \ldots y_{m'}$, where x_i and y_j are a single character, *i.e.*, the lengths of X and Y are m_x and m_y, respectively. At the beginning of the algorithm, it constructs a two-dimensional array $d \in \mathbb{N}^{(m_x+1) \times (m_y+1)}$. Then, the algorithm sets $d_{X,Y}[i, 0] = i$ and $d_{X,Y}[0, j] = j$ for $0 \leq i \leq m$ and $0 \leq j \leq n$, respectively. After that, it computes the edit distance between X and Y in a dynamic programming manner by using the following equation:

$$d_{X,Y}[i, j] = \min\{d_{X,Y}[i-1, j-1] + \sigma(x_i, y_j), d_{X,Y}[i-1, j]+1, d_{X,Y}[i, j-1]+1\}, \tag{1}$$

where $\sigma(x_i, y_j) = 0$ if $x_i = y_j$; otherwise, $\sigma(x_i, y_j) = 1$. The algorithm computes the above equation until all elements of d are filled. Finally, we can obtain $ED(X, Y) = d_{X,Y}[m, n]$.

By letting m be the average sequence length between X and Y, the dynamic programming incurs $O(m^2)$ time for each Edit distance computation. In order to solve kSSPS, we need to invoke Edit ditance computations at least $O(n^2)$ time. Thus, kSSPS totally requires $O(n^2m^2)$ time. To mitigate this expensive cost, Ukkonen proposed a bounding approach, which completes each Edit distance computation in $O(tm)$ time, where t is a user-specified parameter such that $t \leq m$. However, it is still expensive to handle large-scale DNA databases.

3 Proposed Method: Partition-Based Algorithm

3.1 Main Ideas

The basic idea underlying the proposed method is twofold.

(1) Partition-based distance computation: To compute each distance efficiently, our algorithm invokes *partition-based distance computation* Our algorithm partitions each sequence into equal-sized T subsequences. Given a pair of partitioned sequences, it estimates the distance by incrementally computing the Edit distance only between the subsequences at a corresponding position.

(2) Unpromising pair pruning: Our algorithm, then, performs *unpromising pair pruning* to reduce the number of computed pairs of sequences. Given a partitioned sequence pairs, the partition-based distance computation incrementally estimates the Edit distance by comparing the corresponding subsequences one by one. If one of the subsequences has the larger estimated distance than the current top-k candidate, our algorithm excludes such unpromising pairs.

3.2 Partition-Based Distance Computation

Our algorithm first partitions S_i into equal-sized T subsequences; by letting $S_{i,j}$ be the j-th subsequence of S_i, S_i is partitioned into $S_{i,1}, S_{i,2}, \ldots, S_{i,T}$. Based on the partitioned sequences S_i and S_j, our algorithm then obtains a set of regions, each of which is defined as follows:

Definition 2 (Region). *Given two partitioned sequences S_i and S_j, a region $R_{x,y}^{(i,j)}$ is a two-dimensional subarray of $d_{S_i,S_j} \in \mathbb{N}^{(m_i+1)\times(m_j+1)}$ such that*

$$R_{x,y}^{(i,j)} = [d_{S_i,S_j}[i',j']]_{i'\in\{head_i(x),\ldots,tail_i(x)\},j'\in\{head_j(y),\ldots,tail_j(y)\}}, \qquad (2)$$

where $head_i(x) = \frac{m_i}{T}(x-1)+1$ and $tail_i(x) = \frac{m_i}{T}\cdot x$.

Definition 2 indicates that a region $R_{x,y}^{(i,j)}$ is a subarray of d_{S_i,S_j} corresponding to the subsequences $S_{i,x}$ and $S_{j,y}$.

Our approach then computes the distance based on the Eq. (1). Our algorithm tries to reduce the number of computed regions to efficiently approximate $ED(S_i, S_j)$. Given an integer $r \in [1,T]$, our algorithm computes the distances only for the three types of regions: (1) $R_{k,k}^{(i,j)}$ for $1 \leq k \leq r$, (2) $R_{k,k+1}^{(i,j)}$ for $1 \leq k \leq r-1$, and (3) $R_{k+1,k}^{(i,j)}$ for $1 \leq k \leq r-1$. If values in non-computed regions are required, our algorithm skips to refer the values in Eq. (1). By increasing r, our algorithm finally obtains approximated value of $ED(S_i, S_j)$.

3.3 Unpromising Pair Pruning

Here, we employ the unpromising pair pruning [7] based on the partition-based distance computation. Let θ be the k-th largest Edit distance estimated by the partition-based algorithm. Once a sequence pair yields the approximated distance larger than θ, it is not likely to be the top-k similar pair in the database. Based on this observation, Algorithm 1 shows the pseudocode of our pruning algorithm. Once a pair of sequences are specified, our algorithm computes the distances in regions $R_{r,r}^{(i,j)}$, $R_{r,r+1}^{(i,j)}$, and $R_{r+1,r}^{(i,j)}$ using Eq. (1) by increasing r from

1 to T. During this incremental computations, our algorithm stops computing the similarity if the distance exceeds θ (lines 7–8). Our algorithm continues the above steps until all pairs are examined (lines 2–13). Finally, our algorithm outputs the estimated top-k similar pairs P_k (line 14).

Algorithm 1. Proposed Method

Input: A DNA database $S = \{S_1, S_2, \ldots, S_n\}$, integers $k, T \in R$
Output: Top-k similar sequnce pairs P_k
1: $P_k \leftarrow \emptyset$, $\theta \leftarrow \infty$
2: **for each** $\langle S_i, S_j \rangle \in S^2$ **do**
3:      $dist \leftarrow 0$
4:      **for** $r = 1$ to T **do**
5:          Compute distances in $R_{r,r}^{(i,j)}$, $R_{r,r+1}^{(i,j)}$, and $R_{r+1,r}^{(i,j)}$ by Eq. 1
6:          $dist \leftarrow d_{S_i, S_j}[\frac{m_i}{T} \cdot r, \frac{m_j}{T} \cdot r]$
7:          **if** $dist > \theta$ **then**
8:              **break**
9:      **if** $dist < \theta$ **then**
10:         $\theta \leftarrow dist$
11:         $P_k \leftarrow P_k \cup \{\langle S_i, S_j \rangle\}$
12:         **if** $|P_k| > k$ **then**
13:             Remove $(k+1)$-th largest similarity pair from P_k
14: **return** P_k

---

4   Experiments

4.1   Experimental Setup

Methods: We compared our algorithm with the state-of-the-art approach provided by Ukkonen [13]. Hereafter, we refer this algorithm as Ukkonen. We used the best T settings for our proposed algorithm, which were obtained through binary searches. All algorithms examined in the experiments were implemented in C++ using –O2 option. All experiments were conducted on a Linux server with an Intel Xeon 2.7 GHz CPU and 768 GiB RAM.

Datasets: In this experimental analysis, we used three real-world DNA databases provided by [4]. All databases include 20,000 sequences with different average sequence lengths. The statistics are provided in Table 1.

Evaluation Criterion: In order to evaluate accuracy of our proposed algorithm, we employed *Recall*, which shows the fraction of the same top-k sequence pairs between our proposed algorithm and Ukkonen. Recall that we used the setting of Ukkonen so that it outputs the exact results. Thus, Recall indicates that how our algorithm effectively approximates the top-k similar pairs.

Table 1. Datails of the datasets

Datasets	n	Avg. length	Min. length	Max. length
Dataset 1	20,000	1,250	1,207	1,277
Dataset 2	20,000	2,500	2,414	2,554
Dataset 3	20,000	5,000	4,829	5,109

4.2 Efficiency

Figures 1(a), 1(b), and 1(c) show the running time to find top-k similar pairs by varying the size of k. As we can see from the results, Ukkonen achieves smaller running time only for small k settings, e.g., $k = 500$. By contrast, our proposed method outperforms Ukkonen for large k settings. For large k settings, Ukkonen offers longer similarity computation than our proposed algorithm.

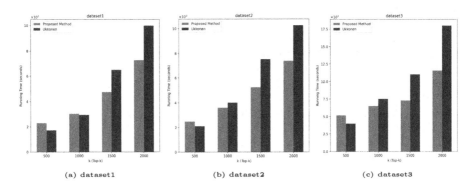

(a) dataset1   (b) dataset2   (c) dataset3

Fig. 1. Running time

4.3 Accuracy

The proposed method approximates the Edit distance, which causes approximated top-k search results. Hence, here we experimentally discuss the accuracy of our proposed algorithm by using the real-world datasets. As described in Sect. 4.1, we used Recall to evaluate the search accuracy. For each dataset, we varied the size of k from 500 to 2,000, and report Recall values in Table 2.

Overall, our proposed algorithm achieves high approximation accuracy, although it drastically drops the distance computations and sequence pairs. Specifically, our algorithm yields almost the same results as Ukkonen for $k = 500$ and $k = 1,000$. For large k settings such as $k = 1,500$ and $k = 2,000$, the accuracy gradually decrease, but our method still achieves accuracy greater than 0.9.

Table 2. Recall of our proposed algorithm

Datasets	$k = 500$	$k = 1,000$	$k = 1,500$	$k = 2,000$
Dataset 1	1.000	1.000	0.950	0.926
Dataset 2	0.998	0.993	0.934	0.913
Dataset 3	0.998	0.987	0.932	0.910

5   Conclusion

We proposed a fast top-k similar sequence search method for DNA databases. Our method reduces the search cost in the Edit distance computation by introducing the partition-based algorithm. Our experimental analysis clarified that our proposed method achieves faster top-k search while keeping high accuracy.

References

1. Li, G., Deng, D., Wang, J., Feng, J.: PASS-JOIN: a partition-based method for similarity joins. Proc. VLDB Endow. **5**(3), 253–264 (2011)
2. Wang, W., Qin, J., Xiao, C., Lin, X., Shen, H.T.: VChunkJoin: an efficient algorithm for edit similarity joins. IEEE Trans. Knowl. Data Eng. **25**(8), 1916–1929 (2013)
3. Zhang, H., Zhang, Q.: EmbedJoin: efficient edit similarity joins via embeddings. In: Proceedings of KDD (2017)
4. Zhang, H., Zhang, Q.: MinJoin: efficient edit similarity joins via local hash minima. In: Proceedings of KDD (2019)
5. Suzuki, Y., Sato, M., Shiokawa, H., Yanagisawa, M., Kitagawa, H.: MASC: automatic sleep stage classification based on brain and myoelectric signals. In Proceedings of ICDE (2017)
6. Wagner, R.A., Fischer, M.J.: The string-to-string correction problem. J. ACM **21**, 168–173 (1974)
7. Shiokawa, H.: Scalable affinity propagation for massive datasets. In Proceedings of AAAI (2021)
8. Deng, D., Li, G., Feng, J., Li, W.-S.: Top-k string similarity search with edit-distance constraints. In: Proceedings of ICDE (2013)
9. Yang, Z., Jianjun, Yu., Kitsuregawa, M.: Fast algorithms for top-k approximate string matching. In Proceedings of AAAI (2010)
10. Yangjun, C., Nguyen, H.-H.: On the string matching with k differences in DNA databases. Proc. VLDB **14**(6), 903–915 (2021)
11. Yangjun, C., Yujia, W.: On the string matching with k mismatches. Theoret. Comput. Sci. **726** (2018). https://doi.org/10.1016/j.tcs.2018.02.001
12. Yangjun, C., Yujia, W.: BWT arrays and mismatching trees: a new way for string matching with k mismatches. In: Proceedings of ICDE (2017)
13. Ukkonen, E.: Algorithms for approximate string matching. Inf. Control **64**, 100–118 (1985)

Graph Data and Knowledge Graph

GN-GCN: Combining Geographical Neighbor Concept with Graph Convolution Network for POI Recommendation

Fan Mo[1(✉)] and Hayato Yamana[2(✉)]

[1] Department of CSCE, Waseda University, Tokyo, Japan
bakubonn@toki.waseda.jp
[2] School of Science and Engineering, Waseda University, Tokyo, Japan
yamana@yama.info.waseda.ac.jp

Abstract. Point-of-interest (POI) recommendation helps users filter information and discover their interests. In recent years, graph convolution network (GCN)–based methods have become state-of-the-art algorithms for improving recommendation performance. Especially integrating GCN with multiple information, such as geographical information, is a promising way to achieve better performance; however, it tends to increase the number of trainable parameters, resulting in the difficulty of model training to reduce the performance. In this study, we mine users' active areas and extend the definition of neighbors in GCN, called active area neighbors. Our study is the first attempt to integrate geographic information into a GCN POI recommendation system without increasing the number of trainable parameters and maintaining the ease of training. The experimental evaluation confirms that compared with the state-of-the-art lightweight GCN models, our method improves *Recall*@10 from 0.0562 to 0.0590 (4.98%) on Yelp dataset and from 0.0865 to 0.0898 (3.82%) on Gowalla dataset.

Keywords: POI recommendation · Graph convolution network · Geographical information · Trainable parameter number-holding

1 Introduction

With the development of mobile internet technology, location-based social networks (LBSN), such as Yelp[1] and Gowalla[2], have attracted many users to share their own experiences and enabled point-of-interest (POI) recommendations. By analyzing the vast amount of users' check-in history, a POI recommendation system helps users filter information and discover their interests to improve their quality of life. To improve users' satisfaction, the accuracy of the recommendation system has always been of great concern. A highly accurate recommendation system is like a close friend who understands a target user's preferences and provides insightful suggestions.

---

[1] http://snap.stanford.edu/data/loc-gowalla.html.
[2] https://www.yelp.com/dataset_challenge.

E. Pardede et al. (Eds.): iiWAS 2022, LNCS 13635, pp. 153–165, 2022.
https://doi.org/10.1007/978-3-031-21047-1_15

In recent years, with the development of neural networks and deep learning techniques, graph convolution network (GCN) recommendation systems [3, 6, 9, 14, 16] have achieved high accuracy as state-of-the-art algorithms. Several works [3, 4, 9] show that collaborative filtered information is learned over the representation of users and items on GCN by aggregating neighbor nodes. When applying GCN models to POI recommendation systems, however, the problem of relationship sparsity arises, which severely impedes extracting the indirect relationships between a target user and POIs and between a target user and other users, depending on their geographical locations. Chang et al. [2] tackled the relationship sparsity problem by preparing multiple GCNs (one is used to mine user preferences and the other to mine geographical information); however, it leads to a significant increase in the number of trainable parameters, making the model training difficult.

In this paper, inspired by the fact [1, 11, 17] that the use of power-law distribution and multi-center Gaussian distribution to model users' geographical information of visited POIs could effectively increase recommendation accuracy, we newly define active area neighbors. Then, we adopt the active area neighbors when adding geographical information of users and POIs to a GCN, enabling the efficient extraction of indirect relationships caused by their locations. Moreover, similar to LightGCN [9], we simplify the design of GCN, which improves the performance of recommendations without increasing both the trainable parameters and the model complexity.

We are the first to propose a lightweight-geographical neighbor concept-based graph convolution network (GN-GCN) model, to integrate geographical information into GCN and keep the model easy to train. The contributions of this work are as follows:

- We propose a new concept called *active area neighbor* to alleviate the problem of relationship sparsity when applying GCN models to POI recommendation systems. We model user-item check-ins and active area neighbors to mine high-order connectivity to improve recommendation accuracy.
- Compared to Chang et al.'s work [2], we do not need to prepare an additional GCN to handle geographical information, enabling no increase in trainable parameters, which improves performance.
- We explore the effect of nonlinear activation functions on geographic aggregation functions because nonlinear activation functions usually have no positive effect on GCN [9]; however, nonlinear functions are often used in POI recommendation systems to model geographic information.

The rest of the paper is organized as follows. First, related work is introduced in Sect. 2. Then, Sect. 3 presents our proposed method, followed by the experiment in Sect. 4. Finally, in Sect. 5, we present our conclusions.

2   Related Work

This section introduces the existing works on both POI recommendation systems and graph convolution networks in the recommendation system.

2.1 POI Recommendation System

In POI recommendation systems, accuracy has always been an important factor. As one of the pioneers in the field of POI recommendation, Ye et al. [15] were the first to suggest that the use of rich geographical information could improve the accuracy. Based on Ye et al.'s work, Baral et al. [1] and Zhang et al. [17] optimized the geographical model to combine POIs' categorical information and users' social information to improve the accuracy. As a simpler approach, Ference et al. [7] proposed a threshold to filter out POIs far away from a target user's current location. Nowadays, the multi-center Gaussian distribution of geographical information [17] has become widely used in POI recommendations; however, the shortcoming is the data sparsity problem that matrix factorization (MF)–based models [8, 10] effectively solve. Compared with the GCN-based models [6, 14, 16], however, MF-based models have a weakness in mining users' high-order connectivity [14], i.e., the indirect relationship between a target user and POIs or between a target user and other users, thereby limiting the model's representation ability and preventing further accuracy improvement.

2.2 Graph Convolution Network in Recommendation System

In recent years, GCN-based models [6, 14, 16] have attracted attention for improving recommendation accuracy to mine users' high-order connectivity. GCNs extract features from connected neighbor nodes using a deep learning model. Wang et al. [14] composed a user-item interaction graph from users' check-in history. By learning a unique representation of each node in the graph, they extracted rich collaborative filtering information to improve the recommendation accuracy. Based on Wang et al.'s work, He et al. [9] simplified the model to improve accuracy. They inferred that the adoption of nonlinear active function does not affect improving the performance of collaborative filtering; thereby, they aggregated the information from neighboring nodes. Similar to He et al.'s work, Chen et al. [3] confirmed that removing the nonlinear active function enhances the recommendation accuracy. They proposed a linear model to form a residual network to learn the complex connections between users and items.

When applying GCN models to POI recommendation systems, the problem of relationship sparsity arises, where the relationships are between a target user and POIs and between a target user and other users, which impedes further performance improvement. To the best of our knowledge, Chang et al. [2] were the first to integrate geographical information into GCN by adopting multiple GCNs (one is for mining user preferences and the other for mining geographical information) to solve the relationship sparsity problem; however, it led to a significant increase in the number of trainable parameters, making the model training difficult.

3 Proposed Method

TO further improve the performance of the POI recommendation system, we propose a lightweight-geographical neighbor concept-based graph convolution network (GN-GCN) model for integrating geographical information on GCNs. First, we extend the definition of neighbor in GCN. In addition to check-in relations (user-checked items and items checked by users), we introduce *active area neighbors* for each user and each POI as newly added relations to solve the relationship sparsity problem. For each user, we define his/her active area neighbors whose active areas in the city are near to his/her active areas. Similarly, for each POI, we define the POI's active area neighbors that are geographically close to the POI. Then, the GCN-based model learns each node's unique representation (embedding) by iteratively aggregating information from the neighbors, similar to LightGCN [9]. Compared to Chang et al.'s model [2], we do not assign additional trainable parameters to mine geographical information because we only have one GCN.

3.1 Preliminary

This section models the POI recommendation and then summarizes the notations in Table 1.

Definition of POI Recommendation: Assume we have M users and N POIs, shown as $U = \{u_1, u_2, \ldots, u_M\}$ and $P = \{p_1, p_2, \ldots, p_N\}$, respectively. POI p_j has a pair of geographical coordinates $\{lat_{p_j}, lon_{p_j}\}$ to represent its latitude and longitude. As we need to mine users' active areas to represent his/her geographical information, we define $A_{u_i} = \{a_{u_i,1}, a_{u_i,2}, \ldots, a_{u_i,m}\}$ as the set of active areas of user u_i. Note that a user may have multiple active areas among cities. A geographical distance-based clustering algorithm sets the number of each user's active areas. For example, check-ins less than 1 km away are merged into the same cluster. Let $N_{u_i}^c = \{p_j | u_i \in U, p_j \in P, u_i \text{ visited } p_j\}$ be the set of POIs checked by user u_i. A POI recommendation system is designed to predict POIs that a target user u_i might visit in the future based on user u_i's historical check-in information $c_{u_i} \in C$, where $C = \{c_{u_1}, c_{u_2}, \ldots, c_{u_M}\}$. We consider a recommendation system to have a good performance if the predicted POIs match the user's real visits. We use $\widehat{r_{u_i,p_j}}$ to indicate user u_i's estimated preference for POI p_j.

Definition of item's check-in set: We define the set of users who visited POI as its check-in set, shown as $N_{p_j}^c = \{u_i | p_j \in P, u_i \in U, u_i \text{ visited } p_j\}$. .

Definition of User's Active area Neighbor: The target user's active area neighbors are set as the users who have close active areas to the target user's active areas, shown as $N_{u_i}^g = \{u_j | u_j, u_i U, j \neq i, u_j's active areas are close to u_i's\}$.

Definition of Item's Active Area Neighbor: We call the POIs that are geographically close to the target POI its active area neighbors, shown as $N_{p_j}^g = \{p_i | p_i, p_j P, i \neq j, p_i \text{ is close to } p_i\}$.

Definition of User's and Item's Representation (embedding): Our proposed GN-GCN learns the unique representation (embedding) of each user and each POI by iteratively aggregating the information of user-item check-ins and neighbors, where e_{u_i} and e_{p_j} are the embeddings of user u_i and POI p_j, respectively. The GN-GCN outputs both e_{u_i} and e_{p_j} at each layer, where the embeddings of user and item at layer k are shown as $e_{u_i}^k$ and $e_{p_j}^k$, respectively.

Table 1. Notations

Notation	Definition
U	Set of users in the dataset
P	Set of POIs in the dataset
lat_{p_j}, lon_{p_j}	Geographical latitude and longitude coordinates of POI p_j
A_{u_i}	Set of active areas $\{a_{u_i,1}, a_{u_i,2}, \dots, a_{u_i,m}\}$ of user u_i
$N_{u_i}^c$	User u_i's check-in set
$N_{p_j}^c$	Set of users that checked POI p_j
$N_{u_i}^g$	User u_i's active area neighbor set
$N_{p_j}^g$	POI p_j's active area neighbor set
e_{u_i}	Final trained embedding of user u_i
e_{p_j}	Final trained embedding of POI p_j
$e_{u_i}^k$	User u_i's embedding output at layer k
$e_{p_j}^k$	POI p_j's embedding output at layer k
$\widehat{r_{u_i,p_j}}$	Estimated preference of user u_i for POI p_j

3.2 Overview

The GN-GCN model, shown in Fig. 1, involves two steps: 1) In addition to user-item check-in interactions, we set the *active area neighbors*. We extract each user's active areas by clustering the POIs that he/she visited. The users who have at least one nearby active area (the distance between active areas is less than λ km) are set to be active area neighbors. Similarly, for the POIs whose geographic distance is less than λ km, we consider them active area neighbors by calculating the distance between all combinations of two POIs; 2) We design the neighbor-aggregation-based neural network to train the representation (embedding) of each user and each POI followed by calculating the inner product similarity between user's embedding and POI's embeddings to score. As shown in Fig. 1, through check-ins (black arrows) and active area neighbors (orange arrows), we aggregate high-order connectivity information to the target user node. As a result, we can enhance a GCN model to adopt geographical information, which can extract high-order connectivity over collaborative filtering information.

3.3 Modeling Active Area Neighbor

User Active Area Neighbor: When analyzing user u_i's check-in history c_{u_i}, we first use the DBSCAN algorithm [5] to cluster user u_i's visited POIs based on POIs' geographical latitude and longitude. Among cities and in a city, users may have multiple active areas where they have frequently checked in, such as the workplace and home. After the clustering, we have a set of active areas A_{u_i} for user u_i. Then, we define user pairs whose active areas' minimum distance is less than threshold λ as active area neighbors, as in Eq. 1.

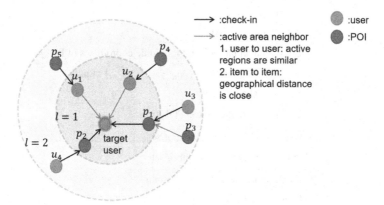

Fig. 1. An example of the proposed GN-GCN model to aggregate high-order information from check-ins and active area neighbors.

$$N_{u_i}^g = \left\{ u_j | u_j U, \ i \neq j, min\_dis_{u_i,u_j} < \lambda \right\} \tag{1}$$

$$min\_dis_{u_i,u_j} = min\left(dis\left(A_{u_i}, A_{u_j}\right) \right)$$

$$dis\left(A_{u_i}, A_{u_j}\right) = \left\{ \begin{array}{c} geodis\left(a_{u_i,k}^c, a_{u_j,l}^c\right) \\ |\forall a_{u_i,k} \in A_{u_i}, \forall a_{u_j,l} \in A_{u_j} \end{array} \right\} \tag{2}$$

where $geodis()$ calculates the geographical distance between two points on the Earth, calculated in radians. $a_{u_i,k}^c$ is the center of POIs located in user u_i's active area $a_{u_i,k}$, where the center position is calculated by the arithmetic mean of latitude and longitude, respectively. Note that we set threshold λ as a small value so that check-ins that are too far away cannot be included in the same active area to prevent center shift problems.

POI Active Area Neighbor: Similar to the user's active area neighbor, we define POI pairs whose distance is less than threshold λ as active area neighbors, shown in Eq. 3.

$$N_{p_j}^g = \left\{ p_i | p_i, p_j P, \ i \neq j, min\_dis_{p_j,p_i} < \lambda \right\} \tag{3}$$

where $min\_dis_{p_j,p_i}$ is calculated by the distance function $geodis()$.

3.4   Geographical Neighbor Concept-Based Graph Convolution Network (GN-GCN)

The basic idea of our proposed GN-GCN model is to extend the definition of the neighbor in a GCN. In addition to user-item check-in interactions, the GN-GCN model also mines rich geographical information from active area neighbors and learns the unique representation (embedding) for each node by smoothing features over the graph.

The architecture of the GN-GCN model is illustrated in Fig. 2. At each layer k, we aggregate information from check-ins and active area neighbors separately. Subsequently, a simple weighted (α and β) addition operation is executed to output the representation (embedding) of each node at the layer.

The representations of users and POIs in the model are calculated by Eq. 4.

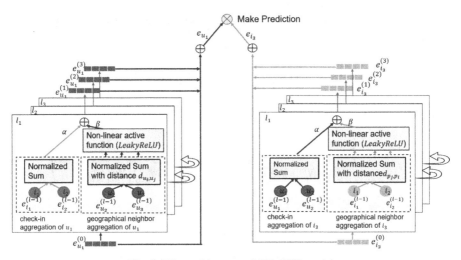

Fig. 2. The architecture of GN-GCN model

$$
e_{u_i}^{k+1} = \alpha * \sum_{p_j \in N_{u_i}^c} \frac{1}{\sqrt{\left|N_{u_i}^c\right| * \left|N_{p_j}^c\right|}} e_{p_j}^k + \beta * \sum_{u_j \in N_{u_i}^g} \frac{1}{\sqrt{\left|N_{u_i}^g\right| * d_{u_i,u_j}}} e_{u_j}^k
$$

$$
e_{p_j}^{k+1} = \alpha * \sum_{u_i \in N_{p_j}^c} \frac{1}{\sqrt{\left|N_{p_j}^c\right| * \left|N_{u_i}^c\right|}} e_{u_i}^k + \beta * \sum_{p_i \in N_{p_j}^g} \frac{1}{\sqrt{\left|N_{p_j}^c\right| * d_{p_j,p_i}}} e_{p_i}^k
$$

(4)

where $1/\sqrt{\left|N_{u_i}^c\right|}\sqrt{\left|N_{p_j}^c\right|}$ is a normalized discount factor as same as the standard GCN-based model [3, 9, 14]; α and β are parameters from 0 to 1; $1/d_{u_i,u_j}$ is the min-max normalized value of $1/min\_dis_{u_i,u_j}$ in the range of 0 to 1; $1/\sqrt{\left|N_{u_i}^g\right|}$ ranges from 0 to 1; $1/d_{p_j,p_i}$ is the min-max normalized value of $1/min\_dis_{p_j,p_i}$ in the range of 0 to 1.

We adopt $1/d_{p_j,p_i}$ instead of the number of neighbors to distinguish the importance of geographic neighbors without increasing trainable parameters.

3.5 Geographical Neighbor Concept-Based Graph Convolution Network (GN-GCN) with Nonlinear Active Function

Both He et al. [9] and Chen et al. [3] mentioned that nonlinear active function has no positive effect on a GCN-based recommendation system. However, in POI recommendation systems, the relationship between user check-in probability and geographic distance is always nonlinear [15, 17], which inspires us to add a nonlinear active function to the integrated information of active area neighbors. Based on the above intuition, our updated user's and POI's representation (embedding) are altered as Eq. 5. Note that "*Active*" means the *LeakyReLU* function. In this paper, we compare Eq. 5 with Eq. 4 to confirm the effect of the nonlinear active function.

$$
e_{u_i}^{k+1} = \alpha * \sum_{p_j \in N_{u_i}^c} \frac{1}{\sqrt{\left|N_{u_i}^c\right| * \left|N_{p_j}^c\right|}} e_{p_j}^k + \beta * Active \left(\sum_{u_j \in N_{u_i}^g} \frac{1}{\sqrt{\left|N_{u_i}^g\right| * d_{u_i,u_j}}} e_{u_j}^k \right)
$$

$$
e_{p_j}^{k+1} = \alpha * \sum_{u_i \in N_{p_j}^c} \frac{1}{\sqrt{\left|N_{p_j}^c\right| * \left|N_{u_i}^c\right|}} e_{u_i}^k + \beta * Active \left(\sum_{p_i \in N_{p_j}^g} \frac{1}{\sqrt{\left|N_{p_j}^c\right| * d_{p_j,p_i}}} e_{p_i}^k \right)
$$

(5)

3.6 Model Prediction for POI Recommendation Task

IT is worth mentioning that, in our GN-GCN model, although the concept of active area neighbor is adopted compared with LightGCN, it does not cause an increase in the number of trainable parameters, which allows our method to maintain the ease of training the GCN model. Same as LightGCN [9], the trainable parameters in our GN-GCN model are the user and the POI representation (embedding) at layer 0.

After we input the embeddings of user and POI at layer 0 to the GN-GCN model and output high-layer embeddings, we adopt a weighted accumulator to calculate the final embedding of each node, shown in Eq. 6.

$$
e_{u_i} = \sum_{k=0}^K \gamma_k e_{u_i}^k, \, e_{p_j} = \sum_{k=0}^K \gamma_k e_{p_j}^k
$$

(6)

where $\gamma_k = 1/(k+1)$, indicating the importance of embedding decreases with the layer increasing. To complete the prediction of user u_i's interest in POI p_j, we use an inner product of the user's and POI's representation (embedding), as shown in Eq. 7.

$$
\widehat{r_{u_i,p_j}} = e_{u_i}^T e_{p_j}
$$

(7)

When the embedding of user and POI are more similar, the POI has a higher prediction rate and is ranked at the top of the recommendation list.

3.7 Model Training

The widely used Bayesian personalized ranking (BPR) loss [3][9][13] is adopted to train the GN-GCN model. BPR loss considers observed user check-ins as positive cases and assigns several negative cases (unobserved counterparts) for each positive one. The BPR loss is trained so that the positive cases are rated higher and rank ahead of negative ones, as Eq. 8.

$$L_{BPR} = -\sum_{u_i=1}^{M} \sum_{p_j c_{u_i}} \sum_{p_k \in P - c_{u_i}} ln\sigma \left(\widehat{r_{u_i,p_j}} - \widehat{r_{u_i,p_k}} \right) + \mu \left\| \theta^2 \right\| \tag{8}$$

where μ controls the importance of L_2 regularization. θ indicates the trainable parameters ($e_{u_i}^0$ and $e_{p_j}^0$ at layer 0) in our model.

4   Experimental Evaluation

This section provides the experimental evaluation to confirm whether the proposed GN-GCN model can improve the performance while keeping the number of trainable parameters the same as LightGCN [9].

4.1 Datasets

We chose two public datasets for offline testing, Yelp and Gowalla, collected by Liu et al. [12]. Both datasets contain geographical information. The Yelp dataset contains many geo-tagged businesses among several cities, including 30,887 users, 18,995 items, and 860,888 check-ins, with a sparsity of 99.86% for the user-item check-in matrix. The Gowalla dataset contains 18,737 users, 32,510 items, and 1,278,274 check-ins, with a sparsity of 99.87% for the user-item check-in matrix. For each dataset, we follow the definition of Liu et al. [12], setting the earliest 70% of check-ins as a training set, using the latest 20% of check-ins as a testing set, and the rest 10% are used as a tuning set.

4.2 Baselines

We chose four state-of-the-art algorithms as baselines – RankGeoFM [10] is based on factorization machines, and LR-GCCF [3], LightGCN [9], and GPR [2] are based on GCNs. We chose RankGeoFM as the best performance model among MF models [12] to confirm a cross-sectional comparison between GCN-based and non-GCN-based models. LR-GCCF is a linear model used to form a residual network to efficiently learn the complex check-in interactions between users and items. LightGCN removes the self-connection to simplify the model, where embedding update at each layer only depends on the neighbor information. Both LR-GCCF and LightGCN are lightweight models. GPR uses additional trainable parameters to integrate geographical information into GCN, where each POI is assigned two trainable embeddings to represent. The comparison with baselines allows us to verify whether the performance of the recommendation is improved with the same number of trainable parameters as LightGCN, i.e., not increasing the parameters like GPR. Note that we do not compare with Elmi et al.s' work [4] due to the different research purposes. They focus on the next POI recommendation. That is, the ground truth contains only the last POI in chronological order of target user.

4.3 Metrics and Hyperparameter Settings

The experiment adopts three widely adopted ranking metrics: *Precision@k*, *Recall@k*, and *NDCG@k* for the top-k recommendation list, where larger values indicate better performance. Hyperparameters were tuned in the predefined ranges and set as shown in Table 2, except for the hyperparameters of RankGeoFM. We used the same parameters of Liu et al. [12] for RankGeoFM. The trainable parameters in our model are the embedding of user and POI at layer 0. We initialized the embedding by using a Gaussian distribution with a mean of 0 and a standard deviation of $1\,e^{-2}$. We also set the hyperparameters for the baseline algorithms by using the same strategy to reach the optimal performance for a fair comparison.

4.4 Experiment Results

Tables 3 and 4 show the experimental results on the Yelp and Gowalla datasets, respectively. We abbreviate *Precision@k* as *P@k*, *Recall@k* as *R@k*, and *NDCG@k* as *N@k*. The proposed methods with and without the nonlinear active function mentioned in Sect. 3.5 are also compared, where GN-GCN represents our method without the nonlinear active function, whereas GN-GCN + Active represents the method with the nonlinear active function. The highest scores are noted boldly. We adopt a two-tailed paired t-test to confirm the statistically significant improvement of our proposed method over the baselines.

Table 2. Grid Search of Hyper-parameters

Algorithms	Hyper-parameters setting		
	Hyper-parameter	Search-range description	Adopted value
DBSCAN	*eps*	$\{0.25, 0.5, 0.75, \ldots, 2\}$	1 km
	minPts	$\{2, 3, 4, 5\}$	2
active area neighbor threshold λ		$\{0.25, 0.5, 0.75, 1\}$	0.75 km
LR-GCCF [3], LightGCN [9], GPR [2], GN-GCN (proposed)	embedding size	same as Chen et al. [3] and He et al. [9]	64
	embedding initialization	same as Chen et al. [3] and He et al. [9]	Gaussian dist. (mean:0, SD:1 e^{-2})
	learning rate	$\{1\,e^{-4}, 1\,e^{-3}, 1\,e^{-2}, 1\,e^{-1}\}$	$1\,e^{-2}$
	regularization coefficient μ	$\{1\,e^{-6}, 1\,e^{-5}, \ldots, 1\,e^{-1}\}$	$1\,e^{-4}$
GN-GCN (proposed)	check-in coefficient α	$\{0, 0.25, 0.5, 0.75, 1\}$	0.5
	geographical coefficient β	$\{0, 0.25, 0.5, 0.75, 1\}$	1

The results show that our proposed model obtains the highest performance for most metrics. Our method successfully improves *Recall*@5 from 0.0453 to 0.0469 (3.53%) and *Recall*@10 from 0.0562 to 0.0590 (4.98%) on the Yelp dataset, while improving *Recall*@5 from 0.0788 to 0.0815 (3.43%) and *Recall*@10 from 0.0865 to 0.0898 (3.82%) on the Gowalla dataset, compared with LightGCN.

On both datasets, comparing GN-GCN + Active and GN-GCN, we cannot confirm a statistically significant difference between GN-GCN + Active and GN-GCN, which concludes that the nonlinear active function cannot affects the performance.

Table 3. Evaluation result on yelp dataset

Algorithms	P@5	R@5	N@5	P@10	R@10	N@10
Baselines	RankGeoFM[10]	0.0320	0.0304	0.0332	0.0273	0.0541	0.0300
	LR-GCCF [3]	0.0286	0.0350	0.0342	0.0252	0.0519	0.0420
	GPR [2]	0.0366	0.0382	0.0386	**0.0321**	0.0577	0.0345
	LightGCN [9]	0.0385	0.0453	0.0468	0.0303	0.0562	0.0507
Proposed	GN-GCN	0.0393*	0.0467*	0.0475 +	0.0311*	**0.0590***	0.0523*
	GN-GCN + Active	**0.0396***	**0.0469***	**0.0486***	0.0312*	0.0588*	**0.0529***

*Statistically significant for p < 0.01 when comparing with all baselines
+statistically significant for p<0.05 when comparing with all baselines.

Table 4. Evaluation result on Gowalla dataset

Algorithm	P@5	R@5	N@5	P@10	R@10	N@10
Baselines	RankGeoFM[10]	0.0684	0.0479	0.0719	0.0559	0.0755	0.0622
	LR-GCCF [3]	0.0640	0.0669	0.0721	0.0504	0.0762	0.0749
	GPR [2]	0.0775	0.0580	0.0671	**0.0640**	0.0881	0.0613
	LightGCN [9]	0.0760	0.0788	0.0859	0.0597	0.0865	0.0870
Proposed	GN-GCN	**0.0784***	**0.0815***	0.0883*	0.0614*	0.0894*	0.0896*
	GN-GCN + Active	0.0782*	0.0812*	**0.0886***	0.0619*	**0.0898***	**0.0900***

*Statistically significant for p < 0.01 when comparing with all baselines.

4.5 Discussion on the Number of Tainable Parameters

Same as LightGCN, the trainable parameters in our GN-GCN model are the embeddings of users and items at layer 0 even with integrating geographic information. Since we set the embedding size to 64, both LightGCN model and our GN-GCN model have

64*($M + N$) trainable parameters, where M and N are the numbers of users and items, respectively. On the contrary, the GPR model has more than 64*($M + 2N$) trainable parameters, which does not include the trainable transformation matrixes (64*64) [2].

To further improve the performance of neural network recommendation systems, integrating multiple information, such as geographical information, is potentially feasible. However, integrating multiple information tends to introduce more trainable parameters, making the model more difficult to train and reducing its practicability. Thus, keeping the number of trainable parameters not increasing is indispensable. As shown in Tables 3 and 4, although GPR integrates geographical information, $NDCG@10$ is smaller than LightGCN which does not integrate geographical information, which shows the difficulty in training.

5 Conclusion

We proposed the GN-GCN to mine users' active areas and integrate geographical information into GCNs in a lightweight manner by adopting a new concept called active area neighbors. Our experimental evaluation confirms that our model outperforms all the baselines. Compared with LightGCN, $Recall@10$ improves from 0.0562 to 0.0590 (4.98%) on the Yelp dataset and from 0.0865 to 0.0898 (3.82%) on the Gowalla dataset. Our future work includes further integrations of the other information, such as time and categorical information, to achieve higher recommendation accuracy.

References

1. Baral, R., Li, T.: Maps: A multi aspect personalized poi recommender system. In: Proceedings of the 10th ACM RecSys, pp. 281–284 (2016)
2. Chang, B., Jang, G., Kim, S., Kang, J.: Learning graph-based geographical latent representation for point-of-interest recommendation. In: Proceedings of the 29th ACM CIKM, pp. 135–144 (2020)
3. Chen, L., Wu, L., Hong, R., Zhang, K., Wang, M.: Revisiting graph based collaborative filtering: a linear residual graph convolutional network approach. In: Proceedings of the AAAI Conference on Artificial Intelligence, pp. 27–34 (2020)
4. Elmi, S., Benouaret, K., Tan, K.L. Social and spatio-temporal learning for contextualized next points-of-interest prediction. In: Proceedings of 2021 IEEE 33rd International Conference on Tools with Artificial Intelligence, pp.322–329 (2021)
5. Ester, M., Kriegel, H.P., Sander, J., Xu, X.: A density-based algorithm for discovering clusters in large spatial databases with noise. In: Proceedings of the 2nd ACM SIGKDD, pp. 226–231 (1996)
6. Fan, W., et al.: Graph neural networks for social recommendation. In: Proceedings of the WWW, pp. 417–426 (2019)
7. Ference, G., Ye, M., Lee, W.C.: Location recommendation for out-of-town users in location-based social networks. In: Proceedings of the 22nd ACM CIKM, pp. 721–726 (2013)
8. Han, P., Shang, S., Sun, A., Zhao, P., Zheng, K., Zhang, X.: Point-of-interest recommendation with global and local context. IEEE Trans. Knowl. Data Eng. (2021). https://doi.org/10.1109/TKDE.2021.3059744

9. He, X., Deng, K., Wang, X., Li, Y., Zhang, Y., Wang, M.: LightGCN: simplifying and powering graph convolution network for recommendation. In: Proceedings of the 43rd ACM SIGIR, pp. 639–648 (2020)
10. Li, X., Cong, G., Li, X., Pham, T., Krishnaswamy, S.: Rank-GeoFM: a ranking based geographical factorization method for point of interest recommendation. In: Proceedings of the 38th ACM SIGIR, pp. 433–442 (2015)
11. Liu, W., Wang, Z.J., Yao, B., Yin, J.: Geo-ALM: POI recommendation by fusing geographical information and adversarial learning mechanism. In: Proceedings of the 28th International Joint Conference on Artificial Intelligence, pp. 1807–1813 (2019)
12. Liu, Y., Pham, T.A.N., Cong, G., Yuan, Q.: An experimental evaluation of point-of-interest recommendation in location-based social networks. Proc. VLDB Endow. **10**(10), 1010–1021 (2017)
13. Rendle, S., Freudenthaler, C., Gantner, Z., Schmidt-Thieme, L.: BPR: Bayesian personalized ranking from implicit feedback. In: arXiv preprint arXiv:1205.2618 (2012)
14. Wang, X., He, X., Wang, M., Feng, F., Chua, T.: Neural graph collaborative filtering. In: Proceedings of the 42nd ACM SIGIR, pp. 165–174 (2019)
15. Ye, M., Yin, P., Lee, W.C., Lee, D.: Exploiting geographical influence for collaborative point-of-interest recommendation. In: Proceedings of the 34th ACM SIGIR, pp. 325–334 (2011)
16. Ying, R., He, R., Chen, K., Eksombatchai, P., Hamilton, W., Leskovec, J.: Graph convolutional neural networks for web-scale recommender systems. In: Proceedings of the 24th ACM SIGKDD, pp. 974–983 (2018)
17. Zhang, J., Chow, C.: GeoSoCa: exploiting geographical, social and categorical correlations for point-of-interest recommendations. In: Proceedings of the 38th SIGIR, pp. 443–452 (2015)

Network Topology to Predict Bibliometrics Indices: A Case Study

Vincenza Carchiolo[✉], Marco Grassia, Michele Malgeri,
and Giuseppe Mangioni

Dipartimento di Ingegneria Elettrica, Elettronica e Informatica, Università degli
Studi di Catania, Catania, Italy
{vincenza.carchiolo,marco.grassia,michele.malgeri,
giuseppe.mangioni}@unict.it

Abstract. Co-authorship networks have been widely studied in recent
years, but today new techniques and increasing computational power
permit performing novel analysis and evaluate larger datasets. One of
the emerging topic is the investigation of the reasons that determine the
success of some people among the others. Researchers and academic community are of interest because the metric to evaluate their performance,
although widely debated, are consolidated and based on bibliometrics
indices, that are quantifiable. Moreover, the paradigm of complex networks added another perspective that, often, allows discovering hidden
behaviors. This paper proposes an analysis of four large datasets related
to Italian academic working for public institutions, and grouped by law
in academic disciplines, using network analysis tools in order to compare
their structure and characteristics highlighting, if any, similarities and
difference. Moreover, applying a machine learning approach, the authors
try to predict some bibliometric indices using network topology.

1 Introduction

Co-authorship networks are an interesting example of social networks that have
been widely studied from different points of view. Firstly, it is worth mentioning
Newman et al. [16,17], Barabási and Albert [5] that, according to many, proposed
this new network based model, however many other authors contributed such as
Vespignani in [22]. The study of co–authorship networks can be considered as
belonging to the wider research topic known as network science. The first studies on
networks focused on topology and structural properties, such as small-worldness,
scale-free property, modularity, fractality, etc., and several models were proposed
to understand both the architecture and the evolution of real-world networks [22].
Recently, the focus shifted to studying what controls the complex networks dynamics [15]. Availability of computing power and massive datasets, machine learning and other novel computational techniques represent a powerful toolbox that
enables researchers to deepen the knowledge of internal mechanism and permit
trying to predict the evolution of the network. One of the more intriguing challenges is to understand the reasons why someone has success and what drives the
evolution of the networks, so the "science of science" comes to light [12,13,24].

E. Pardede et al. (Eds.): iiWAS 2022, LNCS 13635, pp. 166–180, 2022.
https://doi.org/10.1007/978-3-031-21047-1_16

The main contribution of this paper lies in studying how co–authorship network structure impacts on researcher performance both in terms of H-index, document-count, and citation-count. Specifically, we study four different subnetworks of Italian academic researchers enriched with several performance indicators from the Scopus database [4]. In particular, we refer the following Italian Academic belonging to the disciplines defined by the Ministry of Research and University: MAT/05 (A branch of mathematics), ING-INF/05 (computer engineering), INF/01 (informatics), and SECS-P/01 (economics). We show that the four co–authorship networks have different characteristics and that these impact on the predictive performance. We performed the study using both weighted and unweighted co-authorship networks, comparing the results and highlighting the differences when present. This work is based on [10] and [7], that studied some of the correlation between network structure and the interests of the researcher, adding more datasets and increasing the number of the included researchers.

In Sect. 2 we introduce the four co-authorship networks used in this paper, we describe how they have been extracted from Scopus DB and Italian academic lists, and study both their topological properties and the community structure. In Sect. 3 we discuss the dataset used for the prediction, and the prediction results.

2   Co-authorship Networks

A co-authorship network is a graph $G(V, E)$ where the nodes are the authors and an edge $(i, j)|i, j \in V$ exists if the authors i and j are co-authors of at least a publication. In the case of weighted network the weight associated with each edge is the number of co-authored publications.

2.1   Network Extraction

In order to build the co–authorship networks used in this paper, we extracted the information from Elsevier's Scopus Database using the official APIs according to its policies [1,2]. Due to the huge number of authors present in the database, it is necessary to adopt a selection criterion that allows us to create a meaningful dataset but whose dimension is manageable. In this work, we selected the subsets of Italian researchers that are employed by the *Ministero dell'Universitá e della Ricerca (MUR)*[1] [3] and that belong to four *academic disciplines (SSD)* to create the initial seed used to build their co-authorship networks querying Scopus Database. Specifically, we focus on *information processing system* - ING-INF/05 and *information* - INF/01 which belongs to *computer engineering, mathematical analysis* - MAT/05 belonging to *mathematics* and *economics* - SECS-P/01 since they have approximately the same number of researchers, actively refer to Scopus database, research area belongs to scientific matters, although they have different uses. ING-INF/05 and INF/01 were selected since their areas of interest

---

[1] The Italian Ministry of University and Research.

are quite similar (ING-INF/05 and INF/01 belong both to *computer*) in order to investigate if this fact is reflected also in the properties of the co–authorship networks.

The procedure used to craft the co-authorship networks from the Scopus dataset and Ministry's data is described in detail in [8]. Since our goal is to study the property of each co-authorship and their variation as the number of nodes and edges change, we created the following views:

1. depth-zero, that contains only the authors present in the seed and their co-authorship, that means that V contains only Italian researchers belonging to the given academic discipline and employed by public universities;
2. depth-one, that contains all the co-authors of Italian researchers also if they do not belong to original seed, e.g., other Italian researchers working in a private institution.

Table 1 shows the total number of nodes and edges of the full dataset and of the subset of Italian researchers belonging to each academic discipline in addition to the density of the graph. Although the number of nodes stands for Italian researchers are about the same, the other figures are quite different. However, let us note that ING-INF/05 and INF/01 are more comparable than other SSDs, as highlighted, for instance, by their density. Moreover, the ING-INF/05 and INF/01 tends to collaborate more with scientists not belonging to the same SSD as illustrated by the rate between the seed and the nodes/edges in the networks that is 5 times lower in MAT/05 and SECS-P/01. This paper only presents the study of the depth-one network. Figure 1 shows a network representation of the four networks, where you may notice that INF/01 and ING-INF/05 have a very similar shape.

Table 1. Characteristics of the dataset at Depth-one.

SSD	Nodes		Edges		Density
	Total	Italian	Total	Italian	
INF/01	43 339	1 027	78 283	4 327	$8.335 \cdot 10^{-05}$
ING-INF/05	46 879	843	84 127	3 759	$7.656 \cdot 10^{-05}$
MAT/05	10 736	723	13 404	1 990	$44.211 \cdot 10^{-05}$
SECS-P/01	7 891	733	13 764	478	$23.260 \cdot 10^{-05}$

2.2 Networks Analysis

Among the features that characterize the network that help to understand the structure of the networks, we calculated the following: the number of nodes ($|V|$) and edges ($|E|$) of the Largest Connected Component (LCC), the ratio of nodes ($\%pn$) and edges ($\%pe$) that do not belong to the LCC, and the number of Connected Components (N_c); the average node degree ($\overline{k}$), the average path length of the Largest Connected Component (APL_{lcc}), the number of Maximal Cliques

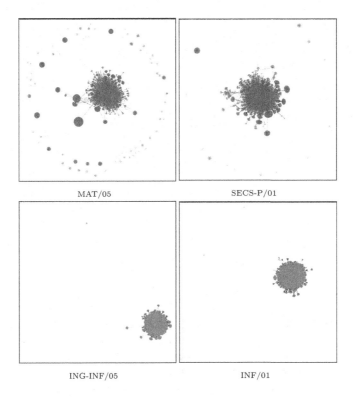

Fig. 1. Co-authorship networks.

(N_{MC}), and the maximum clique size ($|MC|$). In particular, these measures give an insight on how much the co-authorship networks are connected, that is, how tight is the collaboration among groups. For instance, the average node degree represents the average number of co-authors in the same academic discipline, the average path length quantifies the degree of separation between co-authors, etc. The results reported in Table 2 show that ING-INF/05 and INF/01 tend to form a single giant group whilst MAT/05 and SECS-P/01 present a greater number of isolated groups. Moreover, several other metrics are quite similar for ING-INF/05 and INF/01, such as number of components, average degree, and the Average Path Length of LCC (APL_{lcc}), whereas the latter is very high for SECS-P/01. Summarizing, almost all parameters highlight that ING-INF/05 and INF/01 have similar topology.

The most interesting difference shown in Table 2 is clique distribution and the maximum clique size. For instance, the maximum clique size in ING-INF/05, 19, with respect to other SSDS, (INF/01 = 10, MAT/05 = 8, and SECS-P/01 = 5) suggests a higher degree of collaboration. We report the clique size distribution of the four networks in Fig. 2.

Once analyzed the structure of the network, we study the community structure of the co-authorship networks, that often suggests the presence in the net-

Table 2. LCC Network topology analysis.

SSD	$|V|$	$|E|$	%pn	%pe	$\overline{k}$	N_c	APL_{lcc}	N_{MC}	$|MC|$
INF/01	43 324	78 271	0.034%	0.015%	3.6126	4	4.8952	10	51 934
ING-INF/05	46 851	84 101	0.059%	0.030%	3.5891	3	4.8513	19	55 476
MAT/05	7 712	13 599	2.268%	1.198%	3.4885	15	5.4220	8	9 894
SECS-P/01	9 309	12 042	13.291%	10.161%	2.4970	78	7.0010	5	11580

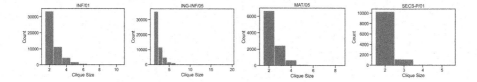

Fig. 2. Clique size distribution of the four networks.

work of some emergent behavior. A network community can be defined as *a subset of nodes within the network such that connections between such nodes are denser than connections with the rest of the network* [11,18]. In this work, the community analysis has been done via stochastic block model (SBM) inference [21] and shows more similarity between ING-INF/05 and INF/01, 99 and 91 groups in the networks respectively, with respect to MAT/05 (26) and SECS-P/01 (15) networks. Table 3 summarizes the community structure of the four networks and Fig. 3 illustrates the adjacency matrix of the communities of edge counts between groups (top) and the resulting groups in the networks (bottom).

In order to evaluate the researcher performance three indices are commonly used: - H-index [14], that is the maximum value of h such that the given researcher has published at least h papers that have been cited at least h times each; - document-count [4], that is the total number of papers published by the researcher; - citation-count [4], that is the total number of citation of paper published by the researcher.

Figure 4 shows the distribution of H-index, document-count, and citation-count (respectively) over the four academic disciplines. At a glance, the higher the collaboration, the higher the value of the bibliometric indices. All three indices have similar distributions in INF/01 and ING-INF/05 and their values are distributed in a wider range than MAT/05 and, in particular, SECS-P/01.

3 Results

In this Section, we introduce and analyze the dataset—derived from the depth-one networks presented in Sect. 2—and used to train a model to predict the H-index, the document-count and the citation-count bibliometrics because the main goal of this work is to assess that network topology affects these indices.

Table 3. Community analysis. # is the number of communities, AS stands for Average Community Size and MCS stands for the average Maximum Community Size.

SSD	#	AS	MCS
INF/01	91	476.09	10366
ING-INF/05	99	473.2	13583
MAT/05	26	296.6	3601
SECS-P/01	15	620.6	6552

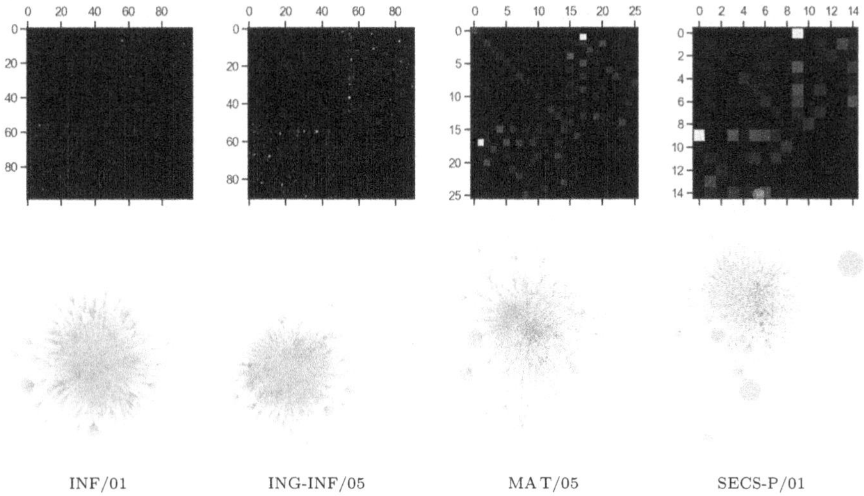

INF/01   ING-INF/05   MAT/05   SECS-P/01

Fig. 3. Community structure of the four networks, adjacency matrix of the communities (above) and the network, where each color correspond to a community.

3.1 Deriving Dataset to Predict Performances

We build four datasets, one for each academic discipline, that contains for each researcher both bibliometrics and node centrality measures, the former are H-index, document-count, citation-count and the latter are Degree (strength) centrality, Local clustering coefficient, Closeness centrality, Betweenness and PageRank Centrality computed in both weighted an unweighted co–authorship networks. More specifically the node centrality measures are:

- **Degree** centrality (D) refers to the total number of direct connections between node i and other $|V| - 1$ nodes in a network with $|V|$ nodes. The higher the degree centrality of a node is, the more nodes this node has contact with it, that means that this node is one of the most important in the network.
- **Local clustering coefficient** (L), as defined in [23], is a measure of the degree to which nodes in a graph tend to cluster together. It gives an indication of the *embeddedness* of single nodes.

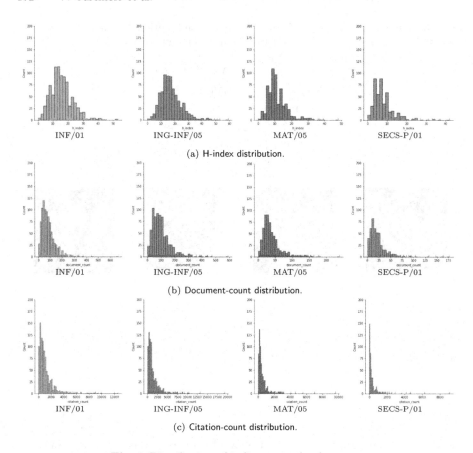

(a) H-index distribution.

(b) Document-count distribution.

(c) Citation-count distribution.

Fig. 4. Distribution of indices over the datasets.

- **Closeness** centrality (C) [19] is a measure of centrality calculated as the reciprocal of the sum of the length of the shortest paths between the node and all other nodes in the graph, thus, it measures how close the i node is close to all the other nodes in the network.
- **Betweenness** (B) [6] quantifies the number of times a node acts as a bridge along the shortest path between two other nodes. Finally, **PageRank** centrality (P) [20] is a measure of the influence of a node in a network.

Once defined the target of our analysis and the needed parameters, we built the datasets as follows:

1. calculate the largest connected component;
2. calculate the centrality measures of all nodes, both in weighted and unweighted networks (let us note that measures depend on all the included authors, than the authors not belonging to SSDs present in depth-one significant impact on the results);
3. extract the subset of Italian researchers (the original seed);
4. extract the performance indices of Italian researchers.

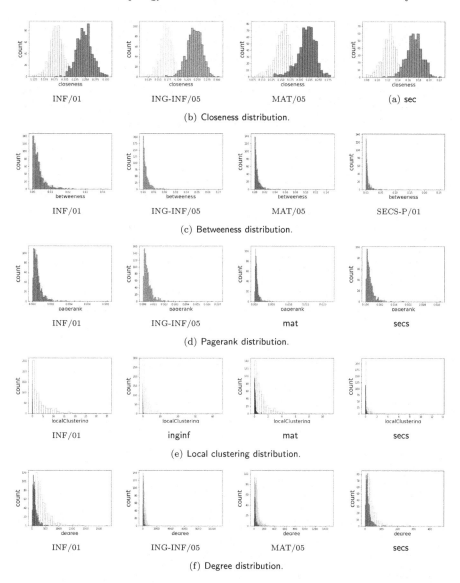

(b) Closeness distribution.

(c) Betweeness distribution.

(d) Pagerank distribution.

(e) Local clustering distribution.

(f) Degree distribution.

Fig. 5. Distribution of all centrality measures, for weighted (fill) and unweighted (clear).

Figure 5 highlights the distribution of centrality measures where each subfigure shows both weighted and unweighted plots. You may notice that the distribution of some centrality metrics (like the closeness C) is way different when the unweighted and weighted measures are considered, thus, we will use both the weighed and the weightless values of centrality to improve the prediction stage performed using Machine Learning tools.

Table 4 shows the Pearson correlation coefficient between and the other features in the four datasets. Once again, the table highlights different behaviors among SSDS with respect to the centrality indices. For example, all three performance indices (document-count and citation-count) seems to poorly depend on the Local centrality while, for example, the Betweenness B is strongly correlated with the performance indices in the case of MAT/05, INF/01, and ING-INF/05, but not for SECS-P/01. The Reader may find a detailed bi-variate analysis in the Appendix of this paper.

Table 4. Pearson's correlation among H-index and bibliometric indices in the academic disciplines, the order of SSDs is: INF/01, ING-INF/05, MAT/05, and SECS-P/01.

	H-index				document-count				citation-count			
C	0.47	0.40	0.31	0.34	0.54	0.47	0.26	0.26	0.41	0.30	0.28	0.24
P	0.60	0.55	0.50	0.60	0.66	0.68	0.62	0.64	0.56	0.58	0.67	0.43
B	0.51	0.49	0.51	0.21	0.66	0.63	0.58	0.23	0.51	0.50	0.65	0.14
L	−0.04	−0.06	−0.11	−0.04	−0.04	−0.07	−0.09	−0.01	−0.07	−0.08	−0.13	−0.06
D	0.43	0.43	0.61	0.67	0.50	0.50	0.75	0.78	0.37	0.35	0.64	0.50

3.2 Bibliometric Index Prediction

In this Section, we try to predict the performance metrics of researchers given their centrality measures in the co–authorship networks described in the previous section. We run a grid search over different various Machine Learning algorithms, hyperparameters, and input features. According to [9], we choose to use classic Machine Learning algorithms, i.e., Support Vector Regression (SVR) models, a Kernel Ridge Regressor (KRR), and Multi-Layer Perceptrons (MLP). We refer the Reader to Table 5 for a summary of the parameters used.

Table 5. Hyper-parameters of the regression model.

Models	Hyper-parameters
SVR linear kernel	$C : [1, 10^1, 10^2, 10^3]$,
	$\gamma : \text{np.logspace}(-2, 2, 10)$
SVR BRF kernel	$C : [1, 10^1, 10^2, 10^3]$,
	$\gamma : \text{np.logspace}(-2, 2, 10)$
Kernel Ridge BRF	$\alpha : [1, 10^{-1}, 10^{-2}, 10^{-3}]$,
	$\gamma : \text{np.logspace}(-2, 2, 10)$
MLP Regressor	$\alpha : [10^2, 10^1, 1, 10^{-1}, 10-2]$,
	$solver : ['lbfgs']$,
	$\text{hidden\_layer\_sizes} : \{(x, y) : x \in (12, 10, 8) \text{ and } y \in (6, 4, 2)\}$

The learning task is a regression, and we use the coefficient of determination (R^2) as performance metric to evaluate the models. We use (R^2) because preliminary studies [9] shows that it reflects the goodness of prediction the better. The best values of R^2 obtained for each learning target are highlighted in bold in Tables 6 (H-index), 7 (document-count) and 8 (citation-count). More in detail, Table 6 shows the results of the H-index prediction on the four datasets, both on the unweighted and weighed networks. We can appreciate that the weighted solution is better than the unweighted except in SECS-P/01 where produce different results. The Betweenness and PageRank are the centralities that most frequently lead to the best result.

Table 6. H-index prediction: Best results of regression through ML and MLP showing the best centrality combination

SSD	ML			MLP		
	Weight	R^2	Model	Weight	R^2	Model
MAT/05	NO	0.5425	PBD	NO	0.5392	PBD
	YES	0.6465	PLD	YES	**0.6487**	$CPBD$
INF/01	NO	0.4777	PBD	NO	0.4940	PBD
	YES	0.6540	BD	YES	**0.6786**	CBD
ING-INF/05	NO	0.5256	CP	NO	0.4904	PB
	YES	**0.6133**	$PBLD$	YES	0.5705	PBL
SECS-P/01	NO	0.3355	CL	NO	0.3262	CL
	YES	0.2659	B	YES	**0.4872**	$CPBD$

Table 7 shows the document-count prediction results, respectively, for both unweighted and weighted networks. The models achieve better R^2 values than predicting the H-index, i.e., the error is lower, and the best results are obtained on the weighted networks.

Table 7. Document-count prediction: Best results of regression through ML and MLP showing the best centrality combination

SSD	ML			MLP		
	Weight	R^2	Model	Weight	R^2	Model
MAT/05	NO	0.6055	CLD	NO	0.6173	CLD
	YES	0.8474	PBD	YES	**0.8381**	PLD
INF/01	NO	0.5615	CPD	NO	0.6082	PBD
	YES	0.6540	BD	YES	**0.8542**	PLD
ING-INF/05	NO	0.7053	PLD	NO	0.6877	PL
	YES	0.8341	CD	YES	**0.8641**	CBD
SECS-P/01	NO	0.3101	CL	NO	0.2668	CPB
	YES	0.3371	LD	YES	**0.5361**	PB

Finally, we perform a regression of citation-count and report the results in Table 8, let us note that the best value of R^2 for SECS-P/01 is reached for unweighted network.

Table 8. Citation-count prediction: Best results of regression through ML and MLP showing the best centrality combination

SSD	ML			MLP		
	Weight	R^2	Model	Weight	R^2	Model
MAT/05	NO	0.5256	$PBLD$	NO	0.5097	$PBBD$
	YES	0.5669	PLD	YES	**0.5839**	LD
INF/01	NO	0.4016	$PBLD$	NO	0.3900	CLD
	YES	0.5522	$CPLD$	YES	**0.5757**	$CPBL$
ING-INF/05	NO	0.5064	PD	NO	0.4578	P
	YES	**0.5190**	P	YES	0.4757	CBD
SECS-P/01	NO	0.1975	CBL	NO	**0.4057**	CBD
	YES	0.1356	B	YES	0.3297	$CBPD$

4   Conclusions and Future Work

In this work, we analyze the impact of co-authorship networks on researcher's performance in terms of H-index, document-count, and citation-count. Our study deals with four co-authorship networks extracted from Scopus and a subset of Italian tenured researchers working in public universities that belong to the same academic disciplines determined by law. We performed topological and community analysis to highlight similarity and differences among these four co-authorship networks, and we use a regression based approach to predict performance indices from centrality measures. As future work we plan to study the generalization of the obtained results to other scientific areas and to other countries. An attractive extension of this work concerns with the study of evolution over time of the co–authorship including also temporary collaborators such as PhD students and postdoctoral researchers.

Acknowledgment. This work has been partially supported by the project of University of Catania PIACERI, *PIAno di inCEntivi per la Ricerca di Ateneo*.

Appendix

Figure 6 shows a bivariate analysis of each centrality measures respect to H-index, Fig. 7 and 8 show a bivariate analysis of document-count and citation-count. In the figures, the cyan refers to MAT/05, yellow to INF/01, green to ING-INF/05, and, finally, orange to SECS-P/01.

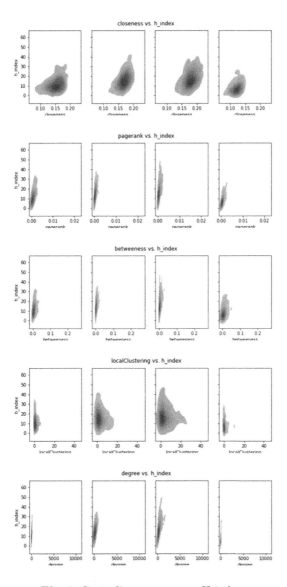

Fig. 6. Centrality measure vs. H-index

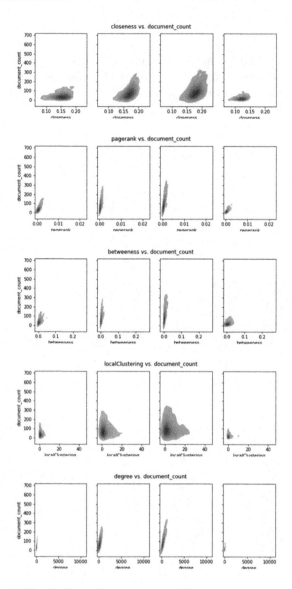

Fig. 7. Centrality measure vs. Document-count

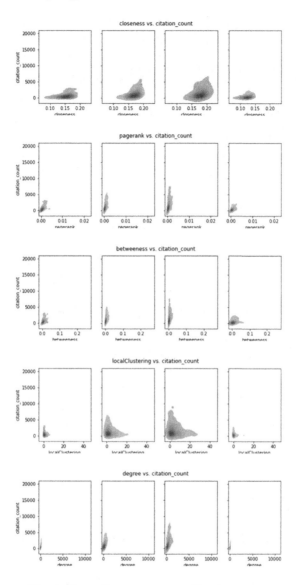

Fig. 8. Centrality measure vs. Citation-count

References

1. Elsevier Developer - Academic Research. Accessed July 2021
2. Elsevier Developer - API Service Agreement. Accessed July 2021
3. Ministero dell'Universitá e della Ricerca - Professori e Ricercatori. Accessed May 2021
4. Scopus fact sheet. www.elsevier.com/__data/assets/pdf_file/0017/114533/Scopus-fact-sheet-2022_WEB.pdf. Accessed April 2022

5. Barabási, A., Jeong, H., Néda, Z., Ravasz, E., Schubert, A., Vicsek, T.: Evolution of the social network of scientific collaborations. Physica A: Stat Mech Appl **311**(3), 590–614 (2002). www.sciencedirect.com/science/article/pii/S0378437102007367

6. Brandes, U.: A faster algorithm for betweenness centrality. J. Math. Sociol. **25**(2), 163–177 (2001). https://doi.org/10.1080/0022250X.2001.9990249

7. Carchiolo, V., Grassia, M., Malgeri, M., Mangioni, G.: Analysis of the co-authorship sub-networks of Italian academic researchers. Stud. Comput. Intell. **1015**, 321–327 (2022)

8. Carchiolo, V., Grassia, M., Malgeri, M., Mangioni, G.: Co-authorship networks analysis to discover collaboration patterns among Italian researcher. Future Internet **14** (2022)

9. Carchiolo, V., Grassia, M., Malgeri, M., Mangioni, G.: Correlation between researchers' centrality and h-index: a case study. In: Intelligent Distributed Computing XV. Springer, Heidelberg (2022)

10. Carchiolo, V., Grassia, M., Malgeri, M., Mangioni, G.: Preliminary characterization of Italian academic scholars by their bibliometrics. In: Camacho, D., Rosaci, D., Sarné, G.M.L., Versaci, M. (eds.) Intelligent Distributed Computing XIV, pp. 343–354. Springer, Cham (2022). https://doi.org/10.1007/978-3-030-96627-0_31

11. Carchiolo, V., Longheu, A., Malgeri, M., Mangioni, G.: Communities unfolding in multislice networks. In: da F. Costa, L., Evsukoff, A., Mangioni, G., Menezes, R. (eds.) CompleNet 2010. CCIS, vol. 116, pp. 187–195. Springer, Heidelberg (2011). https://doi.org/10.1007/978-3-642-25501-4_19

12. Clauset, A., Larremore, D.B., Sinatra, R.: Data-driven predictions in the science of science. Science **355**(6324), 477–480 (2017)

13. Fortunato, S., et al.: Science of science. Science **359**(6379) (2018)

14. Hirsch, J.E.: An index to quantify an individual's scientific research output. Proc. Natl. Acad. Sci. **102**(46), 16569–16572 (2005)

15. Molontay, R., Nagy, M.: Two decades of network science: as seen through the co-authorship network of network scientists. In: Proceedings of the 2019 IEEE/ACM International Conference on Advances in Social Networks Analysis and Mining, ASONAM 2019, pp. 578–583. Association for Computing Machinery, New York (2019)

16. Newman, M.E.J.: Finding community structure in networks using the eigenvectors of matrices. Phys. Rev. E **74**, 036104 (2006)

17. Newman, M.E.J., Girvan, M.: Finding and evaluating community structure in networks. Phys. Rev. E **69**, 026113 (2004)

18. Nicosia, V., Mangioni, G., Carchiolo, V., Malgeri, M.: Extending the definition of modularity to directed graphs with overlapping communities. J. Stat. Mech. Theory Exp. **2009**(03), P03024 (2009)

19. Opsahl, T., Agneessens, F., Skvoretz, J.: Node centrality in weighted networks: generalizing degree and shortest paths. Social Netw. **32**(3), 245–251 (2010). www.sciencedirect.com/science/article/pii/S0378873310000183

20. Page, L., Brin, S., Motwani, R., Winograd, T.: The pagerank citation ranking: bringing order to the web. In: WWW 1999 (1999)

21. Peixoto, T.P.: Efficient monte carlo and greedy heuristic for the inference of stochastic block models. Phys. Rev. E **89**, 012804 (2014)

22. Vespignani, A.: Twenty years of network science (2018)

23. Watts, D.J., Strogatz, S.H.: Collective dynamics of 'small-world' networks. Nature **393**(6684), 440–442 (1998)

24. Zeng, A., et al.: The science of science: from the perspective of complex systems. Phys. Rep. **714**, 1–73 (2017)

A Neural Network Approach for Text Classification Using Low Dimensional Joint Embeddings of Words and Knowledge

Liliane Soares da Costa$^{(\boxtimes)}$ ⓘ, Italo Lopes Oliveira ⓘ, and Renato Fileto ⓘ

Computer Science (PPGCC), Department of Informatics and Statistics (INE),
Federal University of Santa Catarina (UFSC), Florianópolis, SC, Brazil
{liliane.costa,italo.oliveira}@posgrad.ufsc.br, r.fileto@ufsc.br

Abstract. The continuous expansion of textual data collection and dissemination in electronic means has made text classification a crucial task to help exploit, in a variety of applications, massive amounts of digital texts available nowadays. Knowledge Graphs (KGs) or their embeddings can provide additional semantics to improve text classification. However, most proposals from the literature rely solely on words found in the texts to classify them. A few text classification approaches employ knowledge embeddings besides word embeddings, but which are produced separately and not integrated into the same vector space. Different from previous proposals, this work applies an existing solution for generating text and knowledge embeddings in an integrated way to feed neural classifiers. Experiments using these joint embeddings with 50 dimensions yielded results comparable to those of state-of-the-art approaches on the AG News dataset and slightly superior to the BBC news dataset.

Keywords: Text classification · Knowledge graphs · Word embeddings · Knowledge embeddings · Neural networks

1 Introduction

Digital data is growing at an exponential rate, and its use is transforming the way people live and work. The International Data Corporation (IDC)[1] predicts that by 2025 worldwide data creation will grow to 175 zettabytes [22]. However, the complexity is more than just the fast increase in data volumes. Data also originated from multiple sources, exist in multiple models and formats, and are stored in several locations.

Textual data are part of the expanding digital data amount. Despite the availability of these data, their use by applications is hindered by the difficulty

---

Supported by Foundation for Research Support of Santa Catarina (FAPESC), the Print CAPES-UFSC Automation 4.0 Project, and the Brazilian National Laboratory for Scientific Computing (LNCC).

[1] https://www.idc.com/.

E. Pardede et al. (Eds.): iiWAS 2022, LNCS 13635, pp. 181–194, 2022.
https://doi.org/10.1007/978-3-031-21047-1_17

of capturing precise semantics of their contents and identifying documents or text passages that meet particular topics or needs. A trend to circumvent these problems is the use of Artificial Intelligence (AI) techniques, specifically Machine Learning (ML) and Natural Language Processing (NLP), to automatically discover patterns and classify text documents.

Given the large amount and diversity of textual data created daily, their automatic classification, frequently in a variety of possible classes, becomes crucial to screen these data for usage in numerous applications [5]. To do this accurately, syntactic and semantic relations between the words that influence their meaning and, consequently, the general meaning of the text may have to be taken into account. However, traditional models for text representation are limited to words, making it challenging to differentiate documents that express different views of a subject using similar vocabulary and syntax. Conversely, with traditional models, it is difficult to correlate texts that use diverse vocabulary and syntax to express the same idea or very similar ones. Thus, this work is motivated by the complexity of textual contents and the limited use of semantically rich features, particularly joint embeddings of words and knowledge, for text classification.

Currently, some text classification approaches successfully use embeddings as features to classify texts [12,14,21,23,26,27]. The majority of these classification approaches are based on Deep Neural Network (DNN). Word embeddings are rising because they capture in compacted vectors semantic and syntactic properties of words according to the local context in which they usually appear in the texts used to train the embedding model. Consequently, embeddings help to improve the results of text classification while maintaining the scalability of classification approaches for large amounts of text.

Besides word embeddings, additional semantics from knowledge embeddings trained on Knowledge Graphs (KGs) (e.g., DBpedia[2] [1,13], Yago[3] [7]) can also help text classification. According to [19], KGs are relational knowledge representations of Knowledge Bases (KBs). KGs model information as entities and semantic relations between them. The relationships between entities in a KG can express additional knowledge about an entity that is mentioned in a text.

Word embedding and knowledge embedding techniques aim to represent words and entities, respectively, in some n-dimensional continuous vector space. Word embeddings [16] trained with large volumes of text capture relations between words. Knowledge embeddings [24], on the other hand, capture relationships, which can be represented as triples in some KG, between unambiguous entities. Such additional knowledge could benefit text classification. One reason why DNNs have been successfully used with embeddings for text classification, among other tasks, is that they can capture linear and non-linear relations between embeddings. Thus, they could exploit knowledge embeddings as well as text embeddings. However, among the few text classification approaches that employ knowledge embeddings and DNNs [23,27], we have not found works that

---

[2] https://wiki.dbpedia.org.
[3] http://www.yago-knowledge.org/.

exploit the semantics of words and the semantics of KG entities in a combined way for text classification yet.

This work proposes OPHELIA - knOwledge GraPH-augmented tExt cLassIfication Approach. OPHELIA is based on a neural network model that exploits embeddings of words and knowledge in a shared space to tackle the text classification task. Firstly, it jointly trains word embeddings and knowledge embeddings using fastText [8,10]. Then, OPHELIA employs these embeddings to represent ordinary words and entities for each recognized mention in the text documents. Different from other approaches, OPHELIA uses an entity recognition, and linking tool to semantically annotate named entity mentions found in the text and replaces these mentions with their respective entities in a KG. Thus, it uses embedded representations of both words (word embeddings) and entities (knowledge embeddings) as features fed to DNN classifiers. Specifically for this work, we use embeddings with 50 dimensions (which we consider low dimensional embeddings) to allow our model to be used with limited hardware. Experiments with text classification benchmarks based on public datasets of news articles show the viability and the benefits of our approach, which achieves accuracy and F1 measures comparable to those of state-of-the-art approaches on the AG News dataset and outperforms them on the BBC news dataset.

The main contributions of this work are: (i) a process that jointly trains word embeddings and knowledge embeddings by using fastText and semantically enriching text documents with entity embeddings besides word embeddings for text classification; (ii) a neural network model to classify text by exploiting word and knowledge embeddings and; (iii) the evaluation of the proposal performance on public datasets of a text classification benchmark. To the best of our knowledge, OPHELIA is the first text classification approach that employs word and knowledge embeddings jointly trained by fastText.

The remaining of this paper is organized as follows. Section 2 reviews literature about the use of embeddings in text classification approaches. Section 3 details our text classification approach as a process that uses a neural model fed with jointly trained embeddings for words and knowledge. Section 4 reports experiments to evaluate our approach and discusses their results. Lastly, Sect. 5 presents the conclusions and possible future works.

2 Related Works

In this paper, we use the following formal definition for the text classification task, extracted from Deng et al. [5]. Given a set of documents D and a set of predefined categories C, the problem of text classification can be modeled as finding a mapping function F from the Cartesian product $D \times C$ to a set $\{True, False\}$, i.e., $F : D \times C \rightarrow \{True, False\}$. Such a mapping function F is called a classifier. Given a document $d_i \in D$ and a category $c_j \in C$, if $F(d_i, c_j) = True$ based on this mapping, then d_i belongs to category c_j, otherwise d_i does not belong to c_j. Notice that this definition allows the classification to be multi-class ($|C| > 2$) and multi-label [25] (at least one document belonging to more than one label), though it can be restricted to binary and single label classification.

Many recent approaches for text classification use embeddings to represent textual features. Embedding techniques are often lumped into the deep learning field. They were first presented by Bengio [2], but gained popularity with Word2Vec [17]. Nowadays, there are several other competitive word embedding techniques, like GloVe [20], fastText [4], and BERT [6]. They have been the most prominent word embedding models. All of them are unsupervised and take a corpus or a dataset as input to generate the vectors.

Table 1 lists recent work that presented the best performance and that we consider most related to ours, because of their use of embeddings and neural networks for classifying news articles. Most approaches from the literature and also the ones that we list employ traditional word embeddings (e.g., Word2Vec, Glove) or contextual ones (e.g. BERT). Just a few works use KG embeddings (namely KG-BERT and Babel2Vec). However, KGs like DBpedia contain millions of facts that describe entities with well-defined semantics. KG entities and facts can be exploited through knowledge embeddings to improve text classification of text that mention the KG entities. Moreover, as word embeddings and knowledge embeddings are usually trained in independent ways by using different techniques, their respective embeddings are in different vector spaces, hindering their joint use. Existing text classification approaches, to the best of our knowledge, do not employ joint embeddings of words and knowledge as we propose in this work.

Table 1. Classification approaches using embeddings

Work	Domain	Classification technique	Feature representation
Lenc et al. 2017 [14]	News articles	CNN	Word2Vec
Pittaras et al. 2020 [21]	News articles, Biomedical text	DNN	Word2Vec
Zhang et al. 2019 [27]	News articles, All-purpose	CNN	GloVe
Lee et al. 2021 [12]	News articles, Reviews, All-purpose	SVM, BERT	BERT
Zhang et al. 2021 [26]	News articles, Movie review	Bi-LSTM	GloVe, BERT
Zhong et al. 2021 [26]	News articles, All-purpose	BERT	KG-BERT
Sinoara et al. 2019 [23]	News articles, Computer Science Technical Reports, Biomedical text, Sentiment Analysis	Naive Bayes (NB), Sequential Minimal Optimization (SMO), Inductive Modelbased on Bipartite Heterogeneous Net-works (IMBHN)	Word2Vec, Babel2Vec
Our work	**News articles**	**FFNN**	**Jointly trained FastText embeddings of words (entity descriptions) and knowledge (DBpedia KG)**

Word2Vec was the first embedding model used in text classification [14,21]. Lenc et al. 2017 [14] analyzed and evaluated its use to represent long texts for multi-label classification by a neural network that can solve the problem by top-k. The embeddings were used in three convolutional neural network topologies.

The authors analyzed the semantic similarity of the embedding vectors learned during the network training and compared them with the standard Word2Vec vectors. It was concluded that for longer texts better results are achieved using embeddings initialised randomly and trained with the classification network.

Pittarras et al. 2021 [21] applied Word2Vec, WordNet, and semantic features to generate semantic vectors for words and combine them into text embeddings. Then, these embeddings were used for classifying English news from the 20-Newsgroups and Reuters-21578 datasets, using a DNN as a classifier. The accuracy and F-measure obtained were about 75–80%. Error analysis showed that adding semantic information significantly improves classification quality. They concluded that the way of introducing semantic information to the model affected training and the performance of the learned model.

GloVe and BERT have also been successfully used in text classification approaches [12, 26, 27] . Zhang, Lertvittayakumjorn, and Guo 2018 [27] proposed a novel CNN-based two-phase framework together with data augmentation and feature augmentation for recognizing text documents of classes that have never been seen in the learning stage (the so-called zero-shot text classification). It applies GloVe vectors as word embeddings. In fact, four kinds of semantically rich features (word embeddings, class descriptions, class hierarchy, and a general knowledge graph) are incorporated into the proposed framework to deal with instances of unseen classes effectively. Their experiments showed that data augmentation by topic translation improved the accuracy in detecting instances from unseen classes. In contrast, feature augmentation enabled knowledge transfer from seen to unseen classes for zero-shot learning.

Lee and Yu 2021 [12] applied the BERT contextual embedding and out-of-manifold regularization in a contextual embedding space for text classification in the OoMMix proposal. Their motivation is that the embeddings computed from the words only utilize a low-dimensional manifold, while a high-dimensional space is available for the model capacity. Therefore, OoMMix discovers the embeddings that are useful for the target task but cannot be accessed through the words. A discriminator is trained to detect whether an input embedding is located inside the manifold or not, and simultaneously, a generator is optimized to produce new embeddings that can be easily identified as out-of-manifold by the discriminator. In the end, the fine-tuning of the synthesized out-of-manifold embeddings tightly regularizes the contextual embedding space of BERT.

Zhang et al. 2021 [26] also used BERT and incorporated knowledge about class labels into text classification models. In their approach, label-related knowledge is represented by keywords that users can customize. The relatedness between each word in the text sequence and hidden knowledge, such as keywords, is calculated and concatenated with the original model's information. Their proposal showed to be capable of understanding the relationship between sequences and labels, performing well on datasets with many classes.

Zhong et al. 2021 [28] proposed a novel model named BERT-KG, which can classify Chinese short text promptly and accurately and overcome the difficulty of short text classification. BERT-KG enriches short text features by obtaining background knowledge from a knowledge graph and further embeds the triple information of the target entity into a BERT-based model. Experiments conducted on two real-world datasets demonstrate that BERT-KG significantly improves the classification performance compared with state-of-the-art baselines.

Finally, Sinoara et al. 2019 [23] proposed two models to represent document collections based on both words and word senses, having the objective of improving text classification performance by enriching text representations with semantics. They use word sense disambiguation tools and available pre-trained word and word sense models to construct embedded representations of documents. The proposed approach representations are low-dimensional, which helps to speed up the learning and the classification processes. Their experimental evaluation indicates that the use of the proposed representations provides stable classifiers with reliable quantitative results, especially in semantically-complex classification scenarios.

3   Proposed Approach

Our text classification approach, OPHELIA, employs jointly trained word embeddings and knowledge embeddings as semantic features which are fed to a neural classifier. Figure 1 provides an overview of the OPHELIA components and text classification process. The following sections describe its three major modules: Embedding Generation, Semantic Enrichment, and Text Classification.

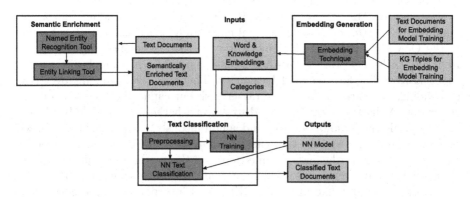

Fig. 1. Overview of OPHELIA main modules and text classification process.

3.1   Embedding Generation Module

The embedding generation in our current implementation is done by using fast-Text [4,9,10], which is available in Github[4].

---

[4] https://github.com/facebookresearch/fastText.

The fastText [10] model used is a simple linear model with ranking constraints. The weight matrix V is used as a look-up table over the discrete tokens, and the weight matrix W for the classifier. The representations of the discrete tokens are averaged into Bag-of-Words (BoW) feature representation. The average representation of the word is fed to the linear classifier. Using a softmax function f to compute the probability distribution over the classes, and N input sets for a discrete token (e.g., sentences), leads to minimizing:

$$-1/N \sum_{n-1}^{N} y_n log(f(WV\mathrm{x}_n)), \tag{1}$$

where x_n is the normalized bag of features of the n-th input set, y_n the label. While BoW models are memory inefficient, their memory footprint can be significantly reduced. The model is trained asynchronously on multiple CPUs with Stochastic Gradient Descent (SGD) optimizer and a linearly decaying learning rate.

As presented in Fig. 1, KG triples and entity abstracts are used as inputs of fastText to jointly train knowledge embeddings and word embeddings in the same vector space. The KG chosen for this work is DBpedia due to its open domain nature, which enables the evaluation of our approach with distinct open domain corpora. We use only the high-quality facts provided by DBpedia[5] to avoid noise in our embedding representation. As textual entity descriptions, we use the long version of the DBpedia entity abstracts[6], which contains the introductory text of each Wikipedia page and provides a summary of the respective entity.

We have combined infobox data triples and long abstracts of entities in a single training file. This allows fastText to jointly produce the knowledge embeddings and word embeddings in the same vector space. The parameters for the fastText model training are detailed and discussed in Sect. 4.

3.2   Semantic Enrichment Module

The Semantic Enrichment Module enriches text documents by performing Entity Linking (EL). It links named entity mentions found in each text document with their respective entity descriptors in KGs like DBpedia. Prior to EL, it is necessary to do Named Entity Recognition (NER), as illustrated in Fig. 1. However, several EL tools also incorporate NER methods. Thus, we just assume that the NER task will always be performed, either by a specific NER tool or by a tool that does NER and EL. In this work, we have used Babelfy[7] [18] to semantically enrich the text documents with links to named entities of DBpedia.

---

[5] http://wiki.dbpedia.org/services-resources/documentation/\datasets#
MappingbasedObjects.

[6] http://wiki.dbpedia.org/services-resources/documentation/\datasets#
LongAbstracts.

[7] http://babelfy.org/.

Semantic enrichment can be done either online or offline. We consider a task to be online when it is integrated into our text classification system, and there is no need for a user to call it manually and take the results into our system. Offline tasks, on the other hand, require text documents to be semantically enriched before the execution of our approach. An example of an offline task in our approach is the *Embedding Generation*, which has to be done beforehand. The semantic enrichment of the textual documents used as the training dataset for the neural network in our experiments is also done offline so that we can submit bulks of text documents at once and, consequently, save time and computational resources. For practical uses of our approach, it is better to adopt online semantic enrichment, as the user is expected to submit just one or a few text documents to be classified at once.

3.3   Text Classification Module

The Text Classification Module first task is preprocessing the semantically enriched texts. Usually, for NLP tasks, preprocessing is the first task to be performed in a text document. However, as shown in Fig. 1, we do the preprocessing after the semantic enrichment of the text document because NER and EL tools already have preprocessing implemented on them. Thus, if we preprocessed the text documents before their semantic enrichment, it could have a negative impact in the results of NER and EL tools.

The main goal of our preprocessing task is to fix words to match their respective embedding representations. To achieve this, we remove capitalization, special characters, apostrophes, and stop words. Capitalization and special characters are removed by using Python built-in functions, like *to_lower()* and *isalnum()*. Stop words are removed by using the list provided by libraries like nltk[8]. Lastly, we remove possessive apostrophes when they appear as "'s". All these preprocessing steps are represented by line 3 in Algorithm 1. Although simple, it is essential to highlight that excessive preprocessing could lead our approach to use incorrect embedded representations. For example, if we transform the verb "died", conjugated in the past, into its infinite "die", the neural network may misinterpret the sentence due to the different embedding representations. The embedded representation of "died" should be more closely related to entities that already have passed away than to the embedded representation of "die".

In the embedded representations of the semantically enriched texts, entity mentions are represented by their respective entity embeddings, while the other words are represented as word embeddings. Remember that all these embeddings are trained in the same vector space by using fastText, before being used as features for training the neural classifier and for classifying documents afterward.

The neural network is the main component of the Text Classification Module. The model is the most traditional for NLP tasks: a Feed Forward neural network (FFNN). The Feed Forward architecture is the most straightforward neural network, as presented in Fig. 2 where information always goes forward.

---

[8] https://www.nltk.org/.

Therefore, the FFNN captures the interactions between the word and knowledge embeddings.

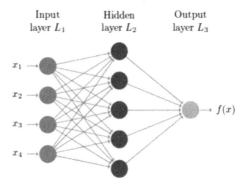

Fig. 2. Feed forward neural network. [3]

Algorithm 1 describes the classification of semantically enriched documents employing the previously described preprocessing and our trained FFNN model.

Algorithm 1. Text classification process

Input: D // List of semantically annotated documents, where $d_i \in D$
    E // Set of word and knowledge embedding, where $e_j \in E$

    C // Set of predefined classes, where $c_k \in C$

Output: $< d_i, c_k >$ # correct class c_k to classify a text document d_i

1: $R = \emptyset$ # Set that will contain the pair $< d_i, c_k >$
2: **for** $d_i \in D$ **do**
3:    $d_i = \text{preprocessing}(d_i)$
4:    $c_k = \text{classification}(\text{NN\_Model}(), d_i, C)$
5:    append(R, $< d_i, c_k >$)
6: **end for**

---

4 Experiments

This section reports the experiments performed to evaluate how well OPHELIA classifies text documents. We compare OPHELIA results with those of state-of-the-art text classification approaches from the literature by using accuracy and F1 score as the comparison metrics. Some approaches use two versions of the F1 score: micro and macro. The micro F1 score calculation considers all true positives, false positives, and false negatives from all documents together, while the macro F1 score is the average of the F1 scores calculated for each document.

4.1   Experimental Setup

As highlighted in Sect. 1, our DNN model obtain the best results using 50-dimensional embeddings. This way, it is possible to train our model in machines with limited hardware. For the training of our model, we use Adam loss optimization [11] with a learning rate of 0.001 and a batch size of 32.

For the embedding generation, we employ fastText with 500 epochs and a context window size of 50. The remaining parameters are set to the default values presented in the fastText GitHub repository[9].

As this work focus on news articles and for the sake of facilitating performance comparison, we use the following datasets: BBC News, AG News, and Reuters21578. Every document of each dataset was semantically enriched using the Babelfy tool [18].

We train a neural network model per dataset. It is necessary because each dataset contains a different number of classes, and their respective text documents present distinct writing styles. We highlight that we, in case the dataset does not present a validation dataset (used to fine-tune hyperparameters), randomly split the training dataset into 80% of training samples and 20% of validation samples. The BBC dataset is a collection of 2225 documents published between 2004 and 2005 and labeled with one of five topical areas: Business, Entertainment, Politics, Sport, and Tech. The dataset has been preprocessed. Stemming (Porter algorithm), stop-word removal (stop word list), and low-term frequency filtering (count < 3) have already been applied to the data. The dataset is divided into 1490 documents for training and 735 for testing.

AG News is a subdataset of AG's corpus of news articles constructed by assembling titles and description fields of articles from the 4 largest classes ("World", "Sports", "Business", "Sci/Tech") of AG's Corpus. The AG News contains 30.000 training and 1.900 test samples per class.

The Reuters-21578 collection is distributed in 22 files. Each of the first 21 files (*reut2-000.sgm* through *reut2-020.sgm*) contain 1000 documents, while the last one (*reut2-021.sgm*) contains 578 documents. The files are in SGML format. The structure of this format is described in [15]

We have used blades of the SDumont supercomputer[10] for embedding generation and neural network training. The embedding generation was done on blades having just CPUs, while the training runs on blades also having GPU. The first blades have 2 CPU Intel(R) Xeon(R) E5-2695v2 @ 2.4 GHz with 12 cores, and 64 GB DDR3 1866MHz RAM memory. The other blades have 2 CPU Intel(R) Xeon(R) E5-2695v2 @ 2.4 GHz with 12 cores, and 64 GB DDR3 1866MHz RAM memory, 2 GPU Nvidia K40, 3584 Cuda cores, and 16 GB of memory. However, we highlight that we were able to run the experiments for evaluating the trained NN performance on text classification in a Dell notebook with 1 CPU Intel(R) Core i3 and 20 GB DD3 1866 MHz RAM memory.

---

[9] https://github.com/facebookresearch/fastText.
[10] https://sdumont.lncc.br/.

Table 2. Accuracy, Micro F1, and Macro F1 on the tested datasets.

Accuracy F1@Micro F1@Macro	BBC	AG News	Reuters
Lenc et al. 2017 [14]	-	-	-
	-	-	-
	-	-	**0.875**
Sinoara et al. 2019 [23]	-	-	-
	0.973	-	-
	0.972	-	
Pittaras et al. 2020 [21]	0.976	-	**0.749**
	-	-	-
	0.976	-	0.378
Zhang et al. 2021 [26]	-	**0.947**	-
	-	-	-
	-	-	-
Lee et al. 2021 [12]	-	0.918	-
	-	-	-
	-	-	-
OPHELIA@50	**0.985**	0.919	0.245
	0.984	**0.918**	0.246
	0.982	**0.918**	0.246
OPHELIA@100	0.956	0.914	0.244
	0.955	0.914	0.243
	0.954	0.914	0.246
OPHELIA@200	0.969	0.914	0.242
	0.969	0.913	0.241
	0.968	0.913	0.242
OPHELIA@300	0.978	0.915	0.232
	0.977	0.915	0.231
	0.978	0.914	0.232

4.2 Results and Discussion

The text classification performance was evaluated with the metrics accuracy and F1 score because they are the most used in text classification approaches that we have considered as baselines [12,14,21,26]. Table 2 presents the accuracy, micro and macro F1 scores of our proposal, and state-of-the-art approaches used as baselines. We experiment Ophelia with different embedding dimensions. The results are expressed as OPHELIA@E, where E is the embedding dimension.

The measures for each dataset are highlighted in bold. Unfortunately, the baselines are not evaluated with all the metrics and datasets in their respective publications. Notice that OPHELIA outperforms all the baselines on the BBC dataset, stays competitive on the AG News dataset, and greatly underperforms on Reuters dataset. We believe that this behavior happens because of the writing styles of the datasets. Both BBC and AG News datasets employ a writing style that uses words present in our embedding representations. However, the

Reuters dataset contains large quantities of acronyms and specific words from the business domain. As we generate our embeddings from DBPedia, they do not have good representations for such words.

Therefore, most of our experimental results are competitive, despite using low dimension embeddings and straightforward neural network architecture. It suggests that text classification using jointly trained word embeddings and knowledge embeddings is promising, though more experiments are still needed to evaluate our proposal with specific vocabulary and particular domains.

5 Conclusion

In this work, we propose OPHELIA, a neural network text classification approach based on joint embeddings of words and knowledge. OPHELIA can produce results comparable with those of state-of-the-art approaches from the literature in news datasets with open domain. The neural network architecture of OPHELIA is relatively simple if compared with other architectures. Thus, OPHELIA has the potential to produce better results with a more sophisticated DNN architecture and a more significant training set.

We plan for future work to propose and use better preprocessing methods for news articles and use distinct corpora and KGs to jointly train word and knowledge embeddings, since we envision that this could improve the performance of our approach. Furthermore, we intend to apply transformer models, like BERT, as our embedding generator and compare the results by using fastText. Lastly, we plan to make our model interpretable by using current algorithms for interpreting black-box models and understanding how the model handles incorrect cases. It can help us understand and optimize our model to better handle those cases, improving its performance.

Acknowledgements. This study was Supported by Foundation for Research Support of Santa Catarina, Fundação de Amparo à Pesquisa e Inovação do Estado de Santa Catarina (FAPESC), the Print CAPES-UFSC Automation 4.0 Project, and the Brazilian National Laboratory for Scientific Computing (LNCC).

References

1. Auer, S., Bizer, C., Kobilarov, G., Lehmann, J., Cyganiak, R., Ives, Z.: DBpedia: a nucleus for a web of open data. In: Aberer, K., et al. (eds.) ASWC/ISWC -2007. LNCS, vol. 4825, pp. 722–735. Springer, Heidelberg (2007). https://doi.org/10.1007/978-3-540-76298-0_52
2. Bengio, Y., Ducharme, R., Vincent, P., Jauvin, C.: A neural probabilistic language model. J. Mach. Learn. Res. (3)(Feb), 1137–1155 (2003)
3. Boehmke, B., Jodrey, J.: UC business analytics R programming guide (2018). https://github.com/uc-r/uc-r.github.io
4. Bojanowski, P., Grave, E., Joulin, A., Mikolov, T.: Enriching word vectors with subword information. Trans. Assoc. Comput. Linguist. **5**, 135–146 (2017)

5. Deng, X., Li, Y., Weng, J., Zhang, J.: Feature selection for text classification: a review. Multim. Tools Appl. **78**(3), 3797–3816 (2019)
6. Devlin, J., Chang, M.W., Lee, K., Toutanova, K.: BERT: pre-training of deep bidirectional transformers for language understanding. In: Conference of the North American Chapter of the ACL, pp. 4171–4186. Association for Computational Linguistics (ACL), June 2019
7. Fabian, M., Gjergji, K., Gerhard, W.: YAGO: a core of semantic knowledge unifying WordNet and Wikipedia. In: 16th International World Wide Web Conference on World Wide Web, pp. 697–706 (2007)
8. Joulin, A., Grave, E., Bojanowski, P., Douze, M., Jégou, H., Mikolov, T.: Fasttext.zip: compressing text classification models. arXiv preprint arXiv:1612.03651 (2016)
9. Joulin, A., Grave, E., Bojanowski, P., Mikolov, T.: Bag of tricks for efficient text classification. In: Proceedings of the 15th Conference of the European Chapter of the Association for Computational Linguistics: Volume 2, Short Papers. pp. 427–431. Association for Computational Linguistics, April 2017
10. Joulin, A., Grave, E., Bojanowski, P., Nickel, M., Mikolov, T.: Fast linear model for knowledge graph embeddings. arXiv preprint arXiv:1710.10881 (2017)
11. Kingma, D.P., Ba, J.: Adam: a method for stochastic optimization. arXiv preprint arXiv:1412.6980 (2014)
12. Lee, S., Lee, D., Yu, H.: OoMMix:out-of-manifold regularization in contextual embedding space for text classification. In: 59th Annual Meeting of the ACL and the 11th International Conference on Joint Conference on Natural Language Processing, pp. 590–599. Association for Computational Linguistics (ACL) (2021)
13. Lehmann, J., et al.: DBpedia - a crystallization point for the web of data. J. Web Seman. **7**(3), 154–165 (2009)
14. Lenc, L., Král, P.: Word embeddings for multi-label document classification. In: International Conference on Recent Advances in Natural Language Processing, RANLP 2017, pp. 431–437. INCOMA Ltd., Varna, Bulgaria , September 2017
15. Lewis, D., et al.: Reuters-21578. Test Collect. **1**, 19 (1987)
16. Li, Y., Yang, T.: Word embedding for understanding natural language: a survey. In: Srinivasan, S. (ed.) Guide to Big Data Applications. SBD, vol. 26, pp. 83–104. Springer, Cham (2018). https://doi.org/10.1007/978-3-319-53817-4_4
17. Mikolov, T., Sutskever, I., Chen, K., Corrado, G.S., Dean, J.: Distributed representations of words and phrases and their compositionality. In: Advances in Neural Information Processing Systems, pp. 3111–3119 (2013)
18. Moro, A., Raganato, A., Navigli, R.: Entity linking meets Word Sense disambiguation: a unified approach. Trans. Assoc. Comput. Linguist. **2**, 231–244 (2014)
19. Nickel, M., Murphy, K., Tresp, V., Gabrilovich, E.: A review of relational machine learning for knowledge graphs. Proc. IEEE **104**(1), 11–33 (2016)
20. Pennington, J., Socher, R., Manning, C.: GloVe: global vectors for word representation. In: 2014 Conference on Empirical Methods in Natural Language Processing (EMNLP), pp. 1532–1543 (2014)
21. Pittaras, N., Giannakopoulos, G., Papadakis, G., Karkaletsis, V.: Text classification with semantically enriched word embeddings. Nat. Lang. Eng. **27**(4), 391–425 (2021)
22. Rydning, D.R.J.G.J., Reinsel, J., Gantz, J.: The Digitization of the World from Edge to Core. Framingham: International Data Corporation 16 (2018)
23. Sinoara, R.A., Camacho-Collados, J., Rossi, R.G., Navigli, R., Rezende, S.O.: Knowledge-enhanced document embeddings for text classification. Knowl.-Based Syst. **163**, 955–971 (2019)

24. Wang, Q., Mao, Z., Wang, B., Guo, L.: Knowledge graph embedding: a survey of approaches and applications. IEEE Trans. Knowl. Data Eng. **29**(12), 2724–2743 (2017)
25. Zha, D., Li, C.: Multi-label dataless text classification with topic modeling. Knowl. Inf. Syst. **61**(1), 137–160 (2019)
26. Zhang, C., Yamana, H.: Improving text classification using knowledge in labels. In: 2021 IEEE 6th International Conference on Big Data Analytics (ICBDA), pp. 193–197 (2021)
27. Zhang, J., Lertvittayakumjorn, P., Guo, Y.: Integrating semantic knowledge to tackle zero-shot text classification. In: 2019 Conference of the North American Chapter of the Association for Computational Linguistics: Human Language Technologies, Volume 1 (Long and Short Papers), pp. 1031–1040. Association for Computational Linguistics, Minneapolis, Minnesota (2019)
28. Zhong, Y., Zhang, Z., Zhang, W., Zhu, J.: BERT-KG: a short text classification model based onKnowledge graph and deep semantics. In: Wang, L., Feng, Y., Hong, Yu., He, R. (eds.) NLPCC 2021. LNCS (LNAI), vol. 13028, pp. 721–733. Springer, Cham (2021). https://doi.org/10.1007/978-3-030-88480-2_58

Tree-Based Graph Indexing for Fast kNN Queries

Suomi Kobayashi[1]([✉]), Shohei Matsugu[1], and Hiroaki Shiokawa[2]

[1] Department of Computer Science, University of Tsukuba, Tsukuba, Japan
{kobayashi,matsugu}@kde.cs.tsukuba.ac.jp
[2] Center for Computational Sciences, University of Tsukuba, Tsukuba, Japan
shiokawa@cs.tsukuba.ac.jp

Abstract. The k nearest neighbor (kNN) query on a graph is a problem to find k nodes having a shortest path distance from a user-specified query node in the graph. Graph indexing methods have the potential to achieve fast kNN queries and thus are promising approaches to handle large-scale graphs. However, those indexing approaches struggle to query kNN nodes on large-scale complex networks. This is because that complex networks generally have multiple shortest paths between specific two nodes, which incur redundant search costs in the indexing approaches. In this paper, we propose a novel graph indexing algorithm for fast kNN queries on complex networks. To overcome the aforementioned limitations, our algorithm generates a tree-based index from a graph so that it avoids to compute redundant paths during kNN queries. Our extensive experimental analysis on real-world graphs show that our algorithm achieves up to 146 times faster kNN queries than the state-of-the-art methods.

Keywords: Graph query · kNN search · Indexing

1 Introduction

Given a graph G, can the k nearest neighbor (kNN) nodes to a user-specified query node be found efficiently? This work presents a novel graph indexing algorithm to efficiently find kNN nodes on large complex networks against the user-specified query nodes.

As social applications advance, complex networks (or graphs) are becoming increasingly important to represent complicated data [24, 25]. To handle such networks, kNN queries [14, 17, 21, 30] are essential building blocks in various applications [2, 4, 5, 11, 16, 18, 19]. Given a query node in a graph, the kNN query explores a set of nodes with the top-k shortest path distances from the query. Unlike traditional distance-based queries [3, 7–9, 21, 22], kNN queries can return a result within a short time because they do not compute the entire graph. Owing to this feature, kNN queries have been employed in various social applications.

This work is partly supported by JST Presto JPMJPR2033, Japan.

Ride-Sharing Services: Ride-sharing services is a popular application of kNN queries, and are used to alleviate travel costs, such as fares, energy consumption, and traffic pressure. Various rider-driver matching algorithms have recently been proposed to increase cost efficiency by using ride-sharing services [5]. For example, Chen et al. proposed DEFC, which is a travelling cost estimation model based on kNN queries, to a rider-driver matching network [5]. By finding the top-k similar drivers from the network, the DEFC effectively predicts the number of passengers and vehicles. Chen et al. experimentally confirmed that their approach, which was based on kNN queries, achieved better cost reductions than competitive approaches in real-world applications.

Spam and Fake News Detection: In recent social networking services, the total number of user accounts has increased significantly. However, in these situations, some malicious users and fake accounts intentionally spread fake news and information on social applications to earn financial gains or political attention, etc. Therefore, spam and fake news detection methods are required to prevent non-malicious users from becoming malicious ones [2,11]. Recently, Alom et al. proposed spam detection model for Twitter [2]. To effectively find malicious user accounts, Alom et al. extracted a set of user features using graph-based kNN queries, and they reported that their proposed model achieved a better performance compared to other state-of-the-art approaches. Analogously, Ankit et al. proposed a similar kNN-based model to detect fake news that were widely spread on social media [11]. They reported that their model achieved more than 79% accuracy on a Facebook news post dataset.

In addition to the above applications, graph-based kNN queries can also be used in other applications, such as malware detection [19], smart city applications [13,18], healthcare data management [16,29], and location-based social networking systems [4].

Although kNN queries are useful in many applications, they have serious drawback when handling real-world complex networks. Specifically, traditional kNN search algorithms [14,17,21,30] are computationally expensive if the given graph is large. Historically, kNN queries have been applied to small graphs such as ego networks and road networks, which have a few thousand nodes at most. By contrast, recent social networking applications must handle large-scale complex networks with a few million nodes [23,27]. In other words, applications suffer from an extensive computation time to query kNN nodes when traditional algorithms run queries. Thus, these algorithms fail to find kNN nodes in large-scale real-world complex networks.

1.1   Existing Approaches and Challenges

Various approaches have been proposed to overcome the expensive costs in kNN queries. *Graph indexing methods* are the most successful to date [1,12,17,28, 30]. Examples include G-Tree [30], G*-Tree [17] and ILBR [1]. These methods construct an index by partitioning the graph and precomputing the shortest path distances between nodes in the graph before kNN queries. G-Tree uses a method called Metis [10] to partition the graph into subgraphs and precompute the distances between all nodes in each subgraph. G*-Ttee [17] is a minor variant of G-Tree. It additionally builds shortcut edges between subgraphs extracted by G-Tree so that those edges reduce the kNN search cost. Similarly, ILBR selects some landmark nodes from among the nodes in the graph and constructs a network Voronoi diagram using these landmarks. It then pre-computes the distances from the landmarks to the nodes in each network Voronoi diagram. These methods process kNN query on the index, avoiding computation of unnecessary nodes and edges and allowing fast processing of kNN query.

Although indexing methods improve kNN query efficiency, they cannot handle large complex networks since a long running time is necessary for a kNN query on complex networks. This is because that complex networks should have multiple shortest paths between two nodes due to the small-world effect [26], which significantly incur kNN search costs. Therefore, a graph indexing algorithm that accelerates kNN queries on complex networks remain elusive.

1.2   Our Approaches and Contributions

In this paper, we propose a novel indexing algorithm for efficient kNN queries on complex networks. The key idea underlying our proposed algorithm is to construct index based on the minimum spanning tree. As we described in Sect. 1.1, complex networks allow multiple shortest paths having the same distance between two nodes. However, existing methods need to compute all of the multiple paths at kNN querying time, which increases the query processing time. By contrast, our tree-based indexing algorithm can avoid to compute the multiple paths during the kNN query time since any two nodes are connected through only a single path. Thus, our algorithm achieves faster kNN queries than existing graph indexing methods.

In summary, we have made the following contributions in this paper:

- **Fast Querying:** Our proposed method is faster than the existing methods in terms of the kNN query time (Sect. 4.2). We experimentally demonstrate that it is up to 146 times faster than existing methods.
- **Correctness:** Our method guarantees to find exact kNN nodes, although it prunes unpromising nodes using the tree-based index.
- **Easy to Deploy:** Our proposed method does not require any user-specified parameters unlike exising methods.

The rest of this paper is organized as follows: We briefly define the problem addressed in this paper in Sect. 2. We then detail the proposed method in Sect. 3, and experimentally discuss the effectiveness of our algorithm in Sect. 4 by using real-world complex networks. Finally, we conclude this paper in Sect. 5.

2   Preliminary

Here, we provide a formal problem definition for the kNN query processing. We first introduce the following definition on a graph $G = (V, E, W)$, where V, E, and W are the sets of nodes, edges, and edge-weights, respectively.

Definition 1 (Shortest path distance). *Let a node path $u = u_0 \rightarrow u_1 \rightarrow u_2 \rightarrow ... \rightarrow u_i = v$ in G be the shortest path between the nodes $u, v \in V$. We denote the shortest path distance between the nodes u and v as $dist(u, v)$, which is defined as follows:*

$$dist(u, v) = \sum_{i=0}^{i-1} w(u_i, u_{i+1})$$

For convenience, given a query node $q \in V$, we use $dist_k(q, V)$ as the k-th smallest distance in $\{dist(q, v)|v \in V\}$.

Based on Definition 1, we define the kNN query processing problem as follows:

Definition 2 (kNN query processing). *Given a graph $G = (V, E, W)$, query node $q \in V$, and integer $k \in \mathbb{N}$, the kNN query is the problem of finding a set of nodes $V_k(q)$ from G, which is defined as follows:*

$$V_k(q) = \{u \in V|dist(q, v) \leq dist_k(q, V)\}$$

3   Proposed Method

We present our indexing method for a fast kNN query on large complex networks. We first explain how to construct our tree-based index in Sect. 3.1. Then, we introduce kNN query processing algorithm using the index in Sect. 3.2.

3.1   Tree-Based Index Construction

Our proposed method constructs an index based on a minimum spanning tree. Thus, we first define the minimum spanning tree as follows:

Definition 3 (*Spanning Tree*). *Given a graph $G = (V, E, W)$ and edge set $T \subseteq E$, we say that T is spanning tree if $G' = (V, T)$ is a tree structure and when G' preserves the connectivity of G.*

Definition 4 (*Minimum Spanning Tree*). *Of all possible spanning trees G can take, the one with the minimum sum of edge weights is called minimum spanning tree.*

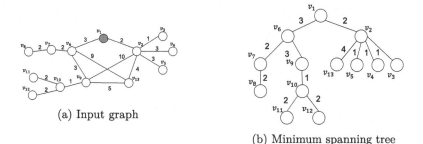

(a) Input graph

(b) Minimum spanning tree

Fig. 1. Minimum spanning tree

Figure 1 shows an example of minimum spanning tree. Given the graph in Fig. 1(a), Fig. 1(b) shows minimum spanning tree when v_1 is the start point. The edge between v_2 and v_9, between v_6 and v_{13} and between v_9 and v_{13} has been removed, but the graph is still connected.

Although the minimum spanning tree works as an index structure, it does not guarantee the exact kNN query results if the tree drops shortest paths for specific two nodes in a graph. Thus, we extends the minimum spanning tree by adding shortcut edges so that the tree ensures to find exact kNN nodes from a query node. To define the shortcut edges to be added into the tree, we first introduce the following definition:

Definition 5 (*TreeDis*). *Let a node path $u = u_0 \to u_1 \to u_2 \to ... \to u_i = v$ in a minimum spanning tree $T(V_T, E_T, W_T)$ be the shortest path between the nodes $u, v \in V_T$. We denote the shortest path distance between the nodes u and v as TreeDis(u, v), which is defined as follows:*

$$TreeDis(u, v) = \sum_{i=0}^{i-1} w(u_i, u_{i+1})$$

Finally, we define the shortcut edges, namely shortcut set SC, as follows:

Definition 6 (Shortcut Set SC). *Given a graph $G(V, E, W)$ and a minimum spanning tree $T(V_T, E_T, W_T)$, a shortcut set SC is computed as*

$$SC = \{\langle e(u, v), w(u, v)\rangle \mid u, v \in V, w(u, v) < TreeDis(u, v)\}.$$

In summary, our tree-based index is composed of two parts: (1) a minimum spanning tree, and (2) a shourtcut set defined in Definition 6. To construct the minimum spanning tree T, we employ the prim method [20]. In the minimum spanning tree construction, the edge-weight between u and v is compared to the *TreeDis(u, v)*, and if the edge satisfies the Definition 6, we add it to SC.

Algorithm: Algorithm 1 is a pseudo-code of our algorithm to generate our tree-based index $\mathcal{I}$. At the beginning of the algorithm, it constructs arrays M and U

Algorithm 1. INDEXING

Input: a graph $G = (V, E, W)$, a node $s \in V$;
Output: a graph index $\mathcal{I}$;
1: $\mathcal{I} \leftarrow \emptyset$, Generate arrays M and U;
2: **for** i from 1 to $|V|$ **do**
3:     $M[i] = \infty$;
4: $M[s] = 0$, $U \leftarrow U \cup \{s\}$;
5: **while** $|U| \le |V|$ **do**
6:     **for each** $u \in V$ and $M[u] < M[v]$ **do**
7:         **if** $U[u] = 0$ **then**
8:             $v \leftarrow u$;
9:     $U[u] \leftarrow 1$;
10:     **for each** $a \in v.adjacent$ **do**
11:         **if** $a \notin U$ **then**
12:             **if** $M[a] > w(a, v)$ **then**
13:                 $M[a] \leftarrow w(a, v)$;
14:                 $\mathcal{I}[a].parent \leftarrow \langle v, w(u, v) \rangle$
15:         **else**
16:             **if** $w(a, v) < TreeDis(a, v)$ **then**
17:                 $\mathcal{I}[v].shortcut \leftarrow \langle a, w(a, v) \rangle$
18: **return** $\mathcal{I}$;

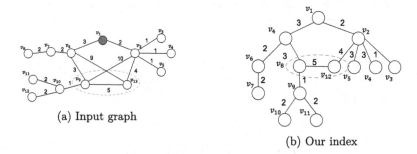

(a) Input graph

(b) Our index

Fig. 2. Index structure

to record the minimum weights and the visited nodes, respectively. In the first step (lines 1–4), our algorithm initializes M and U. In lines 5–18, our algorithm then generates the minimum spanning tree and the shortcut set simultaneously. If node a is an unvisited node, $e(v, a)$ is added the minimum spanning tree, *i.e.*, $\mathcal{I}[a]$. parent (lines 11–14) only when the edge is included in a shortest path from s. Otherwise, our algorithm adds node a into the shortcut set if it satisfies Definition 6 (lines 15–17). Algorithm 1 continues the above processes until all nodes in V are visited.

Figure 2 shows an example of our tree-based index. In a graph shown in Fig. 2(a), we start constructing a minimum spanning tree from v_1. During the minimum spanning tree construction, a shortcut between v_9 and v_{13} is generated

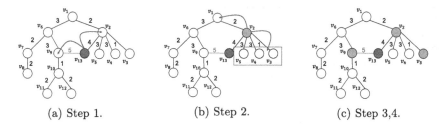

(a) Step 1.   (b) Step 2.   (c) Step 3,4.

Fig. 3. Query processing

since $w(v_9, v_{13}) = 5 < TreeDis(v_9, v_{13}) = 12$. Finally, we obtain the index as shown in Fig, 2(b).

Complexity Analysis: Here, we briefly discuss the space and the time complexity of our indexing method. As described in the above, our index contains $|V|$ nodes, where each node is adjacent to at most $O(|E|/|V|)$ nodes. That is, our index requires the space complexity as $O(|V| + |V|(|E|/|V|)) = O(|V| + |E|)$ in the worst case. Also, the time complexity of our method is $O(|E| \log |V|)$ time since our method completes indexing during the prim method.

3.2 kNN Query Processing

This section explains how a kNN query is computed on the tree-based index $\mathcal{I}$. Given a query $\langle v_q, k \rangle$, where v_q is a query node in V and k is the number of search results. To reduce the number of searched paths, our algorithm explores a set of kNN nodes of v_q by only using the tree-based index $\mathcal{I}$. To this end, we implement kNN query processing on $\mathcal{I}$ by using a priority queue. Specifically, our algorithm first searches for adjacent nodes of the query node on $\mathcal{I}$, and it then inserts the adjacent nodes and their corresponding distances the query node into the priority queue. After that, the algorithm selects a node from the queue, and it continues the above procedures for the selected node. These processes will be repeated until kNN nodes are found. The nature of the priority queue allows the algorithm to search sequentially for nodes with the shortest distance from the query node. Hence, the node inserted in the result list is has the shprtest distance from the query node at that time. Therefore, the algorithm can accurately search for neighboring nodes of the query node. More precisely, we explain the details of our kNN search algorithm in Algorithm 2.

Algorithm: Algorithm 2 shows the pseudo-code of kNN query using $\mathcal{I}$. At the beginning of the algorithm, it initializes a priority queue Q, in which nodes are prioritized by the distance from v_q (lines 1–2). Once $\langle u, dist(v_q, u) \rangle$ is obtained from Q (line 4), it continues the kNN query until $|V_k|$ reaches k (lines 3–15). If $u.parent$ is not searched, the algorithm inserts $u.parent$ into Q. If u has *children* and *shortcut*, it examines SEARCHNODESET (lines 8–9). SEARCHNODESET computes the weights from a node u to every node in the node set N that is not included in V_k.

Algorithm 2. kNN QUERY PROCESSING

Input: an index $\mathcal{I}$, a query node v_q, and the number of results k;
Output: a set of kNN nodes V_k;
 1: $V_k \leftarrow \emptyset$, and priority queue $Q \leftarrow \emptyset$;
 2: $Q \leftarrow \{\langle v_q, 0 \rangle\}$;
 3: **while** $|V_k| \leq k$ **do**
 4:     $\langle u, dist(v_q, u) \rangle \leftarrow Q.dequeue()$;
 5:     **if** $u.parent \notin V_k$ **then**
 6:         $dist(v_q, u.parent) \leftarrow dist(v_q, u) + w(u, u.parent)$;
 7:         $Q.enqueue(\langle u.parent, dist(v_q, u.parent) \rangle)$;
 8:     SEARCHNODESET($u, u.children$);
 9:     SEARCHNODESET($u, u.SC$);
10:     $V_k \leftarrow V_k \cup \{u\}$;
11: **return** V_k;
12: **procedure** SEARCHNODESET($\langle u, nodeset\ N \rangle$)
13:     **for each** $\{n \in N | n \notin V_k\}$ **do**
14:         $dist(v_q, n) \leftarrow dist(v_q, u) + w(u, n)$;
15:         $Q.enqueue(\langle v, dist(v_q, n) \rangle)$;

Example. Consider a query $\langle v_{13}, k = 3 \rangle$ on the graph Fig. 3(a). We now compute the 3NN nodes for v_{13} as follows:

Step 1. Adds adjacent nodes of v_{13} to Q. $Q = \boxed{\langle v_2, 4 \rangle \mid \langle v_9, 5 \rangle}$, $V_k = \phi$'

Step 2. Extracts the first element of the Q $\langle v_2, 4 \rangle$ and adjacent nodes of v_2 are added to Q. Adds v_2 to V_k because the $|V_k| < 3$.
$Q = \boxed{\langle v_3, 5 \rangle \mid \langle v_9, 5 \rangle \mid \langle v_1, 6 \rangle \mid \langle v_4, 7 \rangle \mid \langle v_5, 7 \rangle}$, $V_k = \{v_2\}$.

Step 3. Extracts the first element of the Q $\langle v_3, 5 \rangle$ and adds v_3 to V_k because the $|V_k| < 3$. All of adjacent nodes of v_3 are searched, so no new nodes are added to the Q. $Q = \boxed{\langle v_9, 5 \rangle \mid \langle v_1, 6 \rangle \mid \langle v_4, 7 \rangle \mid \langle v_5, 7 \rangle}$, $V_k = \{v_2, v_3\}$.

Step 4. Extracts the first element of the Q $\langle v_9, 5 \rangle$ and add v_9 to V_k because the $|V_k| < 3$. $|V_k|$ become 3, so no new nodes are added to the Q. $Q = \boxed{\langle v_1, 6 \rangle \mid \langle v_4, 7 \rangle \mid \langle v_5, 7 \rangle}$, $V_k = \{v_2, v_3, v_9\}$.
Finally, 3NN nodes are found for v_{13}, and thus Algorithm 2 terminates.

Complexity Analysis: Finally, we discuss the time complexity of Algorithm 2. Our kNN queries are performed by using the priority queue so as to explore the neighbors of indexed nodes, which entails $O(|E|/|V|)$ time. Since we can find all kNN nodes by performing this process at most $O(k)$ time, our algorithm incurs $O(k|V|/|E|)$ time to obtain the search result in the worst case.

4   Experimental Analysis

Here, we experimentally discuss the efficiency of our algorithm in terms of the kNN querying time.

Table 1. Statistics of real-world datasets.

Name	$|V|$	$|E|$	Type	Source
CAL	21,048	21,693	Road network	[30]
NY	264,346	366,923	Road network	[17]
FLA	1,070,376	2,712,798	Road network	[6]
TV	3,892	17,262	Social network	[15]
GV	7,057	89,455	Social network	[15]
NS	27,917	206,259	Social network	[15]
AT	50,515	819,306	Social network	[15]

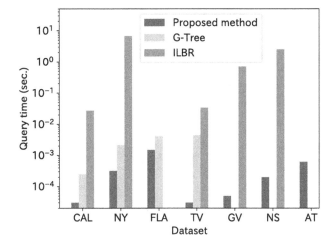

Fig. 4. Example of kNN

4.1 Experimental Setting

Methods: We experimentally compared our method with two state-of-the-art indexing methods: G-Tree [30] and ILBR [1]. For G-Tree, we set $f = 4$ as well as the same setting employed in [30]. All algorithms were implemented by C++ and compiled by gcc 9.2.0 using -O2 option. All experiments were conducted on a server with an Intel Xeon CPU (2.60 GHz) and 128 GiB RAM. We randomly selected 30 query nodes for each dataset. Here, we report their average time. Unless otherwise stated, we set $k = 0.01 \times |V|$.

Datasets: We employed eight real-world graphs, which were published in previous studies [17,30] and several public repositories [6,15] (Table 1). CAL, NY, and FLA denote a road network. All others indicate a social network.

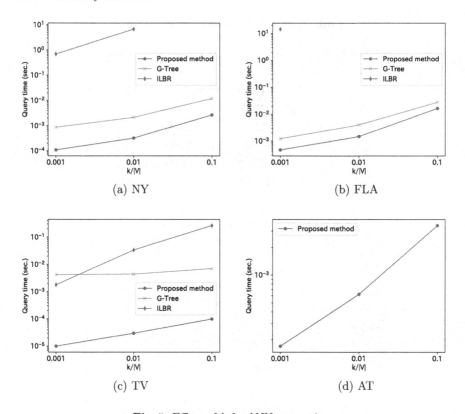

Fig. 5. Effect of k for kNN query time

4.2 kNN Query Efficiency

Figure 4 shows the kNN query time when $k = 0.01 \times |V|$. Results are omitted if the kNN query did not finish within 1 min. Our algorithm significantly outperforms the other methods for social networks. By contrast, its improvements are relatively small for road networks. This is because the number of edges in the road network was originally small. Thus, our proposed algorithm does not reduce the number of indexed paths enough compared to the social networks. By contrast, our algorithm achieves significant speed-ups for social networks. Specifically, our algorithm achieves quick kNN query processing for AT whereas the other methods failed to compute the query. This is because that social networks is a well known instance of complex networks, which incurs so many redundant path searches in existing methods. Thus, our algorithm shows better running time compared to the state-of-the-art algorithms.

In Fig. 5 shows the impact of k for query time. We varied k as $0.001 \times |V|$, $0.01 \times |V|$, and $0.1 \times |V|$. Due to the space limitations, we report results only for NY, FLA, TV, and AT. Results are omitted if the kNN query did not finished within 1 min. Our method is significantly faster than the others on social networks regardless of k. By contrast, its improvements are small for road networks. Consequently, our method is better suited for large-scale complex networks than existing methods.

5 Conclusion

In this paper, we proposed a novel tree-based indexing algorithm for efficient kNN queries on complex networks. By utilizing the minimum spanning tree, our proposed algorithm attempts to reduce the number of redundant shortest path searches explored in the kNN query processing. Our extensive experimental analysis demonstrated that our tree-based indexing algorithm outperforms the state-of-the-art methods up to 2 orders of magnitude in terms of the kNN query time. As for the future studies, it is valuable to extend our indexing method so as to handle dynamic updates of graphs such as node/edge insertions and delitions, and weight replacements.

References

1. Abeywickrama, T., Cheema, M.A.: Efficient landmark-based candidate generation for kNN queries on road networks. In: Proceedings of the 22nd International Conference on Database Systems for Advanced Applications (DASFAA 2017), pp. 425–440 (2017)
2. Alom, Z., Carminati, B., Ferrari, E.: Detecting spam accounts on twitter. In: 2018 IEEE/ACM International Conference on Advances in Social Networks Analysis and Mining (ASONAM), pp. 1191–1198 (2018). https://doi.org/10.1109/ASONAM.2018.8508495
3. Bast, H., Funke, S., Matijevic, D.: Ultrafast shortest-path queries via transit nodes. In: Demetrescu, C., Goldberg, A.V., Johnson, D.S. (eds.) The Shortest Path Problem, pp. 175–392. AMS (2006)
4. Chen, J.-S., Huang, H.-Y., Hsu, C.-Y.: A kNN based position prediction method for SNS places. In: Nguyen, N.T., Jearanaitanakij, K., Selamat, A., Trawiński, B., Chittayasothorn, S. (eds.) ACIIDS 2020. LNCS (LNAI), vol. 12034, pp. 266–273. Springer, Cham (2020). https://doi.org/10.1007/978-3-030-42058-1_22
5. Chen, Z., Li, P., Xiao, J., Nie, L., Liu, Y.: An order dispatch system based on reinforcement learning for ride sharing services. In: 2020 IEEE 22nd International Conference on High Performance Computing and Communications; IEEE 18th International Conference on Smart City; IEEE 6th International Conference on Data Science and Systems (HPCC/SmartCity/DSS), pp. 758–763 (2020). https://doi.org/10.1109/HPCC-SmartCity-DSS50907.2020.00099
6. Demetrescu, C.: The 9th DIMACS Implementation Challenge (June 2010). http://users.diag.uniroma1.it/challenge9/download.shtml
7. Geisberger, R., Sanders, P., Schultes, D., Delling, D.: Contraction hierarchies: faster and simpler hierarchical routing in road networks. In: McGeoch, C.C. (ed.) WEA 2008. LNCS, vol. 5038, pp. 319–333. Springer, Heidelberg (2008). https://doi.org/10.1007/978-3-540-68552-4_24
8. Jing, N., Huang, Y.W., Rundensteiner, E.A.: Hierarchical encoded path views for path query processing: an optimal model and its performance evaluation. IEEE Trans. Knowl. Data Eng. **10**(3), 409–432 (1998)

9. Jung, S., Pramanik, S.: An efficient path computation model for hierarchically structured topographical road maps. IEEE Trans. Knowl. Data Eng. **14**(5), 1029–1046 (2002)

10. Karypis, G., Kumar, V.: Analysis of Multilevel Graph Partitioning. In: Proceedings of the IEEE/ACM SC95 Conference (SC 1995), pp. 29-es (1995)

11. Kesarwani, A., Chauhan, S.S., Nair, A.R.: fake news detection on social media using k-nearest neighbor classifier. In: 2020 International Conference on Advances in Computing and Communication Engineering (ICACCE), pp. 1–4 (2020). https://doi.org/10.1109/ICACCE49060.2020.9154997

12. Kobayashi, S., Matsugu, S., Shiokawa, H.: Fast indexing algorithm for efficient k NN queries on complex networks. In: Proceedings of the 2021 IEEE/ACM International Conference on Advances in Social Networks Analysis and Mining, pp. 343–347 (2021)

13. Komamizu, T., Amagasa, T., Shaikh, S.A., Shiokawa, H., Kitagawa, H.: Towards real-time analysis of smart city data: A case study on city facility utilizations. In: 2016 IEEE 18th International Conference on High Performance Computing and Communications; IEEE 14th International Conference on Smart City; IEEE 2nd International Conference on Data Science and Systems (HPCC/SmartCity/DSS), pp. 1357–1364 (2016)

14. Lee, K.C.K., Lee, W., Zheng, B., Tian, Y.: ROAD: A new spatial object search framework for road networks. IEEE Trans. Knowl. Data Eng. **3**, 545–560 (2012)

15. Leskovec, J., Krevl, A.: SNAP Datasets: Stanford Large Network Dataset Collection (June 2014). http://snap.stanford.edu/data

16. Li, H., Zhang, Q., Lu, K.: Integrating mobile sensing and social network for personalized health-care application. In: Proceedings of the 30th Annual ACM Symposium on Applied Computing, SAC 2015, pp. 527–534. Association for Computing Machinery, New York, NY, USA (2015). https://doi.org/10.1145/2695664.2695767,https://doi.org/10.1145/2695664.2695767

17. Li, Z., Chen, L., Wang, Y.: G*-Tree: An Efficient Spatial Index on Road Networks. In: Proceedings of the 35th IEEE International Conference on Data Engineering (ICDE 2019), pp. 268–279 (2019)

18. Mei, S., Li, H., Fan, J., Zhu, X., Dyer, C.R.: Inferring air pollution by sniffing social media. In: 2014 IEEE/ACM International Conference on Advances in Social Networks Analysis and Mining (ASONAM 2014), pp. 534–539 (2014). https://doi.org/10.1109/ASONAM.2014.6921638

19. Ni, M., Li, T., Li, Q., Zhang, H., Ye, Y.: FindMal: a file-to-file social network based malware detection framework. Knowl. Based Syst. **112**, 142–151 (2016). https://doi.org/10.1016/j.knosys.2016.09.004,https://www.sciencedirect.com/science/article/pii/S0950705116303215

20. Prim, R.C.: Shortest connection networks and some generalizations. Bell Syst. Tech. J. **36**(6), 1389–1401 (1957)

21. Samet, H., Sankaranarayanan, J., Alborzi, H.: Scalable network distance browsing in spatial databases. In: Proceedings of the 2008 ACM SIGMOD International Conference on Management of Data (SIGMOD), p. 43–54 (2008)

22. Sankaranarayanan, J., Samet, H., Alborzi, H.: Path oracles for spatial networks. Proc. VLDB Endow. **2**(1), 1210–1221 (2009)

23. Shiokawa, H.: Fast ObjectRank for large knowledge databases. In: Proceedings of the 20th International Semantic Web Conference (ISWC 2021) (2021)

24. Shiokawa, H.: Scalable affinity propagation for massive datasets. In: Proceedings of the AAAI Conference on Artificial Intelligence (AAAI 2021), vol. 35, 9639–9646, May 2021

25. Shiokawa, H., Amagasa, T., Kitagawa, H.: Scaling fine-grained modularity clustering for massive graphs. In: Proceedings of the Twenty-Eighth International Joint Conference on Artificial Intelligence (IJCAI 2019), pp. 4597–4604, July 2019
26. Shiokawa, H., Fujiwara, Y., Onizuka, M.: SCAN++: efficient algorithm for finding clusters, hubs and outliers on large-scale graphs. Proc. VLDB **8**(11), 1178–1189 (2015)
27. Shiokawa, H., Takahashi, T.: DSCAN: distributed structural graph clustering for billion-edge graphs. In: Database and Expert Systems Applications: 31st International Conference, DEXA 2020, Bratislava, Slovakia, 14–17 September 2020, Proceedings, Part I, pp. 38–54 (2020)
28. Kobayashi, S., Matsugu, H.S.: Indexing complex networks for fast attributed kNN queries. Soc. Netw. Anal. Mining **12**(82) (2022)
29. Suzuki, Y., Sato, M., Shiokawa, H., Yanagisawa, M., Kitagawa, H.: Masc: automatic sleep stage classification based on brain and myoelectric signals. In: 2017 IEEE 33rd International Conference on Data Engineering (ICDE), pp. 1489–1496 (2017). https://doi.org/10.1109/ICDE.2017.218
30. Zhong, R., Li, G., Tan, K.L., Zhou, L., Gong, Z.: G-Tree: an efficient and Scalable Index for spatial search on road networks. IEEE Trans. Knowl. Data Eng. **27**(8), 2175–2189 (2015)

IoT and Machine Learning

An Object Separated Storage Framework Towards Spatiotemporal Point Data Fast Query

Jin Yan[1,2] , Zhiming Ding[1] , and Shuai Zhang[1,2(✉)]

[1] Institute of Software Chinese Academy of Sciences, Beijing 100190, People's Republic of China
zhiming@iscas.ac.cn
[2] University of Chinese Academy of Sciences, Beijing 100049, People's Republic of China
{yvette.yan,zhangshuai191}@mails.ucas.edu.cn

Abstract. Advancement in the Internet of Things (IoT) has become the state-of-the-art technology and marketing trend among researchers due to the availability of the internet everywhere. Beyond the hype, IoT application has shown significant contribution from small to large scale applications in many fields. The IoT involves diverse devices inter-connected and produces vast data in the unit of minutes or even seconds. For the majority of situations, IoT devices produce point data with high timeliness requirements but relatively simple operations. To better cope with IoT point data in actual application scenarios, we propose a design of a two-layer index structure for a quick query of spatiotemporal data, and further reveal a meta-heuristic optimization strategy to overcome the limitations of data skew. The experiments on real-world datasets demonstrate that our method has a good efficiency in handling IoT point data.

Keywords: IoT point data · Spatiotemporal data · Quick query

1 Introduction

With the development of the Internet of Things, personal terminal systems, including our mobile phone terminals, vehicle-mounted systems, smart homes, etc., are constantly generating a large amount of data, the era of big data has entered a new stage of rapid development. Meanwhile, in growing scenarios nowadays such as smart cities [1], E-Commerce [2], Laboratory Monitoring [3] and many other domains [4–6], the Internet of Things has become a new trend. The number of connected IoT devices and sensors is increasing every single day, it will reach 2.3 trillion by 2025 according to Manyika J et al. [7]. These IoT data are producing rapidly, can reach a huge volume in a short time, and show diversity in types due to different sources. These characteristics continue to impact the existing data storage models, and at the same time challenge the management methods. How to further improve IoT data processing methods has become a continuous research topic.

IoT data often shows a high inner connection with both temporal and spatial properties. With the implementation of the Internet of Things (IoT) technology, spatiotemporal

© The Author(s), under exclusive license to Springer Nature Switzerland AG 2022
E. Pardede et al. (Eds.): iiWAS 2022, LNCS 13635, pp. 211–223, 2022.
https://doi.org/10.1007/978-3-031-21047-1_19

data has become the mainstream of IoT data. In most practical application scenarios, IoT data requires efficient write-in and reading without complex operations to satisfy actual needs. This is because almost all IoT sensors work in the pattern that one single sensor acquiesces one single data type (temperature, humidity, GPS location, etc.), and then the sensor sends data in a given frequency (per second, per minute, etc.). Therefore, the value density is relatively low for IoT data but timeliness requirements could be high. Since temporal features and spatial features are nonlinear and weakly related, previous spatiotemporal data management solutions have been carefully designed in indexing and organization. However, the capability could be better with consideration of characteristics of IoT sensing big data and actual scene requirement since the majority of data is in point type, and the efficiency of IoT data retrieval can be further improved.

In view of the above-mentioned shortcomings, this paper proposes a storage model framework design based on the storage object separation mechanism - Hierarchical Storage Framework Based on Storage Object Separation, HSF-SOS. The basic idea of this framework is dividing space and time separately, it provides a fast query method for IoT point data by making full use of the spatiotemporal information collected by IoT sensors combined with IoT scene requirements. The method serves query needs such as range query commonly used in IoT big data, improves query efficiency, realizes real-time query load balancing in various scenarios. For example, using real-time vehicle information, dynamically planning vehicle scheduling and preventing traffic jams; using personnel flow information to record the intersection of time and space between personnel, effectively preventing and controlling the spread of the epidemic, etc.

The paper is organized as follows. Section 2 introduces the previous study and related work in this area. Section 3 presents details of our design of the two-layer index structure for a quick query of spatio-temporal data. In Sect. 4, experiments and results are shown. Then we conclude this paper in Sect. 5.

2   Related Works

IN the area of spatio-temporal data management, the research on indexing technology for spatiotemporal data has been continuously developed to shorten users' retrieval response time and meet the needs of data analysis in a massive data environment [8]. There have been substantial studies and works related to spatio-temporal data storing and querying. However, the existing spatiotemporal databases and various spatiotemporal indexes are sometimes limited by taking care of all types of spatiotemporal data, and cannot achieve their highest efficiency for IoT point data in Euclidean space to meet increasing real-time needs in actual use. General solutions proposed at present are mainly developed based on different types of spatial data indexing. In the introduction of the previous study in this section, we roughly concluded them into two structures and gave a brief introduction: based on R-Tree [9] or Quad-Trees [10], such as 3DR-Tree [11], RT-Tree [12], STR-Tree and TB-Tree [13], HR-Tree [14], MV3R-Tree [15], The SEB-Tree [16], SETI-Tree [17], Overlapped Quad-Tree [18], ST-Tree [19], Traj-Store [20], etc., and based on space-filling curve, such as Geohash-Z2T, MGeohash [21], etc.

R-Tree is a self-balancing tree structure naturally developed from B+-Tree [22], which is specially used for searching spatial objects. The advantages of R-Tree include simple establishment and balanced structure. However, different minimum bounding rectangles (MBRs) will unavoidably have an overlapping and results to lower search efficiency. At the same time, the actual retrieval efficiency of R-Tree will also be significantly impacted by the data volume and data dimension. The basic idea of Quad-Tree which was first proposed by Finkel et al. [10] is plane area dividing. The implementation of Quad-Trees is easy with a quite clear structure. However, as the division process is almost completely based on the total amount of data in a certain area, a Quad-Tree could be unbalanced. The tree will be too deep for areas with massive data but too shallow for areas with sparse data. In extreme cases, the tree structure will even degenerate into a linear structure. Furthermore, the tree structure spatiotemporal index has three groups according to Mokbel M F et al. [23]: 1. Use spatial domain as a priority and temporal domain as secondary; 2. Use time-based multi-version spatial domain to discriminate spatial dimension and temporal dimension; 3. Use trajectory-oriented access method. Under this guideline, 3DR-TREE [11], RT-TREE [12], etc. belong to group one. The effectiveness is highly related to global information and has relatively weak support for real-time requirements. High update cost can either lead to lower efficiency or untimely updates. To deal with this, researchers then proposed solutions such as LUR-TREE [24], which reduced the cost of real-time index update when data was inserted and helped to process real-time data to a certain extent, but there was still a lag. There are arresting methods in group two, such as MR-Tree [25], HR-Tree [14], HR+-Tree [26], MV3R-Tree [15], etc. Although it can be used to process real-time data, redundancy will be generated resulting in less efficiency. Thus, it is still more capable for offline data. For group three, there are typical methods like TB-Tree [13], SETI [17], Traj-Store [20], etc. Since this paper focuses on IoT point data so group three will not be explained in detail.

The space-filling curve is another way of dividing space other than the tree structure. The space filling-line is essentially a dimensionality reduction method that maps high-dimensional space to one-dimensional space. It divides the high-dimensional space and finds a space-filling curve that completely penetrates all the sub-spaces so that the entire high-dimensional space can be encoded under some rules. After a long period of research and development, widely used space-filling include Z-Curve [27, 28], Hilbert-Curve [29, 30], and Gray-Code [31]. The most typical used scenario is GeoHsah encoding based on Z-Curve such as MGeohash [21], which includes Z2, Z3, Z2T, Z3T, and other encoding rules. However, the mutation is a common problem for indexes of the space-filling encoding type, leading to slow query times when querying near mutation points.

3 Methodology of Model Framework

In this section, we introduce the design of a storage model framework based on the storage object separation mechanism - Hierarchical Storage Framework Based on Storage Object Separation, HSF-SOS. For spatiotemporal point data, storage structure is important to avoid frequent global updates during writing and inefficiency query. HSF-SOS has a spatial-temporal two-layer structure as shown in Fig. 1. The Spatial index layer adopted a dynamic space division method based on data volume. In the temporal layer, one table is built for one individual sensor in each subspace in the Spatial layer. The coming data is written to the corresponding table in increasing time order. Due to the mechanism of one device corresponds to one table independently, data between different sensors does not affect each other. In the process of data writing, the relationship between previous and subsequent is not involved, avoiding the use of redundant locks.

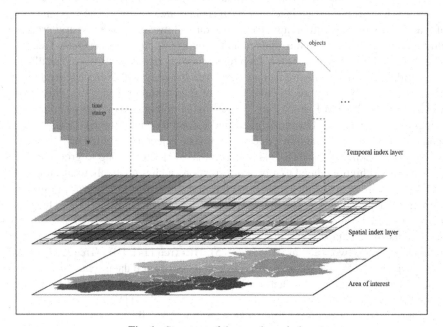

Fig. 1. Structure of the two-layer index.

Within each subspace, the table is retrieved using a B+ tree. Since data is generated by a fixed number of devices in this subspace which is a constant. Therefore, the index to the table is approximately static in size. Within each table, the data is sorted by time since the monotonically increasing of time and data is generated at unique moment.

3.1   Index Design

Spatial Index Layer. When performing spatiotemporal queries, a major request is to extract all required data from a specific area. Intuitively we can tell it must be time-consuming if all data needs to be visited to filter needed for each retrieval, which is not enough for the target of efficient retrieval time requirements under IoT. To shorten the retrieval time based on the idea of reducing the volume of data that needs to be traversed during each query. The Spatial index layer uses the smallest rectangle covered in the area of interest and performs uniform fine-grained spatial division on the rectangle so that the area is divided into grids. Then a Spatial data partition based on graph structure (SDGS) is proposed to prevent data skew. The SDGS will be described in detail in the next sub-section and the spatial unit after applying SDGS is called a block.

Temporal Index Layer. As mentioned above, one table is built for one individual sensor in each grid. For each IoT sensing device, the data is written in its own storage space.

Therefore, for data writing, one table includes the data of a single device of a block. In one single data table, the data is written by appending at the end. For example, we can use $grid^i_{object\_x}$ to represent the data of *object_x* within $i-th\,grid$. Since *object_x* is the only source of data writing, this writing method avoids the lock mechanism and buffer design problems caused by the judgment of arrival time in the multisource write centralized storage mode in the existing storage model.

Storage Structure. The storage organization of HSF-SOS includes the metadata layer, the hash layer and the data layer. The metadata layer is a centralized storage for IoT devices, which mainly includes two parts: the address of each grid in the Spatial layer, and the starting address of all devices globally. The hash layer is in charge of the logical management of the grid in the metadata layer. Through the SDGS method, the space area is dynamically divided according to the data volume, and the dynamic mapping relationship between block and grid is determined. The hash layer is a real-time record of this mapping relationship. In this layer, the data balance result is maintained. The data layer is the actual storage layer for IoT sampling data.

3.2 Prevention of Data Skew

With the development of modern cities, there will inevitably be uneven development between regions due to factors such as population, various types of infrastructure, education, and medical resources resulting in the formation of hotspot areas and relatively sparse areas which also affect the data collection process for all kinds of studies. The amount of collected data is also positively correlated with regional activities density. Obviously, the difference in the size of the generated data will cause the problem of data skew, resulting in the amount of data that needs to be traversed when querying certain hot areas being dramatically larger than querying some other areas.

Figure 2 shows an illustration of the hotspot effect in the city of Beijing, China. In this figure, the area surrounded by the black curve is relatively prosperous with

Fig. 2. A view of city hotspot of Beijing, China (The road map on the right side is from Beijing Urban Plan (2016–2035) appendix 15 http://www.beijing.gov.cn/gongkai/guihua/).

concentrated activities in the city. The degree of density can be seen from the enlarged road network diagram on the right. Outside this hotspot area, infrastructure including roads and buildings are significantly reduced so that human activities are significantly reduced as well.

In response to this problem, we propose a grids integration algorithm based on a meta-heuristic greedy strategy to balance the amount of data between each grid group and reduce the impact of data skew caused by hotspot areas. Algorithm 1 describes the process of grid grouping with a pseudocode illustrated in Table 1. The output of the algorithm will be a set, each element in this set is called a block, which is the grouping of some adjacent grids.

$$B = \{block_1, block_2, block_3, \ldots, block_n\} \tag{1}$$

Equation 1 is the format of an output set B, n depends on how many blocks pre-defined. When querying data, a block is used as the basic unit spatially to achieve load balancing.

Table 1. Algorithm of the process of grid grouping.

Algorithm 1
Input: evenly divided blocks
Output: balanced blocks
Iteratively calculate each region
1.   **while** r > threshold **do**
2.   **for** x in region:
3.   d = judgment_direction(x)
4.   **if** d is not in {left, right, top, bottom}
5.   break
6.   **else**
7.   find the minimum range R in the D direction
8.   adjust the region
9. $r_R = \sum_{i=1}^{R} (num_i - u)^2$
10.   update r use r_R
11.   **end for**
12. **end while**

The key construction steps of the set B are as follows:

Step I. Initialize the target area, combine the grids in the target area into n rectangular grids groups (blocks), where each block contains several grids (not necessarily the same number).

Step II. Initialize the weight of each block using Eq. 2.

$$weight_{block_i} = \sum_{j=1}^{m} nums_{grid_i^j} \tag{2}$$

where $grid_i \in block_i$, $grid_i^j$ is the j-th grid of $grid_i$, m is the number of grids in this block.

Step III. Calculate the ideally target average u using Eq. 3.

$$u = \frac{\sum_{i=1}^{n} weight_{block_i}}{n} \tag{3}$$

Step IV. Calculate the threshold indicator r using Eq. 4.

$$r = \sum_{i=1}^{n} \left(weight_{block_i} - u\right)^2 \tag{4}$$

Step V. Use the greedy strategy combined with the meta-heuristic algorithm to traverse every block. When $weight_{block_i} < u$ is satisfied, there will be a decision-making process for block expansion. For the expansion of a block, the maximum possible direction is four (upward, downward, left, and right). Serval new threshold indicators r_e will be calculated using Eq. 5 for the current block expands along one certain direction while all adjacent blocks connected with the edge shrink. Ideally, we hope that the value of r can be minimized since r represents the degree of difference in the amount of data in each block. However, to avoid falling into the local optimum, we do not choose the direction with the smallest r_e to expand simply in this algorithm. The random strategy of the meta-heuristic algorithm is adopted here to ensure global optimality.

$$r_e = \sum_{i'=1}^{n'} \left(weight_{block_{i'}} - u\right)^2 \tag{5}$$

As the expansion has four possible directions (up, down, left, and right), r_e could have four possible values denoted by $r_{e_1}, r_{e_2}, r_{e_3}$ and r_{e_4} respectively which can be calculated by using Eq. 5 four times. Noted that for blocks beside the edge of rectangle, the potential direction of expansion could go down to minimum two. Thus, the number of r_e could less than four, i.e., for $r_{e_i}, 2 \leq i \leq 4$. Note that only when $r - r_{e_i} > 0$, we consider this r_{e_i} valid, otherwise it will be omitted.

Step VI. Calculate the random operators $p_e(i)$ using Eq. 6.

$$p_e(i) = \frac{r - r_{e_i}}{\sum_{i=1}^{n}\left(r - r_{e_i}\right)}, r - r_{e_i} > 0, 2 \leq i \leq 4, 2 \leq n \leq 4 \tag{6}$$

where p_{e_i} represents the probability of the block expand along this direction.

Figure 3 shows an example of block expansion for the selected block on the right-up corner. First, the algorithm will look at four directions to check which of them can be expanded, here the edge of the block can go down or right since it is at the corner. Thus, only r_{e_2} and r_{e_4} will be calculated. Then the algorithm determines whether every r_{e_i} is greater than zero, and drops those non-positives. Following this step, $p_e(2)$ and $p_e(4)$ are calculated respectively which are the random operators of exploration. Finally, the algorithm performs the expansion randomly according to the calculated probability.

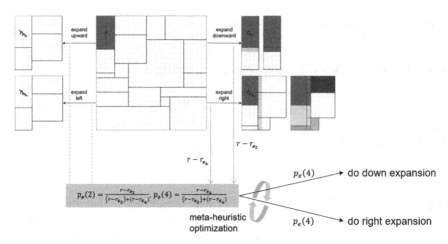

Fig. 3. Sample decision-making process for block expansion.

4   Experiments

4.1   Settings and Data

We conduct our experiments using x86_64 architecture server with Linux version 3.10.0–1160.24.1.el7.x86_64(gcc version 4.8.5 20150623 (Red Hat 4.8.5–44)). The server has 40 Intel(R) Xeon(R) Silver 4210R CPU @ 2.40 GHz CPU, and 2 sockets 10 cores per socket. The experimental environments include Hadoop 2.7.6, Hbase 1.3.6, Geo-Mesa-Hbase 2.1.3, Zookeeper 3.4.14, JDK 1.8.0, and TDEngine 2.1.7.2 as Geomesa is one of the most popular ways dealing with spatiotemporal data.

As a typical application scenario in the Internet of Things, the real-world taxi sensing data of the city of Beijing in December 2012 are selected as the testing data. The data contains nine columns, which are "Time-stamp, Car_ID, WGS84 longitude, WGS84 latitude, Company, Speed, Direction, Status, Event" respectively. The average size of one-day data is approximately vary from 3.5 to 7 GBs with over 1.66 billion available records which is about 150 GB in total after cleaning. The query type we presented for comparison here is range query since it is the most common query for spatiotemporal data and other queries such as temporal query and k-NN query can be performed based on range query.

4.2   Comparison and Analysis of Results

Result of Data Skew Prevention. IN this experiment, we used (115.43, 117.52) as the range of WGS84 longitude and (39.45, 41.06) as the range of WGS84 latitude for the city of Beijing. Figure 4(a) shows the selected area for data cleaning and importing.

Initially, the experimental area is divided into 1080 grids equal in size with 36 rows and 30 columns. The number of grids is determined by the length and width of the area needed. In our experiment, these grids divided the city of Beijing into grids with both

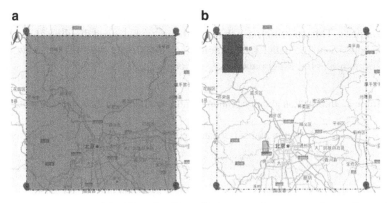

Fig. 4. (**a**) Selected area of the City of Beijing. (**b**) Dense and sparse area by random selection

length and width of no more than five kilometers as a threshold. Figure 5(a) shows the heatmap of 1080 grids representing the area of the city of Beijing, and Fig. 5(b) shows when these 1080 grids are equally divided into 36 blocks with each block contains 6 × 5 grids.

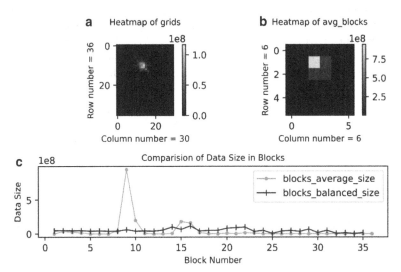

Fig. 5. (**a**) Heatmap of grids. (**b**) Heatmap of even blocks. (**c**) Results of data size comparison between even blocks and balanced blocks

It can be observed that there is an obvious hotspot area in the middle to south-west area. When 1080 grids are evenly divided into 36 blocks, the hotspot area naturally forms a new and larger hotspot area. Figure 5(c) shows the comparison of the amount of data in each block between partition with evenly dividing way and partition with the meta-heuristic balanced dividing algorithm.

Compare to the yellow line, the purple line is a relatively smooth curve shows no significant peak. Thus, partition use the meta-heuristic balanced dividing algorithm can achieve a better result on data load balancing, and effectively prevent data skew. Table 2 gives information about exact data pieces in details.

Table 2. Information about maximum/minimum number of data pieces in units.

	Maximum number of data records	Minimum number of data records
Grids	116,367,600	0
Even Blockc	943,437,473	0
Balanced Blocks	116,367,600	2,070,807

Result of Query Time Cost. The experiments of query time have two parts. The first part we tested the query time with and without the HSF-SOS in TDEngine. The second part we tested the query time for the same queries with the HSF-SOS use TDEngine and use GeoMesa. The reason of choosing GeoMesa to conduct the comparative experiments is that the indexing principle of GeoMesa is also to geographically partition the space. In each experiment, one dense area and one sparse area are selected for testing as shown in Fig. 4(b), the yellow shaded rectangle and the purple shaded rectangle respectively. For both experiments, the end time-stamp is set to "2012–12-28 00:00:00", Sql Query is used for extracting data in a given area within a given duration(24 h to 240 h in a 24 h step). Figure 6 shows the result of query time with and without the HSF-SOS.

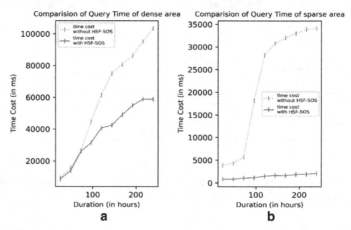

Fig. 6. (a) Line chart of comparison of query time cost between with the HSF-SOS and without HSF-SOS in selected dense area. (b) Line chart of comparison of query time cost between with the HSF-SOS and without HSF-SOS in selected sparse area. (Color figure online)

Figure 6(a) is the result in dense area and Fig. 6(b) is the result in sparse area. It can be observed that for orange lines (time cost without HSF-SOS), the time cost shows similar trend. That is because without HSF-SOS, there will be a global traversal no matter dense or sparse area. For blue lines, we can see the slope of both bule lines are not steep with it in dense area larger than it in sparse area due to the total amount of data is much less in sparse area.

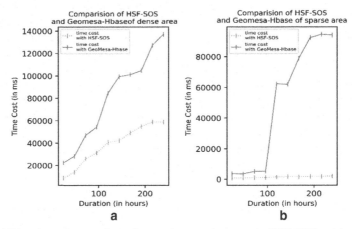

Fig. 7. (**a**) Line chart of comparison of query time cost between the HSF-SOS and the GeoMesa-Hbase in selected dense area. (**b**) Line chart of comparison of query time cost between the HSF-SOS and the GeoMesa-Hbase in selected sparse area.

From Fig. 7, can be seen that the overall trend is similar to Fig. 6. The leap of the bule line in Fig. 7(b) between duration = 96 h and duration = 120 h describes the mutation effect in GeoMesa. Table 3 illustrates some other experimental information.

Table 3. Detail experimental information.

Duration	24 h	48 h	72 h	96 h	120 h
Data Amount (dense)	625,369	1,288,007	2,072,975	2,475,050	3,093,417
Data Amount (sparse)	0	0	1	3	6
Duration	144 h	168 h	192 h	216 h	240 h
Data Amount (dense)	3,725,586	4,238,794	4,653,610	5,090,724	5,519,663
Data Amount (sparse)	148	180	182	190	190

The experimental result shows that with HSF-SOS, the time cost of duration queries are almost remains the same in sparse area while the time cost increases smoothly in dense area. The response time is significantly lower no matter which area is selected in both databases. Thus, HSF-SOS can be considered more suitable when dealing with real-time requirements of IoT point data.

5   Conclusion and Future Work

Compared with traditional indexing and storage methods, the advantages of the HSF-SOS include: The temporal index granularity is coarser than the traditional method, which can point to more data in unit memory, reducing the interaction between memory and disk I/O during retrieval; the strategy of spatial dividing and conquering data processing avoids the effects of data skew and reduces time consumption; data storage in adjacent time/space is continuous, which is convenient for batch reading and reduces addressing consumption. The evaluation shows short response time compare to other methods which verifies again our idea can better serve IoT spatiotemporal point data. Meanwhile, it is worth pointing out that the grids integration algorithm we proposed is rely on historical data so that it is necessary to know in advance the volume of each grid. Which means there is a certain lag in terms of real-time loads. In future research, we would like to explore if some time series model can be used in the algorithm to catch and predict the weight of grids. In this way, the load balancing strategy can dynamically adjust over time to achieve higher efficiency.

Acknowledgements. We would like to thank the National Natural Science Foundation of China (Grant No. 61703013 and No. 91646201), the National Key R&D Program of China (973 Program, No. 2017YFC0803300), the UCAS Scholarship, and the ANSO Scholarship for Young Talents.

References

1. Ahlgren, B., Hidell, M., Ngai, E.C.: Internet of things for smart cities: interoperability and open data. IEEE Internet Comput. **20**(6), 52–56 (2016)
2. Singh, S., Singh, N.: Internet of Things (IoT): security challenges, business opportunities & reference architecture for E-commerce. In: 2015 International Conference on Green Computing and Internet of Things (ICGCIoT), pp. 1577–1581 (2015)
3. Sun, T., Xu, Y., Li, J., Zhang, H.: Research on internet of things middleware technology for laboratory environmental monitoring. In: 2018 International Conference on Virtual Reality and Intelligent Systems (ICVRIS), pp. 544–547 (2018)
4. Hsieh, Y.: Internet of things pillow detecting sleeping quality. In: 2018 1st International Cognitive Cities Conference (IC3), pp. 266–267 (2018)
5. Li, X., Wan, P., Zhang, H., Li, M., Jiang, Y.: The application research of internet of things to oil pipeline leak detection. In: 2018 15th International Computer Conference on Wavelet Active Media Technology and Information Processing (ICCWAMTIP), pp. 211–214 (2018)
6. Rachman, F.A., Putrada, A.G., Abdurohman, M.: Distributed campus bike sharing system based-on internet of things (IoT). In: 2018 6th International Conference on Information and Communication Technology (ICoICT), pp. 333–336 (2018)
7. Manyika, J., Chui, M., Bughin, J.: Disruptive technologies: advances that will transform life, business, and the global economy (2013)
8. Mahmood, A.R., Punni, S., Aref, W.G.: Spatio-temporal access methods: a survey (2010–2017). GeoInformatica **23**, 1–36 (2019)
9. Guttman, A.: R-trees: a dynamic index structure for spatial searching. SIGMOD Rec **14**, 47–57 (1984)
10. Finkel, R.A., Bentley, J.L.: Quad trees a data structure for retrieval on composite keys. Acta Informatica **4**(1), 1–9 (1974)

11. Theodoridis, Y., Vazirgiannis, M., Sellis, T.: Spatio-temporal indexing for large multimedia applications. In: International Conference on Multimedia Computing and Systems, pp. 441–448. IEEE (1996)
12. Xu, X., Lu, J.H.W.: RT-tree: an improved R-tree indexing structure for temporal spatial databases. In: The International Symposium on Spatial Data Handling, pp. 1040–1049 (1990)
13. Pfoser, D., Jensen, C.S., Theodoridis, Y., et al.: Novel approaches to the indexing of moving object trajectories. In: The Proceedings of the VLDB Endowment (PVLDB 2000), pp. 395–406 (2000)
14. Nascimento, M.A., Silva, J.R.: Towards historical R-trees. In: Symposium on Applied Computing, pp. 235–240. ACM (1998)
15. Tao, Y., Papadias, D.: MV3R-tree: a spatio-temporal access method for timestamp and interval queries. In: The Proceedings of the VLDB Endowment (PVLDB 2001), pp. 431–440 (2001)
16. Song, Z., Roussopoulos, N.: SEB-tree: an approach to index continuously moving objects. In: Chen, M.-S., Chrysanthis, P.K., Sloman, M., Zaslavsky, A. (eds.) MDM 2003. LNCS, vol. 2574, pp. 340–344. Springer, Heidelberg (2003). https://doi.org/10.1007/3-540-36389-0_25
17. Chakka, V.P., Everspaugh, A., Patel, J.M.: Indexing large trajectory data sets with SETI. In: The Biennial Conference on Innovative Data Systems Research (CIDR 2003) (2003)
18. Tzouramanis, T., Vassilakopoulos, M., Manolopoulos, Y.: Overlapping linear quadtrees: a spatiotemporal access method. In: International Symposium on Advances in Geographic Information Systems, pp. 1–7. ACM (1998)
19. Liu, H., Xu, J., Zheng, K., Liu, C., Du, L., Wu, X.: Semantic-aware query processing for activity trajectories. In: Proceedings of the Tenth ACM International Conference on Web Search and Data Mining, pp. 283–292. ACM (2017)
20. Cudre-Mauroux, P., Wu, E., Madden, S.: Trajstore: an adaptive storage system for very large trajectory data sets. In: The International Conference on Data Engineering (ICDE 2010), pp 109–120. IEEE (2010)
21. Li, Z., Zhao, Z.: MGeohash: trajectory data index method based on historical data pre-partitioning. In: 2021 7th International Conference on Big Data Computing and Communications (BigCom), pp. 241–246 (2021)
22. Barsky, M., Thomo, A., Toth, Z., Zuzarte, C.: Online update of b-trees. In: Proceedings of the 19th ACM International Conference on Information and Knowledge Management, pp. 149–158. ACM, October 2010
23. Mokbel, M.F., Ghanem, T.M., Aref, W.G.: Spatio-temporal access methods. IEEE Data Eng. Bull. **26**(2), 40–49 (2003)
24. Kwon, D., Lee, S., Lee, S.: Indexing the current positions of moving objects using the lazy update R-tree. In: International Conference on Mobile Data Management (MDM 2003), pp. 113–120. IEEE (2002)
25. Xu, X., Han, J., Lu, W.: RT-tree: an improved r-tree indexing structure for temporal spatial databases. In: Proceedings of the International Symposium on Spatial Data Handling, SDH, pp. 1040–1049, July 1990
26. Tao, Y., Papadias, D.: Efficient historical R-trees. In: The International Conference on Scientific and Statistical Database Management (SSDBM 2001), p. 0223. IEEE (2001)
27. Orenstein, J.: A comparison of spatial query processing techniques for native and parameter spaces. ACM (1990)
28. Bohm, C.: XZ-Ordering: a space-filling curve for objects with spatial extension. In: Proceedings of 6th International Symposium, SSD 1999, Hong Kong, China, July 1999
29. Faloutsos, C., Roseman, S.: Fractals for secondary key retrieval. ACM (1989)
30. Jagadish, H.: Linear clustering of objects with multiple attributes. ACM, New York (1990)
31. Faloutsos, C.: Multiattribute hashing using Gray codes. ACM, New York (1986)

Streaming Augmented Lineage: Traceability of Complex Stream Data Analysis

Masaya Yamada[1,2]([✉]) [iD], Hiroyuki Kitagawa[1,2]([✉]) [iD],
Salman Ahmed Shaikh[2] [iD], Toshiyuki Amagasa[1] [iD], and Akiyoshi Matono[2] [iD]

[1] University of Tsukuba, Tsukuba, Ibaraki, Japan
`yamada@kde.cs.tsukuba.ac.jp`, {`kitagawa,amagasa`}`@cs.tsukuba.ac.jp`
[2] National Institute of Advanced Industrial Science and Technology,
Koto-ku, Tokyo, Japan
{`shaikh.salman,a.matono`}`@aist.go.jp`

Abstract. Data lineage specifies which source tuples contribute to which output tuples and enables us to ensure the traceability of the analysis. Today, innumerable IoT devices and sensors are producing massive amounts of stream data at high velocity. Stream processing is often deployed to continuously process such stream data in realtime. Modern data analysis has become more complex due to the rapid development of AI and machine learning, and stream processing is no exception. Data lineage needs to be enriched to address this increasing complexity. In this paper, we propose *streaming augmented lineage*. *Augmented lineage* presents the reason why AI/ML processing derives the output data along with the ordinary lineage to enhance the traceability of the complex data analysis including AI/ML processing. Streaming augmented lineage provides augmented lineage in complex stream processing. We describe how to implement our scheme on Flink, and show detailed performance evaluations on the prototype system.

Keywords: Streaming augmented lineage · Stream processing · Apache flink · AI

1 Introduction

Today, innumerable IoT devices, such as smartphones and sensors, are continuously producing a massive amount of stream data. Explosion of such stream data is demanding for deployment of stream processing engines (SPEs), enabling us to extract useful information and knowledge in realtime. To realize trustful use of information and knowledge, ensuring the traceability of data analysis is essential. In other words, the users should be able to understand why the analysis results are obtained.

For traceability of analysis, extracting metadata on the derivation of analysis results has been researched in several domains under the topic of data provenance, including database systems, scientific workflow, and big data processing

E. Pardede et al. (Eds.): iiWAS 2022, LNCS 13635, pp. 224–236, 2022.
https://doi.org/10.1007/978-3-031-21047-1_20

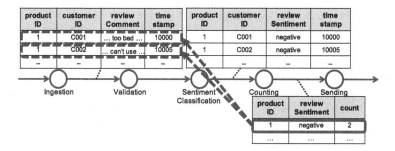

Fig. 1. Product review analysis in stream processing, including a text-sentiment classifier. Tuples surrounded by dashed lines are the data lineage of the output tuple $\langle 1, negative, 2 \rangle$.

systems [1,4,8]. In particular, data lineage has been studied for a long time. The *lineage* of an output tuple means the set of all input tuples which contribute to the derivation of the tuple [2]. It has been well researched in the database field [2,3]. Some past researches also focus on lineage in stream processing [6,12].

Modern data analysis has become more complex since they often incorporate sophisticated AI/ML processing schemes to derive output tuples, and stream processing is no exception. For such complex analysis, the conventional data lineage cannot ensure sufficient traceability, since reasoning inside the AI/ML processing plays an important role in understanding why the outputs are derived. Let us consider the following example.

Example 1. Figure 1 shows the product review analysis using stream processing conducted by a company running an online shopping service. This analysis continuously receives each review as a tuple consisting of four attributes (productID, customerID, reviewComment, timestamp). Then, it validates the source tuple, applies a text-sentiment classifier to the reviewComment attribute, and counts the number of positive reviews and negative reviews for each product. Finally, the output tuple is sent to upstream applications. Let us consider why an output tuple $\langle 1, negative, 2 \rangle$ was derived in this analysis. Using the conventional lineage, we can obtain $\{\langle 1, C001, \text{``... too bad ...''} , 10000 \rangle, \langle 1, C002, \text{``... can't use ...''} , 10005 \rangle\}$ as the source of the output tuple. Although we are given the two source tuples as the origin of the output tuple, we may not understand why the text-sentiment classifier classified these tuples as negative. Namely, in this case, we cannot understand why the output tuple was derived only by the conventional lineage. To resolve this problem, we will include additional information explaining the reason why the text-sentiment classifier regarded these review comments as negative. For example, the classifier can show that the first source tuple with timestamp 10000 was classified as negative because the positive and negative likelihoods are 0.05 and 0.95, respectively. The classifier will show similar information for the second source tuple. If such information is derived along with lineage, we understand why an output tuple of complex analysis was derived.

In our previous work [15], we proposed *augmented lineage*, which provides the reason for complex content analysis like AI/ML processing along with data lineage. However, our previous work considered only static data analysis such as database analysis and file-based data analysis. Our proposed method derives augmented lineage assuming that original data resides as static datasets and is always queriable. Therefore, applying this method to stream processing is impossible since source tuples constantly arrive in stream processing where the source dataset is transient. In this paper, we propose *streaming augmented lineage*, which realizes augmented lineage in the context of stream processing and ensures enhanced traceability for the complex streaming data analysis. We have developed the prototype system implementing streaming augmented lineage on Apache Flink. We have used GeneaLog, the state-of-the-art framework to derive lineage in stream processing [12], as a basis of our development. We explain our implementation and performance evaluation on our prototype. Our evaluation using a real dataset shows that the overhead for deriving streaming augmented lineage with respect to latency and throughput is very small.

The rest of this paper is organized as follows: Sect. 2 overviews related works. Section 3 describes the stream processing model and the abstraction of Genea-Log. Section 4 describes streaming augmented lineage and explains its derivation scheme in our prototype system. Section 5 investigates the performance of our prototype system. Section 6 concludes this paper.

2   Related Work

2.1   Provenance of Database Management System

Many studies have been done on provenance and lineage derivation methods for database queries [3,5,7]. Researches [3,7] focus on the RDBMS queries and derive tuple-level provenance. [3] derives "lineage" of an analysis modeled by the relational operators using reverse queries called tracing queries, and [7] attaches source tuples' identifiers to all in-flight tuples and inherits them to output tuples. For more general queries, [5] proposes the provenance derivation scheme for XQuery. Beyond the database queries, the provenance derivation on big data processing systems also has been researched (e.g., MapReduce [1] and Spark [10]). However, since these works derive only source tuples corresponding to output tuples, such frameworks cannot ensure sufficient traceability for the complex analysis including AI/ML processing. Our previous work [15] proposes augmented lineage, which includes the reason of the complex processing along with the conventional data lineage. However, since [15] assumes the static data analysis, it is not possible to apply the proposed method to stream processing.

2.2   Provenance for Stream Processing

The study of provenance in stream processing is much limited. As early research, [13] showed which source streams contribute to output streams as the coarse-grained provenance. This method cannot track which "tuples" contribute to output tuples. [14] proposed the method which derives provenance depending on rule of operators. Since this approach derives the provenance based on the timestamp of each source tuple, fine-grained provenance can be obtained. However, this method requires that rules be manually defined in advance to specify which input tuples contribute to an output tuple for all operators. This requirement is hard to meet in modern stream processing applications, which usually employ many application-dependent sophisticated operators.

[6] and [12] capture data lineage in stream processing executed on more modern SPEs. Ariadne [6] captures the lineage by the operator instrumentation, and in-flight stream tuples are attached with the annotation for identifying source tuples. However, since the annotation is variable-size data, a huge overhead can occur in ordinary stream processing, as shown in [12]. GeneaLog [12] also uses annotated stream tuples for deriving lineage, but the annotated tuples have only four additional attributes, which makes the size of the annotated tuple fixed. It is shown that it can derive lineage with low overhead compared with [6]. Therefore, our implementation uses GeneaLog as a basis, and we will explain it in more detail in the next section.

3   Stream Processing and Lineage

3.1   Stream Processing Model

Stream S consists of an unbounded sequence of tuples. A tuple t has its timestamp (τ) and attribute values $(t = \langle \tau, a_1, \ldots, a_m \rangle)$. Stream processing consists of a number of operators, which take one or more input streams and return an output stream, and is specified as a DAG structure whose nodes represent operators.

There are three types of operators. The first type, I/O, includes *source* and *sink*. They are responsible for ingesting/feeding tuples from/to external systems. The second type (Transformer) has *map*, *filter*, *union*, *aggregate*, and *join*, which are general operators in SPEs. Note that time-based window instances are generated in the aggregation and join operators, and these operators execute their processing for each window instance. The third type has *send* and *receive*, which communicate tuples between threads.

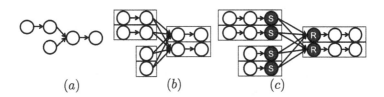

(a) $\qquad\qquad\qquad$ (b) $\qquad\qquad\qquad$ (c)

Fig. 2. Stream processing flow. (a) Logical representation. (b) Physical representation. (c) Insertion of send (S) and receive (R) operators.

Figure 2(a) represents a DAG for stream processing composed of two sources, two transformers, and one sink. This DAG logically models and represents the stream processing flow. When the processing is executed on an SPE running in a multitask processing environment such as a cluster machine, multiple operator instances are instantiated for each node. Figure 2(b) shows the physical representation of Fig. 2(a) when it is executed in parallelism two. A rectangle represents a thread, which is an execution unit in the SPE, and tuples are transmitted among threads. For this purpose, the send operator is inserted after the last operator of the sending thread, and the receive operator is inserted before the first operator of the receiving thread, as shown in Fig. 2(c). Usually, the send and receive also need to take care of serialization and deserialization of transferred tuples, respectively.

3.2 Streaming Lineage Framework: GeneaLog

We describe GeneaLog [12], the state-of-the-art framework to derive lineage in stream processing. We have employed GeneaLog as the basis of our implementation of streaming augmented lineage. In GeneaLog, all tuples generated by any operator are annotated with additional metadata for lineage. The metadata attached to the final output tuple provides clues to trace back to its source tuples. This technique is called *operator instrumentation*. GeneaLog derives lineage of an output tuple by traversing a graph structure implied by the metadata of the output tuple. We will give more details of GeneaLog, explaining 1) additional metadata, 2) operator instrumentation, 3) contribution graph traversal for lineage derivation, and 4) lineage derivation in multitask processing environment.

Additional Metadata: The metadata consists of four attributes (*Type*, *U1*, *U2*, and *Next*). Type identifies the operator which generated the metadata. U1, U2, and Next are pointers used to identify the input tuples which contribute to this output tuple in the operator.

Operator Instrumentation: Each operator is instrumented to generate the metadata based on the input tuple(s). Here, we describe the operator instrumentation taking the aggregate operator as an example.

Instrumented Aggregation: An aggregation operator takes $t_{in_1}, \ldots, t_{in_n}$ in a window instance and returns t_{out}. Under operator instrumentation, the following metadata is attached to the input/output tuples.

(1) $t_{out}.Type = Aggregation$ (2) $t_{out}.U1 = t_{in_n}$ and $t_{out}.U2 = t_{in_1}$
(3) $t_{in_i}.Next = t_{in_{i+1}}$ $(i = 1, \ldots, n-1)$

In the case of the source operator, the instrumented source just assigns "Source" in the output's Type because tuples output from the source are origins themselves. Filter and union do not attach any metadata because they just let input tuples pass through the operators and do not generate new ones. Map and join generate an output tuple from one and two input tuples, respectively. The instrumented map assigns "Map" in the Type and stores a pointer to the input tuple in U1, and the instrumented join assigns "Join" and stores a pair of pointers in U1 and U2.

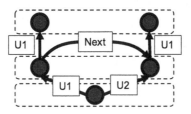

Fig. 3. Contribution graph

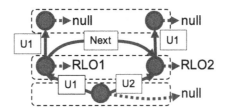

Fig. 4. Extended contribution graph

Contribution Graph Traversal: Given an output tuple t from the stream processing flow, it has metadata pointing to its own immediate input tuples. Then, the input tuples again have metadata pointing to their own immediate input tuples. Therefore, if we recursively trace back the pointers, we get a graph structure (Fig. 3) for the stream processing in Fig. 1. The structure is called *contribution graph*, where each node and edge represent a tuple and pointer to its input tuple, respectively. In Fig. 3, the bottom node represents the final output tuple ($\langle 1, negative, 2 \rangle$), the top nodes represents source tuples which contribute to the output tuple, and intermediate nodes represent output tuples of the map operator. The basic scheme of GeneaLog is to traverse the contribution graph until reaching source tuples and derive them as the lineage.

Lineage Derivation in Multitask Processing Environments: If a tuple is transmitted from a thread to another, U1 and U2 of the transmitted tuple may become invalid because U1 and U2 are pointers to the input tuples, namely addresses in the sender's memory space, and cannot be referred to by the receiver, since the receiver may have its own memory space. To resolve this problem, GeneaLog provides an explicit and an implicit approach. Our implementation employs the implicit approach, which we will elaborate on below.

As mentioned above, the send and receive operators are added for transmitting tuples among threads. In the implicit approach, when the send operator sends a tuple, it assigns "REMOTE" to the tuple and derives its lineage by traversing the contribution graph. Then, it serializes and transmits the source tuples together with the tuple to be sent. When the receive operator receives them, it attaches metadata and constructs a graph using the received tuple and the source tuples as described below.

Instrumented Receive: Let us assume that the receive operator receives t_{out} and source tuples $t_{s_1}, \ldots, t_{s_n}$ of t_{out}. The instrumented receive attaches metadata and constructs a graph as follows. Then, it ships t_{out} to the next operator.

(1) $t_{out}.U1 = t_{s_n}$ and $t_{out}.U2 = t_{s_1}$ (2) $t_{s_i}.Next = t_{s_{i+1}}$ $(i = 1, \ldots, n-1)$

4   Streaming Augmented Lineage

4.1   Definition

This section defines streaming augmented lineage to ensure enhanced traceability for stream processing including AI/ML processing. Streaming augmented lineage of the tuple t is the pair of two types of lineage: *Source lineage* and *Reasoning Lineage*. Source lineage is the set of all source tuples which contributes to the derivation of t. The source lineage is the same as the conventional lineage. Reasoning lineage is the set of reasons which explain how AI/ML processing produces t or its relevant components. Concretely, a reason consists of four attributes (OPid, Input, Output, Reason). OPid identifies the operator involving the AI/ML processing which generated the reason, and Input and Output specify the input and result of the AI/ML processing, respectively. Reason is the information generated by the AI/ML processing to explain why the result is derived from the specified input tuple. Therefore, we can understand what operator, which inputs, and why the output is derived from the reasoning lineage. For example, streaming augmented lineage of the tuple $\langle 1, negative, 2 \rangle$ is shown in Fig. 5. To utilize the reasoning lineage, the designer of the AI/ML processing module needs to provide a code which outputs the reason for each invocation of the AI/ML processing. Our implementation scheme provides the designer with an interface to register the reason for streaming augmented lineage generation.

$$\left[\left\{ \begin{array}{l} \langle\, 1,\ C001,\ ``\ldots\text{too bad}\ \ldots",\ 10000\,\rangle \\ \langle\, 1,\ C002,\ ``\ldots\text{can't use}\ \ldots",\ 10005\,\rangle \end{array} \right\},\ \left\{ \begin{array}{l} \langle\ \text{Map},\ \langle\, 1,\ C001,\ ``\ldots\text{too bad}\ \ldots",\ 10000\,\rangle, \\ \quad \text{negative},\ ``\text{Positive: } 0.05,\ \text{Negative: } 0.95"\ \rangle \\ \langle\ \text{Map},\ \langle\, 1,\ C002,\ ``\ldots\text{can't use}\ \ldots",\ 10005\,\rangle, \\ \quad \text{negative},\ ``\text{Positive: } 0.20,\ \text{Negative: } 0.80"\ \rangle \end{array} \right\} \right]$$

Fig. 5. Streaming augmented lineage of $\langle 1, negative, 2 \rangle$

4.2   Implementation

In this section, we explain how we implemented streaming augmented lineage on top of GeneaLog. We separate the explanation into 1) additional metadata, 2) operator instrumentation, and 3) graph traversal. To simplify the explanation, we assume that the AI/ML processing which generates the reason information is executed in the map operation. However, we can handle other cases similarly where the reason information is generated by other operators.

Additional Metadata: We add a new attribute RL to the original metadata. RL is the pointer to a set of reasoning lineage objects. A reasoning lineage object consists of four attributes (OPid, Input, Output, Reason) as explained in Sect. 4.1.

Operator Instrumentation: The RL value is set when an operator generates an output tuple as well as the other metadata attributes. If we need a reason for output, the map operator is instrumented as shown below.

Instrumented Map for Streaming Augmented Lineage: We assume that the map operator takes t_{in} and returns t_{out} ($t_{out} = Map(t_{in})$), where $t_{out}.v$ is the attribute value derived by AI/ML processing in the map operator for the reason $REASON$. In this case, the instrumented map operator constructs the following output's metadata.

(1) $t_{out}.Type = Map$ (2) $t_{out}.U1 = t_{in}$
(3) $t_{out}.RL = \{\langle Map, t_{in}, t_{out}.v, REASON \rangle\}$

Our system provides the interface for application designers to register the reasoning lineage object for t_{out}. They can easily set the reasoning lineage object by embedding the following code in their map operator before returning t_{out}.

```
// t_in/t_out: Input/output tuples of the map operator
// output/reason: The result value/reason of AI/ML processing
Reason.registerReasonInfo("Map", t_in, output, reason, t_out);
```

We also extend the instrumented send/receive operators to derive the streaming augmented lineage. The extended send operator derives augmented lineage instead of lineage before sending a tuple. The extended receive operator sets the reasoning lineage objects to RL attribute in addition to metadata and graph construction as in the original receive operator.

Contribution Graph Traversal: The new attribute RL values are included in the extended contribution graphs. The extended contribution graph of $\langle 1, negative, 2 \rangle$ in Fig. 1 is shown in Fig. 4. Note that the dotted arrow represents RL pointers. The difference from Fig. 3 is added RL pointers. Over such an extended contribution graph, we can derive streaming augmented lineage by applying Algorithm 1. Note that when the RL attribute is not set in an operator, the value is null. *enqueueIfNotVisited* takes a tuple, a queue (q), and a *visited* set of tuples and checks if the tuple has been already visited. If not, *enqueueIfNotVisited* enqueues the tuple into q and adds it to

---

Algorithm 1 Derive Streaming Augmented Lineage

Input: Output tuple t_{out}
Output: Streaming Augmented Lineage of t_{out}
 1: Initialize q as a queue $\{t_{out}\}$ and *visited*, SL, and RL as empty sets.
 2: **while** q has any element **do**
 3:     $t = q.dequeue()$
 4:     **if** $t.RL \neq null$ and $t.RL.size > 0$ **then**
 5:         $RL = RL \cup \{t.RL\}$
 6:     **if** $t.Type$ is Source **then**
 7:         $SL = SL \cup \{t\}$
 8:     **else if** $t.Type$ is Map **then**
 9:         $enqueueIfNotVisited(t.U1, \ q, \ visited)$
10:     **else if** $t.Type$ is Join **then**
11:         $enqueueIfNotVisited(t.U1, \ q, \ visited)$
12:         $enqueueIfNotVisited(t.U2, \ q, \ visited)$
13:     **else if** $t.Type$ is Aggregate or REMOTE **then**
14:         $t_{tmp} = t.U2$
15:         **while** $True$ **do**
16:             $enqueueIfNotVisited(t_{tmp}, \ q, \ visited)$
17:             **if** $t_{tmp} == t.U1$ **then**
18:                 break
19:             $t_{tmp} = t_{tmp}.Next$
20: **return** $[SL, RL]$

---

visited. Otherwise, it does nothing. This algorithm is based on GeneaLog, and the main extension is lines 4 and 5. These lines mean that if a given tuple has reasoning lineage objects along with other conventional metadata ($t.RL \neq null$ and $t.RL.size > 0$), they are added to RL. By the extension, the algorithm can derive reasoning lineage as well.

5   Experiments

This section evaluates our steaming augmented lineage implementation on a cluster environment. Our experiment consists of two parts: 1) Synthetic data evaluation and 2) Real data evaluation. Both parts are based on Amazon review data [11]. We evaluate the latency and throughput of stream processing in three cases: 1) Execute the processing without lineage (Baseline), 2) Execute the processing with deriving only lineage (Lineage), and 3) Execute the processing with deriving streaming augmented lineage (SAL). Latency and lineage traversing time are measured for each source tuple in one trial. The throughput is measured for five trials. We used a cluster for the evaluation, which consists of a two-node Apache Flink cluster (one Job Manager and one Task Manager with four task slots) and a three-node Apache Kafka cluster (one Zookeeper and two Broker Nodes). Each node has 128 GB of memory and 10 CPU cores.

5.1 Stream Processing Flows

We consider two processing flows: Realtime processing and Window processing flows. Both processing flows ingest a review data stream from Apache Kafka. In the processing flows, we use only productID, productScore, review comment attributes though ingested tuples may have other attributes. Realtime processing applies a text-sentiment classifier to decide whether each review comment is positive or negative, and outputs the result. The processing consists of the following operators: Source-Map-Filter-Map-Sink. Note that the first map operator is just for data transformation, and the second one performs text analysis. The filter operator eliminates tuples with missing values but lets almost all tuples pass through in these experiments. Window processing periodically outputs window-based aggregates counting the numbers of positive and negative comments for each product. The processing consists of the following operators: Source-Map-Filter-Map-Aggregate-Sink.

In the synthetic data evaluation, we employ a dataset slightly modified from the original review dataset and a dummy text classifier to minimize the distortion caused by data skew and fluctuation of the processing time. In the modified dataset, the key values are adjusted to follow the uniform distribution, and all source tuples are set to the equal size. The dummy map operator just idles for a fixed time interval, not actually analyzing the text, and always returns "positive" and the fixed reason string for each input tuple. In the real data evaluation, we employ the original review dataset as source and the text-sentiment classifier provided by IBM [9] is invoked in the map operator.

5.2 Synthetic Data Evaluation

In this evaluation, we measure latency and throughput when the following three properties are changed.

- Processing cost of the dummy text classifier: Idling time interval before output. **Light**: no idling, **Heavy**: 200 milliseconds.
- Source tuple length: Length of the comment attribute value. **Short**: 1 byte, **Long**: 35,094 bytes (the length of the longest comment in the original dataset).
- Window size: **Small**: 1 s window, **Large**: 100 s window.

Each configuration of the three properties is denoted by x/x/x, which shows processing cost, source tuple length, and window size in this order. For example, H/L/S stands for heavy processing cost, long source tuple length, and small window size. In the realtime processing flow, the window size item is "-" (not defined).

Figure 6 shows the average latency and throughput in the synthetic data evaluation. Note that ** suggests statistical difference at a significance level 1 %. In realtime processing, when the processing cost is heavy, the impact of deriving augmented lineage on the latency and throughput is very small. Even though

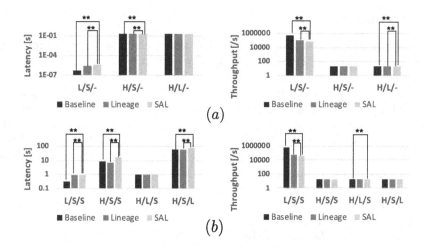

Fig. 6. Latency/Throughput of (a) realtime processing and (b) window processing

there is a statistically significant difference, note that the latency of SAL in H/S/- is x1.0002 of Baseline and x1.0001 of Lineage, and the throughput of SAL in H/L/- is x0.98 of Baseline and x0.99 of Lineage. It means that the overhead of SAL is almost negligible. The reason is that the processing cost of the dummy text classifier is dominant over the whole stream processing, and additional computation caused by the streaming augmented lineage is very small. On the other hand, when the processing cost is light, the performance overhead becomes much evident. The latency of SAL is increased by x8.4 and x1.6 compared to Baseline and Lineage, respectively, and the throughput of SAL becomes x0.14 of Baseline and x0.72 of Lineage. The reason is that traversing the contribution graphs of output tuples takes much cost in this case.

In window processing, when the processing cost is heavy, we can see that the impact of deriving the streaming augmented lineage on the throughput is small. Though there is a statistically significant difference in the throughput in H/L/S, the throughput of SAL is x0.996 of Baseline, which means the impact is very small. The latency is affected by source tuple length. The increase of the latency is negligible when the source tuple length is long, while the increase becomes clear when source tuple length is short. On the other hand, when the processing cost is light, the increase of the latency and throughput becomes more clear compared to Baseline because of the additional cost for streaming augmented lineage. The latency of SAL in L/S/S is x2.8 of Baseline and x1.03 of Lineage.

5.3   Real Data Evaluation

The real data evaluation invokes a neural network-based text classifier with heavy processing cost, and the source tuple length varies a lot in the real review dataset. The window size in the window processing is set to 1 s. Therefore, this

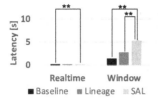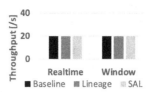

Fig. 7. Latency/Throughput of the real data evaluation

experiment roughly corresponds to H/S/- and H/L/- in realtime processing and H/S/S and H/L/S in window processing.

Figure 7 shows the result. Since this experiment corresponds to the case of the heavy processing cost, the impact for deriving streaming augmented lineage is very small in the realtime processing. Note that the latency of SAL in realtime processing is x0.996 of Baseline. Besides, there is little impact on the throughput in the window processing. The latency in window processing is increased by x3.6 of Baseline and x1.9 of Lineage, because the ratio of short source tuples is high.

6   Conclusions

In this paper, we have proposed the streaming augmented lineage, which derives tuple-level origin and the reason of the derivation in the AI/ML processing for each output tuple online. Streaming augmented lineage can enhance the reliability of data produced by stream processing including AI/ML processing. We described the derivation method for the streaming augmented lineage and implemented it on Apache Flink based on the GeneaLog framework. We evaluated the performance of our scheme using synthetic data and real data, and the result suggests that the proposed method to derive augmented lineage tends to give only small impact on the stream processing when the cost of AI/ML processing is dominant, which is common in real cases.

Future research issues include more intensive evaluations using other datasets and processing flows, deployment in real stream applications, and implementation on other SPEs. Making augmented lineage information persistent, like lineage DB, is also an interesting research topic.

Acknowledgments. This work was partly supported by JSPS KAKENHI Grant Numbers JP19H04114 and JP20K19806, NEDO Grant Number JPNP20006, AMED Grant Number JP21zf0127005, and JST SPRING Grant Number JPMJSP2124.

References

1. Akoush, S., Sohan, R., Hopper, A.: Hadoopprov: towards provenance as a first class citizen in mapreduce. In: 5th USENIX Workshop on the Theory and Practice of Provenance (2013)

2. Cui, Y., Widom, J.: Practical lineage tracing in data warehouses. In: Proceedings of 16th International Conference on Data Engineering, pp. 367–378 (2000)
3. Cui, Y., Widom, J., Wiener, J.L.: Tracing the lineage of view data in a warehousing environment. ACM Trans. Database Syst. **25**(2), 179–227 (2000)
4. Davidson, S.B., Freire, J.: Provenance and scientific workflows: challenges and opportunities. In: Proceedings of the 2008 ACM SIGMOD International Conference on Management of Data, pp. 1345–1350 (2008)
5. Foster, J.N., Green, T.J., Tannen, V.: Annotated XML: queries and provenance. In: Proceedings of the Twenty-Seventh ACM SIGMOD-SIGACT-SIGART Symposium on Principles of Database Systems, pp. 271–280 (2008)
6. Glavic, B., Sheykh Esmaili, K., Fischer, P.M., Tatbul, N.: Ariadne: managing fine-grained provenance on data streams. In: Proceedings of the 7th ACM International Conference on Distributed Event-Based Systems, pp. 39–50 (2013)
7. Green, T.J., Karvounarakis, G., Tannen, V.: Provenance semirings. In: Proceedings of the Twenty-Sixth ACM SIGMOD-SIGACT-SIGART Symposium on Principles of Database Systems, pp. 31–40 (2007)
8. Herschel, M., Diestelkämper, R., Ben Lahmar, H.: A survey on provenance: what for? what form? what from? VLDB J. **26**(6), 881–906 (2017)
9. IBM: Text Sentiment Classifier - IBM Developer. https://developer.ibm.com/exchanges/models/all/max-text-sentiment-classifier/
10. Interlandi, M., et al.: Titian: data provenance support in spark. In: Proceedings of the VLDB Endowment International Conference on Very Large Data Bases, vol. 9, pp. 216–227 (2015)
11. Ni, J., Li, J., McAuley, J.: Justifying recommendations using distantly-labeled reviews and fine-grained aspects. In: Proceedings of the 2019 Conference on Empirical Methods in Natural Language Processing and the 9th International Joint Conference on Natural Language Processing (EMNLP-IJCNLP), pp. 188–197 (2019)
12. Palyvos-Giannas, D., Gulisano, V., Papatriantafilou, M.: Genealog: fine-grained data streaming provenance in cyber-physical systems. Parallel Comput. **89** (2019)
13. Vijayakumar, N.N., Plale, B.: Towards low overhead provenance tracking in near real-time stream filtering. In: Provenance and Annotation of Data, pp. 46–54 (2006)
14. Wang, M., Blount, M., Davis, J., Misra, A., Sow, D.: A time-and-value centric provenance model and architecture for medical event streams. In: Proceedings of the 1st ACM SIGMOBILE International Workshop on Systems and Networking Support for Healthcare and Assisted Living Environments, pp. 95–100 (2007)
15. Yamada, M., Kitagawa, H., Amagasa, T., Matono, A.: Augmented lineage: traceability of data analysis including complex UDFS. In: Database and Expert Systems Applications, pp. 65–77 (2021)

A Web Application for Experimenting and Validating Remote Measurement of Vital Signs

Amtul Haq Ayesha$^{(\boxtimes)}$, Donghao Qiao , and Farhana Zulkernine

Queen's University, Kingston, ON, Canada
{20aha,d.qiao,farhana.zulkernine}@queensu.ca

Abstract. With a surge in online medical advising remote monitoring of patient vitals is required. This can be facilitated with the Remote Photoplethysmography (rPPG) techniques that compute vital signs from facial videos. It involves processing video frames to obtain skin pixels, extracting the cardiac data from it and applying signal processing filters to extract the Blood Volume Pulse (BVP) signal. Different algorithms are applied to the BVP signal to estimate the various vital signs. We implemented a web application framework to measure a person's Heart Rate (HR), Heart Rate Variability (HRV), Oxygen Saturation (SpO$_2$), Respiration Rate (RR), Blood Pressure (BP), and stress from the face video. The rPPG technique is highly sensitive to illumination and motion variation. The web application guides the users to reduce the noise due to these variations and thereby yield a cleaner BVP signal. The accuracy and robustness of the framework was validated with the help of volunteers, and their privacy was protected using face masking techniques.

Keywords: Remote photoplethysmography · Deep learning · Vital signs measurement · Computer vision

1 Introduction

Measurement of vital signs like the HR, HRV, SpO$_2$, BP, stress and temperature are important to understand a patient's health status [26]. Presently, monitoring these vitals requires patients to either visit a clinical facility, or buy multiple devices such as the BP monitor, oximeter, and thermometer which they must learn to use. Wearable sensor devices like smart watches are also available but patients must buy the reliable devices approved by Health Canada. Therefore, an alternative mode of remote vital signs monitoring with a single device (smartphone or web camera) will be beneficial as the users can measure their vitals at the comfort of being at home and without buying additional devices or receiving prior training on device usage.

In the 1930s, Hertzman proposed the principle of Photoplethysmography (PPG) [9]. In PPG method, the skin is illuminated with light and in proportion to the volume of blood flowing through the tissues, a part of the light is absorbed by the tissues and the rest is reflected. From the reflected light, the BVP signal is

E. Pardede et al. (Eds.): iiWAS 2022, LNCS 13635, pp. 237–251, 2022.
https://doi.org/10.1007/978-3-031-21047-1_21

extracted, which is processed further to compute the HR [33]. The first commercial oximeter based on PPG was introduced in 1983 [15]. Oximeters contain a photodiode sensor which measures the intensity of reflected light. Based on this technique, many commercial devices are available today and are widely used to measure the HR and SpO2 [10]. Researchers have used PPG signals obtained from contact PPG sensor devices and analyzed them using machine learning algorithms to calculate the HR and BP [11,29]. With the popularity and wide use of camera based smartphones, researchers have used videos of fingertip and monitored changes in skin color over a period of time to extract the BVP signal [21]. In recent years, the remote Photoplethysmography (rPPG) methods for measuring vital signs based on the principle of PPG have gained momentum, which are referred to as rPPG methods [30]. These methods employ a contactless camera based method to capture the face video for vital signs measurement. The recording is performed under laboratory environment [18,20] with controlled lighting conditions and no subject movements. These good quality videos without real life environmental noises result in clean BVP signals and provide good measurement accuracy. However, many users are hesitant in using online systems to record their face videos. Therefore, the technology needs to be enhanced with privacy measures to work in real world use case scenario and validated using a large sample population having different physical traits and health conditions before it can be deployed in clinical care in Canada.

In this paper, (1) we present a web application framework with a backend server as shown in Fig. 1 for remote web-based measurement of vitals signs namely HR, HRV, SpO$_2$, RR, BP and stress in near real-time using a privacy preserving face video captured with a device camera. (2) We validate the rPPG technology using our web application in the real world environment with different sources of light, varying camera resolutions, multiple browsers, several devices, and networks. (3) Extensive research was done to explore existing rPPG methods [25] and improve the BVP signal by diminishing motion and light noises encountered in real world environment and giving the user appropriate messages to capture a good quality video. In this version of the application, scalability

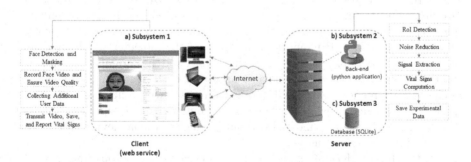

Fig. 1. Overview of the framework. It comprises of three subsystems: (a) front-end HTML application, (b) back-end processing python module and (c) SQLite database.

and load balancing was not addressed. Instead, we focused mainly on validating the accuracy of the framework in the real world.

The rest of the paper is organized as follows. Background and related work are presented in Sect. 2. The web application framework is explained in Sect. 3 and its experimental validation is described in Sect. 4. Finally, Sect. 5 concludes the paper with an outline of future work directions.

2   Background and Related Work

A web application is a software built using client-server architecture with the client side made accessible on the web to communicate with the users and obtain information that is transferred to the back end server for processing. The results can be reported back to the user. It can allow ubiquitous access to a wide range of users, and therefore, is ideal to validate the rPPG technology using a large number of volunteers. In this section we present some required concepts and literature review of the different methodologies we applied to implement a robust rPPG framework.

2.1   Remote Photoplethysmography (rPPG)

rPPG models estimate user vital signs from face videos using signal processing techniques and machine learning models [26]. The complete method consists of the following steps.

1. Detect Region of Interest (RoI)s: Identify face landmarks such as eyes, nose, lips, forehead, cheeks, and segment RoIs in the video frames to obtain the raw signal;
2. Noise reduction: Improve the video quality to reduce the noise due to light and motion and thereby, improve the quality of the raw signal;
3. Signal extraction: From the RoIs of the improved video, BVP signals are extracted based on change in pixel colors representing the periodicity of blood flow under the skin;
4. Vital signs computation: On the BVP signal, different computational pipelines are applied to calculate HR, HRV, SpO_2, RR, BP and stress.

2.2   Literature Review

RoI Detection: The face is detected and suitable RoIs are segmented to extract a periodic BVP signal. This signal is often dampened by motion artifacts owing to involuntary facial movement like blinking, twitching, smiling, and frowning [20,33]. Therefore, it becomes necessary to choose a RoI that includes the least noise and the most cardiac information. Two methods are commonly used for extracting the RoIs on the face [20,33]. The first method uses a face detector to segment the face with a bounding box. The second method predicts the coordinates of the facial landmarks, which can then aid in segmenting the RoIs.

Noise Reduction: Two major sources of noise that result in poor quality BVP signal are, (a) inconsistent illumination and (b) movement [26].

Illumination Noise: In low light environment the skin cardiac data is not clearly visible, which affects the extracted PPG features [20]. Guo et al. [13] applied Histogram Equalization (HE) to the videos and found that the enhanced videos gave larger RoIs than the original ones and also improved the quality of the signal. Qiao et al. [26] used HE to improve the lighting in the video when the background light was low.

Motion Noise: Rahman et al. [27] and Qiao et al. [25] used detrending filter and moving average filter to remove the stationary components and motion artifacts from the signal, respectively. Detrending helps attenuate the background intensity noise from the signal. Moving average filter computes the average of the datapoints between the video frames, thereby reducing the random noise yet retaining a sharp step response. The denoise filter helps in removing the jumps and steps in the signal caused by head movements such as rotation or shaking.

Signal Extraction: The individual face video frames are monitored over a period of time to track the changes in pixel color intensity to generate the BVP signal. All the three-color channels namely red (R), green (G) and blue (B), contain pulsatile data. Wang et al. [34] utilized the data from the green channel while Poh et al. [24] used all the three-color channels.

Vital Signs Computation: The different methods are briefly described below.

HR: The interval between the peaks of the time-domain BVP signal indicates the HR but this method is very sensitive to noise. The BVP signal can be transformed into the frequency domain using Fast Fourier Transform [20]. The highest peak in the frequency spectrum is the fundamental frequency f_{HR}. Qiao et al. [26] calculated HR as $f_{HR} * 60$.

HRV: Inter Beat Interval (IBI) is the time period between the heartbeats. HRV can be computed by calculating the time interval between two successive peaks in the BVP signal [28]. Qiao et al. [25,26] calculated $IBI = t_n - t_{(n-1)}$ where t_n is the time of the n th detected peak. They calculated HRV according to Eq. 1, where N is the number of IBIs in the sequence.

$$HRV = \sqrt{\frac{1}{N-1} \sum_{i=1}^{N-1} (IBI_i - IBI_{i+1})^2} \qquad (1)$$

SpO$_2$: Based on the principle that the absorbance of Red (R) light and Infrared (IR) light by the pulsatile blood changes with the degree of oxygenation [16], SpO$_2$ is calculated from the BVP signal. The extracted BVP signal obtained from the reflected light is divided into two parts: the Alternating Current (AC) component resulting from the arterial blood and the Direct Current (DC) component resulting from the underlying tissues, venous blood, and constant part of arterial blood flow. The SpO$_2$ level in the blood can be calculated using Eq. 2.

$$SpO_2 = A - B \times \frac{AC_R/DC_R}{AC_{IR}/DC_{IR}} \tag{2}$$

where parameters A and B can be calibrated by using a pulse oximeter. Qiao et al. [26] set 1 and 0.04 as the calibration parameters A and B respectively.

RR: Due to its non-stationary nature, estimating RR from PPG is challenging. Park et al. [23] extracted the dominant frequency from the BVP signal, used an infinite impulse response filter to eliminate cardiac component, and then used adaptive lattice notch filter to estimate RR. In this project, we estimated RR by using a bandpass filter to retain frequencies in the range of 0.15–0.35 Hz, and the peak in the resultant signal times 60 was taken as the RR.

BP: Non-linear regression models have shown good accuracy in estimating the BP [17] proving that BP and PPG have a non-linear correlation. Shimazaki et al. [29] used autoencoders to extract the complex features that could be used as input to a four layer neural network. Viejo et al. [31] fed the amplitude and frequency of detected peaks to a regression model comprising a two layer feed forward network. Huang et al. [14] used the results from transfer learning on MIMIC II dataset with k-nearest neighbours for BP prediction from face videos. Qiao et al. used a deep neural network with ResNet blocks and employed transfer learning by first training the network with finger PPG data and then with face video rPPG data. We used this model for BP estimation in this project.

Stress: HR is an indicator of stress level. In this project, we calibrate the stress as follows: relaxed when HR < 67 bpm, normal when 67–75 bpm, low when 75–83 bpm, medium when 84–91 bpm, high when 92–100 bpm, very high when 101–109 bpm and extreme when HR > 109 bpm.

An overview of the commercially available applications for estimating vital signs from face videos is illustrated in Table 1. These applications offer the solution to measure multiple vital signs with a single device which is why we implemented the same approach with improved noise reduction techniques. Additionally, we incorporated face masking for privacy protection.

3   Web Application Framework

The proposed web application framework version 1.0 is a python web framework having a client-server architecture which is composed of three subsystems as

Table 1. Overview of existing commercial applications for remote measurement of vital signs.

App	Technology	Face	Finger	SDK	Free	Vitals measured					
						HR	HRV	RR	SpO$_2$	BP	Stress
Anura [1]	TOI	✓			✓	✓				✓	✓
Happitech [5]	PPG		✓	✓	✓		✓				
Binah.ai [2]	PPG, rPPG	✓	✓	✓		✓	✓	✓	✓	✓	✓
Veyetals [7]	PPG, rPPG	✓	✓	✓	✓	✓	✓	✓	✓	✓	✓

shown in Fig. 1. The server hosts the front-end application, manages resources, and delivers the back-end functionality including data processing, storage, and running the computational models for estimating and returning the vital signs namely HR, HRV, RR, SpO$_2$, BP, and stress from face videos. We specifically focused on the computational models in this version, which will be demonstrated and evaluated through experiments. Load balancing and scalability will be addressed in future work.

We used the Flask framework[1], which is a popular lightweight Python microframework with a built-in development server and support for unit testing. The framework also has a strong community support and excellent documentation which made it our choice for this application. The processes implemented in the framework in each subsystem are briefly described below.

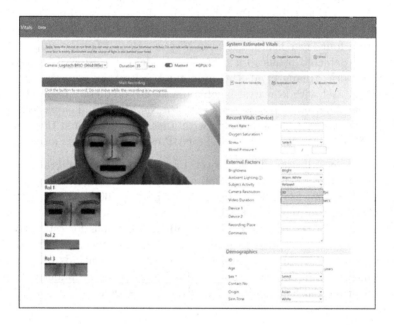

Fig. 2. Front-end web interface

3.1   Subsystem 1: Front-End Web Interface

The front-end web interface shown in Fig. 2 can be accessed on the browser via a public web URL[2]. It is built using HTML5, CSS, jQuery and Bootstrap. The front-end application requests camera access and upon receiving access, it starts capturing user's video. It anonymizes the user video by face masking, monitors

---

[1] https://flask.palletsprojects.com/en/2.0.x/.

[2] https://vital-signs-bamlab.tk/.

the user position, sends the video to the back-end for computing vitals, displays the vitals on the user interface, and collects optional user data such as age, skin color, and other relevant information to enable further analysis as explained below.

1. **Face Detection and Masking:** To protect the user privacy, we apply face masking by detecting face landmarks such as eyes, lips, jawline, and nose, and covering them with another object called the face mask. Three APIs namely Haar-cascade classifier [32], face-api.js [3], and MediaPipe Face Mesh framework JavaScript API [8] were tested for face and facial landmark detection. We used the MediaPipe Face Mesh API as it made real-time predictions and gave superior user experience. We apply a simple mask by covering the mouth and eyes with black strips, and drawing black contour lines on the nose area, eyebrows, and face edges. A button on the user interface allows the user to turn face mask on or off. For experimental analysis we recorded and evaluated both masked and unmasked videos.

2. **Record Face Video and Ensure Video Quality:** The device camera records the user's face video in MP4 format using the MediaRecorder[3] interface of the MediaStream Recording API. A bounding box around the face is computed to determine the face area. User distance from the camera is computed as the ratio of the face area to the video frame area. Tracking of the face landmarks throughout the video allows the system to detect too much movement (beyond 15 units of displacement of the bounding box) and stop the recording. If the user is too far from the camera or moving too much, the User Interface (UI) displays a message to guide the user to reposition or stay steady to obtain a good quality video.

3. **Collect Additional User Data:** To validate the accuracy of the measurements for different parameters, some data is collected from the user using a form on the UI as listed below.

   (a) Ground truth data measurements of HR, SpO_2, stress and BP taken by the user or the researcher using Health Canada approved medical devices. The HRV and RR measurements are sensitive measurements which are typically measured at a clinical facility. In this study we did not record the HRV and RR ground truth values (future study) and used a benchmark dataset containing these values.

   (b) Environmental data such as the brightness of the place (bright/dark), type of ambient lighting (warm white/ cool white/ daylight) causing illumination noise, and subject activity (relaxed/post exercise) causing motion noise, which affect the measurement accuracy.

   (c) User Profile such as name, age, sex, skin tone (white, yellow, brown, dark), and ethnicity (Asian, South-Asian, White Caucasian, African American, Hispanic) can be optionally provided by the user.

4. **Transmit Video, Save, and Report Vital Signs:** Once the noise is acceptable, the recording is transmitted to Subsystem 2 for further processing and calculation of vital signs. Calculated measurements are displayed on the

---

[3] https://developer.mozilla.org/en-US/docs/Web/API/MediaRecorder.

UI in near real time. A *Save* button allows all information to be saved on Subsystem 3, which can be accessed later for further studies.

3.2   Subsystem 2: Back-End Data Processing

The back-end hosts a Python 3.8 application on the server. The videos received from Subsystem 1 are saved on the server, processed and analyzed to extract the raw PPG signals and reduce noises due to changes in light intensity and motion to obtain a robust BVP signal for higher accuracy of vital signs.

After receiving the user video, first the luminance and brightness of the input video are analyzed to ensure that the video quality is good. Otherwise, the user is notified to improve the light condition. Then three RoIs are segmented on the face. Accuracy of measurements is reduced when the face is covered with hair or mask and when the face is excessively illuminated with light. Therefore, three different RoIs are extracted and the best BVP signal from these RoIs is used in further processing and computation of the vital signs.

Each RoI provides a three dimensional array comprising pixel intensities in the three color channels: red, green and blue. The raw PPG signals of each frame are represented by the mean pixel values of the green channel. Hence, the three RoIs generate three raw PPG signals. These signals are further processed by applying various signal processing filters such as denoise filter, detrending filter, and moving average filter to reduce noise due to motion and varying light. This results in three BVP signals $g_1(n)$, $g_2(n)$, and $g_3(n)$ corresponding to the three RoIs. Using Welch's method [22], the Power Spectral Density (PSD) of each BVP is computed and using a bandpass filter, only frequencies in the human HR BVP range of 0.7 Hz–4 Hz are retained. The signal with the highest PSD is selected for calculating the vital signs.

We used the state-of-the-art methods from Qiao et al. [26] for vital sign estimation as explained briefly in Sect. 2.2 and improved the noise filtering techniques (selecting the best RoI, guiding user by UI messaging) while validating the framework in real life environment.

3.3   Subsystem 3: SQLite Database

Due to the ease of installation, usage, and portability, we used the SQLite[4] database version 3.12.2 as the repository on the back-end server to store the experimental data. It consists of a single relational table which saves time stamped data for each user session including the video file name, the vitals calculated by Subsystem 2, and the measured vitals entered by the user in Subsystem 1 along with the additional user and environmental details collected through the UI.

3.4   Application Deployment

To host the framework on a public server accessible by a URL, a Nginx web server and Gunicorn HTTP server is used, as the built-in Flask web server cannot be

---

[4] https://www.sqlite.org/index.html.

used for production. Nginx[5] is a powerful open source web server that can handle reverse proxy, load balancing, security, scalability and HTTP caching. Gunicorn[6] is a Python Web Server Gateway Interface (WSGI) HTTP server for UNIX.

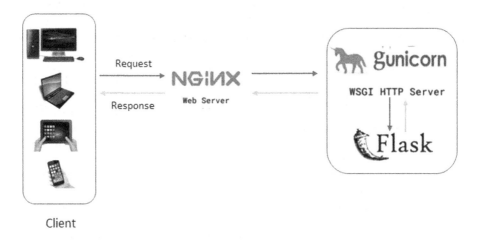

Fig. 3. Application deployment architecture

The deployment architecture is shown in Fig. 3. When the client requests the URL https://vita-signs-bamlab.tk a Domain Name System (DNS) lookup is performed to find the application server's IP address. Once the browser receives the IP address, it establishes a TCP connection with the server and sends a HTTP request with the recorded video. The Nginx engine acts as a reverse proxy server listening on port 80 of the server. Upon receiving an incoming client request, it passes the request to the web socket configured in the Gunicorn service. Gunicorn web socket binds to a WSGI access point which is the entry point to the Flask application. After receiving the request to calculate the vitals from the video, the Flask application processes the video and computes the results. These results are sent back as response to Gunicorn which relays it to the Nginx, and it sends the HTTP response back to the client.

4   Experiments and Results

To demonstrate the usability and performance of the framework, participants were asked to use the application in real life environment. The vitals were measured simultaneously using medical devices Omron HEM-FL31 BP monitor and LOOKEE LK50D1A pulse oximeter. We used the Mean Absolute Error (MAE), System Response Time (SRTime), and Back-end Processing Time (BPTime) as

---

[5] https://www.nginx.com/.
[6] https://gunicorn.org/.

the metric for evaluating the experimental results. The difference between the ground truth vital sign reading measured with a medical device and the vital sign value estimated by the framework, is the error. Average error value computed from multiple measurement sessions is called the Mean Absolute Error (MAE). The SRTime is the total time taken by the application to collect the video and report the results. The BPTime is the time taken by the back-end system to process the videos and report the results. We conducted experiments to validate the framework's:

1. **Accuracy:** Five volunteers in the age group of 13–40 years used the application at different times of the day and in different physical states on the Google Chrome browser of an Acer Aspire A315-55G laptop, with a Logitech UltraHD 4K webcam. The ground truth vital signs readings were in the range of 72–108 bpm, 97–100%, 94–114 mmHg, and 58–76 mmHg for HR, SpO_2, SBP, and DBP respectively. The results of this experiment are shown in Table 2.
2. **Robustness and Performance:** One volunteer used the application for 5 days with multiple sources of light and camera resolutions, and different internet networks, devices and browsers. The application was used three times in a day at 10:00, 13:00, and 16:00 hrs. The experimental results are shown in Table 3 and 4.
3. **Workload Capacity:** The maximum number of users the application can support was tested using Google Chrome browser on different devices starting with 9 participants.

Discussion: From Table 2, it is clear that the system performance improves with face masking because the eyes and mouth movement is completely obscured which avoids the noise due to movement. The participants in the experiment had vital signs measurements in the normal range. In the future, we need to conduct these experiments with patients whose vital signs are above or below the normal medical range. In Table 3, we observed in the experimental results with different light sources that the MAE was the lowest with natural daylight. This clearly indicates that the light sources are adding artifacts to the video resulting in noise in the raw signal. The other experiments with different camera resolutions as listed in Table 3, show that the framework's accuracy does not improve beyond a certain camera resolution. In the future, we will conduct the experiment with many cameras to determine the minimum resolution required for a good accuracy.

Although the performance of the system is comparable on both the networks in Table 4, the BPTime is similar but the SRTime varies for different devices and browsers. This is due to the low frame rate resulting in longer video recordings. SRTime depends on data processing time plus the network data transmission time. The computational complexity, device configuration, and video streaming capability of the device camera affect the data processing time. The frame rate of the camera in a browser depends on video resolution, device memory, and available bandwidth [19]. For example, a camera might capture at 60 fps at 720p resolution but it might only capture 30 fps at 1080p. The number of applications running on a device also affects the frame rate.

We configured the Gunicorn service with 5 worker processes as the official documentation of the service provider mentions that 4–12 worker processes can handle thousands of requests per second [4]. The recommendation is to use $(2 * \#num\_cores) + 1$ as the number of workers. Gunicorn relies on the operating system for load balancing. The Nginx server has efficient load balancing techniques that must be configured properly for faster response times when executing concurrent application [6]. The workload capacity of the framework can be enhanced by appropriate configurations, which is outside the scope of this work.

Table 2. Validating the framework accuracy.

Time	State	Vital	Mask (MAE)	No mask (MAE)
Morning	Rest	HR	9.4 bpm	7 bpm
		SpO$_2$	2.7%	3%
		SBP	8.1 mmHg	10.3 mmHg
		DBP	5.7 mmHg	8.4 mmHg
Morning	Post exercise	HR	6.3 bpm	9.7 bpm
		SpO$_2$	2.3%	2.3%
		SBP	9 mmHg	7.3 mmHg
		DBP	3.6 mmHg	3.3 mmHg
Evening	Rest	HR	5.25 bpm	8.25 bpm
		SpO$_2$	2.7%	2.7%
		SBP	11.75 mmHg	15 mmHg
		DBP	1.5 mmHg	4 mmHg
Evening	Post exercise	HR	6.3 bpm	6.6 bpm
		SpO$_2$	2.3%	2.3%
		SBP	9 mmHg	10.6 mmHg
		DBP	4.3 mmHg	4 mmHg
Mean		**HR**	**6.8 bpm**	**7.9 bpm**
		SpO$_2$	**2.5%**	**2.5%**
		SBP	**9.4 mmHg**	**10.8 mmHg**
		DBP	**3.8 mmHg**	**4.9 mmHg**

Table 3. Validating robustness of the framework with different light sources and camera resolutions.

	Light (MAE)			Camera resolution (MAE)		
	Daylight	Warm tone	Cool tone	0.3MP	2MP	8MP
HR	2.1 bpm	7 bpm	6.2 bpm	13.8 bpm	6.1 bpm	8.2 bpm
SpO2	3%	3%	3%	3%	3%	3%
SBP	5.9 mmHg	9.8 mmHg	5 mmHg	2.1 mmHg	2 mmHg	3.4 mmHg
DBP	4.2 mmHg	6.1 mmHg	5.8 mmHg	6.1 mmHg	1.4 mmHg	3 mmHg

Table 4. Validating the performance of the framework for different networks, devices and browsers.

		Back-end processing time	System response time
Network	Wifi network	47.9 s	84.5 s
	Mobile network	50.1 s	86.0 s
Devices	Acer laptop	50 s	114 s
	Alienware laptop	46.5 s	104.5 s
	Samsung phone	48.7 s	107.5 s
	Redmi phone	47.9 s	116.7 s
	iPhone	48.3 s	111.2 s
	iPad	43 s	198 s
Browser	Google chrome	48 s	84.4 s
	Mozilla firefox	46.5 s	104.55 s
	Microsoft edge	50.9 s	93.47 s
	Safari	46 s	91.2 s

5   Conclusion and Future Work

With the global transition of business processes to online cloud technologies, the medical domain has seen a digital transformation in offering online services to patients. In this regard, the rPPG technology which facilitates measurement of vitals signs remotely from face videos can greatly benefit the online medical consultations. Existing research in rPPG [18,20,21] has shown promising results when used in controlled laboratory conditions. However, their performance degrades when movement or illumination changes affect the videos. Moreover, researchers have usually focused on one or two vitals in validating their experiments [12,31]. We propose a web-based, publicly accessible ubiquitous framework for estimating six vitals namely, Heart Rate (HR), Heart Rate Variability (HRV), Respiration Rate (RR), Oxygen Saturation (SpO$_2$), Blood Pressure (BP), and stress, which handles movement and illumination artifacts prevalent in real life. We validate the accuracy, robustness, usability and functionality of the rPPG models in estimating the vital signs from face videos. Further, we tested the application with different light sources, and camera resolutions. The system performance was also validated on different networks at different times, using multiple browsers and devices. The application framework is compatible with all camera-equipped devices having an internet connection.

As future work, ways to enhance the video quality need to be explored so that low resolution camera devices can be used over weak networks at remote locations. Better camera control can be used to optimize the frame rate for video capture. Videos can be live streamed using WebRTC technology to reduce processing delay instead of recording and uploading to the back end server. Further noise reduction due to facial movements can be explored in the future along with a study design to be executed at the hospital for a wider patient sample having varying vital sign measurements, which can help build a robust technology to deploy at a healthcare setting.

References

1. Anura. https://www.anura.ai/. Accessed 16 Feb 2022
2. Binah.ai. https://www.binah.ai/. Accessed 16 Feb 2022
3. face-api.js. https://justadudewhohacks.github.io/face-api.js/docs/index.html. Accessed 15 Feb 2022
4. Gunicorn 0.16.1 documentation. https://docs.gunicorn.org/en/0.16.1/design.html. Accessed 15 Feb 2022
5. Happitech. https://www.happitech.com/. Accessed 17 Feb 2022
6. Http load balancing. https://docs.nginx.com/nginx/admin-guide/load-balancer/http-load-balancer/. Accessed 15 Feb 2022
7. Veyetals. https://veyetals.com/. Accessed 17 Feb 2022
8. Mediapipe face mesh (2020). https://google.github.io/mediapipe/solutions/face_mesh.html. Accessed 15 Feb 2022
9. Hertzman, A.B.: The blood supply of various skin areas as estimated by the photoelectric plethysmograph. Am. J. Physiol. **124**, 328–340 (1938)
10. Castaneda, D., Esparza, A., Ghamari, M., Soltanpur, C., Nazeran, H.: A review on wearable photoplethysmography sensors and their potential future applications in health care. Int. J. Biosens. Bioelectron. **4**(4), 195 (2018)
11. El-Hajj, C., Kyriacou, P.A.: A review of machine learning techniques in photoplethysmography for the non-invasive cuff-less measurement of blood pressure. Biomed. Signal Process. Control **58**, 101870 (2020)
12. Fan, X., Ye, Q., Yang, X., Choudhury, S.D.: Robust blood pressure estimation using an RGB camera. J. Ambient Intell. Humaniz. Comput. **11**(11), 4329–4336 (2020)
13. Guo, X., Li, Y., Ling, H.: LIME: low-light image enhancement via illumination map estimation. IEEE Trans. Image Process. **26**(2), 982–993 (2017)
14. Huang, P.W., Lin, C.H., Chung, M.L., Lin, T.M., Wu, B.F.: Image based contactless blood pressure assessment using pulse transit time. In: 2017 International Automatic Control Conference (CACS) (2017). https://doi.org/10.1109/cacs.2017.8284275. Accessed 28 Oct 2021

15. Kamshilin A., M.N.: Origin of photoplethysmographic waveform at green light. PNBS (2015)
16. Kanva, A.K., Sharma, C.J., Deb, S.: Determination of SpO 2 and heart-rate using smartphone camera. In: Proceedings of The 2014 International Conference on Control, Instrumentation, Energy and Communication (CIEC), pp. 237–241, January 2014
17. Kim, J.Y., Cho, B.H., Im, S.M., Jeon, M.J., Kim, I.Y., Kim, S.I.: Comparative study on artificial neural network with multiple regressions for continuous estimation of blood pressure. In: International Conference on IEEE Engineering in Medicine and Biology, pp. 6942–6945 (2005)
18. Kumar, M., Veeraraghavan, A., Sabharwal, A.: DistancePPG: robust non-contact vital signs monitoring using a camera. Biomed. Opt. Exp. 6(5), 1565–1588 (2015)
19. Johnston, L.: What are webcam frame rates, July 2020. https://www.lifewire.com/webcam-frame-rates-2640479. Accessed 15 Feb 2022
20. Li, X., Chen, J., Zhao, G., Pietikainen, M.: Remote heart rate measurement from face videos under realistic situations. In: Proceedings of the IEEE Conference on Computer Vision and Pattern Recognition, pp. 4264–4271 (2014)
21. Nemcova, A., et al.: Monitoring of heart rate, blood oxygen saturation, and blood pressure using a smartphone. Biomed. Signal Process. Control 59, 101928 (2020)
22. Welch, P.: The use of fast fourier transform for the estimation of power spectra: a method based on time averaging over short, modified periodograms. IEEE Trans. Audio Electroacoust. 15(2), 70–73 (1967)
23. Park, C., Lee, B.: Real-time estimation of respiratory rate from a photoplethysmogram using an adaptive lattice notch filter. Biomed. Eng. Online 13(1), 1–17 (2014)
24. Poh, M.Z., McDuff, D.J., Picard, R.W.: Non-contact, automated cardiac pulse measurements using video imaging and blind source separation. Opt. Exp. 18(10), 10762–10774 (2010)
25. Qiao, D., Zulkernine, F., Masroor, R., Rasool, R., Jaffar, N.: Measuring heart rate and heart rate variability with smartphone camera. In: 22nd IEEE International Conference on Mobile Data Management (MDM) (2021)
26. Qiao, D., Ayesha, A.H., Zulkernine, F., Masroor, R., Jaffar, N.: Revise: remote vital signs measurement using smartphone video camera (2022). https://arxiv.org/abs/2206.08748
27. Rahman, H., Ahmed, M.U., Begum, S., Funk, P.: Real time heart rate monitoring from facial RGB color video using webcam. In: 9th Annual Workshop of the Swedish Artificial Intelligence Society (SAIS) (2016)
28. Shaffer, F., Ginsberg, J.P.: An overview of heart rate variability metrics and norms, September 2017
29. Shimazaki, S., Bhuiyan, S., Kawanaka, H., Oguri, K.: Features extraction for cuffless blood pressure estimation by autoencoder from photoplethysmography. In: 40th Annual International Conference of the IEEE Engineering in Medicine and Biology Society (2018)
30. Sun, Y., Thakor, N.: Photoplethysmography revisited: from contact to noncontact, from point to imaging. IEEE Trans. Biomed. Eng. 63(3), 463–477 (2015)
31. Gonzalez Viejo, C., Fuentes, S., Torrico, D.D., Dunshea, F.R.: Non-contact heart rate and blood pressure estimations from video analysis and machine learning modelling applied to food sensory responses: a case study for chocolate. Sensors 18(6), 1802 (2018). https://www.mdpi.com/1424-8220/18/6/1802. Accessed 25 Sept 2021

32. Viola, P., Jones, M.: Rapid object detection using a boosted cascade of simple features. In: Proceedings of the 2001 IEEE Computer Society Conference on Computer Vision and Pattern Recognition, vol. 1, pp. 511–518 (2001)
33. Wang, C., Pun, T., Chanel, G.: A comparative survey of methods for remote heart rate detection from frontal face videos (2018)
34. Wang, Z., Yang, X., Cheng, K.T.: Accurate face alignment and adaptive patch selection for heart rate estimation from videos under realistic scenarios. PLoS ONE **13**(5), e0197275 (2018)

Neural Kernel Network Deep Kernel Learning for Predicting Particulate Matter from Heterogeneous Sensors with Uncertainty

Chaofan Li[✉], Till Riedel, and Michael Beigl

Karlsruhe Institute of Technology, Vincenz-Prießnitz-Str. 1,
76131 Karlsruhe, Germany
chaofan.li@kit.edu

Abstract. Modern web technologies allow novel types of sensor networks that collect measurements from different sources ranging from citizen-collected data to official sources. In this paper, we propose a scheme to deal with measurement sources of different quality for time-series prediction of urban particulate matter. Our approach is based on a neural kernel network deep kernel learning model that takes the highly heterogeneous and uncertain measurements provided by a post-hoc hybrid low-cost sensor network as input. And predicts the daily average PM10 mass concentration for the next day. Furthermore, we also validate the contribution of ultra-low-cost sensors in the SmartAQnet sensor network, which reduces the average MAE of our model pipeline from $4.18\,\mu g/m^3$ to $3.67\,\mu g/m^3$ and increases the PCC from 0.589 to 0.665. In contrast to existing approaches, we can model the uncertainty of the prediction based on the quality and quantity of input signals crawled.

Keywords: Machine learning · Gaussian process regression · Time-series prediction · Urban air quality · Low-cost sensor network

1 Introduction

Air pollution causes severe damage to human health. According to the WHO Air Quality Guidelines 2021 [10], outdoor and household air pollution accounted for about 12% of all deaths in 2019. Moreover, even exposure to low concentrations of air pollutants is dangerous, and no thresholds that could be considered safe were observed. Among various air pollutants, Particulate Matter (PM) is causally associated with all-cause mortality and diseases such as acute lower respiratory infections, lung cancer, etc. [6] Individual exposition can vary extremely within the same city. Therefore, fine-grained monitoring and forecasting of PM concentrations in urban areas have become an important task.

In urban air quality modeling, statistical modeling approaches based on machine learning (ML) algorithms are receiving more and more attention as they do not rely on accurate data on emission sources in rapidly changing urban

© The Author(s), under exclusive license to Springer Nature Switzerland AG 2022
E. Pardede et al. (Eds.): iiWAS 2022, LNCS 13635, pp. 252–266, 2022.
https://doi.org/10.1007/978-3-031-21047-1_22

areas. ML algorithms, however, generally require large-scale datasets to capture the relationship between measurements and predictions.

In practical applications, a trade-off must be made between the network size of a sensor network and the average cost of sensors due to budget constraints. Rather than using a dedicated measurement network, post-hoc networks combine the small number of high-precision measurement stations for which government agencies publish data on the internet with low-cost sensors run collaboratively by citizens and researchers [2,9]. However, fusing such heterogeneous information into a large-scale urban air quality measurement network is often characterized by high uncertainty.

This paper proposes a new model pipeline based on a neural kernel network [21] deep kernel learning model. It takes heterogeneous and uncertain data collected from different Internet-connected sources by the "SmartAQnet" [2] as the input. And it predicts the daily average of PM10 concentration readings of the four high-precision PM10 monitoring stations for the next day. As a result, our model pipeline achieved an average mean absolute error (MAE) of $3.67\,\mu g/m^3$ and an average Pearson correlation coefficient (PCC) of 0.665. We also test the effect of different preprocessing strategies and compare our prediction model with other comparison models (baseline, MLP, LSTM, vanilla GPR, etc.). Furthermore, we also validate the contribution of ultra-low-cost sensors in the SmartAQnet sensor network, which reduces the average MAE of our model pipeline from $4.18\,\mu g/m^3$ to $3.67\,\mu g/m^3$ and increases the PCC from 0.589 to 0.665.

2   Background

2.1   Urban Air Quality Data

Historical data with reliable reference measurements is an important asset required for modeling tasks. It provides the ground truth necessary to fit and validate models. Traditional urban air quality data is usually collected by sparsely distributed high-precision measurement stations [5]. These measurement stations provide high-quality measurement data but are expensive to install and maintain. This is why typically only a minimal number of such stations are deployed: typically to comply with regulatory requirements. However, urban areas are highly complex environments, so fine-grained monitoring and modeling of urban pollutants require high temporal and spatial resolution data. To this end, many grassroots, scientific, or even in some cases municipality-driven efforts have been made to simultaneously deploy at much lower price levels to balance the spatial density and cost of deployment [2,8,9,15]. Particularly opportunistically combining the established sensor networks of different local agencies is also a potential way to increase the data scale and resolution [2]. However, for those internet of thing (IoT) enabled methods introduce new difficulties in the data, namely the problem of calibration, heterogeneity and uncertainty.

Heterogeneity in IoT Air Quality Sensor Networks. For data from hybrid sensor networks containing sensors at multiple price levels, the problem of heterogeneity may arise from numerous aspects, such as:

Construction and Maintenance of the Sensor Network. The operational stability of a sensor is often positively related to its cost. When the network contains a large number of medium and low-cost sensors, it becomes almost impossible to maintain the stability of the network. Figure 1 shows the average daily available devices for each month during the operation of the SmartAQnet project [2]. In such a network, both the deployment and the failure of sensors are present throughout the time. Some damaged sensors may eventually be repaired or replenished to work at the former location. However, there are also possibilities that the damaged sensor may never come back to operate, especially when it is a low-cost one.

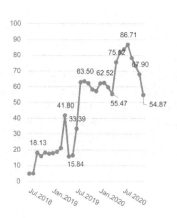

Fig. 1. Average daily available devices for each month

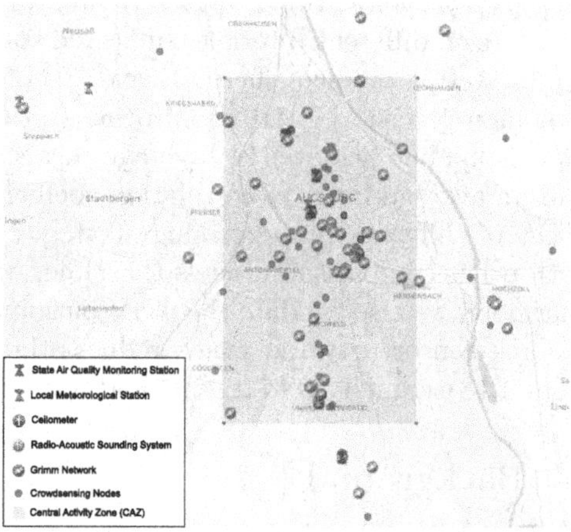

Fig. 2. Sensor deployment map of the SmartAQnet project

Combination of Different Local Sensor Network. Different institutions have different interests in the observed properties, leading them to choose different types of sensors and adopt different spatial and temporal strategies when deploying their own sensor networks. Such differences in strategy will result in differences in the structure of the data sheets, which means there will be a large number of missing values in the merged dataset.

Uncertainty in IoT Air Quality Sensor Networks. Uncertainty issues also come from many different sources in hybrid sensor networks, such as:

Errors of Low-Cost Sensors. The error of low-cost sensors is an essential factor in the uncertainty of the data. For example, Budde et al. analyzed the performance of a popular low-cost PM sensor, SDS011, in [4]. They find out in their experiments that a notable variance between individual sensors can be observed, and the reliability of the sensor's readings is also affected by various environmental factors like humidity. Previous research on citizen weather stations employing also Gaussian process regression, however, to provide spatial interpolation shows the importance but also the complexity of modelling sensor error as uncertainty [1].

Errors of Human Management. The longer the urban air quality sensor network runs, the more likely it is to collect more data across different patterns to help with better modeling. Therefore, such projects tend to last for years and generate hundreds of millions of observational records, posing enormous challenges to project management. In addition, some existing urban air quality projects, such as SmartAQnet [2], Smart Emission [9], and Luftdaten.info, also include citizen science programs, which make human management errors more difficult to detect [3]. No one can guarantee that all human errors are detected and fixed. The associated uncertainty probably still remains in the aggregated data.

2.2 Urban Air Pollutants Modeling

Current urban air pollutant models can be roughly divided into simulation and statistical models. Among them, the simulation model usually makes predictions by simulating the physical and chemical processes of pollutant diffusion and reaction in the atmosphere [16,19]. In comparison, the statistical model makes predictions by summarizing the statistical characteristics from historical observations [13,17,18,20]. Our model pipeline adopts a Gaussian process-based statistical modeling approach.

Gaussian Process Regression. Gaussian Process Regression (GPR) is a classic non-parametric Bayesian regression algorithm. It has the advantage of performing well on small datasets and provides a measure of uncertainty for predictions.

Unlike many popular supervised machine learning algorithms such as MLP and LSTM, Bayesian methods don't just learn an exact value for each parameter in a function. They infer the probability distribution of the parameter over all possible values. The way Bayesian methods work is to specify a prior distribution $p(w)$ for the parameter w and then use the Bayesian rule (Eq. 1) to relocate this probability distribution based on the evidence (that is, observational data).

$$p(w|y, X) = \frac{p(y|X, w) \times P(w)}{p(y|X)} \tag{1}$$

The relocated probability distribution $p(w|y, X)$ is called the posterior distribution, containing information from both the prior distribution and the dataset. When we want to predict the label of a point of interest x^*, the predictive distribution can be calculated by weighting all possible predictions by their posterior distribution (Eq. 2).

$$p(f^*|x^*, y, X) = \int_w p(f^*|x^*, w)p(w|y, X)dw \qquad (2)$$

Instead of calculating a probability distribution over the parameters of a particular function, GPR calculates a probability distribution over all possible functions that fit the data. In GPR, we first assume a Gaussian process prior, which can be defined by a mean function $m(x)$ and a covariance function $k(x, x')$. The training set and the predicted points of interest are joint multivariate Gaussian distributed from the Gaussian process prior (Eq. 3). The training process of GPR is to find suitable parameters for the mean and covariance functions. This is usually done with the help of a gradient-based optimizer by maximizing the log marginal likelihood on the training set.

$$\begin{bmatrix} y \\ f^* \end{bmatrix} \sim \mathcal{N} \left(\begin{bmatrix} \mu \\ \mu^* \end{bmatrix}, \begin{bmatrix} K(X, X) + \sigma_n^2 I & K(X, X^*) \\ K(X^*, X) & K(X^*, X^*) \end{bmatrix} \right) \qquad (3)$$

3   Methodology

3.1   Data Description

The data used in this paper is freely available on the internet and aggregated by the www.smartaq.net website. For reproducibility, we are using a dataset provided by the SmartAQnet project that covers all measurements from January 1, 2017, to December 31, 2021 [14].

SmartAQnet combines meteorology and aerosol measurement data collected by different entities. A considerable portion of the sensors is located in a rectangular area of 6×4 km that covers most of the city of Augsburg, Germany (Fig. 2). The time resolution of the sensor varies by its model. Among them, the high-precision PM10 measuring station generates a record every 1 h, and the temporal resolution of the vast majority of the other sensors is between 5 min and 5 s.

In this study, we treat the data from the above-mentioned 4 high-precision PM10 measurement stations as labels. Other data are treated as input data. Several sensors with remote locations and all height profile data are removed. The considered sensors are all located in a rectangular area of about 16×16 km. Among over 30 observed properties provided in the dataset, we select 9 properties that we believe are highly correlated with PM10 concentration to be input into our model. Namely PM10 mass concentration, PM2.5 mass concentration, temperature, relative humidity, air pressure, precipitation, wind direction, wind speed, and global radiation.

3.2   Model Pipeline

Our model pipeline could be divided into three steps: data preprocessing, feature extraction, and prediction.

Data Preprocessing. The data preprocessing step is responsible for receiving the readings directly from the sensor network and preliminarily eliminating heterogeneity and uncertainty in the input data through methods such as aggregation and interpolation. The data preprocessing step can be further divided into two stages: temporal-spatial aggregation and window generation.

Temporal-Spatial Aggregation. Data aggregation is a simple and effective way to reduce data uncertainty, especially good at dealing with the influence of symmetrically distributed noise and small probability events. Thanks to the high temporal and spatial resolution of the SmartAQnet network, we can aggregate a considerable number of observation records into one. In this stage, the aggregation will be carried out on all input data on the time and space dimensions (Fig. 3). All data from the four high-precision PM10 measurement stations, which will be used as labels, are excluded from data aggregation.

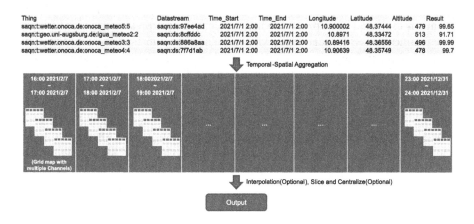

Fig. 3. The workflow of the Temporal-Spatial Aggregation stage

In the time dimension, the aggregation resolution is 1 h, while in the spatial dimension, the spatial extent covered by the dataset (about 16×16 km, as mentioned earlier) is divided into 50×50 grids. That is, The spatial resolution is about 300×300 m. The aggregated data structure is shown in Fig. 3: the data is represented as several 1-hour time slices in the time dimension. Each time slice is defined as a 50×50 grid with 9 channels to reproduce the spatial relationship of the data. Each channel represents one of the above-mentioned 9 observed properties considered relevant to PM10.

After the aggregation, we consider two additional processing operations:

One processing operation is to slice and center the spatial grid. Precisely, we slice each of the above-mentioned 50×50 spatial grids, ensuring that the position we want to predict is in the center of the sliced grid. We're not sure if the model will benefit from this operation. According to Tobler's First Law of Geography [22], everything is related to everything else, but near things are more related than distant things. By slicing, we hopefully help the model exclude interference from distant noise. On the opposite side, in the SmartAQnet sensor network, some observed properties are only collected by a few sensors. An aggressive slicing may cause the input data to lose too much information about these observed properties, resulting in a dramatic decline in model performance. Therefore, we decided to demonstrate whether slicing should be performed through experimental results.

Another processing operation is to perform interpolation on the spatial grid. We think this helps eliminate heterogeneity in the data further. An obvious benefit is that even the most naive interpolation method can help the model distinguish whether an input 0 is a measured value of 0 or we don't know anything about it. Another potential benefit of interpolation is that it promises to alleviate the shortcomings of the slicing step mentioned above. By interpolation, we can generalize the information of observed properties recorded by only a few sensors to the entire grid, which leads to less information loss due to slicing. In addition, a "wonderful" interpolation that can take land use and the wind into account is expected to improve the homogeneity and expressiveness of the input data significantly. But since this problem belongs to another research direction, and its complexity is no less than the time series prediction problem, we plan to take this topic as a future research direction. In this article we only consider Inverse Distance Weighting (IDW) interpolation.

Window Generation. In this stage, we create time windows using the time slices generated in the previous temporal-spatial aggregation stage. After the window generation stage, a piece of training data for predicting the daily average PM10 concentration on day T looks as shown in Fig. 4. It consists of two parts: timestamp and time window.

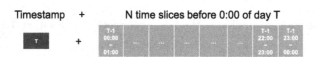

Fig. 4. A piece of training data processed after the window generation stage for predicting the daily average PM10 concentration on day T

For the timestamp part, we use two-dimensional relative timestamps. One dimension represents how many days have passed from the first day of this year until day T. Another dimension means which weekday day T is. We use relative timestamps because, during GPR training, we observed that GPR is difficult to give effective confidence interval estimates in extrapolation tasks. Because GPR does not find any experience from the training set in the corresponding area, thus it does not have any confidence in its prediction. We transform time series prediction into an interpolation problem using relative timestamps, resulting in more reliable predictions and confidence intervals. But this approach also comes at a cost. For example, it completely ignores the difference between different years. In fact, during the operation of the SmartAQnet project, we experienced the coronavirus pandemic. The lockdown policy is likely to lead to the data pattern over the years are not the same, thus affecting the model performance.

As for the time window part, we select N time slices before 0:00 of the day T, which were generated by the previous temporal-spatial aggregation stage. In our experimental setup, N takes a value of 24. That means the time window includes all the time slices of day T-1.

Feature Extraction. The feature extraction step is responsible for receiving the output of the data preprocessing step and performing feature extraction. Feature extraction refers to processing the features that need input to the model through methods such as screening or reorganization to eliminate information redundancy in the input data as much as possible.

In our model pipeline, the feature extraction step mainly has the following two contributions. First, feature extraction reduces the dimension of the input data, making the data more discriminable when the total amount of data is limited. Secondly, during the feature extraction process, the data will lose some unnecessary details (which usually could be treated as noise), which helps further to reduce the impact of data uncertainty on the model.

We tested three feature extraction methods during the model testing phase: Principal Component Analysis (PCA), Convolutional Neural Network (CNN), and Auto-Encoder. Among them, CNN and Auto-Encoder didn't perform well. We believe this is because our dimension reduction task is too heavy (the original input has about 540000 dimensions). At the same time, the total amount of data is too small (only c.a. 1500 available time windows established). PCA, on the other hand, performed well on data generated by all the above-mentioned pre-processing strategies. When set to capture 95% of the variance, PCA can reduce the preprocessed data from 540000 dimensions to 90—240 dimensions (depending on the settings of the preprocessing steps). In addition, PCA maintains some data interpretability. We finally decide to use PCA for feature extraction in the model pipeline.

Prediction Model. The prediction model is a machine learning model for regression tasks. As mentioned above, our pipeline uses a GPR-based prediction model.

Neural Kernel Network. The covariance function (kernel) is essential to the GP models. The choice of kernel determines almost all the generalization properties of a GP model. This is because the kernel incorporates prior assumptions about the characteristics of the data. In Vanilla GPR, the kernel selection relies heavily on the user's experience and prior knowledge of the data, but this is not always feasible. For example, users' prior knowledge of urban air quality prediction tasks is limited. Moreover, the data is often unrecognizable after many preprocessing steps. In addition, with the rise of combination kernel methods [7,11,12,21], it has been found that adding or multiplying multiple kernels can express more complex priors, which further increases the difficulty of choosing a proper kernel. In this context, the concept of compositional kernel learning is introduced. Its idea is to automate the selection and combination of kernels as part of the training process.

The Neural Kernel Network (NKN) [21] is a compositional kernel learning method. It uses a neural network-styled structure to represent the weighted addition and multiplication of kernels. And it can adjust the weights in the network through back-propagation to automatically select the structure of the combined kernel. The following Fig. 5 shows the basic structure of NKN.

First, we need to choose some commonly used kernels (such as RBF kernel, linear kernel, periodic kernel, RQ kernel, etc.) as the basic kernels, and these basic kernels are used as the input layer of the network. After that, each network layer can be divided into two parts, the first part is responsible for weighted addition, and the second is for multiplying adjacent results from the weighted addition step with each other. The last layer of the network has only one output, which can be seen as the result of the final combined kernel.

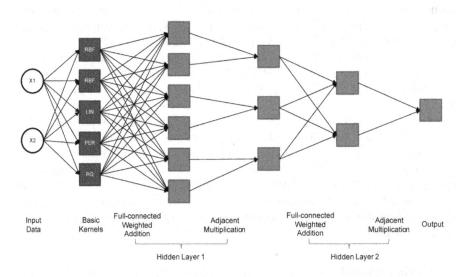

Fig. 5. The structure of a Neural Kernel Network kernel

Prediction Model Design. In our model pipeline, the prediction model consists of MLP and GPR (Fig. 6). We first use an MLP with 2 hidden layer to remap the output from the feature extraction step. Then the data will be input to a GPR model with a constant mean function and an NKN kernel for the regression task. We use RBF kernels, RQ kernels, Cosine kernels, and Matern kernels as the basic kernels of the NKN kernel. In the network part of the NKN kernel, we use two layers: the first layer has 4 outputs and the second layer has 1 output. In addition to this structure, we also implement some other regression models for performance comparison. Detailed information will be discussed in the following Sect. 4.

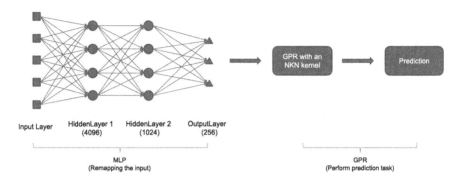

Fig. 6. The structure of the prediction model

4   Experiments

4.1   Model Performance and Comparison

We conducted controlled experiments to determine the optimal model pipeline steps and evaluate our predictive models' performance. As described in Sect. 3, three components need to be tested and assessed: whether interpolation is required, if grid slicing and centering are necessary, and which predictive model to use. For interpolation, we only consider two cases of no interpolation and IDW interpolation. For grid slicing and centering, we consider three cases: no slicing, big slicing (21×21 grid centered on the predicted point), and small slicing (11×11 grid centered on the predicted point). For the prediction model, in addition to the MLP + NKN kernel GPR proposed above, we also tested another five cases, namely MLP, LSTM, RBF kernel GPR, NKN kernel GPR, and MLP + RBF kernel GPR. That is, a total of 36 sets of experiments were carried out.

For each set of experiments, we first do a hyperparameter tuning. After that, we train 2 times for each of the 4 high-precision PM10 measurement stations and then average these 8 training results as the performance of this pipeline setting. We use this metric to decide which pipeline setting is the best for each prediction model. Then we train additional 3 times with the best setting of each model. We compared these results with each other and also with the baseline (using the previous day label as the predicted value). The result of the best performance of each prediction model and in which pipeline settings it was achieved is shown in the following Table 1.

From the results in Table 1, we can draw the following conclusions:

Table 1. The best performance of each prediction model

Model	Best MAE	Best PCC	Best Settings	
			Interpolation	Slice & Center
Baseline	4.71	0.502	-	-
LSTM	4.04 ± 0.07	0.575 ± 0.020	True	Big Slicing
MLP + RBF_GPR	3.89 ± 0.08	0.624 ± 0.015	True	Big Slicing
RBF_GPR	3.87 ± 0.06	0.635 ± 0.007	True	Big Slicing
NKN_GPR	3.80 ± 0.04	0.641 ± 0.006	True	Big Slicing
MLP + NKN_GPR	3.67 ± 0.08	0.665 ± 0.014	True	Big Slicing
MLP	3.66 ± 0.04	0.690 ± 0.001	True	Big Slicing

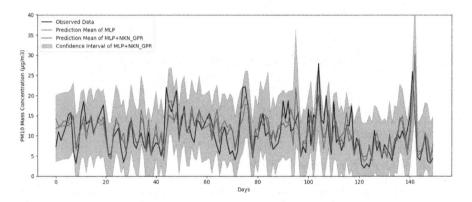

Fig. 7. MLP model (red line) can only give a single-valued prediction, GPR-based model (green line and interval), however, can also give a reasonable confidence interval of prediction through Bayesian theory. (Color figure online)

1. All prediction models give the best results in the experimental setting of interpolation + big slicing, which is consistent with our intuition described in Sect. 3.2.
2. Among all GPR-based models, the MLP + NKN_GPR model is the best-performing one. Overall, MLP achieves the best performance, and surprisingly, LSTM, which is usually considered a better solution to the time series problem, shows the worst result. After analysis, we believe this should be because the recurrent neural network (RNN) design determines that it is better at dealing with short-term dependencies. As an improvement to RNN, although LSTM has gained the ability to deal with long-term dependencies by adding gates mechanisms such as forget gates, the number of hidden units still limits its ability to express long-term memory. On the other hand, we believe that in this specific problem of PM10 forecasting, the short-term dependencies (such as the distribution over the last hour and the distribution of the same day in the previous week) and ultra-long-term periodic dependencies

(such as the same day of the other years) are dominant. In contrast, the more recent long-term dependencies (such as distributions from months ago), which LSTMs are good at handling, have relatively little impact on this problem. Furthermore, it must be pointed out again that MLP and LSTM also has the following shortcomings: MLP and LSTM are uninterpretable model and can only give a single-valued prediction, which means they cannot provide a reasonable confidence interval (Fig. 7, red line). In many scenarios (such as critical decision-making, when people are more reluctant to make mistakes), an uninterpretable single-valued prediction can only provide very limited help. The GPR-based model can give the confidence interval of prediction through Bayesian theory, which means the prediction given by the model is a Gaussian distribution. We can not only obtain the average value of this distribution (as a single-valued prediction) but also the standard deviation of this distribution can also be obtained (as the model's confidence in its predictions) (Fig. 7, green line and interval).

3. NKN kernel can effectively improve GP models' performance without prior knowledge of the dataset with the help of compositional kernel learning methods. Figure 8 shows the prediction results using the NKN kernel, the Matern kernel and the Cosine kernel. Since different kernels represent different prior assumptions about the dataset, their predictions are also entirely different. The NKN kernel can make multiple assumptions through its base kernels and then benefit from all these assumptions by learning the composition structure of these base kernels.

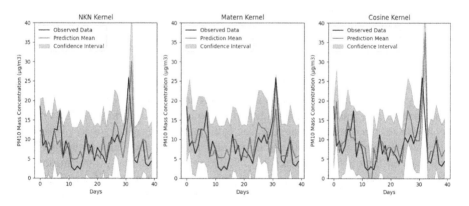

Fig. 8. Sample of the prediction results using the NKN kernel, the Matern kernel and the Cosine kernel

4.2 Evaluating the Role of Low-Cost Sensors in Prediction Tasks

As the first machine learning-based time series prediction study on the SmartAQnet dataset, we are also interested in the contribution that low-cost sensors can make to data analysis. Indeed, to improve sensor networks' temporal and spatial resolution, we must make a trade-off in cost. However, there have still been ongoing discussions about whether introducing ultra-low-cost sensors and citizen science projects into the network could benefit the datasets [3]. For this question, we also set up a set of controlled experiments.

The experimental setup is straightforward. We remove all data collected by ultra-low-cost sensors (84 CrowdSensing Nodes) from the dataset and then train the model pipeline with the same experimental setup as the above-mentioned best practice. It is worth noting that after removing these ultra-low-cost sensors, the entire sensor network still has over 100 sensors, which is still very dense for the spatial extent we model. We run each set of experiment 5 times, the following Table 2 shows the results of the experiments:

Table 2. The contribution that low-cost sensors can make to data analysis

	MAE ± std	PCC ± std
With Ultra-low-cost Sensors	3.67 ± 0.08	0.665 ± 0.014
Without Ultra-low-cost Sensors	4.14 ± 0.04	0.589 ± 0.032
Baseline	4.71	0.502

The results of the experiments are evident: although ultra-low-cost sensors introduce more heterogeneity and uncertainty into the aggregated dataset, they can significantly improve the expressiveness of the data when processed and analyzed appropriately.

5 Conclusions

In this paper, we propose a new model pipeline for time-series prediction of urban particulate matter based on heterogeneous sensor information. The model pipeline takes measurements aggregated from multiple internet sources with high heterogeneity and uncertainty as input and predicts the daily average PM10 mass concentration for the next day. We have experimentally determined the suitable components for the model pipeline: to sequentially perform temporal-spatial aggregation, spatial interpolation, slicing and centering, window generation, PCA dimensionality reduction on the input data, and then use MLP + GP regression with an NKN kernel to perform the prediction task. Ultimately, our model pipeline achieved an average MAE of $3.67\,\mu g/m^3$ and a Pearson correlation coefficient of 0.665.

Furthermore, we experimentally verify the contribution of citizen-run ultra-low-cost sensors in the prediction. Thanks to their meager cost, ultra-low-cost sensors can be large-scale deployed by institutional entities or popularized through citizen science programs. Although these sensors pose challenges such as heterogeneity and uncertainty, they significantly increase the temporal and spatial coverage of the data. We observe that the addition of ultra-low-cost sensor data reduces the average MAE of our prediction model from $4.18 \,\mu g/m^3$ to $3.67 \,\mu g/m^3$ and increases the PCC from 0.589 to 0.665. As long as processed and analyzed appropriately, ultra-low-cost sensors will definitely result in a significant performance improvement. We thus believe that post-hoc sensor networks that fuse different sensor sources in an opportunistic manner can thus advance knowledge in areas into which classical measurement systems cannot scale due to the cost of initial installation and maintenance. Prediction quality, however, can wildly vary based on the quantity and quality of the local sensor. Thus new prediction methods are needed that can derive certainty measures from the available data. We are confident that Gaussian process modeling can be a key component to inter- and extrapolating heterogeneous information sources. Machine learning approaches like neural networks can greatly help to derive fitting kernels that qualify relations between multiple heterogeneous data sources and choose hyperparameters according to the observed data.

Acknowledgments. We would like to give special thanks to Helmholtz European Partnership for Technological Advancement (HEPTA) for supporting this study. This work was also supported by Helmholtz AI Computing Resources (HAICORE) of the Helm-holtz Association's Initiative and Networking Fund through Helmholtz AI.

References

1. Bruns, J., Riesterer, J., Wang, B., Riedel, T., Beigl, M.: Automated quality assessment of (citizen) weather stations. GI-Forum **1**, 65–81 (2018)
2. Budde, M., et al.: Smartaqnet: remote and in-situ sensing of urban air quality. In: Remote Sensing of Clouds and the Atmosphere XXII, vol. 10424, pp. 19–26. SPIE (2017)
3. Budde, M., Schankin, A., Hoffmann, J., Danz, M., Riedel, T., Beigl, M.: Participatory sensing or participatory nonsense? mitigating the effect of human error on data quality in citizen science. Proc. ACM Interact. Mobile Wearable Ubiquitous Technol. **1**(3), 1–23 (2017)
4. Budde, M., et al.: Potential and limitations of the low-cost SDS011 particle sensor for monitoring urban air quality. ProScience **5**, 6–12 (2018)
5. Chen, S.: Beijing Multi-Site Air-Quality Data. UCI Machine Learning Repository (2019)
6. Cohen, A.J., et al.: Estimates and 25-year trends of the global burden of disease attributable to ambient air pollution: an analysis of data from the global burden of diseases study 2015. The Lancet **389**(10082), 1907–1918 (2017)
7. Duvenaud, D., Lloyd, J., Grosse, R., Tenenbaum, J., Zoubin, G.: Structure discovery in nonparametric regression through compositional kernel search. In: International Conference on Machine Learning, pp. 1166–1174. PMLR (2013)
8. English, P., et al.: Performance of a low-cost sensor community air monitoring network in imperial county, CA. Sensors **20**(11), 3031 (2020)
9. Grothe, M., Broecke, J.V., Carton, L., Volten, H., Kieboom, R.: Smart emission-building a spatial data infrastructure for an environmental citizen sensor network. In: Jirka, S., Stasch, C., Hitchcock, A. (ed.) Proceedings of the Geospatial Sensor Webs Conference 2016 (GSW 2016), Münster, Germany, 29–31 August 2016, pp. 1–7. CEUR-WS.org/Vol-1762 (2016)

10. Hoffmann, B., et al.: Who air quality guidelines 2021-aiming for healthier air for all: a joint statement by medical, public health, scientific societies and patient representative organisations. Int. J. Public Health 88 (2021)

11. Jin, S.S.: Compositional kernel learning using tree-based genetic programming for gaussian process regression. Struct. Multidiscip. Optim. **62**(3), 1313–1351 (2020)

12. Kim, H., Teh, Y.W.: Scaling up the automatic statistician: scalable structure discovery using gaussian processes. In: International Conference on Artificial Intelligence and Statistics, pp. 575–584. PMLR (2018)

13. Kuremoto, T., Kimura, S., Kobayashi, K., Obayashi, M.: Time series forecasting using a deep belief network with restricted boltzmann machines. Neurocomputing **137**, 47–56 (2014)

14. Li, C., Budde, M., Tremper, P., Riedel, T., Beigl, M., et al.: Smartaqnet 2020: a new open urban air quality dataset from heterogeneous pm sensors. Proscience **8**, 1–10 (2021)

15. Li, J.J., Faltings, B., Saukh, O., Hasenfratz, D., Beutel, J.: Sensing the air we breathe-the opensense zurich dataset. In: Twenty-Sixth AAAI Conference on Artificial Intelligence (2012)

16. Martilli, A., et al.: Simulating the pollutant dispersion during persistent wintertime thermal inversions over urban areas. the case of Madrid. Atmos. Res. **270**, 106058 (2022)

17. Ong, B.T., Sugiura, K., Zettsu, K.: Dynamically pre-trained deep recurrent neural networks using environmental monitoring data for predicting PM2. 5. Neural Comput. Appl. **27**(6), 1553–1566 (2016)

18. Qin, D., Yu, J., Zou, G., Yong, R., Zhao, Q., Zhang, B.: A novel combined prediction scheme based on CNN and LSTM for urban PM 2.5 concentration. IEEE Access **7**, 20050–20059 (2019)

19. Rivas, E., et al.: CFD modelling of air quality in Pamplona City (spain): assessment, stations spatial representativeness and health impacts valuation. Sci. Total Environ. **649**, 1362–1380 (2019)

20. Suganya, S., Meyyappan, T.: Adaptive deep learning model for air pollution analysis using meteorological big data. In: 2021 2nd International Conference on Communication, Computing and Industry 4.0 (C2I4), pp. 1–6. IEEE (2021)

21. Sun, S., Zhang, G., Wang, C., Zeng, W., Li, J., Grosse, R.: Differentiable compositional kernel learning for gaussian processes. In: International Conference on Machine Learning, pp. 4828–4837. PMLR (2018)

22. Tobler, W.R.: A computer movie simulating urban growth in the detroit region. Econ. Geogr. **46**(sup1), 234–240 (1970)

Ontology and Semantic Web

Comparative Ranking of Ontologies with ELECTRE Family of Multi-criteria Decision-Making Algorithms

Ameeth Sooklall$^{(\boxtimes)}$ (ID) and Jean Vincent Fonou-Dombeu (ID)

School of Mathematics, Statistics and Computer Science, University of
KwaZulu-Natal, Pietermaritzburg, South Africa
ameethsooklall1@gmail.com

Abstract. Ontology selection is an active research topic to date. Essentially, ontology selection is a Multi-Criteria Decision-Making (MCDM) problem, as there are multiple ontologies to choose from whilst considering multiple criteria. The ELimination Et. Choix Traduisant la REalité (ELECTRE) is a family of popular MCDM methods. However, there has been little usage of the methods in ontology ranking to aid ontology selection and the comparisons between them on the same decision problem is missing in the literature. In this study, 4 ELECTRE methods were applied on a dataset of 200 ontologies along with 13 complexity metrics for each ontology. The experimental results show that all 4 ELECTRE methods have successfully ranked each ontology. The performances of the ELECTRE methods were further compared with 3 Statistical Rank Correlation Metrics. The correlation coefficients depicted a high level of agreement amongst the rankings of all ELECTRE versions despite some dissimilarities.

Keywords: Ontology ranking · ELECTRE · Multi-Criteria
Decision-Making · Complexity metrics · BioPortal

1 Introduction

An ontology, defined as an explicit specification of a shared conceptualization [1], is one of the core components facilitating knowledge representation and reasoning in artificial intelligence (AI). Ontologies describe different domains of discourse, and they play an important role in expressing complex knowledge in a form that enables reasoning, dissemination, and computation. It is one of the prominent solutions to managing and advancing knowledge and information overload.

One of the greatest advantages of ontology is its implications to the medical domain. The need for accurate and timely medical knowledge and expertise is of massive importance - it is essentially a matter of life and death. Unfortunately, it is very difficult to acquire medical knowledge, or rather accurate medical knowledge. This is addressed with the usage of ontology and ontological engineering.

© The Author(s), under exclusive license to Springer Nature Switzerland AG 2022
E. Pardede et al. (Eds.): iiWAS 2022, LNCS 13635, pp. 269–281, 2022.
https://doi.org/10.1007/978-3-031-21047-1_23

The BioPortal ontology repository [2] is one such example of an invaluable ocean of medical knowledge. The BioPortal is one of many ontology repositories, stimulating the applications and integration of ontology with other AI technologies - like machine learning, data mining, computer vision, and robotics. Evidently, the ontology is a very powerful tool for human advancement, and it is arguably still in its infancy stages. However, the excellence of ontology is not without its issues and challenges.

Ontologies are complex structures, which make them highly arduous to architect and develop. A wide range of expertise is required for the research and development of an ontology. Accordingly, this process can be time consuming and costly. Whilst some projects may require an ontology to be developed *de novo*, for most projects there is already a massive number of ontologies available to choose from. It is therefore more efficient to reuse [3] an existing ontology, possibly with some modifications, as opposed to developing new ontologies. However, users are often unable to comprehend and analyze existing ontologies. It is therefore evident that there is an urgent need for the development of techniques for selecting ontologies for reuse. This is however, not at all an easy task. There are so many different perspectives and approaches one could consider when selecting an ontology, and therefore a one-size-fits-all approach cannot be taken.

There have been attempts to solve the problem of selecting pertinent ontologies for reuse [4–8]. This generally comprised of users expressing their requirements in search terms or other forms, and the similarity between the users requirements and the ontologies are determined - assigning the most similar ontologies to higher ranks, and the dissimilar ontologies to lower ranks. This has been effective to an extent, however there is also a need to evaluate and rank ontologies according to their inherent characteristics. To this extent, there has been a small amount of research regarding ranking of ontologies in terms of their quality and attributes [9,10]. To evaluate the quality of ontologies researchers have developed different approaches. One effective approach is through the use of complexity metrics [11]. The complexity metrics allow a user to gain insights as to the design and complexity of ontologies. While there has been a vast amount of research related to ontology ranking [4–8], there has been only limited works regarding complexity metrics and ranking of ontologies. This is concerning as it is crucial that techniques be developed that enable thorough evaluation and ranking of ontologies from multi-dimensional perspectives.

Essentially, ontology ranking is a Multi-Criteria Decision-Making (MCDM) problem, as there are multiple ontologies to choose from whilst considering multiple criteria. Concernedly, there has been very little research that has applied decision-making techniques to enhance ontology ranking and selection. The MCDM field has been around for many decades, and it has proven successful in a variety of domains. Arguably one of the most widely used MCDM methods is ELECTRE. The original ELECTRE method was developed as a selection tool, named as ELECTRE I [12]. In subsequent years, researchers have enhanced ELECTRE I, leading to the development of the ELECTRE II [13], III [14], IV [15], and Tri [16] versions.

In this study, the methods of the ELECTRE family are applied to rank 200 biomedical ontologies from the BioPortal repository along with 13 of their complexity metrics, and the performances, pros and cons of ELECTRE methods are compared and discussed. This provides insights on the suitability of the ELECTRE methods in the task of ontology ranking and their potential adoption in decision-making problems in other domains.

The rest of the paper evolves as follows. Section 2 reviews the related studies. The next section presents the methods and materials. Section 4 discusses the results of the experiments, and finally the paper is concluded in Sect. 5.

2   Related Work

Ranking of ontologies has been quite an active research topic in recent years [4–8,17]. In [7], the authors developed the system known as AKTiveRank which uses the search terms of user's as input, and then processes this input in a knowledge engine to output a score. This score is then used to rank ontologies. A range of metrics were employed including the Centrality and the Class Match Measures. This research gave rise to some significant questions which required the subject to be investigated further. For this reason, the authors did a subsequent study [8] where they modified the AKTiveRank system to rank ontologies based on some structural metrics such as the Betweenness, Density and Semantic Similarity Measures. In the same manner as the initial version, an AKTiveRank score is given to each ontology which determines its ranking results.

In another study by Yu et al. [17], the authors devised an approach known as ARRO to rank ontologies. ARRO shares a substantial amount of design with AKTiveRank [8] in that it also performs the ranking based on the relevance of the ontologies to the user's search queries. It makes use of features such as the hierarchy structure to rank the ontologies.

Alipanah et al. [4] performed a study to rank ontologies in which they outlined an algorithm that uses an information theory measurement, Entropy Based Distribution (EBD), as a distance measure to identify similarity between ontology pairs. They used naïve and bisecting k-medoid clustering algorithms along with these similarity pairs to rank the ontologies. The authors also proposed the use of heuristics and pruning methods for future ranking studies.

Another study by Butt et al. [5] developed a framework, namely, DWRank, that performs the ranking of ontologies based on relationships and the retrieval of the top-k concepts. This comprises two phases, an online evaluation and query phase, and an offline phase for learning. DWRank uses concepts of authority and centrality to determine the weights of ontologies.

Subhashini and Akilandeswari [6] proposed a ranking algorithm named Onto-DSB that is based on the internal structure of the ontology and its link to the semantic web. It uses Betweenness, Depthness, and Semantic Informative measures. It was tested on an ontology set from Swoogle [18] and the results outperformed the Swoogle and AKTiveRank techniques. The above studies focus on ranking ontologies but do not employ decision-making techniques.

In recent years, several MCDM methods were applied in ontologies ranking including the Weighted Linear Combination Ranking Technique (WLCRT) [9], the Technique for Order Preference by Similarity to Ideal Solution (TOPSIS), Weighted Sum Model (WSM), and Weighted Product Model (WPM) [10]. Despite the numerous applications of the ELECTRE methods in various domains [21–24], there is extremely little usage of the methods in ontology ranking, or even in the field of ontological engineering in general. The only two studies that applied ELEC-TRE for ontology ranking was in [19] and [20]. Both studies suffer from a significant weakness pertaining to the size of their datasets. Real-world ontology repositories contain a much larger number of ontologies than 12 and 70, and furthermore search engines, recommendation systems, and decision support systems may need to rank hundreds of ontologies. Furthermore, the study in [20] ranked ontologies according to their similarities with users terms, which is essentially taking the same approach as the traditional ontology ranking studies discussed above.

There is a significant gap in the literature regarding the ELECTRE methods applicability to the ranking of large real-world datasets of ontologies. Furthermore, the entire ELECTRE family has not been applied for ontology ranking, and comparisons between the entire ELECTRE family on the same decision problem are rare in the literature. The ELECTRE methods have been applied to a variety of domains [21–24]. The ELECTRE methods have been combined and integrated as components in larger models, frameworks, and methods in a range of studies [22,23]. Furthermore, from [21,24], the ability of ELECTRE to deal with large real-world datasets is affirmed, where the authors apply ELEC-TRE to 100 and 392 alternatives, respectively. These factors provide evidence that the ELECTRE family is an excellent choice for the task of ontology ranking. The materials and methods are presented next.

3   Materials and Methods

3.1   Complexity Metrics of Ontologies

An ontology is fundamentally complex due to the expert knowledge and the underlying logic required for its design. Therefore, researchers have proposed various metrics and measures [11] to enable users or knowledge engineers to better understand the design and complexity of ontologies. In this study, 13 metrics that measure the design complexity of ontology are used as attributes of ontologies criteria to rank them. These complexity metrics are [11]: Average Population (AP), Average Number of Paths (ANP), Average Breadth (AB), Maximal Breadth (MB), Average Depth (AD), Maximal Depth (MD), Attribute Richness (AR), Class Richness (CR), Relationship Richness (RR), Inheritance Richness (IR), Absolute Root Cardinality (ARC), Absolute Leaf Cardinality (ALC), and Equivalence Ratio (ER).

3.2   ELECTRE

All the ELECTRE methods require a decision-maker to specify the decision problem, comprising alternatives, $A = \{a_1, a_2, \ldots, a_m\}$, and criteria, $g_1, g_2, \ldots, g_n$.

The alternatives and criteria form a decision matrix, $D_{m \times n}$. A weight vector, $W = [w_1, w_2, \ldots, w_n]$, is defined, where w_i represents the weight for criterion j. The fifth version of ELECTRE namely ELECTRE Tri was not experimented in this study as it was designed for classification problems [16]. Furthermore, due to space constraints, only a short presentation of each ELECTRE version is given below; more information could be found in the sources provided.

ELECTRE I [12] proceeds by determining the concordance values, $C(a, b)$, and discordance values, $D(a, b)$, between all alternative pairs. Thereafter, a concordance threshold, c, and a discordance threshold, d, must be specified, using which the outranking relation can be determined as aSb if $C(a, b) \geq c$ and $D(a, b) \leq d$. To obtain a complete ranking of alternatives, the difference between the number of alternatives that an alternative a_i outranks and the number of alternatives that outrank alternative a_i is calculated, and the the alternatives are ranked in order of the largest to smallest difference values calculated.

ELECTRE II [13] determines the concordance, $C(a, b)$, and discordance values, $D(a, b)$, as in ELECTRE I. Here five thresholds are required, two discordance thresholds, d_1 and d_2, and three concordance thresholds, c^-, c^0, and c^+. Two outranking relations are determined, a strong outranking relation, S^F, and a weak outranking relation, S^f. To rank the alternatives from best to worst, ELECTRE II develops three pre-orders, V_1, V_2 and $\bar{V}$. V_1 and V_2 are determined by applying iterative approaches, known as the *direct ranking procedure* and the *inverse ranking procedure*, respectively. The final pre-order, $\bar{V}$, is determined by the intersection of V_1 and V_2, resulting in a partial ranking of all alternatives. In this study $\bar{V}$ is determined by taking the mid-point rank of each alternative from both V_1 and V_2, which yielded a complete ranking, rather than a partial ranking.

ELECTRE III [14] requires three sets of thresholds, the indifference thresholds q_j, preference thresholds p_j, and veto thresholds v_j, such that $v_j \geq p_j \geq q_j$. Here the partial and global concordances must be calculated, followed by the discordance values. Following this, the credibility index, $S(a, b)$, is determined. Finally, a technique is applied in order to obtain a ranking. Firstly, a *descending distillation* from best to worst is performed, resulting in a pre-order, Z_1. Thereafter, an *ascending distillation* is performed whereby the alternatives are ranked from worst to best, resulting in a second pre-order, Z_2. To obtain a final ranking, Z_1 and Z_2 are combined using an intersection technique, resulting in a partial ordering of the alternatives. In this study, the alternatives are combined by taking the mid-point of Z_1 and Z_2 to produce a complete ranking.

ELECTRE IV [15], like ELECTRE III, requires the indifference thresholds q_j, preference thresholds p_j, and veto thresholds v_j. ELECTRE IV has 4 parameters, m_p, m_q, m_i, and m_0. These parameters are in-turn evaluated to assign one of five outranking relations for each alternative pair comparison. These are Quasi-Dominance S_q, Canonical Dominance S_c, Pseudo-Dominance S_p, Sub-Dominance S_s, and Veto Dominance S_v. After determining the outranking relations, the degree of credibility is determined in accordance with the outranking relations. Using the similar distillation techniques as in ELECTRE III, the calculated values are applied to produce two pre-orders. The two pre-orders are combined to obtain their average, and are ranked the same as in ELECTRE III.

4   Experimental Results and Discussion

4.1   Dataset

The dataset was composed of 200 ontologies complied from the BioPortal ontology repository. Due to space constraints the dataset was not included in this paper, but it can be accessed in this location[1]. The ontologies in the dataset included various types of knowledge related to the biological and biomedical domains. The thirteen complexity metrics for measuring the quality of the ontologies in the dataset were calculated with the use of the OntoMetrics[2] platform.

4.2   Computer and Software Environment

This study was performed using the Microsoft® Windows® 10 device with 8 GB of RAM. The device had an Intel® Core™ i-5 processor with a speed of 2.30GHz. The software for the ELECTRE I, II, III, and IV algorithms were implemented using the Java 8 programming language, together with the Jet-Brains IntelliJ IDEA Community Edition 2019.1.3 development environment.

4.3   Ranking Results

Initially, the importance of each criterion was determined with the use of the Criteria Importance Through Inter-criteria Correlation (CRITIC) [25] weighting method. The weights were set as follows: $AR = 0.06$, $IR = 0.08$, $RR = 0.14$, $ER = 0.07$, $AP = 0.07$, $CR = 0.10$, $ARC = 0.05$, $ALC = 0.08$, $AD = 0.12$, $MD = 0.07$, $AB = 0.04$, $MB = 0.07$, and $ANP = 0.05$. The thresholds for the ELECTRE I method were set to $c = 0.56$ and $d = 0.11$. The thresholds for ELECTRE II were set to $d^- = 0.2, d^+ = 0.25, c^- = 0.5, c^0 = 0.6, c^+ = 0.7$. The veto, preference, and indifference thresholds for ELECTRE III and IV are displayed in Table 1.

Figure 1 shows the rankings per ELECTRE method, representing each ELECTRE version by a different color plot. ELECTRE I, II, III, and IV are represented by the yellow, red, green, and purple plots, respectively. It can be observed from Fig. 1 that there are some variations in the rankings, but essentially all rankings of ELECTRE methods follow a similar trend. Visually, the ELECTRE III method (green plot) appears to be most dissimilar to the other three methods.

In order to analyze the rankings in terms of the different ELECTRE models, the rank correlation was calculated for every ELECTRE model pair. Three

---

[1] https://bit.ly/3xySKCr.

[2] https://ontometrics.informatik.uni-rostock.de/ontologymetrics/.

Table 1. ELECTRE indifference, preference, and veto thresholds

Criterion	AR	IR	RR	ER	AP	CR	ARC	ALC	AD	MD	AB	MB	ANP
q_j	0.05	0.07	0.05	0.06	0.06	0.06	0.04	0.05	0.06	0.04	0.04	0.04	0.05
p_j	0.08	0.08	0.06	0.08	0.08	0.07	0.07	0.07	0.07	0.07	0.09	0.07	0.08
v_j	0.14	0.10	0.08	0.12	0.12	0.10	0.14	0.10	0.09	0.13	0.17	0.11	0.13

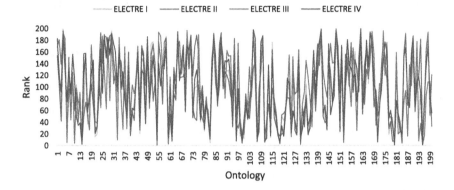

Fig. 1. Plots of ranking results of ELECTRE methods.

statistical techniques were applied, that is, the Spearman's Rho coefficient [26], the Weighted Spearman's Rho coefficient [27], and the WS coefficient [28]. The Spearman's Rho measures the relation between two sets of rankings, by treating all rank positions equally. The Weighted Spearman's Rho is an enhancement of Spearman's Rho that gives more weighting to the ranks at the top, and less importance to the ranks at the bottom. The WS coefficient is similar to the Weighted Spearman's Rho value, in that it also places an emphasis on disagreements that occur at the top as opposed to disagreements that occur at the bottom. The heatmaps in Fig. 2 depicts the three correlation measures applied to the rankings for every ELECTRE pair.

It can be seen that the correlation for the Spearman's Rho (left block of Fig. 2) and the Weighted Spearman's Rho were very similar and the WS coefficients are high as compared to the other coefficients. It can be seen that in all three measures, ELECTRE I had the strongest relationships with the ELECTRE II, III, and IV; this is evidenced by higher correlation coefficients in the top row in Fig. 2. In fact, in all three statistical measures, ELECTRE I had a correlation of at least 0.91 with ELECTRE II and IV. ELECTRE III had the lowest correlations with the other ELECTRE models. Overall, all correlation values from the three statistical measures had a minimum of 0.6 and a maximum 0.99, with more than half of the total 18 correlation measures being at least 0.9. This shows that despite some disagreements, the rankings follow a similar trend. However, it should be emphasized that having a high correlation between two rankings

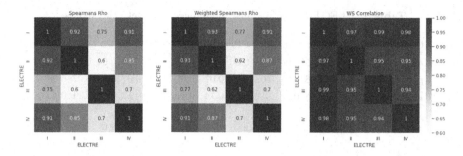

Fig. 2. Heatmaps of statistical correlation values for ELECTRE rankings

does not validate or invalidate either ranking or other rankings, rather it only provides insights regarding the performance of one ranker in light of another.

In order to further compare the rankings of the different ELECTRE methods, the maximum difference in ranks assigned to each ontology is explored. The maximum difference is the distance between the lowest and highest rank assigned to a particular ontology. It signifies the level of agreement amongst the four ELECTRE methods. The maximum differences for all 200 ontologies is shown in the graph in Fig. 3.

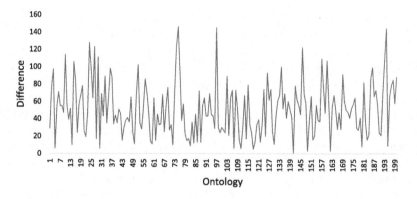

Fig. 3. Maximum difference in ELECTRE rankings

It can be observed from Fig. 3 that most ontologies had a small to moderately sized maximum difference in their rankings. In fact, the average maximum difference for an ontology was 51. There are however, some ontologies that had an unusually large maximum difference. These include O_{10}, O_{24}, O_{27}, O_{29}, O_{52}, O_{74}, O_{75}, O_{97}, O_{146}, and O_{193}. There were also many ontologies that had very small maximum difference values, such as O_{141} having a maximum difference of just 1, O_{149} and O_{162} having maximum differences of 3, O_{118} having a maximum difference of 5, and O_4, O_{30}, O_{107}, and O_{111} having maximum differences of 6. Even though the average maximum difference for an ontology was 51, there were

104 ontologies that had a maximum difference less than 51, of which 32 ontologies had a maximum difference value of less than 20, and 80 ontologies had a maximum difference of less than 40.

The names of the top 10 ontologies ranked by ELECTRE I and II are displayed in Table 2, and the names of the top 10 ontologies ranked by ELECTRE III and IV are displayed in Table 3. Due to space constraints the entire ranking results could not be included in this paper, but can be accessed in this location[3].

Table 2. Top 10 ontologies by each ELECTRE I and II

Rank	ELECTRE I	ELECTRE II
1	planp.owl	Ocmr-merged.owl
2	mro.owl	Cell line ontology v2.0.owl
3	OntolUrgences_v3.0.4.owl	OntolUrgences_v3.0.4.owl
4	Cell line ontology v2.0.owl	MSTDE-FRE.ttl
5	Cmpo.owl	cogat.owl
6	ohpi_merged.owl	ohpi_merged.owl
7	PTS_Revised_Merged_Final.owl	oboe.owl
8	cogat.owl	PTS_Revised_Merged_Final.owl
9	PDO_FullyAnnotated_Final_v1.0.owl	mro.owl
10	STO_v4.0.owl	planp.owl

From Table 2 and 3 it can be observed that many of the ontologies ranked in the top 10 by one ELECTRE version have also been ranked in the top 10 by other ELECTRE versions. The *planp.owl* and *mro.owl* ontologies were given a top 10 rank position by all four ELECTRE methods. The *OntolUrgences_ V3.0.4.owl*, *ohpi_merged.owl*, *PDO_FullyAnnotated_Final_v1.0.owl*, *STO_v4.0.owl*, and *Ocmr-merged.owl* ontologies were given a top 10 rank position by three out of four ELECTRE methods. The *PTS_Revised_Merged_Final.owl*, *cogat.owl* and *Cell line ontology v2.0.owl* ontologies were given top 10 rank positions by two of the four ELECTRE versions. There were only 11 ontologies that were only given a top 10 rank position by one ELECTRE version, these are, *Cmpo.owl*, *MSTDE-FRE.ttl*, *oboe.owl*, *Allergy Detector.owl*, *NCCN-HER.owl*, *cio.owl*, *Pco.owl*, *VO.owl*, *schemaorg-all-layers-3.4-fixes.rdf*, *ohmi_merged.owl*, and *obi.owl*. The top-ranked ontology from each ELECTRE version is discussed further as follows.

The *planp.owl* ontology [2], which represents the Planarian Phenotype Ontology, was ranked as the best ontology by ELECTRE I and III, as the 10th best by ELECTRE II, and the 2nd best by ELECTRE IV. The Planarian Phenotype Ontology comprises phenotypes from the planarian Schmidtea Mediterranean. The ontology had higher values for the IR, ER, AD and ANP metrics. This

---

[3] https://bit.ly/3ObNlXm.

Table 3. Top 10 ontologies by each ELECTRE III and IV

Rank	ELECTRE III	ELECTRE IV
1	planp.owl	mro.owl
2	STO_v4.0.owl	planp.owl
3	PDO_FullyAnnotated_Final_v1.0.owl	STO_v4.0.owl
4	Allergy Detector.owl	VO.owl
5	NCCN-HER.owl	PDO_FullyAnnotated_Final_v1.0.owl
6	OntolUrgences_v3.0.4.owl	schemaorg-all-layers-3.4-fixes.rdf
7	mro.owl	ohmi_merged.owl
8	cio.owl	obi.owl
9	Ocmr-merged.owl	ohpi_merged.owl
10	Pco.owl	Ocmr-merged.owl

implies that the *planp.owl* ontology's structure and contents accurately represent the phenotypes domain [29], better than other ontologies in the dataset.

The *mro.owl* ontology [2] represents the Major Histocompatibility Complex Restriction Ontology, which defines the Major Histocompatibility Complex restriction in experiments. This is an application ontology that includes, exact protein complexes, haplotypes, serotypes, and mutant molecules. The ontology was ranked at first position by ELECTRE IV, and at positions 2, 9, and 7 by ELECTRE I, II, and III, respectively. it had a higher equivalence ratio value, signifying its high accuracy [29] in representing its target domain.

The Ontology of Chinese Medicine for Rheumatism [2], *Ocmr-merged.owl*, was ranked at first place by ELECTRE II. This ontology represents the medical information related to anti-rheumatism Chinese medicines. It had higher values for AD, ANP, IR and MD metrics, implying that it accurately represents the Chinese Medicine for Rheumatism domain [29] better than other ontologies in the dataset. The pros and cons of ELECTRE methods are discussed next.

4.4   Pros and Cons of ELECTRE Methods

This study applied 4 ELECTRE methods to rank ontologies, but in real-world scenarios a decision-maker may only require a single model for ranking. However, it could be difficult to select the appropriate model to apply in a given scenario. Therefore, the pros and cons of ELECTRE methods are discussed in this section to provide some guidelines for selecting the appropriate ELECTRE model for the task of ontology ranking in particular and decision-making problems in general.

ELECTRE I has the advantage of being easier to comprehend compared to other ELECTRE versions. It is therefore easier to implement, as well as to integrate into larger systems, such as recommender and decision support systems. However, the method makes use of only two thresholds, which reduces its modelling capability. ELECTRE I could be ideal for eliminating poor-performing alternatives by selecting a non-dominated kernel from all alternatives.

ELECTRE II is, in some sense, an improvement to ELECTRE I, granted that it is able to better identify differences in performance due to its five thresholds, as opposed to the two thresholds in ELECTRE I. However, this method may also have lower modelling capability than ELECTRE III and IV. Furthermore, ELECTRE II may be less intuitive than ELECTRE I, thereby decreasing its comprehensibility and making it harder to implement.

ELECTRE III allows a decision-maker to define thresholds for the different criteria separately, as opposed to ELECTRE I and II. This enables a richer form of problem modelling and expressiveness. One concern may be the complexity involved in the distillation procedure, which can be less intuitive than the exploitation procedures for ELECTRE I and II. ELECTRE III should be considered for ranking as it is quite expressive and flexible.

ELECTRE IV follows a similar approach to ELECTRE III, but the major difference lies in its ability to function without weights. This may be an advantage and a disadvantage depending on the use case. It is an advantage if a decision-maker is not able to specify weights for the problem, in which case ELECTRE IV would be the only applicable method. However, if a user requires to specify criteria importance weights then ELECTRE IV cannot be used in that instance. The ELECTRE IV method could be applied as a component of a larger system, such as a decision support system, whereby ranking is required without weighted criteria importance.

Overall, this study demonstrated the power of MCDM methods, particularly ELECTRE, in aiding the ontology selection process by performing ontology ranking. The statistical correlation values show that even though the performances of all methods are similar, there still exists differences. This is due to the internal workings of each method. Therefore, the ELECTRE methods can be applied to provide decision support in a range of decision problems, by selecting the appropriate model for the corresponding decision problem.

A factor that may discourage the application of MCDM is the rising trend in the use of machine learning (ML) techniques. However, traditional MCDM methods, like ELECTRE, are still very much needed for their many advantages. For instance, MCDM methods do not need to be trained like ML models, rather they can provide decision support instantly, and MCDM methods typically can be applied to small and large decision problems, whereas ML models require large amounts of data in order to be effective.

5 Conclusion

In this study a prominent branch of MCDM, the ELECTRE family of algorithms, were applied to rank ontologies. A dataset of 200 biomedical ontologies was obtained from the BioPortal repository and 13 complexity metrics were selected and calculated for each ontology. All four ELECTRE methods, namely, ELECTRE I, II, III, and IV, were able to assign a rank to each ontology. In order to compare the performances of the methods, the Spearman's Rho, Weighted Spearman's Rho, and WS correlation values were calculated for each ELECTRE pair. The results depicted that there was a fairly high level of agreement amongst all ELECTRE versions, with ELECTRE I having the highest degree of similarity with the other ELECTRE methods, and ELECTRE III having the highest level of dissimilarity. Thereafter, the top 10 ontologies from each ELECTRE method were analyzed and it was found that many of the top 10 ontologies were given a top 10 rank by more than one ELECTRE version. The top ranked ontology from each method was then analyzed to verify its quality over the other ontologies in the dataset. Lastly, the pros and cons of ELECTRE methods were discussed to provide some guidelines for selecting the appropriate version of ELECTRE for the task of ontology ranking in particular and decision-making problems in general. Future directions of the study may include the application of other MCDM techniques for ontology ranking, as well as MCDM classification techniques, such as ELECTRE Tri, in order to classify ontologies according to their complexity.

References

1. Gruber, T.: A translation approach to portable ontology specifications. Knowl. Acquisit. **5**(2), 199–220 (1993)
2. NCBO BioPortal. https://bioportal.bioontology.org/. Accessed 12 June 2022
3. Uschold, M., Healy, M., Williamson, K., Clark, P., Woods, S.: Ontology reuse and application. In Proceedings of the International Conference on Formal Ontology and Information Systems - FOIS 1998 (1998)
4. Alipanah, N., Srivastava, P., Parveen, P., Thuraisingham, B.: Ranking ontologies using verified entities to facilitate federated queries. In: 2010 IEEE International Conference on Web Intelligence & Intelligent Agent Technology (2010)
5. Butt, A., Haller, A., Xie, L.: DWRank: learning concept ranking for ontology search. Semant. Web **7**(4), 447–461 (2016)
6. Subhashini, R., Akilandeswari, J.: A novel approach for ranking ontologies based on the structure and semantics. J. Theor. Appl. Inf. Technol. **65**(1), 147–153 (2014)
7. Alani, H., Brewster, C.: Ontology ranking based on the analysis of concept structures. In: Third International Conference on Knowledge Capture (K-Cap) (2005)
8. Alani, H., Brewster, C., Shadbolt, N.: Ranking ontologies with AKTiveRank. In: Proceedings of the 5th International Conference on the Semantic Web, Athens, Greece, pp. 1–15 (2006)
9. Fonou-Dombeu, J., Viriri, S.: CRank: a novel framework for ranking semantic web ontologies. In: Model and Data Engineering, pp. 107–121 (2018)
10. Fonou-Dombeu, J.V.: A comparative application of multi-criteria decision making in ontology ranking. In: Abramowicz, W., Corchuelo, R. (eds.) BIS 2019. LNBIP, vol. 353, pp. 55–69. Springer, Cham (2019). https://doi.org/10.1007/978-3-030-20485-3_5
11. Gangemi, A., Catenacci, C., Ciaramita, M., Lehmann, J.: Ontology evaluation and validation: an integrated formal model for the quality diagnostic task (2005)
12. Roy, B.: Classement et choix en présence de points de vue multiples. Revue française d'informatique et de recherche opérationnelle. **2**(8), 57–75 (1968)
13. Roy, B., Bertier, P.: La methode ELECTRE II: Une methode de classement en presence de critteres multiples. SEMA (Metra International), Direction Scientifique, Note de Travail No. 142, Paris, 25 (1971)

14. Roy, B.: ELECTRE III: Un algorithme de classements fonde sur une representation floue des preferences en presence de criteres multiples. Cahiers de CERO. **20**(1), 3–24 (1978)
15. Roy, B., Hugonnard, J.: Classement des prolongements de lignes de metro en banlieue parisienne. Cahiers de CERO **24**(2-3-4), 153–171 (1982)
16. Yu, W.: ELECTRE TRI - Aspects Méthodologiques et Manuel d'utilisation. Document - Université de Paris-Dauphine, LAMSADE (1992)
17. Yu, W., Chen, J., Cao, J.: A novel approach for ranking ontologies on the semantic web. In: Proceedings of the 1st International Symposium on Pervasive Computing and Applications, Xinjiang, China, pp. 608–612 (2006)
18. Ding, L., Finn, T., Joshi, A., Peng, Y., Cost, R., Sachs, J.: Swoogle: a search and metadata engine for the semantic web. In: International Conference on Information and Knowledge Management, pp. 652–659 (2004)
19. Fonou-Dombeu, J.: Ranking semantic web ontologies with ELECTRE. In: 2019 International Conference on Advances in Big Data, Computing and Data Communication Systems (icABCD) (2019)
20. Esposito, A., Tarricone, L., Zappatore, M.: Applying multi-criteria approaches to ontology ranking: a comparison with AKTiveRank. Int. J. Metadata Semant. Ontol. **7**(3), 197 (2012)
21. Bergeron, M., Martel, J., Twarabimenye, P.: The evaluation of corporate loan applications based on the MCDA. J. Euro-Asian Manag. **2**(2), 16–46 (1996)
22. Macary, F., Ombredane, D., Uny, D.: A multicriteria spatial analysis of erosion risk into small watersheds in the low Normandy bocage (France) by ELECTRE III method coupled with a GIS. Int. J. MCDM **1**(1), 25–48 (2010)
23. Achillas, C., Vlachokostas, C., Moussiopoulos, N., Banias, G.: Prioritize strategies to confront environmental deterioration in urban areas: multicriteria assessment of public opinion and experts' views. Cities **28**(5), 414–423 (2011)
24. Augusto, M., Lisboa, J., Yasin, M., Figueira, J.: Benchmarking in a multiple criteria performance context: an application and a conceptual framework. Eur. J. Oper. Res. **184**(1), 244–254 (2008)
25. Diakoulaki, D., Mavrotas, G., Papayannakis, L.: Determining objective weights in multiple criteria problems: the critic method. Comput. Oper. Res. **22**(7), 763–770 (1995)
26. Spearman, C.: The proof and measurement of association between two things. Am. J. Psychol. **15**, 72–101 (1904)
27. da Costa, J.P., Soares, C.: A weighted rank measure of correlation. Aust. New Zealand J. Stat. **47**(4), 515–529 (2005)
28. Sałabun, W., Urbaniak, K.: A new coefficient of rankings similarity in decision-making problems. In: Krzhizhanovskaya, V.V., et al. (eds.) ICCS 2020. LNCS, vol. 12138, pp. 632–645. Springer, Cham (2020). https://doi.org/10.1007/978-3-030-50417-5_47
29. Fonou-Dombeu, J.V., Viriri, S.: OntoMetrics evaluation of quality of e-government ontologies. In: Kő, A., Francesconi, E., Anderst-Kotsis, G., Tjoa, A.M., Khalil, I. (eds.) EGOVIS 2019. LNCS, vol. 11709, pp. 189–203. Springer, Cham (2019). https://doi.org/10.1007/978-3-030-27523-5_14

Machine Learning Selection of Candidate Ontologies for Automatic Extraction of Context Words and Axioms from Ontology Corpus

Mohammed Suleiman Mohammed Rudwan[✉] and
Jean Vincent Fonou-Dombeu

School of Mathematics, Statistics and Computer Science, University of
Kwazulu-Natal, Pietermaritzburg, South Africa
m.suleiman.rudwan@gmail.com

Abstract. Ontology selection for reuse is a challenging task an ontology/knowledge engineer can face due to the diversity and abundance of ontologies on the internet today. This has become an active research area in ontology engineering. In this study, candidate ontologies are selected from a corpus using Skip-gram, a neural networks algorithm. The word embeddings of the vocabulary of 12 ontologies in the corpus were used to train the Skip-gram models. Thereafter, concepts from a text corpus were utilized to test the models and select the candidate ontologies for context words and axioms extraction. The results showed that the proposed method can automatically extract context words, and the URIs and labels of different types of axioms from the candidate ontologies. This gives the knowledge/ontology engineers detailed information about the contents of candidate ontologies so that they can make an informed decision on the parts of the ontologies they would like to reuse.

Keywords: Machine learning · Automatic axioms extraction · Ontology reuse · Skip-gram · NLP

1 Introduction

Thousands of ontologies are being made available on the internet for utilization in several domains and applications including expert systems, decision support systems, etc. This huge number of ontologies in different domains on the web nowadays, represents very significant assets that can be utilized for developing and building new ontologies in similar domains. Therefore, ontology reuse has made this possible. Ontology reuse is the process of making use of existing ontologies to build new ones. It has become an interesting research area since it saves efforts and time that can be devoted to developing new ontologies. The Knowledge/ontology engineer need to carefully determine the objectives and goals of the *to-be* ontology in order to determine the right candidate ontologies from the ontology corpus and reuse the parts that are of interest from these ontologies.

E. Pardede et al. (Eds.): iiWAS 2022, LNCS 13635, pp. 282–294, 2022.
https://doi.org/10.1007/978-3-031-21047-1_24

One of the early tasks that must be performed during the ontology reuse is the ontology selection during which ontologies discoveries, collection, and ontology alignment and evaluation take place. Ontology selection is a critical process since it has consequences on the rest of the development of the new target ontologies. If it is performed right, then it will guarantee the best performance output, that is, better structure and contents. As mentioned earlier, the level of reuse relies mainly on the objectives of the target to-be ontology, and one of the core objectives usually for ontologies development is extracting axioms, and detecting the inferences, that is, the logically related classes. Extraction of the axioms is one of the challenging tasks that ontology engineers face, especially when it comes to logical axioms as it requires high quality direct axioms definition and well-formed ontologies in terms of structure, properties and contents. Axioms play a major role to represent an ontology in a well structure and for practical uses [1].

This study proposes a method for candidate ontology selection from corpus of ontologies. The vocabulary of each ontology in the corpus was built with SPARQL queries. Thereafter, the word embeddings of the ontology vocabularies were computed and used to train the Skip-gram artificial neural network models. The trained models were tested with concepts/terms from a text corpus to select candidate ontologies that match the input terms. The context words and axioms were then extracted from the candidate ontologies. The results obtained showed that the proposed methodology can automatically extract context words as well as different types of axioms and their labels from the candidate ontologies. This enables the knowledge/ontology engineers and decision makers to have a thorough and detailed information about what contents are in the candidate ontologies so that they can make an informed decision on the parts that are of interest for reuse.

The rest of the paper is organized as follows. Section 2 discusses related works. Section 3 presents the materials and methods of the study. Section 4 presents and discusses the results obtained, and Sect. 5 concludes the paper and summarizes future work.

2   Related Works

The majority of studies in the literature have discussed reusing semantic web ontologies by tackling aspects such as ontology modularization [2,3], partial ontology reuse [4], or highlighting guidelines for reuse [5–7]. Other custom approaches which presented the utilization of modern machine learning techniques have recently been proposed as well [8,9].

Other approaches are application-based or customized for a specific purpose such as in [10] in which the authors proposed a 4-steps method to reuse biomedical ontologies with the aid of external tools and applications, i.e., TerMine and BioText. In the first step the corpus's content was collected, and a list of terms was generated. Then, a BioPortal's ontology recommender API was built together with a custom recommender they developed to overcome the limitation of the limited number of terms that BioPortal's API accepts at a time. The purpose was to recommend ontologies based on what information was provided in the first step. A third step maps terms to concepts in ontologies. And finally, recommended ontologies are evaluated. Although the study ignored the possibility of having a difference in the context and semantics of the concepts mapped to the input terms, the results were promising. The current study tackles this issue by providing the user with the context words for the input term from the selected candidate ontologies.

In the study [11] the authors made use of the metadata of the ontologies, such as terminology and ontology structure, to calculate a compatibility metric of ontology suitability for reuse. Thus, the methodology evaluates the degree of their usefulness and decide whether to be considered for reuse or not. A primary ontology was considered as a gold standard, then compared to other candidate ontologies in terms of the similar concepts they have. The process of comparison was performed using an algorithm, the Levensthein, to compare prefixes and suffixes of terms as well as the modified version of the String Metric to compare the terms. Then, the similarity between primary and candidate ontologies is calculated by the combination of the Cosin similarity and Euclidean distance. This process takes a lot of effort, especially in wide domain areas and those with high complexity. In this study, terms are selected by the end-user from a text corpus, and accordingly, the input term is searched for in all the candidate ontologies in the ontology corpus to extract context terms to have a detailed overview of the kind of information contained in that ontologies.

Alani [12] developed a new system that searches online for the representation of certain concepts, ranks the retrieved ontologies, extracts relevant parts of the top-ranked ontologies, and then merges those parts to construct a new ontology automatically. This study can add a massive value in the ontology reuse research when integrated with our proposed methodology. The study did not present details of how the searching for online ontologies takes place, however, the proposed methodology can be integrated with their study to produce a better and more accurate results because context words that define the semantics of the terms are extracted in the proposed methodology. Also the axioms of the candidate ontologies, object and data properties, individuals, etc. that are automatically extracted in the methodology proposed in this study are useful in the building of the target ontology.

Relatively few studies covered the axioms extraction from ontologies in the context of ontology reuse. One study proposed a methodology making use of Fuzzy Description Logics (DLs). They developed a logic-based computational method to automatically induct fuzzy ontology axioms. It followed the approach of the machine learning of inductive logic programming. In another interesting study [8], the authors harnessed machine learning as well to extract axioms. They used deep feed-forward neural network with the cooperation of a logical system to produce a model that can understand logical expressions. The conclusion of their study shows that the more hidden layers their designed network had, the more accurate the results become. Their proposed method works very well for reasoning-based applications. However, logical expressions examples generated can give more reliable results if the examples generated consider the use of specific context terms to learn for custom ontology axioms extraction. In this context, the aim of the purposed methodology is to find the candidate ontologies and extract related axioms. So, it can make a dramatic improvement on the results reported in [8] for custom ontology axioms extraction. The integration between the two approaches will provide a more customized framework that reuses ontologies in a more holistic way.

All in all, there are no standard methods for automated ontology selection and axioms extraction from an ontology corpus. This study proposed a straightforward method of reusing existing ontologies given a term/concept as a user input to nominate related candidate ontologies for reuse, extracting axioms and their labels, as well as statistical information regarding and axioms. This way, the knowledge/ontology engineer can have an overview of what the candidate ontologies are, and what contents they include, to finally decide what to reuse for the building of the new *to-be* ontology.

3   Materials and Methods

The process of selection of the candidate ontologies proposed in this paper utilizes the Skip-gram algorithm, an artificial neural network-based algorithm that mainly perform Natural Language Process (NLP). After discovering the candidate ontologies, a Java API and Python program with related APIs were used to extract axioms, their labels and statistical values.

3.1   Natural Language Processing (NLP)

Natural Language Processing (NLP) is the science of studying and mining a human's natural language in the form of text to extract useful semantic insights. NLP is utilized in several applications across different domains including social media, scientific publishing, robotics, semantic web and many more.

As it is well known that semantic web ontologies are the core of the semantic web, they play a major role in knowledge representation and storage. Since they are semi-structured data in terms of the organization of data and storage, they need some kind of processing and cleanup to prepare for learning. Many NLP algorithms and methods were used in many studies [13,14]. Those algorithms include Latent Semantic Analysis (LSA), Latent Dirichlet Allocation (LDA), Term frequency and inverse document frequency(TF-IDF), Long short-term memory (LSTM), Naive Bayes algorithm, GloVe, and many more. Other recent algorithms that mainly utilize artificial neural networks in their architecture include Word2Vec, Continuous Bag of Word (CBOW) and Skip-gram.

3.2   Skip-gram Algorithm

Skip-gram algorithm is an NLP algorithm that is based on a shallow artificial neural network in its architectural design. It was introduced by Mikolov et al. [15]. It relies mainly on what is called Word2Vec which is a word embedding methodology that transforms text data into numeric values in a form of a vector. Given a text corpus, each word in the text is represented as a vector representing the context of that word given the position and the context it appeared in. By converting the text into vectors, neural networks can process it since the value of each vector is a series of numeric values that represent the features.

Skip-gram algorithm's design is as follows. Given a fixed number of vocabularies, and a specific word as an input, it tries to figure out how surrounding words to the input word (the center word) often appear. In other words, it captures the context of neighboring words to the center word. It skips the actual input word (the center word) and tests the probabilities of the occurrences of the neighboring words to form an individual vector for each one. The vector values representation is performed in Euclidean space for every single word [16]. And from there, the calculations of the probability values for each surrounding word are performed to come up with the most relevant ones. Weights are given to each of the context words. Far-distant words from the center word are likely to have fewer weights as they are considered less relevant.

Skip-gram overcomes the problem of the data sparsity [17] which is one of the major problem we are providing the solution to in this paper by better understanding the ontologies in the corpus, and then pick up the candidate ones.

4   Experiment

4.1   Dataset

The dataset in this study was comprised of two parts. The first part is the text corpus. It is where concepts were taken and tested whether they were represented in the ontology corpus. The second dataset is the ontology corpus which includes several ontologies from which the candidate ontologies are to be selected. The text corpus was searched from the web [18]. Five documents were downloaded on various topics in the Agricultural sciences domain, namely, Leaf vegetable, Agriculture, Soil, Plant genetics, and Organic farming. These topics were carefully chosen from among more than ten different topics in the field. Twelve different ontologies were downloaded from the AgroPortal ontology repository [19]. Both the text and ontology corpuses used in the experiments in this study are available at an online repository [20].

4.2   Tools and Environment

The PyCharm Integrated Development Environment (IDE) and Python language were used for training and testing of Skip-gram models for candidate ontologies selections. The OWLAPI, a Java API was used for context words and axioms extraction from the candidate ontologies. The Owlready2, a Python API was utilized to run SPARQL queries to extract URIs of axioms and their labels from the candidate ontologies. Additionally, a University of Kwazulu-Natal hardware cluster was used to train the Skip-gram models since they consume high computational resources. The computing processors of a regular desktop machine (intel corei7, 3.60 GHz, 16 GB RAM) could not run the Skip-gram models on foodon ontology because of its large size. The Word2Vec was used for words embedding before the training of Skip-gram models.

4.3   Data Pre-processing

For each document in the text corpus, all images, links and tables were removed and the nascent text was moved into a (.txt) document. SPARQL queries were implemented to obtain the information from each candidate ontology, including classes, subclasses, labels and individuals. A separate text document was created to store the data from each candidate ontology. The retrieved data from SPARQL queries were organized and set into the text documents according to the input requirement of the Skip-gram algorithm. In other words, for each ontology, a class label was appended to the document, followed by its subclasses, each written in a separate line. The aim was to make each class and its subclasses contiguous to enable the Skip-gram neural network recognizes the relationship between classes and their subclasses. Thereafter, all individuals extracted were appended at the end of the respective text documents with one individual per line. The files were then saved for the training of the Skip-gram neural network models.

4.4   Skip-gram Setup

Skip-gram was implemented using Numpy Python API. The window size was set to 2, and the embedding size, which represents the number of neurons in the hidden layer in the network, was set to 3. The number of epochs was set to 10. Twelve Skip-gram models were designed and trained for each ontology. Unfortunately, the regular desk-top machine failed to process the $foodon$ ontology due to its large size. Thus, the experiment with the same skip-gram settings was performed on an external high-performance hardware cluster with more than 64 gigabytes of memory. Surprisingly, the cluster also failed during the processing of the $foodon$ because of the memory limitation. To sort out this, a Word2Vec model was designed to convert the vocabulary extracted from $foodon$ ontology into vectors and test whether the input concepts/terms were represented in the $foodon$ ontology.

4.5   Results and Discussion

The number of classes and subclasses, and individuals for each ontology in the ontology corpus is given in Table 1. The largest ontology was $foodon$ with 6,864 indi-viduals and 3,0501 classes and subclasses while the smallest one was $ppeo$ with only 4 classes and subclasses, and individuals. Several ontologies were found to have no individuals at all such as $pato$, $symp$, and po.

Among the concepts that were included in the text corpus, "soil" was a common term that appeared multiple times in several topics. Therefore, it was

Table 1. Statistical overview of ontology corpus

	Ontology	Number of classes & subclasses	Number of individuals
1	agro	3,437	2,4192
2	gao	61	122
3	oboe	9	9
4	po	1,677	0
5	ppo	435	378
6	symp	849	0
7	peco	2428	8622
8	ppeo	4	4
9	pato	4,615	0
10	to	4841	22945
11	vt	3675	4330
12	foodon	3,0501	6,864

selected as the input concept to the skip-gram models. The skip-gram models were then trained. The training time was recorded for the Skip-gram model for each ontology in the ontology corpus. The training times for all the ontologies in the ontology corpus are depicted in Fig. 1. The higher training time was 250.14 s on the *to* ontology while the lower training time was on the *p*peo ontology with only 0.01 s. On the other hand, the testing times of Skip-gram models for the prediction of context words in all candidate ontologies were extremely light as it took only 0.020 s to extract the context words together with their similarity value from the *a*gro ontology.

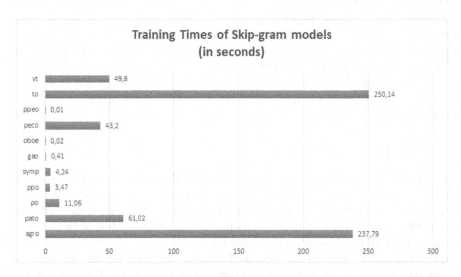

Fig. 1. Time spent to train skip-gram models against each ontology

The $f$oodon ontology could not be processed in the CPU machine used for the experiment. The Word2Vec model developed to test the "soil" concept representation, ran successfully. It was found that the concept is represented in $f$oodon ontology. The reason why Word2Vec succeeded while the skip-gram failed is that Word2Vec looks for the exact term, and uses a low-dimensional vector representation of words to run, whereas, skip-gram looks for surrounding words to the input/center term at a time and compare against others.

Table 2. Context words of the concept "soil" extracted from candidate ontologies

Ontology	Context words	Similarity degree
agro	Clinical	0.99992
	Draft	0.99985
	Pepo	0.99982
	Viroid	0.99920
	Member	0.99873
to	Distribution	0.99576
	Tertiary	0.99510
	Germination	0.99445
	Toxin	0.99443
	Branch	0.99399

The training time of the Skip-gram model on the $f$oodon ontology could not be reported in Fig. 1 due to the failure of execution because of the limited computing resources as explained earlier. Out of the 12 initial ontologies in the dataset, the results show that 4 ontologies represented the concept "soil", namely, $a$gro, $f$oodon, $p$eco, and to. Therefore, these ontologies were selected as candidate ontologies for the context words and axioms extraction. Ten context words with a numeric value for each were extracted per candidate ontology. The numeric value (similarity degree) of each context word is a value between 0 and 1. It represents the degree of closeness to the centre word, the concept "soil". The closest context words have similarity values close or equal to 1. Table 2 shows a sample of context words extracted, and their similarity degrees to the concept "soil" for the candidate ontologies $a$gro, and to.

Table 3. Number of axioms extracted per candidate ontology

Type of axiom	Candidate ontologies			
	agro	peco	to	foodon
Class expressions	6294	3084	5333	9783
Object properties	182	1	17	26
Data properties	5	0	0	0
Individuals	545	0	0	0

In Table 2, sample of context words from some candidate ontologies are presented. Those context words are extracted according to their appearances around the queried centre word "soil" using skip-gram. They might be computationally the closest context words to the given term, however, they might not be semantically related to the objectives of the *to-be* ontology that will be constructed accordingly. To improve those results, other metrics to measure the degree of semantic relatedness of the extracted context words may be considered. These metrics might be making use of external lexical databases, or using competency questions formulated from the objectives of the *to-be* ontology. Considerations of such solutions may take place in future work.

Table 4. URIs of Class expression axioms and corresponding labels for candidate ontologies

Ontology	URI of class expression axiom	Label
agro	\<http://purl.obolibrary.org/obo/TO_0000840\>	collective plant structure morphology trait
	\<http://purl.obolibrary.org/obo/TO_0000860\>	flower length
	\<http://purl.obolibrary.org/obo/ENVO_01001046\>	planetary subsurface environment
	\<http://purl.obolibrary.org/obo/CHEBI_24836\>	inorganic oxide
	\<http://purl.obolibrary.org/obo/ENVO_00000450\>	irrigation reservoir
to	\<http://purl.obolibrary.org/obo/PATO_0000146\>	temperature
	\<http://purl.obolibrary.org/obo/CHEBI_37848\>	plant hormone
	\<http://purl.obolibrary.org/obo/CHEBI_16234\>	hydroxide
	\<http://purl.obolibrary.org/obo/PECO_0007309\>	zinc nutrient exposure
	\<http://purl.obolibrary.org/obo/NCBITaxon_10239\>	viruses
Foodon	\<http://purl.obolibrary.org/obo/NCBITaxon_42528\>	piaractus mesopotamicus
	\<http://purl.obolibrary.org/obo/FOODON_03304834\>	chia seed bread
	\<http://purl.obolibrary.org/obo/FOODON_00002642\>	food (chilled)
	\<http://purl.obolibrary.org/obo/FOODON_00002646\>	food (flavored)
peco	\<http://purl.obolibrary.org/obo/CHEBI_33434\>	elemental halogen
	\<http://purl.obolibrary.org/obo/ENVO_00002005\>	air
	\<http://purl.obolibrary.org/obo/CHEBI_48356\>	protic solvent
	\<http://purl.obolibrary.org/obo/CHEBI_33582\>	carbon group molecular entity
	\<http://purl.obolibrary.org/obo/CHEBI_76946\>	fungal metabolite

After the axioms were extracted in the form of URIs, SPARQL queries were run in Owlready2, a Python API, to retrieve the labels of each axiom. Tables 4, 5, 6, 7 show sample of URIs of some axioms extracted from candidate ontologies with their corresponding labels. In particular, Table 4 presents sample class expression axioms for each candidate ontologies in the form of the URI of the axiom and its corresponding label.

Table 5. URIs of object properties axioms and corresponding labels for candidate ontologies

Ontology	URI of object property axiom	Label
agro	\<http://purl.obolibrary.org/obo/RO_0002329\>	part of structure that is capable of
	\<http://purl.obolibrary.org/obo/RO_0002336\>	positively regulated by
	\<http://purl.obolibrary.org/obo/RO_0002335\>	negatively regulated by
	\<http://purl.obolibrary.org/obo/RO_0002405\>	immediately causally downstream of
	\<http://purl.obolibrary.org/obo/RO_0002162\>	in taxon
to	\<http://purl.obolibrary.org/obo/BFO_0000051\>	has part
	\<http://purl.obolibrary.org/obo/RO_0000052\>	inheres in
	\<http://purl.obolibrary.org/obo/to#from_country\>	from country
	\<http://purl.obolibrary.org/obo/BFO_0000066\>	occurs in
foodon	\<http://purl.obolibrary.org/obo/HANCESTRO_0308\>	hasCountryOfOrigin
	\<http://purl.obolibrary.org/obo/BFO_0000050\>	part of
	\<http://purl.obolibrary.org/obo/FOODON_00001301\>	has food substance analog
	\<http://purl.obolibrary.org/obo/RO_0001025\>	located_in
	\<http://purl.obolibrary.org/obo/FOODON_00001303\>	obsolete - has taxonomic identifier
peco	\<http://purl.obolibrary.org/obo/peco#part_of\>	

Axioms extraction was performed on the candidate ontologies. To extract axioms from the candidate ontologies, the OWLAPI, a Java API, was used. As explained earlier, the axioms extracted were appended to text documents. These documents are available in an online repository [20]

Four types of axioms were extracted from each candidate ontology, namely, class expressions, data properties, object properties, and instances. The number of axioms extracted per candidate ontology are presented in Table 3. The $foodon$ ontology has the largest number of class expressions with 9783 compared to the $peco$ ontology which has the least number with 3084 class expressions. Regarding the instances, none of the candidate ontologies contains instances except the $agro$ ontology which contains 545 individuals. The same applies to the data properties in which the only candidate ontology which has some is $agro$ with only 5 data properties. The $agro$ ontology has the largest number of object properties with 182 compared to the others which have 1, 17 and 26 data properties for $peco$, to, and $foodon$ ontologies, respectively (Table 3).

The object properties' axioms were also successfully extracted from each candidate ontologies. Examples of URIs of object properties' axioms with their corresponding labels are presented in Table 5. As indicated in Table 3, only 1 object property was found in the *peco* ontology; further, the URI of this object property with no label was extracted as show in last row of Table 5.

Table 6. URIs of data properties axioms and corresponding labels for *agro* ontology

Ontology	URI of data property axiom	Label
agro	\<http://purl.obolibrary.org/obo/AGRO_00000418\>	has end date
	\<http://purl.obolibrary.org/obo/AGRO_00000417\>	has start date
	\<http://purl.obolibrary.org/obo/IAO_0000004\>	has measurement value

As reported in Table 3, data properties and individuals were only found in the agro ontology. Therefore, Tables 6 and 7 includes URIs of some data properties' and individuals' axioms and corresponding labels, respectively, for the *agro* ontology only.

Table 7. URIs of individuals' axioms and corresponding labels for *agro* ontology

Ontology	URI of individual axiom	Label
agro	\<http://purl.obolibrary.org/obo/UO_0000314\>	relative fluorescence unit
	\<http://purl.obolibrary.org/obo/UO_0000211\>	plaque forming unit
	\<http://purl.obolibrary.org/obo/UO_0000223\>	watt-hour
	\<http://purl.obolibrary.org/obo/UO_0010033\>	ounce
	\<http://purl.obolibrary.org/obo/UO_0010010\>	hectare

There are other tools that visualize ontologies and give statistical information such as Protégé [21], and the online visualization tool WebVOWL [22]. WebVOWL gets an ontology as an input, and provides a nicely advance visual representation of the ontology's contents. The same can be performed using Protégé which provides not only this, but also detailed statistics on restrictions and actual axioms present in the ontology. The shortcoming of both Protégé and WebVOWL is that they do not provide the flexibility needed to access and handle the URIs of axioms in a process of ontology reuse. This is well covered using our proposed methodology where one can map axioms, types of them, their URIs and their corresponding labels.

5 Conclusion

In this paper, a methodology for candidate ontology selections, and context words and axioms extraction from an ontology corpus was presented. Using the word embedding and Skip-gram algorithm, which are artificial neural networks architectures, different models were trained on agriculture-based ontologies. The model could dis-cover which ontologies in the ontology corpus are representing an input concept, then lists down these candidate ontologies. Thereafter, the context words for the input concept were listed for each candidate ontology in addition to the training times of the models as well as the times spent to extract the context words. Then, axioms and their labels contained in the candidate ontologies were extracted. The extracted axioms could be use by ontology/knowledge engineers to construct new ontologies in the domain concerned. The framework implemented provide flexibility in the access and handling of ontology's axioms better than well-known tools such as Protégé and WebVOWL. The future direction of research will be to integrated the extracted axioms for customization reusing them to build an ontology of the agricultural domain. Additionally, other metrics to measure context words extracted from the ontologies via the Skip-gram algorithm, such as external lexical database, will be considered in future for more accurate measurement of semantic relations to the queried concept and to the objectives of the *to-be* ontology.

References

1. Khadir, A.C., Aliane, H., Guessoum, A.: Ontology learning: grand tour and challenges. Comput. Sci. Rev. **39**, 100339 (2021)
2. Grau, B.C., et al.: Modular reuse of ontologies: theory and practice. J. Artif. Intell. Res. **31**, 273–318 (2008)
3. Grau, B.C., et al.: Modularity and web ontologies. In: International Conference on Principles of Knowledge Representation and Reasoning (2006)
4. Pan, J.Z., Serafni, L., Zhao, Y.: Semantic import: an approach for partial ontology reuse. In: 1st International Conference on Modular Ontologies, vol. 232, pp. 71–84 (2006)
5. Reginato, C.C., et al.: GO-FOR: a goal-oriented framework for ontology reuse. In: 20th International Conference on Information Reuse and Integration for Data Science (IRI), pp. 99–106 (2019)
6. Simperl, E.: Guidelines for reusing ontologies on the semantic web. Int. J. Semant. Comput. **4**(2), 239–283 (2010)
7. Lonsdale, D., et al.: Reusing ontologies and language components for ontology generation. Data Knowl. Eng. **69**(4), 318–330 (2010)
8. Cai, C.-H., et al., Symbolic manipulation based on deep neural networks and its application to axiom discovery. In: International Joint Conference on Neural Networks (IJCNN), May 14, pp. 2136–2143 (2017)
9. Casteleiro, M.A., et al.: Deep learning meets ontologies: experiments to anchor the cardiovascular disease ontology in the biomedical literature. J. Biomed. Semant. **9**(1), 13 (2018)
10. Zulkarnain, N.Z., Meziane, F., Crofts, G.: A methodology for biomedical ontology reuse. In: A Methodology for Biomedical Ontology Reuse, 22 JunE 2016, pp. 3–14 (2016)
11. Trokanas, N., Cecelja, F.: Ontology evaluation for reuse in the domain of Process Systems Engineering. Comput. Chem. Eng. **85**, 177–187 (2016)
12. Alani, H.: Position paper: ontology construction from online ontologies (2006)

13. Casteleiro, M.A., et al.: Ontology learning with deep learning: a case study on patient safety using PubMed. In: SWAT4LS (2016)
14. Buitelaar, P., et al.: Ontology learning from text: an overview. Ontology Learn. Text: Methods Eval. Appl. **123**, 3–12 (2005)
15. Mikolov, T., et al.: Efficient estimation of word representations in vector space. https://arxiv.org/abs/1301.3781. Accessed 21 June 2022
16. Leimeister, M. and Wilson, B.J.: Skip-gram word embeddings in hyperbolic space. https://ui.adsabs.harvard.edu/abs/2018arXiv180901498L/abstract. Accessed 21 June 2022
17. Guthrie, D., et al.: A closer look at skip-gram modelling. http://www.lrec-conf.org/proceedings/lrec2006/pdf/357_pdf.pdf. Accessed 21 June 2022
18. Wikipedia. https://en.wikipedia.org. Accessed 21 June 2022
19. Jonquet, C., et al.: AgroPortal: a vocabulary and ontology repository for agronomy. Comput. Electron. Agric. **144**, 126–143 (2018)
20. Rudwan, M.: Dataset. https://drive.google.com/drive/folders/1sxID7xV-77mtUS2ASm-Se2NgT_fFmpeo?usp=sharing. Accessed 21 June 2022
21. Musen, M.A.: The protégé project: a look back and a look forward. AI Matters **4**(1), 4–12 (2015)
22. Lohmann, S., Link, V., Marbach, E., Negru, S.: WebVOWL: web-based visualization of ontologies. In: Lambrix, P., et al. (eds.) EKAW 2014. LNCS (LNAI), vol. 8982, pp. 154–158. Springer, Cham (2015). https://doi.org/10.1007/978-3-319-17966-7_21

WAPITI – Web-based Assignment Preparation and Instruction Tool for Interpreters

Bartholomäus Wloka[1]([✉]) [ID], Yves Lepage[2] [ID], and Werner Winiwarter[3] [ID]

[1] Department for Translation Studies, University of Vienna, Gymnasiumstraße 50, 1190 Vienna, Austria
bartholomaeus.wloka@univie.ac.at
[2] IPS, Waseda University, 2-7 Hibikino, Wakamatsu-ku 808-0135, Kitakyushu, Japan
yves.lepage@waseda.jp
[3] Faculty of Computer Science, University of Vienna, Währingerstraße 29, 1090 Vienna, Austria
werner.winiwarter@univie.ac.at
https://ufind.univie.ac.at/en/person.html?id=39736,
https://w-rdb.waseda.jp/html/100001079_en.html,
https://ufind.univie.ac.at/en/person.html?id=6309

Abstract. This paper proposes a framework to ease the workload of preparation for interpreters through quick and efficient discovery of relevant material. We describe a software architecture and present arguments why this combination of components and functionalities will result in an ideal assignment preparation tool for interpreters, which they currently are lacking. We draw from the rich professional experience from interpretation experts and teaching staff gathered through interviews and feedback over an extended period of time. We use this experience to add functionalities to enrich, share, and store data; anywhere, be it at home, or on a mobile device while on the go. This results in a multimodal, flexible, easy to use, mobile-ready Web application. The framework allows for incremental extension, export and import of the data collection, keeping in mind accessibility, mobility, interoperability, reusability, and sustainability.

Keywords: Web intelligence · Semantic web · Web technology · Linked open data · Knowledge graphs

1 Introduction

The work of translators and interpreters has undergone significant changes since machine translation made it into everyday use and has been steadily increasing in quality and ease-of-use over the years [4]. However, the benefits were different for translators than for interpreters. Translators enjoy a wide variety of digital help in the form of computer assisted translation tools, which span from text editors that ease the work load of comparing and typing, all the way to intricate translation management tools with the ability to import and align personalized

© The Author(s), under exclusive license to Springer Nature Switzerland AG 2022
E. Pardede et al. (Eds.): iiWAS 2022, LNCS 13635, pp. 295–306, 2022.
https://doi.org/10.1007/978-3-031-21047-1_25

bilingual corpora, store and utilize custom translation memories and extensively take advantage of the newest machine translation systems [3]. While interpreters can also benefit from these tools to some degree, they are not tailored to their specific needs, and digital help for interpreters, though slowly emerging under the term of *Computer Assisted Interpretation* (CAI) as presented in [10], is still scarce and otherwise mostly limited to ergonomic considerations in the booth – the workplace of a simultaneous interpreter – and the use of smart devices as described in "The Digital Booth"[1], by the Knowledge Centre on Interpretation of the European Commission. Apart from existing reports, we considered the observations and feedback from interpreters to create an architecture for a Web-based solution. It will offer help in the process of preparation of terminology and specific sentence structures used in a domain by taking advantage of novel alignment, similarity, and term extraction algorithms.

Since the reader of this paper might not be intimately familiar with the details of the work of translators and especially interpreters, we will summarize some of the key aspects of the training and the preparation for work assignments.

1.1   Background

Generally speaking, there are two ways of interpreting, i.e. transferring spoken information from one language to another. It can be done instantaneously – *simultaneous interpretation* (SI), or in chunks of several sentences or even bigger sequences – *consecutive interpretation* (CI). SI is usually used during official speeches, talks, or presentations where the spoken information is immediately relayed to the listener in a given language. CI is often used in smaller settings, e.g. a meeting of two country representatives, a doctor's appointment with a foreign patient, etc. Translation – the transfer of written information from one language to another – is usually a deliberate task, allowing for breaks, re-thinking, and acquisition of additional information as needed. SI and CI on the other hand need to be well prepared beforehand in anticipation of potential difficulties, such as specific terminology.

Even though translation and interpretation are similar tasks in the sense that they both transfer meaning across languages, and they are usually often mentioned together in academia summarized with the term *translation studies*, they differ fundamentally in the required approach and the necessary skills. Since translation offers the ability to look up different translation options, consider different structures, contemplate style and connotations, the translator puts more emphasis on correctness of the information transfer. Also, the translator can use digital tools *during* the translation process. Since the task of interpretation requires a virtually instantaneous transfer from one language to another, the preparation has to take place beforehand. Therefore, the real-time requirement and the cognitive ability to process several streams of information is clearly more critical than exactness, precision, and the consideration of connotations. Hence,

---

[1] https://ec.europa.eu/education/knowledge-centre-interpretation/digital-booth_en.

the disciplines differ on a procedural level, in terms of results, and in terms of the use of digital assistance.

With these differences in mind, it becomes apparent why the previously mentioned CAT tools are of limited use to an interpretation professional. In contrast to the work of [10], we claim that the interpreter would greatly benefit from help during the preparation of an assignment, hence we propose a framework which will assist interpreters at the stage of preparation, to close the gap in digital assistance in comparison to the translator.

One final general fact about the training of an interpreter remains to be mentioned. The training and preparation for real world assignments requires firstly sharpening the interpreter's cognitive skills to quickly produce language B, while hearing language A. The ability to perceive and automatically and almost instantaneously produce information is practiced over a long time with various special methods. Secondly, they prepare for interpretation assignments by studying the general domain of the prospective conversation, presentation, or talk. While interpreters usually have areas in which they specialize, such as community interpreters, legal interpreters, medical interpreters, they also have to be versatile enough to take an interpretation task that challenges their skills to remain competitive. Especially in this case, a preparation for the given domain of the topic is vital and should be as efficient as possible. This is where our framework is meant to ease their load and offer beneficial effects on several levels, as we describe in Sect. 2. The current style of preparation is usually done with manually looking for sources and reading related articles. In a best case scenario, the interpreter obtains the digital presentation slides. However, some of the terminology or phraseology that has been prepared for a task, might be hazy or completely forgotten when a similar task needs to be prepared some time later.

1.2 Approach

From the above mentioned observations we deduce the necessary requirements for the framework, both at the presentation and the implementation level. Section 2 describes the details of the entire framework (including our algorithms), presents its essential parts, and mentions other resources which can be integrated. The resulting framework offers functionalities tailored to the interpreter's needs. Section 3 then shows a possible application scenario with examples from the data we already obtained from our experiments as a proof of concept. We conclude with a brief summary and an outlook to future work in Sect. 4.

2 Requirements and Proposed Architecture

In this section we describe the architectural requirements derived from the issues, which we collected from the reports and observations in Sect. 1. We describe how we address these issues step by step from the perspective of generic requirement concepts. We explain why and how each concept is crucial and how we propose to address it. Further, we want to ensure that the preparation process for an interpretation assignment is not only efficient, but also improves the quality of work by adding a certain fun-factor through appealing visual exploration and navigation techniques, similar to the gamification component in educational software which proved its merit time and time again. At the same time we have to be careful not to be too intrusive in the attempt to assist the process.

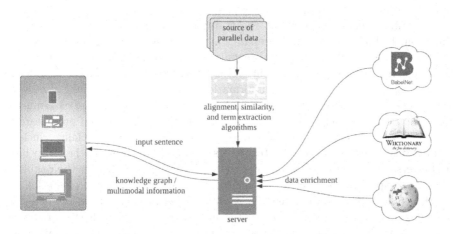

Fig. 1. WAPITI architecture. The input data, at the *top*, which depends on the choice of the interpreter, this could be custom parallel corpora, translation memory, etc., is processed by our algorithms. On the *right*, various resources can enrich the data, which is finally delivered to the interpreter on any type of device – on the *left* – via multi-faceted presentation through augmented browsing.

The following subsections describe each feature, the requirement behind it, and our proposed solution. Figure 1 depicts the planned architecture to illustrate the basic components that enable these features.

Accessibility. When interpreters get their assignment on short notice, they end up having to prepare under a strong time constraint. This happens more often than not, hence preparation must be done very efficiently in general. In addition, interpreters are often not technologically savvy, so solutions which are complicated to set up and to use will hinder, rather than help. They would be perceived as intrusive to their work and hardly efficient. We propose a light-weight Web architecture, which will seamlessly tie into the browser, offering an *augmented browsing* experience. In order to achieve this, we will borrow and extend from our previous work [13]. The computational steps will take place on a server and the resulting data will be presented in an accessible, easy to use way, that can be readily viewed on many different devices, which ties into the next requirement consideration: *mobility.*

Mobility. Since interpreters often get their assignments at a short notice, and sometimes while they are traveling, the preparation often takes place while the interpreter is on the move to the location of the assignment, or in hotels, i.e., places which are not standard office working environments. Hence, a Web-based and mobile-ready front-end is vital for a preparation framework. Additionally, this will enable work on other machines, without the need to install software locally. We plan a server-client architecture, which will outsource intensive calculations to the server, as well as eliminate the problem of data storage on a local device (see middle and left of Fig. 1). Only the currently used data subset will be downloaded to the device. This will help interpreters whilst traveling between assignments, having little time and limited resources staying in hotels between conference talks or speeches. The server-client architecture will also allow for centralized access to data that has been collected previously, which will especially come in handy for organizations and companies which want to share the data among their employees. Further, a mobile interface will allow ad-hoc usage without being intrusive, which very often is a major factor in the popularity of an application.

Sustainability and Interoperability. The architecture will ensure sustainability and interoperability. It will enable sharing of results among colleagues and within institutions. This will increase personal efficiency and productivity, consistency of terminology, terminology management and control on an institutional level. Furthermore, the benefits of the ability to share data go beyond the scope of the company. Standardized export formats, such as *RDF*, enable wide-spread data sharing and more importantly data contributions to a large data collection for common and scientific use, from those who are willing to contribute. While high quality bilingual data is of paramount importance in many multilingual language technologies, the current state of Web-crawled data is rather sobering, as indicated in the study by [5]. We envision that the success in growth and maintenance of such a collection will be possible with minimal effort in the future, thanks to community contribution, similar to other community driven projects, such as the Linux kernel, LRE Map [2], or various Wiki projects. This will inherently ensure sustainability by reducing the environmental carbon footprint since existing data can be reused over a long period of time and the development of the knowledge graph will progress in an incremental fashion. The key points which will facilitate, ease, and encourage this development and participation are: reusability and sustainability of data via exports/imports, use of the RDF format, and straight forward interface to other linked open data resources.

Multimodality. In order to learn and deeply internalize terminology, a multimodal representation is very helpful. Apart from browsing through a knowledge graph by related concepts, the interpreter will be presented with depictions of concepts and additional information, such as Wikipedia or Wiktionary entries. This multimodality enables the connection of the concept with a visual image, which in turn creates a mental association to the word in the other language.

Building such multimodal resources is becoming more and more important in many other applications, such as training of AI in the mushrooming research area of *multimodal artificial intelligence* [6].

Multifaceted Presentation. Adding to and enriching the concept of multi-modality, we plan to enable the interpreter to choose from several perspectives on the information, keeping in mind that the presentation and navigation through the data is at least as important as the content. As mentioned before, the interface must not be intrusive, but at the same time offer as many associative links and connections as possible to maximize the memorization process. In order to optimize the presentation of the output of our alignment and similarity computation algorithms, we plan to make the interface multifaceted, so that the information can be viewed from different perspectives. For example, the content words that are extracted by the alignment algorithm can be displayed in the form of a glossary. This is especially interesting if an interpreter wants to obtain a quick list of words that might be needed, or verify at a glance which words might require additional research. This research could be done using the next presentation type, the navigational component. By clicking on a term, the interpreter is presented with a Wiktionary entry, a Wikipedia entry, and/or an image, depending on the availability for the current word. A third component would be the contextual browsing with a traditional knowledge graph representation, which shows all neighboring terms and concepts. Exploring neighboring concepts will adjust the focus and the graph dynamically, similar to BabelNet [8][2] and other popular applications that include knowledge graph representations, as it is proposed in [9].

Explainability. Our alignment, term extraction, and similarity algorithms from our previous work will serve as the source of information, according to the initial input of the interpreter. These algorithms answer the concern about explainability, being a combination of computational linguistics algorithms and lexical methods that are self-explanatory. They are designed to be traceable and reliable with transparent scoring of the results, much more than contemporary neural networks. By putting emphasis on traceability and efficiency, we create trust by offering transparency to the interpreter.

3 Functionality and Showcase

In this section we describe the functionalities which we have partially implemented and plan to complete to finalize the framework. We describe an envisioned showcase to present a possible path through an assignment preparation. We give examples of relevant data which we have computed by our algorithms, for a possible preparation domain.

---

[2] https://babelnet.org/.

3.1   Preparation for an Assignment

The actual preparation consists of retrieving terminology, structural information, i.e., typical phraseology or frequent patterns, and a general orientation in the domain of the assignment. The input interpreters can enter to initialize our framework might be as short as one sentence, a selected sentence from Wikipedia, or even one domain-specific word. Sometimes, they are provided with a brief summary of the content of the interpretation assignment. Often, they are only told the general domain (e.g., 'military technology', 'medical examinations', 'a presidential speech', 'Nobel prize recipient's speech', etc.) They would like to be presented with actual examples that relate to the initial input. The preparation could be described as exploring random paths from little clues. There is no way to know when preparation is finished.

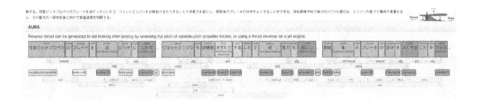

Fig. 2. Selection of a sentence from Wikipedia. On top is the selected Japanese sentence, below that is the English translation, followed by a detailed lexical, syntactical, conceptual, and relational analysis. The displayed title *AURA* stands for AUgmented Reading Assistant.

3.2   Initializing the Framework

The interpreters can approach the framework in three different ways. They can enter sentences, which will serve as the starting point for a query of the existing sentences in the database on the server. This first method of input into the framework operates under the assumption that there exists parallel data on the server. Upon entering a sentence that is exemplary in either terminology or phrase pattern, or both, our algorithms produce documents that are similar. The search is done in the input language, the parallel data delivers the target sentences.

The second method is preferable if there is little or no data present in the database for the given domain. Here the initial input is a selected sentence on Wikipedia, as illustrated in Fig. 2. The terms from this sentence are taken as the starting point for a bilingual crawling process, which results in a bilingual intermediate corpus with scores which indicate the similarity of the sentence in the target and the source language. The basis for this alignment are lexical lookups of content words, hence we are likely to find semantic equivalents in the target language. The interpreter is presented with these parallel results, depending on a choice of an accuracy threshold value that ranges from no match 0.0 to an exact match 1.0. The alignment algorithm is described in detail in [12]. Once a threshold value is set and the selection is satisfactory, the parallel corpus selection can be transferred to the database and the exploration process can be continued. To illustrate such a selection, we show a possible presentation of a terminology-heavy sentence in the domain of "Aviation" from Japanese Wikipedia, its translation, and a linguistic analysis (Fig. 2). Further, selective crawling will produce further examples. The extent and depth of these examples will depend on the choice of the interpreter. This process will take several minutes, depending on the desired output size. The result of this selective crawling is the creation or the enrichment of the above mentioned database on the server.

```
 1 英語 ---English language            26 B-2 (航空機) ---Northrop Grumman B-2 Spirit
 2 飛行 ---                            27 全翼機 ---Flying wing
 3 航空機 ---Aircraft                  28 機体 ---Airframe
 4 推力 ---Thrust                     29 構造 ---Structure (disambiguation)
 5 揚力 ---Lift (force)               30 トラス ---Truss
 6 森鴎外 ---1901 年 ---1901           31 モノコック構造 ---
 7 揚力 ---Lift (force)               32 サンドイッチ構造 (存在しないページ) ---
 8 揚力 ---Lift (force)               33 スポイラー ---Spoiler
 9 空気 ---Atmosphere of Earth#Composition  34 主翼
10 風 ---Wind                        35 垂直 ---Perpendicular
11 力 (物理学) ---Force                36 揚力 ---Lift (force)
12 風 ---Wind                        37 翼型 ---Airfoil
13 風速 ---Wind speed                 38 凸 ---
14 自乗 ---Square (algebra)           39 翼平面形
15 比例 ---Proportionality (mathematics)  40 アスペクト比 ---Aspect ratio
16 迎え角 ---                          41 鈴木真二 (存在しないページ) ---
17 抗力 ---Drag (physics)             42 ライト兄弟 ---Wright brothers
18 失速 ---Stall (fluid mechanics)    43 強度 ---Ultimate tensile strength
19 新幹線 ---Shinkansen               44 抗力 ---Drag (physics)
20 翼 ---Wing                        45 オージー翼 ---
21 推進装置 ---                        46 航研機 ---Gasuden Koken
22 操縦装置 (存在しないページ) ---        47 U-2 (航空機) ---Lockheed U-2
23 胴体 ---Torso                     48 応力 ---Stress (mechanics)
24 降着装置 ---Landing gear            49 戦闘機 ---Fighter aircraft
25 主翼 ---
```

Fig. 3. Part of a glossary output, based on the input "Airplane" spanning over two columns with the line count on the left. Some of the terms do not have equivalents, which is the case when no equivalent English Wikipedia article is found for the Japanese term. Since this is taken directly from the crawling process, some of the terms might be irrelevant and the selection and refinement of the list is left up to the interpreter and his needs for the particular assignment.

The third method is the quickest and simplest way to start the exploration process in a certain domain. Upon entering one or several terms, our crawling algorithm finds related topics and their equivalent in the target language. An example of such output is presented in Fig. 3. This approach is based on the link structure of Wikipedia and can be adjusted to the desired depth by the interpreter. The depth is defined by the distance of links from the starting page, similar to a level in a decision tree, where the root is the initial topic and the leaves are the final level of topic traversal. This algorithm is described in detail in our previous work [12].

Each of these methods present a starting point for further browsing by clicking on selected terms which are connected to enriched presentations, if available. An example of such en enriched presentation is shown in Fig. 4. We plan to extend the presentation by adding a dynamic knowledge graph presentation. The algorithms behind these three methods are elaborated in the following subsections.

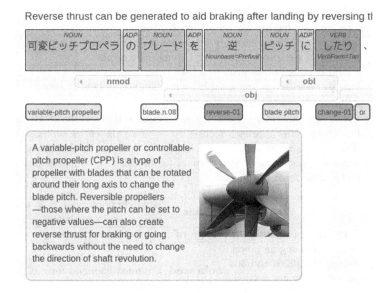

Fig. 4. Multimodal explanation of the term "variable-pitch propeller". On top is the English translation of the input sentence, below that the grammatical decomposition of the Japanese sentence, in the lower part is the conceptual view and a Wikipedia enrichment of the presentation including an illustrative depiction.

3.3 Sentence Retrieval and Enrichment of Data

In order to **retrieve sentences that cover a given sentence**, we utilize parts of our previous work, i.e. the retrieval of sentences which are similar to an input with the twofold objective of maximizing the coverage of the input sentence either in form or in meaning, while minimizing the number of retrieved sentences [7]. An illustrative example from the same domain "Airplane" is depicted in Fig. 5. It shows the difference between matching in form and meaning for the same sentence. Figure 6 illustrates the coverage of an entire sentence from Wikipedia by several sentences from a corpus within the "Aviation" domain.

This is similar to a Keyword-in-Context (KWIC) presentation, but for all parts of a sentence. Applied to bilingual documents, such tools allow to visualize, in the retrieved sentences, the correspondence in translation of the matched parts, in a similar way as a Web interface like Linguee[3] does.

---

[3] https://www.linguee.com/.

Match	several people are exiting a commercial jet aircraft .
Form	**several people are** climbing a snow covered mountain.
	a group of shoppers line the street of **a commercial** district beside a mountain.
	an **aircraft** is standing with a gothic building in the back.
	a group of women **exiting a** obstacle in a race.
	four men are having fun on **jet** ski & apos; s.
Meaning	a man in a uniform carrying a box **exiting the** steps of a plane.
	a crowd of **people is** squeezing through the airport.
	a man is parachuting next to a **jet**.
	two people are riding a ski lift with mountains behind them.

Fig. 5. An input sentence *(top)* and a list of sentences that partly *(boldface)* match in form and meaning. This approach focuses on covering the entire sentence, not only the terms. The input sentence is in the "Aviation" domain. In this particular case, the search space is not specific to this domain (Multi30k [1]), so less than half of the sentences can be considered as relevant.

	This	is so common that it is known as the conventional layout.
This will involve considering the	**type of**	navigation required e.g.
When the available engine power increased during the 1920s and 30s and bracing was no longer needed, the	**unbraced**	or cantilever monoplane became the most common form of powered type.
A shoulder	**wing is**	sometimes considered a subtype of high wing.
Strictly, such a pair of wings	**is called a**	wing plane or just plane.
When the available engine power increased during the 1920s and 30s and bracing was no longer needed, the unbraced or	**cantilever**	monoplane became the most common form of powered type.
A shoulder wing is sometimes considered a subtype of high	**wing.**	

Fig. 6. Visualization of partial matches in retrieved sentences from a selection of articles from Wikipedia in the "Aviation" domain. The sentence covered is: "This type of unbraced wing is called a cantilever wing." The input sentence can be read, vertically, in the middle part of the table. The retrieved sentences are to be read horizontally with the words they cover in the middle, including the domain-specific term "cantilever".

For the **retrieval by similarity**, we find lexical similarities between the sentences of the input language and the existing data in the database. This approach is an extension of our previous work [13]. It produces a transparent score for each of the matches it finds with scores ranging from 0.0 to 1.0, where a larger value denotes more matching components of the sentence. It is the interpreter's choice how much to restrict the output, by raising the threshold value of the search. This retrieval can be combined with the retrieval described in the subsection above by running this search on top of the results of the former one, or vice versa.

The collected parallel data will be **enriched** with existing lexical resources, such as BabelNet, Wiktionary, and Wikipedia and presented in a clear and appealing fashion, as shown in Fig. 4. We plan to enhance this even further by making each term in the output data a starting point for a knowledge graph representation. While browsing this knowledge graph view, the interpreter can add terms as a new starting point for retrieval that can restart the cycle of an iterative and incremental discovery of terminology and phraseology.

4   Conclusion and Future Work

This paper proposes a method to ease the workload of preparation for interpreters. We have built on our close contacts to interpretation professionals and on their feedback and comments to define requirements for the best possible support. We introduce algorithms for quick retrieval of domain-related glossaries and retrieval of similar sentences by content words as well as structure or formal similarity. Such methods provide matching or agreement scores that allow an interpreter to judge the adequacy of the retrieved text to their purpose. We envisage a software architecture which will offer a framework to enrich this data even further by integrating additional content extracted from multilingual resources like BabelNet, Wiktionary, Wikipedia, or the like, in the form of text, pictures, explanations, etc. At the time of writing, we are working on the implementation of the framework for which we will use our existing algorithms.

The finished framework will be realized as a multimodal, integrated interface with a multifaceted, flexible, easy to use, mobile-ready Web application. Its features and architecture should ensure a re-usable, shareable and sustainable framework to meet the requirements of interpreters. It will allow for incremental extension, export and import of the data collection in RDF, keeping in mind reusability, sharing, and extensibility. We plan to disseminate the framework to interpreters for evaluation (see [11]), even in the early stages of development to obtain timely feedback for a user-oriented development.

References

1. Elliott, D., Frank, S., Sima'an, K., Specia, L.: Multi30K: multilingual English-German image descriptions. In: Proceedings of the 5th Workshop on Vision and Language, pp. 70–74. Association for Computational Linguistics, Berlin (2016). https://doi.org/10.18653/v1/W16-3210
2. Gratta, R.D., Goggi, S., Pardelli, G., Calzolari, N.: LREMap, a song of resources and evaluation. In: Proceedings of the Eleventh International Conference on Language Resources and Evaluation (LREC 2018). European Language Resources Association (ELRA), Miyazaki (2018)

3. Han, B.: Translation, from pen-and-paper to computer-assisted tools (CAT tools) and machine translation (MT). MDPI Proc. **63**, 56 (2020). https://doi.org/10.3390/proceedings2020063056

4. Koehn, P.: Computer aided translation. In: Proceedings of the 54th Annual Meeting of the Association for Computational Linguistics: Tutorial Abstracts. Association for Computational Linguistics, Berlin (2016). https://aclanthology.org/P16-5003

5. Kreutzer, J., et al.: Quality at a glance: an audit of web-crawled multilingual datasets. Trans. Assoc. Comput. Linguist. **10**, 50–72 (2022). https://doi.org/10.1162/tacl_a_00447

6. Liang, P.P.: Brainish: formalizing a multimodal language for intelligence and consciousness. CoRR abs/2205.00001 (2022). https://doi.org/10.48550/arXiv.2205.00001

7. Liu, Y., Lepage, Y.: Covering a sentence in form and meaning with fewer retrieved sentences. In: Proceedings of the 35th Pacific Asia Conference on Language, Information and Computation (PACLIC 35), pp. 1–10 (2021)

8. Navigli, R., Ponzetto, S.: Babelnet: the automatic construction, evaluation and application of a wide-coverage multilingual semantic network. Artif. Intell. **193**, 217–250 (2012). https://doi.org/10.1016/j.artint.2012.07.001

9. Nečaský, M.: Štěpán Stenchlák: interactive and iterative visual exploration of knowledge graphs based on shareable and reusable visual configurations. J. Web Semant. **73**, 100713 (2022). https://doi.org/10.1016/j.websem.2022.100713

10. Rodriguez, et al.: SmarTerp: a CAI system to support simultaneous interpreters in real-time. In: Proceedings of the Translation and Interpreting Technology Online Conference. pp. 102–109. INCOMA Ltd. (2021). https://aclanthology.org/2021.triton-1.12

11. Stewart, C., Vogler, N., Hu, J., Boyd-Graber, J., Neubig, G.: Automatic estimation of simultaneous interpreter performance. In: Proceedings of the 56th Annual Meeting of the Association for Computational Linguistics, vol. 2: Short Papers, pp. 662–666. Association for Computational Linguistics, Melbourne (2018). https://doi.org/10.18653/v1/P18-2105

12. Wloka, B., Winiwarter, W.: AAA4LLL - acquisition, annotation, augmentation for lively language learning. In: 3rd Conference on Language, Data and Knowledge (LDK 2021). Open Access Series in Informatics (OASIcs), vol. 93, pp. 29:1–29:15. Schloss Dagstuhl - Leibniz-Zentrum für Informatik, Dagstuhl (2021). https://doi.org/10.4230/OASIcs.LDK.2021.29

13. Wloka, B., Winiwarter, W.: DARE - a comprehensive methodology for mastering kanji. In: 23rd International Conference on Information Integration and Web Intelligence (iiWAS2021), pp. 427–435 (2021). https://doi.org/10.1145/3487664.3487791

Performance and Optimization

Optimization Heuristics for Cost-Efficient Long-Term Cloud Portfolio Allocations

Maximilian Kiessler$^{(\boxtimes)}$, Valentin Haag, Benedikt Pittl, and Erich Schikuta

Faculty of Computer Science, University of Vienna, Vienna, Austria
max.kiessler@gmail.com, valentin.haag94@gmail.com,
{benedikt.pittl,erich.schikuta}@univie.ac.at

Abstract. Today's cloud infrastructure landscape offers a broad range of services to operate software applications. The myriad of options, however, has also brought along a new layer of complexity. When it comes to procuring cloud computing resources, consumers can purchase their virtual machines from different providers on different marketspaces to form so called cloud portfolios: a bundle of virtual machines whereby the virtual machines have different technical characteristics and pricing mechanisms. Thus, selecting virtual machines for a given set of applications such that the allocations are cost-efficient is a non-trivial task.

In this paper we propose a formal specification of the cloud portfolio management problem that takes an application-driven approach and incorporates the nuances of the commonly encountered reserved, on-demand and spot market types. We present two distinct cost optimization heuristics for this stochastic temporal bin packing problem, one taking a naive first fit strategy, while the other is built on the concepts of genetic algorithms. The results of the evaluation show that the former optimization approach significantly outperforms the latter.

Keywords: Cloud economics · Resource portfolio optimization · Human decision support · Stochastic temporal bin packing

1 Introduction

The ever-increasing relevance of cloud computing has brought along a paradigm shift in terms of how modern software applications are developed and operated. While these advancements have certainly made reliable high-performance infrastructure more accessible, they have also added an additional layer of complexity. Heterogeneous cloud portfolio management, where the virtual machines are purchased from different marketspaces, is now concerned with the challenging task of finding cost-efficient resource allocations for a given set of applications.

Nowadays, well-known cloud service providers such as Amazon[1] offer three different types of marketplaces for cloud resources, i.e. the reserved, on-demand and spot marketspace. The reserved resources offers steep discounts, but

---

[1] https://aws.amazon.com/de/ec2/.

© The Author(s), under exclusive license to Springer Nature Switzerland AG 2022
E. Pardede et al. (Eds.): iiWAS 2022, LNCS 13635, pp. 309–323, 2022.
https://doi.org/10.1007/978-3-031-21047-1_26

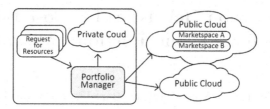

Fig. 1. Portfolio manager creating optimal cloud portfolios by purchasing resources from different providers and marketspaces

clients must purchase resources for a predefined, long time period. On-demand resources, on the other hand, are characterized by their flexibility since providers usually employ a pay-per-use billing method. Finally, on the spot marketplace one can find resources that are heavily discounted. However, resources of this type may be revoked at the service provider's discretion.

The heterogeneous nature of cloud markets as well as the fact, that applications are time-bound are the complexity drivers for this cost optimization problem. Hence, a cost-efficient resource allocation must be found over a longer temporal horizon instead for a single point in time. Furthermore, applications rarely show a constant resource requirement. To our knowledge, scientific literature does not yet provide a cloud portfolio optimization model that combines the concepts of heterogeneous marketplaces, variable resource demands, as well as the temporal character of workloads. However, all three aspects are of integral importance to a realistic depiction of the problem. Thus, with this paper we contribute to this field by i) establishing a formal problem specification that incorporates the aforementioned relevant features of cloud portfolio management, and by ii) proposing and evaluating two distinct optimization heuristics for creating cost-efficient portfolio allocations.

The paper at hand is part of our research on an autonomous Cloud Portfolio Manager as depicted in Fig. 1. It is an entity that creates for a bundle of requested resources an optimal cloud portfolio by purchasing them from different providers and marketspaces. A precondition for creating such an overarching system is the determination of appropriate algorithms for creating cloud portfolios, two different cloud portfolio algorithms are described in the paper at hand.

The structure of the paper is as follows: In Sect. 2 an overview of related work is given. Section 3 introduces the problem formulation while two optimization heuristics are described in Sect. 4. An evaluation of the approaches is introduced in Sect. 5 followed by a conclusion in Sect. 6.

2   State of the Art

In the literature, the spot market has received a lot of attention. So e.g. Sharma et al. focused on preemptible servers and utilized concepts from the domain of financial modelling to construct cost-efficient cloud portfolios while also adhering to the specific requirements of the applications that need to be served [22].

However, since spot instances are preemptible they require special mitigation procedures to avoid the loss of data upon sudden revocation. Jangjaimon and Tzeng tried to address this problem by proposing a sophisticated checkpointing mechanism [9]. The process of checkpointing, i.e. regularly persisting a recoverable state for computational workloads, is quite common when working with transient cloud servers, as also pointed out by Tang et al. In their work the authors propose a biding strategy for spot instances based on the concepts of a constrained Markov decision process. Their research focused on the EC2 Spot market of Amazon Web Services (AWS) and aimed to provide a balanced approach between cost-optimization and revocation mitigation [24]. However, as mentioned by Baughman et al., AWS revised the pricing mechanism of its preemptible servers in 2017. The currently active schema makes prices less volatile, meaning that instead of having high price peaks according to the fluctuating supply and demand, the curve is now flattened [2]. Based on this overhauled pricing mechanism of EC2 spot instances, Zhou et al. developed a long-term price prediction and dynamic task reallocation system. However, their scheduling system again only focuses on the spot market and does not take into account a heterogeneous cloud portfolio [26].

Mireslami et al., on the other hand, incorporated on-demand and reserved instances in their provisioning approach. However, besides the fact that the authors did not consider the spot market, their model also lacks a sophisticated temporal component and thus is not suitable for long-term task scheduling [15]. Li et al. do include time-bound constraints in their dynamic bin packing approach, however, while they do assume that the size of an item may vary from one to another, they do not model the capacity requirements as a random variable. Furthermore, they also do not fully incorporate the heterogeneous nature of cloud markets [10]. Nodari et al. also do not pay attention to the spot market, but instead put an emphasis on reserved and on-demand instances in their stochastic model, to which they apply the concepts of inventory theory [16]. In the research of Haussmann et al. a cost model was presented that incorporated volatile as well as secure instance types. Their research showed that preemptible spot instances can contribute to significantly lower cost in the domain of high performance parallel computing [7]. However, while their model does consider varying execution times, it too is not suitable for long-term job scheduling. Alenizi et al. try to capture the time-bounded nature of workflows by making the remaining expected execution time an integral part of their model. Their approach, however, again only considers reserved and on-demand instances. Further, it also does not consider various starting times of workflows and thus is more geared towards dynamic ad hoc resource allocations [1]. Shen et al. do consider separate arrival and departure times for workflows in their job scheduling model, but also do not incorporate all three of the aforementioned cloud markets. Further, their integer programming problem formulation only considers non-fluctuating resource demands for the individual workflows [23]. A more holistic approach to cloud portfolio management was taken by Pittl et al., who showed that heterogeneous portfolios tend to be more cost-efficient. Furthermore, they also pointed out the importance of right-sizing the server instances to the capacity requirements of the workloads [19].

The task of right-sizing is also highly relevant to the closely-related domain of energy-efficient data center operations. For this field Hwang and Pedram proposed a portfolio-based optimization approach with a probabilistic model, where the assigned workloads have resource demands that are characterised by a normal distribution [8]. Martinovic et al. also use a problem formulation based on probabilities rather than deterministic aspects. They then applied a stochastic bin packing approach to find efficient server allocations [14]. Fatima et al. evaluated a particle swarm optimization algorithm against other approaches in a scenario where the server capacities are assumed to be variable [6]. Wu et al., on the other hand, used a more traditional genetic algorithm concept in their proposed solution for physical and virtual server instance consolidation [25].

As has been shown, while one can find extensive research on the subject of cloud cost optimization, very little work has been done on long-term allocations. Long-term cost-efficient cloud portfolio management requires an emphasis on the temporal component that is inherent to such a problem. Some research tries to capture this time-bound characteristic [1,7,10], however, to the best of our knowledge the scientific literature does not yet provide optimization approaches that adequately capture this constraint, while also incorporating the heterogeneous nature of cloud markets. As mentioned, the research by Pittl et al. performs a more holistic analysis of resource management, i.e. procurement options from reserved, on-demand as well as spot markets are considered, but it can be argued that it does not appropriately address the uncertain nature of capacity demands [19]. As pointed out, researcher that already previously incorporated stochastic problem formulations in their models [14,16], is not suited for the task of long-term resource allocations in heterogeneous cloud market environments.

Based on our past research on resource optimization techniques [17,21] and cloud market analysis [12,18] we try to close this gap. That is, our model not only considers reserved, on-demand and spot instances, it also puts an emphasis on long-term resource allocations. The proposed model and the derived optimization approaches support fine-grained task scheduling over a longer planning horizon, which allows to properly make use of reserved instances. Furthermore, our application driven approach is based on the assumption of uncertain resource requirements and thus also adds a stochastic notion to the problem formulation.

3   Problem Formulation

The problem formulation for cost-efficient long-term cloud portfolio management presented in this section uses the notation as defined in table 1. In the scope of this work a cloud portfolio is defined as a set of *cloud instances I* that are necessary to host a set of *applications A*. The optimization problem, in short, is then concerned with finding a cost-efficient allocation of these applications and instances.

Applications running in the cloud are typically characterized by their resource demands. Following the proposed approach of [8] these capacity requirements are

Table 1. Notation for problem formulation

Parameter	Description
I	A set of selected cloud instances (hosts)
A	A set of applications
T	A set of time slots for which to optimize
x_{ait}	Variable denoting assignments of applications to instances
S_a	The starting time of application a
F_a	The finishing time of application a
U_a	Indicates if application a is preemptible
μ_a	The expected resource demand of application a
σ_a	The std. deviation of the resource demand of application a
R_i	The resource capacity of instance i
C_i	The cost of instance i for one time slot
B_i	The first available time slot of an instance
E_i	The last available time slot of an instance
O_i	Indicates if instance i is suitable for non-preemptible applications
D_{it}	Aggregated resource demand of instance i at time t
Q_{min}	The desired quality of service

assumed to be fluctuating and are therefore represented by an expected demand mean μ_a and corresponding standard deviation σ_a. Furthermore, it is assumed that workloads have varying life spans, which is denoted by the starting time S_a and finishing time F_a of an application. Note that $S_a < F_a$ must apply. Since spot instances are only suitable for very fault-tolerant processes, the binary variable U_a is used to denote whether or not an application can be assigned to such a preemptible server instance.

$$U_a = \begin{cases} 1 & \text{if } a \text{ is preemptible} \\ 0 & \text{else} \end{cases} \tag{1}$$

An instance $i \in I$ has a predefined resource capacity R_i (e.g. CPU, RAM). Moreover, each type of instance is also associated with a certain price per time unit C_i. The total cost incurred by a single host is based on the price per time slot and the overall up-time. The up-time of an instance is given by its starting time B_i and ending time E_i, where $B_i < E_i$ again must hold true. To denote if an instance is considered to be a spot (preemptible) type, the binary parameter O_i is used.

$$O_i = \begin{cases} 1 & \text{if } i \text{ is only suitable for preemptible applications} \\ 0 & \text{else} \end{cases} \tag{2}$$

The aggregated demand of all applications assigned to instance $i \in I$ at time slot $t \in T$ is represented by the parameter D_{it}. This aggregated demand is also a random variable and thus one can only evaluate the probability with which an instance stays within the designated capacity limits. The proposed model assumes that one can specify a desired minimum quality of service, denoted by Q_{min}. In case the probability that the aggregated demand D_{it} stays below the provided capacity of the instance R_i does not satisfy the minimum quality of service Q_{min} for time slot t, then the allocation is invalid.

To formally model the application and instance assignments, while also considering the temporal restrictions of the problem, the approach suggested by Dell'Amico et al. is used. The variable x denotes which hosting instance an application has been assigned to at a specific point in time. The resource demands of an application $a \in A$ are considered to be 0 for any time slot $t \in T$ if $t < S_a$ or $t > F_a$ [4].

$$x_{ait} = \begin{cases} 1 & \text{if application} a \text{ is assigned to instance } i \text{ at time slot } t \\ 0 & \text{else} \end{cases} \tag{3}$$

The cloud portfolio management problem can now be defined as follows:

$$min \sum_{i \in I} C_i * (E_i - B_i) \tag{4}$$

$$s.t. \sum_{i \in I} x_{ait} = 1 \qquad\qquad \forall a \in A, \forall t \in [S_a, F_a] \tag{5}$$

$$\sum_{i \in I} x_{ait} * U_a \geq O_i \qquad\qquad \forall a \in A, \forall t \in [S_a, F_a] \tag{6}$$

$$P(D_{it} < R_i) \geq Q_{min} \qquad\qquad \forall i \in I, \forall t \in [B_i, E_i] \tag{7}$$

$$x_{ait} \in \{0, 1\} \tag{8}$$

$$U_a \in \{0, 1\} \tag{9}$$

$$O_i \in \{0, 1\} \tag{10}$$

$$Q_{min} \in [0, 1] \tag{11}$$

Constraint 5 states that the optimization approach needs to assign each application to an instance. At any given point in the up-time of an application, only one instance can be the dedicated host. Constraint 6 requires the selected host to be from a suitable marketspace. Furthermore, Eq. 7 stipulates that for each time slot an instance is active, the probability that the resource demand stays within the capacity limits of the respective instance is at least the predefined quality of service. This constraint is based on the approach proposed by [8] and assumes applications with load profiles that do not show any correlation and have a normal distribution. With constraints 8 to 11 the auxiliary variables are bound to a valid range. variables are bound to a valid range. variables are bound to a valid range. variables are bound to a valid range.

The mathematical model as described in this section is the foundation of the proposed optimization approaches. Both of the presented algorithms have the objective of minimizing the portfolio cost, while also adhering to the listed constraints.

4   Optimization Approaches

The long-term cost-optimization problem for cloud portfolios, as modeled in Sect. 3, is in essence a multi-dimensional packing problem. Applications with resource demands and up-time requirements need to be fit into instances with varying capacity and temporal availability, such that the incurred cost is minimal. Such bin packing problems are NP-hard and thus complex to solve [11]. As an enumeration of all possible solutions is often not computationally feasible two distinct optimization heuristics are presented.

4.1   The Greedy Optimization Approach

This approach incorporates principles from the well-known first fit decreasing (FFD) approach [3], as well as the proposed portfolio management strategy of [8]. The algorithm outlined in the following, which has been named *Efficient Resource Inference for Cloud Hosting* (ERICH), consists of 4 stages which are described in Algorithm 1 and summarized in the following:

Stage 1: The algorithm expects sets of preemptible and non-preemptible applications, as well as all possible instance types from the three respective marketspaces as input. In the initialization phase applications are sorted according to increasing starting dates and non-increasing resource demand standard deviations. This is based on the proposed idea by [8], who suggested that grouping together workloads with similar resource demand deviation may lead to overall reduced capacity needs. Furthermore, the various instance types are sorted by cost per time slot for the provided capacity in an increasing order, ensuring that the algorithm chooses cost-efficient hosts first.

Stage 2: According to the first fit decreasing approach, the algorithm tries to fit all non-preemptible applications into reserved instances. For each application, it is first checked if a suitable host, i.e. one covering the entire life cycle of the application while also providing the required capacity, already exists in the constructed portfolio. If it does, then the application is assigned to said instance. In case no candidate host exists, a new one is allocated based off the first instance type satisfying the application's requirements.

Stage 3: Although reserved instances usually provide steep discounts compared to the on-demand marketspace, the fact that they have a minimum allocation period means that *stage 2* may result in a cost-inefficient portfolio. To achieve a potentially higher packing density the algorithm iterates over each allocated reserved instance. During each iteration, a new temporary portfolio without the respective reserved instance is created. Applications from the removed reserved host are then assigned to on-demand instances following the same first fit decreasing approach as described in *stage 2*. If the newly created portfolio is more cost efficient, than it replaces the old one in the next iteration.

Stage 4: In the final step, the algorithm is concerned with finding well-fitting allocations for all preemptible applications. Preemptible workloads may be assigned to multiple hosts during their life cycle, which is why the optimization approach allocates these applications not as a whole, but rather on a individual time slot basis. That is, the algorithm first finds all time steps for which a suitable candidate host exists and assigns the app to these instances for the respective periods. In case there are still some assignment gaps in the schedule of the workload the algorithm proceeds with allocating new instances from the input set of spot hosts. This approach ensures that preemptible applications fill up any left-over capacity before new bins are opened.

Algorithm 1: Efficient Resource Inference for Cloud Hosting

Input: A set of non-preemptible apps $A1$; A set of preemptible apps $A2$; A set
      of reserved instance types RES; A set of on-demand instance types
      ON; A set of spot instance types $SPOT$

Result: Packing pattern $portfolio$

sort applications $A1$ and $A2$ by increasing start time and non-increasing σ_a

sort RES, ON and $SPOT$ by non-increasing C_i per R_i and time slot

$portfolio \leftarrow$ empty allocation variable

forall $a \in A1$ **do**
   | assign a to $portfolio$ (FFD) while only considering RES instances

forall $i \in reserved\ instances\ from\ portfolio$ **do**
   | $tmp\_portfolio \leftarrow$ copy of $portfolio$ without instance i
   | **forall** $a \in i$ **do**
   | | reinsert a into $tmp\_portfolio$ (FFD) including ON instances
   | **if** $total\ cost\ of\ tmp\_portfolio < total\ cost\ of\ portfolio$ **then**
   | | $portfolio \leftarrow tmp\_portfolio$

forall $a \in A2$ **do**
   | assign a to $portfolio$ without allocating new instances
   | $gaps \leftarrow$ consecutive time slots where a is not yet assigned to $portfolio$
   | **forall** $gap \in gaps$ **do**
   | | assign a to $portfolio$ for time slots in gap by allocating $SPOT$ hosts

---

4.2 The Evolutionary Optimization Approach

The application of genetic algorithms (GA) to bin packing scenarios is not a new notion, see e.g. [20]. The algorithm presented here has been named *Genetic Optimization of Resource Groupings* (GEORG). In the following its most essential building blocks and genetic operators are presented.

Encoding Scheme: For bin packing problems the grouping of items and their respective bins is an essential piece of information, which is also relevant to the individual genetic operators of a GA [5]. Falkenauer has proposed an encoding scheme, in which the chromosome is an array of bins, each holding a set of items. However, this approach is not well suited for the temporal component of the problem specification. Thus, we propose a temporal group encoding, in which each locus of the chromosome corresponds to a specific time step, with the allele being a set of instances running at the respective point in time. Every host is then mapped to a set of applications, which are assigned to the respective instance at this time slot.

Population Initialization: To ensure a high degree of genetic diversity while also providing initial individuals with comparatively high fitness, a hybrid approach is taken for the creation of an initial set of solutions. Fifty percent of the time applications are assigned in a manner that reduces the number of allocated instances and therefore the overall cost. In the remaining cases, the assignment is at random.

Fitness Evaluation: To evaluate the fitness of an individual, i.e. the quality of a solution, Eq. 4 is used.

Crossover: In each generation a group of individuals is selected based on the fitness proportionate roulette wheel method. The crossover is then applied to a set of two individuals (parents) in order to yield a new offspring. We propose a biased temporal crossover operator that is built on the concepts presented by Quiroz-Castellanos et al. [20] and promotes the transmission of well-fitting genetic material to the next generation. For each time step (gene), active instances are sorted in decreasing order based on their average rate of capacity utilization and cost per time slot. A partial solution is created by zip-merging the instances of both parents. The ranked partial solution is pruned by eliminating hosts of already assigned applications. Instances that result in packing patterns violating the constraints of the problem formulation are ignored in the crossover process of further time steps. The culling of instances may break the chromosome, since applications may end up being partially or fully without any host assignments. To repair the chromosome, a simple heuristic is applied to reinsert any applications that are now considered to be free.

Mutation: Martello and Toth [13] introduced the concept of dominance, which can be used to replace a subset of items with an item of larger or equal size, potentially leading to a tighter packing pattern. For this work the definition of dominance has to be adapted. An application a that is intended to be hosted by instance $i \in I$ for the time slots $[S_t, F_t]$ is said to dominate a partition of apps P from instance i if the time span denoted by $[S_t, F_t]$ encompasses all assignments slots of the partition for the respective host. Furthermore, the expected resource demands of the dominating application must be greater than the aggregated capacity requirements of all elements of the dominated partition. In fact, the probability that the resource demands of the dominating app exceed those of the dominated workloads must be greater than fifty percent. When the mutation operator is applied to an individual a predefined number of instances are removed from the portfolio. For each of the now unassigned applications, candidate hosts from the portfolio are selected. The temporal dominance criterion is checked against partitions of applications of size two for the respective candidate instance. In case the dominance criterion holds true, the unassigned application is swapped with the partition. Similar to the crossover operator, this procedure may leave certain applications unassigned, meaning that the chromosome no

Table 2. Summary of application data sets

App. Set	Non-Pre.	Pre.	Avg. res. dem.	Std. res. dem.	Avg. res. dev.	Std. res. dev.	Avg. alloc. periods	Std. alloc. periods
apps_1	14	6	3.27	1.71	0.53	0.48	43.15	33.4
apps_2	59	41	3.0	2.62	0.53	0.74	63.93	43.94
apps_3	10	10	3.02	2.01	0.71	0.63	212.2	167.88
apps_4	42	58	3.1	2.57	0.5	0.59	237.16	171.57
apps_5	7	13	3.12	2.69	0.6	0.56	2758.55	1996.98
apps_6	41	59	2.78	1.97	0.49	0.57	2871.74	2055.67

longer represents a valid solution. The same aforementioned insertion heuristic is now again used to repair the corrupted individual.

Insertion Heuristic: Equation 5 of the problem specification essentially requires that each application must be assigned an appropriate host for all relevant time slots. During the crossover and mutation processes this constraint might end up being violated, resulting in a broken chromosome. Preemptible applications might have multiple gaps in their packing pattern, where no valid assignment is available. In any case, the insertion heuristic follows a naive first-fit approach, where for each assignment gap of an orphaned application a candidate instance from the existing chromosome is selected. If no candidate host exists, then a new random instance is created to host the respective application. The component of randomness to this rather simple heuristic is intended to mitigate the risk of premature convergence on local optima by ensuring that the genetic diversity is kept at an adequate level.

Termination: Commonly encountered stopping criteria can be employed, such as a maximum number of processed generations or a certain threshold when it comes to the convergence level of the fitness scores among individuals in the population.

5   Evaluation

The evaluation was conducted with three quality criteria in mind: execution speed, packing density and overall cost of the constructed cloud portfolios. The algorithms were implemented using Python 3.9 and the tests were run on a Windows machine with an Intel Core i7-4770 processor (3.4 GHz base clock, 3.9 GHz turbo) and 16 GB of DDR3 memory at 1600 MHz MHz. Table 2 summarizes the key resource demand and allocation characteristics of the application data sets. While the data was synthetically created, careful attention was paid to crafting realistic scenarios based on real-world observations.

The created application data samples were combined with the instance type data sets described in Table 3 to create the following six unique test cases:

Table 3. Summary of instance type data sets

Instance type set	Number of instance types	Avg. capacity	Std. capacity	Avg. res. prc.	Std. res. prc.	Avg. on. prc.	Std. on. prc.	Avg. spot prc.	Std. spot prc.
types_1	500	9.60	8.77	2.27	2.85	3.10	2.16	2.53	2.21
types_2	500	10.32	11.40	2.16	2.38	3.13	2.57	3.15	4.84
types_3	500	9.79	9.91	2.41	3.80	3.10	2.41	2.33	1.74

$case\_1$ ($apps\_1$, $types\_1$), $case\_2$ ($apps\_2$, $types\_1$), $case\_3$ ($apps\_3$, $types\_2$), $case\_4$ ($apps\_4$, $types\_2$), $case\_5$ ($apps\_5$, $types\_3$) and $case\_6$ ($apps\_6$, $types\_3$)[2]

Since wall clock time was chosen as the evaluation metric the test cases for the evaluation of the execution speeds were run a total of 10 times to eliminate any potential side effects of background tasks. It can be seen in Fig. 2 that the execution speeds for the greedy optimization approach ERICH was significantly better across the board. Its deterministic character resulted in more or less static runtime performance. The execution speed of the GA, on the other hand, has proven to be highly volatile due to the stochastic characters of the GA. The most significant factor that contributes to this longer runtime is likely the crossover operator. The temporal component of the problem specification requires a substantial amount of evaluations to be performed to yield a single offspring. Furthermore, it can easily be the case that the crossover results in certain applications not being assigned to any hosts, in which case the insertion heuristic has to reinsert these applications. The same reasoning can be applied to the mutation operator.

The utilization rate of an instance is defined as the total expected resource demand of all assigned applications over the relevant time slots, relative to the absolute capacity provided for the same time period. The results presented in Fig. 3a clearly show the dominance of ERICH over GEORG in terms of the average packing density of the allocation instances. Figure 3b depicts the data for the weighted utilization rate. Instead of simply taking the average utilization rate over all instances within a portfolio, this metric puts an emphasis on those instances with longer allocation periods. The higher the number of time slots for which an instance is assigned to the portfolio, the more it contributes to the overall utilization rate. However, the conclusion that the greedy optimization approach yields tighter-packed portfolios remains unchallenged. It is important to note that both definitions of the utilization rate focus solely on the expected resource demands of the individual applications. The resource demand deviations relevant to the proposed stochastic component of the model are not included in these metrics.

Similar to the analysis of the execution speeds, the evaluation of the overall cloud portfolio cost shows that the naive ERICH outperforms the genetic algorithm by a significant margin, as seen in Fig. 4. However, that is not to say that

---

[2] The full data sets are available publicly: https://gitlab.com/MFJK/optimization-heuristics-for-cost-efficient-cloud-resource-allocations.

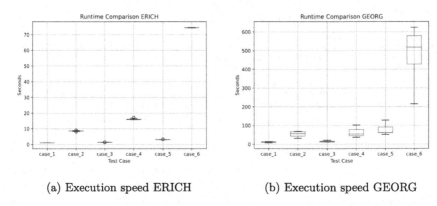

(a) Execution speed ERICH   (b) Execution speed GEORG

Fig. 2. Performance in terms of execution speeds

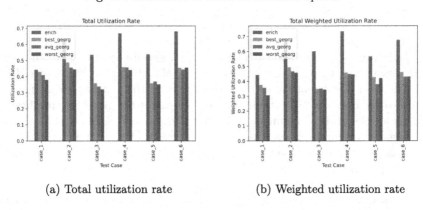

(a) Total utilization rate   (b) Weighted utilization rate

Fig. 3. Instance utilization rates

the GA did not work as intended. Figure 5 depicts the fitness level over multiple generations for the data set *case_6*. Starting from an initial population (generation 0) with a very high degree of genetic diversity, the average fitness score continuously improves as the generations progress. In the end, the average cost has been cut by more than half by the time generation 10 has been processed. However, it is also to note that the fitness levels of the individuals within the general population have converged significantly by the time generation 10 has been concluded. That shows that further significant improvements on the fitness levels would have been unlikely due to the reduced genetic diversity.

The initial population produced by the GA can also serve as a general benchmark for the quality of the yielded solutions of both algorithms. As mentioned, the GA's population initialization has a strong component of randomness to it. Since both algorithms produce results with notably lower costs compared to the initial population, it can be said that either approach significantly improves upon the solutions one would yield from an unplanned allocation of resources.

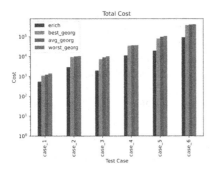

Fig. 4. Overall portfolio cost

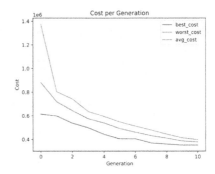

Fig. 5. Cost per generation for data set *case_6*

6   Conclusion

Finding cost-efficient resource allocations is a highly relevant industry problem. In this paper we have presented a formal model for the domain of cloud portfolio management, following an application-centered long-term optimization approach considering uncertain resource demands and incorporating heterogeneous marketplaces. The specification falls into the category of bin packing problems and is characterized by its temporal and stochastic nature. To the best of our knowledge current literature does not provide comprehensive solutions to such long-term probabilistic resource allocation problems. Therefore, the paper at hand introduces two optimization approaches and evaluates them along use cases.

In future research we plan to extend the problem specification and tweak the optimization heuristics. For instance, taking the evaluation results into account, one can consider combining both optimization algorithms to create a hybrid approach. Furthermore, when it comes to adaptations to the problem formulation, we consider it relevant to also look at scenarios where the resource demand of the applications are correlated. Furthermore, in future iterations we also intend to incorporate resource demand load profiles for applications that may change over time. That is, in the current model it is assumed that an application's resource demand is characterized by a normal distribution. More research is necessary to determine the affects on optimization heuristics in case these capacity requirements change over time.

References

1. Alenizi, A., Ammar, R., Elfouly, R., Alsulami, M.: Cost minimization algorithm for provisioning cloud resources. In: 2020 IEEE International Symposium on Signal Processing and Information Technology (ISSPIT), pp. 1–6. IEEE (2020)
2. Baughman, M., et al.: Deconstructing the 2017 changes to AWS spot market pricing. In: Proceedings of the 10th Workshop on Scientific Cloud Computing, pp. 19–26 (2019)

3. Coffman Jr, E., Garey, M., Johnson, D.: Approximation algorithms for bin packing: a survey. In: Approximation Algorithms for NP-Hard Problems, pp. 46–93 (1996)
4. Dell'Amico, M., Furini, F., Iori, M.: A branch-and-price algorithm for the temporal bin packing problem. Comput. Oper. Res. **114**, 104825 (2020)
5. Falkenauer, E.: A hybrid grouping genetic algorithm for bin packing. J. Heurist. **2**(1), 5–30 (1996)
6. Fatima, A.: Virtual machine placement via bin packing in cloud data centers. Electronics **7**(12), 389 (2018)
7. Haussmann, J., Blochinger, W., Kuechlin, W.: Cost-optimized parallel computations using volatile cloud resources. In: Djemame, K., Altmann, J., Bañares, J.Á., Agmon Ben-Yehuda, O., Naldi, M. (eds.) GECON 2019. LNCS, vol. 11819, pp. 45–53. Springer, Cham (2019). https://doi.org/10.1007/978-3-030-36027-6_4
8. Hwang, I., Pedram, M.: Portfolio theory-based resource assignment in a cloud computing system. In: 2012 IEEE Fifth International Conference on Cloud Computing, pp. 582–589. IEEE (2012)
9. Jangjaimon, I., Tzeng, N.F.: Effective cost reduction for elastic clouds under spot instance pricing through adaptive checkpointing. IEEE Trans. Comput. **64**(2), 396–409 (2013)
10. Li, Y., Tang, X., Cai, W.: Dynamic bin packing for on-demand cloud resource allocation. IEEE Trans. Parallel Distrib. Syst. **27**(1), 157–170 (2015)
11. Lodi, A., Martello, S., Vigo, D.: Approximation algorithms for the oriented two-dimensional bin packing problem. Eur. J. Oper. Res. **112**(1), 158–166 (1999)
12. Mach, W., Schikuta, E.: A generic negotiation and re-negotiation framework for consumer-provider contracting of web services. In: Proceedings of the 14th International Conference on Information Integration and Web-Based Applications and Services, IIWAS 2012, pp. 348–351. Association for Computing Machinery, New York (2012)
13. Martello, S., Toth, P.: Lower bounds and reduction procedures for the bin packing problem. Disc. Appl. Math. **28**(1), 59–70 (1990)
14. Martinovic, J., Hähnel, M., Dargie, W., Scheithauer, G.: A stochastic bin packing approach for server consolidation with conflicts. In: Neufeld, J.S., Buscher, U., Lasch, R., Möst, D., Schönberger, J. (eds.) Operations Research Proceedings 2019. ORP, pp. 159–165. Springer, Cham (2020). https://doi.org/10.1007/978-3-030-48439-2_19
15. Mireslami, S., Rakai, L., Wang, M., Far, B.H.: Dynamic cloud resource allocation considering demand uncertainty. IEEE Trans. Cloud Comput. **9**(3), 981–994 (2019)
16. Nodari, A., Nurminen, J.K., Frühwirth, C.: Inventory theory applied to cost optimization in cloud computing. In: Proceedings of the 31st Annual ACM Symposium on Applied Computing, pp. 470–473 (2016)
17. Pittl, B., Mach, W., Schikuta, E.: A negotiation-based resource allocation model in iaas-markets. In: 2015 IEEE/ACM 8th International Conference on Utility and Cloud Computing (UCC), pp. 55–64 (2015)
18. Pittl, B., Mach, W., Schikuta, E.: Bazaar-extension: a cloudsim extension for simulating negotiation based resource allocations. In: 2016 IEEE International Conference on Services Computing (SCC), pp. 427–434 (2016)
19. Pittl, B., Mach, W., Schikuta, E.: Cost-evaluation of cloud portfolios: an empirical case study. In: CLOSER, pp. 132–143 (2019)
20. Quiroz-Castellanos, M., Cruz-Reyes, L., Torres-Jimenez, J., Gómez, C., Huacuja, H.J.F., Alvim, A.C.: A grouping genetic algorithm with controlled gene transmission for the bin packing problem. Comput. Oper. Res. **55**, 52–64 (2015)

21. Schikuta, E., Wanek, H., Ul Haq, I.: Grid workflow optimization regarding dynamically changing resources and conditions. Concurr. Comput. Pract. Exp. **20**(15), 1837–1849 (2008)
22. Sharma, P., Irwin, D., Shenoy, P.: Portfolio-driven resource management for transient cloud servers. In: Proceedings of the ACM on Measurement and Analysis of Computing Systems, vol. 1, no. 1, pp. 1–23 (2017)
23. Shen, S., Deng, K., Iosup, A., Epema, D.: Scheduling jobs in the cloud using on-demand and reserved instances. In: Wolf, F., Mohr, B., an Mey, D. (eds.) Euro-Par 2013. LNCS, vol. 8097, pp. 242–254. Springer, Heidelberg (2013). https://doi.org/10.1007/978-3-642-40047-6_27
24. Tang, S., Yuan, J., Li, X.Y.: Towards optimal bidding strategy for amazon ec2 cloud spot instance. In: 2012 IEEE Fifth International Conference on Cloud Computing, pp. 91–98. IEEE (2012)
25. Wu, G., Tang, M., Tian, Y.-C., Li, W.: Energy-efficient virtual machine placement in data centers by genetic algorithm. In: Huang, T., Zeng, Z., Li, C., Leung, C.S. (eds.) ICONIP 2012. LNCS, vol. 7665, pp. 315–323. Springer, Heidelberg (2012). https://doi.org/10.1007/978-3-642-34487-9_39
26. Zhou, A.C., Lao, J., Ke, Z., Wang, Y., Mao, R.: Farspot: optimizing monetary cost for HPC applications in the cloud spot market. IEEE Trans. Parallel Distrib. Syst. **33**, 2955–2967 (2021)

Latency-Aware Inference on Convolutional Neural Network Over Homomorphic Encryption

Takumi Ishiyama, Takuya Suzuki$^{(\boxtimes)}$ ⓘ, and Hayato Yamana ⓘ

Waseda University, 3-4-1 Okubo, Shinjuku, Tokyo, Japan
{takumi,t-suzuki,yamana}@yama.info.waseda.ac.jp

Abstract. Homomorphic encryption enables privacy-preserving computation in convolutional neural networks (CNNs), keeping their input and output secret from the server; however, it faces long latency because of large overhead of the encryption scheme. This paper tackles shortening the inference latency on homomorphic encryption-enabled CNNs. Since the highest inference accuracy is not always needed depending on real-world applications, finding best-fit combinations of latency and accuracy is also indispensable. We propose a combination of *channel-wise packing* and a *structured pruning technique* besides changing the active functions to shorten the inference latency while allowing accuracy degradation. Our experimental evaluation shows that we successfully tune the latency from 8.1 s to 12.9 s depending on the accuracy of 66.52% to 80.96% on the CIFAR-10 dataset.

Keywords: Homomorphic encryption · Privacy-preserving machine learning · Convolutional neural network · Channel pruning

1 Introduction

Machine learning as a service (MLaaS) has recently emerged like software as a service (SaaS), which enables machine learning (training and/or inference) on third-party servers such as the cloud. However, with the increase of MLaaS, privacy has become a critical issue. To tackle the privacy issue, privacy-preserving machine learning (PPML) has been researched, which trains a machine learning model and/or inferences on input data while maintaining the privacy of the client's input data and its output.

One of the techniques to realize PPML is homomorphic encryption (HE) [1, 2] which allows us to compute over ciphertexts without decryption. Lattice-based HE is mathematically strong and its ciphertexts cannot be decrypted in practical time, even when quantum computers are used. HE can evaluate addition and multiplication over ciphertexts. Our research focuses on an inference protocol adopting HE, as shown in Fig. 1. We assume that a pre-trained model is stored in advance on the computational server as plaintexts, similar to the previous studies.

Previous studies mainly focus on improving the inference accuracy [3–6] to achieve high accuracy by adopting state-of-the-art polynomial approximations of the active functions because the original active functions, such as rectified linear unit (ReLU) and sigmoid function, cannot be implemented as they are due to the limitation of HE. The

E. Pardede et al. (Eds.): iiWAS 2022, LNCS 13635, pp. 324–337, 2022.
https://doi.org/10.1007/978-3-031-21047-1_27

previous studies also compare the accuracy differences among adopted active functions besides investigating pooling layer implementation. Since HE cannot evaluate comparisons or divisions, alternative techniques are applied, which degrades the accuracy. The accuracy of the CIFAR-10 dataset [7] over HE has reached over 80% [6]; however, the inference latency is still long, such as 26 min.

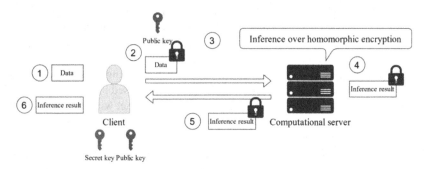

Fig. 1. Protocol of secure inference with homomorphic encryption

Chou et al. [8] first applied pruning techniques to accelerate the inference because the highest inference accuracy is not always needed depending on applications. They used eight-layer CNN with a second-degree polynomial approximation of the ReLU function. As a result, they achieved 76.72% accuracy with a latency of 22,372 s for the CIFAR-10 dataset.

This paper tackles the problem of long inference latency on HE-enabled CNNs. Our contributions include: 1) the adoption of a pruning technique called *channel pruning* [9, 10] with *batch-axis* [3–6] and with *channel-wise packing* [11, 12] to show the effectiveness of shortening the latency, and 2) investigation of different activation functions to tune the inference latency and accuracy in the experiment. Our second contribution is useful for servers and clients to select a best-fit combination of inference latency and accuracy. Since there are two types of packing (aka, SIMD) implementations, we investigate the effectiveness of the pruning technique with either type of packing implementation. Note that *batch-axis packing* packs a pixel of the same position in multiple images into one ciphertext. In contrast, *channel-wise packing* packs one image into a few ciphertexts where the number of ciphertexts is equal to the number of channels, e.g., RGB.

The remainder of this paper is organized as follows: Sect. 2 shows related work. Then, Sect. 3 proposes our latency-aware inference method, followed by the experimental evaluation in Sect. 4. Finally, we conclude this paper in Sect. 5.

2 Related Work

2.1 CNN Inferring

In 2016, Dowlin et al. [3] first implemented the inference of CNN over homomorphic encryption (HE), which adopted a square function as the activation function and a scaled mean-pool function instead of the max-pool function. Since HE cannot compute max-function, they approximated it using summation. Their five-layer CNN achieved 98.95% accuracy for the MNIST dataset [13]. Besides, they used batch-axis packing, which allows inferring 4,096 images simultaneously with a latency of 250 s.

Followed by [3], many studies tackled improving the accuracy. In 2017, Chabanne et al. [4] applied batch normalization before activation functions. Besides, Chabanne et al. adopted the polynomial approximation technique with multiple degrees for the rectified linear unit (ReLU) function because HE cannot calculate the ReLU function. As a result, they achieved 99.30% accuracy with 24 CNN layers and a fourth-degree polynomial approximation of the ReLU function for the MNIST dataset; however, they reported no latency or throughput data. Another approach using GPU to enable faster inference of CNN by adopting batch-axis packing was proposed by Al Badawi et al. [5] in 2018, which achieved 99% accuracy for the MNIST dataset with a latency of 5.16 s and 77.55% accuracy for the CIFAR-10 dataset [7] with a latency of 304.43 s.

In 2020, we [6] combined Al Badawi et al.'s network model [5] and the acceleration techniques proposed in the homomorphic neural network compiler [14] to improve accuracy besides using batch normalization and average pooling. We also unified the coefficients of the layers to reduce the required level[1] to shorten the latency. We achieved 99.29% accuracy for the MNIST dataset with a fourth-degree of polynomial approximation of the Swish function and 81.06% accuracy for the CIFAR-10 dataset with a fourth-degree polynomial approximation of the ReLU function; however, the latencies were long; 21 s for the MNIST dataset and 26 min for the CIFAR-10 dataset.

2.2 Pruning of HE-Based CNN

In 2018, Chou et al. [8] first applied pruning and quantization techniques to accelerate the inference. They evaluated their eight-layer CNN's pruning and quantization techniques with a second-degree polynomial approximation of the ReLU function. They achieved 76.72% accuracy with a latency of 22,372 s for the CIFAR-10 dataset, while the same network model without pruning or quantization achieved 86.76% accuracy. That is, there is a 10.04% accuracy loss after adopting their techniques.

3 Latency-Aware Inference

This paper tackles the problem of long inference latency on homomorphic encryption-enabled CNNs. Researchers have improved the inference accuracy; however, the latency is too long to adapt to real-world problems. Besides, the highest inference accuracy is not always needed depending on applications. As explained in related work, there is research to shorten the latency by pruning and quantization; however, the latency is still long. Besides, the pruning effect when adopted with *batch-axis* [3–6] or *channel-wise packing* [11, 12] is unknown. Thus, this paper proposes to adopt a pruning technique with *batch-axis* and *channel-wise packing* to show the effectiveness of shortening the

---

[1] Level defines the maximum number of applicable homomorphic multiplications. The larger the level is the larger the computational complexity we encounter.

latency with appropriate accuracy. Besides the pruning, we adopt different activation functions to tune the inference latency in the experiment. Note that this paper assumes that the input data to CNNs and the inference result are preserved as secret from the server; however, the CNN model is not encrypted as same in previous research [3–6, 8, 11, 12].

3.1 Preliminary - Batch-Axis Packing and Channel-Wise Packing

WE shorten the inference latency of CNNs by adopting packing [15], which packs multiple plaintexts into one ciphertext to enable SIMD-style calculation. The packing for image inference is classified into *batch-axis packing* and *channel-wise packing*. As shown in Fig. 2, *batch-axis packing* packs pixels in the same position of multiple images into a ciphertext. In contrast, *channel-wise packing* packs pixels in the same channel into a ciphertext, shown in Fig. 3. The number of ciphertexts of *batch-axis packing* is $C \times H \times W$, where H (W) represents the height (width) pixel size of the image and C is the number of channels such as RGB. In contrast, the number of ciphertexts of *channel-wise packing* is C if and only if $H \times W \leq S$ is satisfied, where S is the slot size of ciphertext. In this paper, we assume that the slot size is large enough. Thus, *channel-wise packing* enables $H \times W$ times smaller number of ciphertexts to infer one image than *batch-axis packing*. Note that *batch-axis packing* enables simultaneous image inferring up to S images to increase the inferring throughput when many images are prepared for inferring. Thus, *channel-wise packing* is more suitable for shortening the inference latency than *batch-axis packing*.

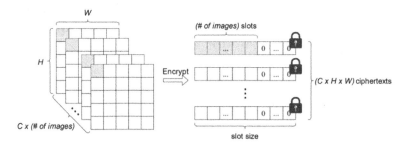

Fig. 2. Batch-axis packing

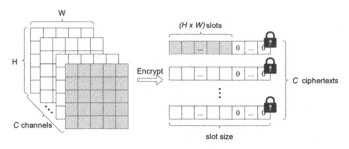

Fig. 3. Channel-wise packing

3.2 Comparison of Number of Homomorphic Operations

Table 1 compares the number of homomorphic operations with *batch-axis packing* and *channel-wise packing*, where HAdd is homomorphic addition, HMulPlain is homomorphic multiplication whose inputs are a ciphertext and a plaintext, and Hsquare is homomorphic multiplication whose inputs are the same ciphertext. Rotation rotates the elements of a ciphertext, which is needed for *channel-wise packing* because one ciphertext consists of whole pixels of one channel. The input for the convolutional and average pooling layer is represented as $IC \times KH \times KW$, and the output as $OC \times OH \times OW$. The kernel height and weight are shown as KH and KW, respectively. Note that $IC = OC$ for average pooling and $IC = OC$, $IH = OH$, and $IW = OW$ for the activation layer. The total number of input units for the convolutional layer is represented as IU, and the total number of output units is shown as OU. S shows the slot size. In Table 1, the number of HAdd for adding bias is omitted because it is negligible. Note that batch normalization is merged in the convolutional layer [6]. As shown in Table 1, we can significantly decrease the number of HMulPlain and HAdd when adopting channel-wise packing. Although the rotation is required for channel-wise packing, we have more decrease in HMulPain.

Table 1. The number of homomorphic operations in each layer

Layer	Operation	# of operation for batch-axis packing	# of operation for channel-wise packing
Convolutional layer	HAdd	$OC \times IC \times KH \times KW \times OH \times OW$	$OC \times IC \times KH \times KW$
	HMulPlain	$OC \times IC \times KH \times KW \times OH \times OW$	$OC \times IC \times KH \times KW$
	Rotation	*none*	$IC \times KH \times KW$
Average pooling	HAdd	$IC \times KH \times KW \times OH \times OW$	$IC \times KH \times KW$
	HMulPlain	$IC \times OH \times OW$	IC
	Rotation	*none*	$IC \times KH \times KW$
Activation	HSquare	$IC \times OH \times OW$	IC
	Rotation	*none*	*none*
Fully connected	HAdd	$OU \times IU$	$OU \times \lceil \log_2 S \rceil - 1$
	HMulPlain	$OU \times IU$	OU
	Rotation	*none*	$OU \times \lceil \log_2 S \rceil - 1$

3.3 Adoption of Structured Pruning

Pruning is one of the model-compaction techniques to reduce the number of parameters and the model's size. We adopt the structured pruning technique, called channel pruning, proposed by Li et al. [10]. We prune the filters in a convolutional layer so that the output channels are reduced based on their priority, where the filter whose L1 norm is smaller has a higher priority. Once x % of filters are pruned, OC and IC in Table 1 decrease as x %, which shortens the inference latency.

4 Experimental Evaluation

We evaluated our latency-aware inference on CNNs by changing activation functions, changing the degree of polynomials, and varying the pruning ratio to show that we can choose a best-fit combination of the CNN model for desired accuracy and latency.

4.1 Experimental Setup

Activation Functions. Before evaluating CNN models over HE, we trained and evaluated the models with different activation functions, including a square function, a second-degree polynomial approximation of ReLU and swish, and a fourth-degree polynomial function of ReLU and swish. We obtained the polynomial approximation using the leastsq function2 from scipy3 in Python. We chose $[-5,5]$ and $[-7,7]$ as the approximation ranges for the leastsq function. Note that the name of an activation function is shown as (activation function)-rg(range)-deg(degree of polynomial approximation). For example, swish-rg5-deg2 means a second-degree polynomial approximation of swish with an approximation range of $[-5,5]$.

Dataset and CNN Network Models. We evaluated each model using the CIFAR-10 dataset [7], a frequently used dataset in this research area. The CIFAR-10 dataset contains 10 classes of images represented by 32×32 pixels in RGB, in which 50,000 training and 10,000 test images are included. As is standard for image dataset preprocessing, we applied data augmentation to the dataset. We added 4 pixels margin on the top, bottom, left, and right to each image and cut it into 32×32 pixels. We also in-verted it horizontally with a 50% probability.

Table 2 and Fig. 4 show our CNN network model [6], except that the first fully connected layer is replaced by global average pooling to reduce the number of parameters. Note that the convolution has (1, 1) strides and (1, 1) padding. Also, the average pooling has (2, 2) strides. We used PyTorch (version 1.1.0) to train the models. The number of epochs was set as 200, and the batch size was set as 128. We used AdamW [16] as the optimization algorithm. The parameter of AdamW was used as a default2 in PyTorch. Then, we prepared three activation functions, ReLU, Swish, and Square, to compare the accuracy without HE. Since ReLU and Swish cannot be implemented with HE, we prepared their polynomial approximated functions.

Table 3 shows the accuracy of the CNN network model with different activation functions. Since the latency when adopting HE depends on the degree of polynomial approximation, we chose the activation function with the highest accuracy in each polynomial degree so that swish-rg5-deg2, swish-rg7-deg4, and Square were chosen as the candidate activation functions.

---

2 https://pytorch.org/docs/stable/generated/torch.optim.AdamW.html.

After training the CNN network models, we performed channel pruning with Torch-Pruning[3] to prune 10%and20% of the whole filters in the second layer. After pruning, we additionally trained each pruned model with 30 epochs. Table 4 compares the accuracy of the non-pruned, and the 10% and 20% pruned models over plaintexts.

Table 2. CNN network model

Layer type	Parameters	# of parameters	Output size
Convolution	32 filters of 3 × 3	896	32 × 32 × 32
Batch normalization	—	64	32 × 32 × 32
Activation	—	—	32 × 32 × 32
Average pooling	2 × 2 pooling size	—	32 × 16 × 16
Convolution	64 filters of 3 × 3	18,496	64 × 16 × 16
Batch normalization	—	128	64 × 16 × 16
Activation	—	—	64 × 16 × 16
Average pooling	2 × 2 pooling size	—	64 × 8 × 8
Convolution	128 filters of 3 × 3	73,856	128 × 8 × 8
Batch normalization	—	256	128 × 8 × 8
Activation	—	—	128 × 8 × 8
Average pooling	2 × 2 pooling size	—	128 × 4 × 4
Global average pooling	—	—	128
Fully connected	10 output units	1,290	10

---

[3] https://github.com/VainF/Torch-Pruning.

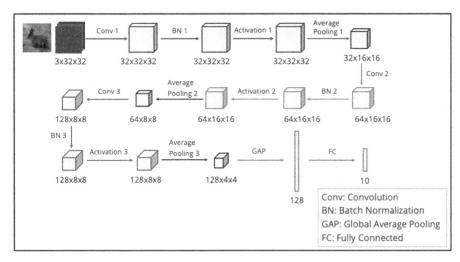

Fig. 4. CNN network model

Table 3. Accuracy of non-pruned network models over plaintext (w/o encryption)

Activation function	Accuracy [%]
ReLU*	85.71
Swish*	85.58
Square*	**79.17**
relu-rg5-deg2	78.79
relu-rg7-deg2	78.29
relu-rg5-deg4	79.48
relu-rg7-deg4	79.95
swish-rg5-deg2	**79.53**
swish-rg7-deg2	78.40
swish-rg5-deg4	80.78
swish-rg7-deg4	**80.91**
* w/o polynomial approximation	

Encryption Parameters. We used version 3.6.6 of Microsoft SEAL6, one of the ho-momorphic encryption libraries implementing the Cheon-Kim-Kim-Song (CKKS) scheme [2], which allows the addition and multiplication of real and complex numbers besides supporting a packing mechanism to pack multiple data into one ciphertext [15]. We set the polynomial degree to 16,384, the number of slots to 8,192, and the scale factor to 30 bits. Table 5 shows the parameters of each model, where Q shows the modulus and the initial level shows the allowed number of multiplications, which affects

Table 4. Accuracy of w/ and w/o pruning of activation function over plaintext (w/o encryption)

Activation function	Accuracy w/o pruning [%]	Accuracy with 10% pruning [%]	Accuracy with 20% pruning [%]
Square	79.17	72.73	66.70
swish-rg5-deg2	79.53	73.93	64.94
swish-rg7-deg4	80.91	76.69	73.18

the computation time, where the larget the level, the longer the computation time. We applied the optimization technique [6, 12] to decrease the required initial level.

Table 5. Parameters

Activation function	Packing method	$\log_2 Q$ [bit]	Initial level
Square function	Batch-axis	260	7
	Channel-wise	290	8
swish-rg5-deg2	Batch-axis	260	7
	Channel-wise	290	8
swish-rg7-deg4	Batch-axis	350	10
	Channel-wise	380	11

Computational Server. Table 6 shows the specification of our computational server used for inference over HE. We use OpenMP7 (version 4.5) and 72 threads for inference without hyper-threading. In order to have stable latency, we execute the inference four times with *batch-axis packing* in the same process, and execute the inference with *channel-wise packing* 10,000 times in the same process. Then, we calculate the average latencies. Note that we omit the first execution latency when averaging *batch-axis packing* latency because the first execution time includes computer architecture-related effects such as cache miss.

Table 6. Specification of our computational server for inference over homomorphic encryption

CPU	Product	Intel Xeon E7-8800 v3
	CPU frequency	2.30 GHz
	# of sockets	4
	# of physical cores per socket	18
Memory		3TB
OS		CentOS 7.6.1810

4.2 Result

Table 7, Table 8, and Table 9 show the inference accuracy, inference latency, used memory size, and the number of major homomorphic operations (multiplication, square, relinearization, rescaling, and rotation) for the three activation functions. We achieved the highest accuracy of 80.96% using swish-rg7-deg4 with a channel-wise packing.

Table 7. Results with square function

Pruning ratio [%]	0		10		20	
Accuracy over plaintexts [%]	**79.17**		72.73		66.70	
Packing method	Batch-axis	Channel-wise	Batch-axis	Channel-wise	Batch-axis	Channel-wise
Accuracy overciphertexts [%]	79.22	79.22	72.14	72.42	66.27	66.52
# of HMulPlain $(\times 10^3)$	9,148	93.2	8,370	84.5	7,592	75.9
# of HSquare $(\times 10^3)$	57.3	0.2	55.8	0.2	54.3	0.2
# of relinearization $(\times 10^3)$	57.3	0.2	55.8	0.2	54.3	0.2
# of rescaling $(\times 10^3)$	114.7	0.6	111.6	0.6	108.5	0.6
# of rotation $(\times 10^3)$	0.0	4.1	0.0	4.0	0.0	3.9
Used memory [GB]	371.1	290.3	355.9	264.4	337.6	238.5
Latency [s]	505.6	9.8	490.5	8.9	447.1	8.1

Channel-Wise vs. Batch-Axis Packing. As we assumed, we confirmed that *batch-axis packing* resulted in longer latency than *channel-wise packing*. The reason is that *batch-axis packing* requires more ciphertexts to infer an image than *channel-wise packing*, which also affects the used memory size. Instead, *channel-wise packing* needs only three ciphertexts to infer an image, i.e., one ciphertext for each channel. On the contrary, the amortized latency is small when adopting *batch-axis packing*. For example, the amortized latency for square function (w/o pruning) was 62 ms when adopting *batch-axis packing*, which is 158 times smaller than *channel-wise packing*.

Table 8. Results with swish-rg5-deg2 active function

Pruning ratio [%]	0		10		20	
Accuracy over plaintexts [%]	**79.53**		73.93		64.94	
Packing method	Batch-axis	Channel-wise	Batch-axis	Channel-wise	Batch-axis	Channel-wise
Accuracy over ciphertexts [%]	79.52	79.55	73.84	73.79	64.40	64.35
# of HMulPlain $(\times 10^3)$	9,205	93.4	8,426	84.7	7,646	76.1
# of HSquare $(\times 10^3)$	57.3	0.2	55.8	0.2	54.2	0.2
# of relinearization $(\times 10^3)$	57.3	0.2	55.7	0.2	54.2	0.2
# of rescaling $(\times 10^3)$	114.7	0.6	111.3	0.6	108.2	0.6
# of rotation $(\times 10^3)$	0.0	4.1	0.0	4.0	0.0	3.9
Used memory [GB]	242.6	290.3	229.2	264.4	216.0	238.5
Latency [s]	526.7	9.6	488.1	8.8	456.5	8.2

Polynomial Approximation Degree. As shown in Table 8 and Table 9, a higher polynomial approximation degree affects higher accuracy, as we expected. The accuracy of swish-rg5-deg4 (w/o pruning) was 1.41% improvement from swish-rg5-deg2 (79.55% to 80.96%); however, the inference latency increased 34.4% (9.6 s to 12.9 s). The significant increase in the latency is because the number of HSquare and relinearization 12 operations increased two times (57.3 M to 114.7 M) besides a 1.5 times increase of rescaling operations (114.7 M to 171.4 M), as shown in Table 8 and Table 9. Therefore, after meeting the required accuracy, choosing the smallest possible polynomial approx-imation degree is advisable.

Comparison Among Activation Functions. SComparing square function with swish-rg5-deg2 (w/o pruning), swish-rg5-deg2 achieved higher accuracy with smaller latency than square function. This relationship is the same when adopting 10% pruning; however, it is not clear in the case of 20% pruning.

Latency-Aware Pruning. Channel pruning affects the accuracy and latency of the inference. Table 7 to Table 9 show that 10% pruning affects 8.3% to 9.3% accuracy degradation with a 5.5% to 8.6% decrease in latency. Besides, 20% pruning affects 15%

Table 9. Results with swish-rg7-deg4 activation function

Pruning ratio [%]	0		10		20	
Accuracy over plaintexts [%]	**80.91**		76.69		73.18	
Packing method	Batch-axis	Channel-wise	Batch-axis	Channel-wise	Batch-axis	Channel-wise
Accuracy over ciphertexts [%]	80.72	80.96	76.34	76.58	72.76	72.85
# of HMulPlain $(\times 10^3)$	9,263	93.6	8,482	85.0	7,701	76.3
# of HSquare $(\times 10^3)$	114.7	0.4	111.6	0.4	108.5	0.4
# of relinearization $(\times 10^3)$	114.7	0.4	111.6	0.4	108.5	0.4
# of rescaling $(\times 10^3)$	171.4	0.8	166.5	0.8	166.5	0.8
# of rotation $(\times 10^3)$	0.0	4.1	0.0	4.0	0.0	3.9
Used memory [GB]	342.2	255.4	324.4	233.4	304.8	211.5
Latency [s]	851.3	12.9	786.3	11.7	727.2	10.5

to 19% accuracy degradation with a 10% to 19% decrease in latency. In sum-mary, active functions, pruning ratio, and approximate polynomial degree affect the accuracy and latency of inference. Figure 4 shows the relationship between accuracy and latency, where the dots connected by lines are the best combination between accuracy and latency. Only if we need the highest accuracy, we can increase the approximate polynomial degree; however, choosing the smallest possible polynomial approximation degree and the smallest pruning ratio is advisable after meeting the required accuracy. Note that the automatic selection of the combination is an open question.

Memory Usage. Table 7 and Table 9 show that a trend of the used memory size where *channel-wise packing* consumes a smaller amount of memory than *batch-axis packing* because *batch-axis packing* needs all the encrypted images on memory simultaneously. However, shown in Table 8, the same trend ccannot be observed with swish-rg5-deg2. Our implementation might cause it; however, this has remained an open question.

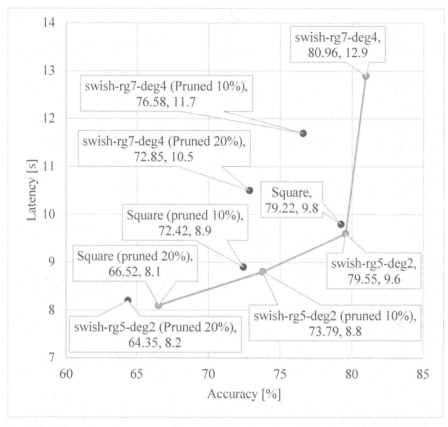

Fig. 5. Inferring time v.s. accuracy. For each data point, the combination of an activation function and pruning ratio is shown as (activation function)-rg(range)-deg(degree of polynomial approximation)-(pruning ratio), besides accuracy and latency.

5   Conclusion

Homomorphic encryption allows us to compute data over ciphertexts, enabling privacy-preserving machine learning; however, the latency becomes high because of large overhead of the encryption scheme. In this paper, we proposed a method that combines *channel-wise packing* and channel pruning to reduce the number of homomorphic operations to shorten the latency. Our experimental evaluation shows that we successfully tune the latency from 8.1 s to 12.9 s depending on the accuracy of 66.52% to 80.96% on the CIFAR-10 dataset by changing the active functions, varying the pruning ratio, and changing the approximate polynomial degrees. Our future work includes automatically tuning the combinations based on a given required accuracy. Another future work is to execute our program with several models and measure memory usage to resolve the curious trend of memory usage.

6 Availability of Data and Materials

Our program is available in https://github.com/yamanalab/latency-aware-cnn-inference.

Acknowledgment. This work was supported by JST CREST Grant Number JPMJCR1503, Japan.

References

1. Gentry, C.: Fully homomorphic encryption using ideal lattices. In: The 41st Annual ACM Symposium on Theory of Computing (STOC 2009), pp. 169–178. ACM, New York (2009)
2. Cheon, J.H., Han, K., Kim, A., Kim, M., Song, Y.: A full RNS variant of approximate homomorphic encryption. In: Cid, C., Jacobson Jr., M. (eds.) Selected Areas in Cryptography – SAC 2018. SAC 2018. LNCS, vol. 11349, pp. 347–368. Springer, Cham (2018). https://doi.org/10.1007/978-3-030-10970-7
3. Dowlin, N., Gilad-Bachrach, R., Laine, K., Lauter, K., Naehrig, M., Wernsing, J.: CryptoNets: applying neural networks to encrypted data with high throughput and accuracy. In: the 33rd International Conference on Machine Learning, vol. 48, pp. 201–210. (2016)
4. Chabanne, H., De Wargny, A., Milgram, J., Morel, C., Prouff, E.: Privacy-preserving classification on deep neural network. In: IACR Cryptology ePrint Archive 2017/035. (2017)
5. Al-Badawi, A., Jin, C., Lin, J., Mu, C.F., Jie, S.J., Tan, B.H.M., et al.: Towards the AlexNet moment for homomorphic encryption: HCNN, the first homomorphic CNN on encrypted data with GPUs. IEEE Trans. Emerg. Top. Comput. **9**(3), 1330–1343 (2021)
6. Ishiyama, T., Suzuki, T. Yamana, H.: Highly accurate CNN inference using approximate activation functions over homomorphic encryption. In: 2020 IEEE International Conference on Big Data, pp. 3989–3995 (2020)
7. Krizhevsky, A., Nair, V., Hinton, G.: CIFAR-10 (Canadian Institute for Advanced Research). http://www.cs.toronto.edu/~kriz/cifar.html. Accessed 7 Jan 2022
8. Chou, E., Beal, J., Levy, D., Yeung, S., Haque, A., Fei-Fei, L.: Faster cryptoNets: leveraging sparsity for real-world encrypted inference. arXiv Preprint arXiv: 1811.09953, pp. 1–15. (2018)
9. He, Y., Zhang, X., Sun, J.: Channel pruning for accelerating very deep neural networks. In: 2017 IEEE International Conference on Computer Vision, pp. 1398–1406. (2017)
10. Li, H., Asim Kadav, H.S., Durdanovic, I., Graf, H.P.: Pruning filters for efficient ConvNets. In: 5th International Conference on Learning Representations (2017)
11. Dathathri, R., et al.: CHET: an optimizing compiler for fully-homomorphic neural-network inferencing. In: Proceedings of the 40th ACM SIGPLAN Conference on Programming Language Design and Implementation, pp. 142–156 (2019)
12. Lou, Q., Jiang, L.: HEMET: a homomorphic-encryption-friendly privacy-preserving mobile neural network architecture. In: Proceedings of the 38th International Conference on Machine Learning, vol. 139, pp. 7102–7110 (2021)
13. LeCun, Y., Cortes, C., Burges, C.J.C.: MNIST handwritten digit database, http://yann.lecun.com/exdb/mnist/. Accessed 7 Jan 2022
14. Boemer, F., Lao, Y., Cammarota, R., Wierzynski, C.: NGraph-HE: a graph compiler for deep learning on homomorphically encrypted data. In: the 16th ACM International Conference on Computing Frontiers, pp. 3–13. ACM, New York (2019)
15. Smart, N.P., Vercauteren, F.: Fully homomorphic SIMD operations. Des. Codes Crypt. **71**(1), 57–81 (2012). https://doi.org/10.1007/s10623-012-9720-4
16. Loshchilov, I., Hutter, F.: Decoupled weight decay regularization. In: arXiv Preprint arXiv: 1711.05101, pp. 1–11. (2019)

PR-MVI: Efficient Missing Value Imputation over Data Streams by Distance Likelihood

Savong Bou[1(✉)] , Toshiyuki Amagasa[1] , Hiroyuki Kitagawa[2,3] ,
Salman Ahmed Shaikh[3] , and Akiyoshi Matono[3]

[1] Center for Computational Sciences, University of Tsukuba, Tsukuba, Japan
{savong-hashimoto,amagasa}@cs.tsukuba.ac.jp
[2] International Institute for Integrative Sleep Medicine, University of Tsukuba,
Tsukuba, Japan
kitagawa@cs.tsukuba.ac.jp
[3] Artificial Intelligence Research Center, AIST, Tokyo, Japan
{shaikh.salman,a.matono}@aist.go.jp

Abstract. Predicting missing attribute values in data streams is useful in boosting the accuracies of analytical results in many applications.
Many algorithms (i.e., Distance Likelihood Maximization (DLM)) have
been proposed for permanently-stored data. They can be used to handle data streams, but the performance is bad when the data streams
have a different distribution from the training data. Some works (i.e.,
Autoregressive Integrated Moving Average (ARIMA)) can deal with data
streams, but they cannot handle categorical data. This paper proposes
Past and Recent neighboring approaches for Missed attribute Value
Imputation by distance likelihood, called "PR-MVI", over data streams.
PR-MVI learns from both past training data and the set of the most
recent complete records. It can handle both numerical and categorical
data streams that have similar and/or different distribution from that of
the past training data. Extensive experiments have shown that PR-MVI
can better predict the missed attribute values over data streams than
other existing approaches.

Keywords: Data cleansing · Data streams · Missed attribute values

1 Introduction

The explosive growth of information from social media, IoT devices, and other
cyber-physical systems compels many opportunities in making use of real-time
data [4–12] for business, science, etc. The missing attribute value is one common
error in data streams, which is caused by many factors, such as device issues, transmission problems in the networks, privacy concerns, etc. An example is in Table 1.

Missing attribute values in data streams could cause serious problems to
many applications, such as wrong weather forecast, inefficient traffic control

---

Savong Bou—Due to name change, Savong Bou is now known as Takehiko Hashimoto.

© The Author(s), under exclusive license to Springer Nature Switzerland AG 2022
E. Pardede et al. (Eds.): iiWAS 2022, LNCS 13635, pp. 338–351, 2022.
https://doi.org/10.1007/978-3-031-21047-1_28

Table 1. Example of missed attribute values (–) in data streams.

Time	Address	Longitude	Latitude
t_1	–	139.83	35.65
t_2	Chuo-ku, Tokyo	138.65	33.87
t_3	Chiyoda-ku, Tokyo	–	36.86
t_4	Chiyoda-ku, Tokyo	137.98	37.98
t_5	–	135.75	36.56
t_6	Chiyoda-ku, Tokyo	136.55	–
t_7	Chuo-ku, Tokyo	–	32.86
...			

systems, inaccurate natural disaster prevention systems, etc. Therefore, repairing missing attribute values of the records from data streams is strongly needed.

Many repairing algorithms for permanently-stored data exist, such as Individual models for Imputation (IIM) [30], Distance Likelihood Maximization (DLM) [24], etc. DLM is the state-of-the-art approach and can deal with both numerical and categorical data. It can deal with data streams that have the same or similar characteristics to the past training data. However, if the data streams have different characteristics from those of the training data, the performance will not be good. A few researches focused on data streams, such as moving-average (MA) model [14], and autoregressive integrated moving average (ARIMA) [19]. They learn from the set of most recent data by ignoring the past training data. Their main bottlenecks are: (1) the inability to handle categorical data, (2) the changing of the correct records, which greatly affects the predicting accuracy, and (3) the recent data might not be sufficient for proper learning.

The past reliable training data (R) and the set of most recent data (W) from data streams are complementary to each other. Specifically, W is useful to instruct the predicting model that the behaviors of data streams have shifted from those of R. Conversely, R provides fundamental yet durable knowledge to the predicting model and could prevent the learning from being too influenced by the noise or temporary shift of the behavior of the data streams. In addition, since DLM can support both numerical and categorical data, DLM is extended so that it can learn from both R and W.

This paper proposes a Past and Recent neighboring-based approach for Missing attribute Value Imputation by distance likelihood, called "PR-MVI", over both numerical and categorical data streams that have similar and/or different distribution from that of the past training data. Extensive experiments over various datasets show that PR-MVI imputes missing attribute values from data streams better than the existing approaches. PR-MVI is about 13% better than ARIMA and about 45% better than DLM for data streams that dynamically change over time. For data streams that have similar distribution to the past training data, PR-MVI achieves comparable performance to DLM and significantly better performance than ARIMA.

This paper is organized as follows. All related works and preliminaries are explained in Sects. 2 and 3 resp. Section 4 elaborates the proposed PR-MVI. Experimental results and the conclusion are in Sects. 5 and 6 respectively.

2   Related Works

Missing value imputation has been extensively studied [3, 13, 22, 23, 25, 26]. A common approach is kNN-based approach [2, 15, 17, 28], which uses a set of k-nearest neighboring records. Specifically, given a record with one or more missing attribute values, the k-NN set of complete records to the incomplete one based on the complete attribute values is first discovered. The missing attribute values are then assigned based on the k-NN. Similar approaches are LOESS [15], kNNE [17], and Missing Categorical Data Imputation Based on Similarity (MIBOS) [28].

Classification-based approaches, such as Gaussian model (GMM) [29] and Clustering-based Imputation (CMI) [31], employ classification to predict missing attribute values. They classify all data into several clusters. Then the cluster closest to the incomplete record based on the complete attribute values is found. The assignment is then made using all complete records in the nearest cluster.

Learning Individual Models (IIM) [30] and DLM [24] use multiple regression models for predicting missing attribute values. DLM [24] is the state-of-the-art approach. It uses the distance likelihood in combination with multiple regressions learned from the k-NN set of complete records to find the best-repaired candidate. This paper is based on DLM, so the detail is explained in Sect. 3.

These existing approaches are specifically designed for permanently-stored data. They are either impossible or too costly to learn in real-time. However, they can be used for dealing with data streams though their performance is poor. Their parameters are learnt from the past training data not from the data streams. Therefore, if the characteristics of data streams are different or shift away from those of the training data, the predicting performance will be worse.

There are a few works suitable for dealing with data streams, such as autoregressive (AR) model [18], moving-average (MA) model [14], autoregressive-moving-average (ARMA) [1], and autoregressive integrated MA (ARIMA) [19]. The models learn the related parameters from the set of most recent complete records from data streams. Their main drawbacks are: (1) the inability to handle categorical data, and (2) the ignorance of the past training data, which could lead to less efficient for missing attribute value imputation for two main reasons: (1) the recent data might not be sufficient for a proper learning, and (2) if there are many recent erroneous and unreliable records, their predicting capability will be badly affected. Another bottleneck is that they sometimes change the original correct records, which greatly affects the predicting accuracy.

3   Overview of DLM and Preliminaries

DLM [24], distance metric, distance predicting model, distance likelihood, and some necessary background knowledge are explained.

3.1 Overview of DLM

DLM relies on multiple regressions learned from the k-NN set of complete records to find the best-repaired candidate by using distance likelihood. It can deal with both numerical and categorical missed attribute values for permanently-stored data. There are two stages to executing DLM: (1) Parameter learning and (2) Missing attribute value imputation. DLM learns the corresponding parameter to predict each attribute value of each record from its k-NN set (Sect. 3.3).

Predicting any missed attribute value of any incomplete record follows four steps: (1) use the complete attribute values of the incomplete record to find its k-NN set; (2) replace the missing attribute values with those of the complete records in the k-NN set to generate all possible repairing candidates; (3) compute the distance likelihoods of all repaired candidates to their corresponding k-NN sets (Sect. 3.4); and (4) choose the repaired candidate with maximum distance likelihood as the repaired solution.

3.2 Distance Metric

Numerical and categorical distance metrics are introduced. The distance from records r_d to r_c on attribute A_m is computed using Eq. 1 if A_m is numerical.

$$\Delta(r_d[A_m], r_c[A_m]) = \frac{r_d[A_m] - r_c[A_m]}{max_{a_i,a_j \in dom(A_m)} |a_i - a_j|} \tag{1}$$

where $dom(A_m)$ is the domain of attribute A_m. The distance is computed using Eq. 2 if the attribute A_m is categorical where $|r[A_m]|$ is the length of the attribute value $r[A_m]$, and $dist()$ is any string similarity measures [20].

$$\Delta(r_d[A_m], r_c[A_m]) = \frac{2dist(r_d[A_m], r_c[A_m])}{|r_d[A_m]| + |r_c[A_m]| + dist(r_d[A_m], r_c[A_m])} \tag{2}$$

3.3 Distance Predicting Model

In DLM, the predicted distance between records is done using the distance regression model [16]. For simplicity, $\Delta_{d,c:l}$ represents $\Delta(r_d[A_l], r_c[A_l])$. The predicted distance from records r_d to r_c on attribute A_m is done using Eq. 3.

$$\Delta_{d,c:m}^p = \phi_0^{c:m} + \sum_{l \neq m}^{|A|} \phi_l^{c:m} \Delta_{d,c:l} = (1, \Delta_{d,c:l}) \phi^{c:m} \tag{3}$$

A_l is an attribute other than attribute A_m and $\phi_l^{c:m}$ is the parameters, and $|A_m|$ is the total number of attributes. Ridge regression [21] is used to learn all parameters $\phi^{c:m}(\phi_0^{c:m}, \phi_1^{c:m}, ..., \phi_{|A|}^{c:m})$ of record r_c by using Eq. 4,

$$\phi^{c:m} = (P^T P + \alpha E)^{-1} P^T Q \tag{4}$$

where α is a regularization parameter, E is an identity matrix, $P = \begin{bmatrix} \Delta_{c,n1:m} \\ \Delta_{c,n2:m} \\ \cdots \\ \Delta_{c,nk:m} \end{bmatrix}$,

$$Q = \begin{bmatrix} 1 & \Delta_{c,n1:1} & \Delta_{c,n1:2} & \cdots & \Delta_{c,n1:|A|} \\ 1 & \Delta_{c,n2:1} & \Delta_{c,n2:2} & \cdots & \Delta_{c,n2:|A|} \\ & & \cdots & & \\ 1 & \Delta_{c,nk:1} & \Delta_{c,nk:2} & \cdots & \Delta_{c,nk:|A|} \end{bmatrix}$$, k is the number of nearest neighbors to

record r_c (represented by k-NN(r_c)), and Q does not contain all elements in P.

3.4 Distance Likelihood

The distance likelihood is computed using the predicted distance. In DLM, the true distance ($\Delta_{d,c:m}$) is assumed to follow normal distribution [27] because it is widely observed in many real data where mean is the predicted distance ($\Delta^p_{d,c:m}$) and variance is $\sigma^2_{c:m}$. Therefore, $\Delta_{d,c:m} \sim \mathcal{N}(\Delta^p_{d,c:m}, \sigma^2_{c:m})$, having Eq. 5.

$$f(\Delta_{d,c:m}|\Delta^p_{d,c:m}, \sigma^2_{c:m}) = \frac{1}{\sigma_{c:m}\sqrt{2\pi}}e^{-(\Delta_{d,c:m}-\Delta^p_{d,c:m})^2/2\sigma^2_{c:m}} \qquad (5)$$

The log-likelihood of distance from r_d to r_c on attribute A_m is in Eq. 6.

$$L(r_d|r_c, A_m) = \log f(\Delta_{d,c:m}|\Delta^p_{d,c:m}, \sigma^2_{c:m})$$
$$= -\frac{\log(2\pi\sigma^2_{c:m})}{2} - \frac{(\Delta_{d,c:m} - \Delta^p_{d,c:m})^2}{2\sigma^2_{c:m}} \qquad (6)$$

$L(r_d|r_c)$ represents the distance likelihood from record r_d to r_c on all attributes. The distance likelihood from record r_d to its k-nearest neighboring records w.r.t. to all attributes is computed using Eq. 7.

$$L(r_d) = \sum_{r_c \in k-NN(r_d)} \sum_{l=1}^{|A|} L(r_d|r_c, A_l) \qquad (7)$$

4 Proposed Approach

4.1 Overview

In contrast to existing approaches that rely on either the past training data or a set of the most recent complete records from streams, the proposed approach uses both data. The overview of the difference is in Fig. 1. Missing attribute value imputation over data streams in this paper is defined in Definition 1.

Definition 1. *Given training data R and data streams DS with user-defined window W and slide S parameters, missing attribute value imputation is to predict all missed attribute values of I incomplete records (I ∈ S) after receiving*

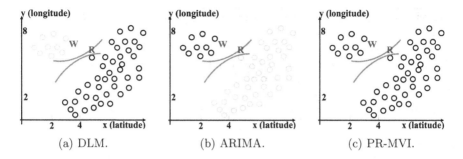

Fig. 1. Overview of existing approaches vs PR-MVI. Each node represents each records, R represents past training data, and W represents the set of most recent complete records from data streams. Nodes in pale-brown color are not used for training the corresponding approaches.

every S records from DS by using both R and W. R is a subset of the received records from DS, which can as much as possible represent the distribution of the future coming records from DS. W is the window that maintains a set of most recent records after receiving every S records from DS.

This paper proposes the Past and Recent neighboring-based approach for Missed attribute Value Imputation (PR-MVI) by extending DLM so that it can learn from both the past training records (R) and the set of most recent complete records (W). There are two main steps for PR-MVI: (1) parameter-learning and (2) imputing the missing attribute values of the incomplete records.

There are two stages for learning the parameters: (1) one-time learning from the training data R prior to receiving records from data streams, and (2) real-time learning from W after receiving every S records from data streams.

After receiving every S records from data streams, missing attribute value imputation of each incomplete records in I is done using following steps: (1) find two sets of k-NN from: (1) W and (2) R by using the values of the complete attributes of each incomplete record, (2) generate the repaired candidates by replacing the missed attribute value by the values of all compete records in the two sets of k-NN in step 1, (3) compute the distance likelihood from each repaired candidate to its corresponding k-NN set, and (4) the repaired candidate that has the biggest distance likelihood is chosen as the repaired solution.

4.2 Proposed Approach (PR-MVI)

Algorithm 1 shows the algorithm of PR-MVI. There are two main stages: (1) parameter-learning (Line 3, 6), and (2) missing-value-imputing (Lines 4–18).

Parameter-learning is divided into two steps: (1) one-time learning of the parameters for all training data (R) (Line 3), and (2) real-time learning of the parameters for all complete records in the set of the most recent records (W) (Line 6). Parameters are learned for each attribute of each complete record as follows (Algorithm 2): (1) find the k nearest neighboring records (k-NN) to each

---

Algorithm 1. PR-MVI: Imputing missing attribute from data streams

---

1: **Input: All training records (R), Data streams (DS)**
2: **Output: Repaired solutions (RS) of I incomplete records**
3: ϕ_R =Param-Learning(R) using Algorithm 2.
4: **for** Every S records from Data Streams DS **do**
5:     $W = Update(W, S/I)$
6:     ϕ_W =Param-Learning(W) using Algorithm 2.
7:     **for** Every missed attribute A_m of each incomplete record $r_m \in I$ from S **do**
8:         $r_{bst} =$"", $Mlkh = -\infty$
9:         $kNN_W = k - NN(W, r_m$ on complete attributes $A_{1,\ldots,|A|\backslash m})$
10:        $RC_W =$ Impute all repaired candidates $(r_{m1}^W, r_{m2}^W, \ldots)$ from kNN_W
11:        $Mlkh, r_{bst}$ =MaxLikelihood($r_{bst}, Mlkh, RC_W, \phi_W$) using Algorithm 3
12:        $kNN_R = k - NN(R, r_m$ on complete attributes $A_{1,\ldots,|A|\backslash m})$
13:        $RC_R =$ Impute all repaired candidates $(r_{m1}^R, r_{m2}^R, \ldots)$ from kNN_R
14:        $Mlkh, r_{bst}$ =MaxLikelihood($r_{bst}, Mlkh, RC_R, \phi_R$) using Algorithm 3
15:        $RS.add(r_{bst})$
16:     **end for**
17: **end for**
18: Return RS

Algorithm 2. Learn all parameters

1: **function** Param-Learning(R)
2:     **for** $r_i \in$ each of all completes records $(R = r_1, \ldots, r_n)$ **do**
3:         **for** $A_l \in$ each of all attributes($A_1, \ldots, A_{|A|}$) **do**
4:             $kNN =$ k-NN(r_i on attributes $A_{1,\ldots,|A|\backslash l})$
5:             $\phi^{il} = ParamLearning(r_i, kNN)$ in Section 3.3
6:             $\phi_R.add(r_i[A_l], \phi^{il})$
7:         **end for**
8:     **end for**
9:     Return ϕ_R
10: **end function**

---

record r_i on all attributes except the target attribute l ($A_{1,\ldots,|A|\backslash l}$) (Line 4), (2) learn the parameters (ϕ^{il}) using ridge regression following distance predicting model in Sect. 3.3 (Line 5), and (3) keep and return all records and their learned parameters (ϕ_R) (Lines 6–9).

Missing attribute value imputation (Algorithm 1) is done after receiving every S records from data streams (DS) (Line 4). We assume that there are I incomplete records with missed attribute values in S where $|I| \leq |S|$. After receiving every S records from streams, we keep a set of W most recent complete records, denoted by $W = Update(W, S/I)$ (Line 5). For all attributes of all records in W, all corresponding parameters ϕ_W are learned ϕ_W =Param-Learning(W) (Line 6) (Algorithm 2).

For each missing attribute value A_m of each incomplete record $r_m \in I$ (Line 7), missing attribute value imputation follows below steps: (1) find the k nearest neighboring records (kNN_W) of the incomplete record based on the complete

---

Algorithm 3. Find repaired candidate with maximum distance likelihood

---

1: **function** MaxLikelihood(r_{bst}, $Mlkh$, RC, ϕ_{Re})
2:    **for** $r_{mi} \in RC$ **do**
3:      $(kNN_{can}, \phi_{can}) = k - NN(\phi_{Re}, r_{mi})$
4:      $Dlkhood = 0$
5:      **for** $(r_{ni}, \phi^{r_{ni}}) \in (kNN_{can}, \phi_{can})$ **do**
6:        $Dlkhood \mathrel{+}= DLikelihood(r_{mi}, r_{ni}, \phi^{r_{ni}})$ by Eq. 7
7:      **end for**
8:      **if** $Mlkh < Dlkhood$ **then**
9:        $Mlkh = Dlkhood$
10:        $r_{bst} = r_{mi}$
11:      **end if**
12:    **end for**
13:    Return $Mlkh, r_{bst}$
14: **end function**

---

attribute values (e.g., $A_{1,...,|A|\backslash m}$) from all records in W (Line 9), (2) enumerate all possible repaired candidates $(r_{m1}^{W}, r_{m2}^{W}, ...)$ by replacing the missed attribute values by those of the records in the kNN_W (Line 10), (3) find the repaired candidate (r_{bst}) with the maximum distance likelihood $(Mlkh)$ using function "MaxLikelihood()" (Line 11) using Algorithm 3, (4) find the k nearest neighboring records (kNN_R) of the incomplete record based on the complete attribute values (e.g., $A_{1,...,|A|\backslash m}$) from all records in R (Line 12), (5) enumerate all possible repaired candidates $(r_{m1}^{R}, r_{m2}^{R}, ...)$ by replacing the missed attribute values by those of the records in the kNN_R (Line 13), (6) find the repaired candidate with the maximum distance likelihood using function "MaxLikelihood()" (Line 14) using Algorithm 3. Specifically, if any repaired candidate has bigger distance likelihood than $Mlkh$ in step (3), r_{bst} and $Mlkh$ are replaced by the respective repaired candidate and its distance likelihood, and (7) return all repaired solutions (RS) of incomplete records in I using both W and R (Lines 15–18).

Function "MaxLikelihood()" in Algorithm 3 finds the repaired candidate with the biggest distance likelihood as follows: (1) for each repaired candidate (r_{mi}), find the kNN_{can} and the corresponding parameters ϕ_{can} (Line 3), (2) retrieve each record r_{ni} and its parameter $\phi^{r_{ni}}$ from the (kNN_{can}, ϕ_{can}) set (Line 5), (3) compute the distance likelihood from r_{mi} to each record r_{ni} in kNN_{can} using the retrieved parameter $\phi^{r_{ni}}$ (Line 6), and (4) return the repaired candidate that has the biggest distance likelihood (Lines 8–13).

Running Example of PR-MVI. Example in Fig. 2 is used to explain PR-MVI. Each data point represents each Geo location with only two dimensions for simplicity. The discussion can also apply to data with more dimensions. All complete records are depicted in the figure. All parameters $(\phi^1, \phi^2, ...)$ of all complete records are learned from R. After receiving S records from data streams, W is updated. All parameters of records in W are learned. In this figure,

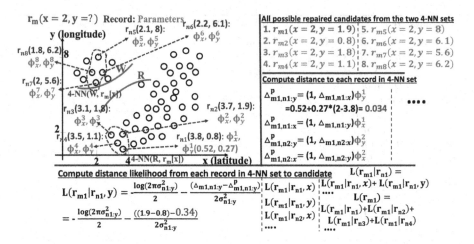

Fig. 2. Example of PR-MVI. $max_{a_i, a_j \in dom(A_m)}|a_i - a_j| = 1$ and number of neighbors is set to four for simplicity. Past training data is represented by R. After receiving S records from data streams, the set of nine most recent complete records is represented by W.

only related parameters are shown for simplicity. For simplicity, the number of neighbors is set to four.

There is one incomplete record r_m with $x = 2$ but its y value is missed. To impute y value, PR-MVI uses the complete attribute value (e.g., x) of r_m to find the 4-NN(R, $r_m[x]$) set $(r_{n1}, ..., r_{n4})$ from R marked by dotted circle, and enumerates all possible repaired candidates $(r_{m1}, ..., r_{m4})$ at the upper right-hand-side. For each repaired candidate, find its 4-NN set of the complete records from R and compute the distance (middle right-hand-side) and distance likelihood (bottom) to its corresponding 4-NN set by using the learnt parameters from each complete record of its 4-NN set $(r_{n1}, ..., r_{n4})$. Similarly, PR-MVI finds 4-NN(W, $r_m[x]$) set $(r_{n5}, ..., r_{n8})$ from W marked by dotted circle, and enumerates all possible repaired candidates $(r_{m5}, ..., r_{m8})$ at the upper right hand-side. Following the same procedure above, PR-MVI computes the distance likelihood of each repaired candidate against W. The best repaired candidate has the biggest distance likelihood.

5   Experimental Evaluation

Two metrics are used to measure the performance: (1) Accuracy (Eq. 8) for categorical data, and (2) Root mean square (RMS) error (Eq. 9) for numerical data where r^p and r^t are respectively the predicted and true records.

$$Accuracy = \frac{truth \cap found}{truth} \quad (8) \qquad RMS = \sum_{l=1}^{|A_m|} \frac{(r^p[A_l] - r^t[A_l])^2}{|A_m|} \quad (9)$$

Two numerical and one categorical datasets are used: (1) Adult[1], (2) Letter[2], and (3) Mushroom[3] respectively. Adult dataset contains census data of the United States in 1994 with 49k records and 14 attributes. Letter dataset is a letter recognition dataset with 20k records and 16 attributes. Mushroom dataset contains features of the mushroom with 5.6k records and 22 attributes.

The past training data (R) and data streams (DS) are 40% and 60% of the datasets respectively. DS is simulated into data streams for experimental purposes. The set of most recent complete records (W) contains 40 records and S is set to 10 records. For experimental purpose, the DS of Mushroom and Letter datasets are chosen to have different distributions from the corresponding R. Specifically, all records in DS are selected so that they have different attribute values as much as possible from all records in R. The DS of the Adult dataset is set to have similar distribution to that of its R. Comparable approaches are explained in Sect. 2. The parameters are: (1) # of incomplete tuples, (2) # of neighbors, and (3) # of attributes with missed values.

5.1 Predicting Accuracy of Missing Attribute Values

The comparison of the predicting accuracy of PR-MVI with other approaches is reported in this section. The results are in Fig. 3 for categorical data.

When increase the # of incomplete tuples and missed attributes, more burden is added to the predicting task. Therefore, the predicting performance gets worse. In contrast, when increasing the # of neighbors, the predicting performances of all approaches get better because more useful information is added to the training data. However, when the # of neighbors is too many, the performance gets worse because more noise and not useful information are added to the learning process.

PR-MVI greatly outperforms other existing approaches when predicting missed attribute values from data streams. DLM and other existing approaches are static in nature and rely on the past training data for learning and predicting. They perform badly when dealing with data streams that have different characteristics from the past training data. PR-MVI learns from both the past training data and the set of the most recent records from data streams, so it is more durable than other existing approaches to the dynamically-changing nature of data streams. As a result, PR-MVI performs much better than the existing approaches.

---

[1] https://sci2s.ugr.es/keel/dataset.php?cod=192.
[2] https://archive.ics.uci.edu/ml/datasets/letter+recognition.
[3] https://sci2s.ugr.es/keel/dataset.php?cod=178.

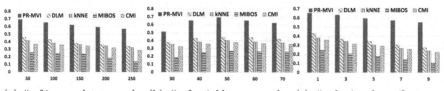

(a) # of incomplete records. (b) # of neighbors records. (c) # of missed attributes.

Fig. 3. Predicting accuracy on mushroom dataset.

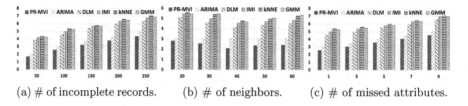

(a) # of incomplete records.   (b) # of neighbors.   (c) # of missed attributes.

Fig. 4. Predicting error (RMS) on letter dataset.

5.2   Predicting RMS Error of Missing Attribute Values

The results are in Fig. 4. Similar trends in Sect. 5.1 can be observed w.r.t. different parameters for predicting numerical dataset. The results show that PR-MVI performs much better than DLM and other approaches for permanently-stored data with similar reasons explained in Sect. 5.1. It is observed that ARIMA performs well when dealing with data streams. ARIMA learns from the set of the most recent records from data streams, so it can flexibly learn from the data streams that are dynamically changed over time. ARIMA performs a little worse than PR-MVI because: (1) Both PR-MVI and ARIMA learn from the set of most recent records from data streams, (2) PR-MVI is based on distance likelihood and the work [24] has shown that when learning from the same set of data, distance-likelihood-based approach is better than ARIMA.

The results in Fig. 5 are for Adult dataset where its DS and R are set to have similar distribution. DLM and other existing approaches for permanently-stored data are very competitive for this kind of dataset and perform significantly better than ARIMA because: (1) DLM and other existing approaches for permanently-

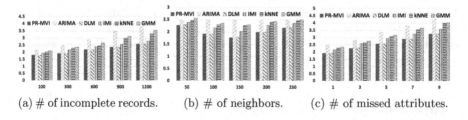

(a) # of incomplete records.   (b) # of neighbors.   (c) # of missed attributes.

Fig. 5. Predicting error (RMS) on adult dataset.

stored data learn from a larger and more reliable training data (R) while ARIMA learns from a smaller subset of data streams (W), (2) DLM adopts distance-likelihood-based approach, which is proven by [24] to be more competitive than autoregressive approaches like ARIMA for this kind of dataset. PR-MVI could achieve comparable performance to DLM because PR-MVI also adopts distance-likelihood-based approach and learns from both R and W from data streams.

6   Conclusion

This paper proposes Past and Recent neighboring approach for Missing attribute Value Imputation (PR-MVI) over data streams by distance likelihood. Existing approaches learn from either the past training data or the set of the most recent records from data streams, but PR-MVI learns from both. PR-MVI could achieve good performance for both numerical and categorical data streams that have similar and/or different distribution from the past training data.

Extensive experiments prove that PR-MVI significantly outperforms other existing approaches for all parameters. PR-MVI is about 13% better than ARIMA and about 45% better than DLM for data streams that dynamically change over time. For conventional data streams that have the same or similar distribution to that of the past training data, PR-MVI achieves comparable performance to DLM and significantly better performance than ARIMA.

Currently, PR-MVI needs to learn from the set of the most recent records (W) after receiving every S records from streams from scratch. The plan is to make PR-MVI be capable of incrementally learning as part of the future work.

Acknowledgements. This work was partly supported by University of Tsukuba Basic Research Support Program Type A, JSPS KAKENHI Grant Number JP19H04114 and JP22H03694, NEDO Grant Number JPNP20006, and AMED Grant Number JP21zf0127005.

References

1. Alengrin, G., Favier, G.: New stochastic realization algorithms for identification of ARMA models. In: IEEE International Conference on Acoustics, Speech, and Signal Processing, Oklahoma, USA, 10–12 April 1978, pp. 208–213. IEEE (1978)
2. Altman, N.S.: An introduction to kernel and nearest-neighbor nonparametric regression. Am. Stat. **46**(3), 175–185 (1992)
3. Alwan, A.A., Ibrahim, H., Udzir, N.I., Sidi, F.: Missing values estimation for skylines in incomplete database. Int. Arab J. Inf. Technol. **15**(1), 66–75 (2018), http://iajit.org/index.php?option=com_content&task=blogcategory&id=126&Itemid=451
4. Bou, S., Amagasa, T., Kitagawa, H.: Filtering XML streams by xpath and keywords. In: Indrawan-Santiago, M., Steinbauer, M., Nguyen, H., Tjoa, A.M., Khalil, I., Anderst-Kotsis, G. (eds.) Proceedings of the 16th International Conference on Information Integration and Web-based Applications & Services, Hanoi, Vietnam, 4–6 December 2014, pp. 410–419. ACM (2014). https://doi.org/10.1145/2684200.2684309

5. Bou, S., Amagasa, T., Kitagawa, H.: Keyword search with path-based filtering over xml streams. In: 2014 IEEE 33rd International Symposium on Reliable Distributed Systems, pp. 337–338 (2014). https://doi.org/10.1109/SRDS.2014.63

6. Bou, S., Amagasa, T., Kitagawa, H.: Path-based keyword search over XML streams. Int. J. Web Inf. Syst. **11**(3), 347–369 (2015). https://doi.org/10.1108/IJWIS-04-2015-0013

7. Bou, S., Amagasa, T., Kitagawa, H.: An improved method of keyword search over relational data streams by aggressive candidate network consolidation. In: Hartmann, S., Ma, H. (eds.) DEXA 2016. LNCS, vol. 9827, pp. 336–351. Springer, Cham (2016). https://doi.org/10.1007/978-3-319-44403-1_21

8. Bou, S., Amagasa, T., Kitagawa, H.: Scalable keyword search over relational data streams by aggressive candidate network consolidation. Inf. Syst. **81**, 117–135 (2019). https://doi.org/10.1016/j.is.2018.12.004

9. Bou, S., Amagasa, T., Kitagawa, H.: Intrans: fast incremental transformer for time series data prediction. In: Strauss, C., Cuzzocrea, A., Kotsis, G., Tjoa, A.M., Khalil, I. (eds.) Database and Expert Systems Applications - 33rd International Conference, DEXA 2022, Vienna, Austria, August 22–24, 2022, Proceedings, Part II. Lecture Notes in Computer Science, vol. 13427, pp. 47–61. Springer, Cham (2022). https://doi.org/10.1007/978-3-031-12426-6_4

10. Bou, S., Kitagawa, H., Amagasa, T.: L-BiX: incremental sliding-window aggregation over data streams using linear bidirectional aggregating indexes. Knowl. Inf. Syst. **62**(8), 3107–3131 (2020). https://doi.org/10.1007/s10115-020-01444-5

11. Bou, S., Kitagawa, H., Amagasa, T.: Cpix: real-time analytics over out-of-order data streams by incremental sliding-window aggregation. IEEE Trans. Knowl. Data Eng. 1 (2021). https://doi.org/10.1109/TKDE.2021.3054898

12. Bou, S., Shiokawa, H., Hayase, Y., Kitagawa, H.: Streamingcube-based analytical framework for environmental data analysis. In: 2019 IEEE International Conference on Big Data and Smart Computing (BigComp), pp. 1–8 (2019). https://doi.org/10.1109/BIGCOMP.2019.8679149

13. Breve, B., Caruccio, L., Deufemia, V., Polese, G.: RENUVER: A missing value imputation algorithm based on relaxed functional dependencies. In: Stoyanovich, J., et al. (eds.) Proceedings of the 25th International Conference on Extending Database Technology, EDBT 2022, Edinburgh, UK, March 29–April 1, 2022. pp. 1:52–1:64. OpenProceedings.org (2022). https://doi.org/10.5441/002/edbt.2022.05

14. Brillinger, D.R.: Time series - data analysis and theory. In: Classics in Applied Mathematics, vol. 36. SIAM (2001)

15. Cleveland, W.S., Loader, C.R.: Smoothing by local regression: principles and methods. In: Härdle, W., Schimek, M.G. (eds.) Statistical Theory and Computational Aspects of Smoothing. Contributions to Statistics. Physica-Verlag HD (1996). https://doi.org/10.1007/978-3-642-48425-4_2

16. Cuadras, C.M., Arenas, C.: A distance based regression model for prediction with mixed data. Commun. Stat. Theor. Methods **19**, 2261–2279 (1990)

17. Domeniconi, C., Yan, B.: Nearest neighbor ensemble. In: Proceedings of the 17th International Conference on Pattern Recognition, vol. 1, pp. 228–231 (2004)

18. Little, R.J.A.: Regression with missing x's: a review. J. Am. Stat. Assoc. **87**(420), 1227–1237 (1992)

19. Liu, C., Hoi, S.C.H., Zhao, P., Sun, J.: Online ARIMA algorithms for time series prediction. In: Schuurmans, D., Wellman, M.P. (eds.) Proceedings of the Thirtieth AAAI Conference on Artificial Intelligence, 12–17 February 2016, Phoenix, Arizona, USA. pp. 1867–1873. AAAI Press (2016)

20. Navarro, G.: A guided tour to approximate string matching. ACM Comput. Surv. **33**(1), 31–88 (2001). https://doi.org/10.1145/375360.375365
21. Rao, C.R.: Linear statistical inference and its applications, 2 edn. Wiley Series in Probability and Statistics, Wiley, Hoboken (1973)
22. Rekatsinas, T., Chu, X., Ilyas, I.F., Ré, C.: Holoclean: holistic data repairs with probabilistic inference. Proc. VLDB Endow. **10**(11), 1190–1201 (2017). https://doi.org/10.14778/3137628.3137631, http://www.vldb.org/pvldb/vol10/p1190-rekatsinas.pdf
23. Samad, M.D., Abrar, S., Diawara, N.: Missing value estimation using clustering and deep learning within multiple imputation framework. Knowl. Based Syst. **249**, 108968 (2022). https://doi.org/10.1016/j.knosys.2022.108968
24. Song, S., Sun, Y.: Imputing various incomplete attributes via distance likelihood maximization. In: The 26th ACM SIGKDD Conference on Knowledge Discovery and Data Mining, Virtual Conference, CA, USA, 23–27 August 2020. pp. 535–545 (2020)
25. Song, S., Sun, Y., Zhang, A., Chen, L., Wang, J.: Enriching data imputation under similarity rule constraints. IEEE Trans. Knowl. Data Eng. **32**(2), 275–287 (2020). https://doi.org/10.1109/TKDE.2018.2883103
26. Sowmya, V., Kayarvizhy, N.: An efficient missing data imputation model on numerical data. In: 2021 2nd Global Conference for Advancement in Technology (GCAT), pp. 1–8 (2021). https://doi.org/10.1109/GCAT52182.2021.9587886
27. Steel, R., Steel, R., Steinberg, D., Torrie, J.: Principles and Procedures of Statistics: With Special Reference to the Biological Sciences. No. 1, McGraw-Hill, New York (1960)
28. Wu, S., Feng, X., Han, Y., Wang, Q.: Missing categorical data imputation approach based on similarity. In: 2012 IEEE International Conference on Systems, Man, and Cybernetics (SMC), pp. 2827–2832 (2012)
29. Yan, X., Xiong, W., Hu, L., Wang, F., Zhao, K.: Missing value imputation based on gaussian mixture model for the internet of things. Math. Probl. Eng. **2015**, 1–8 (2015)
30. Zhang, A., Song, S., Sun, Y., Wang, J.: Learning individual models for imputation. In: IEEE 35th International Conference on Data Engineering, pp. 160–171 (2019)
31. Zhang, S., Zhang, J., Zhu, X., Qin, Y., Zhang, C.: Missing value imputation based on data clustering. Trans. Comput. Sci. **1**, 128–138 (2008)

Discovering Relational Implications in Multilayer Networks Using Formal Concept Analysis

Raji Ghawi[(⊠)][iD] and Jürgen Pfeffer[iD]

School of Social Sciences and Technology, Technical University of Municgh,
Munich, Germany
{raji.ghawi,juergen.pfeffer}@tum.de

Abstract. Many real world networks are multi-relational exhibiting multiple types of relations between nodes. In such complex systems, some of the interaction layers can be dependent on other layers. Unveiling this kind of relational implications among the different layers of a multilayer network is crucial to understand its dynamic properties, and to reveal new non-trivial structural properties. We propose a method, based on Formal Concept Analysis, to discover the implication rules between the different layers in a multilayer network. We demonstrate the usefulness of this method using two large real-world multilayer networks. We also explore how such discovered implications can be exploited in a link prediction task, and the results show that this approach can achieve a good accuracy of 77% for one of the networks.

Keywords: Formal concept analysis · Multilayer networks · Implications · Link prediction

1 Introduction

Network Science is an important tool for describing and analysing complex systems, and has applications in many disciplines including sociology, biology, physics, engineering, economics and information sciences. Originally, network studies employed an abstraction in which systems are represented as ordinary graphs, where the *nodes* (or vertices) of the graphs represent some entity or actor, and a tie between a pair of nodes is represented using an *edge* [20,24]. With advances on research on complex systems, it has become increasingly essential to move beyond simple graphs and investigate more complicated but more realistic frameworks [7,22]. Recently, there have been intensive efforts to investigate networks with multiple types of connections, known as multilayer networks [4,5,13,16,19] (aka. multiplex, multi-dimensional, or multi-relational networks).

Many real world networks are multi-relational by nature, i.e. there might be multiple types of connections between any pair of nodes. Social media networks (e.g., Twitter) exhibit a multiplex of social interactions among users, corresponding to different actions: follow, reply, mention, and retweet. Biological

E. Pardede et al. (Eds.): iiWAS 2022, LNCS 13635, pp. 352–366, 2022.
https://doi.org/10.1007/978-3-031-21047-1_29

networks, such as genetic and protein interaction networks, consider different types of genetic interactions for organisms [8,23]. Collaborative networks can also be treated as multilayer networks, where layers correspond to different working tasks among collaborators. Co-authorship networks are multilayer networks when the different topics of co-authored papers are considered as layers. Therefore, multi-relational analysis is needed to distinguish among different kinds of interactions, or equivalently to look at interactions from different perspectives. A fundamental open question arises then about the structural interdependency of the different layers in a multilayer network. In real world networks, some of the interaction layers considered in the multidimensional representation of a system can be dependent on some other layers. In other words, the presence of a group of edges in some layers imply the presence of that group in other layers. That is, some types of relationships between nodes could be dependent on other types of relations. Unveiling this kind of relational implications among the different layers of a multilayer network is crucial to understand its dynamical properties, and would potentially reveal new non-trivial structural properties about the whole system.

In this paper, we propose a method to discover relational implications between the layers of a multilayer network. The method is based on Formal Concept Analysis (FCA), which is a mathematical framework mainly used for classification and knowledge discovery [11]. FCA is mainly used for deriving implicit relationships between objects described through a set of attributes on the one hand and these attributes on the other. FCA has been used in many practical applications in various fields ([15]), including: data mining [10,12], text mining [21], machine learning [17], knowledge management [18], and semantic web [1]. The utilization of Formal Concept Analysis in Social Network Analysis is not new. Aufaure et al. [2] presented several examples of successful applications of FCA for Social Networks Analysis. FCA has been applied, in a tool called EVARIST [6], to opinion analysis and e-reputation observation on Twitter.

In this paper, we use formal concept analysis to address the open question about unveiling structural interdependency, in terms of relational implications, of the different layers in a multilayer network. We use FCA to efficiently identify comprehensible implications that are implicitly present in a multilayer network. Our proposed method starts with expressing the multilayer network as a formal context, whose set of attributes is the set of layers, and whose set of objects is the set of all pairs of nodes (dyads). In this formal context, the incidence relation expresses which pairs of nodes are connected, through edges, within which layers. Then, our method proceeds with the identification of valid implications in the formal context. This step leads to the discovery of interesting implicational knowledge about the different layers of a multilayer network. Each discovered implication has the form: $X \rightarrow Y$, where X and Y are sets of layers, and it means that all edges that are present in the layers X, are also necessarily present in the layers Y. In other words, any two nodes that are linked through all the relationship types in X, are also linked through all the relationship types in Y.

One promising application of the proposed approach is link prediction. Discovered implications among the network layers can be exploited to predict an edge in a layer based on the co-existence of that edge in other layers.

The contributions of the paper are the following:

- We propose an FCA based method to discover relational implications in multilayer networks.
- We apply our method on two real-world multilayer networks.
- We explore how to exploit discovered implications in link prediction.

The paper is organized as follows. Section 2 provides some preliminaries, and Sect. 3 presents our proposed approach for implication discovery in multilayer networks using FCA. Section 4 is dedicated to the results of applying the proposed approach on empirical datasets; whereas Sect. 5 discusses the exploitation of the approach in link prediction, and Sect. 6 concludes the paper.

2   Preliminary

2.1   Multilayer Networks

Multilayer Networks are networks with multiple kinds of relations. Without lose of generality, we assume that edges are undirected and unweighted. A multilayer network can be defined as $\mathbb{M} = (V, E, \mathcal{L})$, where: V is a set of nodes; $\mathcal{L}$ is a set of labels; E is a set of labeled edges, i.e. the set of triples (u, v, L) where $u, v \in V$ are nodes and $L \in \mathcal{L}$ is a label. Also, we use the term *layer* to indicate label, and we say that an edge belongs to, or appears in, a layer L if its label is L.

Given a layer $L \in \mathcal{L}$, the set of edges that belong to L, denoted $E^{[L]}$, is given by: $E^{[L]} = \{(u, v) \in V \times V \mid (u, v, L) \in E\}$. We assume that given a pair of nodes $u, v \in V$ and a label $L \in \mathcal{L}$, only one edge (u, v, L) may exist. Thus, each pair of nodes in $\mathbb{M}$ can be connected by at most $|\mathcal{L}|$ possible edges.

Given a pair of nodes (edge) $e = (u, v)$, the set of layers to which e belong, denoted $\mathcal{L}^{[e]}$, is given by: $\mathcal{L}^{[e]} = \{L \in \mathcal{L} \mid (u, v, L) \in E\}$.

We assume that the set of nodes V is fixed with respect to the layers; i.e., the nodes across the different layers are identical. Moreover, we assume that edges are intra-layer only (within same layer); that is, we disallow inter-layer edges (between different layers).

2.2   Formal Concept Analysis

Formal Concept Analysis (FCA) is a mathematical framework mainly used for classification and knowledge discovery [11]. FCA starts with a *formal context*, which is a triple $\mathbb{K} = \langle G, M, I \rangle$ where $G = \{g_1, \cdots, g_n\}$ is a set of objects, $M = \{m_1, \cdots, m_k\}$ a set of attributes, and $I \subseteq G \times M$ is a binary relation, called *incidence relation*, with $(g, m) \in I$ (denoted gIm) meaning that object g has attribute m.

Two dual derivation operators, denoted by $(.)'$, are defined as follows:

$$A' = \{m \in M \mid \forall g \in A, gIm\} \text{ for } A \subseteq G,$$
$$B' = \{g \in G \mid \forall m \in B, gIm\} \text{ for } B \subseteq M$$

A' is the set of attributes common to all objects of A; and B' is the set of objects sharing all attributes of B.

The two compositions of the both derivation operators, denoted by $(.)''$, are closure operators. In particular, for $A \subseteq G$ and $B \subseteq M$, we have $A \subseteq A''$ and $B \subseteq B''$. Then A and B are closed sets when $A = A''$ and $B = B''$ respectively.

A *formal concept* is a pair (A, B), where $A \subseteq G$, $B \subseteq M$, whenever $A' = B$ and $B' = A$, where A is closed and called the "extent" of the concept (A, B), and B is closed and called the "intent" of the concept (A, B). The set of all concepts is denoted by $\mathfrak{B}(\mathbb{K})$.

The formal concepts of a given context are partially ordered by the subconcept-superconcept relation as defined by the inclusion of their extents, or equivalently by the inverse inclusion of their intents. An order $\leqslant$ on the concepts is defined as follows: for any two concepts (A_1, B_1) and (A_2, B_2) of $\mathbb{K}$, we say that $(A_1, B_1) \leqslant (A_2, B_2)$ precisely when $A_1 \subseteq A_2$ (or equivalently when $B_1 \supseteq B_2$.) The set of all formal concepts of a context $\mathbb{K}$ together with the order relation $\leqslant$ forms a complete lattice, called the *concept lattice* of $\mathbb{K}$ and denoted by $\underline{\mathfrak{B}}(\mathbb{K})$.

2.3   Implications

FCA also studies attribute dependencies through the notion of *implications*. An implication relates two sets of attributes and expresses that every object possessing each attribute from the first set also has each attribute from the second one. An attribute implication is denoted by $X \rightarrow Y$, where $X, Y \subseteq M$. We say $X \rightarrow Y$ is valid in $\mathbb{K}$ iff $X' \subseteq Y'$. The set of all valid implications for $\mathbb{K}$ on M is called the *attribute implicational theory*.

In general, the theory of a formal context can be exponentially large compared to the size of the context. Thus, one employs an implication base, i.e., a sound, complete, and non-redundant set of implications from which the theory can be inferred. Among the various bases used in FCA, the canonical base (aka Duquenne-Guigues basis) stands out due to its minimal size [14]. The Duquenne-Guigues or canonical basis of implications (w.r.t a closure operator $(.)''$) is the set of all implications of the form $P \rightarrow P''$, where P is pseudo-closed. The best-known algorithm for computing the Duquenne-Guigues basis was developed by Ganter in [9] (see [3] for a performance study). The algorithm is based on the fact that intents and pseudo-intents of a context taken together form a closure system. This makes it possible to iteratively generate all intents and pseudo-intents using Next Closure, a generic algorithm for enumerating closed sets of an arbitrary closure operator. For every generated pseudointent P, an implication $P \rightarrow P''$ is added to the basis.

An implication $X \rightarrow Y$ in a formal context $\langle G, M, I \rangle$ has support:

$$supp(X \rightarrow Y) = \frac{|X'|}{|G|}$$

i.e., the relative number of objects exhibiting the necessary attributes for the rule to be applicable among all objects. A higher support implies that the implication is more relevant to the whole domain of the context. Nevertheless, a valid implication $X \rightarrow Y$ may have a support of zero.

3   Approach

Given a multilayer network, our goal is to discover relational implications among different sets of layers. To do so, we follow a typical FCA pipeline:

– We start by constructing a formal context from a multilayer network, where the objects are the edges and the attributes are the layers.
– Then, using this formal context, we find all formal concepts, which can be organised into a concept lattice.
– Finally, we find the canonical base (Duquenne-Guigues basis) of implications within the formal context.

The crucial step in this approach is the first one: constructing the formal context. Once we construct it, the other two steps are straightforward, as they can be performed using standard algorithms.

3.1   Constructing a Formal Context from a Multilayer Network

Given a multilayer network $\mathbb{M} = (V, E, \mathcal{L})$, we construct a formal context $\mathbb{K}_{\mathbb{M}} = \langle G_{\mathbb{M}}, M_{\mathbb{M}}, I_{\mathbb{M}} \rangle$ for the multilayer network $\mathbb{M}$ as follows:

– the set of objects $G_{\mathbb{M}}$ is the set of pairs of nodes: $G_{\mathbb{M}} = V \times V$
– the set of attributes $M_{\mathbb{M}}$ is the set of layers: $M_{\mathbb{M}} = \mathcal{L}$
– the incidence relation $I_{\mathbb{M}}$ is defined as:

$$(u, v) \; I \; L \Longleftrightarrow (u, v, L) \in E, \text{ for } u, v \in V, \text{ and } L \in \mathcal{L}$$

According to this definition, in the formal context, attributes correspond to network layers, and objects correspond to dyads (pairs of nodes). Let g be an object that corresponds to a pair of nodes (u, v), and let m be an attribute that corresponds to a layer l; then we draw an incidence, gIm, for the object g and attribute m, if and only if there exists an edge between the nodes u and v within the layer L (i.e., $(u, v, L) \in E$).

To illustrate the construction of formal context, we use a toy multilayer network shown in Fig. 1-a. This network comprises 4 layers $\mathcal{L} = \{L_1, L_2, L_3, L_4\}$, each contains the same set of nodes: $V = \{a, b, c, d\}$.

Figure 1-b shows the formal context constructed for this toy network. When we look column-wise at the context, we see, for each layer, how the incidences mark the edges that belong to that layer; and when we look at the context row-wise, we see, for each edge, how the incidences mark the layers that contain that edge. For instance, one can easily observe that the edge (a, b) belongs only to the layer L_3, while the edge (a, c) belongs to two layers: L_2 and L_3.

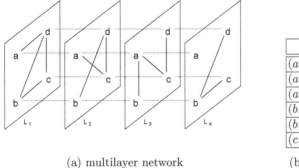

	L_1	L_2	L_3	L_4
(a,b)			×	
(a,c)		×	×	
(a,d)	×			
(b,c)	×			×
(b,d)	×	×		×
(c,d)	×	×	×	

(a) multilayer network   (b) formal context

Fig. 1. A toy example, a 4-layer network and its corresponding formal context.

Following the definition of the formal context, the derivation operators have the following meaning:

- For a set of dyads $A \subseteq V \times V$, the derivation is the set of layers common to all links of A; that is $A' = \{L \in \mathcal{L} \mid \forall(u,v) \in A, (u,v,L) \in E\}$
- For a set of layers $B \subseteq \mathcal{L}$, the derivation is the set of dyads common to all layers of B; that is $B' = \{(u,v) \in V \times V \mid \forall L \in B, (u,v,L) \in E\}$

A major issue with FCA is the large size of lattices generated from realistic data sets. A number of algorithms have been developed to reduce the lattice based on the structure of the lattice itself. These are based on redundant information removal, simplification or selection. A formal context may be redundant in that one can remove some of its objects or attributes and get a formal context for which the associated concept lattice is isomorphic to that one of the original formal context. Two main notions in this regards are that of a clarified formal context and that of a reduced formal context. In this paper, we are interested only in clarified context. A formal context is called *clarified* if the corresponding table does neither contain identical rows nor identical columns.

In our approach, we opt to perform *context clarification*, to reduce the complexity by removing redundancy. Clarification is performed by removing identical rows and columns (only one of several identical rows/columns is left). This step is safe and does not lead to information loss in terms of derived formal concepts, concept lattice or discovered implications.

3.2 Formal Concepts and Implications

The next step is to use this clarified formal context in order to find all formal concepts, which can be then organised in a concept lattice.

A formal concept associates a set of objects A with a set of attributes B, such that the set of attributes that all the objects in A have is identical with B; and the set of objects having the attributes in B is identical with A. In our case, this means that a formal concept comprises a subset A of the edges and a subset B of the layers, where the set of all layers shared by the edges of A is identical with B, and A is also the set of all edges that exist in all layers in B.

The last step, is to find the canonical base (Duquenne-Guigues basis) of implications using the formal context. An implication has the form $X \to Y$ where X and Y are sets of layers, and means that all the edges that belong to all layers in X also belong to all layers in Y. For each implication, we calculate the support, which is basically the number of edges that satisfy the implication rule. For our toy example, two implication rules can be discovered:

- $\{L_4\} \to \{L_1\}$, with support $= 2$
- $\{L_1, L_3\} \to \{L_2\}$, with support $= 1$

The first one says that if an edge belong to the layer L_4 then it belongs to layer L_1. This is supported by two edges (b, c) and (b, d). The second implication says: if an edge belong to the layers L_1 and L_3 then it belongs to layer L_2, and it is supported by 1 edge (c, d).

4 Results on Empirical Datasets

4.1 Datasets

We used two large real-world multilayer networks from the Complex Multilayer Networks collection by CoMuNe Lab (https://comunelab.fbk.eu/data.php).

Auger Collaboration Network. [7] – In this network, nodes represent scientists working at the Pierre Auger Observatory in different research topics on specific tasks. Links indicate collaboration between scientists, and layers represent tasks. It consists of 16 layers, 514 nodes, and 7,153 edges.

ArXiv Co-authorship Network. [7] – This network consists of layers corresponding to 13 categories on ArXiv, a free repository of scientific preprints. All papers containing the word "network" (in the title or in the abstract) were collected up to May 2014 (12,019 articles from 14,488 authors, belonging to 13 categories). The multilayer co-authorship network consists of layers corresponding to different arXiv categories, where each paper is assigned to the corresponding categories, and a link is created between two authors if they co-authored a paper. This multiplex consists of 13 layers, 14,489 nodes, and 59,026 edges.

The characteristics of these networks are shown in Table 1.

Table 1. Networks

	#Layers	#Nodes	#Edges	#Edge-layers
Auger	16	514	6,482	7,153
ArXiv	13	14,489	35,175	59,026

4.2   Construction of Formal Context

For each multilayer network, we construct a formal context (as described in Sect. 3.1). In the formal context, attributes correspond to network layers, and objects correspond to (undirected) edges. We draw an incidence gIm, for a given object g and given attribute m, if the edge $e \in E$ corresponding to the object g belongs to the layer $L \in \mathcal{L}$ corresponding to the attribute m.

To that end, the number of attributes in the formal context equals the number of layers in the network; whereas the number of objects equals the number of distinct edges in the network. The size of the formal context, i.e., number of incidences, is equal to the total number of edges (edge-layer pairs) in the network.

To reduce the complexity, we performed *context clarification* to eliminate redundant rows (i.e., edges); and as mentioned before, this step has no impact on the formal concepts nor on the implications found from the context. Table 2 summarizes the formal contexts constructed from Auger and ArXiv networks.

Table 2. Summary of the formal contexts constructed from the networks

	Original context			Clarified context	
	#Attributes	#Objects	#Incidences	#Objects	#Incidences
Auger	16	6,482	7,153	92	236
ArXiv	13	35,175	59,026	337	1,285

We can see how the clarification step drastically reduces the size of the formal context. For instance, for Auger network, the number of objects (edges) is reduced from 6,482 to 92 only (1.4%) and the number of incidences (edge-layer) is reduced from 7,153 to 236 (3.3%), whereas for ArXiv network, the number of objects is reduced from 35,175 to 337 only (1%) and the number of incidences is reduced from 59,026 to 1,285 (2%).

4.3   Discovered Implications

Using the formal context constructed from each multilayer network, we can infer the formal concepts, and arrange them in a concept lattice. For Auger network, we obtain 115 formal concepts, whereas for ArXiv network we obtain 481 concepts. Recall that each such concept comprises a set of edges (objects) A and a set of layers (attributes) B, such that the set of all layers shared by the edges of A is identical to B, and the set of all edges that belong to all layers in B is identical to A.

Table 3. Number of formal concepts and implications for both networks

	#Concepts	#Implications		
		All	$supp > 0$	$supp > 1$
Auger	115	113	43	24
ArXiv	481	135	91	66

More interestingly, we use the formal context constructed from each multi-layer network, to discover the canonical base of implications. Each implication has the form $X \rightarrow Y$ where X and Y are sets of layers, and means that all the edges that belong to all layers in X also belong to all layers in Y. For each implication, we calculate the support, which is basically the number of edges that satisfy the implication rule. As shown in Table 3, for Auger network, we discover 113 implications, among them 43 have a support> 0 and only 24 implications with a support> 1. On the other hand, for ArXiv we discover 135 implications, among them 91 have a support> 0 with 66 implications having a support> 1.

Table 4 shows some of the discovered implications from both networks (top 5 implications w.r.t support for each network).

For instance, in Auger network, the top implication is:

$$\{\text{Astrophysical-scenarios}\} \rightarrow \{\text{Mass-composition, Spectrum}\}$$

which has support=21. This means that the scientists who are collaborating in the *Astrophysical-scenarios* topic are also collaborating in the topics *Mass-composition* and *Spectrum*. There are 21 such pairs of collaborating scientists who support this implication.

The top implication in ArXiv network (with support = 270) is:

$$\{\text{math.OC, cs.SI, physics.bio-ph}\} \rightarrow \{\text{physics.data-an}\}$$

This implication rule means that the pairs of authors who co-authored papers in the categories math.OC (Optimization and Control), cs.SI (Social and Information Networks), and physics.bio-ph (Biological Physics) also co-authored papers in the category physics.data-an (Data Analysis, Statistics and Probability). There are 270 such pairs of co-authors who support this implication.

5   Application in Link Prediction

In this section, we explore how can we exploit the relational implications discovered in a multilayer network, in a task of link prediction. We want to use those implications to predict whether an edge belongs to a layer or not. The idea is

Table 4. Top implications discovered from the multilayer networks

Auger collaboration network	
Implication	Support
{Astrophysical-scenarios} → {Mass-composition, Spectrum}	21
{Hadronic-interactions, Hybrid-reconstruction} → {Mass-composition}	21
{Magnetic, Mass-composition} → {Spectrum}	18
{Mass-composition, Enhancements, Hybrid-reconstruction} → {SD-reconstruction}	15
{SD-reconstruction, Mass-composition, Hybrid-reconstruction} → {Enhancements}	15
ArXiv network	
Implication	Support
{math.OC, cs.SI, physics.bio-ph} → {physics.data-an}	270
{cs.SI, cond-mat.dis-nn, physics.soc-ph} → {physics.data-an}	116
{math.OC, cs.SI, cond-mat.stat-mech} → {physics.data-an}	116
{math.OC, cs.SI, physics.soc-ph} → {physics.data-an}	82
{cs.SI, cond-mat.stat-mech, cond-mat.dis-nn, physics.bio-ph} → {physics.data-an}	71

to use the implications as "If .., Then .." rules. Given an implication $A \rightarrow B$, where A and B are sets of layers, we can formulate it as the following rule:

If an edge e belongs to all layers in A, then e belongs to every layer in B.

Thus, we can exploit this idea as follows: We can predict whether an edge e belongs to a layer L, by checking whether there is a rule $A \rightarrow B$, such that:

- e belongs to all layers on the rule' left hand side, i.e. $e \in a, \forall a \in A$; and
- the layer L appears on the rule' right hand side, i.e., $L \in B$.

In that case, we conclude that e belongs to L.

5.1 Preparation

To prepare a test dataset, we first exclude the edges that appear in a single layer only (we retain edges that belong to at least two layers). Such edges don't anyway contribute to the discovery of implications, and hence will not be predictable using them[1]. We also opt to use a one-vs-rest approach, where at each time, we try to predict *one* edge-layer pair (predict whether the edge belongs to the layer) using the implication rules discovered using the *rest* of edge-layer instances. In fact, we had to follow this choice, because it is not reasonable to use the typical approach of splitting the instances into training-testing sets; because if we would do so, the set of implication rules that would be discovered using the training set only will not be identical to the entire set of implication rules discovered using the entire dataset. However, with the one-vs-rest approach, we are supposed to perform the implication discovery process, for each test instance, using the rest of instances (which clearly is a very time-consuming step). But, in fact, this is not necessary, as we can always use the same set of implications discovered

---

[1] Notice that even if we conduct the implication discovery using this pruned set of edges, we still obtain the same set of implications.

using all instances. The only modification that we should do is to exclude the implications having support = 1. An implication with support =1 means that there is exactly 1 edge that satisfies this implication, therefore it is necessary to exclude such rule to avoid using it when we predict that only edge used to discover it. In other words, since it is not fair to predict an edge using a rule that was discovered due solely to that exact edge, we should exclude such a rule in the prediction process.

Another necessary preprocessing step is to unfold implication rules that have multiple attributes at the right hand side (RHS), into multiple rules each having a single attribute at the RHS. For instance, if a rule has the form $A \rightarrow \{b_1, \cdots, b_n\}$, we replace it by the rules: $A \rightarrow \{b_1\}, \cdots, A \rightarrow \{b_n\}$.

5.2   Prediction

Given an edge e, let $\mathcal{L}^{[e]}$ denote the set of layers to which e belongs. Out of $\mathcal{L}^{[e]}$, we can create several test instances, each such instance is a triple comprising:

1. the edge e,
2. one of those layers as a ground truth $L_{true}^{[e]} \in \mathcal{L}^{[e]}$, and
3. the rest of those layers as predictors (aka features): $\mathcal{L}_{predictors}^{[e]} = \mathcal{L}^{[e]} \setminus \{L_{true}^{[e]}\}$

Hence, a test instance has the form: $\langle e, L_{true}^{[e]}, \mathcal{L}_{predictors}^{[e]} \rangle$

For example, in our toy example (Sect. 3), the edge (c, d) belongs to 3 layers: $\{L_1, L_2, L_3\}$, thus we create three test instances for this edge:

$$\{ \langle (c,d), L_1, \{L_2, L_3\}\rangle, \ \langle (c,d), L_2, \{L_1, L_3\}\rangle, \ \langle (c,d), L_3, \{L_1, L_2\}\rangle \}$$

Now, the prediction step is conducted as follows:

For each test instance $\langle e, L_{true}^{[e]}, \mathcal{L}_{predictors}^{[e]} \rangle$:

- We first create an empty set of *predicted* layers for edge e: $\mathcal{L}_{pred}^{[e]} = \emptyset$,
- Then, we scan over all the rules, and for each rule $A \rightarrow b$:
  - we check whether the LHS A is a subset of the predictors: $\mathcal{L}_{predictors}^{[e]}$,
  - if yes, we append the RHS b to the set of predicted layers $\mathcal{L}_{pred}^{[e]}$.
- In the case where none of the rules has its LHS as a subset of the predictors, it is not possible to predict the true layer, i.e., the set of *predicted* layers $\mathcal{L}_{pred}^{[e]}$ stays empty, and we say that the instance is *non-predict-able*.

Thus, for each test instance, we obtain a set of *predicted* layers $\mathcal{L}_{pred}^{[e]}$ for the corresponding edge e.

5.3 Evaluation

The evaluation is conducted by simply examining whether the ground truth layer $L_{true}^{[e]}$ is among the predicted layers $\mathcal{L}_{pred}^{[e]}$. If yes, then the prediction is considered as a 'success', otherwise, it is a 'fail'. The overall accuracy can be then assessed by the number of 'success' cases.

However, because it is sometimes not possible to obtain a prediction for a test instance (*non-predict-able* instances), we exclude those cases when we calculate the accuracy. Thus, the accuracy of the prediction is given by the fraction of successful predictions to the number of predict-able instances.

5.4 Results

We have applied the link prediction task on the two multilayer networks, Auger and ArXiv, using the implication rules discovered.

Originally, Auger network comprises 7,153 edge-layer pairs (incidences) with 6,482 unique edges, while ArXiv network comprises 59,026 edge-layer pairs with 35,175 unique edges. After excluding edges belonging to 1 layer only, the number of edge-layer pairs is reduced in Auger network to 1,130 (16%) with 459 unique edges (7%); whereas in ArXiv network, it is reduced to 40,618 (69%) with 16,767 unique edges (48%); see Table 5. Notice that those numbers of edge-layer pairs are the same as the test instances used in the prediction task, since each test instance is made of an edge-layer pair (the true layer).

On the other hand, the number of discovered implications is originally 113 for Auger network, and 135 for ArXiv network. After excluding implications having support=1, we end up with 24 implications for Auger and 66 for ArXiv; and when we unfold the RHS into singletons, we have 29 implications for Auger and 104 for ArXiv.

Now, for Auger network, among the 1,130 test instances, there are only 222 predict-able ones (20%). Clearly, the other instances can not be predicted using the implication rules (for them, there is no rule whose LHS is a subset of their predictor layers). However, among those 222 predict-able instances, 170 instances are predicted correctly (success), giving an accuracy of 0.766. For ArXiv network, there are 1,418 predict-able instances (3.5%), and among them, 689 instances are predicted correctly, giving an accuracy of 0.486. See Table 5.

Table 5. Prediction Results on Auger and ArXiv multilayer networks

	#Instances	#Edges	#Predictable instances	#Success predictions	Accuracy
Auger	1,130	459	222	170	0.766
ArXiv	40,618	16,767	1,418	689	0.486

5.5 Discussion

The above described link prediction task is based solely on the relational impli-cation rules discovered in a multilayer network using FCA. Thus, the ability to predict whether an edge belongs to a layer, is mainly based on the *co-existence* of edges across different layers. The state-of-the-art link prediction methods, however, mainly use different perspectives and are based on the topology of the network and connectivity of nodes. For instance, such approaches broadly make the assumption that nodes with similar network structure are more likely to form a link; and utilize some sort of similarity measures based on common neighbors. Other methods are based on node-similarity to predict the existence of a link based on the similarity of the node attributes.

Therefore, our proposed approach makes an interesting method for link pre-diction tasks, as we have demonstrated its usefulness in this area. However, this method is not intended to replace existing state-of-the-art methods, but rather to be a complementary one, which—when properly integrated with these methods—would certainly improve their performance, and advance the research in the link prediction area.

6 Conclusion

In this paper, we have addressed the problem of discovering relational impli-cations in multilayer networks. We have proposed a method, based on Formal Concept Analysis, to discover the implication rules between the different layers in a multilayer network.

Using two large real-world multilayer networks, Auger and ArXiv, we demon-strated how the proposed approach can be applied, leading to the discovery of interesting implication rules that unveil inter-relational dependencies among the layers of those networks. We have also explored how such discovered implica-tions can be exploited in a link prediction task. This makes an interesting novel method for link prediction, that is based solely on the co-existence of edges across the different layers. We have also applied this approach on the two multilayer networks, Auger and ArXiv, and the results show that this approach can achieve a good accuracy of 77% for Auger network.

This suggests that the proposed method can be an interesting one that com-plements the state-of-the-art topology-based methods for link prediction. Hence, the exploration of how this implications-based method can be integrated with other existing methods would be the main line of future work.

References

1. Alam, M., Buzmakov, A., Codocedo, V., Napoli, A.: Mining definitions from RDF annotations using formal concept analysis. In: Proceedings of the 24th International Joint Conference on Artificial Intelligence, IJCAI (2015)
2. Aufaure, M.-A., Le Grand, B.: Advances in FCA-based applications for social net-works analysis. Int. J. Concept. Struct. Smart Appl. 1(1), 73–89 (2013)

3. Bazhanov, K., Obiedkov, S.A.: Comparing performance of algorithms for generating the duquenne-guigues basis. In: International Conference on Concept Lattices and Their Applications, Nancy, France, pp. 43–57 (2011)
4. Bianconi, G.: Multilayer Networks: Structure and Function. Oxford University Press, Oxford (2018)
5. Cardillo, A., et al.: Emergence of Network Features from Multiplexity. Sci. Rep. **3**(1), 1–6 (2013)
6. Cuvelier, E., Aufaure, M.-A.: A buzz and e-reputation monitoring tool for twitter based on galois lattices. In: Andrews, S., Polovina, S., Hill, R., Akhgar, B. (eds.) ICCS 2011. LNCS (LNAI), vol. 6828, pp. 91–103. Springer, Heidelberg (2011). https://doi.org/10.1007/978-3-642-22688-5_7
7. De Domenico, M., Lancichinetti, A., Arenas, A., Rosvall, M.: Identifying modular flows on multilayer networks reveals highly overlapping organization in interconnected systems. Phys. Rev. X **5**(1), 011027 (2015)
8. De Domenico, M., Nicosia, V., Arenas, A., Latora, V.: Structural Reducibility of multilayer networks. Nat. Commun. **6**(6864), 1–9 (2015)
9. Ganter, B.: Two basic algorithms in concept analysis. In: Proceedings of Formal Concept Analysis, 8th International Conference, ICFCA 2010, Agadir, Morocco, 15–18 March 2010, pp. 312–340 (2010)
10. Ganter, B., Grigoriev, P.A., Kuznetsov, S.O., Samokhin, M.V.: Concept-based data mining with scaled labeled graphs. In: Wolff, K.E., Pfeiffer, H.D., Delugach, H.S. (eds.) ICCS-ConceptStruct 2004. LNCS (LNAI), vol. 3127, pp. 94–108. Springer, Heidelberg (2004). https://doi.org/10.1007/978-3-540-27769-9_6
11. Ganter, B., Wille, R.: Formal Concept Analysis. Springer, Heidelberg (1999). https://doi.org/10.1007/978-3-642-59830-2
12. Ghawi, R., Pfeffer, J.: Characterizing movie genres using formal concept analysis. In: Alam, M., Braun, T., Yun, B. (eds.) ICCS 2020. LNCS (LNAI), vol. 12277, pp. 132–141. Springer, Cham (2020). https://doi.org/10.1007/978-3-030-57855-8_10
13. Ghawi, R., Pfeffer, J.: A community matching based approach to measuring layer similarity in multilayer networks. Soc. Netw. **68**, 1–14 (2022)
14. Guigues, J.-L., Duquenne, V.: Familles minimales d'implications informatives résultant d'un tableau de données binaires. Mathématiques et Sciences humaines **95**, 5–18 (1986)
15. Ignatov, D.I.: Introduction to formal concept analysis and its applications in information retrieval and related fields. In: Braslavski, P., Karpov, N., Worring, M., Volkovich, Y., Ignatov, D.I. (eds.) RuSSIR 2014. CCIS, vol. 505, pp. 42–141. Springer, Cham (2015). https://doi.org/10.1007/978-3-319-25485-2_3
16. Kivela, M., Arenas, A., Barthelemy, M., Gleeson, J.P., Moreno, Y., Porter, M.A.: Multilayer networks. J. Complex Netw. **2**(3), 203–271 (2014)
17. Kuznetsov, S.O.: Machine learning and formal concept analysis. In: Eklund, P. (ed.) ICFCA 2004. LNCS (LNAI), vol. 2961, pp. 287–312. Springer, Heidelberg (2004). https://doi.org/10.1007/978-3-540-24651-0_25
18. Kuznetsov, S.O.: Fitting pattern structures to knowledge discovery in big data. In: Cellier, P., Distel, F., Ganter, B. (eds.) ICFCA 2013. LNCS (LNAI), vol. 7880, pp. 254–266. Springer, Heidelberg (2013). https://doi.org/10.1007/978-3-642-38317-5_17
19. Magnani, M., Micenková, B., Rossi, L.: Combinatorial analysis of multiple networks. CoRR, abs/1303.4986 (2013)
20. Newman, M.: Networks: An Introduction. Oxford University Press Inc, Oxford (2010)

21. Priss, U.: Formal concept analysis in information science. Annual Rev. Info. Sci. Technol. **40**(1), 521–543 (2006)
22. Schoenfeld, M., Pfeffer, J.: Networks and context: algorithmic challenges for context-aware social network research. In: Ragozini, G., Vitale, M.P. (eds.) Challenges in Social Network Research. LNSN, pp. 115–130. Springer, Cham (2020). https://doi.org/10.1007/978-3-030-31463-7_8
23. Stark, C., Breitkreutz, B.J., Reguly, T., Boucher, L., Breitkreutz, A., Tyers, M.: BioGRID: a general repository for interaction datasets. Nucleic Acids Res. **34**(suppl_1), D535–D539 (2006)
24. Wasserman, S., Faust, K.: Social Network Analysis: Methods and Applications. Cambridge University Press, Cambridge (1994)

Inexpensive and Effective Data Fusion Methods with Performance Weights

Qiuyu Xu, Yidong Huang, and Shengli Wu[✉]

School of Computing, Jiangsu University, Zhenjiang, China
swu@ujs.edu.cn

Abstract. Data fusion has been widely used in information retrieval for various tasks. It has been found that two factors impact fusion performance significantly: performance of all component systems and dissimilarity among them. This leads to the classification of data fusion methods into four categories depending on which factors are considered, and methods in different categories are suitable for different situations. In this piece of work, we consider data fusion methods with performance weighting. Both proposed methods assign weights based on performance measured by P@10 for the retrieval system in question, while MAP values are used for such performance weighting in previous studies. Compared with other baseline methods in the same category, our experiment shows that the proposed methods are slightly more effective than the others. Some analysis is also done to justify the rationale for the proposed weighting scheme. Because much less human judgment effort is required for P@10 than for some system-oriented measures such as MAP, the proposed method has higher applicability than all the other methods involved.

Keywords: Data fusion · Information retrieval · Performance weight · Training

1 Introduction

Data fusion has been widely used for different tasks in information retrieval [2,7,9]. It has been found that two factors impact fusion performance significantly: performance of all component systems and dissimilarity among them [18]. Therefore, methods can be divided into four categories: naive methods that consider neither of them (type I), considering component system performance only (type II), considering dissimilarity among component systems/results only (type III), and considering both factors (type IV). CombSum [5], CombMNZ [5], Borda Count [1], Reciprocal Rank Fusion [4], and Condorcet fusion [12] are type I methods, while PosFuse [8], SlideFuse [10], MAPFuse [8] are examples of type II methods, Correlation methods [21] are type III methods, and linear combination with weights trained by regression [18] or by various optimization methods [6,16,22] and weighted Condorcet fusion [19] are type IV methods. Each type of method is appropriate under a certain circumstance.

E. Pardede et al. (Eds.): iiWAS 2022, LNCS 13635, pp. 367–377, 2022.
https://doi.org/10.1007/978-3-031-21047-1_30

This piece of work focuses on type II fusion methods, which are suitable for the situation of equal dissimilarity but inequal performance among component systems/results. Therefore, component systems' performances need to be reflected in their weighting. An analysis of the proposed type II methods such as PosFuse [8], SlideFuse [10], MAPFuse [8] and others, reveals that each deals with the performance issue in a slightly different way. For each component retrieval system, both PosFuse and SlideFuse try to estimate the probability of documents being relevant at each rank. Such a treatment would boost good systems implicitly, while MAPFuse tries to boost those retrieval systems with higher MAP values directly by setting MAP value as weight of the corresponding retrieval system. In this paper, we propose two P@10 related methods, which set P@10 and square P@10 values as weights, respectively. We find that both proposed methods can achieve better fusion performance than MAPFuse, PosFuse and SlideFuse. One desirable property of P@10 is that it requires much less human judgment and computation effort than MAP [15]. For MAP, all relevant documents in the collection need to be identified; while for P@10, only top 10 documents need to be assessed. Both PosFuse and SlideFuse also require relevant documents to be identified at all ranking positions. As a result, the two proposed P@10 related methods have higher applicability than the other methods in the same category.

The rest of this paper is organized as follows: in Sect. 2 we propose two data fusion methods. Some other data fusion methods are also discussed for comparison. A group of data fusion methods including the proposed ones are evaluated in Sect. 3 using four data sets from TREC[1] Then some analysis is done in Sect. 4 to explain why the proposed methods can be good fusion methods. Section 5 concludes the paper.

2   Proposed Methods

In this section we detail the proposed methods P@10Fuse and P@10Fuse2 and also discuss four other methods that will be used as baseline for comparison. In order to apply either of those two methods, we need some training data to set performance weights for all the component retrieval systems ir_i $(1 \leq i \leq n)$ involved. Suppose there is a collection of documents C and a group of queries $Q = (q_1, q_2, ..., q_m)$, all n retrieval systems are used to do the retrieval and their resultant lists are evaluated. Furthermore we assume that ir_i achieves u_i in P@10 for m queries on average, then for P@10Fuse, we let $w_i = u_i$ as ir_i' weight, and for P@10Fuse2, we let $w_i = (u_i)^2$ as ir_i' weight. At the fusion stage, the global score of any document d is calculated by linear combination

$$g(d) = \sum_{i=1}^{m} w_i * s_i(d) \tag{1}$$

---

[1] TREC (Text REtrieval Conference) is an annual event on information retrieval evaluation. Its web site is located at https://trec.nist.gov/.

where w_i is the weight set to ir_i and $s_i(d)$ is the score that d obtains from retrieval system ir_i. After the calculation, all the documents can be ranked by their global score $g(.)$ to obtain the fused results.

P@10Fuse and P@10Fuse2 work in a similar way that both assign heavier weights to better performers. However, the strength of boosting is not the same. Let us look at an example to illustrate this. Suppose we have two systems ir_1 and ir_2 with P@10 values of 0.4 and 0.6, respectively. P@10Fuse will set 0.4 to ir_1 and 0.6 to ir_2, while P@10Fuse2 will set 0.4*0.4 = 0.16 to ir_1 and 0.6*0.6 = 0.36 to ir_2. We can normalize the weights to let them sum to 1. $w(ir_1)$ = 0.16/(0.16+0.36) = 0.31, $w(ir_2)$ = 0.36/(0.16+0.36) = 0.69. Therefore, ir_2 is given heavier weights in P@10Fuse2 than in P@10Fuse, while ir_1 is given lighter weight in P@10Fuse2 than in P@10Fuse1. We can conclude that P@10Fuse2 is more biased to better performers than P@10Fuse does.

MAPFuse [8] is very similar to P@10Fuse and P@10Fuse2 in some ways. Instead of calculating P@10 values, the MAP of each retrieval system is calculated at the training stage and is used as its weight for fusion. For all three, we use the formula $s(d) = 30/(rank(d) + 60)$ to convert the ranking into a score for all the documents involved because it is very good [4], while their raw scores from retrieval systems are not used. Because $s(d) = 30/(rank(d) + 60)$ is the method used by Reciprocal Rank Fusion (RRF), As a type I method, RRF, is a special case of MAPFuse and P@10Fuse with equal weights to all component retrieval systems.

PosFuse [8] and SlideFuse [10] are quite different from the above three type II methods. For the training data set comprising a collection of documents and a group of queries, each retrieval system ir_i performs the retrieval. Then, combining the resultant lists for m queries, the number of relevant documents at each ranking position is determined. For example, if 30 out of 50 documents at ranking position one are relevant, then a score of 30/50 will be given to any document at ranking position one later at the fusion stage, or $s_i(d)$=0.6 if d is top-ranked. The same process applies to documents at any other ranking positions. Instead of calculating scores based on one ranking position, SlideFuse defines a sliding window that includes the position itself and also some neighbouring positions, thus the scores generated from overlapping windows are smoother. We can expect it to achieve better results when the training data set only includes a small group of queries. For both PosFuse and SlideFuse, we may also use Eq. 1 to perform the fusion, with all weights w_i set to 1 and $s_i(d)$ decided by the ranking position of d.

The models used by both PosFuse and SlideFuse are more complex than the models used by the other three, because many parameter needs to be determined and one for each ranking position. P@10Fuse, P@10Fuse2, and MAPFuse are simpler as they require only one parameter, which is the average P@10 or MAP value of all training queries. Their models are much simpler. Usually, more complicated models require more training data to avoid overfitting, while simpler learning models can still be stable even with a small training data set [11].

3   Experiments

In this section we present experimental results to demonstrate the validity of the proposed methods. First we present the experimental setting, which is followed by the experimental results. Some discussion and analysis about the proposed methods and some baseline methods are also given.

3.1   Data Sets Used

In this study, we used four data sets in TREC: the precision medicine track in 2017 [14] and 2018 [13], the deep learning track in 2019 [17], and the health misinformation track in 2020 [3]. In each track, a participant was allowed to submit multiple runs. Because the multiple runs by the same participant usually were generated by the same retrieval system with some difference in optional components, parameter settings, query formats, and so on, it was very likely that those runs submitted by the same participant were more similar than those by different participants. In each data set, we choose six runs for the experiments. In order to consider both performance and diversity at the same time, we try to choose those best performers (in MAP), but with the restriction that only one was chosen from each participant. See Table 1 for the information of four sets of component results (runs).

Table 1. Lists of runs used in experiments (selected by their MAP values)

Track	Run	MAP	Track	Run	MAP
2017 precision medicine	UTDHLTFF	**0.2327**	2018 precision medicine	hpipubboost	**0.3296**
	mugpubbase	0.2050		SIBTMlit4	0.3219
	SIBTMlit4	0.2028		UCASSA2	0.3195
	UDInfoPMSA2	0.1948		imi_mug_abs2	0.3177
	UD_GU_SA_5	0.1932		MedIER_sa13	0.3173
	mRun1Bsl	0.1782		UDInfoPMSA1	0.2831
2019 deep learning	bm25_marcomb	**0.4285**	2020 health misinformation	bm25_marcomb	**0.3832**
	bm25base_rm3	0.3870		bm25base_rm3	0.3640
	idst_bert_v2	0.3852		idst_bert_v2	0.3033
	srchvrs_run1	0.3491		srchvrs_run1	0.2980
	uogTrDNN6LM	0.3156		uogTrDNN6LM	0.1923
	baseline	0.2890		baseline	0.1712

3.2   Experimental Procedures and Results

In each track, top 2, 3, 4, 5, and all 6 result lists in Table 1 are chosen for fusion. Apart from P@10Fuse and P@10Fuse2, PosFuse, SlideFuse, MAPFuse, and Reciprocal Rank Fusion are also involved as baselines for comparison. Two-fold cross-validation was used for all the methods involved. That is to say, 50 queries were divided into odd- and even-numbered queries so that one group was used for training and the other group for testing. Four measures, including MAP, P@10, P@20, and RP, are used for performance evaluation. The average performance of all 50 queries with 2–6 component results is reported in Tables 2, 3, 4 and 5.

From Tables 2, 3, 4 and 5, we can see that all the data fusion methods are quite close in performance. No method is the best in all the cases. However, P@10Fuse2 looks a leading method because it is the best in 7.5 out of 16 cases (4 metrics and 4 data sets). Here .5 means that in one case both P@10Fuse2 and

Table 2. Average performance of all five methods fusing 2–6 runs in the 2017 Precision Medicine Track (% indicates the improvement rate of it over the Reciprocal Rank Fusion).

Method	MAP(%)	P@10(%)	P@20(%)	RP(%)
RRF	0.2737	0.5707	0.4817	0.2625
PosFuse	0.2770(1.21)	0.6513(14.12)	0.5807(20.55)	0.3413(30.02)
SlideFuse	0.2783(1.68)	0.6533(14.45)	**0.5823**(20.88)	0.3615(37.71)
MapFuse	0.3030(10.71)	0.6500(13.90)	0.5687(18.06)	0.3604(37.30)
P@10Fuse	0.3052(11.51)	0.6593(15.52)	0.5750(19.37)	**0.3644**(38.82)
P@10Fuse2	**0.3055**(11.62)	**0.6647**(16.47)	0.5783(20.05)	**0.3644**(38.82)

Table 3. Average performance of all five methods fusing 2–6 runs in the 2018 Precision Medicine Track (% indicates the improvement rate of it over the Reciprocal Rank Fusion).

Method	MAP(%)	P@10(%)	P@20(%)	RP(%)
RRF	0.3615	**0.7012**	0.6354	0.3952
PosFuse	0.3851(6.53)	0.6752(−3.71)	0.6344(-0.16)	0.4136(4.66)
SlideFuse	0.3954(9.38)	0.6752(−3.71)	0.6334(−0.31)	0.4215(6.65)
MapFuse	0.3988(10.32)	0.6792(−3.14)	0.6378(0.38)	0.4248(7.49)
P@10Fuse	0.4033(11.56)	0.6852(−2.28)	0.6428(1.16)	**0.4254**(7.64)
P@10Fuse2	**0.4099**(13.39)	0.6876(−1.94)	**0.6472(1.86)**	0.4253(7.62)

Table 4. Average performance of all five methods fusing 2–6 runs in the 2019 Machine Learning Track (% indicates the improvement rate of it over the Reciprocal Rank Fusion).

Method	MAP(%)	P@10(%)	P@20(%)	RP(%)
RRF	0.4433	0.7344	0.6558	**0.4501**
PosFuse	0.4390(−0.97)	0.7460(1.58)	0.6614(0.85)	0.4390(-2.47)
SlideFuse	**0.4480**(1.06)	**0.7533**(2.57)	0.6642(1.28)	0.4480(−0.47)
MapFuse	0.4432(0.00)	0.7369(0.34)	0.6603(0.69)	0.4489(−0.27)
P@10Fuse	0.4427(−0.14)	0.7395(0.69)	0.6640(1.25)	0.4478(−0.51)
P@10Fuse2	0.4440(0.16)	0.7455(1.51)	**0.6664**(1.62)	0.4490(−0.24)

Table 5. Average performance of all five methods fusing 2–6 runs in the 2020 Health Misinformation Track (% indicates the improvement rate of it over the Reciprocal Rank Fusion).

Method	MAP(%)	P@10(%)	P@20(%)	RP(%)
RRF	0.4239	0.7273	0.6980	0.4477
PosFuse	0.4289(1.18)	0.7504(3.18)	0.7070(1.29)	0.4523(1.03)
SlideFuse	0.4378(3.28)	**0.7557**(3.90)	**0.7148**(2.41)	0.4588(2.48)
MapFuse	0.4293(1.27)	0.7170(−1.42)	0.6978(−0.03)	0.4556(1.76)
P@10Fuse	0.4303(1.51)	0.7209(−0.88)	0.6987(0.10)	0.4575(2.19)
P@10Fuse2	**0.4387**(3.49)	0.7317(0.60)	0.7107(1.82)	**0.4666**(4.22)

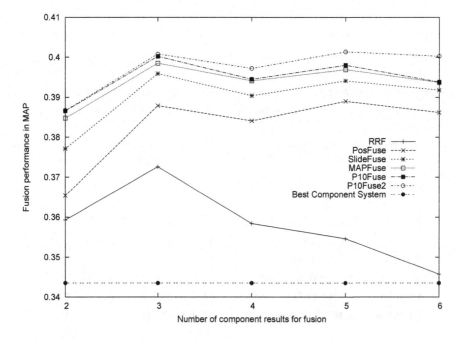

Fig. 1. Comparison of six data fusion methods

another method (which is P@10Fuse) are equally effective and they are better than all the others. SlideFuse, RRF, and P@10Fuse are better than the others in 5, 2, and 1.5 out of 16 cases, respectively. PosFuse and MapFuse do not perform the best in any cases. To have a clear view of their performance from another angle, we consider their average performance grouped by different number of component results. Figure 1 shows their performance in MAP because it is a system-oriented metric.

From Fig. 1 we can see that P@10Fuse2 is the best, which is followed by P@10Fuse, MAPFuse, SlideFuse, and PosFuse, while RRF is the worst. All of them are better than the best component result by a clear margin. It is not surprising that RRF is not as good as the other fusion methods because it is a type I method that treats all component results equally. However, it is a little surprising to see that SlideFuse is not as good as P@10Fuse and MAPFuse. It seems inconsistent with our observations from Tables 2, 3, 4 and 5, which show the results of the four data sets separately. After a close look, we find that in the 2017 Precision Medicine Track, SlideFuse performs much worse than both P@10Fuse and MAPFuse. While in other data sets, the differences are much smaller among them. Thus the average performance of SlideFuse is affected significantly by the results in this data set.

4 Analysis

In information retrieval, many metrics have been used for result evaluation. Among others, Mean Average Precision (MAP), Recall-level Precision (RP), NDCG (Normalized Discounted Cumulative Gain), Precision at 10 document-level (P@10) are some commonly used. Therefore, for performance weighting used in data fusion, there are many choices and it is not always straightforward to decide which metric we should go with.

In some previous studies on performance weighting scheme for data fusion [8,20], MAP is the only metric used for such a purpose. This is mainly because MAP is regarded as a system-oriented metric. Its stability is mainly due to the fact that all relevant documents need to be identified for calculating its value. On the other hand, other metrics have not been investigated. We argue that precision for some top-ranked documents such as P@10 is also a very useful metric. In some situations, it is more favourable than some other metrics such as MAP. For example, in the web environment, it is very often that the users try to find some useful information by browsing through a few top-ranked pages. Related to the data fusion approach, we need to consider two questions:

– Different metrics (such as MAP or P@10) may be used for result evaluation. How does data fusion achieve metric-specific performance improvement?
– Different metrics (such as MAP or P@10) may be used for performance-weighting. Which metric should we use for it?

For Question 2, we have partially answer it by introducing P@10Fuse and P@10Fuse2. It shows both of them can achieve very competitive performance. For Question 1, to our knowledge, no research has been conducted to address it. In this section we try to do some more investigation regarding these two questions. Especially we try to explain why P@10 is a suitable weighting scheme and which factor (MAP values or P@10 values) can better represent component retrieval systems' performance for fusion. We do this through regression analysis.

In Sect. 3, five groups of results were fused in each data set. Now we reconsider the same groups as in Sect. 3. First we define five variables: C-P@10, which is the average P@10 value of all component results; SC-P@10, which is the standard deviation of the P@10 values of all component results; Log(N), which is the logarithm of the number of component results involved for fusion; F-P10, which is the P@10 value of the fused result; and F-MAP, which is the MAP value of the fused result. Then for all those groups in a data set, we list the values of those variables per query. Regression analysis is used to find out the impact of those independent variables on the dependent variable. Either fusion performance in P@10 or MAP is used as the target (dependent) variable, and two groups of variables are used as independent variables for regression analysis. Apart from component result performance either in MAP or P@10, SC-MAP (standard deviation of MAP values), SC-P@10 (standard deviation of

Table 6. Analysis of fusion performance (RRF, 2017)

Dependent variable	Independent variables			R^2
F-P@10	C-P@10	SC-P@10	Log(N)	0.831
F-P@10	C-MAP	SC-MAP	Log(N)	0.350
F-MAP	C-P@10	SC-P@10	Log(N)	0.536
F-MAP	C-MAP	SC-MAP	Log(N)	0.910

Table 7. Analysis of fusion performance (RRF, 2018)

Dependent variable	Independent variables			R^2
F-P@10	C-P@10	SC-P@10	Log(N)	0.860
F-P@10	C-MAP	SC-MAP	Log(N)	0.507
F-MAP	C-P@10	SC-P@10	Log(N)	0.590
F-MAP	C-MAP	SC-MAP	Log(N)	0.953

Table 8. Analysis of fusion performance (RRF, 2019)

Dependent variable	Independent variables			R^2
F-P@10	C-P@10	SC-P@10	Log(N)	0.834
F-P@10	C-MAP	SC-MAP	Log(N)	0.176
F-MAP	C-P@10	SC-P@10	Log(N)	0.374
F-MAP	C-MAP	SC-MAP	Log(N)	0.976

Table 9. Analysis of fusion performance (RRF, 2020)

Dependent variable	Independent variables			R^2
F-P@10	C-P@10	SC-P@10	Log(N)	0.801
F-P@10	C-MAP	SC-MAP	Log(N)	0.521
F-MAP	C-P@10	SC-P@10	Log(N)	0.655
F-MAP	C-MAP	SC-MAP	Log(N)	0.923

P@10 values), and Log(N) (logarithm of the number of component results for fusion) are also used. All those variables affect fusion performance. However, our purpose here is not just to see how accurate the regression estimation can be, but also compare how those different variables impact fusion performance. RRF is the fusion method used here. Because it is neutral to any of the metrics, while MAPFuse and P@10Fuse do not. Tables 6, 7, 8 and 9 shows the results.

In each table, we report the results of four different cases. Note that Log(N) appear in all the cases. It just make the regression more accurate, but does not affect comparison. Using Log(N), rather than N, simply because it can achieve more accurate estimation. R^2 measures how well we can predict the performance knowing only the three independent variables in the model. For example, if the value of R^2 is 0.85, it means that the three variables explain 85% of the variation in the performance of the data fusion method. Not very surprising, using C-MAP, SC-MAP, and Log(N) as independent variables and F-MAP as dependent variable can achieve the most accurate prediction. We observe a R^2 of over 0.9 in all four data sets. On the other hand, using C-P@10, SC-P@10, and LOG(N) as independent variables and F-P@10 as dependent variable can still obtain quite accurate prediction. We observe a R^2 of between 0.8 and 0.9 in all four data sets. It shows that P@10 is very good, but MAP can do better than P@10.

Next let us look at two other cases. Using C-P@10, SC-P@10, and Log(N) to predict F-MAP and using C-MAP, SC-MAP, and Log(N) to predict F-P@10. We find that the prediction is more accurate for the former than the latter case. This is somewhat surprising. It suggests that C-P@10 and SC-P@10 can be more informative than C-MAP and SC-MAP for predicting fusion performance in certain situations. More specifically, to predict fusion performance in P@10, C-MAP and SC-MAP are not very useful. One explanation is that P@10 only concerns those top-ranked documents, higher C-MAP values do not necessarily lead to higher F-P@10 values. On the other hand, higher C-P@10 values can often lead to higher F-MAP values. One straightforward explanation is: for data fusion and result evaluation, top-ranked documents are more important than the others. Therefore, from our above analysis, we can see why C-P@10 and SC-P@10 can be very informative in some situations, and P@10Fuse and P@10Fuse2 can be good fusion methods. Not just because they can be implemented more efficiently than MAPFuse, also they are able to achieve very competitive performance.

5 Conclusion

In this paper, we have presented new type II data fusion methods P@10Fuse and P@10Fuse2. Our experiments with four TREC data sets show that the proposed methods are slightly better than three other fusion methods in the same category. Some regression analysis is also carried out to find why P@10Fuse and P@10Fuse2 are reasonable and good methods. Moreover, the proposed methods require much less human relevance judgment effort than the other baseline methods for determining their weights, so they have higher applicability.

As our future work, we would investigate data fusion methods and related settings that can improve performance especially for top-ranked documents. Metrics such as P@10 are good candidates for this.

References

1. Aslam, J.A., Montague, M.: Models for metasearch. In: Proceedings of ACM SIGIR, pp. 276–284 (2001)
2. Budíková, P., Batko, M., Zezula, P.: Fusion strategies for large-scale multi-modal image retrieval. Trans. Large Scale Data Knowl. Centered Syst. **33**, 146–184 (2017)
3. Clarke, C.L.A., Rizvi, S., Smucker, M.D., Maistro, M., Zuccon, G.: Overview of the TREC 2020 health misinformation track. In: Proceedings of TREC. National Institute of Standards and Technology (2020)
4. Cormack, G.V., Clarke, C.L.A., Buettcher, S.: Reciprocal rank fusion outperforms Condorcet and individual rank learning methods. In: Proceedings of ACM SIGIR, pp. 758–759 (2009)
5. Fox, E.A., Koushik, M.P., Shaw, J., Modlin, R., Rao, D.: Combining evidence from multiple searches. In: The First Text REtrieval Conference (TREC-1), pp. 319–328 (1993)
6. Ghosh, K., Parui, S.K., Majumder, P.: Learning combination weights in data fusion using genetic algorithms. Inf. Process. Manage. **51**(3), 306–328 (2015)
7. Kato, S., Shimizu, T., Fujita, S., Sakai, T.: Unsupervised answer retrieval with data fusion for community question answering. In: Wang, F.L., et al. (eds.) AIRS 2019. LNCS, vol. 12004, pp. 10–21. Springer, Cham (2020). https://doi.org/10.1007/978-3-030-42835-8_2
8. Lillis, D., Zhang, L., Toolan, F., Collier, R., Leonard, D., Dunnion, J.: Estimating probabilities for effective data fusion. In: Proceeding of ACM SIGIR, pp. 347–354 (2010)
9. Lillis, D.: On the evaluation of data fusion for information retrieval. In: FIRE 2020: Forum for Information Retrieval Evaluation, pp. 54–57 (2020)
10. Lillis, D., Toolan, F., Collier, R., Dunnion, J.: Extending probabilistic data fusion using sliding windows. In: Macdonald, C., Ounis, I., Plachouras, V., Ruthven, I., White, R.W. (eds.) ECIR 2008. LNCS, vol. 4956, pp. 358–369. Springer, Heidelberg (2008). https://doi.org/10.1007/978-3-540-78646-7_33
11. Mohri, M., Rostamizadeh, A., Talwalkar, A.: Foundations of machine learning. In: Adaptive Computation and Machine Learning, MIT Press, Cambridge (2012)
12. Montague, M., Aslam, J.A.: Condorcet fusion for improved retrieval. In: Proceedings of ACM CIKM, pp. 538–548 (2002)
13. Roberts, K., Demner-Fushman, D., Voorhees, E.M., Hersh, W.R., Bedrick, S., Lazar, A.J.: Overview of the TREC 2018 precision medicine track. In Proceedings of TREC. National Institute of Standards and Technology, USA (2018)
14. Roberts, K., et al.: Overview of the TREC 2017 precision medicine track. In: Proceedings of TREC 2017. National Institute of Standards and Technology (2017)
15. Sanderson, M., Zobel, J.: Information retrieval system evaluation: effort, sensitivity, and reliability. In: SIGIR 2005: Proceedings of ACM SIGIR, pp. 162–169. ACM (2005)
16. Sivaram, M., Batri, K., Mohammed, A.S., Porkodi, V., Kousik, N.V.: Data fusion using Tabu crossover genetic algorithm in information retrieval. J. Intell. Fuzzy Syst. **39**(4), 5407–5416 (2020)

17. Voorhees, E.M., Ellis, A. (eds.): Proceedings of TREC 2019. National Institute of Standards and Technology (2019)
18. Wu, S.: Linear combination of component results in information retrieval. Data Knowl. Eng. **71**(1), 114–126 (2012)
19. Wu, S.: The weighted Condorcet fusion in information retrieval. Inf. Proc. Manage. **49**(1), 114–126 (2013)
20. Wu, S., Bi, Y., Zeng, X., Han, L.: Assigning appropriate weights for the linear combination data fusion method in information retrieval. Inf. Proc. Manage. **45**(4), 413–426 (2009)
21. Wu, S., McClean, S.: Data fusion with correlation weights. In: Proceedings of ECIR, pp. 275–286 (2005)
22. Xu, C., Huang, C., Wu, S.: Differential evolution-based fusion for results diversification of web search. In: Cui, B., Zhang, N., Xu, J., Lian, X., Liu, D. (eds.) WAIM 2016, Part I. LNCS, vol. 9658, pp. 429–440. Springer, Cham (2016). https://doi.org/10.1007/978-3-319-39937-9_33

GPU Accelerated Parallel Implementation of Linear Programming Algorithms

Ratul Kishore Saha[1]($\boxtimes$), Ashutosh Pradhan[1], Tiash Ghosh[1],
Mamata Jenamani[1], Sanjai Kumar Singh[2], and Aurobinda Routray[1]

[1] Indian Instute of Technology, Kharagpur, India
ratulkishoresaha97@gmail.com
[2] Geodata Processing and Interpretation Centre, Uttarakhand, India

Abstract. Linear Programs are computationally expensive for large constraint matrices. Existing linear programming solvers use serial mode processing using Central Processing Unit (CPU) computation that leads to long execution runtime in real-time. This paper presents, parallel implementation of the Simplex and Interior Point Method using General Purpose Graphical Processing Unit (GPGPU) empowered with a novel Compute Unified Device Architecture (CUDA) for solving multiple LP problems simultaneously. The methods are accomplished by using the concept of parallel kernel map of the algorithms through multiple CUDA threads. The algorithms are implemented in NVIDIA A40 GPU model. The runtime of the algorithms is compared with the standard *Scipy linprog* solvers for the above methods. We also demonstrated the superior performance of the implemented algorithms by varying the size of the linear programming problem.

Keywords: Linear programming · Simplex method · Interior point method · GPGPU · CUDA

1 Introduction

Convex optimization refers to a broad area of optimization problems like Linear programming (LP), least squares (LS), Quadratic programming (QP) and many more [1]. LP is a special kind of optimization problem which has a linear objective function with linear constraints equations. The most exciting application of LP can be in the field of signal processing. Designing finite impulse response (FIR) filter coefficients, compressed sensing, and sparse reconstruction of seismic signals are a few of its remarkable applications. However, the size of the constraint matrix and the number of LPs may vary depending on the application. For example, a three-dimensional seismic volume contains a large number of seismic traces. In [9], the author used LP to invert seismic signal to find reflectivity coefficients which produce promising results over existing algorithms. The major drawback

Supported by organization GEOPIC, ONGC, India.

of [9] is that the size of the LP highly depends on seismic trace length and considered time thickness of the layers. The constrain matrix size is increased with increasing the trace length. Hence, to invert all the seismic traces from a seismic dataset using LP takes unacceptable execution time for real time application. Thus in these types of applications, the optimization must be fast enough to minimize the execution time in real-time and requires massive parallelization of LPs. Moreover, in real-time applications solving a large number of LPs is challenging in CPUs. Researchers developed serial, batched multiprocessing-based LP solvers through multiple CPU cores. But, this implementation is not efficient with few CPU cores machines. Besides, the existing LP solvers like CVXPY, GLPK, and linprog are implemented for CPU architecture. Hence, the increasing size of real LP problems requires more efficient computational mechanisms and parallel computing. In the last few decades, high-performance computing (HPC) is an emerging area of research for large computation in various domains of significant research like image processing, computer vision, machine learning, etc. Recently, the HPC is deployed with the help of GPGPUs having several lightweight streaming multiprocessors. The massive parallel computing is accomplished through the CUDA developed by NVIDIA. Moreover, it is convenient to use matrix computation through several GPGPU threads. Researchers reported that computation time was significantly reduced through parallelization of the algorithm using several streaming multiprocessors available in GPGPU as compared to the CPU programming. The major contributions of this paper are as follows:

1. GPU-based simplex and interior-point method for dense constraint matrix.
2. Implementation of the above algorithms for solving multiple LPs simultaneously in real-time.

The organization of the paper is as follows. The next section describes the related work followed by the proposed methodology and illustrates the efficiency of the proposed GPU implementation of the algorithms. The final section concludes the work by indicating some directions for future work.

2   Related Works

Since the inception of the LP problem, authors in [2] proposed an iterative tabular-based method to solve two equations in every iteration. This simplex algorithm was further improved in [3]. Another gradient-based approach to solve the LP problem is the interior point method (IPM) as described in [4]. With the development of the computational power of CPUs and GPUs, researchers developed several homogeneous (CPU-CPU) and heterogeneous (CPU-GPU) architectures for solving LP. A CPU-GPU-based LP method using IPM is proposed in [5]. Lalami et al. proposed a heterogeneous architecture for parallel implementation [6] of the simplex algorithm. In [6], author implemented heterogeneous simplex method which leads to execution latency due to multiple data transfers between CPU and GPU memory. Shah et al. [7] proposed GPU-based basis update methodology for simplex algorithm. A GPU-based IPM for model predictive control is illustrated in [8].

Note that, in all the above mentioned methods, the GPU-based techniques are applied to a single LP problem. To the best of our knowledge, no parallel implementation for solving multiple LP problems is reported to perform better than sequential solvers. In this paper, we propose an efficient parallel implementation of Simplex and IPM for solving several LPs using GPU.

3   Linear Programming

Linear programming problems refer to the class of convex optimization problems having a linear objective function subject to a set of linear constraints with either inequality or equality constraints. For inequality conditions, the LP problem can be brought into simple equality constraints by scaling the objective function and adding appropriate slack and surplus variables. After the addition of slack and surplus variables the LP problem in its standard equality form can be given as:

$$
\begin{array}{cc}
Primal: & Dual: \\
\underset{x}{min} \; \phi_p = c^T x & \underset{y,\,s}{max} \; \phi_D = b^T y \\
s.t. Ax = b, \forall x_i \geq 0 & s.t. A^T y + s = b, \forall s_i \geq 0
\end{array} \tag{1}
$$

where $A = (A'|I_m) \in R^{m \times (n+m)}$ and $A' = [a'_{ij}]$ is the inequality constraint matrix, where, $a'_{ij}, i = 1, 2, ..., m, j = i, 2, ..., n$ denotes the coefficient of the jth variable in the ith constraint equation. Also note that, $b = (b_1, b_2, .., b_m)^T \in R^m$ and $c = (c_1, c_2, .., c_n, .., 0) \in R^{(n+m)}$. The primal solution is given by $x = (x_1, x_2, .., x_n, x_{n+1} .., x_{n+m}) \in R^{(n+m)}$. Here, $x_k, k = n+1, ..., n+m$ are the basis variables while $x_k, k = 1, ..., n$ represents the non-basis variables.

We consider to solve multiple LPs with the different constraint matrices A, cost vector c, and target vector b. We implement two widely used methods viz. Simplex [2] and IPM [4].

4   Solving Multiple Linear Programs on GPU

We aim to solve a large number of LP problems parallelly through GPU. Let us assume that we intend to solve N number of LPs parallelly. We stack multiple b, A and c in a matrix form. Now, the dimension of b becomes $N \times m$ and A becomes $N \times m \times n$ and c becomes $N \times n$. Also, the number of LPs depends on the available GPU memory. We form the three dimensional simplex tableau, $T \in R^{N \times (m+1) \times (n+1)}$ by combing A, b, c matrices. In CUDA architecture the threads are divided in blocks, grid etc. The grid, blocks may vary upto three dimensional. Next, we transfer the tableau from CPU to GPU memory. We kept suitable threads per block and form one dimensional CUDA grid kernel where each kernel solves one LP using the simplex method individually. Let us consider that each one dimensional block contains 256 threads, so the number of number of blocks per grid in LP formation would be $N/256$. Thus in CUDA, each thread index can be found out as $threadindex = threadIdx.x + blockIdx.x * blockDim.x$.

Hence, each thread index is assigned for each simplex tableau and execute multiple LPs in parallel. Another aspect of parallel computation in GPU is memory management. Latest GPU hardware like TitanX, GeForce series comes with maximum 8GB/12GB /24 GB dedicated GPU memory. Therefore, the number of LPs(N) should be such that the whole 3D tableau ($T \in R^{N \times (m+1) \times (n+1)}$) can be stored in device GPU memory for execution. Again, more frequent data transfer from CPU ram to GPU ram may hamper the overall performance of computation. Thus, N should be such that minimal data transfer is performed to complete the whole computation. So, N majorly depends on the GPU model used for the experimental purpose.

We adopt a slightly different approach for IPM implementation, we launch the 2-D grid kernel with each block mapped to an LP. Each block's particular LP is subjected to additional thread-level parallelization. In contrast to the simplex implementation, we use a heterogeneous computing architecture in IPM, where kernels are started sequentially for each iteration's logical step. The vector operations are subjected to thread-level parallelism in each iteration step when we need to process two vectors. To do this, we start a kernel with several LPs assigned to a block. However, we introduced parallel threading procedures such as batched matrix-vector multiplication and batched matrix-matrix multiplication for stages containing these operations. Solving the linear system is one of the main computational challenges in the IPM. A major computation hurdle in the IPM [4] is to solve large system of equation. we use the batched Cholesky solve routine to compute the solution of the linear system. The detailed block diagram of the proposed methodology is illustrated in Fig. 1.

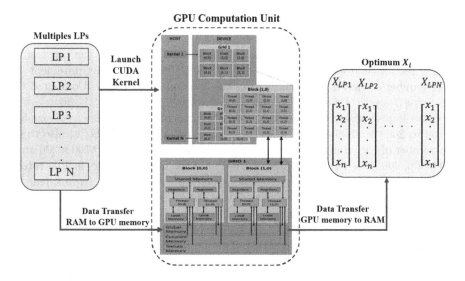

Fig. 1. Block diagram of proposed methodology

5   Experimental Analysis

For executing the proposed CUDA-enabled LP algorithms, we used a machine with 24 physical CPU cores of INTEL Xeon Gold 6252 processor and 64 Gigabytes(GB) RAM along with NVIDIA A40 model with 48 GB dedicated GPU device memory. Here, we evaluate our GPU-based Simplex and IPM for 1000 LPs with different constraint matrices A, cost vectors c and constraint vectors b generated randomly. Note that, all the LP problems satisfied initially feasibility condition. Next, All the 1000 LPs are loaded to the GPU to be solved simultaneously. During the GPU execution, we kept the threads per block as 256. The number of blocks spawned as $1000/256 \approx 4$. Next, we evaluate 1000 LP problems serially using *Scipy* solvers and present a run-time comparison with our GPU implementation in Table 1.

Table 1. Runtime comparison of GPU based Simplex and IPM algorithms with *Scipy Simplex* and *interior − point* solvers respectively.

No of LPs	LP size	Execution time (Seconds)					
		Simplex scipy	Simplex GPU	Speedup	Scipy IPM	GPU IPM	Speedup
1000	50 × 100	41.09	1.16	**38x**	7.38	1.41	**5.23**
	100 × 200	120.30	1.18	**101x**	15.63	3.52	**4.44x**
	200 × 400	389.37	1.23	**316x**	29.89	7.10	**4.21x**
	500 × 1000	2207.38	9.58	**230x**	189.37	47.26	**4.00x**
	1000 × 2000	9628.25	121.28	**79x**	1170.50	217.42	**5.39x**
	2000 × 4000	29120.54	578.82	**50x**	7452.68	1334.61	**5.58x**

It is observed that, for the LP size of 200 × 400, we achieved maximum speed up of **316x** compared with *Scipy Simplex*. Where as, for the constraint matrix 2000 × 4000 we achieved speed up of **50x**. This is due to requirement of more number of iteration for finding out the optimum x_{opt} vector. Compared to the *Scipy Interior Point* solver, our GPU implementation of IPM shows a **5x** (approx) improvement in speed for 1000 LPs with constraint matrices of size 50 × 100 to 2000 × 4000 as shown in Table 1. For extensive analysis, we also vary the number of LPs from 1 to 10^4 for the constrain matrix 50 × 100, 100 × 200 and 200 × 400. The speed-up plot with a variation of the number of LPs is illustrated in Fig. 2. When we vary the batch size, speed up compared to *Scipy* solver is observed for batch sizes greater than 50 as shown in Fig. 2(a). This is due to the overheads of launching kernels and memory transfer to and fro between CPU and GPU. From Fig. 2(b), it is observed that the speed up is much more as compared to the GPU based IPM. This is due to complex computation of IPM through GPU. Hence, it can be concluded that for simultaneous solving of LPs the proposed simplex implementation is recommended over interior point method.

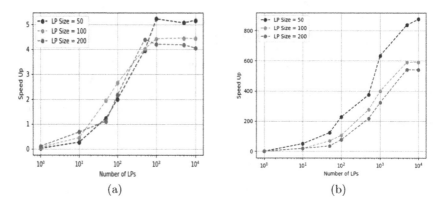

Fig. 2. Speed up vs Number of LPs for (a) Interior points method, (b) Simplex method

6   Conclusion

In this paper, It has been widely researched how to solve a linear programming problem for increased performance on a GPU architecture. To the best of our knowledge, all such studies only note a performance improvement for large-scale linear algorithms. We offer a CUDA-implemented solver that can speed up applications that must solve several small to latge-sized LPs. Our solver uses the simplex and interior point technique to solve the LPs in an application in batches in parallel on a GPU. The results show a significant speedup for both the algorithms compared to the Scipy Linprog library. We also demonstrated the superiority of the proposed implementation with the variation of number of LPs in real-time scenario.

References

1. Mattingley, J., Boyd, S.: Real-time convex optimization in signal processing. IEEE Sig. Process. Mag. **27**(3), 50–61 (2010)
2. Evans, J.P., Steuer, R.E.: A revised simplex method for linear multiple objective programs. Math. Program. **5**(1), 54–72 (1973)
3. Dantzig, G.: Linear Programming and Extensions. Princeton University Press, Princeton (2016)
4. Lustig, I.J., Marsten, R.E., Shanno, D.F.: Computational experience with a primal-dual interior point method for linear programming. Linear Algebra Appl. **152**, 191–222 (1991)
5. Jung, J.H., O'Leary, D.P.: Implementing an interior point method for linear programs on a CPU-GPU system. Electron. Trans. Numer. Anal. **28**(174–189), 37 (2008)
6. Lalami, M.E., Boyer, V., El-Baz, D.: Efficient implementation of the simplex method on a CPU-GPU system. In 2011 IEEE International Symposium on Parallel and Distributed Processing Workshops and PHD Forum, pp. 1999–2006. IEEE, May 2011

7. Shah, U.A., Yousaf, S., Ahmad, I., Rehman, S.U., Ahmad, M.O.: Accelerating revised simplex method using GPU-based basis update. IEEE Access **8**, 52121–52138 (2020)
8. Gade-Nielsen, N.F., Jørgensen, J.B., Dammann, B.: MPC toolbox with GPU accelerated optimization algorithms. In 10th European Workshop on Advanced Control and Diagnosis. Technical University of Denmark, November 2012
9. Palo, P., et al.: Sparse layer inversion using linear programming approach. In: IGARSS 2019–2019 IEEE International Geoscience and Remote Sensing Symposium, IEEE (2019)

Towards Explaining DL Non-entailments by Utilizing Subtree Isomorphisms

Ivan Gocev[(✉)] [iD], Georgios Meditskos [iD], and Nick Bassiliades [iD]

School of Informatics, Aristotle University of Thessaloniki, 54124 Thessaloniki, Greece
{ivangochev,gmeditsk,nbassili}@csd.auth.gr

Abstract. We present our current state of research on explaining non-entailments by finding isomorphic subtrees of $\mathcal{EL}$-description trees. Our approach extends the set of abducible axioms that consist only of concepts to role restrictions as well. We argue how our approach could find solutions to abduction problems in scenarios where other methods cannot, and illustrate this via an example comparing our approach to existing ones.

Keywords: Ontologies · Explanations · Abduction · Non-entailments

1 Introduction

There has been a significant amount of research done on explanations and ontology debugging in the world of OWL and Description Logics (DLs) [1,2]. In particular, research has been focused on methods for explaining entailments (inferences) wrt. some background knowledge. One specific type of explanations are so-called justifications, which represent a minimal subset of an ontology that is sufficient enough for an entailment to hold [3]. Similarly, proofs have also been utilized for explaining DL entailments [4].

However, such methods fall short when explaining non-entailments, i.e. axioms that do not logically follow from a knowledge base. Some classical approaches are based on providing counter examples [5], or using abduction [10]. Recently, this topic has received more attention as seen in [6], where explanations in TBox abduction are formulated by mimicking justifications in ontologies, and [7] in which homomorphisms are used to solve abduction problems. Nonetheless, the problem of explaining non-entailments is infrequently investigated and there is still much to be done.

Explaining non-entailments could aid users when updating a terminology where some new changes can be found not to be entailed by the original knowledge base. For e.g., in medicine, explanations of non-entailments could be used to derive new relationships among drugs or symptoms of diseases. We propose that a combination of DLs and graph isomorphisms could yield a standardized approach. To this end, we investigate using subtree isomorphisms to solve abduction problems in DLs. In this paper, we briefly review some relevant work and analyze limitations of existing approaches. Then, we propose how certain gaps could be filled and illustrate our approach with an example.

© The Author(s), under exclusive license to Springer Nature Switzerland AG 2022
E. Pardede et al. (Eds.): iiWAS 2022, LNCS 13635, pp. 385–390, 2022.
https://doi.org/10.1007/978-3-031-21047-1_32

2 Background and Motivation

Our focus is on the description logic $\mathcal{EL}$ based on two disjoint sets: N_C consisting of atomic concepts (or concept names) denoted by A_i, B_i, and N_R consisting of atomic roles (binary predicates or role names) denoted by r_i, s_i for $i \geq 0$. Complex $\mathcal{EL}$ concept descriptions C, D can be: the top concept ($\top$), atomic concepts ($A \in N_C$), conjunction ($C \sqcap D$), and role restriction ($\exists r.C$). A conjunction of atomic concepts is expressed as $\prod_{i=0}^{n} A_i$, for $n \geq 0$. Let $f(X) = \prod_{i=0}^{n} A_i \sqcap \exists r.(X)$, where X is an $\mathcal{EL}$ concept. Then, $f_0(f_1(f_2(\ldots f_d(X)))) = f_0 \circ f_1 \circ f_2 \circ \cdots \circ f_d(X)$ depicts nesting of role restrictions up to depth d, where $d \geq 0$. For $d = 0$ we have $f_0(X) = \prod_{i=0}^{n} A_i \sqcap \exists r_0.(X)$, for $d = 1$, $f_0(f_1(X)) = \prod_{i=0}^{n} A_i \sqcap \exists r_0.(\prod_{i=0}^{m} B_i \sqcap \exists r_1.(X))$, etc.

A TBox $\mathcal{T}$ represents terminological knowledge and is a finite set of general concept inclusions (GCIs) of the form $C \sqsubseteq D$ (we say "C is subsumed by D" with a meaning "C is included in D" or "D includes C"). We sometimes refer to concept inclusions (CIs) as axioms and denote them as $\alpha_1, \alpha_2, \ldots, \alpha_n$. An observation, η, is a specific GCI (or axiom) that we are interested in. We write $\mathcal{T} \models \eta$ if an observation is entailed by a Tbox $\mathcal{T}$, and $\mathcal{T} \not\models \eta$ if an observation is not entailed by a Tbox $\mathcal{T}$.

The abduction problem we are interested in is defined as following:

Definition 1. *Let $\mathcal{T}$ be an $\mathcal{EL}$ TBox, C_1 and C_2 concepts defined wrt. $\mathcal{T}$. An abduction problem is a tuple ($\mathcal{T}$, $C_2 \sqsubseteq C_1$), where $\mathcal{T}$ is called the background knowledge, $C_2 \sqsubseteq C_1$ the observation, and $\mathcal{T} \not\models C_2 \sqsubseteq C_1$. A solution to the abduction problem is a hypothesis $\mathcal{H}$ of the form:*

$$\mathcal{H} = \{\alpha | \alpha := (\prod_{i=0}^{n_1} A_i \sqsubseteq \prod_{i=0}^{n_2} B_i) \text{ or } (f_0 \circ f_1 \circ \cdots \circ f_{d_1}(X) \sqsubseteq g_0 \circ g_1 \circ \cdots \circ g_{d_2}(X))$$

$$\text{or } (\prod_{i=0}^{n_1} A_i \sqsubseteq f_0 \circ f_1 \circ \cdots \circ f_{d_1}(X)) \text{ or } (f_0 \circ f_1 \circ \cdots \circ f_{d_1}(X) \sqsubseteq \prod_{i=0}^{n_1} A_i)\},$$

and $\forall \alpha \in \mathcal{H}$, $\mathcal{T} \not\models \alpha$ and $\mathcal{T} \cup \mathcal{H} \models C_2 \sqsubseteq C_1$.

Consider some terminological knowledge $\mathcal{T}$, and an observation η s.t. $\mathcal{T} \not\models \eta$. A classical approach to explain this non-entailment is using *abduction* to generate a hypothesis $\mathcal{H}$, i.e. a "missing piece", such that when added to the terminological knowledge the observation becomes entailed. In the case that an observation should logically follow from a knowledge base, abduction allows us to find reasons why the observation is not entailed and fix the non-entailment. Dependent on the context of the observation, abduction could be used to explain why CIs are not entailed by some terminological knowledge (TBox abduction) [6], explain why assertions are not entailed by some assertive knowledge (ABox abduction) [8,9], or a combination of both (knowledge base abduction) [10,11]. Our focus is on the TBox, with the purpose of explaining concept inclusions.

A natural approach to abduction is to determine a set of possible abducibles [6,9,11], i.e. concepts or statements we could abduct. There exist common minimality criteria for constructing solutions to abduction problems, such as subset, size, and semantic minimality [8]. Still, these criteria do not necessarily provide useful information for why an observation is not entailed by a knowledge base. In particular, if we allow abduction of only certain CIs, for e.g. $A \sqsubseteq B$, and exclude CIs with role restrictions such as $A \sqsubseteq \exists r.B$, then a solution to the abduction problem may not be admissible. [6] highlights this challenge and tackles it by abducting all types of CIs found in predefined patters based on justifications. Graph morphisms are also promising in identifying relevant concepts and relations to abduct. [7] addresses this topic and explanations with low explanatory power have been successfully eliminated by utilizing graph homomorphisms. However, homomorphisms capture entailment through axioms such as $A \sqsubseteq B$ and do not explicitly include role restrictions in hypotheses. Our approach differs in that it also allows abduction of role restrictions relevant to the observation of interest, thus covering the cases in which a solution to the abduction problem is not admissible by homomorphisms.

To illustrate this, consider the following TBoxes:

$\mathcal{T}_1 = \{\exists \text{employment.ResearchPosition} \sqcap \exists \text{qualification.Diploma} \sqsubseteq \text{Researcher},$

$\qquad \exists \text{writes.ResearchPaper} \sqsubseteq \text{Researcher}, \text{Doctor} \sqsubseteq \exists \text{qualification.PhD},$

$\qquad \text{Professor} \equiv \text{Doctor} \sqcap \exists \text{employment.Chair},$

$\mathcal{T}_2 = \{\exists \text{employment.ResearchPosition} \sqcap \exists \text{qualification.Diploma}$

$\qquad \sqcap \exists \text{writes.ResearchPaper} \equiv \text{Researcher}, \text{Doctor} \sqsubseteq \exists \text{qualification.PhD},$

$\qquad \text{Professor} \equiv \text{Doctor} \sqcap \exists \text{employment.Chair},$

s.t. $\mathcal{T}_1$ is originally taken from [7] and $\mathcal{T}_2$ is a modified version to exemplify how various CIs can impact the solution of the abduction problem.

Consider first TBox $\mathcal{T}_1$. Here, we have an observation $\eta := \text{Professor} \sqsubseteq$ Researcher, s.t. $\mathcal{T}_1 \not\models \eta$ and $\mathcal{T}_2 \not\models \eta$. To remedy this, the following axioms need to be added to $\mathcal{T}_1$:

$$\mathcal{H}_1 = \{\text{Chair} \sqsubseteq \text{ResearchPosition}, \text{PhD} \sqsubseteq \text{Diploma}\} \tag{1}$$

The axioms in $\mathcal{H}_1$ are the "missing knowledge" for the observation η to become entailed. Such a hypothesis is an explanation for why an observation does not logically follow from a background knowledge, even though, in reality, it should.

$\mathcal{H}_1$ is produced by first representing the concepts in η as $\mathcal{EL}$-description trees (from now description trees or trees) denoted by T_1 and T_2 for Researcher and Professor respectively, which are merely a graphical representation of concept descriptions [12]. Next, a homomorphism $\varphi : T_1 \mapsto T_2$ is found. Since subsumption is characterized via homomorphisms between description trees, they are used to solve the abduction problem and effectively omit arbitrary hypotheses [7].

However, there are some cases in which homomorphisms cannot be used to find a solution to an abduction problem. Let us now consider TBox $\mathcal{T}_2$. A solution to the abduction problem now is the following:

$$\mathcal{H}_2 = \{\text{Chair} \sqsubseteq \text{ResearchPosition}, \text{PhD} \sqsubseteq \text{Diploma},$$
$$\text{Doctor} \sqsubseteq \exists \text{writes.ResearchPaper}\} \tag{2}$$

In the second case the description trees of the concepts in η are not homomorphic due to structural differences, and mapping cannot be performed. Thus, a solution to the abduction problem is not admissible. Structural differences are expressed as axioms in the form of $A \sqsubseteq \exists r.B$, and are a key part in formulating solutions to abduction problems in cases such as this one.

Our main contribution is an approach for abduction of axioms that consist of concepts and role restrictions as well. We argue how *subtree isomorphisms* can extended abduction to include concepts as well as role restrictions in hypotheses, thus confronting the challenges discussed above.

3   Methodology

Our methodology will be described using the example in the previous section. We generate solutions to abduction problems by identifying isomorphic subtrees of concepts represented as description trees originally described in [12].

Definition 2. *A description tree is of the form* $T = (V_T, E_T, v_0, l)$, *where* T *is a tree with root* v_0 *whose nodes* $v \in V_T$ *are labeled with* $l(v) \subseteq N_C$, *and (directed) edges* $vr\omega \in E_T$ *are labeled with role names* $r \in N_R$. *The empty label corresponds to the top concept.*

If we denote the tree with root $T(v_i)$, and the corresponding concept C_T, we have $C_T = C_{T(v_0)}$ and $C_{T(v)} = \bigsqcap_{v \in V} l(v) \sqcap \bigsqcap_{vr\omega \in E} \exists r.C_{T(\omega)}$.

The vertex labels originally contain only atomic concepts and we extend them in the induced subtrees to role restrictions as well. To include role restrictions, we start by obtaining induced subtrees of description trees and join vertex labels.

Definition 3. *Given a description tree of the form* $T = (V_T, E_T, v_0, l)$, *a subtree* $S = (V_S', E_S', v_0, l')$ *is an induced subtree of* T *iff* $V_S' \subseteq V_T$, $E_S' \subseteq E_T$, *and* $\forall v, u \in V_S'$ *if* $vru \in E_S'$ *then* $vru \in E_T$. *The nodes are labeled with* $l'(v) \subseteq N_C \cup \{\exists r.C\}$, *where* $r \in N_R$ *and* C *is an* $\mathcal{EL}$ *concept, and (directed) edges are labeled with role names* $r \in N_R$. *An induced subtree is a description tree itself.*

Induced subtrees are formed by removing vertices from the original tree and embedding them as $\mathcal{EL}$ concepts within their parents' labels. For any $v \in V_T - \{u\}$, if $vru \in E_T$, then $l'(v) = l(v) \cup \{\exists r.(\bigsqcap_{u \in V_T} l(u))\}$.

To construct hypotheses we map induced subtrees as following:

Definition 4. *An isomorphism from an induced subtree* $S_1 = (V_1', E_1', v_0, l_1')$ *to an induced subtree* $S_2 = (V_2', E_2', \omega_0, l_2')$ *is a bijective mapping* $\phi : V_1' \mapsto V_2'$ *such that* $\phi(v_0) = \omega_0$ *and:*

1. $vr\omega \in E_1' \Leftrightarrow \phi(v)r\phi(\omega) \in E_2'$
2. $\forall v \in V_1'$, *and* $\omega \in V_2'$ *s.t.* $\omega = \phi(v)$, $\mathcal{T} \models \bigsqcap_{\omega \in V_2'} l_2'(\omega) \sqsubseteq \bigsqcap_{v \in V_1'} l_1'(v)$

The first point in Definition 4 is a general notion of graph isomorphisms - preserving graph connectivity. On top of this notion, the semantics are added through mapping $\phi(v_0) = \omega_0$, and point 2 of Definition 4 capturing subsumption wrt. a TBox $\mathcal{T}$. If the labels of mapped vertices are not in a subsumption relation as in point 2, then we could potentially abduct that relation. We use this to formulate hypotheses.

Definition 5. *Let $\mathcal{T}$ be a Tbox, $S_1 = (V_1', E_1', v_0, l_1')$ and $S_2 = (V_2', E_2', v_0, l_2')$ induced subtrees of description trees T_1 and T_2 for $\mathcal{EL}$ concepts C_1 and C_2, respectively. Given an abduction problem $(\mathcal{T}, C_2 \sqsubseteq C_1)$ and isomorphism $\phi : V_1' \mapsto V_2'$, the hypothesis is defined as:*

$$\mathcal{H} = \{\textstyle\bigsqcap l_2'(\omega) \sqsubseteq \textstyle\bigsqcap l_1'(v) \mid \omega = \phi(v) \text{ for } v \in V_1'\} \tag{3}$$

The hypothesis in Definition 5 coheres to Definition 1 - the abducted subsumption relations $\bigsqcap l_2'(\omega) \sqsubseteq \bigsqcap l_1'(v)$ are in fact axioms of the forms defined in Definition 1. This is due to the fact they we map vertices of induced subtrees that contain concepts and role restrictions in their labels $l_1'(v)$ and $l_2'(\omega)$.

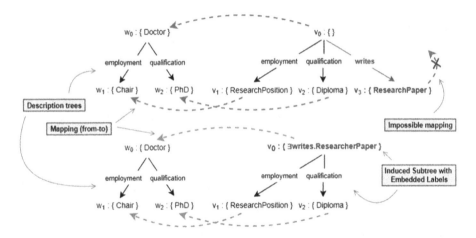

Fig. 1. Description trees of $\mathcal{EL}$ concepts from TBox $\mathcal{T}_2$ (upper part) and induced subtrees with updated labels (lower part). Dashed arcs are potential mappings.

Returning to the example, we discover from the corresponding description trees (T_1 and T_2, respectively) of concepts Researcher and Professor that are neither homomorphic nor isomorphic. This indicates that we cannot map every vertex from T_1 to T_2 wrt. Definition 4. The vertex v_3 from T_1 cannot be mapped to any vertex in T_2, because the structure will not be preserved - the type of role connecting v_0 to v_3 in T_1 does not connect any vertices in T_2 (Fig. 1 (upper part)). However, if we have a look at the induced subtrees of T_1 and T_2, we will discover that they are isomorphic and we can find a mapping $\phi(v_0) = \omega_0, \phi(v_1) = \omega_1, \phi(v_2) = \omega_2$ (Fig. 1 (lower part)). Thus, from Definition 5 we obtain the hypothesis from eq. 2 and $\mathcal{T}_2 \cup \mathcal{H}_2 \models$ Professor $\sqsubseteq$ Researcher.

4   Conclusion

We presented work in progress of an approach for generating solutions to abduction problems, by identifying isomorphic subtrees of graphical representations of $\mathcal{EL}$ concepts. We do this by first generating the description trees of $\mathcal{EL}$ concepts. Further, the induced subtrees are constructed and vertex labels are joined accordingly. Finally, the hypothesis is formulated by discovering isomorphisms between the induced subtrees.

Currently, we are investigating further the use of subtree isomorphisms to obtain solutions to abduction problems. Regarding complexity, in a more general sense the subtree isomorphism problem is NP-complete. On the other hand, in the restricted case of $\mathcal{EL}$-description trees testing for existence of homomorphisms can be done in polynomial time [12], which may indicate that the subtree isomorphism problem could also be solved in polynomial time. This investigation is part of our future steps.

References

1. Schlobach, S., Cornet, R.: Non-standard reasoning services for the debugging of description logic terminologies. IJCAI **3**, 355–362 (2003)
2. Kalyanpur, A.: Debugging and Repair of OWL Ontologies. University of Maryland, College Park (2006)
3. Kalyanpur, A., Parsia, B., Horridge, M., Sirin, E.: Finding all justifications of OWL DL entailments. In: Aberer, K., et al. (eds.) ASWC/ISWC -2007. LNCS, vol. 4825, pp. 267–280. Springer, Heidelberg (2007). https://doi.org/10.1007/978-3-540-76298-0_20
4. Alrabbaa, C., Baader, F., Borgwardt, S., Koopmann, P., Kovtunova, A.: Finding small proofs for description logic entailments: theory and practice (Extended Technical Report) (2020) arXiv preprint arXiv:2004.08311
5. Alrabbaa, C., Hieke, W., Turhan, A.Y.: Counter model transformation for explaining non-subsumption in EL. FCR@ KI pp. 9–22 (2021)
6. Du, J., Wan, H., Ma, H.: Practical TBox abduction based on justification patterns. In: AAAI, vol. 31(1), (2017)
7. Haifani, F., Koopmann, P., Tourret, S., Weidenbach, C.: Connection-Minimal Abduction in EL via Translation to FOL. Proc, IJCAR (2022)
8. Calvanese, D., Ortiz, M., Simkus, M., Stefanoni, G.: Reasoning about explanations for negative query answers in DL-Lite. JAIR **48**, 635–669 (2013)
9. Koopmann, P.: Signature-based abduction with fresh individuals and complex concepts for description logics. Description Logics (2021)
10. Elsenbroich, C., Kutz, O., Sattler, U.: A Case for Abductive Reasoning over Ontologies. In: OWLED, vol. 216 (2006)
11. Koopmann, P., Del-Pinto, W., Tourret, S., Schmidt, R.A.: Signature-based abduction for expressive description logics. In: KR2020 **17**(1), pp. 592–602 (2020)
12. Baader, F., Küsters, R., Molitor, R.: Computing Least Common Subsumers in Description Logics with Existential Restrictions. In: IJCAI **99**, pp. 96–101 (1999)

Query Optimization in NoSQL Databases Using an Enhanced Localized R-tree Index

Aristeidis Karras[1]([✉]) [iD], Christos Karras[1] [iD], Dimitrios Samoladas[1],
Konstantinos C. Giotopoulos[2] [iD], and Spyros Sioutas[1] [iD]

[1] Computer Engineering and Informatics Department,
University of Patras, Patras, Greece
{akarras,c.karras,samoladas,sioutas}@ceid.upatras.gr
[2] Department of Management Science and Technology,
University of Patras, Patras, Greece
kgiotop@upatras.gr

Abstract. Query optimization is a crucial process across data mining
and big data analytics. As the size of the data in the modern applications is increasing due to various sources, types and multi-modal records
across databases, there is an urge to optimize lookup and search operations. Therefore, indexes can be utilized to solve the matter of rapid
data growth as they enhance the performance of the database and subsequently the cloud server where it is stored. In this paper an index on
spatial data, i.e. coordinates on the plane or on the map is presented.
This index is be based on the R-Tree which is suitable for spatial data
and is distributed so that it can scale and adapt to massive amounts of
data without losing its performance. The results of the proposed method
are encouraging across all experiments and future directions of this work
include experiments on skewed data.

Keywords: Big data · NoSQL · Indexes · R-tree · Range queries ·
kNN

1 Introduction

Indexes are data structures that originated from the urge to rapidly locate data
contained within databases. In order to search for all records that belong to a
specific range or to generally fulfil certain criteria, users have to manually retrieve
each item and determine if it meets the parameters entered. For a database
with N items, this would need $\mathcal{O}(N)$ time, which is impractical for the massive
databases existing nowadays due to Big Data era. Consequently, an index is any
data structure that helps speed up the search process. However, to perform so,
additional storage writes and storage space are utilized. There are a number
of indexes that meet the varying requirements of geographical, chronological,
textual, and multidimensional data, among others. Choosing the appropriate
index for a specific use-case is a crucial aspect of the whole procedure since it
might lead to time complications while searching operations can vary between
$\mathcal{O}(logN)$ and $\mathcal{O}(1)$ time.

E. Pardede et al. (Eds.): iiWAS 2022, LNCS 13635, pp. 391–398, 2022.
https://doi.org/10.1007/978-3-031-21047-1_33

2   Related Work and Motivation

The main motivation behind this work is smart query optimizers as the ones presented in [1,6,9–11,13] along with indexing schemes. Moreover, optimized versions of R-tree structures are presented in [3,4] whereas R-tree is used along with machine learning methods to create a learned index which mainly focuses on instance-optimized components. LSM-trees [12] are also of note, while their optimized versions are presented in [2]. Moreover, an LSM index for spatial data is shown in [5]. Spatial analytics require models that are hybrid structures as in [8] utilizing R+ tree. Finally, multidimensional indexes are presented in [7,14].

3   Methodology

Having briefly discussed the efficient query optimizers, our optimized index is presented here which is constructed using the widely-used R-Tree structure.

The distributed implementation comprises the procedure for constructing the distributed R tree, followed by the capacity to conduct searches based on range queries and nearest neighbours. The tree which is produced and stored in HBase is static, meaning that no further input is permitted after its creation. To construct the tree, a MapReduce task is utilized which involves a mapper and a reducer function. The technique here is to separate the dataset and generate local R-Trees for each element and then the trees are then stored within HBase.

The internal structure of an R-Tree record in an HBase database consists of a ROWKEY, the MBR of the node[1]. The children of the node are kept in a family of columns entitled children and each child corresponds to a column entitled child and an index numbers the children. For the leaf nodes, the child0 column always includes the word leaf so that it can be retrieved while traversing the tree, that a leaf is reached. In the proposed method, the data contained in the dataset is saved inside the records. HBase can handle extremely broad rows, therefore it is useful to be able to get all of the entries within a sheet with a single visit to the database rather than sending many GET calls. Obviously, this holds true if the data corresponding to the points in the dataset is not enormous and the values in the sheets include the ROWKEY of a record from the table storing the data.

In order to traverse the tree it is enough to use the values stored in the columns as ROWKEY in subsequent functions of GETs operations. The root in the traditional sense does not exist but there is an external file containing the ROWKEYS (which are a list of MBRs) of its children. To store the R-Trees created by each reducer in HBase, we use two models:

- **A Localized Index**: After partitioning the dataset, the local R-Trees are stored in different HBase tables and the information to access them for searches is stored in a file on the local system.
- **A Global Index**: After partitioning the dataset, the local R-Trees are all stored in an HBase table whereas the information is stored in a local file.

---

[1] which stores the coordinates in ascending order, beginning with the lower left corner of the rectangle and ending with the top left corner.

3.1 Enhanced Range Query for Localized Index

The range query search is based on the initial algorithmic structure whereas the only difference is that we do not have a root in the R-tree but we instead read the MBRs from an index file and check whether there is an element that intersects our search area. This improved version is shown in Algorithm 1. This version uses parallelization among threads to simultaneously search different HBase tables containing local R-Trees. Hence, the search space in the query spans 2 children of the root and thus when used in two tables, the search is optimized. A synchronized method is used for results printing, which prevents it from being executed simultaneously by more than one thread. Moreover, all threads use a single connection to HBase for scalability. Therefore, if a large number of users try to query the index, the system can cope with 1 connection/user. If the same search is performed simultaneously by many users then the load increases significantly but in the Localized Index each thread operates on a different table so the search load is evenly distributed among the tables in the worst case[2].

Algorithm 1. Enhanced Range Query for Localized Index

1: **procedure** range search(search area)
2:   *connection* ⟵ **connectToHBase()**
3:   *file* ⟵ **read file (index file)**
4: **for** each line **in** file **do**
5:     *table, mbr* ⟵ *line*.split()
6:     **if** *mbr* intersects *SearchArea* **then**
7:       **startThread(SearchFunction(***SearchArea, table, connection***)**
8:                        ▷ Default range search algorithm
9:     **end if**
10: **end for**
11: **waitThreads()**
12: **end procedure**

---

4 Experimental Results

In this Section, indexing, range queries, and k-nearest neighbour search performance is evaluated. Three synthetic datasets of 5,000,000, 12,000,000, and 24,000,000 entries are utilised in the experiments. Each consists of a two-dimensional point in Euclidean space and a label. The datasets were created by a Python script that randomly generates user names from a $[-10000, 10000]$ uniformly[3] and separates the lines based on first and last names.

---

[2] Even when many users execute the same query at the same time.

[3] This indicates that there are no thick or sparse regions within the space covered within the datasets and ensures that the burden is dispersed evenly across the reducers.

4.1   Index Construction

To construct the index, two models and a centralised implementation are compared in terms of time for each of the datasets as shown in Fig. 1. The maximum number of children per node $\mathcal{M}$ is set to 100 in all experiments, whereas the number of reducers is set to 6. Note that it was essential to increase the Java memory capacity to at least 4 GBs in order to generate the index in the centralised approach for datasets containing between 12 and 24 million records.

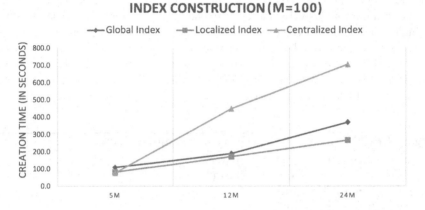

Fig. 1. Indexing functions for Centralized, Global and Localized implementation.

The experiments show that both of the developed models have excellent scalability as the index construction time rises in compact-size as the data size grows[4] compared to the centralised approach, where the duration varies from around 1 min for 5 million records to almost 8 min for 12 million sorted[5] records. In terms of generation speed, the Localized model seems to outperform the Global model as the amount of data grows.

4.2   Range Queries

The range search are compared among the two implemented models and the MapReduce implementation as shown in Fig. 2. In order to evaluate the performance of the different approaches, a comparison is done using range queries on a dataset containing 12 million records and spanning a square-shaped region in the center of the space. For the Localized implementation, six reducers were used, resulting in six partitions along the x axis and six HBase tables. Four queries were executed for each technique with square sides and each query was executed four times. We take the average search time as the evaluation metric.

---

[4] The distributed index contains Terabytes of records.
[5] Because sorting is being done by HBase, PUT functions on a lower table size are substantially quicker than on a much bigger table.

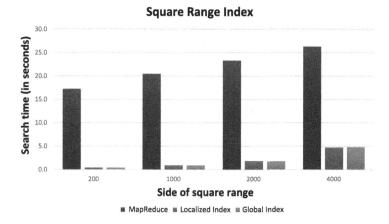

Fig. 2. Square range search times for MapReduce, Localized and Global Indexes.

As we can observe, the MapReduce search solution is unsuitable for tiny datasets and lacks in time due to the additional time necessary to launch a MapReduce job, which consumes at least 40% of the time. Hence, the implementation in MapReduce is not recommended here and is not further discussed. Regarding the two distributed index models, the implementations provide comparable performance, and it seems there is no optimal solution. However, for the Localized technique an enhanced version that parallelizes the operation by separating the index into many arrays is used. In Fig. 3, the improved approach is compared to its predecessors for the specified quadratic ranges.

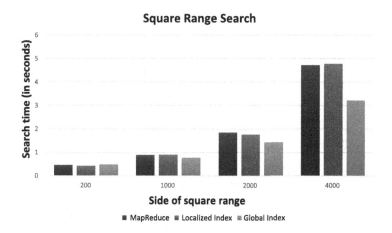

Fig. 3. Simple square range searches with an enhanced version of Localized search.

To improve the lookup version to perform optimally, ranges that cover many tables simultaneously are required. Figure. 3 shows that when the range is very small, the enhanced version shows almost no difference from simple searches, and in the case of 200, it performs lower due to the extra time spent on starting a single thread rather than performing a direct search in a specific table. Due to the fact that index partitioning into arrays is performed using the $\mathcal{X}$-coordinate, the enhanced search is most effective when dealing with long ranges. Hence, the higher the improvement, the longer the search. Due to that, the measurements were repeated with a search length such that searches are performed concurrently on all six tables of the Localized index aforementioned, while we progressively increased the search width. Increasing the search breadth results in increased thread burden as shown in Fig. 4.

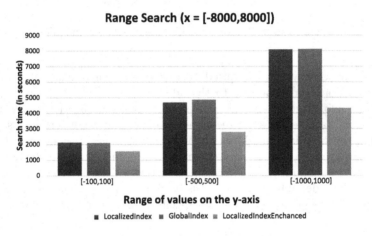

Fig. 4. Lookup times for long-length and variable-width ranges.

The improvement for long-distance searches is significantly larger. In fact, the time required for a search with a breadth in the range $[-1000, 1000]$ is about twice that of typical search techniques. Therefore, we infer that as the number of searches done by each thread rises, the search becomes faster as more searches occur concurrently and parallelism is maximised.

4.3   kNN Queries

Both index models implement the same methods for closest neighbour queries similarly to the centralised implementation. The measurements were performed once again on the dataset consisting of 12,000,000 elements and concerned a position, which we refer to as the Center Point, situated in the centre of the dataset and a point placed outside the dataset, which we refer to as the Remote Point. The searches for the two locations were conducted with progressively increasing k (number of neighbours) to determine the evolution of the two models over time in this form of search. Figure 5 (left) depicts the findings for the Center Point, whereas Fig. 5 (right) depicts the Remote Point.

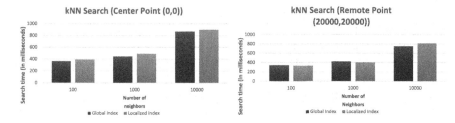

Fig. 5. Nearest neighbor search for the point (0,0) (left) and (2000,2000) (right) located in the center of the space covered by the dataset.

5   Conclusions and Future Work

In the context of this work, an enhanced localized index was created that greatly reduces the time required for different queries compared to basic brute-force searches and MapReduce. In addition, the index can manage increasing data volumes without wildly straining its construction time and performance. This is a useful feature in the era of Big Data, where data is rapidly expanding. However, the index is static, meaning that it cannot be modified after its creation, although this in no way diminishes its use. Data analytics in organisations and identifying the objectives attained by a firm over a given period of time are two examples of activities that demand rapid access to static data gathered over time. This data is hundreds of gigabytes in size and does not change over the course of the investigation. Consequently, the distributed index constructed may be a valuable tool for indexing and searching them quickly and effectively.

In addition to determining the overall utility of the index, the efficiency of the implemented index models must be determined. While both indexes in their traditional form exhibit comparable performance, the Localized index is the correct answer due to its flexibility and room for development. As we have seen, several tables enable us to take use of parallelism in the search without overwhelming a single table. In addition, it was determined that the Localized index derived from the measurements used to construct the index (Fig. 1) scales better in time as the input data of the global index rises.

Additionally, splitting the index into arrays provides an additional level of locality-based data distribution, since each array represents a vast area in space. Generalizing to non-spatial data as well, each of these tables may be a collection of linked texts, sensor readings that happened within a certain time period. This enables us to rank the index depending on the significance of each table and the amount of search traffic it gets. The aforementioned flexibility is lacking in the Global approach, which stores the whole index in a single table and distributes the data depending only on the partitioning performed by HBase in the RegionServers. In order to disseminate this table among multiple network nodes, we must first partition it, a time-consuming and error-prone procedure for large volumes of data. Additionally, a RegionServer may have acquired more popular data, resulting in an unequal distribution of load.

Future directions of this work include the handling of data skew, i.e. the scenarios in which the dataset has highly dense or very sparse portions that result in an unbalanced load distribution among the reducers.

References

1. Babcock, B., Chaudhuri, S.: Towards a robust query optimizer: a principled and practical approach. In: Proceedings of the 2005 ACM SIGMOD International Conference on Management of Data, pp. 119–130 (2005)
2. Dayan, N., Athanassoulis, M., Idreos, S.: Optimal bloom filters and adaptive merging for LSM-trees. ACM Trans. Database Syst (TODS) **43**(4), 1–48 (2018)
3. Gu, T., Feng, K., Cong, G., Long, C., Wang, Z., Wang, S.: A Reinforcement Learning Based R-Tree for Spatial Data Indexing in Dynamic Environments. arXiv preprint arXiv:2103.04541 (2021)
4. Haider, C., Wang, J., Aref, W.G.: The AI+ R-tree: An Instance-optimized R-tree. arXiv preprint arXiv:2207.00550 (2022)
5. He, J., Chen, H.: An LSM-tree index for spatial data. Algorithms **15**(4), 113 (2022)
6. Izenov, Y., Datta, A., Rusu, F., Shin, J.H.: COMPASS: Online sketch-based query optimization for in-memory databases. In: Proceedings of the 2021 International Conference on Management of Data, pp. 804–816 (2021)
7. Langendoen, K., Glasbergen, B., Daudjee, K.: NIR-Tree: A Non-Intersecting R-Tree. In: 33rd International Conference on Scientific and Statistical Database Management, pp. 157–168 (2021)
8. Liu, Y., Hao, T., Gong, X., Kong, D., Wang, J.: Research on hybrid index based on 3D multi-level adaptive grid and R+Tree. IEEE Access **9**, 146010–146022 (2021)
9. Marcus, R., Negi, P., Mao, H., Tatbul, N., Alizadeh, M., Kraska, T.: Bao: Making learned query optimization practical. ACM SIGMOD Rec. **51**(1), 6–13 (2022)
10. Marcus, R., et al.: Neo: A learned query optimizer. In: Proceeding of the VLDB Endow. **12**(11), 1705–1718 (2019). https://doi.org/10.14778/3342263.3342644
11. Markl, V., Lohman, G.M., Raman, V.: LEO: An autonomic query optimizer for DB2. IBM Syst. J. **42**(1), 98–106 (2003)
12. O'Neil, P., Cheng, E., Gawlick, D., O'Neil, E.: The log-structured merge-tree (LSM-tree). Acta Informatica **33**(4), 351–385 (1996)
13. Sellami, R., Defude, B.: Complex queries optimization and evaluation over relational and NoSQL data stores in cloud environments. IEEE Trans. Big Data **4**(2), 217–230 (2017)
14. Sprenger, S., Schäfer, P., Leser, U.: BB-Tree: A main-memory index structure for multidimensional range queries. In: 2019 IEEE 35th International Conference on Data Engineering (ICDE), pp. 1566–1569 (2019)

Handling Exit Node Vulnerability in Onion Routing with a Zero-Knowledge Proof

Nadav Voloch[1]([⊠]) and Maor Meir Hajaj[2]

[1] Ruppin Academic Center, 4025000 Emek Hefer, Israel
voloch@post.bgu.ac.il
[2] University of Haifa, 199 Aba Khoushy Ave. Mount Carmel, Haifa, Israel

Abstract. Onion routing is a method for anonymous data transfer in a communication network. It is mostly used for the deep web via TOR's (The Onion Router) different services such as TOR browser, Atlas, Orbot, and more. In this network, messages are encrypted with several layers, each layer connects only with its predecessor. An anonymity problem arises at the destination point, the exit node, which is the final node in the onion chain of routing. In the exit node the final layer is decrypted, and the message is delivered to the recipient. The possible vulnerability is that if the exit node is compromised in some way, the attacker can receive the raw data that is being delivered, potentially including sensitive or personal information. There are some ways of handling this issue, such as SSL encryption or secure HTTP, but these are not anonymous by nature as certificates include personal verification. This paper suggests a new method for solving the Exit Node Vulnerability issue that keeps the privacy and anonymity of the network. The method uses Zero-Knowledge Proof (ZKP), an encryption scheme in which one party (the prover) can validate specific information to another side (the verifier) without disclosing any additional private information. The paper presents the full scheme that solves the Exit Node Vulnerability in Onion routing.

Keywords: Onion routing · Zero-Knowledge Proof (ZKP) · Deep/Hidden Web · Exit node vulnerability

1 Introduction

The Deep/Hidden web has been thoroughly researched in the last two decades, in several aspects of technology [1], ethics [2], communication [3], and other fields. The most known method of reaching the Deep web is by TOR's (The Onion Router) different services such as TOR browser, Atlas, Orbot, and more Subsequent paragraphs, however, are indented. All of these are based on Onion routing [4], which is a method for anonymous data transfer in a communication network. There are several weaknesses in Onion routing, some of them are described in [5]. One of the most known weaknesses is Exit Node Vulnerability. The exit node is the final node in the Onion chain of routing, in which the final layer of a data packet is decrypted, and the message is delivered. The vulnerability is the possibility of an attacker that gets access to the exit node and receive the raw data that is being delivered, potentially including sensitive information.

© The Author(s), under exclusive license to Springer Nature Switzerland AG 2022
E. Pardede et al. (Eds.): iiWAS 2022, LNCS 13635, pp. 399–405, 2022.
https://doi.org/10.1007/978-3-031-21047-1_34

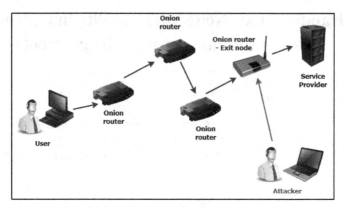

Fig. 1. Exit node vulnerability in onion routing

This process is described in Fig. 1. Some solutions to this weakness have been suggested over the years, such as SSL encryption [6] or secure HTTP [7], but these are not anonymous by nature as certificates include personal verification. This paper suggests a new way for solving this vulnerability issue that keeps the privacy and anonymity of the network. The solution includes a Zero-Knowledge Proof (ZKP), an encryption scheme, described in [8], in which one party (the prover) can validate specific information to another side (the verifier) without disclosing any additional private information.

2   Background and Related Work

Onion Routing was developed in the 1990-s at the U.S. Naval Research Laboratory [9] and then further developed by the Defense Advanced Research Projects Agency (DARPA) and patented by the Navy in 1998 [10]. Onion routing was implemented as a communication protocol with layers of encryption (the Onion layers), which was called The Onion Router [11], which is known till today as TOR. TOR is used for anonymous and private communication for different purposes and by different types of users. It was thoroughly researched and developed in the last two decades. [12] presents a comprehensive study about TOR's hidden services that are a practical solution to protect user privacy against tracking and censorship. The study investigated the lifetime of the different services, that usually do not have a long lifespan because of their nature and uses, such as the darknet. The darknet is an overlay network within the Internet that can only be accessed by TOR or other specific designated software. The darknet has a criminal aspect because of its anonymity [13], but also other important usage [14] that involves fighting censorship in countries that block communication and keeping privacy in cases of whistleblowers [15]. There are several vulnerabilities and weaknesses in TOR. [16] surveys a variety of them, in aspects of structure, design, scalability, security, transport, resource management, congestion control and circuit construction. One of the security weaknesses is Exit Node Vulnerability.

It is described thoroughly also in [17] and [18]. Some solutions to this weakness have been suggested over the years [6, 7], but these are not anonymous by nature.

An encryption scheme that is anonymous by nature is Zero-Knowledge Proof (ZKP), mentioned in the Introduction section and described in [8], in which one party can validate specific information to another side without disclosing any additional private information. Applicative research in zero-knowledge proofs is usually done on authentication systems where one party wants to prove its identity to a second party with some secret information but doesn't want the second party to learn anything about this secret. Such implementations are presented in [19], where the authentication system is group based and users have the option of making decisions on their level of privacy and the amount of resource usages, they are interested in. [20] presents a ZKP authentication protocol that is based also on Chaos. The paper presents a method for protecting servers against attacks such as port scans, and zero-day exploitation.

3   Exit Node Routing in the Onion Network with ZKP

As mentioned above, this research presents a novel method for handling Exit Node Vulnerability in a fully anonymous scheme that uses ZKP instead of non-anonymous methods that are used today that require credentials or authentication such as SSL and HTTPS. For the implementation of ZKP as a communication protocol, the solution uses the Feige-Fiat-Shamir ZKP Scheme [21], denoted here as FFS-ZKP for the exit node, in the communication transfer of the data packet between the exit node and the target node. The combination of a problem of such sort for cryptographic use is similar to the method presented in [22], where a solution for a Multiple Subset problem is used for encryption purposes. The Feige-Fiat-Shamir ZKP Scheme is an efficient protocol that uses ZKP for transferring data without revealing any other unnecessary information about the identity of the sender. The message that is delivered in the exit node of the last Onion router in the router chain encapsulates the FFS-ZKP variables that are used to transmit the data to the destination (service provider or any other end point).

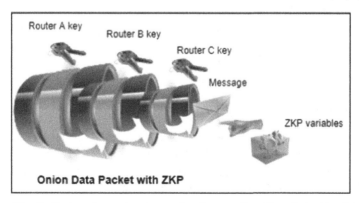

Fig. 2. Design of an onion data packet that uses Zero Knowledge Proof

To build the unique data packet that will support FFS-ZKP exit-node scheme, we need to perform several stages. The general structure of the Onion data packet is presented in Fig. 2, where we can see that every Onion layer of the data packet has its own key, that secures the Onion protocol, and the ZKP variables of the scheme are added to the encapsulated message.

The stages of building the data packet are as follows:

Algorithm 1 – Building Onion-FFS-ZKP data packet (Message msg).

1. For the beginning of the ZKP-FFS setup, choose two large prime integers p and q and compute the product $n = pq$.
2. Create secret numbers $s_1, ..., s_k$ that are coprime to n.
3. Compute $v_i \equiv s_i^2 \ (mod \ n)$.
4. Add to the *msg* header two fields: v_i and s_i.
5. Encapsulate *msg* in Exit Node Router Key.
6. Encapsulate all other onion layers with the router keys.
7. The source node receives the data packet.

After this process we have a unique Onion data packet that can overcome the Exit Node Vulnerability without disclosing any private data of the message sender.

The routing process of the data packet, after its creation is similar to the regular Onion routing protocol throughout the communication path of the Onion routers until the data packet reaches the exit node. At that time, it begins the FFS-ZKP procedure, in which the variables are being transmitted to the service provider from the exit node, that portrays the role of the prover in the ZKP protocol. The whole process is depicted in Fig. 3 and is as follows:

Algorithm 2– Routing Onion protocol with FFS-ZKP.

1. Build the data packet according to **Building Onion-FFS-ZKP data packet** procedure (*Algorithm 1*)
2. Send data packet to the first Onion router
3. While the Onion router is not the exit node:

   a. Use router key to remove onion layer
   b. Continue to next router

4. On the exit node, begin *FFS-ZKP procedure*:

   a. Exit node chooses random integer r, random sign $s \in \{-1, 1\}$
   b. Exit node Computes $s \cdot x \equiv r^2 \ (mod \ n)$.
   c. The Service Provider chooses numbers $a_1, ..., a_k, a_i \in \{-1, 1\}$
   d. The Service Provider sends these numbers to the Exit node.
   e. Exit node Computes $y \equiv rs_1^{a_1}, ..., s_k^{a_k} \ (mod \ n)$.
   f. Exit node sends y to the Service Provider.
   g. The Service Provider checks $y^2 \ (mod \ n) \equiv \pm xv_1^{a_1}, ..., v_k^{a_k}$.

5. *FFS-ZKP procedure* is repeated with different r's and a_i's values until The Service Provider is satisfied that Peggy does indeed possess the modular square roots values s_i of his v_i numbers.
6. The message is decapsulated and transmitted to The Service Provider.

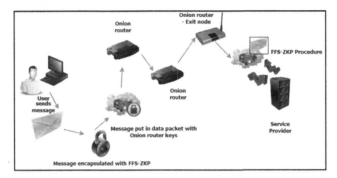

Fig. 3. Routing process of onion protocol combined with FFS-ZKP

4   Proof of Concept

We created a Python software that simulates the communication protocol that is built on TOR and handles Exit Node Vulnerability with ZKP, as described in this paper. The software is based on a public Python implementation of TOR that is called *torpy* [23]. In the preliminary part of data encapsulation, we modify the relevant parts in the message to include the FFS-ZKP variables, and then in the communication between the exit node and the service provider we base the ZKP on an existing Python implementation of FFS [24]. The general code scheme of the combined protocol is presented in Fig. 4. We can see in the figure that the client adds the ZKP variables to the regular TOR communication protocol and then it goes through the regular routing path. Before arriving the service provider, meaning being in the final node, which is the exit node, the ZKP-FFS implementation is added to handle the vulnerability.

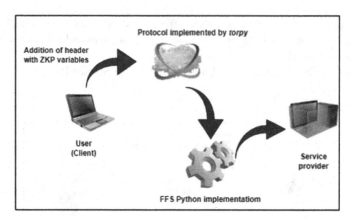

Fig. 4. General implementation scheme of communication via onion with FFS-ZKP

References

1. He, B., Patel, M., Zhang, Z., Chang, K.C.C.: Accessing the deep web. Commun. ACM **50**(5), 94–101 (2007)
2. Li, X., Dong, X.L., Lyons, K., Meng, W., Srivastava, D.: Truth finding on the deep web: Is the problem solved? arXiv preprint arXiv:1503.00303 (2015)
3. Rai, S., Singh, K., Varma, A.K.: A Bibliometric analysis of deep web research during 1997–2019. DESIDOC J. Libr. Inf. Technol. **40**(2), 452–460 (2020)
4. Goldschlag, D., Reed, M., Syverson, P.: Onion routing. Commun. ACM **42**(2), 39–41 (1999)
5. Filiol, E., Maxence Delong, J., Nicolas,: Statistical and combinatorial analysis of the TOR routing protocol: structural weaknesses identified in the TOR network. Journal of Computer Virology and Hacking Techniques **16**(1), 3–18 (2020). https://doi.org/10.1007/s11416-019-00334-x
6. Barker, J., Hannay, P., Szewczyk, P.: Using traffic analysis to identify the second generation onion router. In: 2011 IFIP 9th International Conference on Embedded and Ubiquitous Computing, pp. 72–78. IEEE (2011)
7. Saputra, F. A., Nadhori, I.U., Barry, B.F.: Detecting and blocking onion router traffic using deep packet inspection. In: 2016 International Electronics Symposium (IES), pp. 283–288. IEEE (2016)
8. Rackoff, C., Simon, D.R.: Non-interactive zero-knowledge proof of knowledge and chosen ciphertext attack. In: Feigenbaum, J. (ed.) CRYPTO 1991. LNCS, vol. 576, pp. 433–444. Springer, Heidelberg (1992). https://doi.org/10.1007/3-540-46766-1_35
9. Reed, M.G., Syverson, P.F., Goldschlag, D.M.: Anonymous connections and onion routing. IEEE J. Sel. Areas Commun. **16**(4), 482–494 (1998)
10. US patent 6266704, Reed; Michael G. (Bethesda, MD), Syverson; Paul F. (Silver Spring, MD), Goldschlag; David M. (Silver Spring, MD), Onion routing network for securely moving data through communication networks, assigned to The United States of America as represented by the Secretary of the Navy (Washington, DC)
11. Dingledine, R., Mathewson, N., Syverson, P. : Tor: The second-generation onion router. Naval Research Lab Washington DC (2004)
12. Sanatinia, A., Park, J., Blass, E.O., Mohaisen, A., Noubir, G.: A Privacy-preserving longevity study of Tor's hidden services. arXiv preprint arXiv:1909.03576 (2019)
13. Bancroft, A.: The Darknet and Smarter Crime: Methods for Investigating Criminal Entrepreneurs and the Illicit Drug Economy. Springer Nature (2019)

14. Mirea, M., Wang, V., Jung, J.: The not so dark side of the darknet: a qualitative study. Secur. J. **32**(2), 102–118 (2019)
15. Habbabeh, A., Asprion, P.M., Schneider, B.: Mitigating the risks of whistleblowing-an approach using distributed system technologies. PoEM Workshops pp. 47–58 (2020)
16. AlSabah, M., Goldberg, I.: Performance and security improvements for tor: a survey. ACM Computing Surveys (CSUR) **49**(2), 1–36 (2016)
17. Abbott, T.G., Lai, K.J., Lieberman, M.R., Price, E.C.: Browser-based attacks on Tor. In: Borisov, N., Golle, P. (eds.) PET 2007. LNCS, vol. 4776, pp. 184–199. Springer, Heidelberg (2007). https://doi.org/10.1007/978-3-540-75551-7_12
18. Tan, Q., Wang, X., Shi, W., Tang, J., Tian, Z.: An anonymity vulnerability in Tor. IEEE/ACM Trans. Netw. (01), 1–14 (2022)
19. Rasheed, A.A., Mahapatra, R.N., Hamza-Lup, F.G.: Adaptive group-based zero knowledge proof-authentication protocol in vehicular ad hoc networks. IEEE Trans. Intell. Transp. Syst. **21**(2), 867–881 (2019)
20. Major, W., Buchanan, W.J., Ahmad, J.: An authentication protocol based on chaos and zero knowledge proof. Nonlinear Dyn. **99**(4), 3065–3087 (2020). https://doi.org/10.1007/s11071-020-05463-3
21. Kizza, J.M.: Feige-fiat-shamir zkp scheme revisited. Int. J. Comput. ICT Res. **4**(1), 9–19 (2010)
22. Voloch, N.: MSSP for 2-D sets with unknown parameters and a cryptographic application. Contemp. Eng. Sci. **10**(19), 921–931 (2017)
23. https://github.com/torpyorg/torpy
24. https://github.com/marceleng/Feige-Fiat-Shamir

Privacy and Security

An Accurate, Flexible and Private Trajectory-Based Contact Tracing System on Untrusted Servers

Ruixuan Cao, Fumiyuki Kato[ID], Yang Cao[ID], and Masatoshi Yoshikawa[✉][ID]

Kyoto University, Yoshida-Honmachi Sakyo-ku Kyoto, Japan
{caorx,fumiyuki}@db.soc.i.kyoto-u.ac.jp, {yang,yoshikawa}@i.kyoto-u.ac.jp

Abstract. Infections by the Covid-19 coronavirus have proliferated since the end of 2019, and many privacy-protective contact tracing systems have been proposed to limit infections from spreading. However, the existing Bluetooth-based contact tracking systems lack accuracy and flexibility. In addition, it is desirable to have a contact tracing system that, in the future, can contribute to limiting the proliferation of new coronaviruses and as yet unknown viruses. In this study, we propose a method to extend a contact tracing system to be more flexible, accurate, and capable of dealing with unknown viruses by using trajectory data and infection factor information while protecting privacy. We also implemented the proposed extension method and measured its execution time and confirmed its practicality.

1 Introduction

COVID-19 continues to infect patients with several mutant strains, and there are no signs of complete control of the disease even two years after the outbreak. Many digital contact tracing systems have been developed to automatically record people's close contacts using mobile phones and other devices [2,9,12,15], but nothing definitive has yet been developed. Ideal contact tracing systems must satisfy the mutually contradictory requirements of accuracy, flexibility, privacy protection, and efficiency. A tracing system must be accurate because the results have a significant impact on people's lives. The system must be flexible because it is unknown what kind of mutant strains or viruses will emerge in the future. To meet the accuracy and flexibility requirements, the system should utilize a variety of personal data to determine epidemiologically the likelihood of infection. However, this poses a challenge regarding privacy protection and efficiency. For a system to satisfy accuracy and flexibility requirements, the following two considerations are critical. First, the contact determination method should be flexible enough to calculate the probability accurately of people transmitting future unknown COVID-19 mutants and viruses. It is particularly desirable to allow detecting the possibility of infection by direct contact between two people in close physical proximity, and by indirect contact, i.e., the transmission of the virus to another person via an object such as a doorknob or elevator button. For example, using Bluetooth, DP3T [14], a typical contact tracing system, records

E. Pardede et al. (Eds.): iiWAS 2022, LNCS 13635, pp. 409–414, 2022.
https://doi.org/10.1007/978-3-031-21047-1_35

when two people's mobile phones are in close proximity for a certain time. However, DP3T and other Bluetooth-based contact tracing systems [1,3,4,10], are incapable of detecting indirect contacts. Therefore, at present, a realistic way to record indirect contact is to upload people's trajectories on a central server belonging to a PHA (public health agency). As a second point, it should be noted contact does not necessarily mean that infection will ensue. The contact tracing systems should use other information that is important for determining the likelihood of infection, in addition to spatio-temporal proximity, such as the presence or absence of masks and vaccination histories, if available.

Privacy protection is essential to allow servers belonging to PHAs to collect trajectory data and other personal data because such data [6] is potentially sensitive. Raw trajectory data on the server must be protected even from the sever's administrator. PCT-TEE (trajectory-based Private Contact Tracing system with Trusted Execution Environment) [7] is a privacy-preserving contact tracing system that calculates spatial and temporal proximity from raw trajectory data in a trustworthy operational environment. It determines that contact is made when temporal and spatial proximity thresholds are met. PCT-TEE's program runs under a TEE (Trusted Execution Environment) [11], which can be built using secure Intel SGX hardware. In an isolated TEE, called the *enclave*, access from untrusted software, including the operating system, is prohibited. Therefore, PCT-TEE can realize a contact tracing system on an untrusted central server. However, the following issue has not been fully studied:

- Can TEE-PSI efficiently perform general and flexible infection risk calculations using physical proximity and infection factor information such as mask use and vaccination for a population of metropolitan residents?

In this study, we address this issue and demonstrate that TEE-PSI can be a contact tracing system that satisfies the requirements of accuracy, flexibility, privacy protection, and efficiency, by forwarding diverse personal information to a central server to calculate the probability of infection. This paper's contributions are twofolds:

1. We propose a method to extend PCT-TEE by calculating the probabilities of person-to-person infection by using personal information e.g., whether the user was wearing a mask or how many vaccine doses the user has received, in addition to the trajectory data. We investigate how the PCT-TEE system can be extended using infection factor information, which allows us flexibly to determine the probability of a person being infected while protecting privacy.
2. The proposed extension method was actually implemented, on the PCT-TEE system to include infection factor information, and conduct experiments to demonstrate the feasibility of using the system for a large urban population. The experimental results show that the PCT-TEE system feasibly manages large volumes of diverse personal data including the trajectory data on an untrusted server equipped with TEE hardware.

2   Related Work

Decentralized privacy-preserving proximity tracing (DP3T) [14] and other Bluetooth-based contact tracing systems are widely developed [1,3,4,10,13]. There are two problems with these systems. The first is that they cannot detect indirect contact, such as when a person becomes infected by using a sheet used by an infected person in a restaurant, etc. The second is that Bluetooth-based contact tracing systems cannot flexibly change the criteria of contact time and distance to the infected person. Phong et al. [8] used homomorphic encryption to collect and compute personal data on a untrusted central server in privacy-protecing manner; however, calculation on the server is limited to addition.

3   Privacy-Preserving Calculation of Infection Probability

In this section, we first describe the scope of the contact tracing task problem and explain the possible infection factor information to be acquired and formulate a function to calculate infection probability.

A medical institution registers the infection factor information of a confirmed infected patient on the contact tracing system of a PHA's server whose administrator is not trusted. The infection factor information includes trajectory data. If a user wants to find out if she was infected by an infected person recorded on the sever, She sends her encryped infection factor information to the server as a query. The sever receives the query and secretly calculates the possibility of infection against all patients' data on the server, returning pairs of a patient id and a probability if the probability is larger than zero.

The probability of infection varies depending on the environment and the condition of the user at the time of contact. For example, in the case where the infected person u had already received two doses of COVID-19 vaccine (which claims a reduced likelihood of transmission by vaccinated persons [5]), and if the user v was wearing a mask and no interactions occurred between them, the probability of infection for user v should be negligible. Also, in countermeasures against new coronavirus infections, a mask is more effective in preventing the spread of the virus from you than in reducing the amount of virus inhaled by the other person, and even if you were forced to approach to within 50 cm, it is more effective if only you wear a mask than if only the other person wears a mask. Conversely, for unknown viruses, the mask may be more effective if only the counterpart wears it. To develop a system that can handle unknown viruses, it is necessary to make such assumptions.

Following the advice of an infectious disease specialist, we classified infection factor information A_u of a person u into the following three categories[1] :

---

[1] We note that an exhaustive list of infection factor information or a discussion of the availability of such information is beyond the scope of this paper. Our focus is to confirm that when some or all of such information is available it can be used to efficiently calculate the probability of infection using PCT-TEE. If only partial infection factor information is available, we calculate the probability of infection assuming the worst case scenario.

- A_u^{inf} (factors by which an infected person infects another person): age, days since onset, the number of vaccine inoculations, and so on.
- $A_u^{\text{non-inf}}$ (factors that allow non-infected persons to become infected): age, presence of underlying disease, the number of vaccine inoculations, previous history of infection, and so on.
- A_u^{path} (factors on infection route): wearing a mask or not, duration of contact, space in which contact was made (closed room or not), and so on.

A_u^{inf} and $A_u^{\text{non-inf}}$ include user attributes and individual clinical background factors.

We model the probability $p(u, v)$ that u infected v by using infection factor information as follows:

$$p(u,v) = p^{\text{inf}}(A_u^{\text{inf}}) \times p^{\text{non-inf}}(A_v^{\text{non-inf}}) \times p^{\text{path}}(A_u^{\text{path}}, A_v^{\text{path}}) \qquad (1)$$

The function $p^{\text{inf}}(\cdot)$ in Formula (1) solely dependes on A_u^{inf}, infection factor information of a user u, and is not affected by other users' infection factor information. Let A_u^{inf} be a set of factors $\{a_u^{\text{inf}_1}, a_u^{\text{inf}_2}, \ldots, a_u^{\text{inf}_n}\}$. We simply model $p^{\text{inf}}(A_u^{\text{inf}})$ as:

$$p^{\text{inf}}(A_u^{\text{inf}}) = p^{\text{inf}_1}(a_u^{\text{inf}_1}) \times p^{\text{inf}_2}(a_u^{\text{inf}_2}) \times \cdots \times p^{\text{inf}_n}(a_u^{\text{inf}_n}).$$

The function $p^{\text{non-inf}}(A_v^{\text{non-inf}})$ is modeled analogously.

Our system employs PCT-TEE for judging close contact of u and v. Hence, X_u being the trajectory data of u, we can model $p^{\text{path}}(A_u^{\text{path}}, A_v^{\text{path}})$ as follows:

$$p^{\text{path}}(A_u^{\text{path}}, A_v^{\text{path}}) = p^{\text{nontraj-path}}(A_u^{\text{path}} - \{X_u\}, A_v^{\text{path}} - \{X_v\}) \times p^{\text{traj}}(X_u, X_v) \qquad (2)$$

$p^{\text{traj}}(X_u, X_v)$ is a function which returns 1 if users u and v were in close contact and 0 otherwise.

4   Experiments

In this section, we implement the extended method proposed in Sect. 3 and conduct experiments based thereon. The purpose of this experiment is to verify how much the infection factor information in the trajectory data increases the execution time compared to PCT-TEE, and whether the execution time is acceptable in practical terms.

The trajectory data for the dataset used in the experiments is a real dataset[2] using data on individual's trajectories in a specific region of Japan available from the Joint Usage System of the Center for Spatial Information Science[3] at the University of Tokyo. The real dataset was created using human flow datasets for the Kinki and Tokyo regions of Japan. The length of each trajectory in this dataset is 1440, and the server stores 14,000 trajectories.

---

[2] These human flow datasets are synthetically derived from actual trajectories, but for this study, they are considered to be actual datasets. More details on the specific process of data creation can be found here http://pflow.csis.u-tokyo.ac.jp/data-service/pflow-data/.

[3] https://www.csis.u-tokyo.ac.jp.

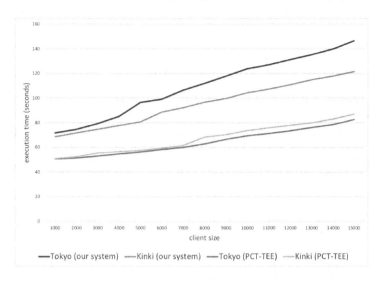

Fig. 1. Relationship between client size and execution time for each method.

Figure 1 shows the overall execution time for each method for all client numbers. As can be seen in the figure, the execution time increases almost linearly as the client numbers increase. This suggests that even when the client numbers become exorbitant, the increase is almost linear, this allows an acceptable execution speed. Put differently, even if infection factor information is added to the trajectory data, the system can be put to practical use as a privacy-protective contact tracking system.

5   Conclusion

Based on a contact tracing system that uses trajectory data while protecting privacy, this study proposes an extended method to realize a contact tracing system that is more flexible, accurate, and able to accommodate unknown viruses by using infection factor information. Future works includes an extension of the system to incorporating identifiers of closed space. If the distance of two users is close but there is an obstruction (e.g. a car and a bus next to each other), the system judges that they have made contact even if they have not. The extension deals with infection factor information that can affect the contact decision result of the system and improve the accuracy of the contact decision.

Acknowledgements. We thank Professor Miki Nagao of Kyoto University Hospital for her thoughtful responses to the authors' questions about the infection probability calculation model. This work was partially supported by JST CREST JPMJCR21M2, JST SICORP JPMJSC2107, JST SICORP JPMJSC2006, Grant-in-Aid for Scientific Research 22H03595, 21K19767, 19K20269, and the KDDI Foundation Research Grant.

References

1. Becker, J.K., Li, D., Starobinski, D.: Tracking anonymized bluetooth devices. Proc. Priv. Enhancing Technol. **2019**(3), 50–65 (2019)
2. Cho, H., Ippolito, D., Yu, Y.W.: Contact tracing mobile apps for COVID-19: privacy considerations and related trade-offs. arXiv preprint arXiv:2003.11511 (2020)
3. Da, Y., Ahuja, R., Xiong, L., Shahabi, C.: React: real-time contact tracing and risk monitoring via privacy-enhanced mobile tracking. In: 2021 IEEE 37th International Conference on Data Engineering (ICDE), pp. 2729–2732. IEEE (2021)
4. Gvili, Y.: Security analysis of the COVID-19 contact tracing specifications by apple inc. and google inc. IACR Cryptol. ePrint Arch. **2020**, 428 (2020)
5. Ministry of Health, L., Welfare: vaccine's effection (2021). https://www.mhlw.go.jp/stf/covid-19/qa.html
6. HUMAN RIGHTS WATCH: mobile location data and COVID-19: Q&A (2020). https://www.hrw.org/news/2020/05/13/mobile-location-data-and-covid-19-qa
7. Kato, F., Cao, Y., Yoshikawa, M.: PCT-TEE: trajectory-based Private contact tracing system with trusted execution environment. ACM Trans. Spat. Algorithms Syst. (TSAS) **8**(2), 1–35 (2022). https://doi.org/10.1145/3490491
8. Phong, L.T., Aono, Y., Hayashi, T., Wang, L., Moriai, S.: Privacy-preserving deep learning via additively homomorphic encryption. IEEE Trans. Inf. Forensics Secur. **13**(5), 1333–1345 (2018). https://doi.org/10.1109/TIFS.2017.2787987
9. Qin, C., et al.: Dysregulation of immune response in patients with coronavirus 2019 (COVID-19) in Wuhan, China. Clin. Infect. Dis. **71**(15), 762–768 (03 2020). https://doi.org/10.1093/cid/ciaa248, https://doi.org/10.1093/cid/ciaa248
10. Rivest, R.L., et al.: The pact protocol specification. Private Automated Contact Tracing Team, MIT, Cambridge, MA, USA, Tech. Rep. 0.1 (2020)
11. Sabt, M., Achemlal, M., Bouabdallah, A.: Trusted execution environment: what it is, and what it is not. In: 2015 IEEE Trustcom/BigDataSE/ISPA, vol. 1, pp. 57–64. IEEE (2015)
12. Salathé, M., et al.: COVID-19 epidemic in switzerland: on the importance of testing, contact tracing and isolation. Swiss Med. Wkly. **150**(11–12), w20225 (2020)
13. Trieu, N., Shehata, K., Saxena, P., Shokri, R., Song, D.: Epione: lightweight contact tracing with strong privacy. arXiv preprint arXiv:2004.13293 (2020)
14. Troncoso, C., et al.: Decentralized privacy-preserving proximity tracing. arXiv preprint arXiv:2005.12273 (2020)
15. Wang, C.J., Ng, C.Y., Brook, R.H.: Response to covid-19 in taiwan: big data analytics, new technology, and proactive testing. JAMA **323**(14), 1341–1342 (2020)

Bilateral Bargaining for Healthcare Data Sharing

Svetlana Boudko$^{(\boxtimes)}$ ⓘ and Wolfgang Leister ⓘ

Norsk Regnesentral, Oslo, Norway
{svetlana,wolfgang}@nr.no

Abstract. The healthcare market demands flexible, and secure solutions for personal health data sharing. For this purpose, we developed a distributed multi-agent system that reinforces a negotiable right management environment. We propose a bilateral bargaining mechanism that facilitates computational negotiation between patients and healthcare stakeholders. The mechanism is evaluated using both open and sealed bids. We show that agents reach an agreement within a feasible number of rounds, even if their bids are kept confidential.

Keywords: Multiagent systems · Computational negotiation · Bilateral bargaining · Secure data sharing · Health data exchange

1 Introduction

Accurate and comprehensive patient-generated health data are highly important for various healthcare stakeholders including healthcare institutions, researchers, pharmaceutical companies, and insurance companies. This information can help healthcare stakeholders to develop better patient-tailored treatments and medications and improve treatment routines [9]. Therefore, sharing personal health data can provide valuable benefits for patients and their treatment. However, unauthorized access to these data can lead to misuse and cause damage if attacked by ransomware, exploited by black market dealers, or accessed by other cybercriminals.

To provide availability and authorized exchange of health data, we develop a distributed multi-agent system that reinforces a negotiable right management environment. The software agents of this system can represent different types of users including patients, their relatives, and various stakeholders. These agents are designed to negotiate data access rights and conditions on data sharing on behalf of the aforementioned users [2].

The multi-agent system is designed as a component of the health democratization platform[1]. Its operation relies on the functionality of several other components: 1) a data provenance layer that collects and manages the health data, 2) an incentive mechanism that evaluates benefits from data sharing, and 3) and a risk assessment component that evaluates risks for data breaches. To facilitate the computational negotiation process, the users preconfigure sets of rules

---

[1] https://www.ntnu.edu/iik/healthdemocratization.

E. Pardede et al. (Eds.): iiWAS 2022, LNCS 13635, pp. 415–420, 2022.
https://doi.org/10.1007/978-3-031-21047-1_36

and parameters that will manage the negotiation. These parameters include various characteristics of patient data, incentives, and possible risks related to data sharing. To assist the users in defining these elements, the configuration process is supported by the risk assessment and incentive components. The details of these two components are beyond the scope of the paper.

Revealing the offer details may be exploited by the opponent, thus, prompting the users to keep their bidding preferences completely private. For this purpose, the system implements a sealed-bid option with all bidding information kept confidential from the opponent. While ensuring the confidentiality of bidding parameters, this solution may slow down the convergence of bargaining routines and result in lower communication efficiency.

Depending on the number of agents that participate in the negotiation process, the system supports 1) bilateral bargaining with strictly one buyer and one seller negotiating the terms of data sharing, and 2) different types of auction, including reverse auction and double auction where several agents can participate in the negotiation. In this paper, we limit our work to bilateral bargaining. We present a bilateral bargaining mechanism for health data sharing. To understand how maintaining confidentiality can influence the effectiveness and communication efficiency of the bargaining process, we evaluate two scenarios in which the amount of information that agents have about their opponent's parameters differs. The evaluation is done for both open-bidding and sealed bidding settings.

2   Related Work

Multiagent Systems (MAS) are referred to as systems of multiple interacting intelligent agents [19,20] that are autonomous entities such as software programs or robots. The complexity of tasks and problems that can be solved by MAS is significantly higher than the complexity of tasks that agents can solve on their own. Such agents may own different information and may have common or conflicting interests. These agents may cooperate in achieving a common goal, or they can be selfish. Intelligent agents also may respond adaptively to changing contexts and situations. To cooperate and to achieve mutually beneficial agreements, negotiation mechanisms, rules and protocols must be implemented and be available for all agents.

Negotiation mechanisms and approaches have been widely studied, including axiomatic bargaining, strategic bargaining, multi-issue negotiations, concurrent negotiations, strategy-proof mechanisms, rational argumentation, auctions, and voting [7,8,12–15,17]. Examples of negotiations may include resolving conflicts over the usage of joint resources, and task assignments [10]. The alternating-offer game initially proposed in [15] uses a non-cooperative game theoretic approach for bilateral single-issue setting with complete information. In the context of complete information, rational negotiators can calculate Pareto-efficient solutions. However, complete information is often not available in practice.

Bargaining with incomplete information has been addressed in several studies [1,6,16]. Automated bilateral multiple-issue negotiation with no information about the opponent's utility function is presented in [21]. The authors used an alternating projection strategy to prove that reaching an agreement is feasible. Using rational negotiators and non-biases mediators in the negotiation process was also proposed in several studies to address the incomplete information problem and optimize the negotiation routines [3,11,18]. A framework for automated multi-attribute negotiation with incomplete information is presented in [11]. A non-biased mediator and a Pareto-optimal mediating protocol were used to implement the negotiation strategy. While relying on non-biases mediators ensures protection of private information, the existence of a trusted third party cannot always be verified in a real-world setting, and, therefore, other privacy-preserving mechanisms should be exploited [4,5].

3   Bilateral Bargaining

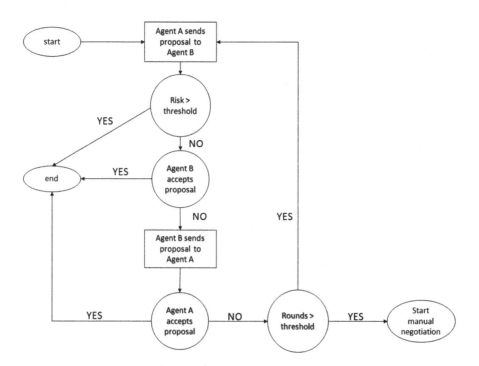

Fig. 1. Bilateral bargaining

To facilitate the bilateral negotiation process, the users of the platform configure their agents by defining bargaining rules and parameters. For each dataset, its duration, and granularity, the user defines acceptable risk levels and upper and lower bounds for incentives. For counteroffers, the user defines bargaining iteration rules.

The bargaining process, depicted in Fig. 1, starts with the lower incentive bound for the buyer and with the upper incentive bound for the seller. When an agent receives an offer, the agent first checks the corresponding risk of data breaches. If the risk exceeds the acceptable level, the process stops. The process also terminates if the offer is satisfying and the agents reach an agreement. Otherwise, the agent sends a counteroffer. The process iterates using predefined bargaining iteration rules. If the number of bargaining rounds exceeds the threshold and the agents do not reach an agreement, the process stops, and the user is notified.

4   Evaluation

To demonstrate the operation of the proposed approach, we consider an evaluation setup. In this setup, two agents negotiate on sharing health data with their corresponding durations, risks, and incentives. The thresholds were 10, 20, 30, 40, 50, 60, 70, and 80 rounds. For each threshold value, we performed 200 simulation runs. The zone of agreement, which is the set of offers acceptable to both agents, was non-empty for all simulation runs.

In terms of information availability, the evaluation was performed using both open bids and sealed bids. In the open-bid setting, the agents had no information about the opponent's preferences, bounds on price settings, or negotiation strategies, however, the offer price was known. In the sealed-bid setting, the offer price was kept confidential. A third-party component was implemented to compute the outcomes of the bidding process, and only these results were provided to the agents.

For each threshold value, we evaluated the percentage of successful bids. The results are depicted in Table 1. Comparing the results of open bidding and sealed bidding, we find that the open bidding process clearly outperforms the sealed bidding process for a lower number of alternations. For a higher number

Table 1. Evaluation results for bilateral bargaining with open bidding and with sealed bidding.

Threshold	Open bidding	Sealed bidding
10	32%	11%
20	38%	19%
30	47%	31%
40	67%	52%
50	82%	71%
60	98%	81%
70	100%	89%
80	100%	100%

of alternations, the results are close. While preserving privacy, the sealed bidding process converges in a feasible number of rounds.

To better interpret the evaluation results, we also computed the average number of rounds required for reaching a mutual agreement. For open bidding, the average number of rounds was 34.3. For sealed bidding, the average number of rounds was 46.1. Thus, preserving privacy resulted in approximately 34% overhead of alternating.

5 Conclusion

We presented and evaluated a bilateral bargaining mechanism for health data sharing. To assess how protecting the privacy of the bids can influence the effectiveness of the bargaining process, the evaluation was performed for open and sealed bidding. We show that the agents can reach an agreement within a reasonable number of iterations, even if they have no information about each other's preferences or bidding parameters. The sealed bidding process was implemented using a trusted third party, which is problematic in a real-world setting. Therefore, we plan to investigate and incorporate homomorphic encryption techniques as our step forward.

Acknowledgements. This work has been carried out in the context of the research project Health Democratization, funded by the Research Council of Norway in the IKTPLUSS program, grant number 288856.

References

1. Ausubel, L.M., Cramton, P., Deneckere, R.J.: Bargaining with incomplete information. In: Aumann, R., Hart, S. (eds.) Handbook of Game Theory with Economic Applications, vol. 3, chap. 50, pp. 1897–1945. Elsevier (00 2002)
2. Boudko, S., Leister, W.: Building blocks of negotiating agents for healthcare data, pp. 635–639. iiWAS2019, Association for Computing Machinery, New York, NY, USA (2019). https://doi.org/10.1145/3366030.3366108
3. Chalamish, M., Kraus, S.: Automed: an automated mediator for multi-issue bilateral negotiations. Auton. Agent. Multi-Agent Syst. **24**, 536–564 (05 2012). https://doi.org/10.1007/s10458-010-9165-y
4. Chaum, D., Damgård, I.B., van de Graaf, J.: Multiparty computations ensuring privacy of each party's input and correctness of the result. In: Pomerance, C. (ed.) CRYPTO 1987. LNCS, vol. 293, pp. 87–119. Springer, Heidelberg (1988). https://doi.org/10.1007/3-540-48184-2_7
5. van Dijk, M., Gentry, C., Halevi, S., Vaikuntanathan, V.: Fully homomorphic encryption over the integers. Cryptology ePrint Archive, Paper 2009/616 (2009). https://eprint.iacr.org/2009/616
6. Fatima, S., Wooldridge, M., Jennings, N.: Bargaining with incomplete information. Ann. Math. Artif. Intell. **44**, 207–232 (07 2005). https://doi.org/10.1007/s10472-005-4688-7

7. Fukuta, N., Ito, T., Zhang, M., Fujita, K., Robu, V.: Recent Advances in Agent-Based Complex Automated Negotiation, 1st edn. Springer, Switzerland (2016)

8. Ito, T., Hattori, H., Zhang, M., Matsuo, T. (eds.): Rational, Robust, and Secure Negotiations in Multi-Agent Systems, Studies in Computational Intelligence, vol. 89. Springer, Berlin, Heidelberg (2008). https://doi.org/10.1007/978-3-540-76282-9

9. Kostkova, P., et al.: Who owns the data? Open data for healthcare. Front. Public Health **21**(6), e13583 (2016). https://doi.org/10.3389/fpubh.2016.00007

10. Kraus, S.: Automated negotiation and decision making in multiagent environments. In: Luck, M., Mařík, V., Štěpánková, O., Trappl, R. (eds.) ACAI 2001. LNCS (LNAI), vol. 2086, pp. 150–172. Springer, Heidelberg (2001). https://doi.org/10.1007/3-540-47745-4_7

11. Lai, G., Sycara, K.: A generic framework for automated multi-attribute negotiation. Group Decis. Negot. **18**(2), 169–187 (03 2009). https://doi.org/10.1007/s10726-008-9119-9

12. Marsa-Maestre, I., Lopez-Carmona, M., Ito, T., Zhang, M., Bai, Q., Fujita, K. (eds.): Novel Insights in Agent-Based Complex Automated Negotiation, Studies in Computational Intelligence, vol. 535. Springer, Tokyo, 1. edn. (2014). https://doi.org/10.1007/978-4-431-54758-7

13. Mas-Colell, A., Whinston, M.D., Green, J.R.: Microeconomic Theory. Oxford University Press, New York (1995)

14. Nash, J.: The Bargaining Problem. Econometrica **18**(2), 155–162 (950). https://ideas.repec.org/a/ecm/emetrp/v18y1950i2p155-162.html

15. Rubinstein, A.: Perfect equilibrium in a bargaining model. Econometrica **50**(1), 97–109 (1982)

16. Rubinstein, A.: A bargaining model with incomplete information about time preferences. Econometrica **53**(5), 1151–1172 (1985). http://www.jstor.org/stable/1911016

17. Sandholm, T.W.: Distributed Rational Decision Making, pp. 201–258. MIT Press, Cambridge, MA, USA (1999)

18. Sarabando, P., Dias, L., Vetschera, R.: Mediation with incomplete information: Approaches to suggest potential agreements. Group Decis. Negot. **22** , 561–597 (01 2009). https://doi.org/10.1007/s10726-012-9283-9

19. Shoham, Y., Leyton-Brown, K.: Multiagent Systems: Algorithmic, Game-Theoretic, and Logical Foundations. Cambridge University Press, New York, NY, USA (2008)

20. Wooldridge, M.: An Introduction to MultiAgent Systems. Wiley Publishing, Hoboken, NJ, USA, second edn (2009)

21. Zheng, R., Chakraborty, N., Dai, T., Sycara, K., Lewis, M.: Automated bilateral multiple-issue negotiation with no information about opponent. In: 2013 46th Hawaii International Conference on System Sciences, pp. 520–527 (2013). https://doi.org/10.1109/HICSS.2013.626

Modifying Neo4j's Object Graph Mapper Queries for Access Control

Daniel Hofer[1,2](✉) ⓘ, Aya Mohamed[1,2] ⓘ, and Josef Küng[1,2] ⓘ

[1] Institute for Application-Oriented Knowledge Processing (FAW),
Faculty of Engineering and Natural Sciences (TNF), Johannes Kepler University
(JKU) Linz, Linz, Austria
{dhofer,amohamed,jkueng}@faw.jku.at,
{daniel.hofer,aya.mohamed,josef.kueng}@jku.at
[2] LIT Secure and Correct Systems Lab, Linz Institute of Technology (LIT), Johannes
Kepler University (JKU) Linz, Linz, Austria

Abstract. A web application without access control is hardly usable. At the same time, we want to avoid boilerplate and use frameworks automating the communication between applications and databases. However, if we use the full potential of the mapper frameworks, the possibilities for access control are getting limited. Consequently, a trade-off between code complexity and mapper functionality must be found. In this work, we use object-graph mapper and at the same time avoid code duplication and entity-type-specific access control implementations. We do so by intercepting and changing the communication between our application code and the mapper framework so it generates queries already containing access-control filters. Thereby, we achieve authorization already on database access. With this approach only entities authorized for the currently active user are loaded, reducing the risk of data leaks. Furthermore, the developers are not required to implement access control on a per-entity-type basis.

1 Introduction

Object-graph mappers (OGMs) are frameworks translating object oriented concepts from and to their serialization in a graph database. They provide automatically generated implementations of database access objects (*DAOs*), sparing developers from implementing them manually. In this paper, we are focusing on *Neo4j OGM*, which is the implementation for the graph database *Neo4j*. This framework offers basic CRUD (*Create, Read, Update, and Delete*) operations out of the box and provides support in creating more complex queries.

In previous work [2], we proposed to enhance object-graph mappers with authorization features by automatically changing the requests on the underlying storage. We proposed using the filtering capabilities of the storage to restrict access to only those entities, a user is authorized to see or modify. Accordingly, we identified an interface and built a wrapper around it, granting us full control on the requests to the storage and entities returned from there.

ⓒ The Author(s), under exclusive license to Springer Nature Switzerland AG 2022
E. Pardede et al. (Eds.): iiWAS 2022, LNCS 13635, pp. 421–426, 2022.
https://doi.org/10.1007/978-3-031-21047-1_37

However, we did not yet consider how to alter the requests on the interface to achieve our goal. In this work, we analyze, which operations are offered out of the box. We then group them into categories and find strategies to enforce access control. We intercept method calls intended for the object-graph mapper, apply the suitable modification and pass the modified version on. The modified requests takes then advantage of the filtering capabilities of the underlying database. This results in a more efficient communication as only authorized entities are returned back to the application and databases are specifically built to do filtering on large amounts of data.

2   Authorization Requirements

In [2], we described how to extend an existing web application with an authoriza-tion layer on an architectural level. We will continue this effort here by providing general approaches for modifying queries to the application's persistent storage. Generally, we want the user to see only authorized entities and prevent them from unauthorized modifications. The extension must remain loosely coupled to the rest of the application and be transparent on collection operations, but notify on insufficient permissions for single-entity operations.

Based on the defined requirements, we can derive our research questions tai-lored to Neo4j's object-graph mapper and its *Session* interface. For our consid-erations, we use the interface *Session.java* for the version 3.2.35 (see GitHub[1]).

RQ1. Which categories of methods are offered by *Session*?
RQ2. Which operations are conducted by each category?
RQ3. How can we filter collections of entities?
RQ4. How can we filter single-entity access and notify the developer or user?

3   Related Work

In scientific literature, Leao et al. [4] focus on the problem of identity propagation from the user through multiple tiers to the backend. The paper [8] by Rizvi et al. proposes a different solution to our problem by using database views. Drawbacks are their platform dependence and their maintenance requirements for the views. A very similar approach is proposed by Jarman et al. [3]. They used virtual private database features to implement dynamic role-based access control. The work [9] by Rosenthal et al. deals with the inference of contextual information in a distributed warehouse context. Bogaerts et al. [1] propose *entity based access control* which not only takes the properties of a single entity into account, but also its relationship to other entities.

There is existing technical related work, partly addressing some of the requirements. For example, Neo4j offers built-in access control capabilities, how-ever, these features are only available for the enterprise versions [6]. Furthermore,

---

[1] https://github.com/neo4j/neo4j-ogm/blob/230029be650f2b15af99caf10de92fd8387a
725d/core/src/main/java/org/neo4j/ogm/session/Session.java.

it only allows role-based access control. This is different to our work as we also plan for decisions based on attributes resulting in attribute based access control.

In addition, *Spring Security* [10] can be used to ensure no unauthorized entity leaves the application, however, it operates solely on the backend at the entity level. To the best of our knowledge, Spring Security is not able to prevent retrieving unauthorized entities from the database. However, there is a project working in this direction [5], but for an outdated version of Spring Security.

Finally, our previous work [2] describes how we intercept the communication between an application and the object-graph mapper in a non intrusive manner.

4   Types of Operations

In this section, we describe the operations offered by the *Session* interface. They consist of several, partly overloaded, functions. All line numbers correspond to the *Session* interface version mentioned earlier.

Read Collection: The *Session* interface defines 40 methods returning collections of entities satisfying some form of filtering. Based on the parameters, we identified 5 subgroups. Each of these groups use a different definition for filtering. However, for each of these definitions, the method is offered multiple times with all combinations of 3 optional parameters (sorting, pagination, query depth), resulting in groups of 8 methods offering the same filtering functionality. In Line 80, we provide a collection of ids (e.g. a list of Long values) and OGM returns the corresponding entities. The next one (Line 168) is similar, however instead of providing the ids directly, the collection already contains the desired objects. The default behavior is to extract the ids and refetch the entities. To retrieve all entities of a specific (Java) class without filtering, the method from Line 251 can be used. Finally, in Line 329 and Line 412, we can provide more complex expressions. These are implemented against another interface (*Filter*). The strategy is to provide an implementation which receives runtime information (e.g., node names) during filter evaluation and returns parts of a Cypher statement. *Filters* are just a boolean concatenation of *Filter* instances.

Single Entity Read: In contrast to the previous operation, reading specific entities (Line 494) is only possible by providing the id of the desired entity. Therefore, we do not have the opportunity to define filters.

Save One Entity: When it comes to persisting entities (Line 511 and 521), the offered methods accept only one entity and an optional depth parameter, so no batch saving operations are supported altogether.

Delete Entities: We can delete a single entity by passing it to the *delete* function from Line 528. However, the whole entity has to be passed - there is no method accepting only the id.

In contrast when deleting multiple entities at once, we can pass collections of entities or delete based on filters (see Lines 535, 545 and 552).

Counting Entities: Features like pagination, require the total number of entities. We must also modify the responsible methods (Lines 658 and 667) to remain consistent with the user's view. Again, like on collection reading, it is possible to define custom filters here.

Free Text Queries: The functions in Lines 613, 625, 637, and 650 accept native Cypher queries and can implement any functionality without the possibility to derive their purpose from the function declaration.

No Access Control Relevance: The remaining methods are without impact on the security of entities and provide functionalities like transaction handling or clearing the query cache.

5   Modifying Queries

Modifying Multi-entity Operations: When working with multiple entities at once (read, delete, and count), at least one function for each operation accepts filters as an argument. This means as a general approach, we redirect the function call and enhance the original filtering semantics (e.g. query by id or name starts with) with our custom one. We have the possibility to return an empty collection in case of no accessible entities.

Modifying Single-Entity Operations: On single-entity operations, the developer or user might know about the existence of an entity, forcing us to provide appropriate denied access notifications. Another difference is that single-entity functions only accept the entity and auxiliary parameters but no filters. Our solution is to craft a (free-text) query asking the database whether all the authorization requirements are satisfied, returning a boolean. Based on this result, we can execute the original request or report denied access by throwing an exception or providing a special return value.

6   Performance

As we are intercepting the usual process flow, we add some overhead. In our previous work [2], we showed that the interception itself is negligible. Therefore, we did not care about this kind of overhead. For performance measurements on our current work, we only compare the execution time of the original requests with the time taken to modify them plus the execution time of the modified version. We do this by loading the whole database (*loadAll**), reading a single entity (*loadOne*) and changing an existing entity (*saveOneExisting*). Requests from administrators or internal actions (e.g. triggered by a schedule) bypass the query alteration, therefore, we use them as our baseline (marked with *admin/internal*). Requests originating from the user are marked with *user*.

The setup of the test consists of a minimal example application. It clears the database and generates 1000 fresh entities and sets up auxiliary structures representing the encoded policies. Each test is then executed 100 times for warmup, followed by another 1000 times for the actual measurements.

Neo4j OGM has some built in caches which we explicitly cleared before performing an operation. This also had a side effect on *saveOneExisting* as the cache is used for dirty checking. Details can be found in the documentation [7].

Table 1. The performance test results

Operation	Mean user [ms] (SD)	Mean unmodified [ms] (SD)	Increase %
loadAll	68.93 (6.73)	57.25 (5.47)	20.4
loadAllNoopFilter	68.58 (4.75)	59.47 (2.71)	15.32
loadAllStartWithF.	69.75 (5.16)	60.85 (3.13)	14.63
loadOne	2.86 (0.87)	0.66 (0.13)	333.33
saveOneExisting	3.09 (1.37)	2.00 (1.25)	54.5

The numbers in Table 1 show our experiments measured in milliseconds, *SD* is the standard deviation. The column *increase in percent* assumes the unmodified request as 100%. The operation *loadAll* fetches all entities, i.e. in the unmodified version, the database does less filtering whereas in the access controlled version, we explicitly added filters resulting in increased overhead. For comparison, the *loadAllNoopFilter* had a filter in place which approved any entity. As this one had approximately the same effect as *loadAllStartWithFilter* (filter based on entity name), we believe adding a filter has an overhead of approximately 5% and our access control logic additionally adds about 15%.

During *loadOne*, we queried the entity by its Neo4j internal id which is probably the fastest possible method. Therefore, we assume that the access control check adds the measured amount of overhead. The write operation uses the same facility to ensure permissions and therefore should show the same absolute overhead. Since the relative overhead for *saveOneExisting* is much less compared to *loadOne*, the write operation must be much slower which is not surprising. However, the calculated absolute overhead increase for *loadOne* and *saveOneExisting* still differs due to the high standard deviation of the write operation samples.

7   Conclusion and Future Work

In this short paper, we extended a web application utilizing an object-graph mapper with an access control layer. Our approach on protecting data from unauthorized access is to offload the filtering into the database and only retrieve authorized data. This saves resources and minimizes the impact of code errors as no data can be leaked if not even loaded. However, we aim to still use the automatically generated queries in the OGM. Therefore, we summarized the methods offered by Neo4j OGM into categories (RQ1). For each category, we identified the performed operation and discussed its security implications (RQ2). For those which provided enough contextual information, we found suitable modifications so the framework would generate queries filtering out unauthorized entities already in the database or prevent unauthorized access by blocking access. Due to differences in the return types, we had to use slightly different approaches for single-entity access (RQ4) than when working with collections of entities (RQ3).

However, we did not consider filtering of free-text queries so far. Our proposed approach relies on the presence of contextual and semantic information. In free-text queries, this information is included in the query string, but not yet accessible. Therefore, we consider parsing these queries and extract the required information in our further research.

Due to space constraints, the content for this short paper had to be reduced. The extended version can be found at https://research.daho.at[2].

Acknowledgements. This research has been partly supported by the LIT Secure and Correct Systems Lab funded by the State of Upper Austria. This work has been supported by the COMET-K2 Center of the Linz Center of Mechatronics (LCM) funded by the Austrian federal government and the federal state of Upper Austria.

References

1. Bogaerts, J., Decat, M., Lagaisse, B., Joosen, W.: Entity-based access control: supporting more expressive access control policies. In: Proceedings of the 31st Annual Computer Security Applications Conference, pp. 291–300 (2015)
2. Hofer, D., Nadschläger, S., Mohamed, A., Küng, J.: Extending authorization capabilities of object relational/graph mappers by request manipulation. In: Strauss, C., Cuzzocrea, A., Kotsis, G., Tjoa, A.M., Khalil, I. (eds.) DEXA 2022. LNCS, vol. 13427, pp. 71–83. Springer International Publishing, Cham (2022). https://doi.org/10.1007/978-3-031-12426-6_6
3. Jarman, J., McCart, J.A., Berndt, D., Ligatti, J.: A dynamic query-rewriting mechanism for role-based access control in databases. In: AMCIS Proceedings (2008)
4. Leão, F., Azevedo, L.G., Baião, F., Cappelli, C.: Enforcing authorization rules in information systems. In: IADIS International Conference Applied Computing (2011)
5. Lecomte, F.: strategy-spring-security-acl (2016). https://github.com/lordlothar99/strategy-spring-security-acl
6. Neo4j Inc: Authentication and authorization. https://neo4j.com/docs/operations-manual/current/authentication-authorization/. Accessed 05 July 2022
7. Neo4j Inc: Reference - OGM Library. https://neo4j.com/docs/ogm-manual/current/reference/#reference:session:configuration. Accessed 08 July 2022
8. Rizvi, S., Mendelzon, A., Sudarshan, S., Roy, P.: Extending query rewriting techniques for fine-grained access control. In: Proceedings of the 2004 ACM SIGMOD International Conference on Management of Data, SIGMOD 2004, pp. 551–562. Association for Computing Machinery, New York (2004). https://doi.org/10.1145/1007568.1007631
9. Rosenthal, A., Sciore, E.: View security as the basis for data warehouse security. In: DMDW, p. 8 (2000)
10. VMware Inc: Spring Security. https://spring.io/projects/spring-security. Accessed 05 July 2022

---

[2] https://research.daho.at/papers/modifying-neo4js-ogm-queries-for-access-control.

Recommendation Systems

A Recommendation Method for Recipes Containing Unskillful Elements Using Naïve Bayes Classifier to Improve Cooking Skills

Xinyu Liu[✉] and Daisuke Kitayama

Kogakuin University, 1-24-2 Nishishinjuku, Shinjyuku-ku, Tokyo 163-8677, Japan
`em21029@ns.kogakuin.ac.jp, kitayama@cc.kogakuin.ac.jp`

Abstract. We cannot acquire cooking skills overnight; although our skills can be improved through repeated practice. This study proposes a method to recommend recipes that amateurs should attempt to turn failures into successes, based on their logs of cooking failures and successes. Initially, the user classifies past recipes and labels them as failures and successes. Next, we use a naive Bayes classifier to find the factors of failures and successes from the recipe's ingredients and cooking actions. By recommending recipes with multiple success factors and some failure factors, we aim to lower the psychological hurdle for attempting recipes with difficult factors that have resulted in failure earlier.

Keywords: Cooking recipe · Unskillful element extraction · Naïve Bayes · Ingredients · Cooking actions

1 Introduction

Recently, recipe submission sites such as Cookpad[1] and Rakuten Recipe[2] have been used to search for recipes that professionals and amateurs can use to cook diverse dishes.

Although users can select their favorite recipes, they may not be able to cook them as they wish due to various reasons, such as the lack of skill in using ingredients and cooking actions. We propose a recipe recommendation method that allows users to practice overcoming the causes of their cooking failures to solve these problems.

Specifically, we use the user's record of failures and successes, extract the necessary unskillful elements from them, and recommend recipes with those unskillful elements and a high success rate. For example, assume that the user is good at cooking salisbury steak and bad at fried chicken. The system extracts the skillful and unskillful elements from the recipes that the user is good at or bad at. If the user can cook "minced meat" well and cannot "fry" something well, the system recommends "meat cutlet" as a recipe that allows the user to practice the weak element based on these factors.

---

[1] https://cookpad.com/.
[2] https://recipe.rakuten.co.jp/.

© The Author(s), under exclusive license to Springer Nature Switzerland AG 2022
E. Pardede et al. (Eds.): iiWAS 2022, LNCS 13635, pp. 429–434, 2022.
https://doi.org/10.1007/978-3-031-21047-1_38

2   Related Work

2.1   Recipe Recommendation

There are many studies related to recipe recommendations. Ueda et al. [8] stated that it is important to consider the user's preferences when recommending recipes, and have proposed a recipe recommendation system that considers the user's likes and dislikes of ingredients. Yajima et al. [9] proposed a method to recommend "easy" cooking recipes by analyzing the content of recipes and considering user's experience level and then develop a recommendation system. Generally, recipe recommendation is based on the user's food preferences. This study addresses recipe recommendation to improve cooking ability, not for recipes that the user wants to eat. Of course, it is important to consider the user's food preferences, and we believe that combining these methods will improve the accuracy of recommendations.

We treat ingredients and cooking actions as simple words, but we believe that it is necessary to treat their structures appropriately. Kiddon et al. [2] are working on automatically extracting the structure of ingredients and actions, and we believe that using them together will enable more advanced recommendation.

2.2   Assistance for Beginner Cooks

We present several studies to assist beginner cooks. Fukumoto et al. [1] proposed a system that displays recipes in a flowchart format in order to reduce cooking errors by inexperienced cooks. Users with little cooking experience can easily understand the recipes with this system. A comparison was made between using a user-contributed recipe site and the proposed system to confirm its effectiveness. Mori et al. [4] proposed a method for automatically generating sentences indicating procedures from flow graphs that display procedures using cooking recipes. They created a template from a training corpus and generated statistical sentences using flow graphs as input. The flow graph was created by tagging "ingredients" and "tools", which are unique expressions in cooking recipes, and treating the extracted words as contact points.

In conventional research, most recipes are flowcharted or supplemented with additional information to make them easier to understand. Our approach differs from conventional methods in that it automatically identifies cooking methods that users have difficulty with and presents recipes for practicing those cooking methods.

3   Proposed Method

3.1   Components of a Cooking Recipe

We treat the factors of users' skillful/unskillful in recipe ingredients and cooking actions.

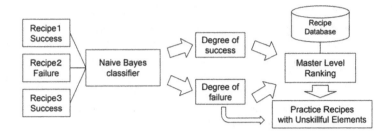

Fig. 1. Process flow of the proposed method

This study used recipes written in Japanese, uses strings of ingredient names as ingredients and verbs as cooking actions. We present these as features, which are vectors of 1 and 0 that are included or excluded in the recipe.

We describe the extraction method of the features. We refer to the pre-processing method in the study by Onita et al. [6] to extract cooking actions. Morphological analysis is performed on the recipe procedure using MeCab [3], and then each action is replaced with a higher-level word using an ontology. As an example of the processing performed, when the action is "add" exists, it is converted to "put." Verbs that are not registered in the ontology dictionary are excluded as "non-cooking actions". The ontology used in this study is the cooking ontology based on the work of Nanba et al. [5] published in the Cooking Ontology Construction Project.

3.2 Overview

Figure 1 shows the process flow of the proposed method. We assume that the user assigns a degree of success to each recipe based on historical cooking. The user labels each recipe a "success" or "failure" based on the assigned degree of success. Next, we extract the failure and success factors from the vector of past cooking recipes and their success/failure labels using a naive Bayes classifier. Finally, we calculate the mastery score of the candidate recipes. Recipes with high scores and failure factors are displayed as recommended results.

3.3 Naïve Bayes Classifier and Calculation of the Mastery Score

The extracted ingredients and cooking actions are analyzed using naïve Bayes in this experiment. We used MultinomialNB[3], a naive Bayesian classifier, to compare the relationship between the ingredients and cooking actions of the features and the subject's skill level. We use this when assuming a multinomial distribution is assumed for the feature vector.

---

[3] https://scikit-learn.org/stable/modules/generated/sklearn.naive_bayes. MultinomialNB.html.

The unskillful element is defined in this study as the cause of failure extracted from the user's cooking history. This study then converts them into successes. Therefore, "success" is defined as the result of analyzing the relationship between each element of the vector and the success label using the naive Bayes classifier. "Failure" is defined as the result of analyzing the relationship between each element of the vector and the failure label. We extract these values as the degree of success and failure by using scikit-learn's attribute of feature_log_prob_. The difference between the degree of success and failure is the degree of mastery. A higher mastery indicates that the feature has been mastered.

3.4   Recipe Recommendation with Unskillful Elements

This section describes the recipe recommendation method. First, the sum of the mastery level assigned to each ingredient and cooking action is calculated as the score of the candidate recipe.

$$score(r) = \sum_{e \in E_r} acq(e) \tag{1}$$

E_r in Eq. 1 is the set of ingredients and cooking actions for recipe r, and acq is a function that returns the mastery level of e.

As the score is the sum of the degrees of mastery, a higher value indicates a higher chance of success. The recipes that are more likely to succeed are more likely to be practiced with unskillful elements. We consider the bottom N elements in the user's history to be unskillful elements and recommend recipes that contain unskillful elements and have high scores.

4   Example of Recipe Recommendation

4.1   Usage Data

This section presents a working example of the method. We used 442,504 recipes from Rakuten Recipes [7]. We selected ten recipes as user's cooking history. Each success label was given by the authors subjectively. The number of unskillful elements was set to $N = 10$.

4.2   Calculation of the Degree of Mastery

Using the extracted ingredients and cooking actions, we calculated the mastery level of the ten culinary characteristics using the MultinomialNB naïve Bayesian classifier described in Sect. 3.3. The left part of Table 1 shows the elements with the highest mastery. The right part of the table shows the elements with the lowest mastery levels. Ten cases are shown for each of them.

In this input, the favorite ingredient and jam only appear in one recipe. It is not clear whether they are truly the users' weak points or not. Therefore, we must calculate a probability based on the general ease of occurrence and the number of occurrences in history.

Table 1. Skillful and unskillful elementss with higher mastery and the degree of mastery

	Feature name	Mastery level		Feature name	Mastery level
Skillful	Draw	1.329	Unskillful	Onion	−1.666
	Cover	1.042		Bake	−1.443
	Chicken leg meat	1.042		Water	−1.155
	Fit in	0.636		Simmer	−1.155
	Shake	0.636		Turn over	−0.749
	Green onion	0.636		Beef rib	−0.749
	King oyster mushroom	0.636		Ground beef and pork	−0.749
	Your choice of ingredients	0.636		Jam of your choice	−0.749
	Grated ginger	0.636		Mustard	−0.749
	Potato starch	0.636		Fruit juice	−0.749

Table 2. Top recommended mastery recipes

Recipe title	Mastery level	Included unskill feature
Fried bean sprouts	6.759	Bake
Easy Crab Croquette	6.597	Onion
Sauteed Chicken	6.528	Bake
Paella	6.528	Bake
Rice omelet with melted cheese	6.528	Bake

4.3   Recipe Recommendation Results

First, recipes with any of the bottom ten mastery levels shown in Table 1 were extracted from the database. Next, the scores of those recipes were calculated. Finally, we ranked the recipes by their scores.

The top five recipes are shown in Table 2. The recipe "Easy Crab Croquette" is recommended as a recipe for practicing "onion". In this recipe, the ingredients that appear in the successful recipes in history, such as "chicken thighs", and the two actions with high learning levels, "sprinkle" and "boil", appear. We checked the procedure of this recipe. "Onion" is used as an ingredient, and we consider it appropriate as a recipe for practice. The weakest element in four of the top five recipes is "baking". For "Sauteed Chicken", "baking" is the main operation, and therefore, it is appropriate as a recipe for practice. However, baking is used only for some of the ingredients in the other recipes, making it an inappropriate recipe for practice. Therefore, we can improve the results by determining if it is a major ingredient or action. We believe this can be done.

5   Conclusion

This study proposed a method for extracting failure and success factors, and a method for recommending recipes to convert failed recipes into successful ones.

Future issues are summarized. First, we plan to conduct evaluation experiments using the comparison method. As a comparison method, we consider ranking by the number of unsuccessful factors. The language used in this work is Japanese, and the possibility of using other languages will be considered in future research.

Finally, this method does not consider the influence of the number of materials on success and failure. Naïve Bayes cannot handle continuous values such as quantities; hence, we must extend it to handle them. We will also conduct an experiment using the aforementioned studies to evaluate the system's effectiveness.

Acknowledgements. This work was supported by ISPS KAKENHI of Grant-in-Aid for Scientific Research(C) Grant Number 21K12147.

References

1. Fukumoto, H., Ohsugi, T., Matsushita, M.: Presenting action-centered recipe to reduce cooking failure for beginners. In: The 34th Annual Conference of the Japanese Society for Artificial Intelligence, no. 1G4-ES-5-02 (2020)
2. Kiddon, C., Ponnuraj, G.T., Zettlemoyer, L., Choi, Y.: Mise en Place: unsupervised interpretation of instructional recipes. In: Proceedings of the 2015 Conference on Empirical Methods in Natural Language Processing, Lisbon, Portugal, pp. 982–992. Association for Computational Linguistics, September 2015. https://doi.org/10.18653/v1/D15-1114. https://aclanthology.org/D15-1114
3. Kudo, T., Yamamoto, K., Matsumoto, Y.: Applying conditional random fields to Japanese morphological analysis. In: Proceedings of the 2004 Conference on Empirical Methods in Natural Language Processing, pp. 230–237 (2004)
4. Mori, S., Maeta, H., Yamakata, Y., Sasada, T.: Flow graph corpus from recipe texts. In: Proceedings of the Ninth International Conference on Language Resources and Evaluation (LREC 2014), pp. 2370–2377 (2014)
5. Nanba, H., Doi, Y., Tsujita, M., Takezawa, T., Sumiya, K.: Construction of a cooking ontology from cooking recipes and patents. In: Proceedings of the 2014 ACM International Joint Conference on Pervasive and Ubiquitous Computing: Adjunct Publication, pp. 507–516 (2014)
6. Oonita, T., Kitayama, D.: Extraction method for a recipe's uniqueness based on recipe frequency and lexrank of procedures. In: Proceedings of the 22nd International Conference on Information Integration and Web-Based Applications & Services, pp. 241–245 (2020)
7. Rakuten Group, Inc.: Rakuten recipe data, August 2012
8. Ueda, M., Takahata, M., Nakajima, S.: User's food preference extraction for personalized cooking recipe recommendation. In: Proceedings of the Second International Conference on Semantic Personalized Information Management: Retrieval and Recommendation, SPIM 2011, vol. 781, pp. 98–105. CEUR-WS.org, Aachen, DEU (2011)
9. Yajima, A., Kobayashi, I.: "easy" cooking recipe recommendation considering user's conditions. In: 2009 IEEE/WIC/ACM International Joint Conference on Web Intelligence and Intelligent Agent Technology, vol. 3, pp. 13–16. IEEE (2009)

Extraction of Complementary Topics Based on Phrase Importance and Co-occurrence in Technical Blogs

Masaru Hakii[✉] and Daisuke Kitayama

Kogakuin University, Tokyo, Japan
em21018@ns.kogakuin.ac.jp, kitayama@cc.kogakuin.ac.jp

Abstract. When acquiring knowledge in a certain field, it is important to obtain comprehensive information. However, it is difficult for users to extract missing information in unknown fields by themselves. Therefore, this study proposes a subtopic extraction method that can supplement missing information step-wise by presenting the user with important unknown phrases related to the topic the user is currently learning about by performing Web searches; the phrases are such that they are highly relevant to the user's browsing history. We then conducted small-scale experiments and found that topic extraction using phrase co-occurrence as a reference for the next search keyword to be entered is effective compared to conventional topic extraction using LexRank.

Keywords: Complementary topics · LexRank · Technical blogs · Search assistance

1 Introduction

In recent years, the improvement in search technology has made it easier for users to obtain the information they seek. Although it is important to obtain comprehensive information when acquiring knowledge, it is difficult for users to extract missing information in an unknown field by themselves. In this study, we propose a subtopic (complementary topic) extraction method that can supplement missing information step-wise by presenting users with unknown phrases that are important to the topic they are currently acquiring information about through Web searches; these phrases are such that they are highly relevant to the browsing history of the user.

In recent years, articles on technical blogs have become increasingly abundant. Qiita[1] and Developers.IO[2] are blogs about programming and other topics. Such blogs often contain systematic articles on various terms and information. Using them, we propose a method for finding unknown phrases that co-occur with the phrases in the articles and extracting phrases that have high co-occurrence and should be learned next. Specifically, the importance of a phrase

---

[1] https://qiita.com.
[2] https://dev.classmethod.jp.

E. Pardede et al. (Eds.): iiWAS 2022, LNCS 13635, pp. 435–440, 2022.
https://doi.org/10.1007/978-3-031-21047-1_39

is calculated using LexRank, and its relevance to browsing history is expressed in terms of phrase co-occurrence.

The contributions of this study are that by using the user's browsing history, we define an acquisition recommendation that implies the priority of acquisition for an unknown topic and experiments reveal that, compared to the simple presentation of important phrases (LexRank method), phrases co-occurrent with viewed phrases are more likely to be judged as valid by humans.

2   Related Work

The purpose of this research is to enable users to efficiently grasp the entire contents of topics for search keywords. The following methods are proposed for learning a topic.

Yumoto et al. [6] proposed the notion of a "page set ranking," which ranks each pertinent set of searched Web pages. Umemoto et al. [5] proposed a method for visualizing unseen information in terms of importance, relevance, and novelty for a search query in a comprehensiveness-oriented task. Nadamoto et al. [4] proposed a method for extracting content holes, which refer to information unknown to users by extracting viewpoints on a certain theme in the Web space and comparing viewpoints.

These related studies do not consider the order of acquisition for the user, as their goal is to obtain a complete picture of the search keywords or topics. This study differs from the aforementioned studies in that it considers the priority of the topic that should be learned next in order to easily obtain a full understanding of the search keywords.

3   Proposed Method

For a set of search results, we present phrases that are missing from the user's past browsing history that contain topics that should be learned next. This study used blogs written in Japanese. As Japanese verbs are located at the end of sentences, this study took this into consideration.

The procedure of the proposed method is as follows. First, obtain an article set based on the search query, second, extract phrases representing the topic from the article set, third, calculate the recommendation for the learning of unknown phrases, finally, eliminate redundancy of unknown phrases and decompose them into keywords

In the acquisition of the article set, it containing the search keyword in the title or body of the article is extracted. If there are multiple search keywords, the product set of articles that can be extracted with each keyword is extracted.

3.1   Extraction of Phrases Representing a Topic from a Set of Articles

Sentences usually contain multiple topics. In this study, it is desirable for each sentence to contain one topic. Therefore, a phrase is defined as a sentence that is analyzed for affiliation and combined until the last word of the affiliation becomes a noun or a verb or the end of a sentence. In addition, there are cases where the words in the last clause of the affix are inappropriate for the phrase to be mastered. For example, the words "OK" and "impression". Since these words are often used in sentences containing opinions, etc. Therefore, if the last clause of the target contains these words, the phrase is not adopted as a phrase that represents the topic. Furthermore, the longer the phrase is, the more likely it is to contain multiple elements. Therefore, phrases whose length exceeds 30 words were not adopted. Examples of phrases that describe topics are "Installing MySQL," "How to connect to a database" etc. The vectors composing each phrase were created using the word vectors learned from the text of all articles and the title sentences, and averaging the product of the vectors of each word and the tfidf value. The word vectors were learned by Word2vec from about 500,000 article titles and the body text on Qiita. The tfidf values were defined by the formula 1. The first term of the formula 1 defines the frequency of occurrence of the word w in the phrase d. In the formula 1, C denotes the number of occurrences of w in d, and L denotes the sum of the number of occurrences of all words in the phrase d. The S in the formula 1 denotes the number of all articles and $S(w)$ denotes the number of articles containing the word w. Only nouns and verbs were used in the vectors, using the morphological analyzer MeCab [3]. For the nouns, personal names, numbers, and pronouns were excluded.

$$TFIDF(d, w) = \frac{C(d, w)}{L(d)} \times log(\frac{S}{S(w) + 1}) \tag{1}$$

3.2   Calculation for Learning of Unknown Phrases

For each phrase in the set of articles that have not yet been viewed, we calculated the degree of recommendation for acquisition, which is the degree to which the phrase should be acquired next. The criteria for a high recommendation are high importance in articles in search results and high co-occurrence in articles containing known phrases. These are based on the concept that what is important should be learned and that, if a phrase contained in an article that is viewed (hereafter referred to as a known phrase) also appears in other articles, the phrase contained in that article is related to the known knowledge and should be learned next. Based on the aforementioned two concepts, the formula for calculating the recommendation for learning is Eq. 2, where F is the importance of the phrase, K is the co-occurrence with known phrases, t is the target phrase, Q are all the articles in the search results by input query, and H is the set of known phrases of the user.

$$rec(t, Q, H) = F(t, Q) \times K(t, Q, H) \tag{2}$$

In this study, we use a summarization algorithm, LexRank [2], to calculate the importance $F(t, Q)$. LexRank is a text summarization method based on PageRank proposed by Erkan et al. The sentences are replaced with phrases, and important and typical phrases have higher values.

The second criterion, $K(t, Q, H)$, is whether the phrase H is likely to appear in articles containing the phrase H that appears in the viewed articles. It is defined as the number of articles containing the known phrase $h \in H$ among the unseen articles Q in which the target phrase t appears.

The procedure is, first, determine known phrases from all phrases. Second, extract a set of articles in which the target phrase appears. Finally, calculate the number of articles in the article set in which the known phrase appears Phrases that are similar to the known and target phrases are treated as known and target phrases in the same way, using the cosine similarity. The similarity threshold is set to 0.7. This value is based on the authors' experience.

3.3 Elimination of Redundancy in Phrases

Next, to eliminate redundancy from the phrases to be learned, we used a document summarization method called MMR [1]. MMR is defined by the formula 3. It is a method that sequentially determines the sentences to be extracted with the goal of eliminating redundancy while maintaining relevance.

$$\arg \max_{t_i \in R/S} \left[\lambda rec(t_i, Q, H) - (1 - \lambda) \max_{t_j \in S} sim(t_i, t_j) \right] \qquad (3)$$

In this method, R is the ranked phrase set, S is the selected phrase set, rec is the next degree to be learned, and sim is the similarity between phrases. In this case, rec is normalized to match the value range of sim. Normalization is performed by subtracting the minimum value from each value and dividing it by the difference between the maximum and minimum values. After eliminating redundancy, words are extracted from the phrases. Words are extracted from the nouns and verbs that make up the vector.

4 Evaluation Experiment

4.1 Experimental Settings

Evaluation experiments were conducted to demonstrate the effectiveness of the proposed method. The value of λ in the formula 3 was set to 0.7. We use two methods for comparison. The first method is only uses the first term of the formula 2, where the degree of phrases including the next topic to be learned is the importance only (hereafter referred to as the LexRank) method. The second method is only uses the second term of the formula 2, where the degree of phrases including the next topic to be learned is only the co-occurrence with known phrases (hereafter called the co-occurrence-oriented) method. The purpose of these two methods was to test the usefulness of a method that combines the importance of a phrase with the degree to which it is related to the user's knowledge.

For each method, the phrases containing the next topic to be learned were calculated, and the percentage of correct answers was calculated for each set of words extracted from each phrase.

Table 1. Experimental results: the percentage of correct answers

Method	$Q1$	$Q2$
LexRank method	39.4%	38.7%
Co-occurrence-oriented method	44.5%	42.4%
Proposed method	53.4%	43.8%

We used approximately 500,000 articles on Qiita as experimental data. The subjects were seven university students studying informatics who were asked to participate in the study so that they could appropriately and adequately understand the topics as written in Qiita. After viewing some articles from the search results, we presented five word sets extracted by each method, and then asked them how many words were included in each word set as reference keywords for the search. The search keywords were $Q1$: "mac mecab" and $Q2$: "python random forest". In the "mac mecab" search, the subjects viewed three articles on how to install mecab on a mac prepared by the experimenter at the beginning of the experiment. In "python random forests," the subjects viewed one article on how to implement random forests using python and one article on the basics of random forests, which were prepared by the experimenter before the experiment began.

Some of the phrases extracted from $Q1$ article include "Installing mecab on a Mac, Preparing mecab" and $Q2$ article include "Belonging to the objective variable" and "Random Forests is an ensemble learning method".

Some of the results of executing the proposed method are "**morphological analysis stopword** for **morphological analysis definition**" by $Q1$ and "The **research** is to **compensate** for this **bias** with and **without** a **teacher**" by $Q2$. The words in bold in the tables are the words extracted from the phrases.

4.2 Results and Discussion

Table 1 shows the experimental results for $Q1$ and $Q2$. The percentage of correct answers is calculated by averaging the percentage of each word set provided by each subject that contains the informative word. The average percentage of correct answers in the table is the average of the percentage of correct answers in each word set by each method.

From the experimental results with two search terms, we found that the proposed method, co-occurrence-oriented method, and LexRank method, in that order, gave better correct answers. This indicates that the proposed method is useful and that co-occurrence is more effective than the importance obtained by the LexRank method in increasing the percentage of correct answers. A one-way ANOVA was conducted under the null hypothesis that there is no difference in the mean percentage of correct answers for the word set calculated by each method. The p values for the $Q1$ and $Q2$ methods were 0.33 and 0.83, respectively. As the null hypothesis could not be rejected owing to $p < 0.05$, it can be concluded that there is no significant difference in the mean percentage of correct answers. As the number of subjects was only 7, we believe that we need to increase the size of the samples to confirm the hypothesis.

5   Summary and Future Issues

As it is difficult for a user with no knowledge of a certain search topic to grasp missing knowledge after browsing articles in a list of search results, we proposed a method to supplement that knowledge. Specifically, we extracted the difference between the topics in the browsing history of technical blogs and the set of search results, and based on the idea that topics that are important and related to known knowledge should be learned, we created an index that should be learned next, and extracted the topics based on this index. We were able to demonstrate the usefulness of the proposed method through evaluation experiments. Future tasks are to conduct experiments on a larger scale.

Acknowledgements. This work was supported by ISPS KAKENHI of Grant-in-Aid for Scientific Research(C) Grant Number 21K12147.

References

1. Carbonell, J., Goldstein, J.: The use of MMR, diversity-based reranking for reordering documents and producing summaries. Association for Computing Machinery, New York (1998). https://doi.org/10.1145/290941.291025
2. Erkan, G., Radev, D.R.: LexRank: graph-based lexical centrality as salience in text summarization. J. Artif. Intell. Res. **22**, 457–479 (2004)
3. Kudo, T., Yamamoto, K., Matsumoto, Y.: Applying conditional random fields to Japanese morphological analysis. In: Proceedings of the 2004 Conference on Empirical Methods in Natural Language Processing, Barcelona, Spain, pp. 230–237. Association for Computational Linguistics, July 2004. https://aclanthology.org/W04-3230
4. Nadamoto, A., Aramaki, E., Abekawa, T., Murakami, Y.: Content hole search in community-type content. In: Proceedings of the 18th International Conference on World Wide Web, WWW 2009, pp. 1223–1224. Association for Computing Machinery, New York (2009). https://doi.org/10.1145/1526709.1526939
5. Umemoto, K., Yamamoto, T., Tanaka, K.: ScentBar: a query suggestion interface visualizing the amount of missed relevant information for intrinsically diverse search. In: SIGIR 2016 - Proceedings of the 39th International ACM SIGIR Conference on Research and Development in Information Retrieval, pp. 405–414 (2016). https://doi.org/10.1145/2911451.2911546
6. Yumoto, T., Tanaka, K.: Page sets as web search answers. In: Sugimoto, S., Hunter, J., Rauber, A., Morishima, A. (eds.) ICADL 2006. LNCS, vol. 4312, pp. 244–253. Springer, Heidelberg (2006). https://doi.org/10.1007/11931584_27

Feature Relevance Analysis of Product Reviews to Support Online Shopping

Fumiya Yamaguchi[1][(✉)], Felix Dollack[1][(✉)], Mayumi Ueda[2,3][(✉)], and Shinsuke Nakajima[1][(✉)]

[1] Kyoto Sangyo University, Motoyama, Kamigamo, Kita-ku, Kyoto 603-8555, Japan
{g1954390,felix,nakajima}@cc.kyoto-su.ac.jp
[2] University of Marketing and Distribution Sciences, 3-1 Gakuen-Nishimachi, Nishi-ku, Kobe, Hyogo 651-2188, Japan
Mayumi_Ueda@red.umds.ac.jp
[3] Cybermedia Center, Osaka University, 1-32, Machikaneyama-cho, Toyonaka, Osaka 560-0043, Japan

Abstract. The number of online shoppers has been increasing in recent years. Online shopping involves the risk that the purchased product may not be what was expected. Recently, the number of product review videos has also been increasing, and more users are using them as a reference because they provide a more accurate understanding of how the product is used than conventional reviews. With this development in mind, we have been developing a review video recommendation system to support online shopping. Our system helps users to know which product review videos they should watch. In this paper, we propose a review video feature analysis method, which is a necessary technology to realize the proposed system, and conduct two evaluation experiments to confirm the effectiveness of the proposed method. The results of the evaluation revealed that the proposed system received good ratings from the users, which confirmed the effectiveness of the proposed method.

Keywords: Comment analysis · Product reviews · Review video · YouTube

1 Introduction

Online shoppers generally can only refer to images of product descriptions and reviews written by users who have purchased the products. If a users purchases a product based only on images of the product whose size cannot be compared or textual information in a review section, there is a risk that the product may not be what they were expecting. Therefore, we have recently seen an increase in the number of product review video postings. However, it is difficult to efficiently listen to only videos that provide the desired information because it is hard to know the contents of the videos in advance. Given this background, we believe that users will be able to watch videos more efficiently if they are informed about which feature of a product each video describes before playing the video. In this paper, we propose a feature analysis method to support online shopping and report the results of evaluation experiments.

E. Pardede et al. (Eds.): iiWAS 2022, LNCS 13635, pp. 441–446, 2022.
https://doi.org/10.1007/978-3-031-21047-1_40

2   Related Work

It is difficult to understand the contents of a video in advance, and it is difficult to efficiently listen to only those video with the desired information. Therefore, previous research has been conducted to classify videos based on the sentiment of video comments [1]. Similarly, Siersdorfer et al. propose a comment analysis method for YouTube using machine learning techniques [2]. In online shopping, reviews and word-of-mouth are important factors in making a decision to purchase a product. However, it is very time consuming to read through all review comments. Therefore, Haque et al. worked on sentiment of reviews using a machine learning method trained on an Amazon dataset [3]. Basani et al. summarized product reviews by classifying them into positive, negative, and neutral categories [4]. Zhang et al. performed sentiment analysis and opinion extraction of product reviews considering textual subjectivity [5]. Furthermore, Matsunami et al. constructed a dictionary of evaluation expressions based on review analysis that specialized in cosmetic items and developed an automatic review scoring method [6]. In addition, Scaffidi et al. proposed an automatic product retrieval that satisfies shoppers' requirements by extracting product features from reviews [7].

Thus, efforts aimed at summarizing the content of videos and reviews are flourishing. However, there have not been enough efforts to conduct feature relevance analysis of product review videos themselves. Against this backdrop, this study aims to conduct feature relevance analysis of product review videos for the purpose of online shopping support.

3   Scoring Method by Features

In recent years, YouTube[1] has become a well-known video-sharing site. A vast number of videos are uploaded to the above site on a daily basis, and product review videos are also actively published and viewed. When viewing product review videos during online shopping, it is important to know whether or not there are reviews of specific features among the multiple features (hereinafter referred to simply as "features") that serve as criteria for making a decision to purchase the product in question.

3.1   Processing Steps of the Feature Analysis Method for Review Videos

First, frequently appearing words in the video were extracted manually and classified to construct a dictionary for each feature of the product, as shown in the center of Fig. 1. The higher the importance score, the more relevant each word is to each feature.

---

[1] YouTube, https://www.youtube.com/.

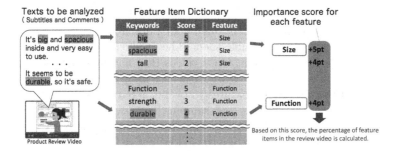

Fig. 1. Feature dictionary and automatic scoring of features in product review videos

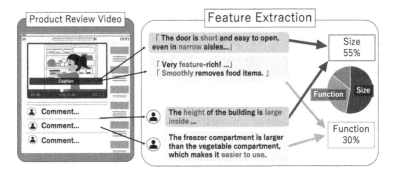

Fig. 2. Analysis method of feature relevance for product review videos

As for the construction of dictionaries, there are previous studies that worked on automatic dictionary creation. Taniguchi et al. have been working on improving dictionaries of evaluation expressions specialized for cosmetic items, and have studied efficient automatic score-rigging by constructing a dictionary of evaluation expressions based on Word2Vec [8]. However, it is difficult to fully automate the process from the viewpoint of accuracy.

Next, the presence or absence of feature expressions in the subtitle and comments attached to the video is checked using the constructed dictionary.

Finally, by totaling the number of sentences extracted for each feature, the ratio or importance of each product feature in the video is calculated. By performing the above processes, we aim to construct a system that enables the presentation of the ratio of features as shown in Fig. 2.

4   Evaluation Experiment

Two evaluation experiments were conducted. The first experiment was to evaluate the accuracy of the proposed method. The second experiment was to evaluate the usability of the proposed system. A total of 11 male participants in their 20s participated in both experiments.

We selected products that are relatively expensive as precision instruments and products that people are cautious about purchasing because they are not sure of the size or how to assemble them. The products selected were (1) Desk, (2) iPad, and (3) Camping Tent. Only videos that had been viewed more than 10,000 times were selected.

We limited the number of features to be extracted to five features per category. For review videos of desks and camping tents, we used the following five feature categories: Size, Function, Design, Cost performance, and Assembly. For review videos about the iPad, we use the following five features: Weight, Camera, Sound quality, Design, and Cost performance.

4.1 Accuracy Evaluation of Feature Analysis Method for Video

Participants were asked to watch product review videos and respond to which extend they perceived the information of each feature was included in the videos. The average of the participants' answers is used as the Ground Truth data. Finally, we compare the feature proportions using Ground Truth and the feature proportions determined by the proposed method to verify the degree of agreement by Pearson correlation coefficient and cosine similarity.

Experimental Results: In the (1) Desk video, the correlation coefficient and cosine similarity of the proposed method when both Ground Truth and subtitles and comments were analyzed were 0.98 and 0.98, respectively, and for subtitles only: 0.97 and 0.98. Thus, the cosine similarity for all other products showed high similarity. Furthermore, taking the average of the correlation coefficients for the three videos, we obtain 0.67 for the subtitle only and 0.47 for the subtitle and comment. Basically, the proposed method shows a strong correlation with Ground Truth, which confirms the effectiveness of the proposed method.

Consideration: The results of the accuracy evaluation experiments confirmed that the proposed method for feature relevance analysis of videos is generally effective. It is considered necessary to improve the accuracy of the proposed method by extending the dictionary or by other means. In addition, the number of videos used for evaluation was small because only one video in each category was used in this experiment. In the future, we would like to expand the number of videos used in the experiment and conduct a larger experiment that is less likely to be influenced by specific videos.

4.2 System Usability Evaluation

In the system usability evaluation experiment, the effectiveness of the proposed system was evaluated using the System Usability Scale (SUS) [9]. The SUS is a questionnaire that enables a numerical evaluation of system usability. The questionnaire consists of 10 questions with alternating positive and negative questions. The respondents were asked to answer on a 5-point scale from 1 (strongly disagree) to 5 (strongly agree). The results of the responses are transformed

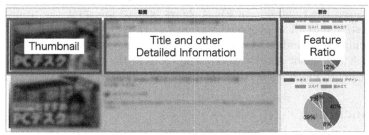

Video Thumbnail Images and Titles   Analysis Results
(Click to Play Video)

Fig. 3. Proposed system to be evaluated

Table 1. System usability scale questions

#	Question	Average score (1–5)
1	I think that I would like to use this system frequently	4.18
2	I found the system unnecessarily complex	1.64
3	I thought the system was easy to use	4.27
4	I think that I would need the support of a technical person to be able to use this system	1.55
5	I found the various functions in this system were well integrated	4.18
6	I thought there was too much inconsistency in this system	1.73
7	I would imagine that most people would learn to use this system very quickly	4.63
8	I found the system very cumbersome to use	1.55
9	I felt very confident using the system	4.45
10	I needed to learn a lot of things before I could get going with this system	1.64

SUS Score		Grade Table		
		SUS score	Grade	Adjective Rating
Average	84.09	> 80.3	A	Excellent
		68 - 80.3	B	Good
Standard Deviation	8.61	68	C	Okay
		51-68	D	Poor
		< 51	E	Awful

Fig. 4. SUS score of the proposed system

and calculated on a 100-point scale to evaluate the usability of the system. The proposed system that was evaluated is shown in Fig. 3.

Experimental Results and Consideration: The SUS question items and the average values of the participants' responses to each question are shown in Table 1. The results of the evaluation experiment show that the score of the proposed system is 84.09. The standard deviation between participants is 8.61.

The table on the right side of Fig. 4 shows how to interpret the results of the SUS questionnaire. The proposed system was rated highly in all the questions. Considering the standard deviation, the proposed system is rated somewhere between A: Excellent and B: Good. The score of the proposed system is much higher than 68, which means that the proposed system has high system usability.

5   Conclusion

In this paper, we propose a feature relevance analysis method for product review videos to support online shopping. The feature relevance analysis of product review videos using a feature dictionary facilitates the judgment of which review videos could be of interest to the user and should be viewed. In the future we aim to improve the accuracy of the feature analysis method by expanding the feature dictionary. Based on the results of the evaluation experiments, we plan to add new features and improve the proposed method.

Acknowledgements. This work was supported by multiple JSPS KAKENHI research grants (19K12243, 20H04293, 22K12281). It is also a product of research activity of the Institute of Advanced Technology and the Center for Sciences towards Symbiosis among Human, Machine and Data which was financially supported by a Kyoto Sangyo University Research Grant (M2001).

References

1. Muhammad, A.N., et al.: Sentiment analysis of positive and negative of YouTube comments using Naïve Bayes - support vector machine (NBSVM) classifier. In: ICOMITEE: International Conference on Computer Science, Information Technology, and Electrical Engineering (2019)
2. Siersdorfer, S., Chelaru, S., Pedro, J.S., Altingovde, I.S., Nejdl, W.: Analyzing and mining comments and comment ratings on the social web. ACM Trans. Web 8(3), 1–39 (2014). Article 17
3. Haque, T.U., et al.: Sentiment analysis on large scale Amazon product reviews. In: IEEE International Conference on Innovative Research and Development (2018)
4. Basani, Y., et al.: Application of sentiment analysis on product review e-commerce. In: International Conference on Advance and Scientific Innovation (ICASI), vol. 1175 (2019)
5. Zhang, Z., et al.: Utility scoring of product reviews. In: The 15th ACM International Conference on Information and Knowledge Management (CIKM 2006), pp. 51–57 (2006)
6. Matsunami, Y., et al.: Explaining item ratings in cosmetic product reviews. In: IMECS 2016 (2016)
7. Scaffidi, C., et al.: Red Opal: product-feature scoring from reviews. In: EC 2007: The 8th ACM Conference on Electronic Commerce, pp. 182–191, June 2007
8. Ueda, M., et al.: A research on constructing evaluative expression dictionaries for cosmetics based on Word2Vec. In: iiWAS 2021, pp. 84–90 (2021)
9. Brooke, J.: SUS—a quick and dirty usability scale. In: Jordan, P.W., Thomas, B., Weerdmeester, B.A., McClelland, A.L. (eds.) Usability Evaluation in Industry. Taylor and Francis, London (1996)

Annotation System for Dialogue Datasets of Older Adult's with Photos and Storytelling

Seiki Tokunaga[ID], Shogo Takata[ID], Kazuhiro Tamura[ID],
and Mihoko Otake-Matsuura[(✉)][ID]

RIKEN Center for Advanced Intelligence Project (AIP), Tokyo, Japan
{seiki.tokunaga,mihoko.otake}@riken.jp
https://www.riken.jp/research/labs/aip/

Abstract. We have developed a state-of-the-art "Dialogue-Based System with Photo and Storytelling" (DBSPS). The system runs automatically when the experimental schedule is on time to reduce cumbersome screen-based operation (e.g., tap) as much as possible for older adults to be ready for home-based use. In this paper, we present an original annotation system that is designed to create a corpus by collecting data with our system. Along with our experimental conditions, it is essential to display the images and stories used as experimental conditions and the user's questions, answers, and responses. Using the system, we conducted three annotations tasks (i.e., *question form annotation, naturalness annotation, and similarity annotation*). First, question form annotation is checking whether the user's utterance is a question form or not. The second is naturalness, which aims to identify how our system could respond naturally. Third, the similarity annotation is designed to check the coverage of our system's prepared datasets. Five annotators could use our system smoothly, and all tasks were completed without system errors. As a result, we identified areas to improve our dialogue system.

Keywords: Annotation system · Web system · Dialogue system for older adults · Crowdsourcing

1 Introduction

Many societies around the globe today are aging rapidly, and thus, maintaining quality of life (QOL) among their older adults, who often suffer from social isolation and loneliness, has become an important concern. To stay mentally and emotionally fit, older adults need positive social interactions and communication [2]. These social activities involve the activation of higher cognitive functions, and have the potential to prevent cognitive decline among the elderly [3]. Research has determined that communication with others balances the sympathetic nerve activity, leading to enhanced emotional well-being [4]. Furthermore, several psychological studies reported that the task of conversation is cognitively simulating [1]. Experiment with conversation that includes various cognitive tasks such as

E. Pardede et al. (Eds.): iiWAS 2022, LNCS 13635, pp. 447–452, 2022.
https://doi.org/10.1007/978-3-031-21047-1_41

attention, speech recognition, verbal comprehension, memory, planning, verbal generation, and speech generation [9].

Dialogue systems and robots which include smart speakers etc. are rapidly become key items for home-based experiment. However to our knowledge, there are few dialogue system which covers the experimental detailed conditions with remote and it's primary target user is older adults.

Hence, our research group has tackled to designed and developed a home-based dialogue system for the cognitive training for older adults. Our research team has proposed a novel dialogue system called Dialogue-Based System Photo and Storytelling (DBSPS). The system has been developed and evaluated in older adult's home [6,7]. We have successfully completed our system full remote experiment under COVID-19 situation in Japan [8]. When we consider the analysis collected data can be analyzed in more detail by adding metadata to interpret the data. Since, In this paper, we report a novel annotation system (AnnoDial) which is s well suited for our data sets and experimental manner. AnnoDial is designed to be an independent and easily operational system. However, the data format is applicable for DBSPS. First we clarify system primary requirements, then we develop and evaluate collected data. Then, we evaluate the datasets along with three research questions one is a categorization of utterance type from the users, second is a naturalness of QA pair and finally the similarity of questions listing from the data set.

1.1   System Architecture

Figure 1 represents the system architecture of the annotation of the dialogue system (AnnoDial). This system mainly consists of two parts: a preprocessor that is built as a data processing system (middle upper center of Fig. 1), which corresponds to the processing raw experimental data to a format compatible with the annotation system. During data processing, the system selects required data for analysis and integration with SimilarityAPI, which, as explained in Section, simulates the response from the dialogue system. The system also assigns a new ID for each question-answer pair to identify for analysis. The other part is a core application system developed as a web-based application (in the middle bottom center of Fig. 1) that serves as the interface for both annotator and administrator. The administrator can assign annotation tasks to the annotators. In addition, the administrator can confirm the progress of tasks assigned to individual annotators. Annotators can conduct annotations aforementioned three perspectives such as to confirm whether the utterance is question-answering, naturalness and the dialogue system contain similar questions.

We introduce a system used for annotator viewpoints. Annotators need to push the button on WebUI to indicate their judgment of each task. User Interface (UI) was built on the single web page; each task is represented as one page to avoid user confusion.

Fig. 1. Left: system architecture of AnnoDial, Right: user interface of AnnoDial

2 Experiment

2.1 Method

In the experiment, 12 topics (favorite things, neighborhood landmarks etc.) were presented to the users, and questions were obtained from the users for each topic. Aforementioned topis are selected based on previous our study [5]. We have prepared a total of 550 QA-pairs for each topic. The data collection procedure is as follows, At first, 50 QA-pairs were prepared, then 10 derivative questions for each question were added to reply to the same question with different expressions. For example, "Where did you buy bread?" is an original question, then we try to create the derivative question such as "Where did you go to buy the bread?". Consequently, 500 questions are derivatives of the original 50 questions. For crowdsourcing, a total of 4383 QA-pairs were used; from here we call them *experimental QA-Pairs*. Each experimental QA-pair belongs to one story with a single theme (e.g., favorite things) [5]. We assigned three kinds of tasks: Task 1: Annotations of whether the utterance is in the form of a question. Task 2: Annotation as to the naturalness of QA-pairs. Task 3: Annotation of whether the question is similar to the list. An annotation task have conducted as follows; on the system pick up a pair of QA from collected QA-Pairs, then the system also pick up five similar QA-Pairs from collected QA-Pairs with SimilarityAPI. Annotators can perform three different annotation tasks on a single dedicated web page. We outsource the abovementioned tasks from companies that provide crowdsourcing services.

2.2 Result

A simple manual of the system was sent in advance to the company, but no additional instructions were required to use the system. The five annotators could use the annotation system smoothly, and all tasks were completed without system errors.

Table 1. Result of annotation of utterance types; the number surrounded by () represents percentage of its breakdown

Type	A question (A1)	Not a question (A1)
A question (A2)	2732 (0.62)	486 (0.11)
Not a question (A2)	55 (0.01)	1110 (0.25)

Table 2. Result of naturalness of QA-pairs for each topic

# topic	Three	Four	Five	Avg
1	30.0	22.6	15.7	24
2	27.6	22.0	18.0	27
3	27.3	19.8	13.6	27
4	26.7	19.8	14.2	30
5	27.2	24.2	22.1	23
6	23.1	18.2	14.2	24
7	25.8	21.0	15.8	35
8	23.4	20.2	15.7	26
9	20.8	16.7	12.3	37
10	24.1	17.1	11.6	28
11	37.7	29.2	19.4	28
12	34.3	26.6	20.7	31
13	33.8	27.5	18.5	35

Table 3. Result of similarity of QA-pairs for each topic

# topic	Three	Four	Five	Avg
1	19.6	16.3	10.5	15.4
2	22.6	17.3	12.1	17.3
3	21.7	15.9	7.5	15.0
4	26.7	22.1	13.4	20.7
5	25.4	20.9	17.9	21.4
6	17.1	13.6	9.5	13.4
7	16.2	13.4	10.3	13.3
8	19.6	16.0	12.2	15.9
9	19.9	15.8	10.1	15.2
10	20.1	14.9	11.0	15.3
11	27.3	24.6	18.0	23.3
12	29.7	22.7	18.4	23.6
13	24.0	18.2	13.0	18.4

We assigned two annotators to judge whether the user's utterance seemed to be a question statement or not. The results of the first annotator (A1) and the second annotator (A2) are represented in Table 1. We confirm that 62% of statements were annotated as questions, while 25% of utterances were categorized as non-questions. Here are examples of annotated questions and non-questions. (Question): What did you buy it? (Answer): Not a question: I feel like adventure is good too (Table 1).

We assigned five annotators to judge the task; each annotator evaluate whether the QA-pair were natural. Each column represents the percentage when three people rated it as natural, when four people rated it as natural, and when five people rated it as natural with unanimous agreement, and the right column of Avg is average of those results. We have confirmed how the system replies naturally to the older adults with annotation. The current data seemed at most 37% was natural; those results imply our dialogue system has currently responded with less than half with unnatural answers.

Table 3 represents the results of the question candidates. Each column represents the cases where three, four, and five people each rated the question as similar to the previous task, and the right column of Avg is the average of those results. It can be observed that the similarity decreases as the number of annotators increases.

3 Discussion and Conclusion

The results of task 1 show that 32% of utterances were categorized as non-questions. As a next step, digging deeper into the non-question statements and separating the question statements into types may be a way to improve the dataset. We have identified patterns that may be able to characterize the data better. The result of naturalness annotation indicates the current system's performance. The results suggest that the current system has a response rate lower than 50% regarding naturalness. Toward various users' utterances may result from the shortage of datasets. Some topics were less spontaneous, indicating that they were not able to successfully answer participants' questions. This indicates that, depending on the topic, many of the questions were outside the scope of the data set we were covering. Therefore we need to consider the more effective approach to improve the coverage of prepared QA-pairs. Considering the results of task 1 and task 2, enriching the dataset can improve the coverage of the dataset and contribute to better performance. Finally, the results of task 3 reveal that a certain percentage of the data had similar content to the statements, as there exist similar utterances between prepared QA-Pairs and collected QA-Pairs. Therefore, we believe that information may contribute to modifying the algorithm or improving the data set. Our future work involves the verification of this improvement.

We consider the result of task 3, our system was designed to return the best answer from the dataset, as described. However, the results of this study confirmed that a certain percentage of similar questions exists among the other candidates. Hence, we may apply the following algorithm: if another candidate exists, and this candidate's similarity is high enough to use, then respond with the other candidate. We gave these statements to the annotators from the list of candidate statements, and assessed the presence of similar questions via annotation. We assigned these tasks to five annotators. We confirmed that similarity questions exist in around 20% of total statements.

Finally, we would like to state the possibility of improving our system perspectives. We have been building a dialogue system for the elderly and have now succeeded in linking those collected data with an annotation mechanism. In the future, we may extend the system to a self-evaluation system in which the participants in the experiment can evaluate the data themselves.

Acknowledgments. We would like to appreciate Fonobono Research Institute. With their help with recruiting participants, we were able to conduct our user study smoothly. We are also grateful for all study participants and staffs. We would like to especially thank to Sachiko Iwata and Kumiko Umemoto in our team. Without their help, we can not conduct home-beased experiment. This research was partially supported by JSPS KAKENHI Grant Numbers JP18KT0035, JP19H01138, JP20H05022, JP20H05574, JP20K19471, JP22H04872, JP22H00544, JP22H04872 and the Japan Science and Technology Agency (Grant Numbers: JPMJCR20G1, JPMJST2168, and JPMJPF2101).

References

1. Dodge, H.H., et al.: Web-enabled conversational interactions as a method to improve cognitive functions: results of a 6-week randomized controlled trial. Alzheimer's Dement. Transl. Res. Clin. Interv. **1**(1), 1–12 (2015). https://doi.org/10.1016/j.trci.2015.01.001. https://www.sciencedirect.com/science/article/pii/S2352873715000025

2. Fingerman, K.L., Huo, M., Charles, S.T., Umberson, D.J.: Variety is the spice of late life: social integration and daily activity. J. Gerontol. Ser. B **75**(2), 377–388 (2019). https://doi.org/10.1093/geronb/gbz007

3. Krueger, K.R., Wilson, R.S., Kamenetsky, J.M., Barnes, L.L., Bienias, J.L., Bennett, D.A.: Social engagement and cognitive function in old age. Exp. Aging Res. **35**(1), 45–60 (2009). https://doi.org/10.1080/03610730802545028. pMID: 19173101

4. Seeman, T.E., Lusignolo, T.M., Albert, M., Berkman, L.: Social relationships, social support, and patterns of cognitive aging in healthy, high-functioning older adults: MacArthur studies of successful aging. Health Psychol. **20**, 243–255 (2001)

5. Tokunaga, S., Seaborn, K., Tamura, K., Otake-Matsuura, M.: Cognitive training for older adults with a dialogue-based, robot-facilitated storytelling system. In: Interactive Storytelling - 12th International Conference on Interactive Digital Storytelling, ICIDS 2019, Little Cottonwood Canyon, UT, USA, 19–22 November 2019, Proceedings, pp. 405–409 (2019)

6. Tokunaga, S., Tamura, K., Otake-Matsuura, M.: A dialogue-based system with photo and storytelling for older adults: toward daily cognitive training. Front. Robot. AI **8**, 179 (2021). https://doi.org/10.3389/frobt.2021.644964. https://www.frontiersin.org/article/10.3389/frobt.2021.644964

7. Tokunaga, S., Tamura, K., Otake-Matsuura, M.: Implementation and evaluation of home-based dialogue system for cognitive training of older adults, pp. 458–461. Association for Computing Machinery, New York (2021). https://doi.org/10.1145/3487664.3487727

8. Tokunaga, S., Tamura, K., Otake-Matsuura, M.: A summary report through home experiment on a dialogue system for older adults. Gerontechnology (2022)

9. Ybarra, O., et al.: Mental exercising through simple socializing: social interaction promotes general cognitive functioning. Pers. Soc. Psychol. Bull. **34**(2), 248–259 (2008). https://doi.org/10.1177/0146167207310454

Evaluation Axes for Automatically Generated Product Descriptions

Kenji Fukumoto[1]([envelope]), Risa Takeuchi[1], Hiroyuki Terada[2], Masafumi Bato[3], and Akiyo Nadamoto[1]

[1] Konan University, Okamoto 8-9-1 Higashinada–ku, Kobe, Japan
{m2124005,s1871056}@s.konan-u.ac.jp, nadamoto@konan-u.ac.jp
[2] Ochanoko-net Inc., Kumoidori 7-1-1 Chuo-ku, Kobe, Japan
terada@ocnk.net
[3] Contact Inc., Kumoidori 7-1-1 Chuo-ku, Kobe, Japan
bato@contact.co.jp

Abstract. We have studied the automatic generation of product descriptions. It is important to evaluate the generated content from the viewpoint of how much the content can motivate people to buy. In this research, we propose the grammar axis, the content axis, and the attribute axis as evaluation axes for product descriptions. The attribute axis has three sub-axes which are the trust sub-axis, the attractive sub-axis, and the polite sub-axis.

Keywords: Evaluation axes · Product description · Deep learning

1 Introduction

With the spread of e-commerce sites, there are many a wide variety of products on the internet. We expect that the product descriptions on the product pages of e-commerce sites are effective in encouraging consumers to purchase the products. However, it is not easy for ordinary sellers to write product descriptions that encourage consumers to buy. Therefore, we have proposed an automatic product description generation method using deep learning [2].

On the other hand, it is important that the product description motivates the person who views the product page (hereinafter referred to as the browsing user) to purchase it. However, the automatically generated product description is not always a document that motivates the browsing user to purchase. Therefore, we consider that it is necessary to evaluate whether the automatically generated product description is a statement that motivated browsing users to purchase.

In general, researchers use BLEU [6] and ROUGE [5] as indicators for evaluating sentences automatically generated by deep learning. These methods evaluate by comparing the automatically generated sentences with the correct sentences. However, since there is no correct answer in the generated product description, we do not know what is correct. Therefore, it is difficult to quantitatively evaluate whether the automatically generated product description is an attractive

E. Pardede et al. (Eds.): iiWAS 2022, LNCS 13635, pp. 453–460, 2022.
https://doi.org/10.1007/978-3-031-21047-1_42

document or not using only BLEU and ROUGE. We regard the attractive product description that makes browsing users want to purchase the product.

In this research, we propose evaluation axes for automatically generating product descriptions that motivate browsing users to purchase. Our proposed axes are the grammar axis, the content axis, and the attribute axis as evaluation axes for product descriptions. We define the evaluation axes as "when evaluating a generated product description, the axis evaluates the browsing user want to purchase the product based on reading the product description."

Currently, various evaluation axes have been proposed [4], and the evaluation results differ greatly depending on the criteria used for evaluation. Therefore, we think that the evaluation axes are important in evaluating the generated product description. Furthermore, to measure the usefulness of the proposed product description evaluation axes, we first conduct a manual evaluation experiment using the product description automatically generated in the previous research [2]. In addition to the product description using Long Short-term Memory (LSTM) and GPT-2, the product description automatically generated in the previous research used here is Rinna[1]. We compare these three types of sentences and show the usefulness of the proposed product description evaluation axes.

2   Related Work

There is much research about the evaluation axes and evaluation methods for the results of Deep Learning. Chris et al. [4] summarise various methods for human evaluation of automatically generated sentences. In this study, we propose evaluation axes for product descriptions based on their proposed evaluation axes. Goodrich et al. [3] propose a method for evaluating the accuracy of the content of generated texts. Zhang et al. [7] propose BERTScore as an automatic evaluation metric for text generation. Their proposed evaluation metric is an automatic evaluation metric for text generation based on pre-trained BERT context embedding. Clark et al. [1] propose Sentence mover's Similarity that evaluates automatically based on the similarity of multi-sentences. Zhu et al. [8] propose Texygen that evaluates open-domain generated texts. The evaluation axes are diversity, quality, and consistency. On the other hand, we propose the evaluation axes for automatically generated product descriptions is different from these researches.

3   The Product Description Evaluation Axes

We consider that when the browsing users read the automatically generated product description, it is a good product description that they are motivated to purchase the product. Therefore, we propose the three evaluation axes of the product description that determine the viewpoint from which the product description is evaluated. Then, we propose three evaluation axes which are the

---

[1] https://rinna.co.jp. This is the GPT-2 Rinna model[2] proposed by /.

grammar axis, the content axis, and the attribute axis. The definition of each evaluation axes is shown below.

Grammar Axis

The grammar axis has three evaluation items: broken, validity, and readability. Evaluate sentences from a grammatical point of view. Specifically, product descriptions that satisfy the following are highly evaluated in terms of content.

- The same word is not repeated multiple times in the product description.
- The product description is not interrupted.
- The product description is not grammatically broken.
- Users can restore the grammar of the product description.

For example, the grammar of the sentences that "The product has a simple design, so it has a simple and simple design." is broken. The reason is that the same word is repeated. The product description has a low evaluation of the grammar axis.

Content Axis

The content axis has four evaluation items: consistency, completeness, fluency, and readability. It evaluates whether the content of the sentence is correct from a semantic point of view. Specifically, product descriptions that satisfy the following are highly evaluated in terms of content.

- The contents of the generated product description are not inconsistent.
- The claim is consistent

For example, "The product is a modern design, you can create a retro atmosphere just by placing it in the room." The first half of the content has a modern design, but the second half has a retro atmosphere. The content of this product description is inconsistent because the claims in the first half and the second half are different. Therefore, the evaluation of the content axis is low.

Attribute Axis

The attribute axis has three sub-axes: trust sub-axis, attractive sub-axis, and polite sub-axis. Even if the product description is grammatically and content-correct, it does not always motivate the browsing user to purchase. Therefore, we propose an attribute axis as an evaluation axis separate from the grammatical and content.

We consider this attribute axis to be an important evaluation axis. The reason is that the sentence that can motivate the browsing user to purchase the product by reading the automatically generated product description is evaluated as a good product description. Therefore, the attribute axis is evaluated from the following viewpoints.

1. The product description contains the correct information and is generated (trust).
2. It is an attractive sentence for browsing users (attractive).
3. Evaluate from the viewpoint that there is a polite expression in the product description (polite).

The three sub-axes of the attribute axis are explained below.

- Trust sub-axis

  The trust sub-axis has two evaluation items: accuracy and appropriateness. It evaluates whether the information entered by the user is correctly included in the item description. For example, if the user enters black as the color, but the product description "The color is brown and the large size makes it a popular sofa for families" is generated. The user input information is not reflected correctly. Therefore, this sentence has a low evaluation of the trust sub-axis.

- Attractive Sub-axis

  The attractive sub-axis has two evaluation items: attractiveness and popularity. It evaluates whether the content or expression of a sentence is attractive to the reader. For example, "This sofa has a simple design." Is a concise product description. However, "This sofa has a simple design. Therefore, you can create a room with a soft impression by coordinating with items with a natural texture." The content and expression of the sentence are more attractive. Therefore, the former is evaluated low and the latter is evaluated high.

- Polite Sub-axis

  The polite sub-axis has only politeness evaluation items. It evaluates whether a product description has been generated that gives a polite explanation that reminds the reader of the usage of the product. For example, "The sofa has a simple design, and it is possible to produce a wide range of styles such as Scandinavian style and vintage style depending on the furniture to be coordinated." This product description gives examples of Scandinavian style and vintage style and makes the reader imagine the usability of the product. Therefore, the polite sub-axis of the product description is highly evaluated.

4   Experiment

To measure whether the proposed product description evaluation axes are effective for the evaluation of the automatically generated product description. When we evaluate our proposed evaluation axis, we used the product descriptions which are generated automatically in the previous research [2].

4.1   Experimental Conditions

Experimental Data

We use 40 product descriptions which are randomly selected from the results of product descriptions generated by the LSTM, GPT-2, and GPT-2 Rinna models. The total number of product descriptions is 120 descriptions. The Table 1 shows an example of the product description used in the experiment. The characteristics of the generated product descriptions for each method as follows:

- LSTM

  The length of the sentence is short, and the characteristics of the sentence are in the form of saying characteristics such as "This product is ...".

- GPT-2

  The length of the sentence is neither so short nor long, and the characteristics of the sentence have the same form as the LSTM.
- GPT-2 Rinna model

  The length of the sentence is long. The generated product descriptions are different from the LSTM and GPT-2. It contains a lot of basic information about the product. For example, "This product is attractive because of ..." and "This product is recommended because of ...".

We experimented with crowdsourcing and had 10 subjects. When we perform the experiment, we randomly extract 8 sentences from each of the 3 methods and make a total of 24 sentences into one set. And prepare a total of 5 sets. As for the order of presentation to the subjects, we randomly displayed the product description generated by the three models.

Table 1. Example of generated product descriptions

Methods	Generated product descriptions
LSTM	The sofa is designed so that the body can relax naturally by angling the backrest.
GPT-2	In addition, <numbser> cushions are included, so it doesn't go well with the furniture, you have at home. You can also use it in the same color as the sofa or in combination with other products, so you can make various combinations depending on the floor plan and taste of the room.
GPT-2 Rinna	The sofa is available in white, so if you coordinate it with a natural-style low table or a natural table, it will be a fashionable cafe-style coordination. I can. Since it is a floor, you can freely change the lay-out. Since it is a sofa with a modern design, you can match it with various interiors such as pnoun> and <pnoun>, mainly in Scan-dinavian style. Cotton is used for the seating surface of the sofa, so you can use it comfortably all year round. This sofa is recommended for families with children, so it is a sofa where the whole family can get along and make memories. The sofa surface is made of fabric, so the cover is removable

Evaluation Method for Each Axis

The subject reads the generated product description and evaluates each axis. In this paper, we evaluate the broken item in the grammar axis, the content axis, the trust sub-axis, the attractive sub-axis, and the polite sub-axis in the attribute axis. The judgment conditions for evaluation for each axis are shown below.

- the grammar axis

  In this experiment, we evaluate the broken evaluation items in the grammar axis. If the sentence is broken, the evaluation is 1, and if the sentence is not broken, the evaluation is 5.

- the content axis
  In this experiment, we evaluate the consistency evaluation items in the content axis. If the content of the item description is inconsistent, the evaluation is 1, and if it is consistent, the evaluation is 5.
- the attribute axis When we evaluate the attribute axis in this paper, we target the trust, the attractive, and the polite sub-axis.
  - the trust sub-axis
    We evaluate whether the generated product description contains basic product information. If the detailed information about the product is not included, the evaluation is 1, and if it is included a lot, the evaluation is 5.
  - the attractive sub-axis
    We evaluate how much readers are motivated to buy the product when they read the product description. When the subject reads the product description and does not want to purchase the item, the evaluation is 1, and if the subject wants to purchase the item, the evaluation is 5.
  - the polite sub-axis
    We evaluate whether the expression method of the generated product description carefully explains the product. If the product description meets the conditions such as containing multiple similar words and phrases, including examples and including grounds, the rating is set to 5.

4.2   Results and Discussion of the Experiment

We conduct experiments with the aim of whether the proposed product description evaluation axis is useful for users who have not specifically decided on the product they want to purchase.

Experimental Procedure

We randomly display 24 sentences per set of product explanations generated by 3 models to the subject. The subject evaluates each of the presented sentences on five product description evaluation axes on a scale of 1 to 5. Repeat the above procedure 5 times.

Results and Discussion

The results of the Experiment are shown in the Table 2. As for the result of the grammar axis, LSTM was the highest evaluation with an average of 3.54. The reason is that since the LSTM consists of one short sentence, there are a few broken parts as a sentence, and the grammatical axis is highly evaluated.

As for the content axis, LSTM received the highest evaluation with an average of 4.01. The reason is that the product description generated by LSTM is made up of one short sentence as well as the grammar axis. On the other hand, the product description generated by GPT-2 is composed of multiple sentences, and the number of words contained in each sentence is large. Furthermore, the product description generated by GPT-2 may have a description in which the assertion changes between the first half and the second half of the sentence. On the content axis, it was found that if there was a contradiction in the content in the product description, the evaluation would be low. Therefore, it is considered that the shorter the sentence is, the higher the evaluation is likely to be for both the grammar axis and the content axis.

Next, we discuss the attribute axis. As for the result of the trust sub-axis, the GPT-2 Rinna model had the highest evaluation with an average of 4.55. The reason is that the GPT-2 Rinna model generates product descriptions for various items such as product types, colors, and materials. Then, it combines all of them, we consider that it contains abundant basic information on the product. Therefore, we find that the trust sub-axis accurately reflects the abundance of categories of words used in the product description and is highly evaluated. As for the results of the attractive sub-axis, the GPT-2 Rinna model had also the highest evaluation value of 3.00. The reason is that many stylistic styles are affirmed in the product description generated by LSTM and GPT-2. On the other hand, the style of the product description generated by the GPT-2 Rinna model is that many sentences recommend products. As a result, we found that the GPT-2 Rinna model was highly evaluated as the attractive sub-axis. Even in the polite sub-axis, the GPT-2 Rinna model was highly evaluated with an average of 4.03. The reason is that the GPT-2 Rinna model generates product descriptions based on various items such as product type, color, and material. Many sentences were in detail. Then, we consider that the GPT-2 Rinna model gives the viewer an accurate image of the product. In addition, we consider that the attractiveness sub-axis and the polite sub-axis are related and that the trigger for purchasing the product affects not only the attractiveness of the text itself but also the way of expressing the polite sub-axis in the text.

From the above results, we confirmed that the proposed product description evaluation axis is suitable for evaluating the product description. In addition, since each proposed product description evaluation axis captured the characteristics of each method, we consider that the proposed product description evaluation axes are effective.

Table 2. Results of Experiment

Method	Grammar	Content	Trust	Attractive	Polite
LSTM	3.54	4.01	2.16	1.77	2.32
GPT-2	2.62	3.11	2.28	1.57	2.22
GPT-2Rinna	2.80	3.01	4.55	3.00	4.03

5 Conclusion

In this study, we proposed the three evaluation axis for the automatically generated product description by using deep learning. The axes are the grammar axis, the content axis, and the attribute axis. The attribute axis are further classified into "the trust sub-axis", "the attractive sub-axis", and "the polite sub-axis".

Then, in order to show the benefits of the proposed axis, we conducted an evaluation experiment by the subjects using the product explanations generated by three types of deep learning.

In the near future, we performed manual evaluation at this time, but we will propose an automatic evaluation method for the evaluation axis.

Acknowledgements. This work was partially supported by the Research Institute of Konan University and by JSPS KAKENHI Great Number 19H04218 and 20K12085.

References

1. Clark, E., Celikyilmaz, A., Smith, N.A.: Sentence mover's similarity: automatic evaluation for multi-sentence texts. In: Proceedings of the 57th Annual Meeting of the Association for Computational Linguistics, pp. 2748–2760 (2019)
2. Fukumoto, K., Suzuki, R., Terada, H., Bato, M., Nadamoto, A.: Comparison of deep learning models for automatic generation of product description on e-commerce site. In: Proceedings of the 23rd International Conference on Information Integration and Web Intelligence (iiWAS2021), pp. 227–235 (2021)
3. Goodrich, B., Rao, V., Liu, P.J., Saleh, M.: Assessing the factual accuracy of generated text. In: Proceedings of the 25th ACM SIGKDD International Conference on Knowledge Discovery & Data Mining, pp. 166–175. Association for Computing Machinery, New York (2019). https://doi.org/10.1145/3292500.3330955
4. van der Lee, C., Gatt, A., van Miltenburg, E., Wubben, S., Krahmer, E.: Best practices for the human evaluation of automatically generated text. In: Proceedings of the 12th International Conference on Natural Language Generation, pp. 355–368. Association for Computational Linguistics, Tokyo, October–November 2019. https://doi.org/10.18653/v1/W19-8643
5. Lin, C.Y.: ROUGE: a package for automatic evaluation of summaries. In: Text Summarization Branches Out, pp. 74–81 (2004)
6. Papineni, K., Roukos, S., Ward, T., Zhu, W.J.: BLEU: a method for automatic evaluation of machine translation. In: Proceedings of the 40th Annual Meeting of the Association for Computational Linguistics, pp. 311–318 (2002)
7. Zhang, T., Kishore, V., Wu, F., Weinberger, K.Q., Artzi, Y.: BERTScore: evaluating text generation with BERT. arXiv preprint arXiv:1904.09675 (2019)
8. Zhu, Y., et al.: Texygen: a benchmarking platform for text generation models. In: The 41st International ACM SIGIR Conference on Research & Development in Information Retrieval, pp. 1097–1100 (2018)

Similarity Measures and Metrics

CISQA: Corporate Smart Insights Question Answering System

Le Duyen Sandra Vu[1]([⊠]) , Jamal Al Qundus[2] , Johannes Jung[1] ,
Silvio Peikert[1] , and Adrian Paschke[1]

[1] Data Analytics Center (DANA), Fraunhofer FOKUS, Berlin, Germany
le.duyen.sandra.vu@fokus.fraunhofer.de
[2] Faculty of Information Technology, Middle East University, Amman, Jordan

Abstract. The development of semantic information systems is a highly topical issue in various domains, e.g., financial news, which both ordinary users and experts deal with. Until now, queries in natural language on open vocabulary from, e.g., query.wikidata.org were hard to answer. The development of such software offers the possibility to make semantic information systems more effective, efficient, and user-friendly. This paper proposes a semantic knowledge-based question answering system called cisqa. It develops entity linking and relation linking approaches that have been experimentally proven to be superior to the state of the art. cisqa also handles question ambiguity, translates natural language questions into SPARQL-queries, and delivers answers to the user in an appropriate manner.

Keywords: Semantic question answering · Natural language processing · Corporate smart insights · Entity linking · Relation linking

1 Introduction

One method of obtaining specific information is to ask questions. Information retrieval (IR) attempts to answer questions by finding and providing lists of documents relevant to the query at hand. However, reading a large number of documents to obtain the desired information proves to be tedious and time-consuming. Question answering (QA) systems try to solve this problem by directly providing the exact answer to a given natural language (NL) question [1,2]. Unlike chatbots, whose responses are limited to NL, QA systems can provide answers in the form of NL, diagrams, lists or tables among others. The most commonly used resource by QA systems is NL text. The disadvantage of working with such "raw data" is that it must be repeatedly analyzed from scratch for each query [2–4] or a context with limited character length has to be given. This is the case with transformer based models such as BERT [5].

Other transformer based models like the GPT models [6–9] do not require context. However, since the "raw data" is converted into a distribution in the GPT models, there is no bijectively correct answer to the query. In other words,

E. Pardede et al. (Eds.): iiWAS 2022, LNCS 13635, pp. 463–475, 2022.
https://doi.org/10.1007/978-3-031-21047-1_43

incorrect answers could be given to queries with little to no traceability. This makes it particularly difficult to update changed data in a verifiable manner.

In the past few years, methods to transform unstructured text into machine suitable formats and the use of knowledge graphs became important resources for countless information retrieval and knowledge discovery tasks [10–13], since curated knowledge supports the efficient use of knowledge artifacts, and thus contributes significantly to the gain of functional quality, data efficiency and reliability [14–16]. This usage efficiency is achieved on two levels. The first level is the increase in quality and quantity of knowledge by semantically curating discovered knowledge. While the second level is the acceleration of data analysis via automation, reuse of discovered knowledge and additional knowledge-based (explorative) analyses [17]. The obtained knowledge is added to knowledge bases (KBs) or knowledge graphs (KGs) and continuously serves as a foundation to derive new knowledge. It should be briefly noted that KGs are considered KBs with a reasoning engine following the definition of [18].

Since machine suitable formats are typically not intuitively human-readable, a query language such as SPARQL is required to access the data [4,19–21]. Furthermore, there is a lack of uniform KBs, leading to dependencies and constraints, allowing little customization of systems based on them [4].

This work proposes a QA system that deals with corporate information to provide further insights. The Corporate Smart Insights (CSI) QA is also called cisqa (CSI phonetically assimilated to CIS). It answers German NL questions on finance by leveraging data from KBs and can be adapted to cover other domains. In this paper we focus on domain-independent translation of NL questions into SPARQL-Queries to perform knowledge based question answering.

The ambiguity of question variants is a challenge to question intent identification, which is usually bounded to a specific context hidden to the system. Another challenge is the variation of a question, e.g., *Where is the company located? What is the address of the company? Where is the company residence?* all ask for the company address.

In order to deal with ambiguities, researchers restrict possible questions within a specific domain relying on approaches such as predefined questions or controlled vocabularies to map questions to a standardised query language (e.g. [22,23]). For example SPARQL can be used to retrieve data from KGs (e.g. Wikidata [24], DBpedia [25], YAGO [26], KnowItAll [27], etc.).

We build on DBpedia as a KB and rely on its structure to create a domain specific RDF triple store. Our approach covers a wider range of question variants and is more flexible in processing free-text questions than existing work (see comparison in the Results and Discussion Sect. 4). A question is processed through a pipeline of approaches i.e., Pattern-Matching and headword extraction (based on [28] definition of headwords) to perform relation linking. Generated SPARQL-Queries are processed by a component with an API4KB[1] interface facilitating the access to underlying KBs. In that way an independence to the KB and its query language is achieved.

---

[1] https://www.omgwiki.org/API4KB/doku.php.

The paper is organized as follows: In Sect. 2 we discuss related work; Sect. 3 gives an overview on the architecture of the cisqa system. Section 4 presents our results, which are concluded and discussed in Sect. 5.

2   Related Work

Semantic parsing-based QA systems rely on entity linking and relation linking tasks, where key phrases have to be linked to their respective concept (i.e., RDF triples) in KBs. These form a basic pipeline to measure semantic similarity. We studied state-of-the-art work such as AskNow [29], Qsearch [30], GQA [31] that are based on entity linking, and IQA [32], KBPearl [33], EARL [35], Falcon [36] that consider both tasks.

AskNow [29] as an information retrieval system is in its core a rule-based system that relies on a KG to translate free-text NL questions to a formal query language. It performs entity linking to DBpedia and proposes an intermediary canonical syntactic form for NL, which is called Normalized Query Structure (NQS). Questions in NL are mapped to this structure, which acts as a syntactic template, before translating them to SPARQL-Queries. NQS builds on part-of-speech (POS) tagging to extract the "query desires" such as noun phrases.

Qsearch [30] is a QA system that considers quantity conditions (e.g., high, much, low) in questions. A rule-based parser associates input questions with Qqueries, then a deep neural network is used to extract and process quantity-centric so-called Qfacts, which are assigned a score reflecting relevance to the mapped Qquery. In contrast to QSearch, GQA [31] highlights grammar instead of quantity conditions. GQA is a Grammatical QA system allowing queries in English over DBpedia. It proposes a set of conceptual grammars derived from a Grammatical Framework (GF). These grammars are used to parse questions of complex syntactic constructions.

IQA [32] proposes an approach based on user interaction. It follows an interaction scheme for a semantic QA pipeline (PL) to incorporate user feedback into a question answering process. That is, given a user question and after the entity recognition phase, the PL generates a large number of entity-related questions that the user can answer to interpret the original question. The authors propose a metric called "Option Gain" to efficiently integrate user feedback.

KBPearl [33] addresses the KB population (KBP) problem by constructing KBs from unstructured text, supported by joint entity linking and relation linking. The authors point out the limitation of inconsistencies caused by redundancy and ambiguity when generating facts for KBP in related approaches. The work starts with an incomplete KB and a set of documents. It utilises extraction methods from Open Information Extraction [34] to decompose the documents into facts and side information, i.e., metadata derived from the source text. Since not all source texts provide such metadata, e.g. timestamps, this approach is limited to certain types of data.

EARL [35] establishes a pipeline of entity linking and relation linking as a joint task and pursues two solution strategies. First, it formalises both tasks as an

Table 1. summarizes relevant work that inspired the proposed cisqa system. It shows that some types of queries with multiple keywords are difficult to disambiguate using relationship linking tools.

	AskNow[29]	EARL[35]	Falcon[36]
Approach	Separate Entity & Relation Linking	Combined Entity & Relation Linking	Combined Entity & Relation Linking
Language models	word2vec	fasttext	-
EvaluationDataset: Precision/ Recall/ F1	Accuracy: QUALD-5: .63/.60/.61	Entity Linking: QALD-7: .58/.60/.58 LC-QuAD: .53/.55/.53 Relation Linking: QALD-7: .27/.28/.27 LC-QuAD: .17/.21/.18	Entity Linking: QALD-7: .78/.79/.78 LC-QuAD: .81/.86/.83 Relation Linking: QALD-7: .58/.61/.59 LC-QuAD: .42/.44/.43
Advantage/ Disadvantage	– Returns complete SPARQL-Query – Language model necessary – Difficult to customize	– Flexible SPARQL-Query – Language model necessary	– Flexible SPARQL-Query – Easy customizable code

instance of the Generalized Travelling Salesman Problem (GTSP), which is NP-hard. Second, it employs machine learning to utilize the connectivity densities of the KB nodes. It uses Shallow Parsing to extract keywords and a KB to resolve entities and relations by examining the relation and its context around the entity.

Falcon [36] and Falcon 2.0 [37] are approaches that jointly perform entity linking and relation linking from questions in NL to DBpedia and to Wikidata [24], respectively. Falcon's key idea is to use a background KG created from several knowledge sources to examine the context of the extracted entities in order to find the relation. Therefore, Falcon performs well on short questions. In addition, the output of Falcon 2.0 includes a ranked list of entities and relations annotated with their Internationalized Resource Identifier (IRI) in Wikdata.

In addition to AskNow [29], the last two works (EARL [35] and Falcon [36]) inspired cisqa. Table 1 summarizes our experiments with them. cisqa aims to create a QA system, which is able to integrate arbitrary knowledge and is not dependent on a large NL corpus or a language model, as is the case for AskNow [29], EARL [35], Qsearch [30], IQA [32], and KBPearl [33].

It also aims to offer similar functionality to GQA [31] and Falcon [36] while allowing more flexibility regarding linguistic variation of questions and adapting the rules to the German language. Morever, cisqa enables the adoptions to general domain KBs such as Wikidata, but also to domain specific data bases.

3 System Overview

At the core of cisqa is a processing pipeline consisting of three major stages. In the first stage NL queries are analysed and translated into machine processable SPARQL queries. The second stage executes these queries in multiple KBs using a component based on API4KB. The retrieved results are presented and can be edited in the final curation stage (see Fig. 1).

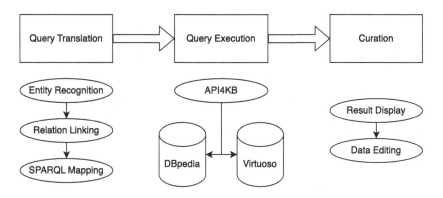

Fig. 1. gives an overview of the system components of cisqa.

3.1 Query Translation

The system distinguishes between 2 NL query types, each of which is processed using different approaches. Sentences that do not fall under a specific syntactic pattern, but instead can be easily classified by a phrase or a word are processed using symbolic pattern matching. For example, "News about Adidas", where "news" is the keyword. This approach allows for fast processing, but is dependent on pre-chosen keywords.

In order to be less reliant on keywords, the second approach is based on entity recognition and relation linking. For entity recognition, a combination of a pre-trained language model[2]) from Spacy[3] and direct token comparison to a list of relevant entities from the underlying KG is used. For relation linking an approach based on headwords extraction is applied as follows. First the question is tokenized, lemmatized, and POS-tagged using a language model. This annotated text is parsed using predefined grammar rules resulting in a set of partial grammar trees also called shallow syntax tree. In general, such Shallow Parsing covers approaches of partial or incomplete parsing. In that way Shallow Parsing is able to handle variations with a small set of rules. Shallow parsers use the output of morphological analysers, such as POS-taggers, to add dependency relations [38]. In our implementation, the query will be chunked into prepositional phrases (PP), adjective phrases (AP), noun phrases (NP) and verb phrases (VP). This shallow parser was implemented using NLTK chunker[4]. The construction rules are:

```
PP: {<ADP><PROPN>}              NP: {<PROPN><PP>}        NP: {<ADJ><NOUN>}
PP: {<ADP><DET>?<ADJ>?<NOUN>}   NP: {<NOUN><PP>}         NP: {<DET><NOUN><PP>}
PP: {<ADP><NUM><NOUN>}          NP: {<DET><NOUN>}        VP: {<VERB>}
AP: {<ADV><ADJ>}                NP: {<AP>}               VP: {<PP>?<PP><VERB>}
AP: {<ADV><DET><ADJ>?<NOUN>}    VP: {<ADV><PP><VERB>}
```

*A question mark in a rule denotes the optionality of the element preceding it.

---

[2] de_core_news_lg-2.3.0 https://spacy.io/models/de#de_core_news_lg.

[3] https://spacy.io/.

[4] https://www.nltk.org/.

To extract relevant headwords the shallow parse trees will be traversed. This will detect interrogatives such as 'wo' (where), 'wer' (who), 'wann' (when), adverbs and verbs in VPs as well as determiners like 'viel' (much), 'wenig' (few), 'mehrere' (several), adjectives, nouns and numerals in NPs. The extracted verbs and nouns are compared to relation labels in the KG. This comparison is done using the cosine similarity of the phrase vectors to the label vectors. Each word has a word-embedding, which is a word vector retrieved from a trained language model. The phrase vectors are the arithmetic mean of its word vectors. The similarity score of the headwords "Ort gründen" (found place) and the label "Gründungsort" (foundation place) is 0.75, while the similarity to the label "Ort" (place) is only 0.48. Therefore dbo:foundationPlace is ranked higher than dbo:Place.

The highest ranked relation and the identified entity are inserted into the following SPARQL template:

```
?search
WHERE {
 ?iri a dbo:Company; dbo:abstract ?description; rdfs:label ?lbl .
 ?lbl bif:contains "'ENTITY'"@en  .
 FILTER(langMatches(lang(?description),"de"))
 FILTER(langMatches(lang(?lbl),"de"))
 OPTIONAL {?iri RELATION ?search FILTER langMatches(lang(?search),"de")}}
```

Words with other word categories than verbs or nouns are used to assign alternative SPARQL-Query templates. For example, the determiner 'viel' (much) turns ?search to count(?search) as the headword suggests that the query asks for a quantity.

If that approach does not yield a valid result, the input question was likely misspelled. Therefore a spelling correction[5] based on [39] is applied in that case. In general, spelling correction would be the first step of pre-processing. However, in order to avoid a system bias that causes over-correction, it is only run if the plain query did not yield a result.

3.2   Query Execution

To retrieve the data necessary for answering the questions asked by users, multiple KGs are considered. "API for Knowledge Bases" (API4KB) is used as a common interface. It is a reference implementation of the "API for Knowledge Platforms" specification [40], which is a standard that is based on a model driven architecture and combines different specifications to build a platform and technology independent Knowledge Based System. We use API4KB to facilitate the process of storing, managing and requesting data in different knowledge resources.

Our extension of API4KB adds an endpoint to API4KB that receives SPARQL-Queries. The endpoint works similar to a standard SPARQL endpoint in the sense that a SPARQL-Query is received and a success message, error

---

[5] https://github.com/jdlauret/SpellChecker.

(a) UI view of the question "Wo befindet sich adidas?" ("Where is adidas located?"). It shows the address of the company and a map.

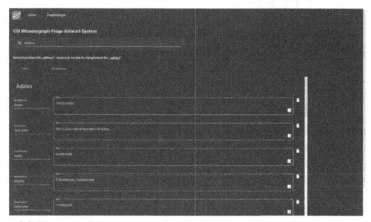

(b) UI view of the question "adidas?". It shows the editing mode.

Fig. 2. cisqa UI landing (a) and editing (b) pages

message or table (for e.g. a select query) is returned. In our case the API4KB endpoint will also distribute the query to two different KBs in the following way:

First the query will be sent to a local virtuoso store. If the request was successful such that a non empty table in json format is returned, it will be forwarded to the endpoint user. If instead an empty result was returned, the same query will be sent to DBpedia and the response will be forwarded to the endpoint user. In that way the contents of public KGs can be updated and extended. The local database is prioritized over the DBpedia database because it is assumed that it holds information that is extended, more recent or not contained in DBpedia.

3.3 Curation

The results will be presented to the user by a Web UI. Based on the detected intent of a given question 3 types of result views can be displayed. If the question gets classified as a location request, a map will be displayed. Accordingly tables will be displayed for sets of items (such as latest news) and info cards are used to display detailed information on entities. An example is shown in Fig. 2 (a).

It is possible for users to edit or extend information in info cards. The edited content will be then sent to an API4KB endpoint that will update the content in the local database such that at a later request the updated content will appear. An example view of the editing feature is displayed in Fig. 2 (b). In that figure one can also see the handling of a misspelled entity. Instead of searching for "adidass" the system recognizes the misspelled entity and searches for "adidas", while it notifies the user about it.

4 Results and Discussion

In order to compare our system to related approaches, we have tested various questions, which aim to retrieve detailed information on companies from news and DBpedia, against three implementations. Since financial reports mostly consist of tables and charts rather than continuous text, approaches that require a large NL corpus were not considered. Unfortunately, the GQA [31] approach could not be replicated because the code was not accessible. Of the two Falcon implementations, Falcon [36] and Falcon 2.0 [37], the first is used as a baseline compared to the headword approaches using deep and shallow parse trees. Falcon 2.0 uses Wikidata instead of DBpedia and is, therefore, less comparable. The results of the experiments are summarised in Table 2.

Falcon fails on about half of the questions. The following variants of questions illustrate the problems:

1. Which year was adidas founded? → -, {dbo:alias, dbo:foundationPlace}
2. Which year was Adidas founded? → Adidas, dbo:foundingYear
3. Which place was Adidas founded? → Adidas, {dbo:place, dbo:foundingYear}

In Sentence 1 Falcon fails to identify the entity because Adidas is written in lower case. It also links Adidas to the relation dbo:alias. This could be avoided by improving entity recognition. In 2 entity and relation are linked correct, while Sentence 3 links place with dbo:place and founded with dbo:foundingYear. The correct relation, however, would be dbo:foundingPlace.

The headword approach with deep parsing performs better than Falcon, since on the one hand more syntactic dependencies are taken into consideration to find the words necessary for relation linking and on the other hand entity linking is solved independent from relation linking.

The best performance is achieved using Shallow Parsing, which gives the following results on the questions above:

1. Which year was adidas founded? → adidas, dbo:foundingYear

Table 2. results of our experiment comparing our two implementations of Headword Deep Parsing and Headword Shallow Parsing, as well as comparing the two approaches with Falcon.

Original question in German	Translated question into English	HW Deep	HW Shallow	Falcon
Wer ist der Grnder von Adidas?	Who is the founder of Adidas?	✓	✓	✓
Grnder von Adidas?	Founder of Adidas?	o	✓	✓
Wer grndete Adidas?	Who founded Adidas?	o	✓	✓
Wer sind die CEOs von Adidas?	Who are the CEOs of Adidas?	✓	✓	✓
Wer ist der CEO von Adidas?	Who is the CEO of Adidas?	✓	✓	✓
CEO von Adidas?	CEO of Adidas?	o	✓	✓
Wer hat Adidas gegrndet?	Who founded Adidas?	✓	✓	o
Wann wurde Adidas gegrndet?	When was Adidas founded?	✓	✓	o
Wo wurde Adidas gegrndet?	Where was Adidas founded?	✓	✓	o
In welchem Jahr wurde Adidas gegrndet?	In which year was Adidas founded?	✓	✓	o
An welchem Ort wurde Adidas gegrndet?	In which place was Adidas founded?	✓	✓	o
Welche Produkte bietet Adidas an?	What products does Adidas offer?	✓	✓	✓
Was ist der Slogan von Adidas?	What is the slogan of Adidas?	✓	✓	✓
Wie viele Mitarbeiter hat Adidas?	How many employees does Adidas have?	✓	✓	✓
Wie viele CEOs hat Adidas?	How many CEOs does Adidas have?	✓	✓	o
Was ist das Eigenkapital/der Vermgenswert/die Aktiva von Adidas?	What is the equity/asset/assets of Adidas?	✓	✓	✓
Wie hoch ist das Eigenkapital/der Vermgenswert/die Aktiva von Adidas?	What is the equity/assets/assets of Adidas?	✓	✓	✓
Umsatz Prognose fr 2020?	Revenue forecast for 2020?	✓	✓	o
Umsatz von Pseudo gmbh?	Revenue of Pseudo gmbh?	✓	✓	o
Aktuelle Nachrichten zu Nemetschek	Current news on Nemetschek	✓	✓	o
Wo befindet sich adidas?	Where is adidas located?	✓	✓	o

2. Which year was Adidas founded? → Adidas, dbo:foundingYear
3. Which place was Adidas founded? → Adidas, dbo:foundationPlace

Falcon, furthermore, struggles to disambiguate interrogatives such as *Where was Adidas founded?, When was Adidas founded?, Who founded Adidas?, How many founders does Adidas have?* all are linked to "http://dbpedia.org/ontology/ foundationPlace". Our solution, which incorporates relation similarity ranking between extracted headwords and the obtained labels, shows the following results: For the question *An welchem Ort wurde Adidas gegründet?* (In which place was Adidas founded?) with the extracted headwords *Ort gründen*, the correct label "Gründungsort" has a similarity score of 0.75, while the incorrect label "Ort" has a lower score of 0.48. The same holds true for *In welchem Jahr wurde Adidas gegründet?* (In which year was Adidas founded?) with the extracted headwords *Jahr gründen* where the correct label "Gründungsjahr" achieves a score of 0.78, while the incorrect label "Jahr" has a lower score of 0.63.

Lastly, Falcon maps quantifiers incorrectly e.g. *Wie viele CEOs hat Adidas?* (How many CEOs does Adidas have?). Our solution applies query templates to map quantifiers, i.e., *viel* (much) → (count(?x) as ?x). In that way such questions are correctly interpreted.

Besides better performance regarding question disambiguation, the proposed system offers means to update, correct and extend data form the underlying KG by incorporating a local triple store. For example that triple store contains data which was crawled from a German website that publishes financial news and announcements. These announcements include changes of shareholder voting rights, merge and acquisition offers, director's dealings and general financial news about a company. In that way the proposed system is able to respond to questions with visualizations made up from up-to-date information beyond the data in public KGs. An example is shown in Fig. 3.

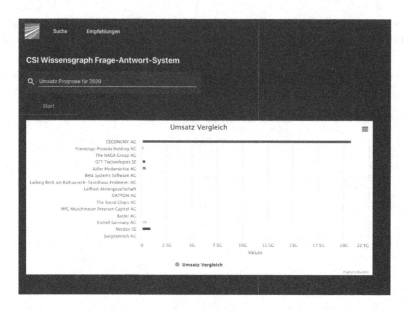

Fig. 3. UI view of the question "Umsatz Prognose für 2020?" ("Revenue forecast for 2020?"). It shows company revenues for the year 2020.

5   Conclusion and Future Work

cisqa is a modular domain adaptable QA system providing a natural language interface. It has been implemented and tested on an example use case related to financial information from DBpedia and crawled news websites. Similarly to existing approaches cisqa is able to understand questions using entity recognition and relation linking techniques.

Considering that most related work focuses on English language and is not easily adaptable to other languages, cisqa focuses on German. In detail cisqa made the following contributions:

- Advanced modular infrastructure for a QA system featuring a spellchecker, API4KB, and data curation. This provides adaptability to other domains and data customization.
- A pipeline of AI components for classifying question intent that is more resistant to question variations than comparable systems while it allows for more linguistic flexibility.
- Translation component translating NL questions into SPARQL-Queries for more flexible use of a Semantic Web infrastructure (e.g. triple stores) that supports formulation of questions.
- Syntax trees for syntactic dependency information to find headwords required for relation linking.

In future work we plan to add more experiments using benchmark datasets to compare cisqa with baseline systems. Moreover, the implementation of cisqa for further domains besides financial data, e.g., legal or medical knowledge is planned. In that context the rule set for shallow parsing will be tested on additional questions and may be extended. Other KBs and more complex queries, such as aggregations, may be included as well.

Acknowledgment. The research presented in this article is partially funded by the German Federal Ministry of Education and Research (BMBF) through the project PANQURA, grant no. 03COV03F https://qurator.ai/panqura/

References

1. Laurent, D., Séguéla, P., Nègre, S.: QA better than IR?. In: Proceedings of the Workshop on Multilingual Question Answering-MLQA 2006 (2006)
2. Quarteroni, S., Manandhar, S.: A chatbot-based interactive question answering system. DecaLog **2007**, 83 (2007)
3. Al-Zubaide, H., Issa, A.A.: OntBot: ontology based chatbot. In: International Symposium on Innovations in Information and Communications Technology, pp. 7–12 (2011)
4. Baksi, K.D.: Recent advances in automated question answering in biomedical domain. ArXiv, abs/2111.05937 (2021)
5. Devlin, J., Chang, M.W., Lee, K., Toutanova, K.: BERT: pre-training of deep bidirectional transformers for language understanding. arXiv preprint arXiv:1810.04805 (2018)
6. Radford, A., Narasimhan, K., Salimans, T., Sutskever, I.: Improving language understanding by generative pre-training (2018)
7. Radford, A., Wu, J., Child, R., Luan, D., Amodei, D., Sutskever, I.: Language models are unsupervised multitask learners. OpenAI Blog **1**(8), 9 (2019)
8. Brown, T., et al.: Language models are few-shot learners. In: Advances in Neural Information Processing Systems, vol. 33, pp. 1877–1901 (2020)
9. Liu, J., Shen, D., Zhang, Y., Dolan, B., Carin, L., Chen, W.: What makes good in-context examples for GPT-\$3 \$?. arXiv preprint arXiv:2101.06804 (2021)
10. Shahapure, K.R., Nicholas, C.: Cluster quality analysis using silhouette score. In: 2020 IEEE 7th International Conference on Data Science and Advanced Analytics (DSAA), pp. 747–748. IEEE (2020)
11. Qundus, J.A., Paschke, A.: Investigating the effect of attributes on user trust in social media. In: Elloumi, M., et al. (eds.) DEXA 2018. CCIS, vol. 903, pp. 278–288. Springer, Cham (2018). https://doi.org/10.1007/978-3-319-99133-7_23
12. Al Qundus, J., Paschke, A., Kumar, S., Gupta, S.: Calculating trust in domain analysis: theoretical trust model. Int. J. Inf. Manage. **48**, 1–11 (2019)
13. Al Qundus, J., Paschke, A., Gupta, S., Alzouby, A.M., Yousef, M.: Exploring the impact of short-text complexity and structure on its quality in social media. J. Enterprise Inf. Manag. (2020)
14. Cerone, A., Naghizade, E., Scholer, F., Mallal, D., Skelton, R., Spina, D.: Watch 'n' Check: towards a social media monitoring tool to assist fact-checking experts. In: 2020 IEEE 7th International Conference on Data Science and Advanced Analytics (DSAA), pp. 607–613. IEEE (2020)
15. Yousef, M., Qundus, J.A., Peikert, S., Paschke, A.: TopicsRanksDC: distance-based topic ranking applied on two-class data. In: Kotsis, G., et al. (eds.) DEXA 2020. CCIS, vol. 1285, pp. 11–21. Springer, Cham (2020). https://doi.org/10.1007/978-3-030-59028-4_2

16. Al Qundus, J., Peikert, S., Paschke, A.: AI supported topic modeling using KNIME-workflows. arXiv preprint arXiv:2104.09428 (2021)
17. Rehm, G., et al.: QURATOR: innovative technologies for content and data curation. arXiv preprint arXiv:2004.12195 (2020)
18. Ehrlinger, L., Wöß, W.: Towards a definition of knowledge graphs. SEMANTiCS (Posters, Demos, SuCCESS) **48**(1–4), 2 (2016)
19. Purkayastha, S., Dana, S., Garg, D., Khandelwal, D., Bhargav, G.P.: Knowledge graph question answering via SPARQL silhouette generation. ArXiv, abs/2109.09475 (2021)
20. Unger, C., Bühmann, L., Lehmann, J., Ngonga Ngomo, A. C., Gerber, D., Cimiano, P.: Template-based question answering over RDF data. In: Proceedings of the 21st International Conference on World Wide Web, pp. 639–648 (2012)
21. To, N.D., Reformat, M.Z: Question-answering system with linguistic terms over RDF knowledge graphs. In: 2020 IEEE International Conference on Systems, Man, and Cybernetics (SMC), pp. 4236–4243. IEEE (2020)
22. Diefenbach, D., Both, A., Singh, K., Maret, P.: Towards a question answering system over the semantic web. Semantic Web **11**(3), 421–439 (2020)
23. Dubey, M., Banerjee, D., Abdelkawi, A., Lehmann, J.: LC-QuAD 2.0: a large dataset for complex question answering over Wikidata and DBpedia. In: Ghidini, C., et al. (eds.) ISWC 2019. LNCS, vol. 11779, pp. 69–78. Springer, Cham (2019). https://doi.org/10.1007/978-3-030-30796-7_5
24. Vrandečić, D.: Wikidata: a new platform for collaborative data collection. In: Proceedings of the 21st International Conference on World Wide Web, pp. 1063–1064 (2012)
25. Auer, S., Bizer, C., Kobilarov, G., Lehmann, J., Cyganiak, R., Ives, Z.: DBpedia: a nucleus for a web of open data. In: Aberer, K., et al. (eds.) ASWC/ISWC -2007. LNCS, vol. 4825, pp. 722–735. Springer, Heidelberg (2007). https://doi.org/10.1007/978-3-540-76298-0_52
26. Suchanek, F.M., Kasneci, G., Weikum, G.: YAGO: a core of semantic knowledge. In: Proceedings of the 16th International Conference on World Wide Web, pp. 697–706 (2007)
27. Etzioni, O., et al.: Web-scale information extraction in KnowitAll: (preliminary results). In: Proceedings of the 13th International Conference on World Wide Web, pp. 100–110 (2004)
28. Silva, J., Coheur, L., Mendes, A.C., Wichert, A.: From symbolic to sub-symbolic information in question classification. Artif. Intell. Rev. **35**(2), 137–154 (2011)
29. Dubey, M., Dasgupta, S., Sharma, A., Höffner, K., Lehmann, J.: AskNow: a framework for natural language query formalization in SPARQL. In: Sack, H., Blomqvist, E., d'Aquin, M., Ghidini, C., Ponzetto, S.P., Lange, C. (eds.) ESWC 2016. LNCS, vol. 9678, pp. 300–316. Springer, Cham (2016). https://doi.org/10.1007/978-3-319-34129-3_19
30. Ho, V.T., Ibrahim, Y., Pal, K., Berberich, K., Weikum, G.: Qsearch: answering quantity queries from text. In: Ghidini, C., et al. (eds.) ISWC 2019. LNCS, vol. 11778, pp. 237–257. Springer, Cham (2019). https://doi.org/10.1007/978-3-030-30793-6_14
31. Zimina, E., Nummenmaa, J., Järvelin, K., Peltonen, J., Stefanidis, K., Hyyrö, H.: GQA: grammatical question answering for RDF data. In: Buscaldi, D., Gangemi, A., Reforgiato Recupero, D. (eds.) SemWebEval 2018. CCIS, vol. 927, pp. 82–97. Springer, Cham (2018). https://doi.org/10.1007/978-3-030-00072-1_8
32. Zafar, H., Dubey, M., Lehmann, J., Demidova, E.: IQA: interactive query construction in semantic question answering systems. J. Web Semant. **64**, 100586 (2020)

33. Lin, X., Li, H., Xin, H., Li, Z., Chen, L.: KBPearl: a knowledge base population system supported by joint entity and relation linking. Proc. VLDB Endowment **13**(7), 1035–1049 (2020)
34. Etzioni, O., Banko, M., Soderland, S., Weld, D.S.: Open information extraction from the web. Commun. ACM **51**(12), 68–74 (2008)
35. Dubey, M., Banerjee, D., Chaudhuri, D., Lehmann, J.: EARL: joint entity and relation linking for question answering over knowledge graphs. In: Vrandečcić, D. (ed.) ISWC 2018. LNCS, vol. 11136, pp. 108–126. Springer, Cham (2018). https://doi.org/10.1007/978-3-030-00671-6_7
36. Sakor, A., et al.: Old is gold: linguistic driven approach for entity and relation linking of short text. In: Proceedings of the 2019 Conference of the North American Chapter of the Association for Computational Linguistics: Human Language Technologies, vol. 1 (Long and Short Papers), pp. 2336–2346 (2019)
37. Sakor, A., Singh, K., Patel, A., Vidal, M.E.: Falcon 2.0: an entity and relation linking tool over Wikidata. In: Proceedings of the 29th ACM International Conference on Information & Knowledge Management, pp. 3141–3148 (2020)
38. Federici, S., Montemagni, S., Pirrelli, V.: Shallow parsing and text chunking: a view on under specification in syntax (2021)
39. Norvig, P.: Natural language corpus data. Beautiful Data, pp. 219–242 (2009)
40. Athan, T., Bell, R., Kendall, E., Paschke, A., Sottara, D.: API4KP metamodel: a meta-API for heterogeneous knowledge platforms. In: Bassiliades, N., Gottlob, G., Sadri, F., Paschke, A., Roman, D. (eds.) RuleML 2015. LNCS, vol. 9202, pp. 144–160. Springer, Cham (2015). https://doi.org/10.1007/978-3-319-21542-6_10

Symmetry Metrics for Pairwise Entity Similarities

Alex Romanova(✉)

Melenar, LLC, McLean, VA 22101, USA
sparkling.dataocean@gmail.com

Abstract. Outstanding success of Convolutional Neural Network (CNN) image classification made it an instrument for many data mining domains. However highly accurate CNN image classification methods that are based on supervised machine learning require labeling of huge volumes of input data. One of the ways to resolve this problem is unsupervised learning model that transforms pairwise entities to Gramian Angular Fields (GAF) images and classifies them to symmetric and asymmetric classes. In this study we will extend benefits of this model by introducing Symmetry Metrics—a probability for pairwise entity converted to GAF image to get into the symmetric class. In this paper we will demonstrate on several scenarios how to use symmetry metrics to measure differences between vectors and compare their values with cosine similarities.

Keywords: Embedded vectors · Deep learning · Gaf images · Vector similarity · Image classification · Symmetry metrics

1 Introduction

Huge success of deep learning image classification techniques in the last few years [1,2] inspired using them as a powerful instrument for various techniques such as vector classification. One of such techniques is based on encoding vectors as Gramian Angular Fields (GAF) images and classifying GAF images by CNN image classification methods [3–5]. CNN image classification methods are getting high accuracies but being based on supervised machine learning, they require labeling of huge volumes of data. As it's impossible to label everything in the world, supervised learning is a bottleneck for building more intelligent generalist models [6].

In paper [7] we introduced unsupervised machine learning model that classifies pairs of vectors as similar or dissimilar. In that model pairs of vectors are concatenated by reversing right vectors and joint vectors are transformed to GAF images. As illustrated on Fig. 1, in plot picture self-joined vectors look like mirror vectors and corresponding GAF images look as symmetric squares. Based on this we can expect that pairs of similar vectors will be transformed to GAF images that are closed to symmetric images and pairs of dissimilar vectors to asymmetric GAF images. As you can see on training data example (Fig. 2),

© The Author(s), under exclusive license to Springer Nature Switzerland AG 2022
E. Pardede et al. (Eds.): iiWAS 2022, LNCS 13635, pp. 476–488, 2022.
https://doi.org/10.1007/978-3-031-21047-1_44

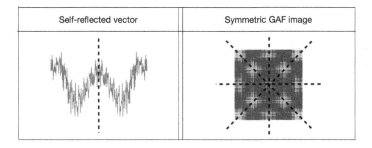

Fig. 1. Self-reflected vectors transformed to GAF images create symmetric squares.

GAF images of training data can visually be split to image sets of symmetric and asymmetric squares.

The process of approximately classifying images to symmetric or asymmetric classes acts as dimensionality reduction that might help to ease the distance concentration problem of high dimensional data [8] and therefore it is expected to work better than more complex image classification methods. We were inspired by geometric deep learning study to focus on symmetry as a powerful principle of solving the curse of dimensionality problem [9].

Techniques of classifying pairwise vectors transformed to GAF images to symmetric and asymmetric classes seems to be easier then techniques of classifying images of specific types, like cats and dogs. Potentially pairwise entity classification model can be trained on heterogeneous data domains and used for classifications of pairwise entities taken from a variety of data domains. This hypothesis, being conceptually analogical to ImageNet model [2] that is widely used for image classification or Natural Language Processing (NLP) models (like BERT [10]) that are used for word classification, opens a new area for data mining.

Unsupervised pairwise entity classification model described above was introduced on high level as a backbone for a pairwise entity classification. The model was trained on time series climate data and was applied to experiments with data from the same data domain. In paper [11] we examined a possibility to train pairwise entity classification model on one data domain and apply it to classification of entity pairs from another data domain. The model was trained on time series climate data domain and applied to data from NLP data domain to uncover unexpected word pairs in text documents. This allowed us to evaluate whether pairwise image classification model trained on one data domain is applicable to classifying entity pairs taken from different data domains.

In this study we will look at pairwise entity classification model from a different angle—we will investigate how to apply it to measure vector similarities. Vector similarity measures are essential in solving many data mining problems such as classification, clustering, information retrieval, graph mining and other. Methods that are commonly used to compare vectors are cosine similarities or dot products. In this paper we will introduce a method to distinguish between similar and dissimilar entity pairs as probabilities for GAF images of pairwise vectors to be classified as symmetric. We will call these vector similarity measures Symmetry Metrics.

In this paper we will describe:

– How to create pairwise vectors for two different data domains, time series data and NLP data
– How to transform pairwise vectors to GAF images
– How to train the model
– How to interpret image classification results through symmetry metrics

As a new challenge, in this paper will demonstrate how to use symmetry metrics to measure similarities between vectors and compare symmetry metrics values with cosine similarities. In this comparison we do not expect to get computationally better or worse results for symmetry metrics than for cosine similarities. In fact, through symmetry metrics we expect to get new insights for data mining.

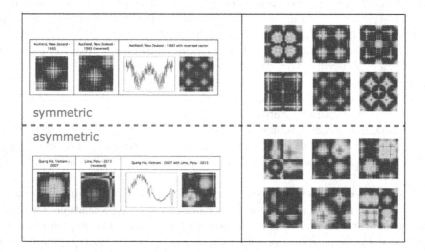

Fig. 2. Training data examples. Symmetric images demonstrate 'same' class for self-reflected vectors converted to GAF images. Asymmetric images demonstrate 'different' class for pairs of different vectors converted to GAF images.

Unsupervised pairwise entity classification model has some limitations. In the paper where we introduced this model we also indicated that the model is not reliable for classification of entity pairs with two-way relationships [7]. Based on these limitations, we recommend to consider symmetry metrics as applicable only to entity pairs with one-way relationships.

In this study we will demonstrate how to use symmetry metrics to measure differences between vectors and compare effectiveness of symmetry metrics with traditional cosine similarity metrics. As a basic model we will use a model trained on daily temperature history data. We will examine scenarios on climate time series data domain and NLP data domain.

For climate data domain scenarios we will compare temperatures between city pairs in one-way relationships. In one scenario we will compare city yearly temperature with central city and in another scenario we will compare city yearly temperatures with average of all yearly city temperatures.

For NLP scenario we will detect dissimilar pairs of words from text documents and compare statistical distributions and semantic graph clusters based on symmetry metrics and cosine similarities.

2   Related Work

In the last few years, after the evolutionary model AlexNet was created in 2012, deep learning demonstrated great success outperforming previous state-of-the-art machine learning techniques in various domains [1,2]. It influenced usage of CNN image classification as an instrument for other techniques, specifically for classification of embedded vectors transformed to two-dimensional matrices. In study [12,13] authors suggested time series transformation to Recurrence Plots (RP) and in studies [4,5] to Gramian Angular Fields (GAF) and Markov Transition Fields (MTF) images. In one of our studies we showed higher accuracy metrics of CNN image classification model with vector to GAF image transformation than accuracy metrics of models with plot pictures [14].

The idea of that model came from one of fast.ai forum presentations [3] that shows how to take advantages of both vector to GAF image transformation and CNN transfer learning image classification. Author of that study, Ignacio Oguiza translated Olive Oil time series data to GAF images [4,5] and demonstrated how to use fast.ai CNN transfer learning image classification model [12,13] for time series classification.

CNN image classification methods are getting high accuracies but being based on supervised machine learning, they require labeling of huge volumes of data. Self-supervised representation learning has made significant progress over the last years, almost reaching the performance of supervised baselines on many downstream tasks [6,15]. The closest to our method are discriminative self-supervised methods or contrastive methods that are based on direct comparison between training samples [16]. As our method categorizes pairs of entities to classes of similar pairs and not similar pairs, it is conceptually comparable with a combination of Siamese Nets [17] and self-supervised contrastive methods [16]. Siamese nets were first introduced in 1993 by Bromley and LeCun to solve signature verification as an image matching problem [17].

Another beneficial technique that we use it our study is transfer learning that allows to deal with comparatively small sets of training data. Fine-tuning a network with transfer learning usually works much faster and has higher accuracy than training CNN image classification models from scratch [18].

3   Methods

Symmetry metrics represent probabilities for GAF images of pairwise vectors to get to symmetric image class and therefore define how similar are pairs of vectors to each other. For data processing, model training and interpreting the results we will use techniques that are described in details in our technical blog: data preparation process [19,20,22], model training procedure [20] and interpretation approach [20–22].

3.1   Transform Pairs of Vectors to Joint Vectors

To generate training data for entity pair classification we will create vector pairs of the 'same' class by concatenating vectors with themselves and vector pairs of the 'different' class by concatenating vectors of different entities.

To predict pairwise vector similarity by symmetry metric we will concatenate left vectors with reversed right vectors. Code for data preparation process is described in [19] for climate time series data domain and in [22] for NLP data domain.

3.2   Transform Joint Vectors to GAF Images

As a method of vector to image translation we will use Gramian Angular Field (GAF), a polar coordinate transformation based technique [4,5]. Code and techniques are described in our technical blog [19]. Python code in details can be found in Github [23].

3.3   Train CNN Image Classification Models

Training data for this model is illustrated on Fig. 2. It shows similar entities being represented as self-reflected mirror vectors and symmetric GAF images and dissimilar entities represented as asymmetric GAF images. Model accuracy was estimated as the proportion of the total number of predictions that were correct. The training model accuracy was about 0.965.

To deal with comparatively small sets of training data, instead of training the model from scratch, we followed ResNet-50 transfer learning model: loaded the results of model trained on images from the ImageNet database and fine tuned it with data of interest [18].

Fast.ai CNN transfer learning image classification can be used for both supervised and unsupervised machine learning. Methods of transforming vectors to GAF images and fine tuning ResNet-50 model are described in fast.ai [3,12,13] and Python code in details can be found in Github [23].

3.4   Get Similarity Metrics by Interpreting Trained Model Results

To calculate how similar are vectors to each other we will combine them as pairwise reflected vectors and transform joint vectors to GAF images. Then we will run GAF images through trained image classification model and predict vector similarities. Symmetry metrics will be calculated as probabilities of GAF images to get to the 'same' class. Model training and interpretation techniques are described in details on our technical blog [20–22].

4   Experiments

4.1   Climate Time Series Data for Training the Model and Data Analysis

Data Source. Climate time series raw data was taken from kaggle.com: "Temperature History of 1000 cities 1980 to 2020" [24]. This data represents average daily temperatures in Celsius degrees for 1000 most populous cities in the world. Based in this data we will train the unsupervised pairwise entity classification model and examine two vector similarity prediction scenarios.

Training the Model. Training of this model was described in the paper where this model was introduced [7]. On the high level, time series classification model training was processed based on fast.ai transfer learning method. This method is described in study [12] and coding in [23].

Training data for this model is illustrated on Fig. 2. It shows symmetric and asymmetric GAF images that represent similar and dissimilar entity pairs. Model accuracy was estimated as the proportion of the total number of predictions that were correct. The training model accuracy was about 0.965.

Compare City, Year Temperature Vectors with Central City. For the first climate scenario we will select daily temperature data for years 2008 and 2016 for 66 cities located in Western Europe and compare them with Stuttgart (Germany) - the centrally located city. To calculate symmetry metrics we will create pairwise vectors by concatenating temperature vector pairs [City, Stuttgart], transform joint vectors to GAF images, and run those images through the trained image classification model. We will calculate symmetry metrics as probabilities for images to get to the 'same' class.

As expected, for both years, cities located close to Stuttgart have high cosine similarities and high probabilities of getting into the 'same' class. For most cities located far from Stuttgart daily temperature vectors have higher 'different' probabilities and lower cosine similarities (detail information about statistics is represented in our technical blog [21]). However it is not easy to predict which cities have similarities with Stuttgart temperatures on the border between 'different' and 'same'. To find such cities, we order the table by formula:

ABS (0.5 - same probability for 2008) * ABS (0.5 - same probability for 2016)

Table 1. Examples of city, year temperature time series 'on the border'.

		2008	2008	2016	2016
City, Country	Distance (km)	Cosine sim.	'Same' prob	Cosine sim.	'Same' prob.
Stockholm (Sweden)	1308	0.955	0.586	0.937	0.539
Genoa (Italy)	486	0.956	0.380	0.951	0.543
Nice (France)	582	0.951	0.321	0.948	0.443
Florence (Italy)	578	0.964	0.674	0.968	0.349
Oslo (Norway)	1242	0.937	0.942	0.906	0.498

Data in the table (Table 1) shows a data mining example where symmetry metrics work much better then cosine similarity metrics.

Compare City, Year Temperature Vectors with Average of All Yearly Temperatures. For another scenario we will calculate average vector for 2640 daily temperature time series - for years from 1980 to 2019 for 66 Western European cities and compare this vector with yearly daily temperature vectors for all cities.

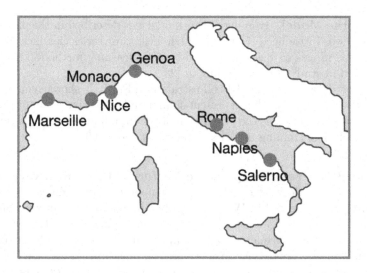

Fig. 3. Cities located on Mediterranean Sea have high similarities to 'average of average' smooth line.

As the average vector of all city-year temperature time series provides a very smooth line, we do not expect many city-year temperature vectors to be similar to it. With symmetry metrics we found that most of cities with high similarities to a smooth line are located on Mediterranean Sea not far from each other. The Fig. 3 shows a clockwise city list: Marseille (France), Nice (France), Monaco (Monaco), Genoa (Italy), Rome (Italy), Naples (Italy), and Salerno (Italy).

4.2   Dissimilar Word Pair Detection

For this experiment to analyse NLP data we will use the same trained model that we used for climate data experiments – unsupervised pairwise entity classification model trained on climate time series data. As we showed on paper [11], unsupervised pairwise entity classification model can be trained on one data domain and be used to classify pairwise entities taken from another data domain.

In this experiment we will demonstrate how to predict word pair similarities by symmetry metrics and cosine similarities. In both scenarios, using data about Psychoanalysis from Wikipedia, we will extract co-located word pairs from text document and transform words to vectors through Glove model. To compare word vectors via cosine similarities we will just calculate cosines between co-located pairs of word. Coding for these techniques are described in detail in our technical blog [22].

Cosine similarity metrics are valid for word pair classifications with both one-way and two-way relationships, but as we mentioned above [7], unsupervised pairwise entity classification model is only valid for entity pairs with one-way relationships and it is not reliable for classifying entity pairs with two-way relationships.

Table 2. Distributions of Word Pair Similarity Statistics: Symmetry Metrics and Cosine Similarities

Symmetry metrics		Cosine similarities	
Count	**2244**	Count	**2234**
Mean	**0.706**	Mean	**0.304**
Std	**0.270**	Std	**0.214**
Min	**0.001**	Min	**−0.470**
25%	**0.538**	25%	**0.165**
50%	**0.793**	50%	**0.321**
75%	**0.932**	75%	**0.459**
max	**1.000**	Max	**0.988**

To compare word vector similarities based on symmetry metrics we will extract from the document co-located pairs of word in the order that they are presented in the document, i.e. we will apply the model to word pairs with one-way relationships. To create pairwise vectors we will concatenate left vectors with reversed right vectors and transform joint vectors to GAF images. Corresponding pairwise vectors with low similarities will represent dissimilar word pairs. To find dissimilar word pairs we will look at word pairs with low symmetry metrics. As we mentioned above, as trained model we will use the same model that we used from climate data experiment: pairwise entity classification model trained on climate time series data. To calculate word vector similarities we classified GAF images through the trained model and used probabilities of getting to the 'same' class as metrics.

Distribution of Word Pair Similarity Statistics. The distribution of statistics on word pair similarities represented on Table 2 shows the following:

– On cosine similarity scenario there is high proportion of dissimilar word pairs.
– On symmetry metrics scenario there is low proportion of dissimilar word pairs.
– On symmetry metrics scenario there is much lower proportion of dissimilar word pairs then proportion of dissimilar word pairs in cosine similarity scenario.

Examples of Word Pairs. For this experiment we are looking for dissimilar pair of words and as examples we will show the lowest sets of word pairs with left and right neighbors for the word 'infant'. On Table 3 we present the most dissimilar neighbors based on cosine similarities and on Table 4 the most dissimilar neighbors based on symmetry metrics. Word pair exampled are represented in two directions: 'other word' to 'infant' pairs and 'infant' to 'other word' pairs. Word pairs are ordered from semantically less similar pairs to more similar pairs.

Comparison of vector similarities between cosine similarities and symmetry metrics corresponds with the distribution of statistics. As cosine similarity measurements are much lower than symmetry metric measurements (Table 2), we can see that the most dissimilar neighbors calculated by cosine similarities have much lower entity similarity measures (Table 4) than dissimilar neighbors uncovered through symmetry metrics (Table 3).

Table 3. Examples of word pairs around the word 'infant' represented in two directions calculated by symmetry metrics.

Other word – infant		Infant – other word	
Word pair	Metric	Word pair	Metric
likewise – infant	0.017	infant – phantasies	0.157
response – infant	0.087	infant – mind	0.254
focus – infant	0.094	infant – completely	0.570
prior – infant	0.158	infant – structure	0.576
example – infant	0.397	infant – internalization	0.707
frustrated – infant	0.562	infant – able	0.761

Table 4. Examples of word pairs around the word 'infant' represented in two directions calculated by cosine similarities.

Other word – infant		Infant – other word	
Word pair	Cosine	Word pair	Cosine
comprehended – infant	−0.0671	infant – fairbairn	−0.0803
maintains – infant	0.0075	infant – phantasies	−0.0321
persecuted – infant	0.0493	infant – internalization	0.0210
individuality – infant	0.0657	infant – resolves	0.0304
frustrated – infant	0.0771	infant – paranoid	0.0527
phantasy – infant	0.0796	infant – interact	0.1418

Semantic Graph Clusters to Uncover Topics of Documents. Finally, we will compare values of cosine similarity and symmetry metrics for uncovering document topics based on semantic graph mining. Document topics can be discovered by identifying semantic graph clusters. For both cosine similarity and symmetry metric scenarios we will build semantic graphs by selecting pairs of words based on thresholds. As we are looking for dissimilar word pairs, we will select pairs of word vectors with similarities lower than threshold.

To uncover clusters we will use a simple graph clustering method - graph connected components. Graph connected components are subgraphs where every two nodes have path between them and none of the nodes is related to nodes outside of this subgraph. In dense graphs the largest connected component usually contains large amount of graph nodes and therefore connected components method is not useful for community detection in dense graphs. On the contrary, community detection via connected components method works well for sparse graphs [25].

In consequence of our observations, the proportion of co-located dissimilar words is documents is not high and we can expect to get sparse semantic graphs. Based on our statistics (Table 2) we defined the following graph thresholds: for cosine similarities we took words pairs with metric lower than −0.1 and for symmetry metrics – word pairs with metric lower than 0.2.

Figure 4 represents top three connected components for corresponding semantics classes. As for symmetry metrics we observed lower proportion of dissimilar word pairs then for cosine similarities, we can expect semantic graph for symmetry metrics to be sparser than semantic graph based on cosine similarities. Illustration on Fig. 4 confirms this expectation: sizes of top connected components of symmetry metrics semantic graph change much slower than sizes of top connected components of cosine similarities semantic graph.

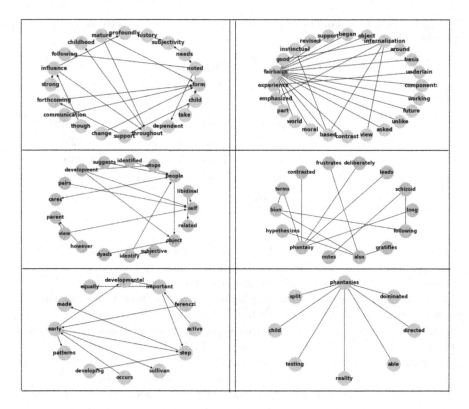

Fig. 4. Document topics calculated based symmetry metrics less than 0.2 (left) and cosine similarities less than −0.1 (right)

5   Conclusion

In this study we extended the benefits of unsupervised pairwise entity classification model by building a new method of measuring vector similarities—symmetry metrics. An ability to apply symmetry metrics relies on transforming concatenated entity pair vectors to GAF images and trained unsupervised pairwise entity classification model. In this paper we described how to convert entity pairs to joint vectors, how to train the model and how to calculate symmetry metrics by interpreting GAF image classification results.

With experiments based on climate time series data domain and NLP data domain we compared effectiveness of symmetry metrics with cosine similarity metrics and demonstrated how the symmetry metrics provide a complementary view for entity pair data analysis.

Symmetry metrics can be applied to a variety of embeddable entity pairs such as words, documents, images, videos, etc. For example, symmetry metrics can be used for unsupervised outlier detection in finding stock prices that are very different from average stock price. Potentially it opens a possibility to train pairwise entity classification model on heterogeneous data domains and use it for classifications of entities from a very big variety of embeddable data domains such as described in *2Vec [26].

References

1. LeCun, Y., Bengio, Y., Hinton, G.: Deep learning. Nature **521**(7553), 436–444 (2015)
2. Krizhevsky, A., Sutskever, I., Hinton, G.E.: ImageNet classification with deep convolutional neural networks. In: Advances in Neural Information Processing Systems, pp. 1097–1105 (2012)
3. Time series/sequential data study group (2019). https://forums.fast.ai/t/time-series-sequential-data-study-group/29686
4. Wang, Z., Oates, T.: Encoding time series as images for visual inspection and classification using tiled convolutional neural networks. In: Association for the Advancement of Artificial Intelligence (2015). www.aaai.org
5. Wang, Z., Yan, W., Oates, T.: Time series classification from scratch with deep neural networks: a strong baseline. In: International Joint Conference on Neural Networks (IJCNN)(2017)
6. LeCun, Y., Misra, I.: Self-supervised learning: the dark matter of intelligence (2021). https://ai.facebook.com/blog/self-supervised-learning-the-dark-matter-of-intelligence/
7. Romanova, A.: Unsupervised time series classification for climate data. In: Proceedings of the Northern Lights Deep Learning Conference (NLDL 2022) (2022)
8. Aggarwal, C., Hinneburg, A., Keim, D.: On the surprising behavior of distance metrics in high dimensional space. Paper presented at the Database Theory - ICDT 2001, Proceedings, 1973, pp. 420–434, (2001)
9. Bronstein, M., Bruna, J., Cohen, T., Veličković, P.: Geometric deep learning: grids, groups, graphs, geodesics, and gauges (2021). https://doi.org/10.48550/arXiv.2104.13478
10. Devlin, J., Chang, M.-W., Lee, K.: Kristina Toutanova: BERT: pre-training of deep bidirectional transformers for language understanding (2018). https://doi.org/10.48550/arXiv.1810.04805
11. Romanova, A.: Unsupervised pairwise entity classification model to detect free associations. Proceedings of the International Conference on Electrical, Computer and Energy Technologies (ICECET 2022), 20–22 June 2022, Prague-Czech Republic (2022). https://doi.org/10.1109/ICECET55527.2022.9872922
12. Howard, J., Gugger, S.: Deep Learning for Coders with fastai and PyTorch. O'Reilly Media, Inc. (2020)
13. Practical Deep Learning for Coders (2020). https://course.fast.ai/
14. Kotsis, G., et al. (eds.): DEXA 2021. CCIS, vol. 1479. Springer, Cham (2021). https://doi.org/10.1007/978-3-030-87101-7
15. Bardes, A., Ponce, J., LeCun, Y.: VICReg: variance-invariance-covariance regularization for self-supervised learning. ArXiv, abs/2105.04906 (2021). arXiv: 2105.04906
16. Chen, T., Kornblith, S., Norouzi, M., Hinton, G.: A simple framework for contrastive learning of visual representations. ArXiv, abs/2002.05709 (2020). PMLR119: 1597-1607

17. Bromley, J., Guyon, I., LeCun, Y., Sickinger, E., Shah, R.: Signature verification using a Siamese time delay neural network. J. Pattern Recogn. Artif. Intell. **7**(04), 669–688 (1993). https://doi.org/10.1142/S0218001493000339
18. Yosinski, J., Clune, J., Bengio, Y., Lipson, H.: How transferable are features in deep neural networks? In: Advances in Neural Information Processing Systems, pp. 3320–3328 (2014)
19. sparklingdataocean.com: CNN image classification for climate data (2021). http://sparklingdataocean.com/2021/04/04/cityTempCNN/
20. sparklingdataocean.com: Unsupervised deep learning for climate data analysis (2021). http://sparklingdataocean.com/2021/08/01/unsupervisdCityTempCNN/
21. sparklingdataocean.com: Symmetry metrics for high dimensional vector similarity. http://sparklingdataocean.com/2022/02/22/symmetryMetrics/
22. sparklingdataocean.com: Find unexpected word pairs by symmetry metrics (2022). http://sparklingdataocean.com/2022/04/22/symmetryMetricsNLP/?
23. Oguiza, I.: Time series - olive oil country (2019). https://gist.github.com/oguiza/c9c373aec07b96047d1ba484f23b7b47
24. kaggle.com: Temperature history of 1000 cities 1980 to 2020 (2021). https://www.kaggle.com/datasets/hansukyang/temperature-history-of-1000-cities-1980-to-2020
25. Romanova, A.: Semantics graph mining for topic discovery and word associations. Int. J. Data Mining Knowl. Manag. Process (IJDKP) (2021). https://doi.org/10.5121/ijdkp.2021.11401
26. Something2Vec (2016). https://gist.github.com/nzw0301/333afc00bd508501268fa7bf40cafe4e

A New Method to Measure Similarity of Words in Japanese Twitter Based on Related Images

Zhelin Xu[1]([✉]), Atsushi Matsumura[2], and Tetsuji Satoh[2]

[1] Doctoral Program in Informatics, University of Tsukuba, Tsukuba, Ibaraki, Japan
`zhelin@ce.slis.tsukuba.ac.jp`
[2] Faculty of Library, Information and Media Science, University of Tsukuba,
Tsukuba, Ibaraki, Japan
`matsumur@slis.tsukuba.ac.jp`, `satoh@ce.slis.tsukuba.ac.jp`

Abstract. Twitter, as a popular form of social media in Japan, has emerged as a valuable data resource for various important social network analysis tasks. However, Japanese tweets often contain nonstandard words and variant notations, owing to which several words with the same meaning may be written differently. The use of such words will generate the sparsity problem and decrease the accuracy of similarity measures between users. Furthermore, the performance of user or tweet recommendations may be deteriorated. Therefore, words with the same meaning must be unified in the preprocessing step. In this research, assuming that words with the same meaning have similar or common related images, we propose a method to use word-related images to measure the similarity between words. A manually annotated Japanese data set is created to evaluate the proposed method. Experimental results indicate that the proposed method outperforms the existing methods in most cases.

Keywords: Social media processing · Similarity measures · Related images · Japanese tweets

1 Introduction

Social media has transformed into an essential part of daily life. Twitter is a popular form of social media that currently has 54.15 million users in Japan [26]. Twitter users typically post event updates and ideas in real time. However, owing to the casual writing style usually employed on Twitter, the tweets are noisy and contain many nonstandard words [10] such as "PS4" for "PlayStation4." Moreover, the Japanese language has more characters than other languages such as English, and it includes four character sets: Kanji, Hiragana, Katakana, and the Roman alphabet. Kanji is one of the oldest and complex scripts worldwide, and thousands of kanji elements are used in the Japanese language (e.g., "鴨," duck in Japanese, written in kanji). The hiragana and katakana scripts were created by the Japanese. Each of these scripts includes 46 characters, and the individual character does not have an independent semantic meaning but carries phonetic

E. Pardede et al. (Eds.): iiWAS 2022, LNCS 13635, pp. 489–503, 2022.
https://doi.org/10.1007/978-3-031-21047-1_45

information [5]. Hiragana is used for expressing grammatical elements and words (e.g., subject markers and inflections), while katakana represents loanwords [23]. The Roman alphabet is used to transcribe Japanese words. As a result, a word has many types of variant notations in Japanese sentences [19]. For example, a word may be composed of one type of character (e.g., "Nintendo" (a video game company, written in the Roman alphabet) has three variant notations: "任天堂" (written in kanji), "にんてんどー" (written in hiragana), and "ニンテンドー" (written in katakana)). A word may also be composed of two character types (e.g., "たまねぎ" (onion in Japanese, written in hiragana) can be written as "玉ねぎ", which contains two characters, as "玉" is written in kanji, and as "ねぎ" is written in hiragana).

This aspect poses a challenge for natural language processing tools [1], because they cannot easily identify the semantic equivalence of these words in tweets (e.g., PS4 and PlayStation4), and thus treat these words differently. Consequently, the sparsity problem is generated, and the accuracy of similarity measures between users is decreased [34]. These aspects adversely influence the performance of several important social network analysis tasks, such as the identification of potential communities, and its application to user or tweet recommendations.

To solve this problem, the semantic equivalence can be determined by calculating the similarity between words. Word embedding models such as the Word2Vec [17] use vectors to represent words in a low-dimensional space to compute the semantic similarities between them. Notably, training an embedding model on a large-scale corpus is time and cost-intensive. Moreover, the embedded vector is unreliable if words do not appear in the training set. In contrast, calculating the similarity between words based on visual content is a more human-like behavior. As indicated by the adage "A picture is worth a thousand words," it is not necessary to explain the meaning of the two words because the visual content represents their meaning. For instance, even if the meanings of "スターバックス" and "スタバ" are unknown, as shown in Fig. 1 , we can determine that they have the same meaning based on the image content. Consequently, if "スターバックス" and "スタバ" have the same meanings, the related images are expected to be similar, and thus, the distance between "スターバックス" and "スタバ" is smaller than that between "スターバックス" and "bike".

Based on this assumption, in this research, we focus on the nonstandard words and variant notations in Japanese tweets and propose a method to measure the similarity between words by calculating the similarity between related images. Our main goal is to identify words with the same meaning as those of the target and unify these words. The proposed method exhibits two key advantages: 1. Images contain visual content that directly represents word meanings, and thus, it is not necessary to infer the meaning of words via a large-scale corpus, and 2. Since some Japanese words have variant notations, one word can represent by kanji or the Roman alphabet, which can be regarded as calculating the similarity between Chinese and English. Thus, the proposed method may be adaptable to calculate the word similarity in languages other than Japanese, because only the similarity of the images needs to be determined, which is not relevant to the language.

(b) スタバ   (a) スターバックス   (c) bike

Fig. 1. Images of "スタバ", "スターバックス", and "bike", obtained by Bing https://
www.bing.com/images/

2 Related Work

Several methods are proposed to calculate the similarity between words. The
Normalized Google Distance (NGD) [4] is a concurrency-based similarity measurement method. When two words have a higher probability of occurring
together in a large number of web pages, the NGD distance is smaller, which
means that the two words are similar. The assumption underlying the concept
of orthographic similarity is that two words have the same meaning if they
appear similar. Several researchers have used the longest common subsequence
and edit distance to calculate the orthographic similarity between words [32].
However, closely related words do not always look alike. For example, "nite"
looks more similar to "note" than to "night" [31]. Moreover, the edit distance
does not always effectively indicate the similarity between two words. Therefore, [8] extended this work by constructing an exception dictionary of strongly
associated word pairs. The phonetic similarity is also used to calculate the similarity between words, which based on the assumption that two words have the
same meaning if they sound similar. The challenge pertains to the conversion
of words into phonetic code. The Soundex algorithm is a promising tool for
decoding pronunciation [24]. In addition, the double metaphone algorithm can
be used to measure the phonetic edit distance, which can be used as a feature
to capture the morphophonemic similarity between two words [9]. Notably, several phonetic matching algorithms such as the Soundex distance are designed
for English. Although the English-based algorithms can be used if the Japanese
characters are transformed to the Latin alphabet, several input characters may
be lost, leading to transliteration errors [33].

Orthographic similarity or phonetic similarity can be used to evaluate the
similarity of two words, both similarity metrics exhibit several limitations. Therefore, several researchers have recommended the combination of these two similarity metrics to enhance the performance. The edit distance and Refined Soundex
technique have been used to represent word-level similarity [1]. Moreover, [31]
assumed that people tend to first segment a word into syllables, and identify
the corresponding standard word with syllables, such as "t-m-r" and "to-mor-
row". In this context, syllables are chosen as the basic unit, and an exponential
potential function is used to combine the orthographical distance and phonetic
distance to measure the syllable similarity as a reflection of word similarity.

However, the abovementioned word similarity metrics do not consider semantic information. The semantics of words must be considered because if two words look alike or sound alike, they may be considered to have the same meaning. But it is still necessary to recall the meanings of the two words to confirm this aspect. Thus, a semantic similarity measurement method can likely help evaluate the similarity between two words as a human would.

Knowledge-based methods and corpus-based methods are frequently used to measure the semantic similarity [37]. Knowledge-based semantic approaches measure the semantic similarity between words based on a large lexical database, such as WordNet. Two words are considered more similar if they are located nearby in the given lexical database [2]. However, knowledge-based methods exhibit three limitations. First, because people define the words in the lexical database and the definitions are highly subjective, the meanings of several words may be incorrect. Second, many new words have not been added to the lexical database. Third, we cannot measure the similarity between a Japanese word and an English word with a lexical database.

Word embedding method, a representative corpus-based method, was introduced in 1986 [12]. This approach involves using a corpus to represent the semantic information at the word level and mapping this information into a low-dimensional continuous space while ensuring that semantically similar words also have similar values in this space [16]. In an ideal situation, "PS4" and "PlayStation4" can be encoded as $(1,1,1)$ and $(1,1,2)$, respectively, and the semantic similarity between the two words can be calculated using two real-valued vectors. Word embedding has been popularized with the introduction of the Word2Vec model. Subsequently, fastText [18] and BERT [6] were developed. However, as mentioned in Sect. 1, word embedding methods are highly dependent on the size of the training data set. The vector associated with a small data set may not correctly represent the words. Moreover, BERT currently shows good performance on the sentence classification task, but often worse than averaging Glove [21] embeddings on sentence embedding for other downstream tasks [22]. Besides, some researchers have proposed hybrid methods that combined linguistic features (e.g., obtained from the Word2Vec model) and visual features which aim to enhance word embedding [11,14]. Our method is different from these existing methods in two aspects: 1. According to the experiment results, the hybrid methods slightly outperform word embedding methods. Thus, how to combine linguistic features and visual features is a challenge for hybrid methods. On the other hand, the proposed method is inspired by the adage "A picture is worth a thousand words," we only use visual features to represent word meaning, and 2. The existing methods collect related images from image data sets. However, images in some data sets are generally noisy [11], and some word-related images cannot retrieve from image-text data sets such as ImageNet. Therefore, in order to process more words like those that exist in Twitter, we proposed a method to retrieve word-related images.

3   Framework

This section describes the proposed framework (Fig. 2) for measuring the similarity between words in Japanese tweets. Section 3.1 describes the representation of a word as a set of fixed-length vectors with image characteristics by collecting related images. Section 3.2 describes the method for calculating the similarity between images, which helps determine whether a pair of words have the same meaning.

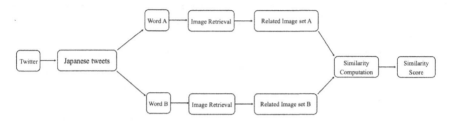

Fig. 2. Framework for measuring the similarity between words in Japanese tweets

3.1   Retrieval of Related Images

The Bing image search engine uses the TBIR approach, however, the performance of TBIR is limited owing to the noisy nature of manually labeled tags [30]. Consequently, several images collected by Bing may not be relevant to the query. Moreover, we consider that related images can be divided into main and minor visual contents. For example, in the case of images related to the "PS4", the main visual content pertains to the PS4 game console, and the minor content includes the PS4 controller or certain game software. In this case, when calculating the similarity between "PS4" and "PlayStation4", more accurate results can be obtained using only the images of the game console. If a word having main visual content, we consider most images represent this content, and they are similar to one another. By clustering the images collected by Bing, we aim to achieve the following two objectives: 1. To narrow the number of related images to those containing the main visual content; and 2. To increase the proportion of related images. Figure 3 shows the process of related image retrieval. Subsequently, we describe the method to cluster the images in four phases.

Phase 1 is visual feature selection. Generally, the visual features can be classified into: "global features" and "local features." Global features are used in combination with local features [35]. Scale-invariant feature transform (SIFT) is a representative local feature with the following advantages: 1. A large number of SIFT features can be generated from a single image; and 2. this feature exhibits robust invariance to rotation, scale, and intensity changes. Notably, although the color feature is a key global feature of images [28], SIFT features are calculated from the standard gray space, owing to which, the color information of an image

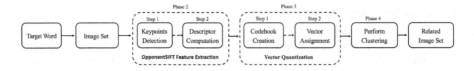

Fig. 3. Process of related image retrieval

may be ignored. To overcome this limitation, OpponentSIFT [29] extends the basic SIFT by using the SIFT descriptor to describe key points in the opponent color space. Therefore, we use the OpponentSIFT feature with color information to describe the image content.

Phase 2 is OpponentSIFT feature extraction. The feature extraction is performed through the following two steps: step 1 is the key point detection. Key point detection aims to detect the location of unique points in an image. We use a difference-of-Gaussian detector to extract the key points; and step 2 is the descriptor computation. After a key point is detected, the image is first converted to the opponent color space using equation (1). Next, the SIFT descriptor is used to compute the feature vector that describes the key point in each channel. Finally, the vectors are concatenated to produce the OpponentSIFT vector (384-dimensional). Commonly, hundreds of OpponentSIFT features can be extracted from a single image. However, this computation involves the following problems: 1. Classification cannot be performed at the image level; and 2. Because the similarity of two images is determined by matching visual features, the amount of computation significantly increases when the image contains many features. Vector quantization is performed to solve these problems.

$$O_1 = \frac{R - G}{\sqrt{2}}$$
$$O_2 = \frac{R + G - 2B}{\sqrt{6}} \tag{1}$$
$$O_3 = \frac{R + G + B}{\sqrt{3}}$$

Phase 3 is vector quantization. All OpponentSIFT feature vectors calculated from an image are quantized to obtain a fixed-length vector, which is used to describe the image content. Typically, the following steps are performed to transform a set of OpponentSIFT features of an image into a fixed-length vector using the bag-of-visual-words model. Step 1 is codebook creation. Before quantizing the vector, it is necessary to construct a codebook. The center of each cluster of the OpponentSIFT features extracted from the images is known as a visual word, which can be seen as representative feature. We use the MiniBatchKMeans algorithm for clustering as it can converge more rapidly than the K-means technique on large-scale data, and the results are only slightly inferior to those of the standard algorithm [7]. Because all features are expected to be quantized into visual words in the codebook, the codebook size affects the performance of fixed-length vectors. [20] recommends using a codebook size of 1,000. However, if hundreds of thousands or millions of features are used to create a codebook, the number of representative features increases accordingly. Therefore, we create two codebooks sized 1,000 and 10,000 to ensure that as many unique features become visual words as possible. Step 2 is vector assignment. Vector assignment is converts each feature to the closest visual word. To decrease the computational cost, we first convert the codebook into a k-d tree and calculate the Euclidean distance between each feature and visual word [36]. After vector assignment, a histogram of the visual words is obtained, which is used as the fixed-length vector of the image.

Phase 4 is clustering method. As mentioned above, we consider that the images containing the main visual content are highly similar. Furthermore, the main visual content should correspond to the largest number of images. Since the largest cluster contains the maximum number of similar images, the images containing the main visual content are most likely to be found in this cluster. Therefore, the largest cluster obtained by clustering the set of fixed-length vectors corresponding to each word is used as the set of related images of the word. We adopt the mean shift algorithm as the clustering algorithm for two reasons [15]: 1. The mean shift algorithm is an unsupervised clustering algorithm. Thus, it is unnecessary to select the number of clusters for each image set manually as the optimal number of clusters for each image set is not known. 2. The algorithm can select the optimal number of clusters without manual specification.

3.2   Similarity Computation

As described in Sect. 3.1, the related images are inferred and each fixed-length vector represents the content of each image. The similarity between images is determined by computing the distance between vectors.

Word vectors can be average to determine the degree of matching between two text sequences [25]. Following this method, the word is considered as text and the related image is considered as a word in the text, calculate the average of the fixed-length vector. Subsequently, the distance between the related image sets can be measured based on the L_1-norm (equation (2)) between mean vectors. Here, $\mathbf{A}$ and $\mathbf{B}$ are the mean vectors, expressed as $[A_1, ..., A_n]$ and $[B_1, ..., B_n]$ respectively, and n denotes the vector dimension, which is equal to the codebook size.

$$\|\mathbf{A} - \mathbf{B}\|^1 = \sum_i |A_i - B_i|^1 \tag{2}$$

Finally, since the reciprocal of the distance can be used to measure the similarity [13], the similarity between related image sets can be computed using equation (3). This similarity score can be used to determine the similarity between words.

$$S(\mathbf{A}, \mathbf{B}) = \frac{1}{1 + \|\mathbf{A} - \mathbf{B}\|^1} \tag{3}$$

4 Data

Evaluation Data. To evaluate the proposed method, it is necessary to use a manually annotated reliable data set, and each group in the data set consists of two or more words with the same meaning. Lexical normalization data such as LexNorm1.2 [32] and LexNorm2015 [3] are frequently used. However, the focus of this research is Japanese tweets. Because the abovementioned data sets are composed of English data, variant notations unique to Japanese do not appear. Therefore, we create a manually annotated Japanese data set. First, we used data collected from Twitter in 2020 and 2021. Next, the experimental objects are manually collected from the twitter data set by three people. In this research, the type of experimental object shows in Table 1. Several groups are formed if both the objects exist in the tweet data set. Otherwise, we use the Wikipedia Redirect tool[1] to find words with the same meaning as the objects. For example, if the official name of "桃鉄" (acronym of a Japanese game software) does not exist in the tweet data set, the Wikipedia Redirect tool is used to find the official name "桃太郎電鉄シリーズ." Although the Wikipedia Redirect tool can find words with the same meaning as the object, only some of the synonyms are two object types on which we focused on. Therefore, we manually select the words that match the criteria to make some groups. Finally, our Japanese data set contains 401 groups collected from 1,667 tweets, while each group has two or more words, pertaining to 786 words. Moreover, the characteristics of the groups in the data set can be divided into five categories: 1. Sub culture (44% of the total groups, e.g., game, movie, anime, etc.); 2. Famous person (19% of the total groups); 3. Food (19% of the total groups); 4. Company (12% of the total groups); 5. Others (6% of the total groups, e.g., SNS, animal, electronic goods, etc.).

Table 1. Type of Experimental Objects

No.	Types	Examples
1	Acronyms	(スタバ , スターバックス)
2	Variant notations (one character)	(Nintendo, 任天堂 , にんてんどー , ニンテンドー)
	Variant notations (two characters)	(たまねぎ , 玉ねぎ)

Image Sets. In our Japanese data set, each word is used as a query, and 100 images are collected using Bing API. However, owing to unknown factors, 77,493 images are included in our image sets. In addition, we set the image size as 224×224 to decrease the computational cost. As indicated in Phase 3 (vector quantization), to quantize each image into a fixed-length vector, it is necessary to create a codebook. First, we process all the images in the image sets to obtain 28,844,505 OpponentSIFT vectors. Subsequently, 3,000,000 random vectors are used to create two codebooks sized 1,000 and 10,000.

---

[1] Japanese Wikipedia dump data : https://dumps.wikimedia.org/jawiki/20210901/.

5   Experiment

5.1   Experimental Setup

First, we experimentally evaluate the effectiveness of the proposed method by comparing it with three baseline methods: (A) Word2Vec trained model for Japanese [27]; (B) fastText trained model for Japanese [18]; and (C) BERT pre-trained model for Japanese[2]. Next, one word is randomly extracted from each group in the Japanese data set as an experimental object to obtain 401 objects. Then, the similarity between each experimental object and other words in the Japanese data set is computed using the four methods. The total number of word pairs for each method is $786 \times 401 - ((1 + 401) \times 401)/2 = 234,585$. Note that the proposed method generated two codebooks, we refer to the proposed method with codebook sizes of 1,000 and 10,000 as Proposed_a and Proposed_b, respectively, in the experimental section. Finally, five ranked lists based on the similarity scores are obtained.

In this research, our goal is to find more words with the same meaning as the target word appear in the top-N list through the proposed method. The following metrics are considered to evaluate the performance of each method: 1. Top-10 similarity ranking: Number of words that appear in the top-10 similarity ranking with the same meaning as that of the experimental objects; 2. Precision, recall, and F1-score. Note that only 154 embedding of experimental objects can be generated using the Word2Vec model. Since we do not retrain the Word2Vec model in this research, we get the following two experimental results: (a) results for 154 experimental objects, and (b) results for all 401 experimental objects.

5.2   Results

Top-10 Similarity Ranking. Figure 4 shows the results of the top-10 similarity ranking, in which the horizontal axis represents each ranking position, and the vertical axis represents the number of words with the same meaning as that of the experimental object at each rank. Figure 4(a) shows that Proposed_a finds 83 words in the highest position (@1), outperforming both baseline methods and Proposed_b. In terms of the second position, the performance of Proposed_a is comparable to that of the Word2Vec and superior to that of the fastText and BERT. However, the Word2Vec outperforms the proposed method from the third position in the ranking list. In the results shown in Fig. 4(b), Proposed_a outperforms the other methods in all cases except for the third and eight position, in which the performance of the fastText and BERT is slightly superior. Nevertheless, Proposed_a significantly outperforms the fastText and BERT by achieving 178 words in the highest position and 40 words in the second position.

Precision, Recall, and F1-score. Table 2 summarizes the precision@N, recall@N, and F1-score@N (N = 1,2,...,5) values of the four methods with 154

---

[2] https://github.com/cl-tohoku/bert-japanese.

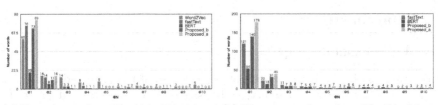

(a) Experimental results with 154 objects (b) Experimental results with 401 objects

Fig. 4. Results of top 10 similarity ranking

experimental objects. The results show that proposed_a outperforms three baseline methods except the top-5 positions. In particular, in the highest position (@1), the performance of Proposed_a is 9%, 36% and 315% higher than that of the fastText, Word2Vec and BERT, respectively. In the top-5 positions, the performance of Proposed_a is comparable to that of the Word2Vec model and superior to that of the fastText and BERT.

Table 2. Results of Precision@N, Recall@N, and F1-score@N with 154 objects

Model	Precision					Recall					F1-score				
	@1	@2	@3	@4	@5	@1	@2	@3	@4	@5	@1	@2	@3	@4	@5
Proposed_a	**0.540**	**0.321**	**0.216**	**0.164**	0.131	**0.500**	**0.596**	**0.602**	**0.608**	0.608	**0.519**	**0.418**	**0.318**	**0.258**	0.216
Proposed_b	0.474	0.273	0.184	0.140	0.112	0.440	0.506	0.512	0.518	0.518	0.456	0.354	0.271	0.220	0.184
Word2Vec	0.390	0.247	0.195	0.159	**0.139**	0.361	0.458	0.542	0.590	**0.645**	0.375	0.321	0.287	0.251	**0.228**
fastText	0.494	0.299	0.206	0.161	0.130	0.458	0.554	0.572	0.596	0.602	0.475	0.388	0.303	0.253	0.214
BERT	0.130	0.08	0.063	0.048	0.039	0.120	0.157	0.175	0.181	0.181	0.125	0.110	0.092	0.077	0.064

Table 3 presents the precision@N, recall@N, and F1-score@N ($N = 1, 2,...,$ 5) values of three methods with 401 experimental objects. The results show that Proposed_a outperforms the other methods in all cases, and in the highest position (@1), the Proposed_a outperforms the fastText and BERT by 49% and 229%, respectively.

Table 3. Results of Precision@N, Recall@N, and F1-score@N with 401 objects

Model	Precision					Recall					F1-score				
	@1	@2	@3	@4	@5	@1	@2	@3	@4	@5	@1	@2	@3	@4	@5
Proposed_a	**0.444**	**0.272**	**0.188**	**0.145**	**0.120**	**0.388**	**0.475**	**0.492**	**0.508**	**0.523**	**0.414**	**0.346**	**0.226**	**0.227**	**0.195**
Proposed_b	0.349	0.213	0.149	0.115	0.094	0.305	0.373	0.390	0.403	0.410	0.326	0.271	0.215	0.179	0.153
fastText	0.302	0.178	0.128	0.100	0.082	0.264	0.312	0.336	0.351	0.359	0.281	0.227	0.185	0.156	0.134
BERT	0.135	0.084	0.062	0.049	0.040	0.118	0.146	0.161	0.172	0.176	0.126	0.106	0.089	0.077	0.066

5.3   Analysis

According to the experimental results, the performance of the proposed method with a codebook size of 1,000 is superior to that when the codebook sized 10,000 is adopted. This finding indicates that after resizing the images, the OpponentSIFT features from the images (each image contains an average of 372 features) are quantized into a high-dimensional sparse vector, which deteriorates the performance significantly. Besides, for using BERT to convert a word into a vector, we input the target word into BERT and derive subword token embeddings, then average the subword token embeddings. As mentioned in Chap. 2, BERT do not always do well in some downstream tasks. According to the experimental results, using the output of BERT directly leads to quite poor performance. Therefore, we think that original BERT model does not apply to the word embedding task. Moreover, although satisfactory results are obtained in the experiments, the proposed method exhibits a deteriorated performance in some cases. Next, we will discusses the reasons why the proposed method with a codebook size of 1,000 outperforms the baseline methods and why its performance deteriorates significantly in some cases.

We present two examples to explain why the proposed method outperforms the three baseline methods in most cases. First, for the experimental object "有吉," the proposed method identifies the formal name "有吉弘行 (Japanese famous entertainer)" in the highest position. By examining the set of related images of these two words, we note that the proposed method can successfully extract the images containing the main visual content (portrait) from the images collected by Bing as well as eliminate most of the images not related to the two words (Fig. 5 shows several unrelated images). This finding indicates that the proposed method uses the main visual content as the related image by clustering and can identify more words with the same meaning than the baseline methods. Moreover, in the two related image sets, most of the images are similar, and some images are identical. Thus, for words with the same meaning, it is reasonable to assume that the related images are similar or common if main visual content consists, which enhances the accuracy of word similarity calculation.

Fig. 5. Sample images unrelated to "有吉弘行 " collected from Bing https://www. bing.com/images/

As the second example, we consider five experimental objects. Table 4 lists the correct words and their meanings for these experimental objects, as well as the ranking results for Proposed_a, Word2Vec, fastText and BERT. For these five objects, Proposed_a identifies the correct word in the highest position, while BERT does not do well in most cases, fastText performs extremely poorly, and Word2Vec cannot convert some of these words into vector. The reason for this result can likely be attributed to the low frequency of these words appearing in the training data used by the baseline methods. Although these methods use Wikipedia dump data for training, data are not publicly available. Therefore, the numbers in parentheses in Table 4 lists the frequencies of the words obtained using the latest Wikipedia dump data[3]. The results indicate that one or both of the five word pairs have low frequencies. Consequently, Word2Vec cannot handle these words unless the model is retrained because these words do not exist in the training corpus. Although fastText and BERT can handle these words, the performance of these model are not well because adequate resources are not available for these words. In contrast, when images are used to calculate similarity between low-frequency words, if these words have main visual content, then the proposed method can also handle low-frequency words.

Table 4. Ranking for five experimental objects; the numbers in parentheses assigned to the experimental objects and correct words are the frequency of occurrence in the latest Wikipedia dump data

Experimental object	Correct word in our groups	Meaning	Ranking			
			Proposed_a	Word2Vec	FastText	BERT
メガネ(1706)	目がね (4)	Glasses	1	NaN	734	487
Amazon (3148)	あまぞん (2)	An American technology company	1	NaN	753	457
任天堂 (4152)	にんてんどー (1)	A Japanese video game company	1	NaN	668	524
きゃりぱみゅ (2)	きゃりーぱみゅぱみゅ (215)	A Japanese singer and model	1	NaN	529	1
Tiktok (468)	ティックトック (8)	A video-focused social networking service	1	NaN	678	70

Subsequently, we use two examples to discuss the reasons for the degradation of the performance of the proposed method. After checking the proposed_a ranking results, we found that 40 words with the same meaning as that of the experimental objects appear after the 600th rank. For example, for the experimental object "SideM (a Japanese game)," the official name "アイドルマスターSideM " appears in the 765th position when using the proposed method. The reason is due to the meaning of these words can be described by many factors (e.g., different characters), which word meaning cannot represent by the visual content directly. Therefore, related images contain several different visual contents, such as characters, backgrounds, and clothes, and no main visual content exists. This leads to the similarity between the images being low, and the size of the largest cluster being extremely small. In this case, the probability that two words with the same meaning are not similar in the corresponding cluster of related images is high, which leads to the similarity between the two words being extremely low. This aspect represents a limitation of the proposed method:

---

[3] "jawiki-20210901-pages-articles-multistream.xml.bz2". Containing 1 billion words, download fromhttps://dumps.wikimedia.org/jawiki/20210901/.

the accuracy of the word similarity decreases dramatically when the meaning of word can be described by many factors (which means there is no main visual content exists).

Consider another example: for the experimental object "鬼滅 (a Japanese manga series)," the official name "キメツノヤイバ" appears in the 403rd position. These two words contain four meanings (animation, comics, movies, and anime-themed items). Because our method do not identify the meaning of word before images collection, each word as a input query and use Bing to collect images directly. Finally, Bing determines the image that correspond to words with polysemy. For example, the images for "鬼滅" include many images related to comics and animation, whereas the images for "キメツノヤイバ" include many peripheral anime-themed items. Therefore, the largest clusters of images associated with "鬼滅" and "キメツノヤイバ" are from different categories, and the similarity between them is low. Thus, the proposed method has another limitation: it cannot handle words with polysemy.

6 Conclusions and Future Work

This paper proposes a method for measuring the similarity between words by computing the similarity between related images. Specifically, OpponentSIFT features are extracted from each image and transform these features into a fixed-length vector by using the bag-of-visual-words model. We subsequently find related images by clustering images using the mean shift algorithm based on fixed-length vectors. Then, compute the similarity between word-related images. Finally, an annotated Japanese data set is created to evaluate the proposed method. According to the experimental results, the proposed method outperforms all baseline methods in most cases. In particular, it significantly outperforms the baseline methods in terms of the top-1 ranking. Future work can be focused on enhancing the proposed approach to handle polysemy and words that do not have main visual content.

Acknowledgments. This work was supported by JST SPRING, Grant Number JPMJSP2124.

References

1. Ahmed, B.: Lexical normalisation of twitter data. In: 2015 Science and Information Conference (SAI), pp. 326–328. IEEE (2015)
2. Araque, O., Zhu, G., Iglesias, C.A.: A semantic similarity-based perspective of affect lexicons for sentiment analysis. Knowl.-Based Syst. **165**, 346–359 (2019)
3. Baldwin, T., De Marneffe, M.C., Han, B., Kim, Y.B., Ritter, A., Xu, W.: Shared tasks of the 2015 workshop on noisy user-generated text: twitter lexical normalization and named entity recognition. In: Proceedings of the Workshop on Noisy User-generated Text, pp. 126–135 (2015)
4. Cilibrasi, R.L., Vitanyi, P.M.: The google similarity distance. IEEE Trans. Knowl. Data Eng. **19**(3), 370–383 (2007)

5. Clanuwat, T., Lamb, A., Kitamoto, A.: Kuronet: pre-modern japanese kuzushiji character recognition with deep learning. In: International Conference on Document Analysis and Recognition (ICDAR), pp. 607–614. IEEE (2019)
6. Devlin, J., Chang, M.W., Lee, K., Toutanova, K.: Bert: pre-training of deep bidirectional transformers for language understanding. arXiv preprint arXiv:1810.04805 (2018)
7. Fitriyani, S.R., Murfi, H.: The k-means with mini batch algorithm for topics detection on online news. In: 4th International Conference on Information and Communication Technology (ICoICT), pp. 1–5. IEEE (2016)
8. Gouws, S., Hovy, D., Metzler, D.: Unsupervised mining of lexical variants from noisy text. In: Proceedings of the First workshop on Unsupervised Learning in NLP, pp. 82–90 (2011)
9. Han, B., Baldwin, T.: Lexical normalisation of short text messages: makn sens a# twitter. In: Proceedings of the 49th Annual Meeting of the Association for Computational Linguistics: Human Language Technologies, pp. 368–378 (2011)
10. Han, B., Cook, P., Baldwin, T.: Automatically constructing a normalisation dictionary for microblogs. In: Proceedings of the 2012 Joint Conference on Empirical Methods in Natural Language Processing and Computational Natural Language Learning, pp. 421–432 (2012)
11. Hasegawa, M., Kobayashi, T., Hayashi, Y.: Incorporating visual features into word embeddings: a bimodal autoencoder-based approach. In: 12th International Conference on Computational Semantics (IWCS) (2017)
12. Hinton, G.E., et al.: Learning distributed representations of concepts. In: Proceedings of the Eighth Annual Conference of the Cognitive Science Society, Amherst, MA, vol. 1, p. 12 (1986)
13. Keskin, C., Kıraç, F., Kara, Y.E., Akarun, L.: Hand pose estimation and hand shape classification using multi-layered randomized decision forests. In: Fitzgibbon, A., Lazebnik, S., Perona, P., Sato, Y., Schmid, C. (eds.) ECCV 2012. LNCS, vol. 7577, pp. 852–863. Springer, Heidelberg (2012). https://doi.org/10.1007/978-3-642-33783-3_61
14. Kiela, D., Bottou, L.: Learning image embeddings using convolutional neural networks for improved multi-modal semantics. In: Proceedings of the 2014 Conference on empirical methods in natural language processing (EMNLP), pp. 36–45 (2014)
15. Li, P., Que, M., Jiang, Z., Hu, Y., Tuzhilin, A.: Purs: personalized unexpected recommender system for improving user satisfaction. In: Fourteenth ACM Conference on Recommender Systems, pp. 279–288 (2020)
16. Li, Y., Yang, T.: Word embedding for understanding natural language: a survey. In: Srinivasan, S. (ed.) Guide to Big Data Applications. SBD, vol. 26, pp. 83–104. Springer, Cham (2018). https://doi.org/10.1007/978-3-319-53817-4_4
17. Mikolov, T., Chen, K., Corrado, G., Dean, J.: Efficient estimation of word representations in vector space. arXiv preprint arXiv:1301.3781 (2013)
18. Mikolov, T., Grave, E., Bojanowski, P., Puhrsch, C., Joulin, A.: Advances in pre-training distributed word representations. In: Proceedings of the International Conference on Language Resources and Evaluation (LREC) (2018)
19. Murata, M., Kojima, M., Minamiguchi, T., Watanabe, Y.: Automatic selection and analysis of Japanese notational variants on the basis of machine learning. Int. J. Innov. Comput. Inf. Control 9(10), 4231–4246 (2013)
20. Olaode, A.A., Naghdy, G., Todd, C.A.: Bag-of-visual words codebook development for the semantic content based annotation of images. In: 11th International Conference on Signal-Image Technology & Internet-Based Systems (SITIS), pp. 7–14. IEEE (2015)

21. Pennington, J., Socher, R., Manning, C.D.: Glove: global vectors for word representation. In: Proceedings of the 2014 Conference on Empirical Methods in Natural Language Processing (EMNLP), pp. 1532–1543 (2014)
22. Reimers, N., Gurevych, I.: Sentence-bert: sentence embeddings using siamese bert-networks. arXiv preprint arXiv:1908.10084 (2019)
23. Samimy, K.K.: Teaching Japanese: consideration of learners' affective variables. Theory Pract. **33**(1), 29–33 (1994)
24. Satapathy, R., Guerreiro, C., Chaturvedi, I., Cambria, E.: Phonetic-based microtext normalization for twitter sentiment analysis. In: IEEE International Conference on Data Mining Workshops (ICDMW), pp. 407–413. IEEE (2017)
25. Shen, D., et al.: Baseline needs more love: on simple word-embedding-based models and associated pooling mechanisms. arXiv preprint arXiv:1805.09843 (2018)
26. statista: Leading countries based on number of twitter users as of April 2021 (2021). https://www.statista.com/statistics/242606/number-of-active-twitter-users-in-selected-countries/. Accessed 27 July 2021
27. Suzuki, M., Matsuda, K., Sekine, S., Okazaki, N., Inui, K.: A joint neural model for fine-grained named entity classification of wikipedia articles. IEICE Trans. Inf. Syst. **101**(1), 73–81 (2018)
28. Tian, D.P., et al.: A review on image feature extraction and representation techniques. Int. J. Multimedia Ubiq. Eng. **8**(4), 385–396 (2013)
29. Van De Sande, K., Gevers, T., Snoek, C.: Evaluating color descriptors for object and scene recognition. IEEE Trans. Pattern Anal. Mach. Intell. **32**(9), 1582–1596 (2009)
30. Wu, L., Jin, R., Jain, A.K.: Tag completion for image retrieval. IEEE Trans. Pattern Anal. Mach. Intell. **35**(3), 716–727 (2012)
31. Xu, K., Xia, Y., Lee, C.H.: Tweet normalization with syllables. In: Proceedings of the 53rd Annual Meeting of the Association for Computational Linguistics and the 7th International Joint Conference on Natural Language Processing, vol. 1: Long Papers, pp. 920–928 (2015)
32. Yang, Y., Eisenstein, J.: A log-linear model for unsupervised text normalization. In: Proceedings of the 2013 Conference on Empirical Methods in Natural Language Processing, pp. 61–72 (2013)
33. Yasukawa, M., Culpepper, J.S., Scholer, F.: Phonetic matching in Japanese. In: OSIR@ SIGIR, pp. 68–71 (2012)
34. Zhang, F., Qi, S., Liu, Q., Mao, M., Zeng, A.: Alleviating the data sparsity problem of recommender systems by clustering nodes in bipartite networks. Expert Syst. Appl. **149**, 113346 (2020)
35. Zhang, S., Yang, M., Cour, T., Yu, K., Metaxas, D.N.: Query specific fusion for image retrieval. In: Fitzgibbon, A., Lazebnik, S., Perona, P., Sato, Y., Schmid, C. (eds.) ECCV 2012. LNCS, vol. 7573, pp. 660–673. Springer, Heidelberg (2012). https://doi.org/10.1007/978-3-642-33709-3_47
36. Zhou, W., Li, H., Tian, Q.: Recent advance in content-based image retrieval: a literature survey. arXiv preprint arXiv:1706.06064 (2017)
37. Zhu, G., Iglesias, C.A.: Computing semantic similarity of concepts in knowledge graphs. IEEE Trans. Knowl. Data Eng. **29**(1), 72–85 (2016)

Topic and Text Matching

Hybrid Phishing URL Detection Using Segmented Word Embedding

Eint Sandi Aung[1][(⊠)] and Hayato Yamana[2]

[1] Department of Computer Science and Communications Engineering,
Waseda University, Tokyo, Japan
eintsandiaung@toki.waseda.jp
[2] Faculty of Science and Engineering, Waseda University, Tokyo, Japan
yamana@waseda.jp

Abstract. Phishing is a type of cybercrime committed by attackers to steal sensitive information. This paper focuses on URL-based phishing detection, i.e., detecting phishing webpages by analyzing the URL. Previously proposed methods tackled this problem; however, insufficient word tokenization of URLs arises unknown words, which degrades the detection accuracy. To solve the unknown-word problem, we propose a new tokenization algorithm, called *URL-Tokenizer*, which integrates BERT and WordSegment tokenizers, besides utilizing 24 NLP features. Then, we adopt the URL-Tokenizer to the DNN-CNN hybrid model to leverage the detection accuracy. Our experiment using the Ebbu2017 dataset confirmed that our word-DNN-CNN achieves an AUC of 99.89% compared to the state-of-the-art DNN-BiLSTM with an AUC of 98.78%.

Keywords: Phishing URL detection · Word segmentation · Word embedding

1 Introduction

Phishing is a crime where phishers trick users to steal confidential data ranging from passwords to bank information. For the past two years, there has been significant growth in phishing attacks. The quarterly reports of the Anti-Phishing Working Group (APWG) analyzed phishing attacks and found that the attacks have been increasing dramatically over the past 20 months (July 2020 to December 2021). The fourth-quarter report of 2021 showed that the number of unique phishing webpages (approximately 890,000) was twenty times larger than the number of unique phishing emails (approximately 43,000), emphasizing the importance of phishing webpage detection.

Phishing detection techniques are generally classified into five approaches: whitelist-[1], blacklist- [2], content- [3], visual similarity- [4], and Uniform Resource Locator (URL)-based approaches. The URL-based approaches adopt character embedding [5], word embedding [6], or word and character embeddings [7]. This paper focuses on the URL-based approach, i.e., detecting phishing webpages by retrieving features from the URL. The most significant advantage of the URL-based approach is that we do not need to access the webpages, which results in malware attack-free detection. On the contrary,

E. Pardede et al. (Eds.): iiWAS 2022, LNCS 13635, pp. 507–518, 2022.
https://doi.org/10.1007/978-3-031-21047-1_46

malicious software may be installed unintentionally when adopting a content-based app-roach. In addition, the URL-based approach is time-effective compared to content- and visual similarity-based approaches. Furthermore, the URL-based approach can undoubt-edly classify zero-day phishing attacks, while blacklist and whitelist approaches fail to detect newly created phishing URLs. In summary, URL-based phishing detection techniques are indispensable because of the advantages, including malware attack-free, time-effectiveness, and zero-day detection.

A URL comprises different parts, including protocol, host, path, and query. In phish-ing URL detection, phishers bait a trap using synthetic URLs with straightforward techniques such as swapping letters, replacing letters with similar digits, adding ran-dom letters and/or digits, and legitimate keywords in different parts of a URL (e.g., www.amazon.com → amaz0n.co.jp.zvrqz64.cn). These facts lead us to have an idea that highly accurate word segmentation of the URL may help distinguish phishing URLs from legitimate URLs yet challenging in URL-based phishing detection.

An existing problem in URL segmentation is insufficient tokenization that cannot accurately segment URLs to meaningful words. Unlike the tokenization in NLP, using special characters as a delimiter does not work because the URL is composed of a com-bination of characters/words without any whitespaces, which results in many unknown words [7]. Maneriker et al. [6] proposed to handle unknown words using Byte Pair Encod-ing (BPE); however, they cannot extract meaningful English words (e.g., bankofamerica → [bank, ##of, ##ame, ##rica], instead of [bank, of, america]).

Our contributions in this paper include 1) tackling the unknown word problems to reduce the number of unknown words by constructing a new URL-Tokenizer that integrates Bert and WordSegment tokenizers, and 2) detecting character swapping to solve the problem of replacing letters with similar digits, which decomposes a URL to a sequence of consecutive letters/digits/symbols.

The rest of the paper is organized as follows. Section 2 introduces related work in phishing detection. Section 3 details our proposed algorithm, followed by the adopted features, and model architecture in Sect. 4. Section 5 presents the experimental evaluation and comparison with the previous work. Finally, Sect. 6 concludes our work.

2   Related Work

Researchers have engaged in various feature handling techniques to analyze URLs, extracting diverse features from URLs, including lexical features (NLP features [6]). However, phishers always upgrade their sophisticated attacks to bypass such hand-crafted lexical features; thus, researchers have shifted to discover complicated fea-tures extracted from raw URLs, i.e., characters and words, with the help of competitive performance in text classification and natural language processing (NLP).

In 2017, Le et al. [7] proposed the URLNet using CNN to detect URLs referring to malicious websites. URLNet considers three levels of embeddings, i.e., character-level, word-level, and character-level word embeddings, to capture the semantic meaning of words and sequential patterns of characters. They also proposed advanced word embed-ding to solve the problem of infrequently observed words in the dataset. After tokenizing URLs with special characters (described in Sect. 3.1), they transform infrequent words that appear less than 100 times among millions of word corpus into unknown words. However, this technique results in a considerable number of unknown words. Besides, the complexity of the word-level CNN is relatively high because they perform character-level word embedding instead of naïve word embedding such that word embedding = [https, www, google, com] and character-level word embedding = [[h, t, t, p], [w, w, w], [g, o, o, g, l, e], [c, o, m]].

Ozcan et al. [5] in 2021 proposed a hybrid deep learning model to detect phishing URLs. The hybrid deep learning model is based on long short-term memory (LSTM) and deep neural network algorithms (DNN-LSTM and DNN-BiLSTM) using character embedding and manually extracted NLP features. The limitation of Ozcan et al.'s model is the model complexity and training time, as they applied the BiLSTM using character embedding. Moreover, character embedding has the disadvantage of overwhelming unnecessary symbols (e.g., "%2B" or "%21") without URL decoding, which affects phishing URL detection accuracy.

Maneriker et al. [6] in 2021 proposed URLTran using a transformer model with Byte Pair Encoding (BPE) tokenizers to handle character subsequences. Their fine-tuned transformers using the standard BERT work well to detect phishing URLs. However, they used the dataset collected from Microsoft's Edge and Internet Explorer browsing telemetry, which makes it difficult to compare their results to other works without implementing the same model. Furthermore, segmented words from BPE cannot be able to form meaningful words (e.g., bankofamerica → bank, ##of, ##ame, ##ri, ##ca).

The works above decomposed raw URLs into character- or word-embeddings; however, unknown words cannot be tokenized correctly. Additionally, the BERT tokenizer, inherited from BPE, tokenizes a URL into a sequence of words, in which only the first appearing word is the meaningful word; however, the rest are a continuation of words that are not well tokenized. Thus, this paper proposes a URL-Tokenizer to overcome the unknown-word problem in Sect. 3.

Unlike our previous work [8], we not only evaluate our URL-tokenizer on URL-based features but additionally utilize NLP-based features described in Sect. 4.1 to improve the detection accuracy of our previous work. Our work focuses on the unknown-word problems: 1) previous studies [7] adopting traditional word-level detection tokenized by special characters result in a great number of unknown words, and 2) BPE with word-level embedding [6] does not retrieve meaningful English words. To tackle these problems, we aim to segment meaningful words from URLs while reducing the unknown words. Then, we compare our new hybrid DNN-CNN model equipped with our 24 NLP features with the state-of-the-art works [5, 7].

3 Segmentation-Based Phishing URL Detection

This section presents our proposed URL-Tokenizer and Recursive-Tokenizer algorithms, then explains how to solve the unknown-word problems.

3.1 Overview

In phishing URL detection, traditional tokenization techniques using special characters (shown below) have been adopted to extract words from URLs [7]. However, such tokenization produces many unknown words because URLs do not consist of whitespace but consist of a combination of words without delimiters (e.g., bankofamerica). Meanwhile, common tokenization techniques cannot extract meaningful words from URLs.

Therefore, we propose a novel URL-Tokenizer to decompose a URL into meaningful words. The URL-Tokenizer inherits WordSegment (https://pypi.org/project/wordsegment/) in the initial stage of the tokenizer to take advantage of its successful decomposition of standalone words (e.g., knowledge application to knowledge and application) or alphabetic words (e.g., webhostapp to web, host, and app). Undoubtedly, WordSegment cannot decompose a complex combination of letters and numbers, i.e., alphanumeric words (e.g., 000webhostapp and web000host). To overcome this, we recursively tokenize with the Recursive-Tokenizer in the next stage.

The Recursive-Tokenizer adopts the Bert tokenizer (https://pypi.org/project/bert-tokenizer/) to segment the first word because the Bert tokenizer can tokenize the first-appearing word as a meaningful word. For instance, "bankofamerica" to [bank, ##of, ##ame, ##rica]. However, the Bert tokenizer does not correctly tokenize all the word combinations of the URL because of its "##" prefixing technique to recognize the continuation of a word sequence. Thus, the Recursive-Tokenizer will repeatedly decompose a combination of words until the words can no longer be split, while using the prefixing when the decomposed word is neither the first word nor exists in the English dictionary. This study uses PyEnchant (https://pypi.org/project/pyenchant/), an English spell-checking package, to validate whether the decomposed words are meaningful, i.e., English words or not.

Special Characters. The common special characters are colon [:], forward slash [/], dot [.], dash [-], underscore [_], semicolon [;], comma [,] equals [=], at [@], dollar [$], ampersand [&], question mark [?], plus [+], hash [#].

3.2 URL-Tokenizer

In Algorithm 1, the input of the URL-tokenizer is shown as τ, which is a fragment of the URL (URL string) tokenized by the special characters. For example, if the original URL is www.bankofamerica.com, τ becomes {www, bankofamerica, com}. Then, the URL-Tokenizer further decomposes τ to a list of consecutive letters/digits, shown as w, to confirm if τ contains malicious character swapping (e.g., amaz0n $\rightarrow$ [amaz, 0, n]). Then, WordSegment segments w; however, WordSegment cannot segment a combination of alphanumeric words such as 000webhostapp and web000host. Thus, for each segmented word $w_i \in w_{ws}$, we validate if w_i is included in the English word corpus $D_{enchant}$. If w_i is not an English word, we recursively apply the Recursive-Tokenizer until w_i can no longer be decomposed. We then prefix the output word list w_{pre} with "##" if it is neither the first word nor included in $D_{enchant}$. This prefixing is adopted based on the concept of the Bert tokenizer.

ALGORITHM 1: URL-Tokenizer

Input τ ▶ *URL strings tokenized by special characters*
Output W ▶ *tokenized word list*
$W \leftarrow \emptyset, w \leftarrow \emptyset$
for each $i \in \tau$ **do**
  if i = alphanumeric **then**
    $w \leftarrow w \cup$ decompose (i) ▶ *Decompose alphanumeric words to consecutive letter/digit*
  else $w \leftarrow w \cup i$
  end if
end for
$w_{ws} \leftarrow WordSegment(w)$ ▶ *Segments w by WordSegment*
for each $w_i \in w_{ws}$ **do**
  $w_{tok} \leftarrow \emptyset$
  if $w_i \in D_{enchant}$ **then**   ▶ *English word case (included in English disctionary)*
    $w_{tok} \leftarrow w_{tok} \cup w_i$
  else   ▶ *Non English word case*
    $w_{tok} \leftarrow w_{tok} \cup Recursive\text{-}Tokenization(w_i)$
  endif
  for each $w_{pre} \in w_{tok}$ **do**
    if $(w_{pre} \neq$ the first word in $w_{tok})$ **AND** $(w_{pre} \notin D_{enchant})$ **then**
      ▶ *prefixing w_{pre} so that neither the first word nor an English word is prefixed by ##*
      like Bert tokenizer to indicate the continuation of words
      $W \leftarrow W \cup \#\# w_{pre}$
    else
      $W \leftarrow W \cup w_{pre}$
    endif
  endfor
endfor
return W

3.3 Recursive-Tokenizer

ALGORITHM 2: Recursive-Tokenizer

Input w_i ▶ *a word (not null)*
Output w_{seg} ▶ *tokenized word list (no longer segmentable word list)*
$w_{seg} \leftarrow \emptyset$
$\acute{\omega} = bert\_tokenizer.tokenize(w_i)$ ▶ *applying Bert tokenizer*
$w_{seg} \leftarrow w_{seg} \cup \acute{\omega}_1$ ▶ *extracting the first word $\acute{\omega}_1$ as a tokenized word*
if length of $\acute{\omega} > 1$ **then**   ▶ *validating plural words or not*
  ▶ *recursively applying Recursive-Tokenizer for $\acute{\omega}_{\neq 1}$, i.e., the rest of $\acute{\omega}$ except for $\acute{\omega}_1$*
  return $w_{seg} \cup Recursive\text{-}Tokenization(\acute{\omega}_{\neq 1})$
else
  return w_{seg}
endif

The recursive-tokenizer, shown in Algorithm 2, tokenizes w_i to return the no longer segmentable word list w_{seg}. The recursive-tokenizer applies the Bert tokenizer to extract the first meaningful word from the input word. The remaining words, $\acute{\omega}_{\neq 1}$, are later returned from the recursive function to be segmented further.

To sum up, we develop the URL-tokenizer to solve the problem of many unknown words by taking advantage of WordSegment and Bert tokenizers.

4   NLP Features and Hybrid Model Architecture

This section explains the enhancement of our previous work [8] by applying additional NLP features and constructing a hybrid DNN-CNN model to improve phishing URL detection accuracy.

4.1   NLP Features

We extract the following 24 NLP features used on the hybrid model to achieve robust detection accuracy compared to our previous work [8]. Note that the URL is divided by domain part, path part, and query part which is after "?" in the path part.

Previously Proposed Features. Previous papers [9–15] proposed the following NLP features. Note that we decompose the number-related features, i.e., the number of letters, digits, and symbols, to express more concrete characteristics. That is, we adopt maximum and minimum lengths of consecutive-letters, consecutive-digits, and consecutive-symbols for each part, i.e., domain and path. Besides, we decompose the domain length into TLD (Feat_tld) and the length of the subdomains (Feat_len_subdomain). The features are explained below.

Feat_tld (Integer) in Domain
Feat_tld is the Top-Level Domain (TLD) name (such as jp and com) in the domain part. Each TLD is encoded to a distinct Integer. We hypothesize that phishing sites are biased towards certain TLDs (e.g., xyz).

Feat_ip (binary) in Domain

Feat_ip is a binary identifier to show the URL is represented by IP-address or domain name. We hypothesize that phishing and malicious webpages often use an IP address in the domain part (e.g., http://47.74.231.192/).

Feat_max_letter & Feat_min_letter (Integer) in Domain and Path
Feat_max_letter (Feat_min_letter) shows the maximum (minimum) length of consecutive-letters in the domain part and path part, respectively (e.g., amaz0n has Feat_max_letter $= 4$ and Feat_min_letter $= 1$). We hypothesize that the length of consecutive-letters in the path part of legitimate webpage is shorter than that of phishing webpage. We also hypothesize that the length of consecutive-letters in the domain part of phishing webpage becomes short because the letters in the domain part of phishing webpage tend to be replaced with visually similar digits.

Feat_max_digit & Feat_min_digit (Integer) in Domain and Path
Feat_max_digit (Feat_min_digit) shows the maximum (minimum) length of consecutive-digits in the domain part and path part, respectively (e.g., a111.1ks1.com has Feat_max_digit = 3 and Feat_min_digit = 1). We hypothesize that the number of digits appearing in the domain part is smaller than the number in the path part because legitimate webpages tend not to use digits in the domain part, but instead use the brand names.

Feat_max_symbol & Feat_min_symbol (Integer) in Domain and Path
Feat_max_symbol (Feat_min_symbol) represents the maximum (minimum) length of consecutive-symbols in the domain and path parts, respectively. We hypothesize that the length of consecutive-symbols in legitimate webpage is less than that in phishing webpage (e.g., xn----72-6kcdg1cujbrmlb.xn--p1ai.com has Feat_max_symbol = 4 and Feat_min_symbol = 1).

Feat_dnan in Domain & Feat_pnan in Path (Real number)
Feat_dnan and Feat_pnan show the entropy of non-alphanumeric (NAN) characters in the domain and path part [10], respectively. The hypothesis is that the distribution of NAN characters in legitimate URLs is significantly different from that in phishing URLs. If no NAN characters exist, it is set to zero.

$$\text{Entropy} = -\sum\nolimits_{i \in T}^{n} P_i \log P_i \tag{1}$$

where T represents the set of NAN characters in the domain/path part, n = |T|, and P_i is the probability the i-th NAN character appears.

Feat_at (binary) in Path
Feat_at is a binary identifier to show whether an embedded redirection symbol at [@] exists in the path part. The hypothesis is that at [@] is the character most used by phishers to redirect to a different web address (e.g., https://jflkp.csb.app/index.html#a@b.com).

Feat_dslash (binary) in Path
Feat_dslash indicates whether the path part contains a double slash [//] or not. The double slash tends to be used to redirect to a phishing webpage. We hypothesize that phishers deceive users with [//] for redirection by ignoring the content before [//] (e.g., https://despertardoshormonios.club/ccm/Updated//ampt.html).

Feat_link (binary) in Query
Feat_link indicates whether there is an internal link in the query part. We hypothesize that phishers usually embed internal links in the query part (e.g., https://l.w.co/l?u=https://wanzane.com/071YGXy).

Feat_len_subdomain (Integer) in Domain
Feat_len_subdomain represents the length of characters in subdomain of eTLD + 1 where eTLD represents effective top-level domain (e.g., in the case of www.abc.ac.uk, ac.uk is eTLD and in case of abc.edu, edu is eTLD). Thus, eTLD + 1 is the main-domain that may be registered by the domain registry organization. We use a public suffix dataset to distinguish eTLD. It returns 0 for no subdomains of the main-domain and -1 for an IP

address occurrence in the domain part (e.g., in the case of "https://www.spare-parts.san iflo.co.uk/," Feat_len_subdomain = 15 (www.spare-parts) characters. We hypothesize that phishers tend to use too-long or too-short subdomains to confuse users.

Feat_sus_pattern (Integer) in Domain
Feat_sus_pattern defines the number of suspicious words in the domain part. After tokenizing the domain part by special characters, each extracted word is measured as suspicious if and only if the extracted words are neither lettered nor numeric, but the alphanumeric word (e.g., in the case of amazon.wang-we1.com, Feat_sus_pattern = 1, and in the case of ec-1re-paypal07.serveftp.com, Feat_sus_pattern = 2). This idea comes from [9], where they measured the number of occurrences of suspicious words.

Additional Features. We newly propose the following three features to represent more characteristics of the domain part because domain-based features are crucial to improve the phishing webpage detection accuracy.

Feat_long_word (Real number) in Domain
Feat_long_word indicates the ratio of the longest word length to the total length of the domain part, as shown in Eq. 2. Note that words are extracted by tokenizing the domain part by special characters. We hypothesize that phishing domains use a longer consecutive word to trick users by adding keywords/brand names in the domain part (e.g., https://www.amazonlogistics-ap-northeast-1.amazonlogistics.jp).

$$Feat\_long\_word = (Length\_of\_the\_Longestword)/(Total\_Length) \qquad (2)$$

Feat_subdomain (Integer) in Domain
Feat_subdomain shows the number of subdomains of eTLD + 1 in the URL. It returns 0 for no subdomains or -1 for an IP address occurrence in the domain part. We hypothesize that phishers often use subdomains to deceive users with brand names in the subdomains (e.g., in the case of http://www.amazon.com.supportsbooks.fun, Feat_subdomain = 3 {www, amazon, com} because eTLD + 1 is supportsbooks).

Feat_sp (Integer) in Domain
Feat_sp indicates the number of special characters used in the subdomains of eTLD + 1. We hypothesize that as phishing URLs contain more special characters in the subdomains to insert keywords/brand names of legitimate URL. (e.g., in the case of http://www.amazon-login.freenbyuvazcety.club, Feat_sp = 3 {., -, .}). It returns -1 for an IP address occurrence in the domain part; otherwise, the number of special characters in the subdomains of eTLD + 1.

4.2   Hybrid Model Architecture

Figure 1 illustrates our hybrid model architecture combining CNN and DNN. The CNN trains the URL features, where the inputs to the CNN are word-vectors padded with a maximum length of 200 words [7]. We prepare 128 embedding dimensions EM_w for each URL_w. The DNN model adopts 24 NLP features as the input of n dimensions where we have *m* number of URLs. Note that the model was chosen after varying the different number of layers. Then, we combine the DNN with the CNN to improve the performance. We tune hyper-parameters of learning rate [0.01, 0.001, 0.0001], dropout [0.0–0.6] (by 0.1 increment), batch-size [32, 128], and epoch [5, 10, 20, 50] on training data. In summary, the hybrid DNN-CNN model was constructed for simpler complexity compared to DNN-BiLSTM [5].

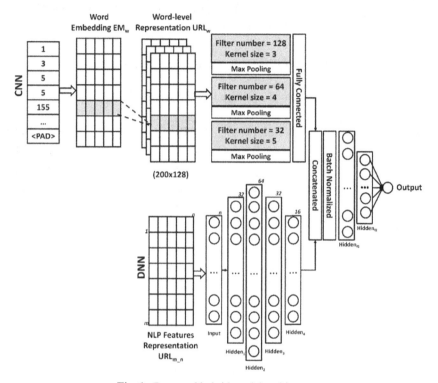

Fig. 1. Proposed hybrid model architecture

5 Experimental Evaluation

We used two neural network models (CNN and DNN) to conduct the performance comparison on word-level and character-level embeddings with the two state-of-the-art baselines: Le et al.'s model [7] as a baseline of word-level segmentation and Ozcan et al.'s model [5] as a baseline of character-level segmentation. Note that the results of Le et al.'s model were obtained using their program, and the results of Ozcan et al.'s model are cited from [5]. We performed 10-fold cross-validation with the balanced dataset Ebbu2017 (36,400 legitimate and 37,175 phishing webpages) as same as [5].

Table 1 shows the performance comparison using AUC, ACC, and F1 as metrics. Our proposed model successfully achieved the highest AUC when compared in each comparison category: character-segmentation models, word-segmentation models, and hybrid models. The result, where our *word*-CNN performs the best among single models, confirms that our URL-Tokenizer works well with word-embeddings.

Our proposed hybrid word-DNN-CNN achieved the best AUC of 99.89%, compared to Ozcan et al.'s best model (char-DNN-BiLSTM) with an AUC of 98.78%. As for ACC and F1, a small degradation was observed compared to Ozcan et al.'s model; however, AUC is the most important metric in phishing URL detection [6] because the phishing URL detection must have a very low FPR (false positive ratio) with higher TPR (true positive ratio), which only could be shown as AUC.

Table 1. Performance evaluation with two baselines on Ebbu2017.

Model (*char/word*: segmentation scheme)	Single/Hybrid	Feature	AUC	ACC	F1
char-CNN [5]*	*Single*	URL	0.9326	0.9325	0.9339
char-RNN [5]*	*Single*	URL	0.9718	0.9717	0.9720
char-LSTM [5]*	*Single*	URL	0.9826	**0.9824**	**0.9828**
char-BiLSTM [5]*	*Single*	URL	0.9759	0.9758	0.9761
char-CNN (Our)	*Single*	URL	**0.9983**	0.9806	0.9807
word-CNN [7]	*Single*	URL	0.9741	0.9739	0.9735
word-CNN (Our)	*Single*	URL	**0.9986**	**0.9855**	**0.9857**
char-DNN-LSTM [5]*	*Hybrid*	URL + NLP	0.9864	0.9862	0.9865
char-DNN-BiLSTM [5]*	*Hybrid*	URL + NLP	0.9878	**0.9879**	**0.9881**
char-DNN-CNN (Our)	*Hybrid*	URL + NLP	0.9984	0.9812	0.9814
word-DNN-CNN (Our)	*Hybrid*	URL + NLP	**0.9989**	0.9864	0.9865

* Results are cited from [5] on Ebbu2017.

To confirm the best model among our proposed models, we evaluated our single and hybrid models in terms of TPR w.r.t FPR. Table 2 shows that the word-DNN-CNN model achieves the best in the range of FPR = [0.001, 0.01, 0.1]. Figure 2 shows the mean ROC curves of 10-fold cross-validated results.

Table 2. Performance evaluation among our proposed models on Ebbu2017.

Our Models	Feature	TPR@FPR0.0001	TPR@FPR0.001	TPR@FPR0.01	TPR@FPR0.1
char-CNN	URL	0.5902	0.8369	0.9695	0.9982
word-CNN	URL	0.3997	0.7926	0.9800	0.9988
char-DNN-CNN	URL + NLP	**0.6779**	0.8379	0.9731	0.9979
word-DNN-CNN	URL + NLP	0.5826	**0.8399**	**0.9817**	**0.9991**

6 Conclusion

This paper first proposed a novel URL-Tokenizer for the URL segmentation to reduce the unknown words by extracting accurate and meaningful English words from URLs. Besides word-level embedding, we applied character-level embedding to confirm the effectiveness of our proposed hybrid models. We further extracted a set of NLP features to utilize in the DNN model, which we later combined with the word-level CNN to construct a new hybrid model (DNN-CNN). Our experimental results show that the URL-Tokenizer works well with word-embeddings in single and hybrid models, obtaining AUCs of 99.86% and 99.89% on the balanced Ebbu2017 dataset, respectively.

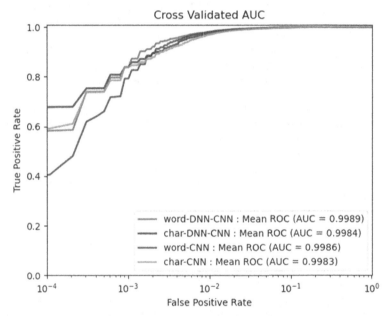

Fig. 2. Mean ROC curves of proposed models.

Acknowledgement. This work was partially supported by JST SPRING Grant Number JPMJSP2128.

References

1. Cao, Y., Han, W., Le, Y.: Anti-phishing based on automated individual white-list. ("Phishing Detection with Popular Search Engines: Simple and Effective"). In: Proceedings of the 4th ACM Workshop on Digital Identity Management (DIM), pp. 51–60. ACM (2008)
2. Prakash, P., Kumar, M., Kompella, R.R., Gupta, M.: PhishNet: predictive blacklisting to detect phishing attacks. In: Proceedings of IEEE INFOCOM, pp. 1–5. IEEE (2010)

3. Zhang, Y., Hong, J.I., Cranor, L.F.: Cantina: a content-based approach to detecting phishing web sites. In: Proceedings of the 16th International Conference on World Wide Web (WWW), pp. 639–648. ACM (2007)

4. Fu, A.Y., Wenyin, L., Deng, X.: Detecting phishing web pages with visual similarity assessment based on earth mover's distance (EMD). IEEE Trans. Dependable Secure Comput. **3**(4), 301–311 (2006). https://doi.org/10.1109/TDSC.2006.50

5. Ozcan, A., Catal, C., Donmez, E., Senturk, B.: A hybrid DNN–LSTM model for detecting phishing URLs. Neural Comput. Appl., 1–7 (2021). https://doi.org/10.1007/s00521-021-064 01-z

6. Maneriker, P., Stokes, J.W., Lazo, E.G., Carutasu, D., Tajaddodianfar, F., Gururajan, A.: URLTran: improving phishing URL detection using transformers. In: Proceedings of IEEE Military Communications Conference (MILCOM), pp. 197–204. IEEE (2021)

7. Le, H., Pham, Q., Sahoo, D., Hoi, S.C.: URLNet: learning a URL representation with deep learning for malicious URL detection. In: arXiv preprint arXiv:1802.03162 (2018)

8. Aung, E.S., Yamana, H.: Segmentation-based phishing URL detection. In: Proceedings of IEEE/WIC/ACM International Conference on Web Intelligence and Intelligent Agent Technology, pp. 550–556. ACM (2021)

9. Lin, M.S., Chiu, C.Y., Lee, Y.J., Pao, H.K.: Malicious URL filtering—a big data application. In: Proceedings of IEEE International Conference on Big Data, pp. 589–596. IEEE (2013)

10. Aung, E.S., Yamana, H.: URL-based phishing detection using the entropy of non-alphanumeric characters. In: Proceedings of the 21st International Conference on Information Integration and Web-based Applications & Services (iiWAS), pp. 385–392. ACM (2019)

11. Hong, J., Kim, T., Liu, J., Park, N., Kim, S.-W.: Phishing URL detection with lexical features and blacklisted domains. In: Jajodia, S., Cybenko, G., Subrahmanian, V.S., Swarup, V., Wang, C., Wellman, M. (eds.) Adaptive Autonomous Secure Cyber Systems, pp. 253–267. Springer, Cham (2020). https://doi.org/10.1007/978-3-030-33432-1_12

12. Christou, O., Pitropakis, N., Papadopoulos, P., McKeown, S., Buchanan, W.J.: Phishing URL detection through top-level domain analysis: a descriptive approach. arXiv preprint arXiv: 2005.06599 (2020)

13. Sadique, F., Kaul, R., Badsha, S., Sengupta, S.: An automated framework for real-time phishing URL detection. In: Proceedings of the 10th Annual Computing and Communication Workshop and Conference (CCWC), pp. 0335–0341. IEEE (2020)

14. Abutaha, M., Ababneh, M., Mahmoud, K., Baddar, S.A.: URL phishing detection using machine learning techniques based on URLs lexical analysis. In: Proceedings of the 12th International Conference on Information and Communication Systems, pp. 147–152. IEEE (2021)

15. Lakshmi, L., Reddy, M.P., Santhaiah, C., Reddy, U.J.: Smart phishing detection in web pages using supervised deep learning classification and optimization technique ADAM. Wireless Pers. Commun. **118**(4), 3549–3564 (2021). https://doi.org/10.1007/s11277-021-08196-7

A Scheme for News Article Classification in a Low-Resource Language

Hailemariam Mehari Yohannes[1,2(✉)] and Toshiyuki Amagasa[1,2]

[1] Graduate School of Science and Technology, University of Tsukuba, Tsukuba,
Ibaraki, Japan
s2030154@s.tsukuba.ac.jp, amagasa@cs.tsukuba.ac.jp
[2] Center for Computational Sciences, University of Tsukuba, Tsukuba, Ibaraki, Japan

Abstract. This paper proposes a scheme for classifying news articles in Tigrinya, a language spoken in northern Ethiopia and Eritrea,
and is known for its lack of extensive and readily available data. We
present the first publicly available news article dataset for Tigrinya,
containing 2396 articles. In addition, we propose a data augmentation
method for text classification. Furthermore, we explore the performance
in text classification using traditional machine learning methods (support vector machine, logistic regression, random forest, linear discriminant analysis, decision tree, and Naive Bayes), a neural network-based
model (bidirectional long short term memory), and a transformer-based
model (TigRoBERTa). The experimental results show that the proposed
method performs better in accuracy than the comparative methods up
to nine points. The codes and the dataset are open to the research community (https://github.com/mehari-eng/Article-News-Categorization).

Keywords: Low-resource language · Text classification · Machine
learning · Data augmentation

1 Introduction

In the world, more than 7000 languages used[1], and the distribution of the population is biased to some of the major languages, such as English, Chinese,
Spanish, etc. Consequently, most of the existing research activities in natural
language processing (NLP) tend to focus on such major languages, leading to
the large discrepancy in the language resources in different languages, and most
of the state-of-the-art methods are dedicated to English or other resource-rich
languages. For this reason, there have been growing demands to develop NLP
resources, including text corpus and tools, for low-resource languages to address
the ever-growing digital divide.

Despite its morphological richness, Tigrinya is considered one of the low-
resource languages, i.e., there are limited language resources for conducting NLP

---

[1] https://www.infoplease.com/world/social-statistics/how-many-languages-are-
there.

E. Pardede et al. (Eds.): iiWAS 2022, LNCS 13635, pp. 519–530, 2022.
https://doi.org/10.1007/978-3-031-21047-1_47

research. For this reason, we have developed a dataset and a scheme for named-entity recognition (NLP) for Tigrinya [23]. However, to our knowledge, there have been few existing works for text classification.

Document classification is one of the fundamental and popular tasks in which documents are classified into predefined categories, and there have been many approaches to address this problem, such as traditional machine learning methods [1, 16], neural network classifiers [10], and transformer-based models [3, 13]. Note that most of these methods deal with resource-rich languages. The situation is similar in other NLP tasks, such as machine translation [6], named entity recognition [2], and part of speech tagging [4]. Hence, most of the techniques and datasets are dedicated to resource-rich languages.

Besides, several attempts have already been made to create datasets in the Tigrinya language. For example, a work reported in [7] created a dataset for Tigrinya text classification with six different classes. However, the dataset is not publicly accessible. Furthermore, [20] introduced a 72,080-token POS tagging dataset for Tigrinya. Similarly, [23] created a 69,309-token Tigrinya dataset for named entity recognition. As can be observed, there has been no dataset for text classification that is publicly available.

For this reason, we introduced a new dataset in Tigrinya for news article classification. Our dataset comprises 2396 news articles obtained from local news. It is divided into seven categories: agriculture, business, health, politics, religion, sport, and technology. To mitigate the dataset's problem that the number of documents is limited and the expensive cost of manually annotating documents, we propose a scheme of data augmentation for the Tigrinya where some words are replaced by their synonyms and the order of sentences is shuffled.

We propose a transformer-based model for classifying the documents using the pre-trained language model for Tigrinya, TigRoBERTa [23]. We compare the performance of the model with traditional machine learning methods (support vector machine, logistic regression, random forest, linear discriminant analysis, decision tree, and Naive Bayes) and a neural network-based model (bidirectional long short term memory). The experimental result shows that the proposed data augmentation method is useful in improving the classification accuracy by up to 9 points.

The contribution of this paper can be summarized as follows:

- We present the first publicly available news article dataset in Tigrinya language with seven categories.
- We propose a data augmentation technique to augment text documents in Tigrinya to mitigate the low-resource problem.
- We test the classification accuracy with different classifiers to compare the classification accuracy.
- We make all our code and datasets available to the public[2].

The remainder of this paper is organized as follows: Section 2 briefly reviews previous NLP works on Tigrinya and related low-resourced language. Section 3

---

[2] https://github.com/mehari-eng/Article-News-Categorization.

shows the development of our dataset. Section 4 Illustrates the proposed method of data augmentation. Section 5 describes the algorithms used for text classification. Section 6 examines the experimental evaluation and results obtained by different classifiers. Finally, Sect. 7 presents the conclusions and directions of future work.

2 Related Work

2.1 Techniques for Low-Resource Languages

Many researchers have proposed deep learning-based methods for different NLP tasks, such as text classification, text summarization, and machine translation. Meanwhile, there have been a few attempts at deep learning-based methods for Tigrinya language. A paper reported in [7] demonstrates a text classification scheme for Tigrinya using a convolutional neural network (CNN) and word embedding. They introduced 30,000 Tigrinya news documents from various sources, analyzing and categorizing them into six classes: sport, agriculture, politics, religion, education, and health, but the dataset has not been publicly available. The authors built CNN models with and without word2vec and fasttext embedding. According to their experimental result, CNN with word2vec outperformed comparative methods.

Similarly, [5] proposed a deep learning model for categorizing 3,600 document news articles using six categories in the Amharic language. They utilized fasttext to generate vector representations for texts reflecting inherent semantics. Then, the text vectors are fed into the embedding layer of the CNN, thereby pulling the features automatically.

Another investigation by [11] examined the possibilities of categorizing Amharic text news using *learning vector quantization* (LVQ) for the Amharic language. In addition, the effectiveness of text news classifiers was investigated using the TF and TF*IDF weighting algorithms. Moreover, a stemmer for Tigrinya words was proposed by [15] to facilitate information retrieval. To improve the information retrieval performance over Tigrinya texts, a stemmer was designed to represent different forms of Tigrinya words as a canonical form. As for their experiment, they used a hybrid approach that combines rule-based and dictionary-based stemming. The rule-based method was used to remove affixes, and the dictionary-based method was used to reduce the stemming errors.

The study by [20] addressed the POS (part of speech)-tagging task for Tigrinya language using 72k tokens of a dataset manually annotated from 4,656 sentences for POS task. They employed the CRF (conditional random field) and SVM (support vector machine) for predicting POS tags in the experiment. The author claimed that the CRF algorithm achieved the highest accuracy.

The work reported in [21] investigated the effectiveness of deep neural network classifiers (i.e., feed-forward neural network, LSTM, BiLSTM, and CNN) using pretrained word2vec neural embeddings. Their experiments used the POS tagging dataset developed by Nagaoka [20]. Their finding stated that an overall 91% of accuracy has been achieved. Similarly, our work [23] created a manually

Table 1. Distribution of the dataset.

Category	Number of samples
Agriculture	270
Business	346
Health	300
Politics	354
Religion	337
Sport	452
Technology	337
Total	2396

annotated dataset for Tigrinya language tagged with named entity recognition (NER) and proposed a language model trained on RoBERTa architecture using the Tigrinya dataset. The proposed model's performance was evaluated by fine-tuning in two separate tasks, POS and NER.

To our knowledge, so far, no existing research has addressed the problem of news article classification for Tigrinya language using the state-of-the-art (transformer-based) model.

2.2 Data Augmentation for Texts

Recent works show that data augmentation has become a common technique for training a neural network in the field of computer vision [18]. Hence, applying those techniques to NLP is difficult and not straightforward. The authors in [6] proposed a machine translation data augmentation for low resourced languages. Their work proposes translation data augmentation (TDA), which enhances the training data by changing existing sentences in the parallel corpus. Similar work by [19] using back-translation, they obtain large-scale pseudo parallel corpora, then examine the impact of back-translation on context-aware neural machine translation performance. However, these technique depends on a parallel corpus. Another study by [22] proposed four different methods for text classification tasks, i.e., synonym replacement, random insertion, random swapping, and random deletion. Hence their method affects only words in a sentence.

3 Dataset

Tigrinya is written left to right and uses Ge'ez script for its writing system. There are 231 characters in Ge'ez script, categorized into 33 letters, each denoting seven characters[3]. An example of Ge'ez (Tigrinya) script is shown in Fig. 1.

This paper presents a news article dataset for Tigrinya language categorized into seven classes: agriculture, business, health, politics, religion, sport,

---

[3] http://ethiopiantreasures.co.uk/pages/language.htm.

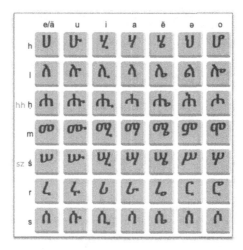

Fig. 1. Ge'ez (Tigrinya) characters example.

and technology. The dataset consists of 2396 news articles. The distributions of our dataset are shown in Table 1. To our knowledge, this is the first dataset publicly available for Tigrinya article news categorization collected from Tigrinya news. The minimum and the maximum number of sentences in the news article, which range from one to seventeen, are, respectively. Moreover, each news article contains four sentences on average.

4   Data Augmentation

It is well known that machine learning models consume a lot of data. Therefore, the more training data we provide, the better the model performs and the more robust it becomes. Unfortunately, access to high-quality data continues to be a challenge for many applications. Either there is a lack of data, or it is too expensive to gather. This problem can be solved by generating new training examples from existing ones using data augmentation.

Data augmentation is a class of techniques for artificially augmenting the amount of data by applying different operations to the original data and is useful when dealing with datasets with small samples or low-resource languages. We can expect a reduced cost for dataset construction. Several data augmentation methods have been suggested in the field of natural language processing (NLP), including data augmentation using language models [12], synonym replacement from word embedding [9], synonym replacement from Word-Net [22], machine translation [6], back translation [19], and paraphrasing [8].

In this work, we propose a data augmentation technique for the text classification task for texts in Tigrinya by considering the language characteristics. Specifically, our method combines synonym word replacement, sentence random substitution, and sentence shuffling. In the following, we give more detailed explanations.

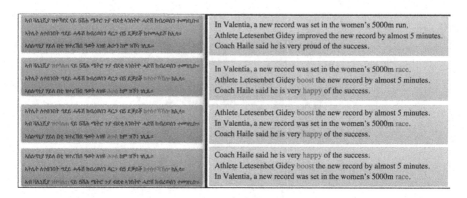

Fig. 2. An example of the original and augmented news article. The left side shows Tigrinya text. Similarly, the right side of the figure shows a translation of Tigrinya into English. The first paragraph shows the original before applying the data augmentation mechanism. In the second paragraph, words with red color are replaced with their synonym from word2vec embedding (embedding trained on Tigrinya text). The third and fourth paragraphs show the sentences' shuffling (changing position). Note that '::' indicates the end of the sentences. (Color figure online)

Synonym replacement. We randomly select 15% of the words in the sentences except for stop words. Then, we replace each of these words with randomly chosen synonyms. We use word2vec [14] embedding trained on Tigrinya text to choose synonyms.

Random shuffling. In this step, we randomly shuffle the sentences to generate text with different sentence orders.

Random substitution. For an article, we replace randomly selected sentences with those ones taken randomly from the articles in the identical category. E.g, let us assume a couple of article in the same category, i.e., agriculture.

Agriculture <sent A1>, <sent A2>, <sent A3>, <sent A4>.
Agriculture <sent B1>, <sent B2>, <sent B3>, <sent B4>.

We can generate the following articles.

Agriculture <sent A1>, <sent A2>, <sent B3>, <sent A4>.
Agriculture <sent B1>, <sent B2>, <sent B3>, <sent A2>.

In this work, we applied the above technique against our dataset as follows. We applied each step to generate augmented article, and applied the next step to the augmented dataset, including the original and augmented articles. Specifically, our first step generated 4792 articles in total. Subsequently, we obtained 7187 articles and finally generated 9582 articles. Figure 2 shows before and after applying the proposed method.

5   Text Classification Using a Pre-trained Language Model

Recently, it has been shown that state-of-the-art transformer-based models, like BERT [3] and RoBERTa [13], are very efficient for language understanding and can produce high-quality results. A *pretrained language model* (PLM) is trained using a large-scale unsupervised corpus with masking language model (MLM) and next sentence prediction objectives [3]. Having trained, a PLM can be fine-tuned for different downstream tasks using task-specific training data datasets, in many cases with smaller sizes. To our knowledge, no previous study used transformer-based architecture for Tigrinya text classification.

In this work, we exploit a transformer-based pretrained language model, TigRoBERTa [23], for the news article classification task. As described above, it is based on RoBERTa [13] and trained using Masked Language Modeling (MLM) task on a Tigrinya corpus. More precisely, it used a Byte Pair Encoder (BPE) tokenizer with a vocabulary size of 50,265 units and was trained in an unsupervised manner using 4.3 million sentences. With the help of the BPE tokenizer, the model can encode inputs without encountering "unknown" tokens by learning a sub-word vocabulary. TigRoBERTa has 12 blocks, 768 hidden dimensions, 12 attention heads, and a maximum sequence length of 512.

The fine-tuning process of TigRoBERTa in text classification can be seen in Fig. 3. First, the input text was tokenized, and then certain words that are not found in the TigRoBERTa vocabulary were handled using the BPE tokenizer. Next, the data was sent to the embedding layer to obtain a vector representation. Finally, the model is trained and can predict the labels that correlate to the dataset. The following hyper-parameter settings are used for this experiments: batch size is 4; learning rate is 2e-5; optimizer is Adam; and # of epochs is 10.

6   Experimental Evaluation

To assess the effectiveness and validity of the proposed data augmentation method and text classification method, we have conducted a set of experiments.

6.1   Experimental Setup

Dataset. We have used the Tigrinya news article dataset described in Sect. 3, and applied pre-processing, i.e., removal of stopwords, punctuation, and special characters. Specifically, we removed 129 stopwords – some examples can be found in Fig. 4. Then, we removed symbols, special characters, and punctuation's as Tigrinya (Ge'ez) script has its own punctuation's such as (፡፡) used to mark the end of a sentence, and (፡) uses to separate words, ideas, or phrases within a sentence. Note that the dataset contains augmented articles that have been generated by the method described in Sect. 4.

Methodology. We partitioned the dataset into 80% for training, 10% for test, and the rest 10% for validation. All experiments were performed using Google Colab environment, Tesla V100-SXM2-16 GB.

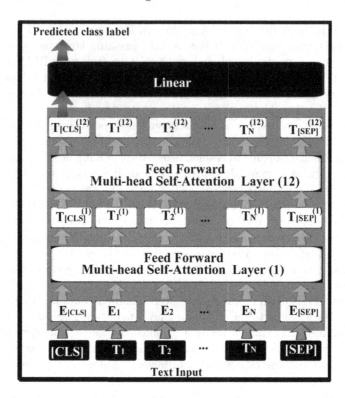

Fig. 3. Fine-tuning TigRoBERTa on text classification task. The model has 12 layers. [CLS] is placed at the beginning of the input sentences. (T) refers to the input token, (E) refers to the embedded of that token. And [SEP] is used for separating the following sentence.

Comparative Methods. To evaluate the classification accuracy of the proposed method, we use several existing methods for text classification.

Non-neural network classifiers. We employ Logistic Regression (LR), Naive Bayes (NB), Support Vector Machine (SVM), Random Forest (RF), and Linear Discriminant Analysis (LDA). To extract feature vectors from the news articles, we utilized BOW (bag-of-words) uni-gram characteristics, mapping each word to a vector representation using the TF-IDF.

Neural-network classifiers. We employ BiLSTM [17], where its inputs flow in forward/backward, which is known to perform well for text data. Specifically, we use word2vec [14] embedding trained on Tigrinya to initialize the BiLSTM followed by softmax, which is used to decide the output of BiLSTM whether it should be activated or not based on each neurons input. Our experiments are conducted with the following settings for hyper-parameters: embedding dimension: 100, learning rate: 0.00001, dropout: 0.3, batch size: 64, epoch: 40, optimizer: Adam, and activation function: softmax.

ከምቶም : እቶም : ከምዘለኔ : ነበሩ
እዚ : ዝኾነ : ኸዓ : እዛ : ኣይኮነን
ኣብቲ : ማለት : እዩ : ከም : ነቲ : ኣብ
ከማኸ : ከምዘለኺ : ከምዘለዎ : እቲ
ወይ : ድማ : ከሳብ : መን : ኣቢይ
እምበር : በቶም : ነዚ : ይኹን : ኣሎ
እንታይ : እታ : ካብ : ነይርም : ኩሉ
ከምዘለኩም : እውን : ውን: ኣብዚ

Fig. 4. An example of Tigrinya stopwords.

6.2 Experimental Results

All experiments are conducted on four distinct datasets with different number of augmented articles, i.e., 2,396, 4,792, 7,187, and 9,852. Note that 2,396 articles do not contain augmented articles.

Table 2 shows the experimental results of the classification accuracy for the proposed method and the comparative methods. In our investigation, LR and LDA achieved the highest accuracy of 84%, followed by SVM 78%, NB 73%, and DT with 58% accuracy in our initial trial with 2,396 articles. If we augment the articles to 4,792, we observe a 1–8% gain in accuracy except for LDA, and the highest gain is obtained by logistic regression. When the number of articles is 7,187, we did not observe any significant improvement in accuracy, but LR and LDA showed the best accuracy with 9,582 articles. Overall, we can say that the proposed data augmentation method is useful to improve the classification accuracy, but the size of best-performing dataset varies depending on the classifier.

Table 2. Classification accuracy.

# articles	2,396	4,792	7,187	9,582
SVM	78	**81**	78	79
LR	84	**87**	84	**87**
LDA	84	84	83	**85**
DT	58	**66**	62	63
NB	73	**74**	72	71
BiLSTM	81	85	85	**90**
TigRoBERTa	87	92	92	**94**

Regarding the neural-network based method (BiLSTM) and the proposed transformer-based model (TigRoBERTa), we obtained 81% and 87% accuracy, respectively, i.e., the proposed method performed the best without data augmentation. Moreover, if we augment the size of dataset, unlike non-neural network

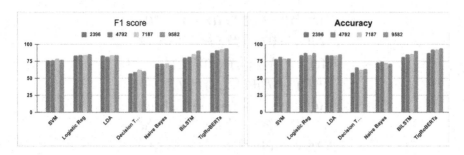

Fig. 5. Performance on news article classification with and without the proposed method for various dataset sizes used for training. All results are presented in terms of accuracy, and f1 score.

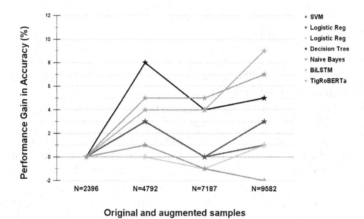

Fig. 6. Performance gain of the proposed method across all classifiers on various training set sizes. N = 2396 is the original dataset while N = (4792,7178, and 9582) are the augmented.

methods, the performance was consistently improved, and the best performance was observed at the largest dataset size. The proposed TigRoBERTa showed the best accuracy of 94% with 9,582 sample sizes; similarly, the BiLSTM obtained a 90% with the maximum number of samples.

Figure 5 depicts different results, which are summarized in terms of accuracy, and f1 score for all classifiers. In Fig. 6, we examine the effect of the number of augmented articles generated per original. Increasing the amount of training data impacted the performance to some classifiers, such as NB, which resulted in a decline as more samples were generated. TigRoBERTa and BiLSTM, on the other hand, showed performance improvements as the number of samples increased.

7   Conclusions

In this work, we have addressed the problem of news article classification for Tigrinya language. To address the problem of low-resource of NLP tasks, we have built a new news article dataset in Tigrinya language, containing 2,396 articles, for news article classification task with seven classes, namely, agriculture, business, health, politics, religion, sport, and technology. Furthermore, we proposed a data augmentation technique for text data in Tigrinya. Our method combines word synonym replacement and sentence shuffling to generate a new synthetic article. Besides, we have proposed a text classification method based on a pre-trained language model, TigRoBERTa. To test the effectiveness of our proposals, we have conducted a set of experiments where the classification accuracy is compared with some comparative methods, containing traditional machine learning models and neural-network based model. The experimental results have shown that the data augmentation method is useful for improving classification accuracy. Besides, our method improves 1–8 % accuracy over traditional machine learning approaches, similarly 1–9 % and 5–7 % accuracy gain over the neural network and transformer-based model, respectively. In the future, we plan to extend our method to other low-resource languages.

References

1. Breiman, L.: Random forests. Mach. Learn. **45**(1), 5–32 (2001)
2. Dernoncourt, F., Lee, J.Y., Szolovits, P.: NeuroNER: an easy-to-use program for named-entity recognition based on neural networks. arXiv preprint arXiv:1705.05487 (2017)
3. Devlin, J., Chang, M.W., Lee, K., Toutanova, K.: BERT: pre-training of deep bidirectional transformers for language understanding. arXiv preprint arXiv: 1810.04805 (2018)
4. Dos Santos, C., Zadrozny, B.: Learning character-level representations for part-of-speech tagging. In: International Conference on Machine Learning, pp. 1818–1826. PMLR (2014)
5. Endalie, D., Haile, G.: Automated Amharic news categorization using deep learning models. Comput. Intell. Neurosci. **2021** (2021)
6. Fadaee, M., Bisazza, A., Monz, C.: Data augmentation for low-resource neural machine translation. arXiv preprint arXiv:1705.00440 (2017)
7. Fesseha, A., Xiong, S., Emiru, E.D., Diallo, M., Dahou, A.: Text classification based on convolutional neural networks and word embedding for low-resource languages: Tigrinya. Information **12**(2), 52 (2021)
8. Gao, S., Zhang, Y., Ou, Z., Yu, Z.: Paraphrase augmented task-oriented dialog generation. arXiv preprint arXiv:2004.07462 (2020)
9. Hazem, A., Daille, B.: Word embedding approach for synonym extraction of multiword terms. In: Proceedings of the Eleventh International Conference on Language Resources and Evaluation (LREC 2018) (2018)
10. Hochreiter, S., Schmidhuber, J.: Long short-term memory. Neural Comput. **9**(8), 1735–1780 (1997)
11. Kelemework, W.: Automatic Amharic text news classification: Aneural networks approach. Ethiop. J. Sci. Technol. **6**(2), 127–137 (2013)

12. Kumar, V., Choudhary, A., Cho, E.: Data augmentation using pre-trained transformer models. arXiv preprint arXiv:2003.02245 (2020)
13. Liu, Y., et al.: RoBERTa: a robustly optimized BERT pretraining approach. arXiv preprint arXiv:1907.11692 (2019)
14. Mikolov, T., Chen, K., Corrado, G., Dean, J.: Efficient estimation of word representations in vector space. arXiv preprint arXiv:1301.3781 (2013)
15. Osman, O., Mikami, Y.: Stemming Tigrinya words for information retrieval. In: Proceedings of COLING 2012: Demonstration Papers, pp. 345–352 (2012)
16. Rish, I., et al.: An empirical study of the Naive Bayes classifier. In: IJCAI 2001 Workshop on Empirical Methods in Artificial Intelligence, vol. 3, pp. 41–46 (2001)
17. Schuster, M., Paliwal, K.K.: Bidirectional recurrent neural networks. IEEE Trans. Signal Process. **45**(11), 2673–2681 (1997)
18. Shorten, C., Khoshgoftaar, T.M.: A survey on image data augmentation for deep learning. J. Big Data **6**(1), 1–48 (2019)
19. Sugiyama, A., Yoshinaga, N.: Data augmentation using back-translation for context-aware neural machine translation. In: Proceedings of the Fourth Workshop on Discourse in Machine Translation (DiscoMT 2019), pp. 35–44 (2019)
20. Tedla, Y.K., Yamamoto, K., Marasinghe, A.: Nagaoka Tigrinya corpus: design and development of part-of-speech tagged corpus. Nagaoka University of Technology, pp. 1–4 (2016)
21. Tesfagergish, S.G., Kapociute-Dzikiene, J.: Deep learning-based part-of-speech tagging of the Tigrinya language. In: Lopata, A., Butkienė, R., Gudonienė, D., Sukackė, V. (eds.) ICIST 2020. CCIS, vol. 1283, pp. 357–367. Springer, Cham (2020). https://doi.org/10.1007/978-3-030-59506-7_29
22. Wei, J., Zou, K.: EDA: easy data augmentation techniques for boosting performance on text classification tasks. arXiv preprint arXiv:1901.11196 (2019)
23. Yohannes, H.M., Amagasa, T.: Named-entity recognition for a low-resource language using pre-trained language model. In: Proceedings of the 37th ACM/SIGAPP Symposium on Applied Computing, pp. 837–844 (2022)

Expertise Computation for Automatic Reviewer Assignment

Divya Kwatra[1]([⊠]) and Vasudha Bhatnagar[2]

[1] Department of Computer Science, Hansraj College, University of Delhi, Delhi 110007, India
divya@hrc.du.ac.in
[2] Department of Computer Science, University of Delhi, Delhi 110007, India
vbhatnagar@cs.du.ac.in

Abstract. Assigning effective and accurate reviewers is a crucial step in the peer-reviewing process to ensure high-quality publications. Automatic reviewer assignment problem, which aims to assign experts for rating the submitted research, relies critically on determining the expertise of the reviewers in the topics covered in the manuscript and assigning them so that all research topics covered in the manuscript are rated by proficient reviewers.

In this paper, we consider research expertise as a commixture of *interest* and *proficiency* of the reviewers in the topics that span the manuscript. We take reviewers' recent publications and self-declaration about the areas of research interest as input. Lexical variations in the topics declared by reviewers are leveled using sentence transformers and the research publications. Similarity between the semantic content of the manuscript and the research topics is also matched using the sentence transformer framework. Subsequently, we quantify the reviewers' *interest* in each topic along with their *proficiency* in that topic based on the number of authored publications. Reviewers are scored for *expertise*, which is a function of the two computed quantities. Top scoring reviewers are assigned the manuscript for review ratings.

We evaluate the effectiveness of the proposed method using topic coverage and review confidence as metrics. We observe that the proposed algorithm for expertise computation and reviewer assignment performs better than the baseline method.

Keywords: Reviewer expertise · Reviewer proficiency · Reviewer interest · Topic matching · Sentence transformers

1 Introduction

Robust peer reviewing is a critical step in research for advancement of the body of knowledge. Identifying reviewers with apt expertise for submitted manuscripts is highly desirable as it directly impacts the review quality, which has a direct bearing on the prestige of the venue. Assigning reviewers for critiquing the submitted

© The Author(s), under exclusive license to Springer Nature Switzerland AG 2022
E. Pardede et al. (Eds.): iiWAS 2022, LNCS 13635, pp. 531–547, 2022.
https://doi.org/10.1007/978-3-031-21047-1_48

manuscripts is a complex task for a publishing venue. It requires ascertaining from a pool of reviewers those who are not only *proficient* with the subject matter of the manuscript but *interested* in reviewing it. With the increase in the number of submissions in conferences and journals and given short turnaround times, manual matching of the subject matter of the submitted research articles and suitable reviewers is infeasible. This has driven research in the area of automatic reviewer assignment problem with systems used in real scenario [2, 7–9, 15, 18, 27].

Identifying and assigning reviewers is a two-step problem. Given a pool of reviewers, the first step is to quantify reviewers' expertise with respect to the subject matter of the manuscript. This is followed by the assignment of reviewers who best match the manuscript. Quantification of expertise entails creating reviewers' research profiles, which are typically based on information either volunteered by the reviewers, collected from publication lists available on internet, and reviewers' authority that can be estimated from impact factor of publication venue, H-index, citation relations, and time of publications [6, 11, 13, 15, 20, 22]. After the research profiles have been suitably created, reviewers are scored for the manuscript in question and assignment is effected either by ranking method [1, 13, 20, 26] or by solving a constrained assignment problem [5, 6, 8, 10–12, 14, 16].

Research profile of the reviewer is often derived from the set of recent research articles authored (or co-authored) by the reviewer, from which relevant information about the subject of research (topics) is retrieved. Thus recent research publications proxy for reviewer's research interest(s) as well as proficiencies. Retrieval-based methods are used to extract similar information from the submitted manuscript, and similarity between the reviewers' articles and the manuscripts using cosine similarity is computed. This score is typically the basis of scoring a reviewer's expertise for rating the manuscript. Natural Language Processing (NLP) and Information Retrieval (IR) techniques for topic modeling, like Latent Dirichlet Allocation (LDA) and Latent Semantic Index (LSI) are commonly used to infer topics from the documents [9, 11, 12, 18, 19, 22]. Since computing semantic similarity between the reviewers' publications and the manuscript is a computationally expensive process, an alternate strategy is to compute the reviewers' expertise using their research experience and research impact, which are combined dexterously to produce a score that is interpreted as affinity of the reviewer for the manuscript [6, 11, 13, 15, 20, 22].

Subsequent to the reviewer scoring step, the prime focus is to assign reviewers to assess the manuscript. Reviewer assignment can be performed either by ranking the reviewers in order of their expertise or by solving an optimization problem with the objective to maximize the expertise of the reviewers for the manuscripts [5, 6, 8, 10]. Assignment may be constrained by either the load of the reviewer minimum and maximum papers assigned for reviewing [5, 6, 8, 11] local or global fairness [10]. The *manuscript coverage* constraint restricts the number of reviewers to be assigned to a manuscript.

In this work, we focus on quantification of expertise of the reviewers and make the assignment based on ranking method (as in [13, 20, 26]). Expertise computation is the first novelty of our work, which is based on the (i) interest of the reviewer relative to all other research interests of the reviewer, and (ii) proficiency of the reviewer in the topic (of the manuscript) relative to that of all other reviewers in the set of potential reviewers. The second novelty of our proposal lies in the use of sentence transformers (RoBERTa Model [17]) to perform topic match between the topics contained in the documents. Based on the match score, we create reviewer-topic matrix and manuscript-topic vector, aggregated to realize reviewer expertise. Preliminary experimentation shows promise. Specifically, our contributions are as follows.

i. We propose a novel method to quantify reviewers' expertise by simultaneously considering their interest and proficiency in all topics of the manuscript to be reviewed.
ii. We show the effectiveness of our method by demonstrating the impact of variation in number of assigned reviewers on the coverage of reviewers.
iii. We experiment to showcase the impact of increasing number of matched topics on the topic coverage and review confidence of manuscript.
iv. We demonstrate that considering reviewers' proficiency along with their interest improves the quality of reviewer assignments.

The remainder of this paper is organized as follows. We outline the related research work in Sect. 2. The problem is formally defined in Sect. 3. Section 4 explains the proposed methodology. Section 5 describes the experimental setup, dataset used, evaluation metrics, and the results. Finally, Sect. 6 concludes this paper.

2   Related Work

In this section, we review and compare the existing work published for reviewer assignment problem based on two aspects: (i) extracting reviewer and manuscript topics, and (ii) creating reviewer profile. We mention that the main focus of our research is to score reviewer expertise and use ranking for automatic reviewer assignment. Therefore, we omit discussion of several creditable works, which consider automatic reviewer assignment as unconstrained or constrained assignment problem.

Extracting Reviewer and Manuscript Topics: The main challenge is to extract the research areas of the reviewers from the past publications. Natural language processing (NLP) techniques like Latent Semantic analysis (LSA) and Latent Dirichlet allocation (LDA) have been used extensively for information retrieval [2,9,18,22,23]. Rule-base classification for revealing *disciplines* has been attempted in [27]. Recent advances in NLP related to large language models have been well exploited towards this goal. Word embedding, which carry rich semantic information, have been found effective for accurate retrieval of research topics spanning reviewer publications and manuscript [4,19,21,28].

Creating Reviewer Profile: Diverse facets of the reviewers' professional information have been used to create their profiles, in addition to the reviewers' publications. These include reviewers' self assessments in terms of bids to express their level of interests [2], relevance between the manuscript and reviewer [15], expertise, authority (reviewer's recognition in the scientific community), diversity (reviewer's diverse research background) [16], H-index, affiliations etc. [22]. Reviewer's topic interests, quality and recency of publications are used to score reviewers [20]. Seniority aspects of the reviewers to assess their suitability for the manuscript has been considered in [13].

Reviewer profile, thus elicited, is either directly matched with the manuscript for ascertaining suitability, or is used to compute expertise of the reviewers for use in assignment algorithm.

3   Problem Definition

Let M be the manuscript submitted for review, and $R = \{R_1, R_2, ..., R_r\}$ be a pool of r potential reviewers. Let $P = \{P_1, P_2......P_r\}$ be the repository of publications of the reviewers, where $P_i = \{p_1, p_2.....p_{n_i}\}$ is the set of recent publications of reviewer R_i. Let $T_i = \{t_1, t_2, ..., t_{m_i}\}$ denote the set of topics of research interests declared by R_i. Assuming that the publication venue has identified reviewers in consonance with the topics that fall with in the aims and scope of the venue, define set $T = \cup T_i, (1 \leq i \leq r)$ as the complete topic set that covers the scope of publication at the venue. The underlying motivation to construct set T is to cover the clause "not limited to", commonly used in all publication venues. The problem is to retrieve the top-k experts as reviewers for the submitted manuscript such that:

1. each reviewer has *high interest* in at least one topic of the manuscript, *relative* to other research interests,
2. each reviewer has *high proficiency* in at least one topic of the manuscript, *relative* to other potential reviewers, and
3. all topics of the manuscript are collectively covered to the *best* possible extent by the k reviewers.

Table 1. List of frequently used notations

Symbol	Description
M	Submitted Manuscript
R	Pool of reviewers $\{R_1, R_2...R_r\}$
P_i	Set of publications of reviewer R_i
P	Repository of reviewers' publications, $\{P_1, P_2,...P_r\}$
T_i	Set of research topics declared by reviewer R_i
T	Complete set of research topics, $(\cup T_i)$
$\mathbb{R}$	Reviewer-topic matrix representing the research topics of reviewers

Assuming that the current research interest is revealed by recent publications authored by the researcher, we aim to quantify reviewers' expertise as a composite of current research interest and proficiency in the research topics covered in the manuscript M, and assign top ranking reviewers for reviewing it. To the best of our knowledge, no existing works consider *interest* and *proficiency* of reviewers in the topics simultaneously to quantify their expertise. Table 1 lists the notations used in rest of the paper.

4   Methodology for Expertise Computation

In this section, we detail the proposed method to compute the expertise of reviewers in the topics that span the manuscript M. The objective is to identify the best k reviewers among the available r, such that the technical content for each research topic covered in M is graded by the best available expert(s) in that area. Our method is based on the premise that expertise of a researcher is characterized by *interest* and *proficiency* in a topic, and both attributes can be elicited from the number of authored publications in which that topic is dominant.

We first identify the prominent research topics spanning the manuscript and the reviewers' publication using the topic set T as the benchmark. Recall that T is the exhaustive set of topics divulged by the experts. Matching the research publications of the reviewers against T to extract dominant research topics in each publication, despite self-declaration of expertise, is apparently an extravagant computation. However, this step is essential to instill standardization of semantically related topics. Topic matching is followed by creation of the reviewer profile, which is exacted by the number of publications for each matched research topic. Deft use of the publications and reviewers' expertise declaration distills important information about the reviewers' research profiles and aids quantification of interest and proficiency of the reviewer for matching the research topics covered in the submitted manuscript M. We describe the detailed methodology in the following subsections.

4.1   Matching Manuscript Topics with Reviewer Publications

Identifying common topics between the submitted manuscript and reviewer publications is a crucial preparatory step for assigning suitable reviewers for the manuscript. Generally, the author given keywords in research articles are subjective, and specific for the work. They may overlap, to varying extents, with one or more topics of research interest for the publication venue . Analogously, individual interest declarations by the reviewers may have significant semantic similarity with the topics mentioned by the venue even though the terms used may be different. Therefore, it is prudent to standardize research topics before proceeding to identify suitable reviewers. Furthermore, in case a publication does

not specify keywords[1], this step is imperative for extracting information about
the research topics covered by the publication.

Recent advances in NLP techniques come handy in leveling the differences
among the keywords mentioned in research publications and revealing latent
semantic similarity between self-declarations of reviewers' research interest.
Kreutz et al. demonstrated that the use of embeddings are more effective than
the traditional NLP methods for exposing the semantic similarity between the
reviewers' publications and the submitted manuscripts [13]. We advance the
method by using Sentence Transformers framework proposed in [25]. The state-
of-the-art framework is exploited to compute text embedding of the complete
topics set (T), the reviewer publications (P) and the manuscript (M). Subsequently, semantic similarity is computed between the embeddings to match
the topics in the manuscript and reviewer publications against the benchmark
topic set T. We employ RoBERTa (Robustly optimized BERT approach) model,
which is a robustly optimized large language model advancing the state-of-the-
art BERT model [3], as the sentence transformer to realize the embeddings. The
embeddings preserve the semantic information contained in the text without
concerning the lexical information therein. The choice of RoBERTa model is
motivated by the improved performance as reported in [17,24].

We retrieve RoBERTa embeddings for all topics in T and conserve them for
matching against reviewers' publications and the manuscript. Instead of matching the entire text, which are typically long, we use only the abstracts of the
publications and manuscript because of efficiency and efficacy. Subsequently,
we compute cosine similarity between the embedding of the article abstract
(manuscript/reviewer publication) with each topic in the topic set T. The computation captures the extent to which the abstract is semantically close to the different topics in the benchmark topic set T. For a well written abstract, topics that
bear high semantic similarity with the text are considered to be the prominent
topics in the research article. Thus we overcome the lingual and morphological
variations in the author declared keywords present in the reviewer publications
and self-declared research topics of interest, while mapping the semantic content
of the submitted manuscript to the exhaustive topic list declared collectively by
all experts.

Let A_j^i denote the abstract of the jth publication of reviewer R_i. The abstract
is submitted to the sentence transformer and its 1024 dimensional embedding θ_j^i
is retrieved. Similarly, embedding β_k of the same dimension is retrieved for each
topic $t_k \in T$. Cosine similarity $(\sigma_j^i(k) = Cosine(\theta_j^i, \beta_k))$ between the abstract
A_j^i and topic t_k is computed. We thus generate a vector of size $|T|$, in which
each element signifies the semantic proximity between the abstract and the corresponding topic. Depending on the user's discretion, t topics corresponding to
the top scores are construed to be prominently discussed in the research article. Thus, the use of sentence transformer facilitates discovery of notable latent
topics in the research article. Figure 1 pictorially depicts this step. Selecting the
optimal value of t is important here and requires calibration. Matching with

---

[1] For example, ACL publications do not contain keywords.

too few topics results in missing important topics in the paper, which may lead to inadequate reviewer assignment and there may remain some topics in the manuscript which are not adequately evaluated. Such a situation is undesirable as it may deteriorate the quality of the review. On the other hand, matching with *too many* topics may introduce noise in the discovered topics, which again lowers the coverage as revealed by our experiments.

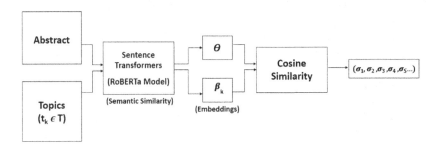

Fig. 1. Matching the semantic content of an article with the topics to identify dominant topics in the paper. θ : embedding of the abstract, β_k : embedding of the topic t_k, $\sigma_k : Cos(\theta, \beta_k)$

4.2   Create Reviewer Profile

Once the subject area of all the reviewers' publications is identified, we proceed to create the reviewer profile, aggregating the number of publications authored by the reviewer for each topic in T. Thus, a profile for reviewer R_i is created by taking into consideration the reviewer's knowledge in all technical areas designated by the set of topics T, derived from the list of publications (P_i).

After matching the publications of reviewer R_i, a topic vector of size $|T|$ is obtained in which each element is the count of publications of the reviewer for the corresponding topic, and the topic is a dominant topic in the publication. Combining the topic vectors of all reviewers yields the reviewer-topic matrix $\mathbb{R}$, of size $r \times |T|$, which summarizes the profile of all r reviewers. Element j in row i of $\mathbb{R}$, ρ_j^i, is the number of publications for reviewer R_i in topic t_j.

4.3   Consolidating Reviewer Expertise

Subsequent to reviewer profiling, reviewer expertise computation is carried out. Reviewers should not only have a high level of proficiency in topics spanning the manuscript that she is expected to review but additionally must have a keen interest in these topics.

Current *interest* of reviewer R_i is evident from her publication profile P_i. Effectively, top-t topics extracted from the set of reviewers' publications indicate t areas of current research interest of the reviewers. Having extracted top-t

current interests from the publications set P_i, we assess relative interest in those t topics for R_i. The motivation is to ensure that the reviewer is assigned a manuscript, which has topics that are of high interest to the reviewer currently.

The second component of expertise, i.e. *proficiency*, is also important to assess before the reviewers are assigned. Proficiency entails in-depth knowledge and awareness about the current state of the art for the topic(s) that is(are) to be reviewed. It is reasonable to assume that the proficiency of a reviewer in a topic is proportional to the number of her publications on that topic. Since proficiency in a topic varies across reviewers, analyzing the number of publications on a topic relative to the publications of other reviewers on the same topic enables inference about the relative *proficiency* of a reviewer for a given topic. Furthermore, considering relative competence of the reviewers in the topics of manuscript ensures appropriateness of the assignment to the manuscript for review.

Based on these ideas we compute *Topic-Interest* and *Topic-proficiency* matrices, $\mathcal{I}$ and $\mathcal{P}$ respectively, for all reviewers and topics.

Definition 1. *Topic-Interest matrix $\mathcal{I}$, of size $r \times |T|$, is matrix of real number in range $[0, 1]$ where the element (ι_j^i) indicates the interest of a reviewer in a topic, relative to all other topics in T. It is computed as follows.*

$$\iota_j^i = \frac{\rho_j^i}{\sum_j \rho_j^i} \tag{1}$$

Row i of $\mathcal{I}$ corresponds to reviewer R_i, and captures her relative interest in each of the benchmark topics. Note that the each row sums to 1.

Definition 2. *Topic-Proficiency matrix $\mathcal{P}$, of size $r \times |T|$, is matrix of real number in range $[0, 1]$ where the element (ψ_j^i) indicates the proficiency of a reviewer in a topic, relative to all other potential reviewers in the pool. It is computed as follows.*

$$\psi_j^i = \frac{\rho_j^i}{\sum_i \rho_j^i} \tag{2}$$

In matrix $\mathcal{P}$, the columns are of interest. Column j of this matrix corresponds to topic t_j and denotes relative proficiency of reviewers in topic t_j. Note that the each column in this matrix sums to 1.

Next, we compute the expertise of the reviewers in the manuscript. Recall that we identify the top-t topics in the manuscript by matching against the topic set T in Step 1. We compute the expertise of reviewers in manuscript M as per the following definitions.

Definition 3. *Manuscript-Interest: Given the manuscript M, the interest of reviewer R_i in M is the sum of her interest in topics that match the topics in M.*

$$\hat{\iota}_i = \sum_{j \in m} \iota_j^i, \tag{3}$$

where m is the list of topics common to M and R_i. Manuscript-interest quantifies how much is the reviewer R_i interested in the topics that span M, based on her current research interests divulged by her publications.

Definition 4. *Manuscript-Proficiency: Given the manuscript M, the proficiency of reviewer R_i in M is the sum of her proficiency in topics that match the topics in M.*

$$\hat{\psi}_i = \sum_{j \in m} \psi_j^i \tag{4}$$

where m is the list of topics common to M and R_i. Manuscript-proficiency quantifies how much is the reviewer R_i proficient in the topics that span M, based on her number of research publications.

Definition 5. *Expertise score (E): Given the manuscript M, Expertise score of reviewer R_i is the Hadamard product of her interest score $(\hat{\iota}_i)$ and proficiency score $(\hat{\psi}_i)$ for M.*

$$\epsilon_i = \hat{\iota}_i \otimes \hat{\psi}_i \tag{5}$$

Expertise score, which is the critical computation for reviewer assignment, integrates the relative interest of the reviewers and relative competence of the reviewers in the manuscript topics. Assuming recentness of the list of publications of reviewers, from which both these attributes are distilled, the expertise score ϵ_i for reviewer R_i is an apt criterion for reviewer assignment. The complete algorithm for computing the expertise score of reviewers and retrieving top-k reviewers for reviewing the manuscript M is shown in Algorithm 1.

Algorithm 1: Algorithm for Expertise Computation and Reviewer Assignment

---

Input: Set of reviewer publications P, set of reviewers' research areas T, and manuscript M
Output: Top-k reviewers for manuscript M

Step 1: Matching topics with reviewer publications and manuscript
(i) Obtain embeddings of all topics in the topic set T.
(ii) Obtain the embeddings of abstract of manuscript M.
(iii) Obtain the embeddings of abstracts of reviewer publications.
(iv) Find cosine similarity between the embeddings of reviewers' publications and embeddings of topic set to match each publication with top-t topics.
(v) Similarly, obtain top-t topics matching with manuscript M.

Step 2: Create Reviewer Profile
(i) Construct an abstract-topic vector for each publication of the reviewer.
(ii) Aggregate all the abstract-topic vectors to build a Reviewer-Topic matrix.

Step 3: Consolidating Reviewer Expertise
(i) Compute interest of a reviewer in topic t_j in all topics of M as in Eq. (3).
(ii) Compute proficiency of a reviewer in topic t_j in all topics of M as in Eq. (4).
(iii) Compute the expertise of a reviewer as in Eq. (5).

Step 4: Rank the reviewers in descending order of their expertise, and select the top-k suitable reviewers for manuscript M.
Return: Top-k reviewers for manuscript M

4.4 Expertise Computation Algorithm

Step 1 of algorithm retrieves the embedding of topic set, research publications of reviewers, and the manuscript using sentence transformers. Semantic similarity between the topics and the research texts is computed using cosine function, and topics corresponding to top-t scores are noted. Thus, publications and manuscript are mapped to the prominent topics among the set of common research topics. Reviewer profile for each reviewer is an abstract-topic vector for all publications of the reviewer, which is created in Step 2. These vectors are aggregated to create reviewer-topic matrix that defines reviewer's profile. Subsequent to reviewer profiling in Step 2, it is important to quantify two critical aspects of a reviewer, viz. *interest* and *proficiency* in the topics spanning the manuscript M. Finally, reviewers' expertise is computed as the function of her interest and proficiency in M. In the last step, the reviewers are ranked according to their expertise score for the manuscript M, and top-k reviewers are selected for reviewing the submitted manuscript.

5 Experimental Evaluation

In this section, we present the performance evaluation of the proposed method of expertise computation. We aim to examine the effectiveness of the proposed method on a public dataset with ground-truth. Specifically, we investigate

  i) to what extent does the expertise of the assigned reviewers cover all the research topics in the manuscript?
 ii) are all topics in the manuscript reviewed with adequate expertise? Is the review rigorous?
iii) does increasing the number of reviewers improve the coverage of research topics in the manuscript?
 iv) how does the proposed method perform in comparison to the baseline?
  v) does reviewers' proficiency in conjunction with their interest improve quality of reviewer assignments?

Since t, the number of matched topics and k, the number of assigned reviewers is user specified, we also study the variation in the quality of reviewer assignment with varying number of matched topics and assigned reviewers. We first briefly describe the dataset and metrics, and then present the results in Sec. 5.1.

Data Set: Challenges associated with datasets for evaluation of automatic reviewer assignments have been outlined by researchers in [13, 22]. Datasets used in several earlier works are not available, which makes it infeasible to compare our work with these methods [1, 7, 13, 20]. Tan et al. published three different datasets with varying number of manuscripts, reviewers, reviewers' details including their publications [26]. However, none of these carry the ground truth, and hence are not useful for our performance evaluation.

Patil et al. recently published a dataset consisting of title, authors, abstract, introduction, and conclusion of 100 accepted papers in AAAI19 [22]. The dataset[2] also includes similar information of 107 reviewers including their areas of research. The datatset also provides the five reviewers (k=5) for each manuscript assigned by the algorithm, which we use as the ground truth to evaluate our method.

Evaluation Metrics: The reviewer assignments made by the proposed method are evaluated against the ground truth assignment. Since this ground truth is also the outcome of the method proposed in [22], we use this as baseline for comparison. Some earlier works use human experts to evaluate the algorithmic assignments [1,13,16,20,23]. Due to the expense involved in evaluation by human experts, we use the following two metrics for evaluation.

i) *Topic Coverage*: This metric gauges the extent to which the topics of experts match with those of the manuscript [18]. Topic coverage is computed as the summation of ratio of total number of topics covered by each reviewers to the top-t topics in M. Let T_i be the set of topics for which reviewer R_i is designated as an expert, then the topic coverage (Cov) is computed as shown below.

$$Cov = \sum_i \frac{|T_i \cap T_M|}{|t|} \tag{6}$$

Note that $0 \leq Cov \leq k$. Ideally, automatic assignment of reviewers should result into the coverage value of k, which is achieved if all the reviewers are experts in all research topics dealt in the manuscript.

ii) *Review Confidence:* This metric quantifies the rigour of the review by checking out the number of reviewers who are experts for each topic [18]. The computation of review confidence averages the fraction of reviewers (out of k) who have expertise in one topic, over all the topics covered in M. Let k_i be the number of reviewers who have expertise in topic t_i of M, review confidence ($Conf$) for manuscript M is given as:

$$Conf = \frac{1}{|t|} \sum_i \frac{k_i}{k} \tag{7}$$

Intuitively, it is prudent to assign reviewers such that the expertise for each manuscript topic is maximum, which leads to possibly high quality reviews.

---

[2] https://www.kaggle.com/datasets/abolihpatil/dataset-reviewer-paper-assignment-2-ahp-pnm.

5.1   Results

We find that one manuscript in the data set (paper id 3806) doesn't have the content. Thus we test our method on 99 manuscripts and report the results. We describe the details of experiments and discuss the results below.

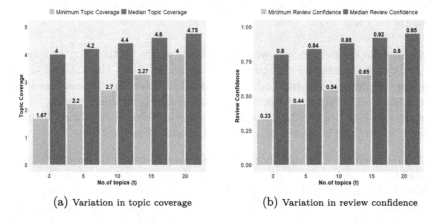

(a) Variation in topic coverage   (b) Variation in review confidence

Fig. 2. Variation in evaluation metrics with varying number of matched topics.

Sensitivity Analysis. We first assess the sensitivity of expertise computation to the number of topics (top-t) matched for the manuscript and reviewers' publications. As mentioned in Sec. 4.1, extreme values of the number of top matching topics deteriorate the quality of reviews. Since the dataset provides five reviewers for each manuscript as ground truth, we assign 5 reviewers for each manuscript while varying number of matching topics ($t = 3, 5, 10, 15, 20$). We compute the five-number summary of Cov and $Conf$ and plot the minimum and median values of the two evaluation metrics (Fig. 2). It is evident from Fig. 2a that the minimum coverage improves significantly with increase in the number of matching topics. Median, which is already high at ≈ 4, also shows slight improvement. However, the improvement plateaus when the number of topics increases beyond fifteen. Figure 2b also exhibits similar pattern for minimum and median review confidence. The minimum review confidence gains impressively as the number of topics increase up to fifteen. The gain in median is not as considerable. Increasing the number of topics leads to more overlapping between the manuscript and reviewers' topics, resulting in an increase in number of reviewers for each topic. This generally boosts the overall review confidence. However, if the number of matched topics increases beyond fifteen, some noisy and improper topics also get included, thereby deteriorating the topic coverage and review confidence.

Effectiveness of Expertise Computation.
Next we study the effectiveness of proposed
algorithm by analyzing the effect of variation
in number of assigned reviewers on coverage.
We match top-10 topics and observe the coverage with increasing number of reviewers. Note
that the topic coverage is bound by the number of reviewers k. In this experiment we vary
the value of k, and average the metric value
for fair comparison. Thus, the metric value for
all values of k now lies in the interval $[0, 1]$. It
is observed from Fig. 3 that the median value
of coverage increases with increasing number
of reviewers assigned. This completely matches
the expectation because each reviewer brings in
her personal expertise, which may be diverse for
different reviewers.

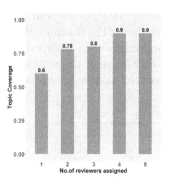

Fig. 3. Variation in median topic
coverage with varying number of
reviewers

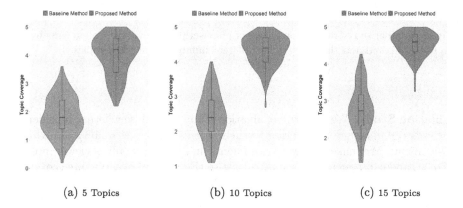

(a) 5 Topics   (b) 10 Topics   (c) 15 Topics

Fig. 4. Comparison of topic coverage by the reviewer assignment by the proposed
method and the baseline method for different number of matched topics.

Comparison with Baseline. We assign five reviewers for all the manuscripts,
while matching varying number of top$-t$ topics and compare the topic coverage
and review confidence with those of the ground-truth assignments. We display
the distribution of the metrics as violin plots, with a box-plot for further clarity in
Fig. 4. It is noticeable that the proposed method of reviewer assignment provides
superior topical coverage than the baseline for minimum, median and maximum
values. Smaller variation in the distributions for all topics also suggests higher
consistency. Deeper investigation is warranted for confirming this. Similarly, it
is evident from Fig. 5 that rigour in the automatic assignment is more than the

baseline. In this case also the variation in review confidence is significantly less than that of the baseline. Width of the violin at top indicates that there are more manuscripts with high value of confidence. There are more reviewers assigned for each topic of the manuscript, which suggests that the expertise computation is focused and ranking is suitable methods of assignment in the current context.

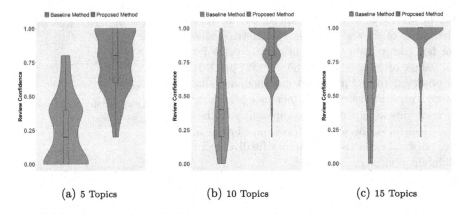

(a) 5 Topics   (b) 10 Topics   (c) 15 Topics

Fig. 5. Comparison of review confidence of manuscript for reviewer assignments by the proposed method and the baseline for different number of matched topics.

Ablation Study. We perform an ablation study to analyse whether considering reviewers' *proficiency* in addition to their *interest* improves quality of reviewer assignments. We make reviewer assignments first based on only reviewer interest (Eq. 3), and subsequently based on expertise (Eq. 5), and observe topic coverage and review confidence of the manuscript. We show the results for two scenarios, each with t=10 and 15, in Fig. 6 and 7. It is evident that topic coverage and review confidence of a manuscript increase when proficiency is taken into account along with the reviewers' interest in topics spanning the manuscript. The wider shape of the two distributions at higher score indicates higher probability that a manuscript has high topic coverage and review confidence. The longer length of the plot, when only interest is taken into account, indicates higher variation in topic coverage and review confidence of the manuscripts. The plots assert that the reviewer assignments are better when reviewers' proficiency is considered in conjunction with their subject-interest to compute reviewers' expertise.

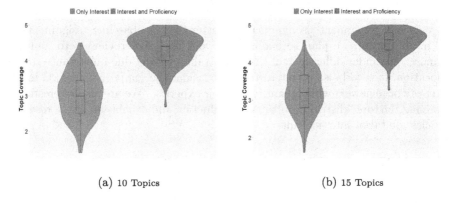

Fig. 6. Comparison of topic coverage of manuscript for reviewer assignments when only Interest is considered and when Interest and Proficiency are considered for different number of matched topics.

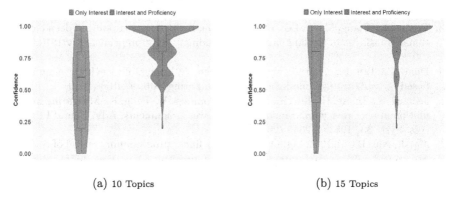

Fig. 7. Comparison of review confidence of manuscript for reviewer assignments when only Interest is considered and when Interest and Proficiency are considered for different number of matched topics.

6   Conclusion

In this paper, we propose a method for determining top-k reviewers for a submitted manuscript using a combination of semantic similarity between the topic set, reviewer publications, and manuscript. To compute their expertise, we introduce two critical aspects of a reviewer viz., *interest* and *proficiency* in the subject area of the manuscript.

   We use *topic coverage* and *review confidence* to evaluate the performance of the reviewer assignments by the proposed algorithm. We find that the expertise computation is sensitive to the number of topics matched with the reviewers' publications and manuscripts. We also observed that the quality of review assignments improves with the increase in the number of reviewers. The quality of reviewers assignments is significantly better that the baseline assignments.

In the future, we plan to extend our work to assign reviewers to multiple manuscripts under different real-time constraints, giving due importance to fair allocation. It would also be interesting to consider the temporal variation in the interests of reviewers while quantifying their expertise. We are also interested in studying the topic distribution when introduction and conclusion of the research articles are taken into account.

References

1. Anjum, O., Gong, H., Bhat, S., Hwu, W.M., Xiong, J.: PaRe: a paper-reviewer matching approach using a common topic space. In: Proceedings of the 2019 Conference on EMNLP-IJCNLP, pp. 518–528. ACL, Hong Kong, China (2019)
2. Charlin, L., Zemel, R.: The toronto paper matching system: an automated paper-reviewer assignment system. In: Proceedings of the 30th International Conference on Machine Learning, Atlanta, Georgia, USA, 2013 (2013)
3. Devlin, J., Chang, M.W., Lee, K., Toutanova, K.: Bert: pre-training of deep bidirectional transformers for language understanding. arXiv preprint arXiv:1810.04805 (2018)
4. Duan, Z., Tan, S., Zhao, S., Wang, Q., Chen, J., Zhang, Y.: Reviewer assignment based on sentence pair modeling. Neurocomputing **366**, 97–108 (2019)
5. Jecmen, S., Zhang, H., Liu, R., Shah, N., Conitzer, V., Fang, F.: Mitigating manipulation in peer review via randomized reviewer assignments. Adv. Neural Inf. Process. Syst. **33**, 12533–12545 (2020)
6. Jin, J., Niu, B., Ji, P., Geng, Q.: An integer linear programming model of reviewer assignment with research interest considerations. Ann. Oper. Res. **291**(1), 409–433 (2020)
7. Karimzadehgan, M., Zhai, C.: Constrained multi-aspect expertise matching for committee review assignment. In: Proceedings of the 18th ACM CIKM, pp. 1697–1700 (2009)
8. Karimzadehgan, M., Zhai, C.: Integer linear programming for constrained multi-aspect committee review assignment. Inf. Process. Manag. **48**(4), 725–740 (2012)
9. Karimzadehgan, M., Zhai, C., Belford, G.: Multi-aspect expertise matching for review assignment. In: Proceedings of the 17th ACM CIKM, pp. 1113–1122 (2008)
10. Kobren, A., Saha, B., McCallum, A.: Paper matching with local fairness constraints. In: Proceedings of the 25th ACM SIGKDD, pp. 1247–1257 (2019)
11. Kou, N.M., U, L.H., Mamoulis, N., Gong, Z.: Weighted coverage based reviewer assignment. In: Proceedings of the 2015 ACM SIGMOD, pp. 2031–2046 (2015)
12. Kou, N.M., U, L.H., Mamoulis, N., Li, Y., Li, Y., Gong, Z.: A topic-based reviewer assignment system. Proc. VLDB Endow. **8**(12), 1852–1855 (2015)
13. Kreutz, C.K., Schenkel, R.: Revaside: assignment of suitable reviewer sets for publications from fixed candidate pools. In: The 23rd International Conference on Information Integration and Web Intelligence, pp. 57–68 (2021)
14. Li, B., Hou, Y.T.: The new automated IEEE infocom review assignment system. IEEE Netw. **30**(5), 18–24 (2016)
15. Li, X., Watanabe, T.: Automatic paper-to-reviewer assignment, based on the matching degree of the reviewers. Procedia Comput. Sci. **22**, 633–642 (2013)

16. Liu, X., Suel, T., Memon, N.: A robust model for paper reviewer assignment. In: Proceedings of the 8th ACM RecSyS, pp. 25–32 (2014)
17. Liu, Y., et al.: Roberta: a robustly optimized bert pretraining approach. arXiv preprint arXiv:1907.11692 (2019)
18. Mimno, D., McCallum, A.: Expertise modeling for matching papers with reviewers. In: Proceedings of the 13th ACM SIGKDD, pp. 500–509 (2007)
19. Mirzaei, M., Sander, J., Stroulia, E.: Multi-aspect review-team assignment using latent research areas. Inf. Process. Manag. **56**(3), 858–878 (2019)
20. Nguyen, J., Sánchez-Hernández, G., Agell, N., Rovira, X., Angulo, C.: A decision support tool using order weighted averaging for conference review assignment. Pattern Recogn. Lett. **105**, 114–120 (2018)
21. Ogunleye, O., Ifebanjo, T., Abiodun, T., Adebiyi, A.: Proposed framework for a paper-reviewer assignment system using word2vec. In: Covenant University Conference on E-Governance in Nigeria (2017)
22. Patil, A.H., Mahalle, P.N.: Multi-label reviewer profile building and ranking based on expertise, recency, authority and h-index: vital module of reviewer paper assignment. Turk. J. Comput. Math. Educ. (TURCOMAT) **12**(6), 3026–3035 (2021)
23. Peng, H., Hu, H., Wang, K., Wang, X.: Time-aware and topic-based reviewer assignment. In: Bao, Z., Trajcevski, G., Chang, L., Hua, W. (eds.) DASFAA 2017. LNCS, vol. 10179, pp. 145–157. Springer, Cham (2017). https://doi.org/10.1007/978-3-319-55705-2_11
24. Rajapaksha, P., Farahbakhsh, R., Crespi, N.: Bert, xlnet or roberta: the best transfer learning model to detect clickbaits. IEEE Access **9**, 154704–154716 (2021)
25. Reimers, N., Gurevych, I.: Sentence-bert: sentence embeddings using siamese bert-networks. arXiv preprint arXiv:1908.10084 (2019)
26. Tan, S., Duan, Z., Zhao, S., Chen, J., Zhang, Y.: Improved reviewer assignment based on both word and semantic features. Inf. Retr. J. **24**(3), 175–204 (2021). https://doi.org/10.1007/s10791-021-09390-8
27. Xu, Y., Ma, J., Sun, Y., Hao, G., Xu, W., Zhao, D.: A decision support approach for assigning reviewers to proposals. Expert Syst. Appl. **37**(10), 6948–6956 (2010)
28. Zhao, S., Zhang, D., Duan, Z., Chen, J., Zhang, Y.P., Tang, J.: A novel classification method for paper-reviewer recommendation. Scientometrics **115**(3), 1293–1313 (2018)

Detection of Hot Topics Using Multi-view Text Clustering

Maha Fraj[✉], Mohamed Aymen Ben Hajkacem, and Nadia Essoussi

Université de Tunis, Institut Supérieur de Gestion de Tunis, 41, Rue de la Liberté,
Cité Bouchoucha, Le Bardo 2000, Tunisia
maha.fraj.m@gmail.com

Abstract. Clustering tweets aims to obtain topically coherent grouping of documents i.e. clusters of tweets that can be exploited for multiple
applications such as topic detection, news extraction, etc. However, handling such data is considered challenging due to its noisy aspect, the
lack of context and the length constraint on one hand, and the natural
aspect of text regarding its different interpretations and representations
on the other hand. In fact, a single representation model cannot capture
the various aspects of text which leads to losing valuable information.
Targeting these issues, we propose a multi-view tweets clustering method
that exploits various representation models in order to improve the clustering results. The experimental results show that the proposed method
enhances the clustering quality.

Keywords: Microblog clustering · Multi-view learning · Topic
detection · Self-organizing map

1 Introduction

Twitter presents a colossal repository of user-generated data and raises the interest of multiple research studies. Consequently, multiple machine learning methods were proposed in order to exploit this data as presented in [4,6,17,24]. Tweets
are micro-blogs restricted to a limited number of characters [8]. This length constraint makes users thrifty with words and usually resort to abbreviations and
hashtags i.e. terms preceded by the "#" symbol to indicate relevance to an event,
a topic, etc. Due to the richness and wide range of discussed subjects in twitter
data, numerous clustering algorithms have emerged [16,20,21]. Generally, text
clustering consists of two main steps: pre-processing first, then running a clustering algorithm. In the pre-processing step the data is converted into a structured
and more manageable form. To this end, text representation models are used,
such as the Vector Space Model [19], topic models [2] and more recently word
embeddings [14]. However, in the absence of an optimal representation model for
text and considering the noisy aspect of tweets, tackling such data becomes challenging especially for clustering algorithms, where data is unlabeled. In addition,
one representation method is unable to capture the different aspect of text. To

E. Pardede et al. (Eds.): iiWAS 2022, LNCS 13635, pp. 548–558, 2022.
https://doi.org/10.1007/978-3-031-21047-1_49

this end, multi-view clustering presents a solution to integrate those aspects and enrich the feature space. Furthermore, the clustering performance can be more accurate by considering multiple perspectives i.e. views. The work of [1] shows that the multi-view versions of K-means and EM outperformed their single-view equivalents. Furthermore, outliers and data noise which exist in one view may be compensated by other views. Hitherto, multiple research works were put forward to improve the performance of existing machine learning algorithms under a multi-view framework [3,10,11,13].

In the literature, three categories of multi-view based methods are distinguished. The first category, centralized fusion methods, integrates the views directly in the objective function of the clustering algorithm [3,10]. The second category is priori fusionn methods, where all views are mapped into the same space on which the algorithm is applied [5,25]. The third category is the posteriori fusion, in which one or more algorithms are performed on each view individually and then the obtained partitions are integrated into one final partion [7,22,23]. Admittedly, the exisiting methods have shown improvements in the clustering results. However, the different aspects of text are not fully exploited. The proposed methods rely only on the syntactic representation of text i.e. terms occurrences. In addition, views are represented with a single model, most commonly the Term Frequency weighting [18]. Although such representation gives an insight into a word's relative importance in a document, it is unable to capture the semantic relationships, which affects the quality of obtained clusters especially in the case of clustering noisy data such as tweets.

To deal with these issues, we propose in this paper a new multi-view text clustering method which exploits different text representation models to capture and integrate information from each view and maintain both syntactic and semantic aspects of text. Moreover, the proposed method uses the Self-Organizing Map to not only overcome the issue of high dimensionality by mapping the different views onto a low-dimensional space, but also to represent the intrinsic structure of the multi-view data by preserving the topology of each view.

The remainder of this paper is organized as follows: Sect. 2 reviews related work to subspace based methods for multi-view clustering. The proposed multi-view approach for text clustering is presented in Sect. 3. The experimental results are discussed in Sect. 4. Conclusions are given in section 5.

2   Detection of Hot Topics Using Multi-view Text Clustering

The proposed multi-view method is based on different representation models of text. When documents are clustered based on the traditional Vector Space Model, and the tf-idf scheme in particular which only considers the occurrence of a word in a document, identifying semantically related documents becomes hard. Consequently, our method intends to enrich the pre-processing step by incorporating other representation schemes such that each representation corresponds to a view that captures a particular aspect of the text. Hence, each document will have three distinct vector representations. The views are then presented as parallel layers, and mapped onto a low-dimensional subspace using SOM architecture in order to uncover a latent structure. Finally, we run a clustering algorithm to obtain distinct documents clusters. After the generation of views in three different feature space, each document is represented by three vectors: traditional representation with tf-idf, topical vector with LDA, and vector based on semantic cliques with Skip-gram. These vectors constitute the inputs to the SOM neural network, such that each view is an input layer. We first recall the basic concepts of SOM, then we adapt the SOM architecture for multi-view document clustering.

2.1 Basic Concepts of SOM

Self-organizing map is an unsupervised neural network model also know as Kohonen network, that projects high dimensional input vectors of data onto a low-dimensional sapce [9]. The obtained feature space is a topological map that enables the partitioning of the input data into similar groups. Generally, SOM consists of two layers: the input layer contains the input vector as represented in their original space, and the output layer consists of the nodes of the map. Moreover, each node i.e. neuron on the map corresponds to a set of inputs. The learning algorithm of SOM is as follows:

1. *Initialization:* Start with random values for initial weights w_i
2. *Matching*: Determine the winning neuron c, at a time index t according to the smallest Euclidean distance

$$c = \arg\min_i ||x_j - w_i||, \ i = 1, 2, \cdots, M \tag{1}$$

where x_j is an input vector, M is the number of neurons.
3. *Weights Updating*: Adjust the weights of the winning neuron and its neighbors, such that:

$$w_i(t+1) = w_i(t) + \epsilon(t) \times h_{ci}(t) \times (x_j(t) - w_i(t)) \tag{2}$$

$$h_{ci} = \exp\left(-\frac{||r_c - ri||^2}{2\sigma^2(t)}\right) \tag{3}$$

where $h_c i$ is the neighborhood kernel function, $\epsilon(t) \in [0, 1]$ is the learning rate and $\sigma(t)$ defines the width of the kernel, both value decrease monotonically at each time index, r_c and r_i are the position vectors of nodes c and i on the map.

2.2 Multi-view Mapping Using SOM

the SOM neural network in order to handle multi-view data. Figure 1 illustrates an example of mapping multi-view documents using SOM. The generated views represent parallel input layers to the SOM such that each input tweet is represented with three numeric vectors $\mathbf{x} = \{\mathbf{x}^1, \mathbf{x}^2, \mathbf{x}^3\}$, corresponding to each view.

Given l nodes of the SOM network, tweets are mapped onto the output layer, such that each tweet $\mathbf{x}_i$ is assigned to a specific node. Consequently, each node of the output layer is defined by three vectors $\{\mathbf{w}^1, \mathbf{w}^2, \mathbf{w}^3\}$ each is associated to a specific view. First, the learning process consists in generating random SOM weights $\mathbf{W}^v$ connected to each view. Secondly, an overall distance is calculated for each document $\mathbf{x}_i^v$ in the view v and SOM nodes $\mathbf{c}_j$ with $j = 1, \ldots, l$, such that:

$$D(\mathbf{x}_i, \mathbf{c}_j) = \sum_v \lambda_v D(\mathbf{x}_i^v, \mathbf{w}_j^v), \ v = 1, 2, 3 \tag{4}$$

where λ_v is a scaling parameter fixed to $\lambda = \frac{1}{m}$ where views are considered equally important. The node with the smallest distance is considered the Best Matching Unit BMU to which the document $\mathbf{x}_i$ is assigned. This step is detailed in Algorithm 1. Finally, the network parameters σ and α representing respectively the radius of the neighborhood and the learning rate are updated. Algorithm 2 describes the main steps of **SOMMVT**.

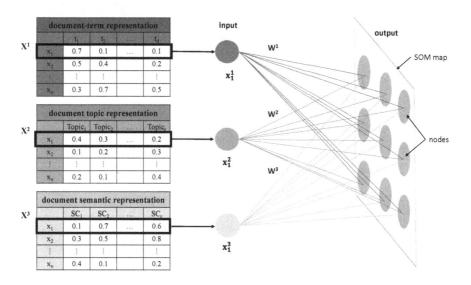

Fig. 1. The mapping of a multi-view documents

Once the training step of SOM is finished, the output layer gives the clustering of documents, such that each node on the output map represent a cluster of a set of documents. Since the mapping using SOM preserves the topological order of data, neighboring nodes are similar and indicate a particular pattern of the data. Moreover, the layout of nodes can be exploited such that similar documents are appointed to the same node or nodes that are located in neighboring regions of the map.

Algorithm 1: Find Best Matching Unit

Input: multi-view document $\mathbf{x}^v$, SOM prototypes $\mathbf{W}^v$,
Output: Best Matching Unit BMU

1 **for** $j = 1$ **to** l **do**
2 | $dist \leftarrow 0$
3 | **for** $v = 1$ **to** m **do**
4 | | $dist \leftarrow dist + \left\| \mathbf{x}^v - \mathbf{w}_j^v \right\|$
5 | **end for**
    // Update BMU
6 | **if** $(dist < min\_dist)$ **then**
7 | | $BMU \leftarrow j$
8 | | $min\_dist \leftarrow dist$
9 | **end**
10 **end for**

Algorithm 2: Self-Organizing Map for multi-view text clustering

---

Input: multi-view documents $\mathbf{X}^v$, number of SOM neurons l, learning rate α_0, radius σ_0
Output: SOM prototypes of each view $\mathbf{W}^v$

1 $t \leftarrow 1$
2 **repeat**
3 | **for** $v = 1$ **to** m **do**
4 | | Initialize random SOM prototypes $\mathbf{W}^v$
5 | | **for** $i = 1$ **to** n **do**
6 | | | determine Best Matching Unit BMU for document $\mathbf{x}_i$ using Algorithm 1
    // Update SOM prototypes
7 | | | **for** $j = 1$ **to** l **do**
8 | | | | $\mathbf{w}_j^v \leftarrow \mathbf{w}_j^v + h \times \alpha \times \left(\mathbf{x}_i^v - \mathbf{w}_j^v \right)$
9 | | | **end for**
10 | | **end for**
11 | **end for**
    // Update radius of the neighborhood
12 | $\sigma \leftarrow \sigma_0 \exp\left(\frac{t}{tmax}\right)$
    // Update the learning rate
13 | $\alpha \leftarrow \alpha_0 \exp\left(\frac{t}{tmax}\right)$
14 | $t \leftarrow t + 1$
15 **until** $t > tmax$

2.3   Merging and Splitting

The previous step allows a clustering of documents given by the SOM output layer, where each node represents a centroid of a set of documents that were assigned to it. The number of nodes on the output map is set empirically to boost the performance of the SOM learning, the number however may not coincide with the desired number of clusters which is usually less important. Moreover, nodes on the map can be associated to a single document or to a set of documents, while other nodes may be "empty" and have no documents assigned to them. To this end, the last step of our method consists in the merging of the SOM nodes into the required number of clusters, and then splits the documents appointed to each node onto the final clustering assignment.

Since the SOM network preserves the topology of data, neighbouring nodes are similar while distant nodes are dissimilar. Hence, the merging step consists in applying agglomerative hierarchical clustering on the map, in which close nodes are merged into the same cluster. Finally, to obtain the final clustering assignment of documents, a splitting step is performed, where each document is assigned to the same cluster as its corresponding SOM node. Algorithm 3 summarizes this process.

Algorithm 3: Merging and splitting

Input: SOM clusters $\mathbf{C} = \{\mathbf{C}_1, \mathbf{C}_2, \ldots \mathbf{C}_l\}$, number of clusters **k**

Output: Final clustering assignment of documents **X**

    `// Merging step`

1 $\chi = \{\}$

2 **for** $j = 1$ ***to*** l **do**

3 | $\chi \leftarrow \chi \cup C_i$

4 **end for**

5 **repeat**

6 | Compute similarity distance between each pair of centroids of the SOM clusters

       `// Merge the two most similar SOM clusters`

7 | $(i^*, j^*) = \arg\min_{i,j \in \{1 \ldots |\chi|\}, i \neq j} Dist(C_i, C_j)$

8 | $C' = C_i \cup C_j$

9 | $\chi = \chi - \{C_i, C_j\} \cup C'_k$

10 | $k \leftarrow k + 1$

11 **until** $|\chi| = \mathbf{K}$

    `// Splitting step`

12 **for** $j = 1$ ***to*** l **do**

13 | **for** $i = 1$ ***to*** $|\mathbf{C}_j|$ **do**

14 | | assign document $\mathbf{x}_i$ to the cluster χ_k, where $\mathbf{C}_j \in \chi_k$

15 | **end for**

16 **end for**

---

3   Experimental Results

3.1   Data Set Description

To evaluate the performance of our approach, we collected tweets using Twitter REST API which enables the access to real Twitter data. With the number of tweets collected, we were able to create four data sets DS 1, DS 2, DS 3 and DS 4, each containing 1000; 3000; 5000 and 8000 tweets, respectively. Furthermore, to evaluate the quality of the clustering, we followed the work in [20] by manually annotating the tweets into K different topics, creating a gold standard classes. For each data set, there are 7 topics forming the gold standard classes: Politics, Technology, Sports, Fitness, Movies, Music and Entertainment. Before applying the clustering algorithms, a pre-processing step is performed on the data sets including stop words removal. Stop words removal consists in eliminating common words that appear frequently but offer no additional value in deciphering what a text is about, for example words like "the", "and", "to", etc.

3.2   Evaluation Measures

To measure the quality of the clustering and compare it with existing methods, three evaluation measures are utilized: the F-measure [12], the Normalized Mutual Information (NMI) [26], and Purity [15]. Given a set of clusters $C = \{c_1, c_2, \ldots, c_k\}$ and the gold standard classes $G = \{g_1, g_2, \ldots, g_j\}$:

F-measure is a trade-off between *Precision* and *Recall* such that:

$$F - measure(c_k, g_j) = 2 * \frac{Precision(c_k, g_j) \times Recall(c_k, g_j)}{Precision(c_k, g_j) + Recall(c_k, g_j)} \tag{5}$$

$$Precision(c_k, g_j) = \frac{|c_k \cap g_j|}{|c_k|} \tag{6}$$

$$Recall(c_k, g_j) = \frac{|c_k \cap g_j|}{|g_j|} \tag{7}$$

Normalized Mutual Information (NMI) measures the quality of clustering with regards to the number of clusters and their sizes. NMI is defined as:

$$NMI(C, G) = \frac{I(C, G)}{[E(C) + E(G)]/2} \tag{8}$$

where I is the mutual information and $E(C)$ is entropy.

$$I(C, G) = \sum_k \sum_j \frac{|c_k \cap g_j|}{N} \log \frac{N|c_k \cap g_j|}{|c_k||g_j|} \tag{9}$$

$$E(C) = -\sum_k \frac{|s_k|}{N} \log \frac{|s_k|}{N} \tag{10}$$

Purity: measures the number of correctly assigned documents, where each cluster is assigned to the dominant class in that cluster. The larger the number of clusters is, the higher is the Purity. Unlike NMI, Purity cannot trade off the quality of the clustering against the number of clusters

$$Purity(C, G) = \frac{1}{N} \sum_k \max_j |c_k \cap g_j| \tag{11}$$

For all measures, the values range from 0 to 1, such that values closer to 0 represent poor quality

Table 1. Performance of multi-view vs single view methods

		F-measure	NMI	Purity
DS1	LDA	0.344	0.226	0.315
	VSM	0.287	0.206	0.228
	SG	0.463	0.354	0.430
	LDA+VSM	0.346	0.230	0.336
	LDA+SG	0.553	0.416	0.531
	SG+VSM	0.540	0.456	0.520
	All views	**0.573**	**0.460**	**0.565**
DS2	LDA	0.603	0.477	0.598
	VSM	0.700	0.544	0.687
	SG	0.727	0.553	0.722
	LDA+VSM	0.705	0.544	0.691
	LDA+SG	0.728	0.546	0.733
	SG+VSM	0.733	0.565	0.735
	All views	**0.748**	**0.582**	**0.742**
DS3	LDA	0.390	0.217	0.347
	VSM	0.286	0.227	0.248
	SG	0.560	0.435	0.520
	LDA+VSM	0.392	0.297	0.350
	LDA+SG	0.589	0.461	0.552
	SG+VSM	0.594	0.491	0.537
	All views	**0.674**	**0.561**	**0.639**
DS4	LDA	0.397	0.287	0.370
	VSM	0.288	0.218	0.228
	SG	0.519	0.357	0.503
	LDA+VSM	0.423	0.25	0.382
	LDA+SG	0.559	0.396	0.535
	SG+VSM	0.564	0.408	0.545
	All views	**0.599**	**0.454**	**0.573**

3.3   Experimental Results

The proposed method is evaluated against the single view based clustering. Each view correspond to a single text representation model which are the VSM, the LDA model, and the Skip-gram model. We use classic SOM for all single view methods. Furthermore, we evaluate the performance of pairwise combination of views. In addition, we compare the proposed method to existing multi-view clustering methods, Multi-view Kmeans (MVKM) [1], and ensemble methods for text clustering (MVEM) where views are represented based on TF-IDF and TF-ICF weightings [7]. Given the results in Table 1, the proposed approach outperforms the single view-based clustering by yielding better results for F-measure, NMI and Purity. This confirms that combining information extracted from the different views of the data improves the learning and the clusters quality. Furthermore, we notice that although the single view clustering based on the Skip-gram model always gives better results than LDA and VSM, the combination of the three did not cause any deterioration in the clustering quality. This only validates the fact that each representation model corresponding to a view is capable of capturing an aspect of the text that is missing in other views. Despite not giving the best results in the single view context, the LDA and VSM based views contributed to achieving better clustering in multi-view context. Furthermore, the evaluation results against existing multi-view text clustering methods are given in Table 2. We notice that all three methods performed better with larger data sets. Nonetheless, our method scored the highest F-measure with 0.748, NMI with 0.582 and Purity with 0.742. The yielded results show that the different text representations of each view affect considerably the quality of the obtained clusters.

Table 2. Performance against existing methods

Data set	Method	F-score	NMI	Purity
DS1	MVEM	0.504	0.334	0.485
	MVKM	0.523	0.444	0.437
	Proposed	**0.573**	**0.460**	**0.565**
DS2	MVEM	0.610	0.491	0.652
	MVKM	0.618	0.478	0.605
	Proposed	**0.748**	**0.582**	**0.742**
DS3	**MVEM**	**0.537**	**0.417**	**0.472**
	MVKM	0.485	0.346	0.416
	Proposed	**0.674**	**0.561**	**0.639**
DS4	MVEM	0.522	0.387	0.523
	MVKM	0.501	0.336	0.486
	Proposed	**0.599**	**0.454**	**0.573**

4   Conclusion

In this paper, we have proposed a novel method for multi-view text clustering. Different from existing works, our method explores the use of three representation models i.e., VSM, LDA, Skip-gram to generate different views that respectively capture syntactic, topical, and semantic aspects of text. Moreover, we exploit the SOM neural network for multi-view clustering, which not only ensures the preservation of the topological properties of each view, but also helps uncover the intrinsic structure of the multi-view data. The conducted experimentation on tweets shows that, in comparison to single view-based clustering, using multiple views improves the clustering quality. The experiments also show that the proposed method yields better results compared to other multi-view clustering methods.

References

1. Bickel, S., Scheffer, T.: Multi-view clustering. ICDM **4**, 19–26 (2004)
2. Blei, D.M., Ng, A.Y., Jordan, M.I.: Latent dirichlet allocation. J. Mach. Learn. Res. **3**, 993–1022 (2003)
3. Blum, A., Mitchell, T.: Combining labeled and unlabeled data with co-training. In: Proceedings of the Eleventh Annual Conference on Computational Learning Theory, pp. 92–100. ACM (1998)
4. Dilrukshi, I., De Zoysa, K., Caldera, A.: Twitter news classification using SVM. In: 2013 8th International Conference on Computer Science & Education, pp. 287–291. IEEE (2013)
5. Guo, Y.: Convex subspace representation learning from multi-view data. In: AAAI, vol. 1, p. 2 (2013)
6. Hachaj, T., Ogiela, M.R.: Clustering of trending topics in microblogging posts: a graph-based approach. Future Gener. Comput. Syst. **67**, 297–304 (2017)
7. Hussain, S.F., Mushtaq, M., Halim, Z.: Multi-view document clustering via ensemble method. J. Intell. Inf. Syst. **43**(1), 81–99 (2014). https://doi.org/10.1007/s10844-014-0307-6
8. Java, A., Song, X., Finin, T., Tseng, B.: Why we twitter: understanding microblogging usage and communities. In: Proceedings of the 9th WebKDD and 1st SNA-KDD 2007 Workshop on Web Mining and Social Network Analysis, pp. 56–65. ACM (2007)
9. Kohonen, T.: The self-organizing map. Proc. IEEE **78**(9), 1464–1480 (1990)
10. Kumar, A., Daumé, H.: A co-training approach for multi-view spectral clustering. In: Proceedings of the 28th International Conference on Machine Learning (ICML-11), pp. 393–400 (2011)
11. Kumar, V., Minz, S.: Multi-view ensemble learning: an optimal feature set partitioning for high-dimensional data classification. Knowl. Inf. Syst. **49**(1), 1–59 (2016)
12. Larsen, B., Aone, C.: Fast and effective text mining using linear-time document clustering. In: Proceedings of the Fifth ACM SIGKDD International Conference on Knowledge Discovery and Data Mining, pp. 16–22. Citeseer (1999)
13. Liu, J., Wang, C., Gao, J., Han, J.: Multi-view clustering via joint nonnegative matrix factorization. In: Proceedings of the 2013 SIAM International Conference on Data Mining, pp. 252–260. SIAM (2013)

14. Mikolov, T., Chen, K., Corrado, G., Dean, J.: Efficient estimation of word representations in vector space. arXiv preprint arXiv:1301.3781 (2013)
15. Nie, F., Cai, G., Li, X.: Multi-view clustering and semi-supervised classification with adaptive neighbours. In: AAAI, pp. 2408–2414 (2017)
16. Rangrej, A., Kulkarni, S., Tendulkar, A.V.: Comparative study of clustering techniques for short text documents. In: Proceedings of the 20th International Conference Companion on World Wide Web, pp. 111–112. ACM (2011)
17. Rosa, K.D., Shah, R., Lin, B., Gershman, A., Frederking, R.: Topical clustering of tweets. In: Proceedings of the ACM SIGIR: SWSM 63 (2011)
18. Salton, G., Buckley, C.: Term-weighting approaches in automatic text retrieval. Inf. Process. Manag. **24**(5), 513–523 (1988)
19. Salton, G., Wong, A., Yang, C.S.: A vector space model for automatic indexing. Commun. ACM **18**(11), 613–620 (1975)
20. Tsur, O., Littman, A., Rappoport, A.: Efficient clustering of short messages into general domains. In: Seventh International AAAI Conference on Weblogs and Social Media (2013)
21. Vicient, C., Moreno, A.: Unsupervised topic discovery in micro-blogging networks. Expert Syst. Appl. **42**(17–18), 6472–6485 (2015)
22. Xie, X., Sun, S.: Multi-view clustering ensembles. In: Machine Learning and Cybernetics (ICMLC), 2013 International Conference on, vol. 1, pp. 51–56. IEEE (2013)
23. Xu, Z., Sun, S.: An algorithm on multi-view adaboost. In: Wong, K.W., Mendis, B.S.U., Bouzerdoum, A. (eds.) ICONIP 2010. LNCS, vol. 6443, pp. 355–362. Springer, Heidelberg (2010). https://doi.org/10.1007/978-3-642-17537-4_44
24. Zhao, W.X., et al.: Comparing twitter and traditional media using topic models. In: Clough, P., et al. (eds.) ECIR 2011. LNCS, vol. 6611, pp. 338–349. Springer, Heidelberg (2011). https://doi.org/10.1007/978-3-642-20161-5_34
25. Zhao, X., Evans, N., Dugelay, J.L.: A subspace co-training framework for multi-view clustering. Pattern Recogn. Lett. **41**, 73–82 (2014)
26. Zhuang, F., Karypis, G., Ning, X., He, Q., Shi, Z.: Multi-view learning via probabilistic latent semantic analysis. Inf. Sci. **199**, 20–30 (2012)

Virtual Reality/Augmented Reality

Interactive Visualization of Comic Character Correlation Diagrams for Understanding Character Relationships and Personalities

Kanna Miyagawa, Yutaka Morino, and Mitsunori Matsushita$^{(\boxtimes)}$

Kansai University, 2-1-1 Ryozenji, Takatsuki,Osaka 569-1095, Japan
{k399699,k790414,m_mat}@kansai-u.ac.jp
http://mtstlab.org/

Abstract. Comic character relationships are an essential aspect of understanding comic content. These relationships are often expressed in a character correlation diagram. However, existing diagrams with complex relationships can confuse users, and simple correlation diagrams do not show information on character personalities. Therefore, it is necessary to 1) make these diagrams more visually clear and 2) to display character personality information in addition to relationships without increasing the diagram complexity. This paper presents an interactive visualization system for character correlation diagrams that display complex character relationships and personalities. We propose a relationship labeling method based on FOAF and implement a user selection function to emphasize specified relationships visually. This paper also provides visualizations of character personalities chosen by the user. Consequently, users can understand both comic character personalities and relationships. This paper verified whether users could correctly find a specific relationship when asked.

Keywords: Comic character correlation diagrams · Visualization of relationship · Comic computing

1 Introduction

With the recent increase in the number of comics published, users have more choices. While this increase in choice is beneficial to the user, it has been noted that there is concern that too many choices may increase the psychological burden on the user [1].

Since comic characters provide essential clues for understanding story lines [7], there has been much research on automatic computational detection for comic characters, although users cannot understand comic contents from only detecting comic characters; the relationships among comic characters are also crucial to the development of the story. However, often many comic characters

E. Pardede et al. (Eds.): iiWAS 2022, LNCS 13635, pp. 561–567, 2022.
https://doi.org/10.1007/978-3-031-21047-1_50

appear in a work, leading to complex character relationships that can be difficult to follow. This paper proposes a visualization system that interactively presents the relationships among comic characters to the user to make their relationships easier to understand.

Several studies have examined to visualize the relationships among comic characters. Murakami [5], for instance, proposed a method for creating comic character relationships for comic content visualization. They developed correlation diagrams by identifying the main characters using the frequencies of characters and their relatedness and then added semantic relations to these diagrams. This diagram enables us to grasp the relationships among characters. However, it does not allow the users to know each character's personality, and it is still challenging to understand their complex relationships with the method. Since character personalities are one of the characteristics of comic characters that express internal characteristics (e.g., cheerful, inhuman) and play an important role in content creation, differences in character personality often affect story development even in comics that follow the same concept [6]. It implies that it would be more beneficial to simultaneously present the characters' personalities and relationships in a relationship diagram to understand the content of the comic. In addition, if the diagram shows too much information at once, it may become too complicated, hindering the user's understanding. It implies that allowing the user to narrow down to the relationships he or she wants to confirm is desirable.

From these considerations, this paper proposes an interactive visualization method of the characters' relationships interactively.

2   Data Set Creation

Various relationship types appear in a comic. To perform relationship categorization, we created relationship labels with reference to RELATIONSHIP[1] that expand the FOAF (Friend of a Friend) Vocabulary[2]. FOAF [2] is a metadata type that explains a human relationship by connecting people through acquaintance relationships. Our method refers to the RELATIONSHIP [4] to create relationship labels for describing more precise relationships (e.g., lover or rival). We created nine relationship labels and categorized relationships that appeared in comics as those. We also created a relationship dictionary made from words with similar meanings to the labels. We assembled a dataset of comic character personalities and relationships from 25 works of romance comics at Mangazenkan.com[3]. Since Wikipedia entries describe character activities and features, we extracted them from these entries. The targeted characters were selected by referring to the official website of each work. We extracted character personalities that matched the words in the "MOE elements dictionary" after extracting nouns and adjectives from Wikipedia using the Japanese morphological analyzer MeCab[4]. The

---

[1] https://vocab.org/relationship/.

[2] http://xmlns.com/foaf/spec/.

[3] https://www.mangazenkan.com/.

[4] https://github.com/jordwest/mecab-docs-en.

MOE elements dictionary is a list of frequently appearing words in Anime culture that describe character appearance or personality [3]. Next, we analyzed the dependency structure of sentences in Wikipedia describing manga characters using CaboCha[5], a Japanese dependency structure analyzer; a modifying word and its modifier words are extracted pairwise for each sentence. From these pairs, relationships were determined by focusing on character names and words registered in the relationship dictionary as clues. In total, 209 words of character personalities and 340 words of relationships were extracted.

3   Visualization Method

This study proposes a system that visualizes a correlation diagram of comic characters. Figure 1-(a) shows the appearance of this system. The correlation diagram was created using the vis.js[6] JavaScript library.

The proposed system categorizes relationships and produces a correlation diagram with each relationship type shown by a different color to aid user comprehension. The system displays characters as nodes and their relationship as edges. In this system, nodes are colored in blue and red for men and women to let users know the characters' genders. For characters of unknown gender, the node color is the default color, light blue. Nodes for main characters, such as the hero or heroine, are displayed more extensively than other characters to indicate their importance. The edges also have particular colors for each relationship type (e.g., yellow for Friend Of, blue for Enemy Of).

This system intends to enable users to identify desired information about the relationships or personalities in a comic. The system enables this requirement by providing two functions to the user: showing detailed information and highlighting specific relationships on demand.

The user can see information about the character's personality by hovering the mouse over a node (see Fig. 1-(b)) and the relationship between them by hovering the mouse over an edge between characters(see Fig. 1-(c)). This function prevents showing much information simultaneously to the user. It helps users recognize comic characters' personalities and relationships on demand.

The system also has a checkbox to emphasize the relationship selected by the user. The checkbox lists the relationship labels, and when users select a checkbox label, the edge for the corresponding relationship is emphasized. The system can show relationships between multiple comics on the same screen and simultaneously apply the emphasizing function to all of them (see Fig. 2). In this figure, the relationships are visualized for two comics when the "Would Like To Know" label has been selected. Using this function, users can compare the comics' relationships and understand the similarities and dissimilarities of the comics' contents. This function lets users easily understand where the selected relationship appears between comic characters, even for complex relationship

---

[5] https://rpubs.com/auroratsai/440718.
[6] https://visjs.org/.

diagrams, and promotes user understanding of the correlation diagram. Relationship emphasis helps users to discover the links between selected characters. Users can find specific relationships using these two features, such as calm and passionate characters being best friends.

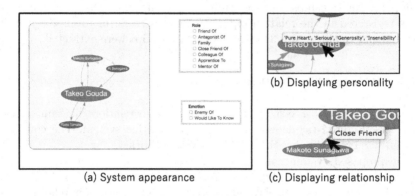

(a) System appearance

(b) Displaying personality

(c) Displaying relationship

Fig. 1. System appearance

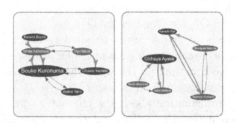

Fig. 2. Emphasizing the edges of the designated relationship

4   Experimental Validation

We tested whether the proposed visualization system enables people to understand relationships, including comic character personalities, easily. Eleven participants were involved in the experiment.The automatic placement of comic characters sometimes resulted in the main characters being placed at the edge of the screen. As the main characters are essential story elements, we manually positioned these nodes at the center of the screen.

First, we taught the participants how to operate the system. Next, we presented them with correlation diagrams for four works and they answered five questions. As the correlation diagram presented, we used the following four

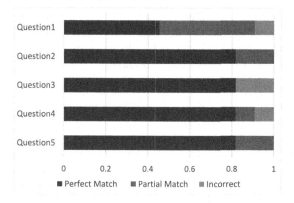

Fig. 3. Results from experimental questions: Love Triangle, Same Gender Love, One Woman Is Favored By Many Men, Irritable Character And Positive Character are Rivals, Have Hostility To The Main Character

works, "Nisekoi" (by Naoshi Furumi, Shueisha Inc.), "Touch" (by Mitsuru Adachi, Shogakukan Inc.), "What Did You Eat Yesterday?" (by Fumi Yoshinaga, Kodansha LTD.), and "Card Capture Sakura" (by CLAMP, Kodansha LTD.). Since some users may have prior knowledge of these works that could affect their answers, we presented the diagrams without naming the work to remove this factor. We asked the users to select all works with the relationships such as "love triangle", "same gender love", "one woman is favored by many men", "irritable character and positive character are rivals," and "have hostility to the main character" from the four options. We recorded how they used this system and checked whether the operations they performed to select an item matched the asked relationship before answering the question and whether they confirmed the node and edge contents before answering the question. We also conducted an open-ended questionnaire regarding the usability and visibility of the system.

Figure 3 shows the result of the questions. Each question may have multiple answers. A perfect match means the participant selected all relationships correctly, and a partial match means they selected some relationships correctly. The remaining option indicates incorrect answers. We found that 74.5%, 18.2%, and 7.3% of the results were perfect matches, partial matches, and incorrect, respectively.

We confirmed two operating tendencies from user observation. First, those whose answers were perfect matches checked the edge and node contents after emphasizing the edge. Second, those whose answers were partial matches only checked the contents of node and edge. We received feedback from the open-ended questionnaire that, "It is easy to check the relationship because each of the selected edges is emphasized." The operation tendency showed that users emphasized the edge to search for the requested relationship and checked the contents of both the node and edge. The percentage of perfect and partial matches combined was as high as 92.7%. Therefore, the results show that using the correlation diagram to check comic character relationships and personalities helped the participants to find specific relationships. We also received a negative feedback that "It is hard to check the edge because the edge crowd some of the nodes, and it was hard to find the comic character personalities."

5   Discussion

The experimental results indicate that our interaction system, presenting character personalities and emphasizing relationships in correlation diagram, is effective to find specific relationship even if there are complex relationships. However, the open-ended questionnaire pointed out a problem with the system. When one character has many relationships, it becomes difficult for the user to see nodes and edges simultaneously. In such a case, we can solve that by displaying edges dynamically in chronological order or by volumes, thereby reducing the number of edges and making it easier to understand the content. As the character personality information does not have the emphasizing function used for relationships, it is difficult for them to compare or find similar personalities. In order to emphasize the personality, the system should give visual clue to the nodes, such as the color of presenting the principal personality trait for each character.

6   Conclusion

In this study, we built an interactive visualization system that users can use to discover the personality and relationships of comic characters. We verified the system utility for the experiment. The results confirmed the utility of displaying the contents of character personalities and relationships by emphasizing visualizations. On the other hand, checking content was difficult for crowded edges, and that personality information requires a visual effect similar to that for edges. Our future work will improve the information display for character personalities and characters with multiple relationships.

Acknowledgement. This work is supported by JSPS KAKENHI Grant Number #22K12338.

References

1. Barry, S.: The Paradox of Choice: Why More is Less. Ecco Press, New York (2004)
2. Graves, M., Constabaris, A., Brickley, D.: FOAF: connecting people on the semantic web. Cataloging Classif. Q. **43**(3–4), 191–202 (2007)
3. Kobayashi, T., Matsushita, M.: Search for similar characters by adding or subtracting personality and appearance factors. In: ARG WI2, vol. 16, pp. 106–111 (2020)
4. Matsuo, Y., Hamasaki, M., Mori, J., Takeda, H., Hasida, K.: Ontological consideration on human relationship vocabulary for FOAF. In: Proceedings of the 1st Workshop on Friend of a Friend, Social Networking and Semantic Web (2004)

5. Murakami, H., Nagaoka, Y., Kyogoku, R.: Creating character networks with kinship relations from comics. Int. J. Serv. Knowl. Manag. **4**(1), 1–26 (2020)
6. Park, B., Ibayashi, K., Matsushita, M.: Classifying personalities of comic characters based on egograms. In: Proceedings of the ISASE2018, No. B3–2 (2018)
7. Sun, W., Burie, J.C., Ogier, J.M., Kise, K.: Specific comic character detection using local feature matching. In: Proceedings of the ICDAR2013, pp. 275–279 (2013)

Two Case Studies on Guiding Human Behavior Using Virtualization Technologies in Distributed Virtual Shopping Malls

Taku Watanabe, Yuta Matsushima, Risa Kimura, and Tatsuo Nakajima[✉]

Waseda University, Tokyo, Japan
{taku.watanabe,y.matsushima,r.kimura,tatsuo}@dcl.cs.waseda.ac.jp

Abstract. This paper reports two case studies that use virtualization technologies on guiding human behavior for supporting distributed virtual shopping malls. The first case study is to portray a virtual crowd in front of exhibitions and stores to guide human behavior by creating interest in the exhibitions and stores. The second case study is to investigate whether it is possible to change a customer's interest in a target store by displaying an alternative stores' advertisements. We investigate the opportunities to adopt virtualization technologies in our future real world digital services from these two case studies.

Keywords: Virtual reality · Bandwagon effect · Behavior economics

1 Introduction

Recent advances in virtual reality technology have led to a variety of new developments in which actual facilities, services, stores, etc. are represented in the 3D virtual world [17]. These direction suggests a virtual world as social infrastructures and extend them as places for daily activities [2, 3, 18]. Virtual reality will become more common as a social infrastructure in the future. It will be the foundation to support human activities, enabling people to perform more activities in the virtual world than they do in the real world currently. Digital media forms can deliver more information to customers than conventional analog media forms when a variety of methods of inducing human behavior, such as advertising and recommendation activities, are implemented in virtual society [16]. For example, when information is disseminated in a shopping mall, analog media forms such as posters and voice guidance are common in the real world. On the other hand, objects in the virtual world can be presented alternatively by using digital technologies. Therefore, when information is delivered in the virtual world, a more flexible technique can be chosen for appealing customers.

This paper reports two case studies of guiding human behavior in distributed virtual shopping malls using virtualization technologies. Virtualization technologies are effective digital technologies that change human behavior by synthesizing virtual worlds with different properties from the real world through virtual reality or augmented reality technologies, or by modifying the meaning of the real world by adding virtually synthesized

E. Pardede et al. (Eds.): iiWAS 2022, LNCS 13635, pp. 568–574, 2022.
https://doi.org/10.1007/978-3-031-21047-1_51

objects [7]. The first example is to induce human behavior by drawing a virtual crowd in front of an exhibition or store to arouse customers' interests in the exhibition or store. This case study intends to facilitate the induction of human behavior based on the theory of behavioral psychology that people generally want to identify with what many people support. The second case study investigates whether it is possible to change customers' interests in a target store by inducing them to visit the store while hiding advertisements for alternative stores. The case is an investigation of whether it is possible to change their interests in the target store by directing them to the target store while hiding advertisements for alternative stores. According to the theory of behavioral economics, people generally do not choose those stores if they are simultaneously shown advertisements for multiple alternative stores other than the intended target store. Therefore, displaying advertisements for alternative stores when approaching an actual store can make that store appear more attractive and increase the likelihood of being chosen.

2 Background and Related Work

2.1 Bandwagon and Snob Effects

Behind the first case study to advertising effectiveness is the theory of the bandwagon effect [11]. The bandwagon effect is usually studied in behavioral psychology and it is a psychologic phenomenon. People tend to believe that something that many other people support are more valuable. This effect is typically used in economic marketing, and can be incorporated as advertising effects for selling more products to customers [14]. Political researches have also suggested a relationship with voter rate in elections [12]. On the other hand, a psychological phenomenon of wanting to maintain the perception of scarcity exists. The effect make people not to want to own something that many people support. This phenomenon is referred to as the snob effect. Both effects are explained without contradictions in behavioral psychology [10].

2.2 Behavior Economics

The theory behind the second case study is the nudge theory [19]. The theory is developed in behavioral economics. This theory exploits the behavioral economics characteristics of humans by having people voluntarily, rather than forcibly, choose desired behaviors [6]. Behavior change through nudging has been used by governments and marketing in various countries. The authors in [9] proposed the use of nudging to control obesity in the U.S. In the second case study, the default option strategy [19], one of the methods to implement nudging, is used. This method takes advantage of the human psychological characteristic of not wanting to change the initial path taken when making a choice about something. By applying this technique, it is possible to design scenarios in which a certain option is set as the default option and is intentionally chosen.

2.3 Guiding Human Behavior Through Digital Technologies

Several past studies have also been conducted to investigate the impact of bandwagon effects on IoT-based systems [4], where recommended systems incorporating bandwagon effects are investigated based on customer selection history. In recent years, systems in which customers operate digitally without thinking have become popular. This study is an example of research related to persuasion without customer attention [5]. In [1], the authors propose a solution to a bottleneck in public institutions by providing information about the surrounding environment and presenting it to customers. In this way, the research is being conducted to enrich daily life by providing information about the everyday world in which people live.

Augmented reality technologies are a powerful approach to enhance the meaning of the real world. One promising direction to enhance human perception. Some researchers proposed several different augmentation methods to change a user's food taste experience [15]. Altering one sensory channel like the visual appearance of a food can affect the taste experience of the food. This direction can be generalized to improve the experience in shopping malls.

3   Guiding Human Behavior Through Visualizing a Virtual Crowd

The first case study proposes a technique of displaying virtual crowds as a way of guiding customers. The aim of this technique is to depict a thriving situation by placing several virtual persons in front of a store, exhibition, event, or object that wants to be advertised. Figure 1 shows an example to display a virtual crowd in front of a shop. We believe that this technique will allow the service to advertise more favorably to the target situation than conventional text-based advertising.

Fig. 1. Sparse (upper) and crowded (lower) situations

It is effective to examine human behavioral psychology theory and some studies that apply the theory as an approach to inducing people [19]. In this case study, we propose an advertising technique of virtually portraying a store as one that many people support as a way to guide customers to the target stores. Especially, as shown in the lower figures of Fig. 1, a virtual crowd is displayed in front of a store to express that it is supported by many people in a virtual world. By using the technique that places a virtual crowd in stores in a virtual shopping mall, customers feel more comfortable. The technique may be effective for customers who are strongly disposed to join bandwagons in this case study, as it emphasizes the support of the majority. Also, it needs to consider responses when the same approach is attempted with the customer who is highly oriented toward the snob effect. The evaluation of the technique can be found in [20].

4 Guiding Human Behavior Through Presenting Nudges

The second case study proposes another advertising technique to engage users while navigating them in virtual stores. This case study examines whether the default option strategy can be used as nudges explained in Sect. 2.2 to guide people to their favorite stores in a virtual shopping mall. We conducted studies to compare advertisements that adopted the default option strategy to the approach that did not adopt the strategy.

Fig. 2. Guidance in default option and no nudge

In an advertising technique that does not adopt the default option strategy, the store's advertisement is shown at the first stage in the guidance. This technique is defined as No Nudge, where the recommended shops are presented at the bottom of the guidance as shown in the right figure of Fig. 2, and a user can choose the recommend shops when he/she is interested. On the other hand, in the advertising technique using the default option strategy, advertisements are placed near alternative stores while people are on their way to the desired store. The default option is then to see information about the store where the advertisement is placed. This option is defined as Default Option and is displayed in front of the store where the advertisement is recommended, as shown in the left figure of Fig. 2. As explained in Sect. 2.2, it is hypothesized that studies using Default Option are more likely to induce user interest. The evaluation of the technique can be found in [13].

5 Conclusion: Towards a Generic Framework for Virtualizing the Real World

In this paper, we reported two case studies to guide human behavior based on virtualization technologies that are used to developing a distributed virtual shopping mall. Finally, we discuss a generic framework to virtualize the real world from the experiences with the case studies described in the previous sections. Virtualizing the real world is usually realized by changing the line of sight or replacing one of the five senses with another for making our world interactive by implicitly influencing human attitudes and behaviors.

The framework offers a model that guides the analysis of the real world and the design for virtualizing the real world [8]. The framework models the world by categorizing the real world into seven abstract components and considering their meaning: the seven components are living things, physical objects, landscapes, informative cue, institutional mechanisms, and symbols, and are a way to redefine the real world as shown in the left part of Fig. 3. By examining each component in the real world, a designer can systematically examine the refinement of the real world based on the model. The designer considers introducing cyber parts of the digital twin to each dimension of the real world in order to achieve an alternate reality.

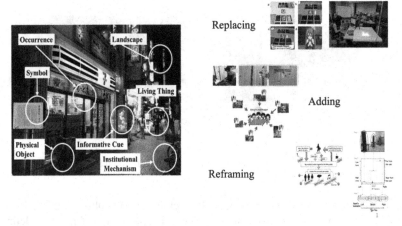

Fig. 3. A generic framework for virtualizing the real world

The right of Fig. 3 shows three approaches to considering digital extensions of the real world to incorporate virtuality into the real world. In this framework, we would like to examine how each of the components classified in several categories shown above be modified by the following three approaches. The first approach is "replacing". This approach involves replacing real-world components with fictitious components. To select the components to be replaced, the designer needs to find out what the value of each component is. The second approach is "adding". This approach adds fictional elements to the real world. This is the most typical use case for virtualization in this framework. The last approach is "reframing". The typical use is to add new regulations to govern the real world commons through an abstract structure (or set of rules).

In the next step, we like to investigate how the proposed framework can be used to more systematically enhance distributed virtual shopping moles.

References

1. Boehm, G.: Ambient persuasive guidance. In: Proceedings of the Fifth International Conference on Tangible, Embedded, and Embodied Interaction, pp. 431–432 (2011)
2. Boulos, M.N., Hetherington, L., Wheeler, S.: Second Life: an overview of the potential of 3-D virtual worlds in medical and health education. Health Info. Libr. J. **24**(4), 233–308 (2007)
3. Brutzman, D.P., Macedonia, M.R., Zyda, M.J.: Internetwork infrastructure requirements for virtual environment. In: The unpredictable Certainly: White Papers, pp. 110–122 (2000)
4. Choi, S., Lee, H., Han, Y., Man, K.L., Chong, W.K.: A recommendation model using the bandwagon effect for E-marketing purposes in IoT. Int. J. Distrib. Sensor Netw. **11**(7), 475163 (2015)
5. Ham, J., Midden, C., Beute, F.: Can ambient persuasive technology persuade unconsciously?: using subliminal feedback to influence energy consumption ratings of household appliances. In: Proceedings of the 4th International Conference on Persuasive Technology, Article No. 29, pp. 1–6 (2009)
6. Kahneman, D.: Thinking, Fast and Slow, Farrar, Straus and Giroux (2011)
7. Kimura, R., Nakajima, T.: Gamifying human behavior in urban crowdsourcing for a sustainable smart city. In: Proceedings of the 21st International Conference on Information Integration and Web-based Applications & Services (iiWAS2019) (2019)
8. Kimura, R., Nakajima, T.: Digitally enhancing society through structuralism: virtualizing collective human eyesight and hearing capabilities as a case study. In: Streitz, N., Konomi, S. (eds.) Distributed, Ambient and Pervasive Interactions: 8th International Conference, DAPI 2020, Held as Part of the 22nd HCI International Conference, HCII 2020, Copenhagen, Denmark, July 19–24, 2020, Proceedings, pp. 400–414. Springer International Publishing, Cham (2020). https://doi.org/10.1007/978-3-030-50344-4_29
9. Kraak, V.I., Englund, T., Misyak, S., Serrano, E.L.: A novel marketing mix and choice architecture framework to nudge restaurant customers toward healthy food environments to reduce obesity in the United States. Obesity Rev. **18**(8), 852–868 (2017)
10. Kuwashima, Y.: Structural equivalence and cohesion can explain bandwagon and snob effect. Ann. Bus. Adm. Sci. **15**(1), 1–14 (2016)
11. Leibenstein, H.: Bandwagon, snob and veblen effects in the theory of consumers' demand. Q. J. Econ. **40**(2), 183–207 (1950)
12. McAllister, I., Studlar, D.T.: Bandwagon, underdog, or projection? opinion polls and electoral choice in Britain, 1979–1987. J. Polit. **53**(3), 720–741 (1991)
13. Matsushima, Y., Gushima, K., Nakajima, T.: Human behavior guidance methods in distributed virtual shopping malls. In: Proceedings of the IEEE 3rd Global Conference on Life Sciences and Technologies (LifeTech), pp. 195–197 (2021)
14. McBride, N.: Business use of the internet: strategic decision or another bandwagon? Eur. Manag. J. **15**(1), 58–67 (1997)
15. Radoslaw, N., Eleonora, C., Gijs, H., Gualtiero, V., Maurizio, M.: Computational commensality: from theories to computational models for social food preparation and consumption in HCI. Front. Rob. AI **6**(119), 1–19 (2019)
16. Shankar, A., Horton, B.: Ambient media: advertising's new media opportunity? Int. J. Advert. Rev. Mark. Commun. **18**(3), 305–321 (2015)
17. Speicher, M., Cucerca, S., Krüger, A.: VRShop: a mobile interactive virtual reality shopping environment combining the benefits of on- and offline shopping. In: Proceedings of the ACM on Interactive, Mobile, Wearable and Ubiquitous Technologies, vol. 1, no. 3, Article No. 102 (2017)
18. Taylor, T.L.: Life in virtual worlds: plural existence, multimodalities, and other online research challenges. Am. Behav. Sci. **3**(3), 436–449 (1999)

19. Thaler, R., Sunstein, C.: Nudge: Improving Decisions about Health, Wealth, and Happiness (2009)
20. Watanabe, T., Tsukamoto, K., Matsushima, Y., Nakajima, T.: A new advertisement method of displaying a crowd. In: Proceedings of the Twelfth International Conference on Advances in Multimedia (2020)

Central Figures in the Climate Change Discussion on Twitter

Anil Can Kara[✉] ⓘ, Ivana Dobrijevic ⓘ, Emre Öztas ⓘ, Angelina Mooseder ⓘ,
Raji Ghawi ⓘ, and Jürgen Pfeffer ⓘ

School of Social Sciences and Technology, Technical University of Munich, Munich,
Germany
{anil.kara,ivana.dobrijevic,emre.oeztas,
angelina.mooseder,raji.ghawi,juergen.pfeffer}@tum.de

Abstract. Climate change is vividly discussed on social media platforms. In this study, we analyse the central figures in the climate change discourse on Twitter. We identify the most mentioned people, brands and groups. We then evaluate how users tweet about them, regarding stances and co-mentions. Our results indicate that tweets about media outlets, institutions and companies are dominating the climate change debate on Twitter, and that their role in shaping the public perception of climate change should not be underestimated. Moreover, we can show that politicians receive much more user attention than other groups and that Joe Biden and Greta Thunberg are the most mentioned actors in the discourse. Our research provides new insights on the driving actors behind the climate change discussion. This can help further researchers to develop effective measures for climate change communication.

Keywords: Climate change · Twitter data · Social network analysis

1 Introduction

Climate change is one of the biggest threats to human civilization. In the past, some celebrities, politicians and other popular people have raised their voices to increase public awareness of climate change [1], while others have expressed scepticism or even denied the existence of human caused climate change [3]. As individuals with great impact and reach, they can draw attention to the topic of climate change, act as role models [1], and influence behavioral intentions of others [7]. This does not only account to people, but also to brands, as stances of companies regarding climate change might influence how consumers think about the topic. Considering their impact, it is crucial to study the main actors in the climate change discussion, to better understand perceptions of climate change and to develop effective measures for increasing public attention on the topic.

Climate change discourse has been observed on multiple social media platforms [5]. We focus on Twitter as it has become an important instrument for political debates and crisis communication [12]. There are several studies about climate change discussion on social media, each of which with a different focus on various aspects of the topic [6]. Cann, 2021 [2] explores the ideological biases and polarization via URL sharing. They argue that political opinion and environmental stance correlate, which leads to a strong polarization in climate change discussion. Camarillo, 2021 [4] analyses how the dynamics of the climate change discussion have changed over the pandemic. Proskurnia, 2016 [9] investigates the strategies of public campaigns on Twitter. These studies and others provide good insights into the topic. Yet, we think that an extensive analysis of influential actors, meaning people who receive much public attention regarding climate change, is missing in the literature. Therefore we focus on the most mentioned people in the climate discourse on Twitter.

We do not only assess who they are, but also in which ways the public talks about them: Veltri, 2017 [10] used sentiment analysis to study the emotions expressed in tweets regarding climate change. Similarly, we use sentiment analysis to assess the stances expressed towards the most famous people in the climate discourse. In addition, we analyse the co-mentioning network of these actors. Walter, 2019 [11] already investigated the network of scientists in the climate change discussion. In our study we include all popular people and brands mentioned in the debate. Moreover, we classify the main actors according to their professions to analyse which groups tend to be popular in the discussion.

In this study, we analyse important groups and figures in the climate change discussion on Twitter. We evaluate the polarity and subjectivity of tweets about them as well as the co-mentioning connections between them. In this way, we aim to answer following research questions: Which actors receive the most attention regarding climate change? In which ways does the general public talk about them? We find that brands and politicians play an important role in the climate change debate on Twitter. In addition, we show that Joe Biden and Greta Thunberg are the most mentioned figures in the discourse. Our research helps to obtain a bigger picture of driving actors in the climate change discussion. In this way, we aim to provide a skeleton for further researchers to develop effective strategies for climate change communication.

2   Methods

2.1   Data Collection and Preprocessing

Using Twitter's Academic API [8] from 29. March 2022 to 30. March 2022 we collected all tweets published in 2021, excluding retweets, containing the hashtag "climatechange". We collected a total number of 982,008 tweets.

For each tweet we gathered the unique tweet id, unique tweet author id, tweet text, hashtags, user mentions, date and stored the context annotations created by Twitter. This annotation gave us information about whether a mentioned account was a brand, a famous person in general, a politician, actor, musician, athlete, entertainment personality, sports personality, coach, digital creator, fictional character, video game personality, e-sport player or journalist. A person could have been annotated by Twitter with multiple labels. To be able to compare different (groups of) actors in the climate change discourse, we calculated per person the number of tweets mentioning this person as well as for each group the number of tweets mentioning at least one member of the group. We repeated the process for brands and obtained the number of tweets mentioning any brand and how many times each brand was mentioned.

To gain an understanding of the emotions in tweets related to individuals, groups, and brands, we applied sentiment analysis using TextBlob.[1] We calculated the polarity and subjectivity for each tweet. Polarity ranges between 0 and 1 and describes the valence of a text chunk (-1 = most negative, 1 = most positive). Subjectivity ranges between 0 and 1 and describes whether a statement refers to a personal opinion, emotion or judgement (1 = most subjective) or rather to factual information (0 = most objective). In the data, there was a positive correlation between subjectivity and the absolute value of polarity ($r = .73$, $\mathbf{p} < .001$), indicating that objective tweets included rather neutral sentiments.

2.2   Network of Co-mentions

We built two different co-mentioning networks, one for actors and one for brands. In both cases we restricted our analysis to the top 50 actors/brands that were mentioned in the most tweets. If two actors/brands were mentioned in the same tweets, an edge was established between them. After filtering the top 50 for the people network, two nodes (BST and Critical Role) were removed since they were not individuals but a music band and TV series cast. To simplify the network structure, we omitted all edges with a weight less than or equal to 20 in both networks. The threshold of 20 was decided by plotting a histogram of edge weights and looking at where there is a significant jump. We visualized each network using *Visone*[2], a powerful graph visualization tool.

3   Results

3.1   Data Overview

In our dataset, 3,753 unique accounts were mentioned. By far the most mentioned group was *brand* (130,854 tweets), followed by *popular persons* (106,610) and *politicians* (77,221), and all other groups were mentioned in less than 5000 tweets. The most mentioned brands were the UN (23,093) and Tesla Motors (12,194), the most mentioned famous people Joe Biden (20,968) and Greta Thunberg (11,010), and the most mentioned politicians Joe Biden and Scott Morrison (7,400).

We compared the subjectivity and polarity values of groups by analysing all tweets mentioning at least one group member. Brands were mentioned mostly in a neutral and objective way. The majority of tweets mentioning a person had

---

[1] https://textblob.readthedocs.io/en/dev/.
[2] https://visone.ethz.ch/.

a neutral to slightly positive and a slightly objective tone, with every group having an average polarity score between [0, 0.20] and an average subjectivity scores between [0.25, 0.45]. The only group outstanding was "video games personalities", which was mentioned quite positively (0.46) and highly subjectively (0.82).

3.2 Network of People

Figure 1 gives an overview of the most mentioned people in the climate change discussion on Twitter. The politicians Yoweri Museveni (0.59) and Jair Bolsonaro (0.56) showed the highest subjectivity scores in the network, indicating that they were mentioned on Twitter in a way that is not based on facts, but rather subjective. The most objectively mentioned actors were Sylvester Stallone (0.11), Kamala Harris (0.19) and Arnold Schwarzenegger (0.19).

The most positively mentioned people were Jair Bolsonaro (0.27) and Chuck Schumer (0.24), both having also high subjectivity scores. While tweets about the most mentioned actors tend to be positive on average, there were three people mentioned in negative tweets on average: Naomi Klein (−0.05), George Floyd (−0.03), who was often mentioned in calls for political action regarding climate change and the Black Lives Matter movement, and Doug Ford (−0.02).

In terms of weighted degree centrality, Joe Biden (0.24) is clearly the most central person in the network, meaning that he is mentioned together with many other actors, and has most of the thickest edges in the network, as he is mentioned together with others considerably many more times than other actors.

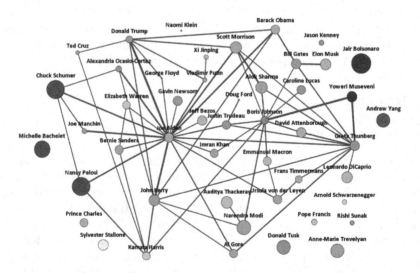

Fig. 1. Network of top 48 most mentioned people. Two actors are connected if they were mentioned in the same tweets. Node sizes correspond to the average polarity score (larger nodes indicating more positivity) and node colours correspond to the average subjectivity (darker colours indicating higher subjectivity). Edge thickness is proportional to the (logarithm of the) number of common mentioning tweets.

3.3   Network of Brands

Figure 2 shows the network of top 50 brands that are mentioned in 2021, and can be read in a similar way as Fig. 1. The food companies Trader Joe's (0.46) and Whole Foods (0.45) are the most subjectively mentioned brands and car companies Ford (0.17) and Tesla Motors (0.18) the most objectively mentioned ones. Similar to the top actors, top brands also tend to have neutral values in polarity scores, with tweets mentioning Aposto (0.19) and Amazon (0.16) being the most positive in average and with only the NGO Oxfam being mentioned in rather negative tweets in average (−0.05).

Figure 2 is depicted by placing densely connected nodes close to each other. This sheds light on several structures, e.g. a cluster of news companies at the top right. Interestingly, Greenpeace is connected to multiple clusters, indicating that users mention it together with various topics related to media, technology and international institutions. The news outlets New York Times (0.08) and CNN (0.08), are the most central brands in the network regarding weighted degree centrality scores.

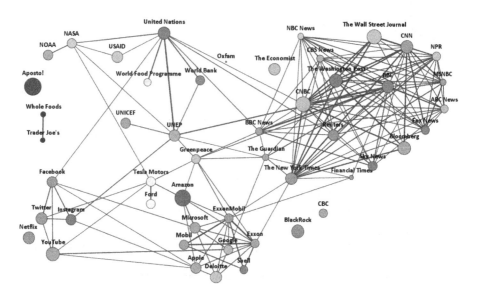

Fig. 2. Network of top 50 most mentioned brands. Visualization according to Fig. 1.

4   Discussion and Conclusion

This study aimed to analyse the most mentioned personalities, brands and groups in the climate change discussion. Our exploration showed that Joe Biden and Greta Thunberg are the most mentioned people in the climate change discussion on Twitter and that tweets about politicians are dominating the climate change debate on Twitter. This indicates that their attitudes and actions regarding climate change are observed by a great audience and thus might have a high impact on the public perception of climate change. Nevertheless, it should be noted that we relied on Twitter annotations for analysing the professions of mentioned people and the quality of these annotations might impact our results.

We found that brands are by far the most mentioned category, almost two times more than politicians. On the one hand, this might be an indicator of how much attention brands can generate with their policies and actions regarding climate change. On the other hand, this could be due to many news brands reporting current incidents on climate change and thus being mentioned on Twitter. Hence, news companies are an important driver for the discussion and should be encouraged to spread information about climate change.

Our research helps to obtain a bigger picture of the most famous actors in the climate change discussion. These results can be used by further research to understand how important personalities and institutions can affect the discussion and influence public attitudes regarding climate change.

References

1. Anderson, A.: Sources, media, and modes of climate change communication: the role of celebrities. WIREs Clim. Change **2**(4), 535–546 (2011)
2. Cann, T.J.B., Weaver, I.S., Williams, H.T.P.: Ideological biases in social sharing of online information about climate change. PLoS ONE **16**(4), 1–25 (2021)
3. De Pryck, K., Gemenne, F.: The denier-in-chief: climate change, science and the election of Donald J. Trump. Law Critique **28**, 119–126 (2017)
4. Gaytan Camarillo, M., Ferguson, E., Ljevar, V., Spence, A.: Big changes start with small talk: Twitter and climate change in times of coronavirus pandemic. Frontiers Psychol. **12**, 661395 (2021)
5. León, B., Bourk, M., Finkler, W., Boykoff, M., Davis, L.: Strategies for climate change communication through social media: objectives, approach, and interaction. Media Int. Aust. (2021)
6. Loureiro, M., Alló, M.: How has the covid-19 pandemic affected the climate change debate on Twitter? Environ. Scie. Policy **124**, 451–460 (2021)
7. Park, S.: How celebrities' green messages on twitter influence public attitudes and behavioral intentions to mitigate climate change. Sustainability **12**, 7948 (2020)
8. Pfeffer, J., Mooseder, A., Hammer, L., Stritzel, O., Garcia, D.: This sample seems to be good enough! Assessing coverage and temporal reliability of Twitter's academic API (2022)
9. Proskurnia, J., Mavlyutov, R., Prokofyev, R., Aberer, K., Cudré-Mauroux, P.: Analyzing large-scale public campaigns on Twitter. In: Spiro, E., Ahn, Y.-Y. (eds.) SocInfo 2016. LNCS, vol. 10047, pp. 225–243. Springer, Cham (2016). https://doi.org/10.1007/978-3-319-47874-6_16
10. Veltri, G.A., Atanasova, D.: Climate change on Twitter: content, media ecology and information sharing behaviour. Public Underst. Sci. **26**(6), 721–737 (2017)
11. Walter, S., Lörcher, I., Brüggemann, M.: Scientific networks on Twitter: analyzing scientists' interactions in the climate change debate. Public Underst. Sci. **28**(6), 696–712 (2019)
12. Weller, K., Bruns, A., Burgess, J., Mahrt, M., Puschmann, C.: Twitter and Society. Peter Lang (2014)

E-Tracer: A Smart, Personalized and Immersive Digital Tourist Software System

Alexandros Kokkalas[1(✉)], Athanasios T. Patenidis[1],
Evangelos A. Stathopoulos[1], Eirini E. Mitsopoulou[1], Sotiris Diplaris[1],
Konstadinos Papadopoulos[2], Stefanos Vrochidis[1], Konstantinos Votis[1],
Dimitrios Tzovaras[1], and Ioannis Kompatsiaris[1]

[1] Information Technologies Institute, CERTH, Thessaloniki, Greece
{akokkalas,apatenidis,stefanos,emitsopou,diplaris,stefanos,
kvotis,dimitrios.tzovaras,ikom}@iti.gr
[2] LINK Technologies SA, Thessaloniki, Greece
info@link-tech.gr

Abstract. This paper describes a system that discovers and semantically unifies information from multiple sources, allowing the end user to organize and implement integrated tourist itineraries and tours by utilizing innovative spatio-temporal interconnection technologies of multiple spaces and events of environmental, cultural, and tourist interest. Moreover a user evaluation from the pilot tests is included in the study.

Keywords: Semantics · Reasoning · Augmented reality · User experience · Personalized route recommendation system · User evaluation

1 Introduction

To support and promote places and events of environmental, cultural and tourist interest many digital applications have been developed. The majority of these applications are for specific areas with static content and predefined routes. For this matter there has been a lot of research in route planning and recommendation systems [2,5] and it was not until recently, that these systems could offer the user personalized content and routes and augmented/virtual reality features. Several study areas are under the scope of the proposed system, from the initial data collection and processing through the end-user-served product. The system uses innovative methods and techniques, such as real-time (semi-)automatic search and knowledge mining from online sources, open data and sensors, automated discovery points of interest (POIs), events and movement, semantic integration, classification and prioritization of information from different sources, spatial representation of the content, personalized user experience, augmented reality (AR) for interconnecting the virtual and real world. The application and

E. Pardede et al. (Eds.): iiWAS 2022, LNCS 13635, pp. 581–587, 2022.
https://doi.org/10.1007/978-3-031-21047-1_53

evaluation of the system is set on the axis of Egnatia motorway, that connects all Northern Greece and is linked to the neighboring countries. The first versions of e-tracer have been evaluated in pilot trials that took place in the museums of Silversmithing in Ioannina and of Silk in Soufli Greece and are presented in the paper.

2   Related Work

There are numerous applications that can recommend spatial content to users. Apps like tripadvisor [10] and google maps provide location suggestions based on user overall ratings and thematic filters, while other applications provide route recommendations [4,9]. Different ontologies and methods have been created [6,8,11] to manage heterogeneity, cultural heritage and POIs. Concerning AR technology, there are applications [1] as CHESS [3] used in the museums of Acropolis Greece and Cite de l'Espace France, which aims to project personalized stories guiding visitors to the museum. The innovation in our work is the integration of all the various services and technologies into a single system that utilize semi-automatically retrieved data to offer the end user personalized automatic route suggestions as well as connected AR applications that provide a unique experience.

3   E-Tracer System

The e-tracer system consists of multiple individual components, each with a specific purpose, that connect and interact with each other (Fig. 1). It has two different synchronized databases designed for storing and analyzing triplets, spatial and non-spatial data, i.e. a Semantic Graph Database developed with GraphDB that follows W3C Standards and an object-relational database developed in PostgreSQL with PostGIS and pgRouting extensions for spatial and route calculations. Custom web crawlers and scrapers developed in Java collect POIs from various online sources in a selected map area, and store the retrieved data in the databases. The web platform developed in Django and OpenLayers uses all the separate components to allow the end user access all the different services through an interactive map.

The semantic web technologies have manifold usability, spanning from homogenizing heterogeneous incoming data, semantically annotating pieces of information, forming the knowledge graph of e-Tracer, to smart querying the knowledge base and perform reasoning on the graph patterns via SPARQL. More specifically, apart from maintaining and serving knowledge to other components, semantics are utilized to intelligently filter out POIs as a pre-processing stage of the routing algorithm via multiple constraints based on euclidean distance, time and accessibility.

The personalization component consists of a recommender engine that generates suggestions for touristic destinations, according to user's needs, preferences and trip constraints such as time or distance availability, weather and accessibility options. Recommender engine breaks down the process of proposing attractions into the following two stages:

1. Stage 1: The candidate destinations are subjected to a knowledge-based filtering that takes into account user constraints, in order to remove non-functional per user POIs and produce a more condensed list of recommendations.
2. Stage 2: The resulting list of destinations then fuels a hybrid technique that combines a content-based and a collaborative filtering component with the intention of offering tailored recommendations of new locations that have been selected by similar users and are in line with the user's preferences.

The routing component developed with pgRouting using data collected from OpenStreetMap [7], generates routes based on a combination of user preferences, geographical attributes and rating system. A main route with no stops is computed using the user-provided start and destination locations and exported as geoJSON. Subsequently the POIs in a buffer zone around the main route are collected and sent to semantic and personalization components, to be filtered, grouped and ranked. Finally, the ranked POIs are used by the routing component first to calculate their optimal path for visiting order and then calculate and create the personalized suggested route (Fig. 2).

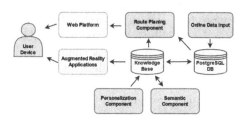

Fig. 1. High level system architecture

Fig. 2. Suggested alternative route

The web platform grants the user that interacts with it, access to all the individual components as a single unit. An interactive map showing the collected POIs with filters and multiple base layers, allows users to enter personal preferences, examine details of each point as well as plan a personalized route. The web platform also has an administrator back-end interface that can be accessed only by the curator, with options to create and update POIs, user accounts as well as semi-automatically retrieve new online data through the use of customized website crawlers.

Three AR applications were created as part of the project e-tracer, one for exploring urban and outdoor landscapes and the other two for exploring the inside of two museums, of Silversmithing in Ioannina and of Silk in Soufli. The outer space AR app seeks to provide the user with the most effective and simple navigation possible within these areas of interest by providing additional virtual information that is included in the project e-tracer. The application makes advantage of the position and orientation data that the smart device's GPS and compass sensors give, allowing the user to see the locations of nearby attractions on the device screen. The second AR application was designed to provide the user additional information about the museum exhibits, as well as rich multimedia material that includes text, images, animation with information of each exhibit that the user observes and a 3D virtual object (identical to the actual exhibit). Without having to touch or directly come into contact with the exhibit, the user is given the chance to examine it in great detail from all available viewing angles, rotate it, magnify it, and minimize it. After the user has finished their museum tour, they use the third AR app, a serious quiz game for self-evaluation. This program loads 10 distinct questions each time it is launched, the first seven of which are multiple-choice or one-choice questions, and the latter three of which are AR questions. The user must search the museum for the required exhibit in order to find the answers to the AR questions.

4   User Evaluation

Evaluation of interactive systems refers to the activity that tests the degree of goal satisfaction for the system, from the perspective of users. More specifically, usability assessment is a major factor for the acceptance of the product or system by the users and is linked with nearly every product, system or service. Usability is defined as a combination of the following: learnability, efficiency, memorability, error avoidance and recall and personal (user) satisfaction. A common and reliable method for measuring the usability of a system or product, is through the use of questionnaires, which have been used in this case. The scale used in the questionnaires is the Likert scale. The samples are random, independent of age or sex. This user evaluation process concerns the following three (3) applications for the e-tracer system: web platform for route recommendation, AR for an indoor environment, AR for an outdoor environment. Users had the opportunity to interact with the systems in real environments of cultural and environmental interest, and then proceeded to answering the questionnaires, under the supervision of specialized personnel. Concerning the web platform the results show that users were fully or mostly satisfied with the app and that the app fully covered their needs on a percentage of more than 90%. More than 95% agreed that the app is useful for finding POIs and for scheduling their trips. Approximately 90% of the users agreed that the app is easy to use and that the suggested POIs correspond with their interests. Furthermore 95% of the users were interested or somewhat interested in searching for more alternative routes, after using the app. 90% of the users agreed that the response time of the app is satisfactory. Similarly 90% of the users agreed that the actual times of the suggested routes, are satisfactory. 88% of the users were satisfied when asked about the suggested distances of the routes. 86% of the users were satisfied or mostly satisfied when asked about the response of the app and 88% were satisfied or mostly satisfied when asked about the efficiency of the app. Finally 97% of the users agreed that they would use or were likely to use the app again and 100% of the users agreed that they would suggest or would likely suggest the app to a friend.

The evaluation results of AR for indoor environment are compiled from two different surveys that took place on different dates and locations. The users agreed that they were fully or mostly satisfied by the AR app, on a percentage of approximately 97% at the first location and 95% at the second location. 92% of the users agreed that the app fully or mostly corresponds to their needs at the first location and 80% at the second location. 97% of the users agreed or mostly agreed that the app is useful for getting more information about their selected subject on the first location, while 80% agreed on the second location. When asked about the simplicity and ease of use of the app 95% of the users were fully or mostly positive at the first location, 87% at the second location. Finally 95% of the users agreed or mostly agreed that they would use the app again and 95% that they would certainly or most likely suggest the app to a friend, on the first location. The percentages were 90% and 90% for the second location.

Concerning the user evaluation of AR for outdoor environment the results are compiled from two different surveys that happened on different dates and locations, similarly to the two surveys for the indoor environment. The users were fully or mostly satisfied by the AR app, 83% at the first location, 90% at the second. When asked whether the app satisfies their needs, they were fully or mostly positive, with 85% at the first location and 83% at the second location. The responses to whether the app helped them to discover more POIs at the location they were at were fully or mostly positive, with percentages of 85% for the first location and 90% for the second location. Similarly the responses were fully or mostly positive for the question of the app being useful for getting more information about POIs, 92% at the first location and 77% at the second location. 90% of the users answered that the app was useful in locating more POIs at the location it was used. In both instances users agreed that the app was very or mostly easy to use, with percentages of 82% and 94% respectively. When asked if they would use the app again, the percentages were 92% and 86% respectively. Some questions exclusive to the second location, e.g. concerning whether the users would suggest the app to a friend or whether the app was needlessly complicated, provided positive results, with the users indicating that they would suggest the app to a friend (86%) and that the app was not needlessly complicated (85%) (Fig. 3).

The results overall show that the majority of users have a positive feedback to the e-tracer application. For every question the majority of the answers provide positive or mostly positive responses, which indicate the high level of usability, as defined at the start of this section.

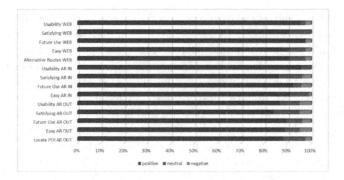

Fig. 3. Evaluation outcome

5   Conclusion and Future Work

The system and components presented in this paper describe the current version and interconnections of each module in the e-tracer platform. The results of the user evaluation indicate that the system pleased the majority of users, alongside showing the weak points that needed to be addressed. The e-tracer platform is designed as an open architecture tool, therefore with the appropriate space-time limitations it can be adapted to operate in other touristic domains as well, such as routing for island-hopping or railway traveling.

Acknowledgments. This research was co-financed by the E.U. and Greek national funds via the Operational Program Competitiveness, Entrepreneurship and Innovation, under the call RESEARCH-CREATE-INNOVATE (project code: T1EΔ K-00410).

References

1. Berlino, A., Caroprese, L., Vocaturo, E., Zumpano, E.: A mobile application for the enhancement of POIs in Calabria. In: VIPERC@IRCDL, pp. 13–25 (2020)
2. Borràs J., Moreno A., Valls A.: Intelligent tourism recommender systems: a survey. Exp. Syst. Appl. **41**(16), 7370–7389 (2014)
3. Katifori, A., Karvounis, M., Kourtis, V., et al.: CHESS: personalized storytelling experiences in museums. In: International Conference on Interactive Digital Storytelling (ICIDS) 2014, pp. 1247–1275 (2014)
4. Kurashima, T., Iwata, T., Irie, G., Fujimura, K.: Travel route recommendation using geotags in photo sharing sites. In: Proceedings of the 19th ACM International Conference on Information and Knowledge Management (CIKM 2010) (2010)
5. Lim, K.H., Chan, J., et al.: Tour recommendation and trip planning using location-based social media: a survey. Knowl. Inf. Syst. **60**, 1247–1275 (2019)
6. Lodi, G., Asprino, L., Nuzzolese, A., et al.: Semantic web for cultural heritage valorisation. Data Anal. Digit. Hum., 3–37 (2017)
7. OpenStreetMap Data Extracts. https://download.geofabrik.de. Accessed 1 July 2022

8. Palumbo, R., Thompson, L., Thakur, G.: SONET: a semantic ontological network graph for managing points of interest data heterogeneity. In: Proceedings of the 3rd ACM SIGSPATIAL International Workshop on Geospatial Humanities, pp. 1–6 (2019)

9. Su, H., Zheng, K., et al.: CrowdPlanner, a crowd-based route recommendation system. In: IEEE 30th International Conference on Data Engineering, pp. 1144–1155 (2014)

10. Tripadvisor. https://www.tripadvisor.com. Accessed 1 July 2022

11. Yu, F., McMeekin, D.A., Arnold, L., West, G.: Semantic web technologies automate geospatial data conflation: conflating points of interest data for emergency response services. In: LBS 2018: 14th International Conference on Location Based Services, pp. 111–131 (2018)

Author Index

Alawneh, Heba   90
Aldumaykhi, Abdullah   98
Alkofahi, Hamza   90
Alsudais, Abdulkareem   98
Amagasa, Toshiyuki   224, 338, 519
Araujo, Jean   75
Aung, Eint Sandi   507
Ayesha, Amtul Haq   237

Barracchia, Emanuele Pio   60
Bassiliades, Nick   385
Bato, Masafumi   453
Beecks, Christian   119
Beigl, Michael   252
Berns, Fabian   119
Bhatnagar, Vasudha   531
Bou, Savong   338
Boudko, Svetlana   415

Cao, Ruixuan   409
Cao, Yang   409
Carchiolo, Vincenza   166
Chaturvedi, Ritu   126
Comai, Sara   45

da Costa, Liliane Soares   181
Dantas, Jamilson   75
De Troyer, Olga   104
Ding, Zhiming   211
Diplaris, Sotiris   581
Dobrijevic, Ivana   575
Dollack, Felix   441
dos Santos Mello, Ronaldo   31
Draheim, Dirk   137
Düsterhus, Tim   119

Essoussi, Nadia   548
Ezeife, C. I.   126

Fileto, Renato   181
Finocchi, Jacopo   45
Fonou-Dombeu, Jean Vincent   269, 282
Fraj, Maha   548

Fugini, Maria Grazia   45
Fukumoto, Kenji   453

Ghawi, Raji   110, 352, 575
Ghosh, Tiash   378
Giotopoulos, Konstantinos C.   391
Gocev, Ivan   385
Grassia, Marco   166

Haag, Valentin   309
Hajaj, Maor Meir   399
Hajkacem, Mohamed Aymen Ben   548
Hakii, Masaru   435
Hofer, Daniel   421
Huang, Yidong   367
Hüwel, Jan David   119

Impedovo, Angelo   60
Ishiyama, Takumi   324

Jenamani, Mamata   378
Jung, Johannes   463

Kangur, Katrin   18
Kara, Anil Can   575
Karras, Aristeidis   391
Karras, Christos   391
Kasuk, Tiina   18
Kato, Fumiyuki   409
Kaushik, Minakshi   137
Kiessler, Maximilian   309
Kimura, Risa   568
Kitagawa, Hiroyuki   224, 338
Kitayama, Daisuke   429, 435
Kobayashi, Suomi   195
Kokkalas, Alexandros   581
Kompatsiaris, Ioannis   581
Küng, Josef   421
Kwatra, Divya   531

Leister, Wolfgang   415
Leoste, Janika   18
Lepage, Yves   295

Li, Chaofan   252
Linxen, Andrea   119
Liu, Xinyu   429

Malgeri, Michele   166
Mangioni, Giuseppe   166
Manjunath, Vinay   126
Mastos, Theofilos   45
Matono, Akiyoshi   224, 338
Matsugu, Shohei   195
Matsumura, Atsushi   489
Matsushima, Yuta   568
Matsushita, Mitsunori   561
Meditskos, Georgios   385
Meyer, João Vicente   31
Mitsopoulou, Eirini E.   581
Miyagawa, Kanna   561
Mo, Fan   153
Mohamed, Aya   421
Mooseder, Angelina   575
Morino, Yutaka   561

Nadamoto, Akiyo   453
Nakajima, Shinsuke   441
Nakajima, Tatsuo   568
Nasir, Mahreen   126

Oliveira, Italo Lopes   181
Otai, Saad   98
Otake-Matsuura, Mihoko   447
Öztas, Emre   575

Papadopoulos, Angelos   45
Papadopoulos, Konstadinos   581
Paschke, Adrian   463
Patenidis, Athanasios T.   581
Peikert, Silvio   463
Peious, Sijo Arakkal   137
Pereira, Luis F.   75
Pfeffer, Jürgen   110, 352, 575
Pittl, Benedikt   309
Pradhan, Ashutosh   378

Qiao, Donghao   237
Qundus, Jamal Al   463

Riedel, Till   252
Rizzo, Giuseppe   60
Rocha, Rodrigo   75

Romanova, Alex   476
Routray, Aurobinda   378
Rudwan, Mohammed Suleiman Mohammed
    282

Saha, Ratul Kishore   378
Samoladas, Dimitrios   391
Satoh, Tetsuji   489
Schikuta, Erich   309
Schlake, Georg Stefan   119
Shahin, Mahtab   137
Shaikh, Salman Ahmed   224, 338
Sharma, Rahul   137
Shiokawa, Hiroaki   145, 195
Singh, Sanjai Kumar   378
Sioutas, Spyros   391
Soni, Kushal   104
Sooklall, Ameeth   269
Stathopoulos, Evangelos A.   581
Suzuki, Takuya   324

Takata, Shogo   447
Takeuchi, Risa   453
Talisainen, Aleksei   18
Tamura, Kazuhiro   447
Terada, Hiroyuki   453
Tokunaga, Seiki   447
Tolmos, Piedad   18
Tzovaras, Dimitrios   581

Ueda, Mayumi   441
Umphress, David   90

Vanderlei, Igor   75
Vieira, José   75
Virkus, Sirje   18
Voloch, Nadav   399
Votis, Konstantinos   581
Vrochidis, Stefanos   581
Vu, Le Duyen Sandra   463

Watanabe, Taku   568
Winiwarter, Werner   295
Wloka, Bartholomäus   295
Wrembel, Robert   3
Wu, Shengli   367

Xu, Qiuyu   367
Xu, Zhelin   489

Yagi, Ryuichi   145
Yamada, Masaya   224
Yamaguchi, Fumiya   441
Yamana, Hayato   153, 324, 507
Yan, Jin   211

Yohannes, Hailemariam Mehari   519
Yoshikawa, Masatoshi   409

Zhang, Shuai   211
Zulkernine, Farhana   237

Printed in the United States
by Baker & Taylor Publisher Services